THE PERSON

Readings in Human Nature

William O. Stephens

Creighton University

Upper Saddle River, New Jersey 07458

Library of Congress Cataloging-in-Publication Data

The person : readings in human nature / [edited by] William O. Stephens.—1st ed.
p. cm.
ISBN 0-13-184811-9
1. Personalism. 2. Agent (Philosophy) I. Stephens, William O.
B828.5.P37 2006
126--dc22

2005014031

VP/Editorial Director/Acquisitions Editor: Charlyce Jones Owen
Editorial Assistant: Carla Worner
Production Liaison: Marianne Peters-Riordan
Manufacturing Buyer: Christina Helder
Cover Art Director: Jayne Conte
Cover Design: Bruce Kenselaar
Cover Photo: iStockphoto.com
Manager, Cover Visual Research & Permissions: Karen Sanatar
Composition/Full-Service Project Management: Bruce Hobart/Pine Tree Composition, Inc.
Printer/Binder: Courier Companies, Inc.
Cover Printer: Courier Companies, Inc.

Credits and acknowledgments borrowed from other sources and reproduced, with permission, in this textbook appear on appropriate page within text.

Pearson Education LTD.
Pearson Education Singapore, Pte. Ltd
Pearson Education, Canada, Ltd
Pearson Education–Japan
Pearson Education Australia PTY, Limited
Pearson Education North Asia Ltd
Pearson Educación de Mexico, S.A. de C.V.
Pearson Education Malaysia, Pte. Ltd
Pearson Education, Upper Saddle River, New Jersey

10 9 8 7 6 5 4 3 2 1
ISBN 0-13-184811-9

CONTENTS

*indicates a more difficult reading.

TOPICAL UNITS FOR CONSTRUCTING SYLLABI*

I. Conceptual History

1. Plato, *Phaedo, Phaedrus, Republic* (1)
2. Aristotle, *On the Soul* (2)
3. Cicero, *On Obligations* (3)
4. Charles Taylor, "The Concept of a Person" (31)
5. Mary Midgley, "Persons and Non-Persons" (34)
6. A. O. Rorty, "Persons and Personae" (36)
7. Troels Engberg-Pedersen, "Stoic Philosophy and the Concept of the Person"★ (38)
8. William O. Stephens, "Masks, Androids, and Primates: The Evolution of the Concept 'Person'" (41)

II. Personology

1. Cicero, *On Obligations* (3)
2. Epictetus, *The Discourses* and *The Handbook* (4)
3. René Descartes, *Treatise on Man* (10)
4. Thomas Hobbes, *Leviathan* (11)
5. J. O. de la Mettrie, *Man a Machine* (13)
6. Immanuel Kant
   a. *Religion within the Boundaries of Mere Reason* (16b)
   b. *The Doctrine of Virtue*★ (16c)
7. Søren Kierkegaard, *Sickness unto Death* (17)
8. Auguste Comte, *Positive Philosophy* (18)
9. F. W. Nietzsche, *The Gay Science, Beyond Good and Evil, The Will to Power* (19)
10. Simone Weil, "Human Personality" (20)
11. Jean-Paul Sartre, "Existentialism" (21)
12. Daniel C. Dennett, "Conditions of Personhood" (27)

III. Identity of Persons

1. John Locke, *An Essay Concerning Human Understanding* (12)
2. G. W. Leibniz, *New Essays on the Human Understanding* (14)
3. David Hume, *A Treatise of Human Nature* (15)

*Some essays appear under more than one heading; ★indicates a more difficult reading; number following title (in parentheses) indicates chronological number of reading

IV. (Christian) Divine Persons

V. Nonhuman Persons and Human Non-Persons

VI. Persons and Non-Western Cultures

PREFACE

What is a person? The history of this concept (πρόσωπον = *prosōpon* in Greek, *persona* in Latin, *Person* in German, *personne* in French) intertwines with the histories of such concepts as *human being, individual, soul, subject, self, ego,* and *mind*. But while these comprise a constellation of interconnected and sometimes overlapping ideas, each has its own conceptual history, its own distinct evolution. Consequently, *person* does not admit of a clumsy, ham-handed semantic reduction to more basic concepts. This selection of readings attempts to trace in outline one trajectory in the philosophical history of the idea of the person. It is, of course, not intended even to approach a comprehensive study. While not disguising preferences, I try to avoid indulging in idiosyncrasy. My goal is to offer a group of stimulating readings that revolve around a single rich, widely debated, and seemingly indefeasible concept. I hope that this book proves useful to students and teachers of philosophy in a variety of courses in which the concept of the person figures, including courses on the Philosophy of Mind, the Philosophy of Human Nature (Philosophical Anthropology), and Personal Identity. The reader will judge the extent to which I have succeeded in weaving together these diverse selections with continuous thematic threads. If the net result is closer to a coherent whole than a hodgepodge, I will be satisfied.

A topical grouping of the readings accompanies the chronological table of contents so as to allow flexibility in designing courses or units of a course. Topics are grouped under six headings: (I) conceptual history, (II) personology (meaning "account of the person"), (III) identity of persons, (IV) divine persons in the Christian tradition, (V) nonhuman persons and human non-persons, and (VI) persons viewed from outside Christian, Euro-American culture. Some readings appear under more than one heading. Instructors are invited to experiment with grouping the readings to serve the particular needs of each course.

For ease of reference, the readings appear in chronological sequence. They begin with the prehistory of the concept of the person in Plato and Aristotle. The inception of the concept in ancient Stoicism (Cicero and Epictetus) follows. Medieval discussions of the divine persons of the Trinity lead to key texts on the concept in the Renaissance, the Enlightenment, and 19th century European philosophy, which show an increasing emphasis on theories of personal identity. Selections from 20th century Anglo-American males are balanced with contributions by women philosophers (Simone Weil, Mary Anne Warren, A. O. Rorty, and Mary Midgley). The perspectives of Taoism (Raymond Smullyan), Buddhism (Richard Taylor, Derek Parfit), and Islam (Gary Legenhausen), alongside the texts in Christian theology, provide religious pluralism. The following overview sketches a few key thematic continuities and tensions reflected in the readings.

PREHISTORY

Plato (through the character of Socrates) identifies the self with the non-physical soul, rather than the physical body and bodily desires of a human being. More specifically, he sees the calculating, rational part of the soul as the guide to the true good of a human being. Indeed, the success of reason in subordinating (or, in the *Phaedo,* eliminating) carnal desires determines how the immortal soul will fare after liberation from the encumbrance of the body. Plato's dualist conception of what a human being is and his tripartite view of the human soul provided the philosophical setting in which the idea of the person was to arise.

Aristotle, Plato's most accomplished student, conceived of the soul in terms of levels of potentiality and classified types of souls by their powers or functions. The human soul contains both the vegetative powers of self-nourishment and reproduction and the animal powers of sensation and locomotion, and uniquely includes the power of *logos*. The capacity for rational utterance (*logos*) and thought is so special a power of the soul that Aristotle believed it could exist separately from the soul's other capacities. He further distinguishes two parts of the mind or intellect (*nous*): One thinks by becoming the form of the object of thought; the other has an essence of active productivity. This "productive mind" never ceases to think, and only this part of the mind is separable, impassible, pure, and immortal. When Aristotle says in the *Nicomachean Ethics* that each human being "would seem to be the part that understands, or that most of all" (viii, 116621–23), it seems that he identifies the self with the intellect.

BIRTH OF THE CONCEPT

The philosophy of mind in the Greek classical period supplied the conditions for the appropriation of a term used in Greek theater, the *prosōpeion* or dramatic mask (Latin: *persona*), into the philosophical vocabulary of the Stoics in the first and second centuries BCE. Thus one can argue that the concept "person" originated with the Stoics. Scholars agree that the Stoic Panaetius is Cicero's source in *On Obligations,* and so the four-*personae* theory articulated there can be credited to him. Cicero follows the Platonic-Aristotelian view that nonhuman animals lack minds and so are inferior to human beings. The natural endowment of reason dictates the four kinds of roles (*personae*) that we are obliged to act out in life. Reason in general, our individual mental bent and emotional make-up (or what we today might call our peculiar "personality"), the reasonable response to the chance circumstances thrust upon us, and our own studied choice of the career that suits us, constitute these four roles.

Epictetus illustrates how people's judgments of what is rational and appropriate vary. Each individual is the judge of his own self-worth and his own character (*prosōpon*). One person's intolerable indignity is another's sensible strategy to avoid a beating. Epictetus' concept of the faculty of choice or volition (*prohairesis*) is another key moment in the philosophical history of the self because Epictetus explicitly identifies an individual with his *prohairesis.* He reiterates the point made by Cicero in his third *persona* that chance, not choice, forces many of our roles upon us. Yet Epictetus emphasizes that how well we perform a particular role (*prosōpon*) is entirely up to us, and we can take pride in acting our assigned parts well. Choosing roles beyond our ability is foolish and shameful. Clement of Alexandria uses this same vocabulary in describing Jesus assuming the mask (*prosōpeion*) of a human being when performing the leading role of the drama of human salvation. Jesus *personified* God. Thus in the early Christian tradition, God was understood as revealing the truth and manifesting his salvific power *as* a person.

MEDIEVAL PERIOD

Three centuries later Boethius employs the originally Aristotelian concepts of substance and accident to argue that a *persona* must be a substance. He reasons that "person" applies only to particular individuals. His conclusion: A person must be defined as "an individual substance of a rational nature." Armed with this definition, Boethius argues for the Trinity. God is substantial Being, subsisting in absolute independence from all other things. Therefore, God is *one* essence and *three* persons (*hypostases*). Moreover, Boethius insists that Christ has both divine and human natures, but remains an individual comprising one person. So began centuries of debate on how best to understand the Trinity of persons which is God.

St. Anselm of Canterbury steers away from heretical interpretations of the Trinity by explaining that the Father, the Son, and the Holy Spirit are not three substances, but three different *relations.* God is one unique, simple, partless nature and three persons. St. Thomas Aquinas and most medieval philosophers agree with Anselm that the persons of the Trinity are constituted by relations. While not rejecting this view, John Duns Scotus proposes an alternative: The Divine Persons are constituted by something absolute.

EARLY MODERN PERIOD

René Descartes' dualistic conception of a human person as a rational soul in a machine made of earth is overtly Platonic in flavor. The relentless clocklike mechanism of his speculative physiology is striking because it displays his staunch materialism as regards everything but the rational soul. Descartes' rejection of an Aristotelian appeal to a vegetative and sensitive soul is explicit.

Thomas Hobbes contributes to the history of the person by distinguishing a *natural* person, whose words or actions are his own, from an *artificial* person, whose words or actions represent another. To personate, Hobbes explains, is to act or represent oneself or another. He thinks that God can be personated by Moses, Jesus, or the Holy Ghost. Hobbes seminally introduces the notion of a corporate person by observing that when every member of a group consents to be represented by one individual, that group makes one person.

The modern history of the concept person arguably begins with John Locke for several reasons. First, for centuries subsequent thinkers will return to his definition for their point of departure. Second, Locke's emphasis on the continuity of memory and consciousness in establishing the identity of the person sets the stage for the next three centuries of debate. His analysis of the case of the soul of a prince entering the body of a cobbler, for example, ushers in a popular tradition of using such imaginative cases in theories of personal identity. In the 20th century, Derek Parfit is an example. Finally, Locke's view that person is a forensic term continues to be invoked by philosophers today, as with Raymond Martin.

While J. O. de la Mettrie claims to reject the materialist view that matter can think, which he attributes to Locke, he also rejects the spiritualist dualism of Descartes. Nevertheless, de la Mettrie's view of a human being as a machine which food fuels clearly seems to anticipate elements of later materialist theories of the person represented by Richard Taylor. Moreover, the similarity de la Mettrie observes between the brains of certain mammals and human brains gives rise to the sensibility that humans and other animals importantly share much in common. This sensibility resurfaces in Auguste Comte and figures prominently in Mary Midgley, W. O. Stephens, and members of the Boyd Group.

G. W. Leibniz draws on Plato and responds to Locke in his unusual philosophy of the person. He holds that the soul's body is continuously reshaped over time, but that no soul ever completely lacks a body. Leibniz thinks that memory can connect the different *personae* which are made by the same soul in order to constitute sufficient moral identity—for punishment and reward—in a single person. Most curiously of all, perhaps, he defends the view that nature establishes a pre-existing harmony of perfect correspondence between the mind and the body.

Descartes and Leibniz' lush speculations about the soul are met by David Hume's austere skepticism. Though philosophers like Leibniz imagine that at every moment we are intimately conscious of an identical, simple self, Hume denies this outright. When Hume introspects, all he finds are fleeting perceptions and impressions, each quickly being replaced by the next. Hume rejects the notion of a simple, identical self as pure fiction. Personal identity, he believes, is *discovered* by memory, which reveals the causal relations among our various perceptions.

NINETEENTH-CENTURY ENLIGHTENMENT PERIOD

Immanuel Kant responds to Hume's skepticism by distinguishing consciousness of numerical identity over time which we find in our soul (the person as *noumenon*) from how other people perceive us as external objects (the person as *phenomenon*). Kant further contributes to the evolution of the concept of a person by identifying three tiered predispositions of a human being—animality (as a living being), humanity (as a living and *rational* being), and personality (as a rational and morally *responsible* being). Thus as a *phenomenon,* a human being is a rational animal in the world of sense. But, Kant explains, as a *noumenon,* a human being is an end in itself that possesses dignity and demands respect from all other rational beings.

Søren Kierkegaard's Christian idea of despair universally forced upon every self by eternity contrasts sharply with F. W. Nietzsche's philosophy of the future. Comte and Nietzsche criticize their predecessors who subordinated the passions to a controlling, unified, intellectual, and impartial self. Instead they see humans possessed of multiple competing drives, not a single uniform nature. Nietzsche also questions Descartes' use of the *cogito* ("I think"). Personality is a rare achievement rather than a birthright, Nietzsche believes.

TWENTIETH-CENTURY ANGLO-AMERICAN PERIOD

Weil attacks the philosophy of personalism and the notion of natural rights that anchors it. She insists that personality is no noble achievement. For her, the personal is profane. Truth, beauty, justice, and love dwell in the impersonal and anonymous realm.

P. F. Strawson argues that person is a primitive concept, one which cannot be analyzed into simpler ones. This account is a key moment in the philosophical history of the person. Harry Frankfurt and subsequent Anglo-American philosophers in the analytic tradition adopt Strawson's coinage of M(aterial)-predicates and P(ersonal)-predicates.

The essays of C. D. Broad and Legenhausen return to the theology of the person inherited from Boethius, Anselm, Aquinas, and Scotus. Legenhausen wants to transcend the controversy between Christians and Muslims by suggesting that God is neither personal nor impersonal, but transpersonal or suprapersonal. Broad offers the idea that personhood is a matter of degree: The more fully one's mental states are unified, and the more fully one recognizes this unity, the more personal one is. Daniel Dennett echoes this notion that personhood is an ideal that entities only aspire to approximate. In African thought, as described by I. A. Menkiti, personhood is again conceived of as a matter of degree. He explains that on the African view, a human baby begins life as a nameless "it" that slowly matures and grows into the social fabric of the community whose excellences it absorbs. In this view a person emerges through a gradual process of socialization and participation in cultural traditions.

Just as Broad, Dennett, and Menkiti all agree that human infants are not persons, Mary Anne Warren argues that a fetus unquestionably lacks the traits of a person. Frankfurt falls into this same camp, since he describes all nonhuman animals and all young children as "wantons." A Frankfurtian person is an entity for whom the freedom of its will may be a problem. Wantons are not concerned with the desirability of their desires, and so do not count as persons.

Dennett thinks the notion of a metaphysical person and the notion of a moral person are not separate concepts, but two different and unstable resting points on the same continuum. The importance of intentions in Dennett's philosophy of the person is also reflected in Peter French's essay. French distinguishes four notions of personhood: metaphysical, moral, legal, and sociological. He defines a moral person as a non-eliminatable subject of a responsibility ascription. For instance, corporations have reasons for what they do and can be ascribed intentions. Thus they are moral persons.

Richard Taylor argues that his materialist view that a person simply is his body is in keeping with the Buddha's denial of the self. Parfit too believes that his Reductionist view of the person conforms to the Buddhist view. Smullyan offers a neo-Taoist view reminiscent of Kant's distinction between the noumenal self and the phenomenal self. Smullyan, through the character of God, suggests that human beings can be viewed either as *personal* (conscious beings who choose) or as *impersonal* (collections of atoms under physical laws). So too can God be viewed either as personal (a conversational partner) or as impersonal (the scheme of things, the very process of enlightenment).

Charles Taylor thinks that persons are a subclass of agents, and that animals are in some sense agents, but not persons. For Midgley, Stephens, and the Boyd Group, the more urgent question is not whether animals like great apes and dolphins are full-blown metaphysical *agent*-persons, but whether they count as moral *patients* that deserve appropriate treatment at the hands of responsible moral agents. Midgley, for example, discards Kant's all-or-nothing dichotomy between *persons* possessed of dignity and worthy of respect as ends in themselves and *things* that are mere means and tools for use. What entitles creatures to basic consideration, she argues, is not intellectual or linguistic capacity but emotional fellowship. Highly sensitive social beings like apes, dolphins, and whales count morally, but computers do not.

Related concerns motivate Martin, who is reacting to the view of Nicholas Rescher. Martin worries that Rescher's seven necessary and jointly sufficient conditions of personhood set the bar much higher than Locke did, since they are not couched exclusively in an individual's capacities, but also in terms of an individual's beliefs, attitudes, and values. The unwelcome result, Martin argues, is that Neanderthals, dolphins, great apes, the mentally retarded, psychopaths, sociopaths, misanthropes, fatalists, determinists, and amoralists like Spinoza, all fail to qualify as Rescherian persons. Rescher defends distinguishing humans, intelligent beings, and persons from one another.

R. G. A. Dolby appears to question the confidence with which Midgley says computers do not worry us with moral claims. Dolby imagines that technologically sophisticated computer-operated robots may well one day be accepted into our society as persons. Oswald Hanfling is of a similar mind. He reasons that skepticism about the feelings of artificial people (like the Replicants in *Blade Runner*) would be no better than skepticism about the feelings of natural (biologically human) people. A different kind of skepticism is the concern of Troels Engberg-Pedersen. He criticizes the modern understanding of individuality and subjectivity. This view threatens to erode the traditional concept of the person derived from Stoic philosophy and the doctrine of *oikeiōsis.* Engberg-Pedersen defends the Stoic conception of the person, which viewed human beings and human reason as bound to the world and saw human freedom as the exercise of our capacity to understand the world and ourselves better. Thus his essay brings us full circle back to Cicero and Epictetus.

How is the reader to understand these ongoing debates on the identity, character, and types of persons—human, divine, animal, artificial, and corporate? Rorty's essay is instructive about this rich and diverse philosophical history. Her analysis yields two possible conclusions: (1) there is no such thing as the concept of personhood; there are only seven separate and independently functioning regional conceptions that cannot be unified; and (2) the various functions of the concept sometimes conflict and the concept itself cannot provide decision procedures for resolving conflicting claims for rights and obligations because it embeds and expresses just those conflicts. She sees appeals to the various conceptions of the person as *rhetorical*.

* * *

How should this book be used? The reader's task is to engage with and philosophically scrutinize each reading on its own terms. The discussion questions provided can be used both to stimulate classroom participation and for writing assignments. The introduction to each reading includes some biographical information about each author and a summary of the reading itself. The former is intended to personalize each reading and interest the reader. The latter is designed to help navigate the reader through the denser, more intellectually demanding selections. (More difficult readings are marked with a star in the Contents.) Students can orient themselves by reading the summary and alerting themselves to the discussion questions before tackling a reading. They can then return to the summary and discussion questions to prepare to discuss the reading in class.

So we return to my initial question: What is a person? These selections equip the reader with tools to craft the answer.

ACKNOWLEDGMENTS

I have many persons to thank for helping to bring this book to fruition. Useful suggestions on the preface came from Greg S. Bucher, John B. Stephens, and Michael A. Brown, who also led me to de la Mettrie. Patrick Murray provided the Kierkegaard. Jeff Hause helped with the Aquinas and generously supplied the Scotus. Randy Feezell's skepticism about the very idea of this book was a challenge that spurred me to see it through, for better or worse, to the end. He also helped me locate the selection from Sartre. For both, I thank him. Editing and photocopying assistance was provided by Fran Minear, Peggy Troy, Creighton's Philosophy Department's work study students, Joan Behrens, and Georgia A. Szkolny. Mary Nash and her staff of reference librarians at Reinert Alumni Library assisted with various chores. Creighton's Graduate School funded the book purchases in November and December 2003. I thank Jack Dudley and my other Creighton colleagues for their help and the reviewers, Darin Davis, St. Norbert College; Andrew P. Mills, Otterbein College; Svetlana Correa, College of Mount Saint Joseph; Michael Henry, St. John's University in Jamaica; and Brian Clayton, Gonzaga University, for their suggestions. I much appreciate my students in the Spring 2003 Honors God and Persons course for gamely trying out the prototype photocopy packet of these readings. I am grateful for the release time provided by Creighton College of Arts & Sciences Fall Semester 2003. I also wish to thank my mother, Professor Emerita M. Irene Stephens, both for her constant emotional support and for her cheerful patience in waiting out the long hours I spent laboring in my office during the week of Christmas 2003. My deepest gratitude goes to my research assistant, Christopher Hogrefe. The tasks he stalwartly performed to help realize this book are legion. I thank my darling Susan for her support, equanimity, and practical wisdom in dealing with my crashed hard drive in August 2004. Four rudimentary persons provided inspiration and fur during this project: Davy, Doreen, and, *in memoria,* Bryseis and Chryseis; their felinity reliably soothes my humanity. I dedicate this book to the memory of Douglas M. Weber; I sorely miss our friendliest meeting of minds battling on the chessboard.

William O. Stephens
Creighton University

PLATO

Plato (c. 429–347 BCE*) was an Athenian aristocrat deeply influenced by Socrates. His philosophy in general, and his conception of the human being and the soul in particular, have exerted enormous influence in the history of philosophy. Thus the prehistory of the concept of the person can reasonably enough begin with Plato, since his thought left a strong mark on the philosophy of the Stoics. In these selections from three of Plato's dialogues, Socrates is the principal dramatic character insofar as he seems to direct the arguments.*

The scene of the first reading is the prison cell where Socrates, who is awaiting his execution, discusses with his friends the nature of death and the fate of the human soul. He says that the soul that has been completely purified of physical desires by practicing philosophy will, when freed from the cage of the body, travel to an invisible, divine realm (Hades) where it will dwell immortal with good and wise gods. Pains and pleasures, on the other hand, pollute the soul and nail it to the body, making it corporeal, so that soon after bodily death it sinks again into a new body.

In the second reading Socrates likens the human soul to a pair of winged horses, one ugly and base, the other beautiful and good, and a charioteer to control them. The bad horse represents lust, the good horse modesty, and the charioteer reason. Similarly in the third reading, Socrates divides the soul in three: (1) the part that desires food, drink, and sex, (2) the "spirited" part (the thumos*) that feels anger, and (3) the part that reasons.*

Phaedo (80c–84b)

You realize, he said, that when a man dies, the visible part, the body, which exists in the visible world, and which we call the corpse, whose natural lot it would be to dissolve, fall apart, and be blown away, does not immediately suffer any of these things but remains for a fair time, in fact, quite a long time if the man dies with his body in a suitable condition and at a favorable season? If the body is emaciated or embalmed, as in Egypt, it remains almost whole for a remarkable length of time, and even if the body decays, some parts of it, namely bones and sinews and the like, are nevertheless, one might say, deathless. Is that not so?—Yes.

Will the soul, the invisible part which makes its way to a region of the same kind, noble and pure and invisible, to Hades in fact, to the good and wise god whither, god willing, my soul must soon be going—will the soul, being of this kind and nature, be scattered and destroyed on leaving the body, as the majority of men say? Far from it, my dear Cebes and Simmias, but what happens is much more like this: If it is pure when it leaves the body and drags nothing bodily with it, as it had no willing association with the body in life, but avoided it and gathered itself together by itself and always practiced this, which is no other than practicing philosophy in the right way, in fact, training to die easily. Or is this not training for death?

It surely is.

A soul in this state makes its way to the invisible, which is like itself, the divine and immortal and wise, and arriving there it can be happy, having rid itself of confusion, ignorance, fear, violent desires, and the other human ills and, as is said of the initiates, truly spend the rest of time with the gods. Shall we say this, Cebes, or something different?

This, by Zeus, said Cebes.

But I think that if the soul is polluted and impure when it leaves the body, having always been associated with it and served it, bewitched by physical desires and pleasures to the point at which nothing seems to exist for it but the physical, which one can touch and see or eat and drink or make use of for sexual enjoyment, and if that soul is accustomed to hate and fear and avoid that which is dim and invisible to the eyes but intelligible and to be grasped by philosophy—do you think such a soul will escape pure and by itself?

Impossible, he said.

It is no doubt permeated by the physical, which constant intercourse and association with the body, as well as considerable practice, has caused to become ingrained in it?

Quite so.

We must believe, my friend, that this bodily element is heavy, ponderous, earthy, and visible. Through it, such a soul has become heavy and is dragged back to the visible region in fear of the unseen and of Hades. It wanders, as we are told, around graves and monuments, where shadowy phantoms, images that such souls produce, have

---

Source: Plato, excerpt from *Phaedo* (80c–84b). G. M. A. Grube translation revised by John Cooper, Hackett (2002), pp. 119–122. Reprinted by permission of Hackett Publishing Company, Inc. Line numbers have been deleted.

been seen, souls that have not been freed and purified but share in the visible, and are therefore seen.

That is likely, Socrates.

It is indeed, Cebes. Moreover, these are not the souls of good but of inferior men, which are forced to wander there, paying the penalty for their previous bad upbringing. They wander until their longing for that which accompanies them, the physical, again imprisons them in a body, and they are then, as is likely, bound to such characters as they have practiced in their life.

What kind of characters do you say these are, Socrates?

Those, for example, who have carelessly practiced gluttony, violence, and drunkenness are likely to join a company of donkeys or of similar animals. Do you not think so?

Very likely.

Those who have esteemed injustice highly, and tyranny and plunder, will join the tribes of wolves and hawks and kites, or where else shall we say that they go?

Certainly to those, said Cebes.

And clearly, the destination of the others will conform to the way in which they have behaved?

Clearly, of course.

The happiest of these, who will also have the best destination, are those who have practiced popular and social virtue, which they call moderation and justice and which was developed by habit and practice, without philosophy or understanding?

How are they the happiest?

Because it is likely that they will again join a social and gentle group, either of bees or wasps or ants, and then again the same kind of human group, and so be moderate men.

That is likely.

No one may join the company of the gods who has not practiced philosophy and is not completely pure when he departs from life, no one but the lover of learning. It is for this reason, my friends Simmias and Cebes, that those who practice philosophy in the right way keep away from all bodily passions, master them and do not surrender themselves to them; it is not at all for fear of wasting their substance and of poverty, which the majority and the money-lovers fear, nor for fear of dishonor and ill repute, like the ambitious and lovers of honors, that they keep away from them.

That would not be natural for them, Socrates, said Cebes.

By Zeus, no, he said. Those who care for their own soul and do not live for the service of their body dismiss all these things. They do not travel the same road as those who do not know where they are going but, believing that nothing should be done contrary to philosophy and their deliverance and purification, they turn to this and follow wherever philosophy leads.

How so, Socrates?

I will tell you, he said. The lovers of learning know that when philosophy gets hold of their soul, it is imprisoned in and clinging to the body, and that it is forced to examine other things through it as through a cage and not by itself, and that it wallows in every kind of ignorance. Philosophy sees that the worst feature of this imprisonment is that it is due to desires, so that the prisoner himself is contributing to his own incarceration most of all. As I say, the lovers of learning know that philosophy gets hold of their soul when it is in that state, then gently encourages it and tries to free it by showing them that investigation through the eyes is full of deceit, as is that through the ears and the other senses. Philosophy then persuades the soul to withdraw from the senses insofar as it is not compelled to use them and bids the soul to gather itself together by itself, to trust only itself and whatever reality, existing by itself, the soul by itself understands; and not to consider as true whatever it examines by other means, for this is different in different circumstances and is sensible and visible, whereas what the soul itself sees is intelligible and invisible. The soul of the true philosopher thinks that this deliverance must not be opposed and so keeps away from pleasures and desires and pains as far as he can; he reflects that violent pleasure or pain or passion does not cause merely such evils as one might expect, such as one suffers when one has been sick or extravagant through desire, but the greatest and most extreme evil, though one does not reflect on this.

What is that, Socrates? asked Cebes.

That the soul of every man, when it feels violent pleasure or pain in connection with some object, inevitably believes at the same time that what causes such feelings must be very clear and very true, which it is not. Such objects are mostly visible, are they not?

Certainly.

And doesn't such an experience tie the soul to the body most completely?

How so?

Because every pleasure and every pain provides, as it were, another nail to rivet the soul to the body and to weld them together. It makes the soul corporeal, so that it believes that truth is what the body says it is. As it shares the beliefs and delights of the body, I think it inevitably comes to share its ways and manner of life and is unable ever to reach Hades in a pure state; it is always full of body when it departs, so that it soon falls back into another body and grows with it as if it had been sewn into it. Because of this, it can have no part in the company of the divine, the pure and uniform.

What you say is very true, Socrates, said Cebes.

This is why genuine lovers of learning are moderate and brave, or do you think it is for the reasons the majority says they are?

I certainly do not.

Indeed no. This is how the soul of a philosopher would reason: It would not think that while philosophy must free it, it should while being freed surrender itself to pleasures and pains and imprison itself again, thus laboring in vain like Penelope at her web. The soul of the philosopher achieves a calm from such emotions; it follows reason and ever stays with it contemplating the true, the divine, which is not the object of opinion. Nurtured by this, it believes that one should live in this manner as long as one is alive and, after death, arrive at what is akin and of the same kind, and escape from human evils. After such nurture there is no danger, Simmias and Cebes, that one should fear that, on parting from the body, the soul would be scattered and dissipated by the winds and no longer be anything anywhere.

Phaedrus (246a–b, 253d–256e)

"That, then, is enough about the soul's immortality. Now here is what we must say about its structure. To describe what the soul actually is would require a very long account, altogether a task for a god in every way; but to say what it is like is humanly possible and takes less time. So let us do the second in our speech. Let us then liken the soul to the natural union of a team of winged horses and their charioteer. The gods have horses and charioteers that are themselves all good and come from good stock besides, while everyone else has a mixture. To begin with, our driver is in charge of a pair of horses; second, one of his horses is beautiful and good and from stock of the same sort, while the other is the opposite and has the opposite sort of bloodline. This means that chariot-driving in our case is inevitably a painfully difficult business. . . .

. . . "Remember how we divided each soul in three at the beginning of our story—two parts in the form of horses and the third in that of a charioteer? Let us continue with that. One of the horses, we said, is good, the other not; but we did not go into the details of the goodness of the good horse or the badness of the bad. Let us do that now. The horse that is on the right, or nobler, side is upright in frame and well jointed, with a high neck and a regal nose; his coat is white, his eyes are black, and he is a lover of honor with modesty and self-control; companion to true glory, he needs no whip, and is guided by verbal commands alone. The other horse is a crooked great jumble of limbs with a short bull-neck, a pug nose, black skin, and bloodshot white eyes; companion to wild boasts and indecency, he is shaggy around the ears—deaf as a post—and just barely yields to horsewhip and goad combined. Now when the charioteer looks in the eye of love, his entire soul is suffused with a sense of warmth and starts to fill with tingles and the goading of desire. As for the horses, the one who is obedient to the charioteer is still controlled, then as always, by its sense of shame, and so prevents itself from jumping on the boy. The other one, however, no longer responds to the whip or the goad of the charioteer; it leaps violently forward and does everything to aggravate its yokemate and its charioteer, trying to make them go up to the boy and suggest to him the pleasures of sex. At first the other two resist, angry in their belief that they are being made to do things that are dreadfully wrong. At last, however, when they see no end to their trouble, they are led forward, reluctantly agreeing to do as they have been told. So they are close to him now, and they are struck by the boy's face as if by a bolt of lightning. When the charioteer sees that face, his memory is carried back to the real nature of Beauty, and he sees it again where it stands on the sacred pedestal next to Self-control. At the sight he is frightened, falls over backwards awestruck, and at the same time has to pull the reins back so fiercely that both horses are set on their haunches, one

Source: Plato, excerpts from *Phaedrus* (246a–b, 253d–256e). Alexander Nehamas & Paul Woodruff translation, Hackett (1995), pp. 30–31, 43–48. Reprinted by permission of Hackett Publishing Company, Inc. Line numbers have been deleted.

falling back voluntarily with no resistance, but the other insolent and quite unwilling. They pull back a little further; and while one horse drenches the whole soul with sweat out of shame and awe, the other—once it has recovered from the pain caused by the bit and its fall—bursts into a torrent of insults as soon as it has caught its breath, accusing its charioteer and yokemate of all sorts of cowardice and unmanliness for abandoning their position and their agreement. Now once more it tries to make its unwilling partners advance, and gives in grudgingly only when they beg it to wait till later. Then, when the promised time arrives, and they are pretending to have forgotten, it reminds them; it struggles, it neighs, it pulls them forward and forces them to approach the boy again with the same proposition; and as soon as they are near, it drops its head, straightens its tail, bites the bit, and pulls without any shame at all. The charioteer is now struck with the same feelings as before, only worse, and he's falling back as he would from a starting gate;[1] and he violently yanks the bit back out of the teeth of the insolent horse, only harder this time, so that he bloodies its foul-speaking tongue and jaws, sets its legs and haunches firmly on the ground, and 'gives it over to pain.'[2] When the bad horse has suffered this same thing time after time, it stops being so insolent; now it is humble enough to follow the charioteer's warnings, and when it sees the beautiful boy it dies of fright, with the result that now at last the lover's soul follows its boy in reverence and awe.

"And because he is served with all the attentions due a god by a lover who is not pretending otherwise[3] but is truly in the throes of love, and because he is by nature disposed to be a friend of the man who is serving him (even if he has already been set against love by schoolfriends or others who say that it is shameful to associate with a lover, and initially rejects the lover in consequence), as time goes forward he is brought by his ripening age and a sense of what must be to a point where he lets the man spend time with him. It is a decree of fate, you see, that bad is never friends with bad, while good cannot fail to be friends with good. Now that he allows his lover to talk and spend time with him, and the man's good will is close at hand, the boy is amazed by it as he realizes that all the friendship he has from his other friends and relatives put together is nothing compared to that of this friend who is inspired by a god.

"After the lover has spent some time doing this, staying near the boy (and even touching him during sports and on other occasions), then the spring that feeds the stream Zeus named 'Desire' when he was in love with Ganymede begins to flow mightily in the lover and is partly absorbed by him, and when he is filled it overflows and runs away outside him. Think how a breeze or an echo bounces back from a smooth solid object to its source; that is how the stream of beauty goes back to the beautiful boy and sets him aflutter. It enters through his eyes, which are its natural route to the soul; there it waters the passages for the wings, starts the wings growing, and fills the soul of the loved one with love in return. Then the boy is in love, but has no idea what he loves.[4] He does not understand, and cannot explain, what has happened to him. It is as if he had caught an eye disease from someone else, but could not identify the cause,[5] he does not realize that he is seeing himself in the lover as in a mirror. So when the lover is near, the boy's pain is relieved just as the lover's is, and when they are apart he yearns as much as he is yearned for, because he has a mirror image of love in him—'backlove'—though he neither speaks nor thinks of it as love, but as friendship. Still, his desire is nearly the same as the lover's, though weaker: he wants to see, touch, kiss, and lie down with him; and of course, as you might expect, he acts on these desires soon after they occur.

"When they are in bed, the lover's undisciplined horse has a word to say to the charioteer—that after all its sufferings it is entitled to a little fun. Meanwhile, the boy's bad horse has nothing to say, but swelling with desire, confused, it hugs the lover and kisses him in delight at his great good will. And whenever they are lying together it is completely unable, for its own part, to deny the lover any favor he might beg to have. Its yokemate, however, along with its charioteer, resists such requests with modesty and reason. Now if the victory goes to the better elements in both their minds, which lead them to follow the assigned regimen of philosophy, their life here below is one of bliss and shared understanding. They are modest and fully in control of themselves now that they have enslaved the part that brought trouble into the soul and set free the part that gave it virtue. After death, when they have grown wings and become weightless, they have won the first of three rounds in these, the true Olympic Contests. There is no greater good than this that either human self-control or divine madness can offer a man. If, on the other hand, they adopt a lower way of living, with ambition in place of philosophy, then pretty soon when they are careless because they have been drinking or for some other reason, the pair's undisciplined horses will catch their souls off guard and together bring them to commit that act which ordinary people would take to be the happiest choice of all; and when they have consummated it once, they go on doing this for the rest of their lives, but sparingly, since they have not approved of what they are doing with their whole minds. So these two also live in mutual friendship (though weaker than that of the philosophical pair), both while they are in love and after they have passed beyond it, because they realize they have exchanged such firm vows that it would be forbidden for them ever to break them and become enemies. In death they are wingless when they leave the body, but their wings are bursting to sprout, so the prize they have won from the madness of love is considerable, because those who have begun the sacred journey in lower heaven may not by law be sent into darkness for the journey under the earth; their lives are bright and happy as they travel together, and thanks to their love they will grow wings together when the time comes.

NOTES

1. "Starting gate": *husplēx*. This is the most likely meaning of the word. It probably consisted of a rope across the starting line, which would pose great danger to horses that were champing at the bit to cross the gate before the proper time.
2. "Gives it over to pain": a Homeric expression; cf. *Iliad* 5.397 and *Odyssey* 17.567.
3. "Not pretending otherwise": The speaker in Socrates' first speech was a lover pretending not to love.
4. In the classical pattern, the one who is loved does not love in return. After all, he is the only beautiful one in the picture. Hence Plato's coinage of the word "backlove" to refer to the emotion that is returned by the loved one (255e1). By contrast, friendship (*philia*) is supposed to be reciprocated.
5. The ancient Greeks thought you could catch an eye disease merely by making eye contact with an infected person.

Republic (Book 4, 439c–442b)

SOCRATES: Now, would we assert that sometimes there are thirsty people who don't wish to drink?

GLAUCON: Certainly, it happens often to many different people.

SOCRATES: What, then, should one say about them? Isn't it that there is something in their soul, bidding them to drink, and something different, forbidding them to do so, that overrules the thing that bids?

GLAUCON: I think so.

SOCRATES: Doesn't that which forbids in such cases come into play—if it comes into play at all—as a result of rational calculation, while what drives and drags them to drink is a result of feelings and diseases?

GLAUCON: Apparently.

SOCRATES: Hence it isn't unreasonable for us to claim that they are two, and different from one another. We'll call the part of the soul with which it calculates the rational part and the part with which it lusts, hungers, thirsts, and gets excited by other appetites the irrational appetitive part, companion of certain indulgences and pleasures.

GLAUCON: Yes. Indeed, that's a reasonable thing to think.

SOCRATES: Then, let these two parts be distinguished in the soul. Now, is the spirited part by which we get angry a third part or is it of the same nature as either of the other two?

GLAUCON: Perhaps it's like the appetitive part.

SOCRATES: But I've heard something relevant to this, and I believe it. Leontius, the son of Aglaion, was going up from the Piraeus[1] along the outside of the North Wall when he saw some corpses lying at the executioner's feet. He had an appetite to look at them but at the same time he was disgusted and turned away. For a time he struggled with himself and covered his face, but, finally, overpowered by the appetite, he pushed his eyes wide open and rushed towards the corpses, saying, "Look for yourselves, you evil wretches, take your fill of the beautiful sight!"

GLAUCON: I've heard that story myself.

SOCRATES: It certainly proves that anger sometimes makes war against the appetites, as one thing against another. Besides, don't we often notice in other cases that when appetite forces someone contrary to rational calculation, he reproaches himself and gets angry with that in him that's doing the forcing, so that of the two factions that are fighting a civil war, so to speak, spirit allies itself with reason? But I don't think you can say that you've ever seen spirit, either in yourself or anyone else, ally itself with an appetite to do what reason has decided must not be done.

GLAUCON: No, by god, I haven't.

SOCRATES: What happens when a person thinks that he has done something unjust? Isn't it true that the nobler he is, the less he resents it if

---

Source: Plato, excerpt from *Republic* (Book 4, 439c–442b). G. M. A. Grube translation revised by C. D. C. Reeve, Hackett (1997), pp. 1071–1073. Reprinted by permission of Hackett Publishing Company, Inc.

he suffers hunger, cold, or the like at the hands of someone whom he believes to be inflicting this on him justly, and won't his spirit, as I say, refuse to be aroused?

GLAUCON: That's true.

SOCRATES: But what happens if, instead, he believes that someone has been unjust to him? Isn't the spirit within him boiling and angry, fighting for what he believes to be just? Won't it endure hunger, cold, and the like and keep on till it is victorious, not ceasing from noble actions until it either wins, dies, or calms down, called to heel by the reason within him, like a dog by a shepherd?

GLAUCON: Spirit is certainly like that. And, of course, we made the auxiliaries[2] in our city like dogs obedient to the rulers, who are themselves like shepherds of a city.

SOCRATES: You well understand what I'm trying to say. But also reflect on this further point.

GLAUCON: What?

SOCRATES: The position of the spirited part seems to be the opposite of what we thought before. Then we thought of it as something appetitive, but now we say that it is far from being that, for in the civil war in the soul it aligns itself far more with the rational part.

GLAUCON: Absolutely.

SOCRATES: Then is it also different from the rational part, or is it some form of it, so that there are two parts in the soul—the rational and the appetitive—instead of three? Or rather, just as there were three classes in the city that held it together, the money-making, the auxiliary, and the deliberative, is the spirited part a third thing in the soul that is by nature the helper of the rational part, provided that it hasn't been corrupted by a bad upbringing?

GLAUCON: It must be a third.

SOCRATES: Yes, provided that we can show it is different from the rational part, as we saw earlier it was from the appetitive one.

GLAUCON: It isn't difficult to show that it is different. Even in small children, one can see that they are full of spirit right from birth, while as far as rational calculation is concerned, some never seem to get a share of it, while the majority do so quite late.

SOCRATES: That's really well put. And in animals too one can see that what you say is true. Besides, our earlier quotation from Homer bears it out, where he says,

> *He struck his chest and spoke to his heart.*[3]

For here Homer clearly represents the part that has calculated about better and worse as different from the part that is angry without calculation.

GLAUCON: That's exactly right.

SOCRATES: Well, then, we've now made our difficult way through a sea of argument. We are pretty much agreed that the same number and the same kinds of classes as are in the city are also in the soul of each individual.

GLAUCON: That's true.

SOCRATES: Therefore, it necessarily follows that the individual is wise in the same way and in the same part of himself as the city.

GLAUCON: That's right.

SOCRATES: And isn't the individual courageous in the same way and in the same part of himself as the city? And isn't everything else that has to do with virtue the same in both?

GLAUCON: Necessarily.

SOCRATES: Moreover, Glaucon, I suppose we'll say that a man is just in the same way as a city.

GLAUCON: That too is entirely necessary.

SOCRATES: And we surely haven't forgotten that the city was just because each of the three classes in it was doing its own work.

GLAUCON: I don't think we could forget that.

SOCRATES: Then we must also remember that each one of us in whom each part is doing its own work will himself be just and do his own work.

GLAUCON: Of course, we must.

SOCRATES: Therefore, isn't it appropriate for the rational part to rule, since it is really wise and exercises foresight on behalf of the whole soul, and for the spirited part to obey it and be its ally?

GLAUCON: It certainly is.

SOCRATES: And isn't it, as we were saying, a mixture of music and poetry, on the one hand, and physical training, on the other, that makes the two parts harmonious, stretching and nurturing the rational part with fine words and learning, relaxing the other part through soothing stories, and making it gentle by means of harmony and rhythm?

GLAUCON: That's precisely it.

SOCRATES: And these two, having been nurtured in this way, and having truly learned their own roles and been educated in them, will govern the appetitive part, which is the largest part in each person's soul and is by nature most insatiable for money. They'll watch over it to see that it isn't filled with the so-called pleasures of the body and that it doesn't become so big and strong that it no longer does its own work but attempts to enslave and rule over the classes it isn't fitted to rule, thereby overturning everyone's whole life.

GLAUCON: That's right.

SOCRATES: Then, wouldn't these two parts also do the finest job of guarding the whole soul and body against external enemies—reason by planning, spirit by fighting, following its leader, and carrying out the leader's decisions through its courage?

GLAUCON: Yes, that's true.

NOTES

1. Athens' port city.
2. The "auxiliaries" are the class of the soldier-police.
3. Spoken by Odysseus at *Odyssey* xx.17–18.

DISCUSSION QUESTIONS

1. In the *Phaedo* reading, Socrates describes philosophy as "training to die easily." Do you agree with this view of philosophy? Explain.
2. Compare and contrast the views of sexual desire in the readings from the *Phaedo* and the *Phaedrus*. Do you share Socrates' worries about the dangers of sex? Explain.
3. In the *Republic* reading, Socrates tells the story of Leontius shouting at his eyes having lost the battle to defeat his desire to look at the corpses. Is this story effective in showing that there is a third part of the soul separate from the part that desires food, drink, and sex and the rational part? Explain.
4. Socrates says that the appetitive part is "the largest part in each person's soul." What could he mean by this?
5. Socrates says that the appetitive part "is by nature most insatiable for money." Do you agree? Explain.

Chapter 2

ARISTOTLE

Aristotle (384–322 BCE*) was born in Stagira in northeast Greece, the son of the court physician to the king of Macedon. At the age of seventeen he entered Plato's Academy in Athens where he studied and later taught for the next 20 years until Plato's death. He then traveled, tutored Alexander the Great for several years, and returned to Athens in 335 to found his own school, the Lyceum. The role of Aristotelian ideas in the history of philosophy, science, and logic cannot be exaggerated. His theory of the soul deeply influenced St. Thomas Aquinas and other major thinkers, and his ethical theory continues to be influential today.*

De Anima *is the Latin title of the work excerpted here. Aristotle explains that the soul (*psychē*) is the source of, and is characterized by, the powers of nourishment (in plants, animals, and humans), perception (in animals and humans), understanding (only in humans), and locomotion (in humans and in some animals). He believes that only the power of understanding admits of being separated from all other psychic powers. The soul is not a body, but is present in and belongs to a body of a definite kind. Aristotle affirms that the soul requires a body. Yet the part of the soul that understands, the intellect, is capable of receiving the form of any object of thought, so it can have no nature or quality of its own. Hence, Aristotle reasons, the intellect cannot be mixed with the body, but rather is separable from it. The intellect is in a way potentially any intelligible object (including itself), but it is actually nothing before it understands that object. At the end of this reading Aristotle notoriously distinguishes between the destructible intellect that corresponds to matter by becoming all things and the intellect that produces all things, always understands, is separable, unaffected, immortal, and everlasting.*

On the Soul (Book 2, Chapter 2; Book 3, Chapters 4 and 5)

[CRITERIA FOR A DEFINITION]

2

Since what is perspicuous and better known from the point of view of reason emerges from what is less perspicuous but more evident, we must start again and apply this approach to the soul. For the defining account must not confine itself, as most definitions do, to showing the fact; it must also include and indicate its cause. The accounts that are customarily stated in formulae are like conclusions, so that if we ask, for instance, what squaring is, we are told that it is making an equilateral rectangle equal to an oblong rectangle. This sort of formula is an account of the conclusion, whereas the one that defines squaring as the finding of the mean states the cause of the fact.

[DIFFERENT FORMS OF LIFE]

To begin our examination, then, we say that living is what distinguishes things with souls from things without souls. Living is spoken of in several ways—for instance, understanding, perception, locomotion and rest, and also the motion involved in nourishment, and decay and growth. And so whatever has even one of these is said to be alive.

This is why all plants as well <as animals> seem to be alive, since they evidently have an internal potentiality and principle through which they both grow and decay in contrary directions. For they grow up and down and in all directions alike, not just up rather than down;[1] they are continually nourished, and they stay alive as long as they can absorb nourishment. This <sort of life> can be separated from the others, but in mortal things the others cannot be separated from it. This is evident in the case of plants, since they have no other potentiality of the soul.

This principle, then, is what makes something alive. What makes something an animal is primarily perception; for whatever has perception, even without motion or locomotion, is said to be an animal, not simply to be alive. Touch is the primary type of perception belonging to all animals, and it can be separated from the other senses, just as the nutritive <potentiality> can be separated from touch and the other senses.

Source: Aristotle, *Selections;* translated with notes by Terence Irwin and Gail Fine, Hackett (1995), pp. 179–182, 198–202. Line numbers have been deleted.

[THE PARTS OF THE SOUL]

The part of the soul that belongs to plants as well as to animals is called nutritive; and all animals evidently have the sense of touch. Later we will state the explanation of each of these facts.[2] For now let us confine ourselves to saying that the soul is the principle of the <potentialities> we have mentioned—for nutrition, perception, understanding, and motion—and is defined by them.

Is each of these a soul or a part of a soul? And if a part, is it the sort that is separable only in account, or is it also separable in place? In some cases the answer is easily seen, but some parts raise a puzzle. For some plants[3] are evidently still alive when they are cut <from one plant> and are separated from each other; for, we assume, the soul in each plant is actually one but potentially more than one. And we see that the same is also true of other differentiae of the soul. <This is clear> in the case of insects that are cut in two. For each part has both perception and locomotion; if it has perception, then it also has appearance and desire. For if it has perception, then it has pain and pleasure,[4] and if it has these, then it necessarily also has appetite.

So far, however, nothing is evident about understanding and the potentiality for theoretical study. It would seem to be a different kind of soul,[5] and to be the only part that admits of being separated,[6] just as the everlasting <admits of being separated> from the perishable.

It evidently follows, however, that the other parts of the soul are not separable, as some say they are. But they evidently differ in account; for perceiving is different from believing, and hence being the perceptive part is different from being the believing part, and so on for each of the other parts mentioned.

Further, animals are differentiated by the fact that some of them have all of these parts, some have some of them, and some have only one; we should investigate the reason for this later. Practically the same is true of the senses: some animals have all of them, some have some of them, and some have only the most necessary one, touch.

[ANOTHER APPROACH TO THE DEFINITION OF THE SOUL]

When we say we live and perceive by something, we speak in two ways,[7] just as we do when we say we know by something. For we say we know either by knowledge or by the soul, since we say we know by each of these; and similarly, we are healthy in one way by health, in another way by some part or the whole of the body. In these cases, knowledge or health is a sort of shape and form, i.e., an account[8] and a sort of actuality of what is receptive of knowledge or health; for the actuality of the agent seems to occur in the thing that is acted on and suitably disposed.

Now the soul is that by which we primarily[9] live, perceive, and think, and so it will be an account and a form, not matter and subject. For substance, as we said, is spoken of in three ways, as form, matter, and the compound of both; of these, matter is potentiality, form actuality. Since, therefore, the compound of body and soul is ensouled, body is not the actuality of soul, but the soul is the actuality of some sort of body.[10]

[THE RELATION OF SOUL TO BODY]

This vindicates the view of those who think that the soul is not a body but requires a body; for it is not a body, but it belongs to a body, and for that reason it is present in a body, and in this sort of body. Our predecessors were wrong, then, in trying to fit the soul into a body without further determining the proper sort of body, even though it appears that not just any old thing receives any old thing. Our view, however, is quite reasonable, since a thing's actuality naturally comes to be in what has the potentiality for it, i.e., in the proper matter.

It is evident from this, then, that the soul is a certain sort of actuality and form, of what has the potentiality to be of this sort.

[UNDERSTANDING COMPARED WITH PERCEPTION]

4

Now we must consider the part by which the soul has knowledge and intelligence, and ask whether it is separable, or it is not separable in magnitude but only in account; and what its differentia is, and how understanding comes about.

Now, if understanding[11] is like perceiving, it consists either in being affected by the object of intellect or in something else of the same sort. Hence the intellect must be unaffected, but receptive of the form; it must have the quality <of the object> potentially, not actually; and it must be related to its object as the perceiving part is related to the objects of perception.

Hence the intellect, since it understands all things,[12] must be unmixed, in order, as Anaxagoras says, to 'master' them (i.e., to know them); for the intrusion of any foreign thing would hinder and obstruct it. And so it has no nature except this—that it is potential. Hence the part of the soul called intellect (by which I mean that by which the soul thinks and supposes) is not actually, before it understands, any of the things there are. It is also unreasonable, then, for intellect to be mixed with the body, since it would then acquire some quality (for instance, hot or cold) or even, like the perceiving part, have some organ, whereas in fact it has none.

And so those who say that the soul is a place of forms are right, except that it is the intellectual soul, not the whole soul, which is—potentially, not actually—the forms.

The condition of the sense-organ and of the faculty of perception makes it evident that the perceiving part and the intellectual part are unaffected in different ways. For after a sense perceives something very perceptible, it cannot perceive; after hearing very loud sounds, for instance, it cannot hear sound, and after seeing vivid colors or smelling strong odors, it cannot see or smell. But whenever intellect understands something that is very intelligible, it understands more, not less, about inferior objects; for intellect is separable, whereas the perceiving part requires a body.[13]

When the intellect becomes each thing <that it understands>, as it does when someone is said to have actual knowledge (this comes about whenever someone is able to actualize his knowledge through himself), even then it is still potential in a way, though not in the same way as before it learned or discovered; and then it is capable of understanding itself.[14]

[THE OBJECTS OF UNDERSTANDING]

Magnitude is different from being magnitude and water from being water,[15] and the same applies in many other cases too, though not in all, since in some cases the thing is the same as its being.[16] It follows that to discriminate being flesh we use something different, or something in a different state, from what we use in discriminating flesh; for flesh requires matter, and, like the snub, it is this <form> in this <matter>. Hence to discriminate the hot and the cold and the things of which flesh is some sort of form, we use the perceptive part; but to discriminate being flesh, we use something else that is either separable <from body> or related to it as a formerly bent line is related to the straight line it has become.

Further, if we turn to things whose being depends on abstraction, the straight is similar to the snub, since it requires something continuous. But if being straight is different from the straight, then so is the essence of straight (duality, let us say) different from the straight, and therefore to discriminate it we use something different, or something in a different state. In general, then, the <separability> of intellect corresponds to the way in which objects are separable from matter.

[PUZZLES ABOUT INTELLECT AND UNDERSTANDING]

A puzzle arises. If intellect is simple and unaffected, having, as Anaxagoras says, nothing in common with anything, then how can it understand, if understanding consists in being affected? For it seems that two things must have something in common if one is to affect the other. Again, is intellect itself an object of intellect? For if nothing other <than itself> makes it an object of intellect, and if all objects of intellect are one in species, then the other objects of intellect will also be intellect; alternatively, it will need something mixed into it, to make it an object of intellect in the same way as the other objects of intellect are.[17]

On the other hand, our previous discussion of ways of being affected because of something in common has shown that the intellect is in a way potentially the objects of intellect, but before it understands them, it is none of them actually. Its potentiality is that of a writing tablet with nothing actually written on it—which is also true of intellect.

Further, intellect itself is an object of intellect in the same way as its objects are. For in the case of things without matter, the understanding part and its object are one,[18] since actual knowledge[19] and its object are the same. (We should investigate why it is not <engaged in the activity of> understanding all the time.) In things that have matter, each object of intellect is potentially present; hence intellect will not be in them (since it is a potentiality for being such things without their matter), but it will be an object of intellect.

[PASSIVE V. PRODUCTIVE INTELLECT[20]]

5

In the whole of nature each kind of thing has something as its matter, which is potentially all the things in the kind, and something else as the cause and producer, which produces them all—for instance, the craft in relation to its matter. These differences, then, must also be found in the soul. One sort of intellect corresponds to matter, by becoming all things. Another sort corresponds to the producer by producing all things[21] in the way that a state,[22] such as light, produces things—for in a way light makes potential colors into actual colors. This second sort of intellect is separable, unaffected,[23] and unmixed, since its essence is actuality.

For in every case the producer is more valuable than the thing affected, and the principle is more valuable than the matter. Actual knowledge is the same as its object; potential knowledge is temporally prior in an individual <knower>, but in general it is not even temporally prior. But <productive intellect> does not understand at one time and not at another.

Only when it has been separated is it precisely what it is, all by itself. And this alone is immortal and everlasting. But <when it is separated>[24] we do not remember, because this <productive intellect> is unaffected,[25] whereas the intellect that is affected is perishable. And without this <productive intellect>[26] nothing understands.

NOTES

1. **For they . . . than down:** Hence the motion involved in growth cannot simply be explained by reference to the motion of the material elements constituting the organism.
2. **explanation . . . facts:** A final-causal explanation is given in iii 12.
3. **For some plants . . . :** This paragraph gives evidence to suggest that some parts of the soul cannot be separated in place.
4. **then . . . pleasure:** If it has these it must have appearance.

5. **different kind of soul:** Or perhaps 'different kind (*genos*) of thing from soul'.
6. **and the . . . separated:** Read *endechesthai,* 413b26. OCT: 'and it is the only part that admits of being separated'.
7. **two ways:** These refer to the formal and to the efficient cause.
8. **account:** *logos.* Here Aristotle actually seems to refer to what the account is an account of.
9. **primarily:** This corresponds to the formal cause illustrated above, since being alive is a functional, not a material, property.
10. **Since, therefore . . . of body:** Since the soul is what primarily (as formal cause) makes the body alive, and since it is actuality, it is form.
11. **understanding:** In this chapter *noein* is rendered 'understand', and the term for the relevant faculty, *nous,* by 'intellect'. 'Thought' and 'thinking' are reserved for *dianoia* and *dianoeisthai.* See *APo* 100b8n.
12. **understands all things:** i.e., is capable of understanding all kinds of things (it is not restricted to knowledge of birds as opposed to numbers).
13. **For after a sense . . . inferior objects:** We do not, for instance, find it more difficult to measure a room after thinking about complex geometry.
14. **understanding itself:** Reading *de hauton.* OCT: 'it is capable of understanding through itself'.
15. **being water:** This translates to *einai* with the dative. In this chapter 'essence' renders *to ti ēn einai.*
16. **the thing is the same as its being:** See *Met.* 1036a1.
17. The next two paragraphs set out the account of thinking and being affected that is meant to solve the puzzles of this paragraph.
18. **the understanding . . . are one:** Cf. *Met.* 1072b18–21.
19. **actual knowledge:** Lit. 'attending (or 'contemplating', *theōrētikē*) knowledge', when we are actually attending to what we know; see 412a11n, 22, 417b5.
20. The text, translation, and interpretation of this chapter are all extremely doubtful. There are disputes about whether a numerically distinct productive intellect belongs to each individual soul or there is one productive intellect common to all souls, about the role of productive intellect in thought, and about its dependence on or independence of the senses and the body.
21. **One sort . . . producing all things:** Lit. 'One intellect is such by becoming all things, one by producing all things'.
22. **a state:** A state, *hexis,* is contrasted with some process of change. Light makes things visible simply by shining on them, not by undergoing any change in the course of shining on them. Aristotle may suggest that productive intellect is more like a permanent feature of intellect than like a potentiality that is activated at one time and not at another.
23. **unaffected:** Or perhaps 'impassible' (i.e., incapable of being affected).
24. **<when it is separated>**: Or perhaps: <when it is embodied>.
25. **this <productive . . . unaffected:** We cannot remember without being affected.
26. **without this <productive intellect>**: Or perhaps 'without this <passive intellect>'.

DISCUSSION QUESTIONS

1. What different meanings of "alive" does Aristotle distinguish?
2. How does Aristotle define what soul is?
3. Why does Aristotle think the part of the soul that understands must be "unaffected" and "unmixed"?
4. How is one kind of intellect like a writing tablet?
5. How is another kind of intellect like a state such as light?
6. In what sense is the productive intellect "separable"?
7. Why does Aristotle think the productive intellect is immortal?

CICERO

Marcus Tullius Cicero (106–43 BCE) was the greatest of Roman orators, a politician, and a prolific author. In this selection from his work De Officiis, *"On Obligations," Cicero borrows from the Stoic philosopher Panaetius. Whereas nonhuman animals are moved only by pleasure, Cicero argues that human minds are nurtured by learning and reflection, which make human nature superior to that of other animals. Our obligations arise from four roles nature has endowed us with. The first role, common to all human beings, is reason; we use reason to judge what is honorable and fitting and to assess our obligations in general. The second role is the mental make-up distinctive of and peculiar to each individual; this varies from Socrates' affable wit, to Pericles' seriousness, to Hannibal's guile and adeptness at concealment, to the candid and open character of others. Just as actors opt not for the best plays but for those most suited to their talents, Cicero urges us to work hardest at the tasks and projects for which we are individually best suited. Chance or circumstance can demand a third role. Chance may thrust upon us a kingship, a military command, a noble birth, a public office, or their opposites, and our role is to adapt to these circumstances and fulfill the special obligations attached to each of them. The fourth role, in contrast to the third, is prompted by our own choice—our studied choice of career; philosophy, civil law, oratory, and soldiering are examples.*

On Obligations (Book 1, §§105–118)

It is relevant to every aspect of obligation always to focus on the degree to which the nature of man transcends that of cattle and of other beasts. Whereas animals have no feeling except pleasure, and their every inclination is directed towards it, human minds are nurtured by learning and reflection; and enticed by delight in seeing and hearing, they are constantly investigating something or performing some action. Indeed, if a person is a little too prone to seek sensual gratifications—always assuming that he is not an animal (for certain men are human only in name, and not in practice), and that he stands rather more upright than the beasts—even if he is in the grip of base pleasure, he seeks to cloak and disguise his appetite for such pleasure because he is ashamed of it. We infer from this that base pleasure of the body is insufficiently worthy of man's superior status, and that it should be despised and rejected. But if an individual does lend countenance to such pleasure, he must be careful to observe a limit in its enjoyment. So the nurture and cultivation of our bodies should be directed towards health and strength rather than to pleasure. Moreover, if we are willing to reflect on the high worth and dignity of our nature, we shall realise how degrading it is to wallow in decadence and to live a soft and effeminate life, and how honourable is a life of thrift, self-control, austerity and sobriety.

We must also grasp that nature has endowed us with what we may call a dual role in life. The first is that which all of us share by virtue of our participation in that reason and superiority by which we rise above the brute beasts; from this the honourable and fitting elements wholly derive, and from it too the way in which we assess our obligation. The other is that which is assigned uniquely to each individual, for just as there are great variations in physical attributes (for we see that some can run faster and others wrestle more strongly, or again, one has an imposing appearance, while another's features are graceful), so our mental make-up likewise displays variations greater still. So Lucius Crassus and Lucius Philippus had abundant wit, and Gaius Caesar, Lucius' son, had it in greater measure and applied it more deliberately, whereas their contemporaries Marcus Scaurus and the young Marcus Drusus were notably serious. Gaius Laelius was the most genial of men, but his close friend Scipio nursed greater ambition, and his life was more austere. Amongst the Greeks, so we are told, Socrates was an affable and witty man, amusing in conversation, exhibiting feigned ignorance in everything he said (what the Greeks indeed call an 'ironical' man), but by con-

---

Source: Cicero, *On Obligations* (Book 1, §§105–118) P. G. Walsh translation, Oxford University Press (2000), pp. 36–40. By permission of Oxford University Press. In this reading "role" translates the Latin word *persona*. Line numbers have been deleted.

trast Pythagoras and Pericles attained their supreme influence without recourse to gaiety. Tradition has it that among Carthaginian generals Hannibal, and amongst our own Quintus Maximus, were men of guile, adept at concealment, tight-lipped, dissemblers, laying traps, and forestalling the stratagems of the foe. The Greeks reckon Themistocles and Jason of Pherae as supreme examples in this category; and that trick of Solon was especially crafty and clever, when he pretended to be insane so as to attain greater personal safety and to enhance his service to the state.

In stark contrast to these, other men are candid and open, believing that nothing should be hidden or underhand; they cherish the truth, and abhor deceit. Others again would stoop to anything and kowtow to anyone to achieve their ends, as we saw with Sulla and Marcus Crassus. The most guileful and submissive Spartan of this type by all accounts was Lysander, whereas Callicratidas, his successor as admiral of the fleet, was the very opposite. Again, we find that the most eminent of individuals makes himself out in social discourse to be one of the common run; we saw this in the cases of the Catuli, father and son, and of Quintus Mucius [Mancia]. I am told that the same was true in an earlier generation of Publius Scipio Nasica, whereas his father, the man who punished the heinous forays of Tiberius Gracchus, was never genial in conversation, and this very trait lent him stature and celebrity. There are countless other variations in men's natures and habits which should not in the least be criticized.

We should each of us stick closely to the characteristics peculiar to us as long as they are not flawed; this is how we can more easily maintain that element of the fitting which we are investigating. We must follow this course so as not to resist the general sway of nature, and so as to follow our natural bent in conforming with this. Thus even if there are pursuits more important and better than ours, we can assess those which we ourselves follow by the criterion of our own nature. It is pointless to go to war with nature and to aim at something which we cannot achieve. This is a truth which lends greater clarity to the nature of the fitting; for nothing is fitting if it flies in the face of Minerva, as the saying goes, in other words if nature confronts and conflicts with it. If the concept of the fitting means anything at all, it is surely nothing more than keeping our whole life and all our activities on an even keel within it, and we cannot achieve this if we forsake our own nature by mimicking that of others. In conversation we should use the language familiar to us so as not to attract deserved derision by inserting Greek words, as some do, similarly we should not contaminate our activities and our entire lifestyle with any incongruities.

Indeed, this variation between natural temperaments has such force that sometimes one individual is driven to suicide while another in the same circumstances is not. We can hardly say that Marcus Cato's situation was different from that of the rest who surrendered to Caesar in Africa. Yet if those others had killed themselves, it would perhaps have been regarded as a fault because their manner of life was less exacting and their behaviour more easy going. But Cato had been endowed by nature with a seriousness of purpose beyond belief; he had reinforced this unfailing steadfastness, and remained always true to his principles and the policy which he adopted, and for this reason he had to die rather than meet the tyrant face to face.

Think of the many hardships which Ulysses endured in his lengthy wanderings. Though he was at the beck and call of women (if 'women' is the right word for Circe and Calypso), he strove to be courteous and pleasant in all his dealings with everyone; and again, once he reached home he bore the insults even of slaves and maidservants in order finally to attain the goal which he sought. On the other hand, Ajax with that fabled temper of his would have preferred to face death a thousand times rather than endure such treatment. As we reflect on these exemplars, we must each of us assess our own characteristics and regulate them, without seeking to experiment with how others' traits may suit us, for a person's most distinctive characteristics are what suit him best.

So we should each be aware of our own abilities, and show ourselves to be keen judges of our merits and failings. Otherwise actors on stage may appear to be more farsighted than we are. They do not opt for the best plays, but for those most suited to their talents. Those who pride themselves on their voices choose *Epigoni* and *Medus;* those who rely on gesture go for *Melanippa* and *Clytaemestra;* Rupilius by my own recollection always played in *Antiope,* while Aesopus did not often appear in *Ajax.* So will the wise man in real life not grasp what the actor grasps on the stage?

We must therefore work hardest at the things for which we are best suited. But if at some time the need forcibly diverts us to undertake tasks unsuited to our talents, we must devote all our attention, thought, and concentration to be able to perform them if not fittingly, at least as little unfittingly as possible. Our effort should be directed not so much at attaining good results beyond our abilities as at avoiding pitfalls.

To the twin roles which I mentioned earlier, a third is added when some chance or circumstance demands it; and there is also a fourth which we attach to ourselves by our own studied choice. Regal powers, kingships, military commands, noble birth, magistracies, riches, resources—and the opposites of these—are a matter of chance, depending on circumstances. On the other hand, the role which we should like to play is prompted by our own choice. So some devote themselves to philosophy, others to civil law, and others again to eloquence; and even in the practice of the virtues different people prefer different ones at which to excel. Men whose fathers or forebears achieved outstanding fame in some capacity are often eager to obtain celebrity in the same field; for example, Quintus Mucius, son of Publius, in civil law, and Africanus, son of Aemilius Paulus, in soldiering. Some sons complement the distinctions taken over from their fathers with some additional glory of their own; for example, the same Africanus crowned his fame in war with eloquence. Timotheus, the son of Conon, did the same; not only did he not fall below his father in military renown, but he reinforced that renown with the fame of his learning and intellect. But from time to time some sons forgo imitation of their forebears to strike out on a path of their own; men of high ambition whose ancestors are little known often work particularly hard at this.

So when investigating the notion of the fitting, we must mentally grasp and reflect on all these aspects. But above all we must establish who and what kind of person we wish to be, and what pattern of life we wish to adopt. This is the most difficult decision of all to reach, for it is when we are on the threshold of manhood, at a time when our powers of judgement are at their weakest, that we each opt for the kind of lifestyle which appeals to us most. So the individual becomes trapped in a fixed pattern and career in life before he is able to assess what is best.

According to Xenophon, Prodicus states that when Hercules was reaching maturity, the time designated by nature for choosing one's future path in life, he retired into the wilderness, and sat there for a long time. He saw ahead two paths, one of Pleasure and one of Virtue, and he pondered long and hard which it was better to take. This could perhaps have been possible for Hercules, 'sprung from the seed of Jupiter' as he was, but it is not an option for us, for we each imitate those who take our fancy, and we are drawn towards their enthusiasms and practices. Very often we are steeped in the injunctions of our parents, and are propelled towards their routines and habits. Others are borne on the wind of popular opinion, and they aspire chiefly to what seems most attractive to the majority. But some by a kind of blessed fortune or innate virtue follow the right path of life without constraint from their parents.

DISCUSSION QUESTIONS

1. How might Cicero's account of the second role relate to how people select their friends or spouses?
2. Is there a virtue in working hard to improve your skills in an activity at which you are not naturally gifted? Would such an endeavor conflict with Cicero's view of the second role?
3. When do people opt for activities that they enjoy and when does reason dictate their pursuits? Would Cicero consider the pursuit of enjoyable activities—whether or not you excel in them—bestial, subhuman gratification? Explain.
4. Cicero worries that adolescents, despite their immature powers of judgment, opt for the kind of lifestyle which appeals to them most, and that this traps them in a fixed pattern in life before they can assess what is best for them. Does this worry apply to undergraduates selecting majors and planning postgraduate careers? Explain.
5. Do you agree with Cicero that the life paths of most people are propelled by popular opinion and their parents' habits? Why does Cicero think this is bad? What do you think?

EPICTETUS

Epictetus (c. 50–c. 130 CE*) was born into slavery in the city of Hierapolis in Phrygia, located in what is today central Turkey. His name means "acquired." He travelled to Rome, where his master allowed him to study Stoic philosophy with the great teacher Musonius Rufus. After being freed, Epictetus founded a school in the city of Nicopolis in northwest Greece. There he taught Stoicism for many years, primarily to adolescent males ambitious for political careers, but also to various visitors to his prominent school. One of his students, Flavius Arrian, recorded Epictetus' lectures into eight books of discourses, four of which survive.* The Handbook *is a compendium of these discourses.*

*In Chapter 2 Epictetus argues that individuals have different standards about what is reasonable or unreasonable for them to do and to suffer. Each person is the judge of his own self-worth, his own character (*prosōpon*). Most people avoid pain and death at the cost of being humiliated, and Epictetus suggests that they conform to mediocrity. But a few are like the purple stripe in the toga Roman senators and equestrians wore; they stand out as a beautiful example to the rest. They value the integrity of their bodies more than living at any cost. The bull who protects the herd, Socrates, fast horses, and excellent hunting dogs are great exemplars.*

*In Chapter 29 Epictetus argues that if I identify myself with my (faculty of) choice (*prohairesis*) and its correct opinions, then nobody can threaten what I care about, but only the material things—including my body—that are not truly under my control, that are nothing to* me. *Epictetus urges his students to embrace challenges that test their mettle and to use well the bodies, parents, and positions (governor, beggar, or citizen) they happen to be given. Most people, however, are slaves to the masters of death, life, pleasure, and pain.*

In Handbook §17 *Epictetus reminds us that how well we act out the role (*prosōpon*) assigned to us is ours, but selecting that assigned role is not. In* Handbook §37 *he urges us to take up only those roles that we can successfully carry out.*

The Discourses, Book 1

CHAPTER 2

HOW IS ONE TO PRESERVE ONE'S TRUE CHARACTER IN EVERYTHING?

To a rational creature, only what is contrary to reason is unendurable: but everything rational he can endure. Blows are not by nature unendurable.—'How so?'—See how the Spartans bear a whipping, after they have learned that it is a reasonable thing. 'But to be hanged—is that not unendurable?' Even so, when a man feels that it is reasonable, he goes off and hangs himself. In short, we shall find by observation, that by nothing is the rational creature so distressed as by the irrational, and, conversely, to nothing is he so drawn as to the rational.

But it happens that these concepts of rational and irrational, as well as good and bad, and advantageous and disadvantageous, mean different things to different people. This is the principal reason why we need an education, to teach us to apply our preconceptions of rational and irrational to particular cases in accordance with nature. But to judge what is rational and irrational, we make use not only of a due estimation of the value of external things, but of what relates to each person's particular character. Thus, it is reasonable to one man to hold another's chamber-pot for him, since he considers only that if he does not submit to this, he will be beaten and lose his dinner, whereas if he does hold it, he will have nothing harsh or distressing to suffer; whilst to some other man it appears insupportable, not merely to hold the pot himself, but to allow anyone else to do so. If you ask me, then, 'Shall I hold the pot or not?', I will tell you, it is a more valuable thing to get a dinner than not; and a greater disgrace to be given a thrashing than not to be: so that, if you measure yourself by these things, go off and hold the pot.

'Yes, but that would be beneath me.'

It is you who are to consider that, not I: for it is you who know yourself, and what value you set upon yourself, and at what rate you sell yourself: for different people sell themselves at different prices.

Hence Agrippinus, when Florus was considering whether he should go to Nero's shows, so as to perform some part in them himself, said to him, 'Go.'—'So why do you not go yourself?' said Florus. 'Because', replied Agrippinus, 'I do not even consider doing so.' For as soon as a person even considers such questions, comparing and calculating the values of external things, he draws close to those who have lost all sense of their proper character.* Now what are you asking me?

*'Character' translates the Greek word *prosōpon.* [Ed.]

Source: The Discourses of Epictetus, translated by Robin Hard, pp. 8–11 and 65–71, is reprinted with the permission of J.M. Dent, a division of The Orion Publishing Group. Line numbers have been deleted.

'Is death to be preferred, or life?' I answer, life. 'Pain or pleasure?' I answer, pleasure.—'But if I do not act a part in the tragedy, I shall lose my head. Go and act it then, but I for my part will not.—'Why?'—Because you regard yourself as just a single thread of the many that make up the garment.—'And then?'—You should give thought as to how you can be like all other men, as one thread desires not to be distinguished from the others. But I want to be the purple, that small and shining band, which gives lustre and beauty to all the rest. Why do you bid me resemble the multitude, then? In that case, how shall I still be the purple?

Helvidius Priscus saw this too, and acted accordingly: for when Vespasian had sent word to him not to attend the Senate, he answered, 'It is in your power not to allow me to be a senator; but as long as I am one, I must attend.'—'Well, then, if you do attend, at least be silent.'—'Do not ask for my opinion, and I will be silent.'—'But I must ask it.'—'And I must say what seems right to me.'—'But if you do, I will put you to death.'—'Did I ever tell you that I was immortal? You will do your part, and I mine: It is yours to kill, and mine to die without trembling; yours to banish me, mine to depart without grieving.'

What good, then, did Priscus do, who was but a single person? Why, what good does the purple do to the cloak? What else than standing out in it as purple, and setting a fine example to others? Another man perhaps, if Caesar had told him in such circumstances not to go to the Senate, would have said, 'I am obliged to you for excusing me.' But Caesar would not have tried to prevent such a man from going in the first place, well knowing that either he would sit there like a jug or, if he spoke, he would say what he knew Caesar wanted him to say, and then pile on still more.

In this manner also did a certain athlete act, who was in danger of dying unless his genitals were amputated. His brother, who was a philosopher, came to him and said, 'Well, brother, what do you intend to do? Are we going to cut this part of you off, and return again to the gymnasium?' He would not submit to that, and awaited his death with courage.

Someone asked: 'How was it that he did so? As an athlete or as a philosopher?' As a man, said Epictetus; but as a man who had contended at Olympia and been proclaimed a victor; who had spent a good deal of time in such places, and not merely been rubbed with oil in Bato's training-school. Yet another person would have had his very head cut off, if he could have lived without it. This is what I mean by respect for one's true character; and such is its power with those who have acquired the habit of deliberately introducing this consideration when examining how they should behave.

'Come now, Epictetus, shave off your beard.'—If I am a philosopher, I answer, I will not shave it off.—'Then I will have you beheaded.'—If it will do you any good, behead me.

Somebody asked, 'How shall each of us perceive what is appropriate to his true character?' How is it, replied Epictetus, that the bull alone, when the lion attacks, is aware of its own powers, and puts itself forward to protect the entire herd? Is it not clear that the possession of these powers is at the same time accompanied by an awareness of them also? And with us, too, whoever has such powers will not be ignorant of them. But neither a bull nor a noble-spirited man comes to be what he is all at once: he must undertake hard winter training, and prepare himself, and not propel himself rashly into what is not appropriate to him.

Only consider at what price you sell your own will and choice, man: if for nothing else, that you may not sell it cheap. But what is great and exceptional perhaps belongs to others, to Socrates and those who resemble him.

Why, then, if we are born to this, do not all or many of us become like him?

Why, do all horses become swift? Are all dogs keen at the scent? What, then: because I am not naturally gifted, shall I neglect all care of myself? Heaven forbid! Epictetus will not be better than Socrates; but if I am not worse, that is enough for me. I shall never be a Milo, and yet I do not neglect my body; nor a Croesus, and yet I do not neglect my property: nor, in general, do we cease to take pains in any area, because we despair of arriving at the highest degree of perfection.

CHAPTER 29

ON STEADFASTNESS

The essence of the good is a certain disposition of our choice, and essence of evil likewise.

What are externals, then?

Materials for the faculty of choice, in the management of which it will attain its own good or evil.

How, then, will it attain the good?

If it does not admire the materials themselves: for its judgements about the materials, if they are correct, make our choice good, and if they are distorted and perverse, make it bad.

This law has god ordained, who says, 'If you want anything good, get it from yourself.' You say, 'No, but from another.'—Rather, you must get it from yourself. So, when a tyrant threatens and sends for me, I say, What does he threaten? If he says, 'I will chain you', I say, 'He is threatening my hands and my feet.' If he says, 'I will cut off your head', I say, 'He is threatening my neck.' If he says, 'I will throw you into prison', I say, 'He is threatening all of my poor flesh'; and, if he threatens me with exile, I reply the same.

Then it is not really you that he is threatening?

If I am persuaded that these things are nothing to me, not at all; but, if I am afraid about any of them, it is me that he threatens. Who is there left for me to fear? The man with power over what? Of things in my own power? Of these no one is the master. Of things not in my power? And what are those to me?

What, then! do you philosophers teach us contempt for kings?

Heaven forbid. Who of us teaches any one to contend with them about things of which they have authority? Take my poor body, take my possessions, take my reputation, take those who are about me. If I persuade any one to contend for these things as his own, accuse me with justice.—'Yes, but I want to control your judgements too.'—And who has given you that authority? How can you conquer another's judgement?—By the application of fear I will conquer it.—You fail to see that it was a person's own judgement that conquered itself, it was not conquered by another. Nothing else can overcome the power of choice but that itself. For that reason too the law of god is most excellent and just, that the better should always prove superior to the worse.

'Ten people are superior to one', you say. In what? In chaining, killing, dragging people away where they please and taking away their property. Thus ten people can overcome one only in that in which they are superior.

In what, then, are they worse?

If the one has right judgement and the others have not. For can they conquer him in this? How can they? If we are weighed in a balance, must not the heavier drag down the scales?

So that Socrates should suffer in the way that he did at the hands of the Athenians?

Slave! what do you mean by 'Socrates'? State the matter as it really is: that the paltry body of Socrates should be arrested and dragged to prison by those who were stronger than he: that someone should give hemlock to the poor body of Socrates and that it should expire; do these things appear marvellous to you, these things unjust, is it for such things as these that you accuse god? Had Socrates, then, no compensation for them? In what, then, to him did the essence of good consist? Whom shall we listen to, you or him? And what does he say? 'Anytus and Meletus can kill me, but they cannot harm me.' And again: 'If this is what god wills, so be it.' But prove to me that one who holds inferior judgements can prevail over a man who is superior in his judgements. You never will prove it, nor anything like it: for the law of nature and of god is this: Let the better always be superior to the worse.

In what?

In that in which it is better. One body is stronger than another, a number of people are stronger than a single person, and a thief is stronger than one who is not a thief. Thus I, too, lost my lamp because the thief was better at keeping awake than I. But he bought a lamp at the price of being a thief, a rogue, and a brute. That seemed to him a good bargain.

Very well; but now someone has seized me by my cloak and drags me to the market-place, and then others shout at me 'Philosopher, what good have your judgements done you? See, you are being dragged off to prison: see, you are going to lose your head!'—And pray what kind of 'Introduction to Philosophy' could I have studied, that when a stronger man than myself seizes my cloak, I should not be dragged off? Or that when ten men pull me at once and throw me into prison, I should not be thrown there? But have I learned nothing, then? I have learned to see that whatever happens, if it be outside the sphere of choice, is nothing to me. So have you gained no benefit in this respect? Why do you seek your benefit in anything other than that in which you have claimed it is to be found? And so I sit in prison and say: 'The person who shouts at me in this way does not hearken to what is meant, does not follow what is said, and has made no effort at all to know what philosophers say or how they act. Away with him, then.' 'Come out of prison again.' If you have no further need for me in prison, I will come out; if you need me again, I will return. For how long? Just as long as reason requires I should continue in this paltry body: when reason does so no longer, take it and good health to you. Only, let me not abandon it without due reason, or from mere feebleness, or on some casual pretext; for that, again, would be contrary to the will of god: for he has need of such a world and such creatures to live on earth. But if he gives the signal for retreat as he did to Socrates, we should obey his signal as that of our general.

Well, should such things to be said to all and sundry?

For what purpose? Is it not sufficient to be convinced oneself? When children come to us clapping their hands and saying: 'Today is the good Saturnalia', do we say to them, 'There is no good in that'? By no means; but we clap our hands along with them. Thus, when you are unable to change a person's views, recognize that he is a child, and clap your hands with him; or if you do not wish to do that, merely keep your silence.

These things we ought to remember, and when we are called to meet some such difficulty, we should know that the time has come to show whether we have been well educated. For a young man who goes from his studies to confront such a difficulty is like a person who has practised the analysis of syllogisms, and if somebody proposes an easy one, says, 'Give me, rather, a fine intricate one, that I may get some exercise.' So also are wrestlers displeased when matched with lightweight young men. 'He cannot lift me', one says, 'now there is a fine young man.' But no—when the crisis calls, he has to weep and say, 'I wanted to go on learning.'—Learn what? If you did not learn these things to demonstrate them in practice, why did you learn them at all? I imagine there must be someone amongst those who are sitting here that feels secret pangs of impatience, and says: 'When will such a difficulty befall me as has befallen him? Must I sit wasting my life in a corner when I might be crowned at Olympia? When will any one bring me news of such a contest?' Such should be the disposition of you all. Even among the gladiators of Caesar there are some who bear it very ill because no one brings them out or matches them in combat, and they pray to god, and go up to their managers, begging to fight. And will none of you show such spirit? I would willingly sail off just for that purpose, to see how some athlete of mine is acting and how he treats his task. 'I do not want such a task', say you. Is it in your power, then, to take on what task you choose? Such a body is given you; such parents, such brothers, such a country, and such a rank in it; and then you come to me and say:

'Change my task.' Besides, have you not abilities to deal with that which is given you? What you should say is, 'It is your business to propose; mine to practise it well.' No, but you say instead, 'Do not propose such an argument to me; but such a one: do not offer such an objection to me; but such a one.'—There will come a time, I suppose, when tragic actors will fancy that their masks* and buskins and long robes are their real selves. Man, you have these things as your materials and your rule of action. Say something, so that we may know whether you are a tragic actor or a buffoon: for, save their words, these hold everything else in common. If any one, therefore, should take away his buskins and his mask, and bring him on stage like a ghost, is the tragic actor lost or does he hold good? If he has a voice he holds good. So also in life. 'Take this governorship.' I take it; and, taking it, I show how a person who has been properly educated behaves. 'Lay aside your senatorial robe, put on rags, and come on the stage in that character.[†]—What of it? Is it not in my power to deploy a fine voice? 'In what character do you now appear?'—As a witness called by god. 'Come you, then, and bear witness for me, for you are worthy to be brought forth as my witness. Is anything outside the sphere of choice, either good or evil? Do I harm anyone? Have I placed the advantage of each individual in anyone but in himself? What is the witness that you bear for god?' I am in a miserable condition, lord; I am undone; no mortal cares for me; no mortal gives me anything; all blame me, all speak ill of me.—Is this the evidence you are to give? And will you bring disgrace upon the appeal that he has made to you, who has thus conferred such an honour upon you, and thought you worthy of being produced as a witness in such a cause?

But he who has authority has declared, 'I judge you to be impious and unholy.' What has happened to you?—I have been judged to be impious and unholy. Nothing else?—Nothing. Suppose he had passed his judgement upon a hypothetical proposition, and declared 'I judge the proposition, "if it be day, there is light" to be false', what would have happened to the proposition? Who is being judged here? Who has been condemned? The proposition, or he who is utterly mistaken about it? So who on earth is this man who has authority to pass such judgement on you? Does he know what piety or impiety is? Has he made a study of it, or learned it? Where? From whom? A musician would pay no heed to him if he pronounced the lowest string to be the highest: nor a mathematician, if he passed sentence that lines drawn from the centre of a circle to the circumference are not equal. So shall the truly educated man pay any heed to an uneducated one when he passes judgement on what is holy and unholy, just and unjust?

How wrong of the educated that would be! Is that, then, what you have learned here? Are you not willing to leave quibbles about such things to others, to trivial men of no endurance, so that they can sit in a corner and accept their paltry fees or grumble that nobody gives them anything? You, though, should come forward and practise what you have learned. For it is not quibbles that are wanted now—the books of the Stoics are full of them. What is wanted, then? The man who will properly apply his arguments and bear witness to them in his actions. This is the character I would have you assume, so that we may no longer make use of old examples in the school, but may have some example of our own.

Whose concern is it, then, to contemplate these matters? The concern of the man who has leisure. For man is an animal fond of contemplation. But it is shameful to contemplate these things as runaway slaves do. We are to sit free from distractions and listen, sometimes to the tragic actor, and sometimes to the musician, and not to do as runaway slaves do, for at the same time as one of those is paying attention and praising the

---

*'Masks' translates the Greek word *prosōpeia.* [Ed.]

[†]'Character' translates the Greek word *prosōpon.* [Ed.]

actor, he is looking around on every side: and then if somebody mentions the word 'master', he is all at once disturbed and alarmed. It is shameful for philosophers thus to contemplate the works of nature. For, what, in fact, is a master? It is not another man who is the master of a man, but death, and life, and pleasure, and hardship: for, without these, bring Caesar to me and you will see how steadfast I shall be. But if he comes in thunder and lightning along with these, and I am frightened of them, what else am I doing but, like the runaway slave, recognizing my master? But so long as I have any respite from these, I too am like the runaway slave watching in the theatre; I bathe, drink, sing; but all in fear and wretchedness. But if I free myself from my masters, that is, from such things as render a master terrible, what trouble, what master do I still have?

What, then, are we to proclaim these things to all men?

No. We must show indulgence to laymen and say: This man is advising for me what he thinks good for himself. I excuse him. For Socrates, too, excused the gaoler who wept when he was about to drink the poison, and said, 'How nobly he has wept for me.' Was it to him that Socrates said, 'That is why we sent the women away'? No; but to his friends, to those who could understand; the gaoler he treated with indulgence as though he were a child.

The Handbook

§ 17

Remember that you are an actor in a play, which is how the Playwright wishes it; if He wishes it short, it is short; if long, it is long; if He wishes you to play the beggar, then play even this skillfully; and similarly if a cripple, a public official, or a private citizen. For this is yours, to play the assigned role [*prosōpon*] well; but the selection of it is Another's.

§ 37

If you undertake some role [*prosōpon*] beyond your capability, you both disgrace yourself in that one, and you neglect the one which you might have been capable of successfully filling.

DISCUSSION QUESTIONS

1. Why do we need education, according to Epictetus? How does education affect our preconceptions of what is reasonable and unreasonable?
2. Under what circumstances would *you* hold a chamber-pot for someone to urinate in? Would you consider it unworthy of yourself or would you rather avoid being beaten and going hungry? Explain.
3. Is Epictetus right to think that most people succumb to threats of death while only a few refuse to humiliate themselves preferring to risk being killed?
4. Why might Epictetus refuse to be coerced into shaving off his beard? Is he silly to care so much about his facial hair?
5. Would it be in keeping with your character to keep silent when others speak or act wrongly? If given an ultimatum to shave your head or be harmed, what would it be in keeping with your character to do?
6. Which parts of your body would you be willing to have amputated to avoid dying of an infection? Do you respect the decision of the athlete Epictetus tells about? Explain.
7. What can conquer the body, according to Epictetus? What can conquer one's *prohairesis?*
8. Do you identify yourself with your body and your material possessions or your volition, reason, beliefs, judgments, and decisions? Is Epictetus right that you cannot realistically expect to prevail in *both* the mental *and* the physical?
9. Which of our roles does Epictetus seem to think are assigned to us and which do we choose for ourselves? Do you agree?

Source: Editor's translation.

Chapter 5

CLEMENT OF ALEXANDRIA

Clement (c. 150 to c. 213 CE) was born of pagan parents, converted to Christianity and travelled widely seeking instruction from Christian teachers. He eventually studied with Pantaenus, head of the Catechetical School of Alexandria. Clement was very familiar with the Platonic and Stoic philosophers, Homer, Hesiod, and Greek literature in general. In this text Clement speaks of Jesus assuming the "mask" (prosōpeion) *of a human being and acting the drama of salvation for humanity. The sense of* prosōpeion *as a personified dramatic role follows the usage of Epictetus.*

Protrepticus (10.110.2.2)

[. . .] For not without divine care could so great a work have been accomplished, as it has been in so short a time by the Lord, who to outward appearance is despised, but in very deed is adored; who is the real Purifier, Savior and Gracious One, the Divine Word, the truly most manifest God who is made equal to the Master of the universe, because He was His Son and "the Word was in God."

When at the first His coming was proclaimed the message was not disbelieved; nor was He unrecognized when, having assumed the mask of a human being and received fleshly form, He began to act the drama of salvation for humanity. For He was a true champion, and a fellow-champion with His creatures; and, having been most speedily published abroad to all men,—for swifter than the sun He rose from the very will of the Father—He readily lighted up God for us.

DISCUSSION QUESTIONS

1. How does Clement's use of *prosōpeion* relate to the discussion of the *persona* of Christ in the Trinity by later medieval philosophers?
2. Is Clement's description of Christ's *prosōpeion* consistent with Boethius' definition of *persona?*

Chapter 6

BOETHIUS

Boethius (480–524 CE) was an accomplished Hellenist who became consul in 510. While in prison under suspicion of treason, he wrote his famous work On the Consolation of Philosophy. *His ambition was to write a Latin translation of Aristotle and Plato with reconciling commentaries.*

In this selection, he argues that (1) "Person" cannot exist apart from a nature. (2) Natures are either substances or accidents. (3) A person cannot come into being from accidents (e.g., white, black, size). (4) Hence, a person is a substance. He then reasons that substances are either corporeal or incorporeal, and are either universal (e.g., genus, species) or particular (e.g., individual specimen). "Person" cannot be applied to universals but only to particular individuals, Boethius holds, so he concludes that a person must be defined as "an individual substance of a rational nature." The Greeks named the individual subsistence of a rational nature hypostasis, *while the Latins call it* persona *(from the Greek term* prosōpon*). Boethius then advances an argument for the Trinity of God: (1) God is. (2) The being of all things subsists from God. (3) Hence, God is essence* (ousia)*. (4) God is substantial Being. (5) Hence, God subsists in absolute independence. (6) Therefore, God is* **one** *essence (subsistence), but* **three** hypostases *(substances, persons). If Christ has both divine and human natures, then wouldn't Christ be two persons? Boethius insists that Christ is, so Christ is a unity. Moreover, the Scriptures never equivocate the name Christ. So the substance of God and man in Christ comprise one person, according to Boethius.*

Contra Eutychen (§§2–4)

II

But the proper definition of Person is a matter of very great perplexity. For if every nature has person, the difference between nature and person is a hard knot to unravel; or if person is not taken as the equivalent of nature but is a term of less scope and range, it is difficult to say to what natures it may be extended, that is, to what natures the term person may be applied and what natures are dissociate from it. For one thing is clear, namely that nature is a substrate of Person, and that Person cannot be predicated apart from nature.

We must, therefore, conduct our inquiry into these points as follows.

Since Person cannot exist apart from a nature and since natures are either substances or accidents and we see that a person cannot come into being among accidents (for who can say there is any person of white or black or size?), it therefore remains that Person is properly applied to substances. But of substances, some are corporeal and others incorporeal. And of corporeals, some are living and others the reverse; of living substances, some are sensitive and others insensitive; of sensitive substances, some are rational and others irrational. Similarly of incorporeal substances, some are rational, others the reverse (for instance the animating spirits of beasts); but of rational substances there is one which is immutable and impassible by nature, namely God, another which in virtue of its creation is mutable and passible except in that case where the Grace of the impassible substance has transformed it to the unshaken impassibility which belongs to angels and to the soul.

Now from all the definitions we have given it is clear that Person cannot be affirmed of bodies which have no life (for no one ever said that a stone had a person), nor yet of living things which lack sense (for neither is there any person of a tree), nor finally of that which is bereft of mind and reason (for there is no person of a horse or ox or any other of the animals which dumb and unreasoning live a life of sense alone), but we say there is a person of a man, of God, of an angel. Again, some substances are universal, others are particular. Universal terms are those which are predicated of individuals, as man, animal, stone, stock and other things of this kind which are either genera or species; for the term man is applied to individual men just as animal is to individual animals, and stone and stock to individual stones and stocks. But particulars are terms which are never predicated of other things, as Cicero, Plato, this stone from which this statue of Achilles was hewn, this piece of wood out of which this table

---

Source: Boethius, *Contra Eutychen* (in *The Theological Tractates*), §§2–4, H. F. Stewart & E. K. Rand tr., Loeb Classical Library, Harvard University Press (1962): 80–99. Reprinted by permission of the publishers and the Trustees of the Loeb Classical Library.

was made. But in all these things person cannot in any case be applied to universals, but only to particulars and individuals; for there is no person of a man if animal or general; only the single persons of Cicero, Plato, or other single individuals are termed persons.

III

Wherefore if Person belongs to substances alone, and these rational, and if every nature is a substance, existing not in universals but in individuals, we have found the definition of Person, viz.: "The individual substance of a rational nature." Now by this definition we Latins have described what the Greeks call ὑπόστασις. For the word person seems to be borrowed from a different source, namely from the masks which in comedies and tragedies used to signify the different subjects of representation. Now *persona* "mask" is derived from *personare,* with a circumflex on the penultimate. But if the accent is put on the antepenultimate the word will clearly be seen to come from *sonus* "sound," and for this reason, that the hollow mask necessarily produces a larger sound. The Greeks, too, call these masks πρόσωπα from the fact that they are placed over the face and conceal the countenance from the spectator: παρὰ τοῦ πρὸς τοὺς ὦπας τίθεσθαι. But since, as we have said, it was by the masks they put on that actors played the different characters represented in a tragedy or comedy—Hecuba or Medea or Simon or Chremes,—so also all other men who could be recognized by their several characteristics were designated by the Latins with the term *persona* and by the Greeks with πρόσωπα. But the Greeks far more clearly gave to the individual subsistence of a rational nature the name ὑπόστασις, while we through want of appropriate words have kept a borrowed term, calling that *persona* which they call ὑπόστασις; but Greece with its richer vocabulary gives the name ὑπόστασις to the individual subsistence. And, if I may use Greek in dealing with matters which were first mooted by Greeks before they came to be interpreted in Latin: αἱ οὐσίαι ἐν μὲν τοῖς καθόλου εἶναι δύνανται · ἐν δὲ τοῖς ἀτόμοις καὶ κατὰ μέρος μόνοις ὑφίστανται, that is: essences indeed can have potential existence in universals, but they have particular substantial existence in particulars alone. For it is from particulars that all our comprehension of universals is taken. Wherefore since subsistences are present in universals but acquire substance in particulars they rightly gave the name ὑπόστασις to subsistences which acquired substance through the medium of particulars. For to no one using his eyes with any care or penetration will subsistence and substance appear identical.

For our equivalents of the Greek terms οὐσίωσις οὐσιῶσθαι are respectively *subsistentia* and *subsistere,* while their ὑπόστασις ὑφίστασθαι are represented by our *substantia* and *substare.* For a thing has subsistence when it does not require accidents in order to be, but that thing has substance which supplies to other things, accidents to wit, a substrate enabling them to be; for it "substands" those things so long as it is subjected to accidents. Thus genera and species have only subsistence, for accidents do not attach to genera and species. But particulars have not only subsistence but substance, for they, no more than generals, depend on accidents for their Being; for they are already provided with their proper and specific differences and they enable accidents to be by supplying them with a substrate. Wherefore *esse* and *subsistere* represent εἶναι and οὐσιῶσθαι, while *substare* represents ὑφίστασθαι. For Greece is not, as Marcus Tullius[1] playfully says, short of words, but provides exact equivalents for *essentia, subsistentia, substantia* and *persona*—οὐσία for *essentia,* οὐσίωσις for *subsistentia,* ὑπόστασις for *substantia,* πρόσωπον for *persona.* But the Greeks called individual substances ὑποστάσεις because they underlie the rest and offer support and substrate to what are called accidents; and we in our term call them substances as being substrate—ὑποστάσεις, and since they also term the same substances πρόσωπα, we too may call them persons. So οὐσία is identical with essence, οὐσίωσις with subsistence, ὑπόστασις with substance, πρόσωπον with person. But the reason why the Greek does not use ὑπόστασις of irrational animals while we apply the term substance to them is this: This term was applied to things of higher value, in order that what is more excellent might be distinguished, if not by a definition of nature answering to the literal meaning of ὑφίστοσθαι = *substare,* at any rate by the words ὑπόστασις = *substantia.*

To begin with, then, man is essence, *i.e.* οὐσία, subsistence, *i.e.* οὐσίωσις, ὑπόστασις, *i.e.* substance, πρόσωπον, *i.e.* person: οὐσία or *essentia* because he is, οὐσίωσις or subsistence because he is not accidental to any subject, ὑπόστασις or substance because he is subject to all the things which are not subsistences or οὐσιώσεις, while he is πρόσωπον or person because he is a rational individual. Next, God is οὐσία or essence, for He is and is especially that from which proceeds the Being of all things. To Him belong οὐσίωσις, *i.e.* subsistence, for He subsists in absolute independence, and ὑφίστασθαι, for He is substantial Being. Whence we go on to say that there is one οὐσία or οὐσίωσις, *i.e.* one essence or subsistence of the Godhead, but three ὑποστάσεις or substances. And indeed, following this use, men have spoken of One essence, three substances and three persons of the Godhead. For did not the language of the Church forbid us to say three substances in speaking of God, substance might seem a right term to apply to Him, not because He underlies all other things like a substrate, but because, just as He excels above all things, so He is the foundation and support of things, supplying them all with οὐσιῶσθαι or subsistence.

IV

You must consider that all I have said so far has been for the purpose of marking the difference between Nature and Person, that is, οὐσία and ὑπόστασις. The exact terms which should be applied in each case must be left to the decision of ecclesiastical usage. For the time being let that distinction between Nature and Person hold which I have affirmed, viz. that Nature is the specific property of any substance, and Person the individual substance of a rational nature. Nestorius affirmed that in Christ Person was twofold, being led astray by the false notion that Person may be applied to every nature. For on this assumption, understanding that there were in Christ two natures, he declared that there were likewise two persons. And although the definition which we have already given is enough to prove Nestorius wrong, his error shall be further declared by the following argument. If the Person of Christ is not single, and if it is clear that there are in Him two natures, to wit, divine and human (and no one will be so foolish as to fail to include either in the definition), it follows that there must apparently be two persons; for Person, as has been said, is the individual substance of a rational nature.

What kind of union, then, between God and man has been effected? Is it as when two bodies are laid the one against the other, so that they are only joined locally, and no touch of the quality of the one reaches the other—the kind of union which the Greeks term κατὰ παράθεσιν "by juxtaposition"? But if humanity has been united to divinity in this way no one thing has been formed out of the two, and hence Christ is nothing. The very name of Christ, indeed, denotes by its singular number a unity. But if the two persons continued and such a union of natures as we have above described took place, there could be no unity formed from two things, for nothing could ever possibly be formed out of two persons. Therefore Christ is, according to Nestorius, in no respect one, and therefore He is absolutely nothing. For what is not one cannot exist either; because Being and unity are convertible terms, and whatever is one is. Even things which are made up of many items, such as a heap or chorus, are nevertheless a unity. Now we openly and honestly confess that Christ is; therefore we say that Christ is a Unity. And if this is so, then without controversy the Person of Christ is one also. For if the Persons were two He could not be one; but to say that there are two Christs is nothing else than the madness of a distraught brain. Could Nestorius, I ask, dare to call the one man and the one God in Christ two Christs? Or why does he call Him Christ who is God, if he is also going to call Him Christ who is man, when his combination gives the two no common factor, no coherence? Why does he wrongly use the same name for two utterly different natures, when, if he is compelled to define Christ, he cannot, as he himself admits, apply the substance of one definition to both his Christs? For if the substance of God is different from that of man, and the one name of Christ applies to both, and the combination of different substances is not believed to have formed one Person, the name of Christ is equivocal and cannot be comprised in one definition. But in what Scriptures is the name of Christ ever made double? Or what new thing has been wrought by the coming of the Saviour? For the truth of the faith and the unwontedness of the miracle alike remain, for Catholics, unshaken. For how great and unprecedented a thing it is—unique and incapable of repetition in any other age—that the nature of Him who is God alone should come together with human nature which was entirely different from God to form from different natures by conjunction a single Person! But now, if we follow Nestorius, what happens that is new? "Humanity and divinity," quoth he, "keep their proper Persons." Well, when had not divinity and humanity each its proper Person? And when, we answer, will this not be so? Or wherein is the birth of Jesus more significant than that of any other child, if, the two Persons remaining distinct, the natures also were distinct? For while the Persons remained so there could no more be a union of natures in Christ than there could be in any other man with whose substance, be it never so perfect, no divinity was ever united because of the subsistence of his proper person. But for the sake of argument let him call Jesus, *i.e.* the human person, Christ, because through that person God wrought certain wonders. Agreed. But why should he call God Himself by the name of Christ? Why should he not go on to call the very elements by that name? For through them in their daily movements God works certain wonders. Is it because irrational substances cannot possess a Person enabling them to receive the name of Christ? Is not the operation of God seen plainly in men of holy life and notable piety? There will surely be no reason not to call the saints also by that name, if Christ taking humanity on Him is not one Person through conjunction. But perhaps he will say, "I allow that such men are called Christs, but it is because they are in the image of the true Christ." But if no one Person has been formed of the union of God and man, we shall consider all of them just as true Christs as Him who, we believe, was born of a Virgin. For no Person has been made one by the union of God and man either in Him or in them who by the Spirit of God foretold the coming Christ, for which cause they too were called Christs. So now it follows that so long as the Persons remain, we cannot in any wise believe that humanity has been assumed by divinity. For things which differ alike in persons and natures are certainly separate, nay absolutely separate; man and oxen are not further separate than are divinity and humanity in Christ, if the Persons have remained. Men indeed and oxen are united in one animal nature, for by genus they have a common substance and the same nature in the collection which forms the universal. But God and man will be at all points fundamentally different if we are to believe that distinction of Persons continues under difference of nature. Then the human race has not been saved, the birth of Christ has brought us no salvation, the writings of all the prophets have but beguiled the people that believed in them, contempt is poured upon the authority of the whole Old Testament which promised to the world salvation by the birth of Christ. It is plain that salvation has not been brought us, if there is the same difference in Person that there is in Nature. No doubt He saved that humanity which we believe He assumed; but no assumption can be conceived, if the separation abides alike of Nature and of Person. Hence that human nature which could not be assumed as long as the Person continued, will certainly and rightly appear incapable of salvation by the birth of Christ. Wherefore man's nature has not been saved by the birth of Christ—an impious conclusion.

But although there are many weapons strong enough to wound and demolish the Nestorian view, let us for the moment be content with this small selection from the store of arguments available.

NOTES

1. *Tusc.* ii. 15.35.

DISCUSSION QUESTIONS

1. Boethius says that "person" cannot be affirmed of a horse or ox or any other nonhuman animal because they all lack mind and reason. What do you think about this claim?
2. Boethius says that there is a person of a human being, of God, and of an angel. How does his conception of "person" compare to yours?
3. Discuss Boethius' accounts of God and man. What powers and attributes does each have?
4. Are human beings more closely related to animals or to God? In what sense does God have a *personal* relationship to human beings?

Chapter 7

ST. ANSELM

Saint Anselm (1033–1109) was born of a noble family in Aosta, northern Italy and became a Benedictine monk against his father's wishes. He travelled to Bec in Normandy and entered the order in 1060, where he succeeded his teacher Lanfranc as Prior in 1063, and became Abbot in 1078. On his death-bed, William the Conqueror wanted Anselm to come console him. He was Archbishop of Canterbury and Primate of England from 1093 until his death. Anselm may have been canonized as early as 1163, or as late as 1494. He was declared a Doctor of the Church in 1720 by Clement XI. Because he believed strongly that rational understanding helped to clarify faith, Anselm is often considered to be the father of scholasticism.

It seems that if the three persons in God are only one thing, then either God the Father and God the Holy Spirit were incarnated with the Son, or there is a plurality of gods. In this selection, Anselm tries to solve this dilemma by offering a third alternative. He argues that since God is the Supreme Good and there can only be one Supreme *Good, there is consequently only one God, not several. The Father, the Son, and the Holy Spirit are not three things in the sense of three substances, but rather three differently named* relations. *God is one unique, individual simple nature that is not composed of parts. Anselm argues that just as in God one nature is several persons, and the several persons are one nature, so in Christ one person is several natures and the several natures are one person. God, Anselm believes, is that nature which is above all other things and is free from every law of place, time, and composition of parts. He likens the Trinity to the Nile, which is the spring, the river, and the lake; each is the* whole *Nile. Finally, God is eternity, Anselm believes, so there can be no plurality of gods.*

The Incarnation of the Word (§§8–16)

8

[. . .] That there is only one God and no more than one is easily proved from the consideration that either (1) God is not the Supreme Good or else (2) there is more than one Supreme Good or else (3) instead of there being several gods there is only one God. (~1) But no one denies that God is the Supreme Good, because whatever is less than something else is not at all God, and whatever is not the Supreme Good is less than some other because it is less than the Supreme Good. (~2) And, assuredly, it is not the case that the Supreme Good admits of plurality and thus that there are several Supreme Goods. For if there were several Supreme Goods, they would be equal. But, indeed, the Supreme Good is that which so excels other goods that it has neither an equal nor a superior. Therefore, there is only one Supreme Good. (3) Hence, instead of there being several gods, there is only one God—just as there is only one Supreme Good and [only one] Supreme Substance, Supreme Being, or Supreme Nature, which, by a process of reasoning exactly similar to that in the case of the Supreme Good, is proved to be unable in any respect to be spoken of plurally.

9

Although this one and only God is three persons—Father, Son, and Holy Spirit—it is not necessary (as my opponent thinks) for the other persons to be incarnate when the Son is incarnate; on the contrary, it is impossible. For [my opponent] concedes that since they are different from one another they are several persons. Indeed, if they were not different from one another, they would not be more than one. (In order to explain more briefly and easily what I want to, I will continue to speak, as I have done above, only of the Father and the Son; for by considering them it will be clear what must be understood about the Holy Spirit.) Accordingly, because the Father and the Son are not two substances it is not with respect to substance that they are different from each other and are more than one. The Father is not one substance and the Son another; rather, the Father and the Son are one and the same substance. But because the Father and the Son are two persons and are different from each other (rather than being one and the same person) it is with respect to person that they are more than one and are different from each other.

Source: The Incarnation of the Word in *Anselm of Canterbury*, J. Hopkins & H. Richardson tr., Toronto: The Edwin Mellen Press (1976) Vol. 3: 25–37. Reprinted by generous permission of The Edwin Mellen Press. Nowhere in their text does The Edwin Mellen Press acknowledge a previously published source of all or part of the material reprinted here.

So [my opponent] says: "If the Son was incarnate, and if the Son is not a different thing from the Father but is numerically one and the same thing as the Father, then it must be the case that the Father also was incarnate. For it is impossible that a thing which is numerically one and the same both be and not be, at the same time, incarnate in the same man." I reply that if the Son was incarnate and if the Son is not numerically one and the same person as the Father, but is another person, then it does not follow that, necessarily, the Father also was incarnate. For it is possible that one person be incarnate in a given man and that at the same time another person not be incarnate in this man.

But [my opponent will perhaps say]: "If God the Son was incarnate and if God who is the Son is not other than, but is numerically one and the same as, God who is the Father, then even though the Father and the Son are different persons, the necessity that the Father also be incarnate with the Son because of the unity of deity seems to outweigh the possibility that because of the diversity of persons the Father was not incarnate at the same time." Notice how he who says this is lame in both feet regarding the incarnation of the Son of God. For whoever rightly understands His incarnation believes that He assumed a human nature [*homo*] into a unity with His person, rather than into a unity with His nature. But [my opponent] dreams that a human nature was assumed by the Son of God into a unity of nature rather than into a unity of person. For if this were not his view, he would not have said that the necessity that the Father be incarnate with the Son because the Father and the Son are one God outweighs the possibility that because they are more than one person the Father was not incarnate at the same time. Therefore, regarding the incarnation of the Son of God, who is one nature with the Father and a different person from the Father: whoever thinks that this incarnation so accords with the unity of nature that the Son cannot be incarnate apart from the Father, and whoever does not understand that the incarnation so accords with the unity of person that the Father cannot be incarnate with the Son, is lame in both feet, i.e., in both respects.

Indeed, God assumed a human nature not in such way that the divine nature and the human nature were one and the same but in such way that the person of God and the person of the man were one and the same. But this [assumption of a human nature] can only occur in the case of one person of God. For it is incomprehensible that different persons be one and the same person with one and the same man. For if one man were one person with several other distinct persons, then [here would be an instance in which] a plurality of persons who are different from one another would have to be one and the same person—something impossible. Therefore, when God is incarnate with respect to any one of His persons, it is impossible that He be incarnate with respect to another of His persons as well.

10

Although it was not my purpose [to explain] in this letter why God assumed a human nature into a unity of person with the Son rather than into a unity with either of the other persons, nevertheless since mention of the matter has been made, I think that an explanation must be given.

Assuredly, if the Holy Spirit had been incarnate—just as the Son was incarnate—the Holy Spirit would have been the son of a human being. Hence, there would be two sons in the Divine Trinity, viz., the Son of God and the son of a human being. Thus, a certain confusing ambiguity would arise when we would speak of God the Son. For both [of the persons] would be God and a son, though one would be the Son of God, the other the son of a human being. Moreover, since the one son would excel by virtue of the dignity of His greater parent, and since the other son would be subordinate because of the lowliness of His lesser parent, there would occur—with respect to their being sons—a seeming inequality in two persons who ought in every respect to be equal. For the greater the nature of God is than the nature of a man, the more becoming it is to be the Son of God than to be the son of a human being. Therefore, if the Holy Spirit had been begotten of a virgin, then since the Son of God would have had a uniquely more excellent birth (viz., from God), and since the Holy Spirit would have had only a lesser birth (viz., from a human being), the one person would be greater and the other lesser with respect to the dignity of birth—an inadmissible consequence.

On the other hand, if the *Father* had assumed a human nature into a unity with His own person, the plurality of sons would have produced not only the same unbefittingness in God but also an additional one. For if the Father were the son of a virgin, then two persons in the Trinity would have the name "grandson"; for the Father would be the grandson of the parents of the virgin, and His son would be the grandson of the virgin (even though His son would have received nothing from the virgin).

Therefore, since it is impossible for there to be even any small unbefittingness in God, no person of God other than the Son ought to have been incarnate. For if *He* is incarnate nothing inadmissible follows. As for the fact that the Son is said to be less than the Father and the Holy Spirit from the point of view of His humanity: these two persons do not excel the Son, because even the Son has that very majesty by which these two persons are greater than His humanity and by which He Himself, with them, excels His own humanity.

There is another reason why incarnation befits the Son more than another [of the persons]. He who was to be incarnate was going to pray on behalf of the human race. And the human mind understands it to be much more suitable for the Son to supplicate the Father than for either of the persons other than the Son to make supplication to either of the persons other than the Father—even though this supplication is made not by the Son's divinity but by His humanity to His divinity. The Son of God makes this supplication [on behalf of the human race] because by virtue of a unity of person the Son of God is a man.

Furthermore, the one who was going to assume a human nature was going to come in order to war against the Devil and to intercede, as I have said, on behalf of man. Now, by an act of robbery both the Devil and man willed to make themselves like unto God when they exercised an autonomous will [*propria voluntas*]. And because by an act of robbery they [thus] willed, they willed only by falsehood, inasmuch as they could only [thus] have willed unjustly. Now, the will of an angel or of a man is autonomous when it wills contrary to the will of God. For when someone wills that which God forbids him to will, he has no author of his will except himself; so his will is autonomous. Now, even though a man might at some time submit his will to the will of another man, still this willing is autonomous if it is in opposition to God. For he only submits his will in order to obtain something that he wants, and thus he himself is the author of the reason why he submits his will to another will. Hence, his will is an autonomous will and is not [in one sense] submitted to another will. Yet, it is the prerogative of God alone to have an autonomous will—i.e., a will which is subject to no other will. Therefore, whoever else exercises an autonomous will tries to attain unto the likeness of God by an act of robbery, and is convicted of depriving (as far as it lies in his power to do so) God of His proper dignity and unique excellence. For if there were another will which were subject to no other will, then the will of God would not be superior to all other wills, nor would it be that will which no other will excels. Therefore, none of the three persons of God more fittingly "emptied Himself and took on the form of a servant" (in order to vanquish the Devil and to intercede on behalf of man, who by an act of robbery had presumed unto a false likeness of God) than did the Son, who, being the brilliance of the eternal light and the true image of the Father, "thought it not robbery to be equal to God" but by virtue of a true equality and likeness said, "I and the Father are one" and "He who sees me sees the Father also."

Indeed, no one can more justly vanquish or punish a criminal, or more mercifully spare him or intercede on his behalf, than someone against whom the wrong is shown to be the more specifically committed. Nor can anything be more fittingly opposed to falsehood in order to vanquish it, or more fittingly applied to it in order to cure it, than is truth. Now, those who have presumed unto a false likeness to God are seen to have sinned the more specifically against Him who is believed to be the true likeness of God the Father. But the Son assumed a human nature into a unity with His person, as I have said, in order that two natures—one divine and one human—would be one person.

II

Nevertheless, because an argument can be given on the basis of which Christ can seem (to those viewing the matter too carelessly) to exist of and in two persons, I think it valuable to say something about this unity of person, which we most steadfastly believe *not* to be a unity of two persons in Christ. For there are those who argue:

> How is it that we do not say that in Christ there are two persons even as there are two natures? For even before the assumption of human being [*homo*] God was a person; and after the assumption of human being He did not cease to be a person. Moreover, the human being that was assumed (*homo assumptus*) is a person because every individual human being is known to be a person. Therefore, the person of God who existed before the incarnation is one person, and the person of the assumed human being is another. Hence, just as Christ is both God and a man, so there are seen to be two persons in Him.

This argument seems to prove—because of the fact that God is a person and the assumed man (*homo assumptus*) is a person—that there are two persons in Christ. But the argument is not sound. For just as in God one nature is several persons, and the several persons are one nature, so in Christ one person is several natures and the several natures are one person. For just as the Father is God and the Son is God and the Holy Spirit is God, and yet there is one God and are not three gods, so in Christ the divine being (*deus*) is a person and the human being (*homo*) is a person, and yet there is one person and are not two persons. For in Christ the divine being is not one [individual] and the human being another (even though in Christ the divine being is one thing and the human being another). On the contrary, the same [individual] who is human is also divine. For the "Word made flesh" assumed another nature, not another person. Now, when the word "man" ("*homo*") is used, only the nature which is common to all men is signified. But when we say, demonstratively, "this man," or "that man," or use the proper name "Jesus," we designate a person—who has not only a nature but also a collection of distinguishing properties by which the common human nature is individuated and marked off from other individuated human natures. When this designation occurs, not just any man at all is understood [to be referred to] but only [the individual] who was announced by the angel— [the individual] who is both divine and human, Son of God and Son of the Virgin (and whatever else it is true to say about Him in accordance with His deity and His humanity). For it is not possible to designate personally or to name personally the Son of God without designating or naming the Son of man; nor is it possible to designate or name the Son of man without designating or naming the Son of God. The reason for this impossibility is (1) that the same [individual] who is the Son of man is also the Son of God and (2) that the Word and the assumed man have the same collection of distinguishing properties. Now, it is impossible for two different persons to have the same collection of distinguishing properties or for these persons to be called by each other's name. For Peter and Paul do not have the same collection of distinguishing properties; and Peter is not called Paul, nor is Paul called Peter.

Therefore, when the "Word was made flesh," He assumed a nature. And only this nature is signified by the word "man"; moreover, it is always a different nature from the divine nature. The Word did not assume another person, because the Word has the same collection of distinguishing properties as does the assumed man. For man and the man-as-assumed-by-the-Word (viz., Jesus) are not the same thing. For the word "man" (as I have said) signifies only [human] nature; but the phrase "the assumed man" or the name "Jesus" signifies not only [human] nature (i.e., humanity) but also a collection of distinguishing properties which is the same for the Word and the assumed man. Therefore, lest we be saying that that man is no more personally identical with the Word than is any other man, we do not say that the Word and man, in an unrestricted sense, are the same person. Rather, we say that the Word and the assumed man, viz., Jesus, [are the same person]. Similarly, lest we seem to be confessing that the assumed man is the same person as the Father and the Holy Spirit, we do not believe that the assumed man is the same person as God, in an unrestricted sense. Rather, [we believe that the assumed man is the same person] as the person who is Word and Son. But since the Word is God and since the assumed man is human, it is true to say that God and man are the same person. Yet, by "God" must here be understood the Word; and by "man" must here be understood the Son of the Virgin.

Except for the statement I quoted above, I have had access to nothing from the writings of the opponent to whom I am responding in this letter. Nonetheless, I think that the truth of the matter has been made so evident by what I have said that anyone who is intelligent will plainly recognize that nothing said against this truth contains the force of truth.

12

But if when recalled from [subscribing to] a multiplicity of gods [my opponent] rejects the plurality of persons in God, he does so because he does not know what he is talking about. He has in mind not God or His persons but something like a plurality of human persons; and because he sees that it is not possible for one man to be several persons, he denies that God is several persons. But we speak of three persons in God not because they are three separate things as are three men but because they have a certain likeness [*similitudo*] to three separate persons. Let us consider this point in regard to the Father and the Son, and let the same consideration be understood [to apply to] the Holy Spirit.

Accordingly, let us take the case of a man who is only a father without being a son, and of his son, who is only a son without being a father (viz., the case of Adam and Abel). We say, then, of Adam the father and of Abel the son that the father is not the son and the son is not the father. For Adam and Abel are two men and are separate persons; and there is not anyone of whom Adam is the son or anyone of whom Abel is the father. Similarly, then, even though there are not two gods, we confess that, in God, the Father is not the Son and the Son is not the Father, because the Father does not have a father and the Son does not have a son. Similarly, the Holy Spirit is not the Father or the Son, because there is no one whose father He is or whose son He is. Therefore, the Father and the Son and the Holy Spirit are called three persons not because they are three separate things but simply because they are three, and are different from one another, and cannot be called by one another's names (just as I have shown about the father and the son in the case of different human persons).

13

But suppose that—on the ground that he cannot understand it in God and does not see any instance of it in other things— [my opponent] denies that something *one* can be called something *three* and that something *three* can be called something *one* (in such way that the three are not called by one another's respective name) as we do in the case of the one God and His three persons. In that event, let him tolerate something which his intellect cannot comprehend to be in God. And with things that are enclosed by place or time or are composed of parts let him not compare that Nature which is above all other things and is free from every law of place, time, and composition of parts. Instead, let him believe that something holds true of this Nature which cannot hold true of those things; and let him submit to Christian authority without contending against it.

However, let us see whether among created things, which are subject to the law of place, time, and composition of parts, we can to some extent find that which [my opponent] denies to hold true of God. Suppose that there is a spring from which originates and flows a river that later accumulates into a lake; and let its name be the "Nile." Accordingly, we speak so separately of the spring, the river, and the lake that we do not call the spring "river" or "lake," nor call the river "spring" or "lake," nor call the lake "spring" or "river." And yet, the spring is called the Nile, the river is called the Nile, and the lake is called the Nile. Moreover, the spring and the river taken together are called the Nile, the spring and the lake taken together are called the Nile, and the river and the lake taken together are called the Nile. Furthermore, the spring, the river, and the lake—all three taken together—are called the Nile. Nevertheless, whether the name "Nile" is applied to each separately or to two in combination or to all three together, there are not different Niles; there is one and the same Nile. Hence, the spring, the river, and the lake are three; and they are one Nile, one stream, one nature, one body of water—none of which can be said to be something three, for there are not three Niles or three streams or three bodies of water or three natures. Nor are there three springs or three rivers or three lakes. Here, then, is an example in which something three is called something one and something one is called something three, without the three being called by one another's respective name.

But if [my opponent] objects that the spring, the river, or the lake neither singularly nor in combinations of two are the complete Nile but are only parts of the Nile, then let him think of this whole Nile, from when it began until when it shall end, as its whole lifespan, so to speak. For it does not exist as a spatial or a temporal whole at once but exists through parts and will not be complete until it ceases to exist. In this respect it is like a statement, which is not complete as long as it issues from the fountain of the mouth, so to speak; and when it *is* complete it no longer exists. Now, if anyone considers the matter in this way and understands it carefully, he will realize that the whole Nile is the spring, the whole Nile is the river, and the whole Nile is the lake, and that the spring is not the river or the lake, the river is not the lake or the spring, and the lake is not the spring or the river. For the spring is not the same as the river or the lake, even though the river and the lake are the same thing that the spring is, viz., the same Nile, the same stream, the same body of water, the same nature. Therefore, here is a case in which one complete whole is called something three and something three is called one complete whole, without these three being called by one another's respective name. However, in the case of that Nature which is perfectly simple and perfectly free from the law of all space and time, the foregoing kind of predication occurs in quite a different manner and much more perfectly. Nevertheless, if this kind of predication is seen [to occur] to some extent with respect to something which is composed of parts and is spatial and temporal, then it is not beyond belief for it to occur perfectly in the case of that Nature which is supremely free [of spatial and temporal parts].

Here we ought also to take into consideration—even as we speak [in a similar fashion] of the Father and the Son and the Holy Spirit—that the spring does not exist from the river or from the lake; but the river so exists only from the spring (and not from the lake), and the lake so exists from both the spring and the river, that the whole river exists from the whole spring, and the whole lake exists both from the whole spring and the whole river. Furthermore, we ought to take into consideration that the river exists from the spring in one way, whereas the lake exists from the spring and the river in another way, so that the lake is said not to be the river—just as in His own way the Word exists from the Father, whereas the Holy Spirit exists from the Father and the Word in another way, so that the Holy Spirit is not the Word, or the Son, but is the one who proceeds.

14

In addition, I want to mention a comparison which is not without some resemblance to the incarnation of the Word, even though the dissimilarity is great. Perhaps one who reads this comparison will treat it with disdain; nonetheless, let me say that I would not altogether disdain the comparison should someone else make it: If the river ran from the spring to the lake through a pipe, then even though the river is not a different Nile from the spring and the lake, is it not the river alone that is "en-piped," so to speak—just as the Son alone is incarnate, even though He is not a different God from the Father and the Holy Spirit?

15

But since these earthly things are very far removed from the Supreme Nature, let us with the help of that Nature lift up our minds to it, and with regard to it let us consider briefly some aspects of what we mean.

God is nothing other than simple eternity itself. But a plurality of eternities is unintelligible. For if there were a plurality of eternities, they would be either outside or inside one another. Now, nothing is external to eternity. Therefore, it is not the case that eternity is external to eternity. Likewise, if they were outside one another, they would exist in different places or times—something incompatible with eternity. Therefore, there is not a plurality of eternities outside one another. On the other hand, if we say that there is a plurality of eternities within one another, we ought to know that however often eternity is repeated within eternity, it is only one and the same eternity. For a nature which, when repeated within itself, always integrates into a perfect unity with itself is of greater worth than a nature which admits of plurality. For where there is plurality there is diversity; and where there is diversity there is not perfect harmony. Indeed, perfect harmony is that which integrates into a unified identify and identical unity. Therefore, if perfect harmony is better than imperfect harmony, and if it is impossible for anything imperfect to exist in the Supreme Good (which is eternity itself), then it is not possible for the nature of eternity to admit of plurality. Hence, however often eternity is repeated within eternity, it is always only one and the same eternity.

In a similar way, the foregoing remarks also apply to many other things. For example, omnipotence within omnipotence is only one omnipotence. Or to cite one of those things which do not have a divine nature but in which the case is similar: a point within a point is only one point. For a point (such as the middle point of the world or a point of time, e.g., the present moment) has some similarity to eternity and is of no small use for the investigation of eternity. This issue must be discussed more fully elsewhere. Here let it suffice [to note] only that, like eternity, a point is simple (i.e., without parts) and indivisible; and so a point together with a point, without an interval, is only one point—just as eternity together with eternity is only one eternity.

Therefore, since God is eternity, there is no plurality of gods; for God is not external to God, nor does God within God add numerically to God. Thus, there is always and only one and the same God. Hence, when God is begotten of God, then since what is begotten is not outside of that from which it is begotten, the offspring is in the parent and the parent in the offspring, i.e., there is one God, who is Father and Son. And when God proceeds from God, who is Father and Son, and does not go outside of God, God (i.e., God the Holy Spirit) remains in God from whom He proceeds; and there is one God, who is Father, Son, and Holy Spirit. And since this begottenness and this procession do not have a beginning—Were it otherwise, then an eternity which is begotten and an eternity which proceeds would have a beginning (a consequence which is false)—we absolutely ought not, and absolutely cannot, think that God ever began to be the Father, the Son, or the Holy Spirit.

16

However, just as the divine substance preserves its eternal and singular unity, so the nature of these relations (viz., of the Father and of the Son; of the one proceeding and of Him from whom He proceeds) retains its inseparable plurality. For just as it is necessary that God always be one and the same rather than many, so with respect to these relations the Father is never identical with His Son, and He who proceeds is never identical with Him from whom He proceeds. Rather, the Father is always different from the Son, and He who proceeds is always different from Him from whom He proceeds; and no one of the three can ever be called by either of the others' names. Therefore, when God is begotten of God or when God proceeds from God, the substance cannot lose its singularity nor the relations their plurality. For this reason, in God the one thing is three things and the three things are one thing, and yet the three are not called by one another's respective name. Now, in a Nature which is above all other things and is unlike all other things, it ought not to be preposterous that there is something of which an example cannot perfectly be found in other things. Now, the Latins call these three things *persons,* whereas the Greeks call them *substances.* For just as we say that in God one substance is three persons, so they say that one person is three substances. By the word "substance" they signify in God exactly what we signify by the word "person"; and they are not at all at variance with us in faith.

As for how the Son is begotten of the Father, and how the Holy Spirit proceeds from the Father and the Son without being a son: since in this life we cannot behold [this truth] "as it is," Blessed Augustine, "as through a glass, darkly," has studied [the matter] carefully in his book *On the Trinity;* and to the best of my ability I also have discussed [it] in my *Monologion,* which I alluded to earlier. Now, if anyone wants to know why, although there is no sexual distinction in the Supreme Being, the parent in the Supreme Being is called father rather than mother, or the offspring called son rather than daughter, or why only the Father is called unbegotten, only the Son called begotten, and only the Holy Spirit called neither begotten nor unbegotten, then he will find [the answers] clearly [stated] in this same small book of mine.

DISCUSSION QUESTIONS

1. Anselm speaks of Jesus as one and the same individual who is human in nature and also divine in nature. Can you think of any other individual thing that could be argued to have two different natures?
2. How adequate is Anselm's analogy of the Nile as the spring, the river, and the lake to God as a trinity of persons? Explain. How much weight does Anselm himself put on this analogy?
3. Anselm concludes that since God's nature is above and unlike all other things, it is not preposterous that no perfect example of a trinitarian nature can be found elsewhere. Is this a satisfactory defense of the Trinity? Explain.

Chapter

ST. THOMAS AQUINAS

Born in Roccasecca, Italy around 1225, Aquinas joined the Dominican order in 1244 and studied under Albert the Great for four years in Cologne, where he entered the priesthood. He lectured in Paris until he was granted the full privileges of master of theology in 1257. Aquinas' philosophy and theology are strongly inspired by Aristotle, "the Philosopher." Aquinas defended his speculative theology against those more skeptical about the value of Aristotelian thought in theology and against radical Aristotelians. A large man and powerful thinker blessed with a tremendous memory, Saint Thomas was called "the dumb ox" by his enemies. He produced a prodigious body of writings before his death in 1274, and was canonized by John XXII in 1323.

In Questions 29 and 30 Aquinas discusses the definition, number, and relations of the divine persons of God. He invokes Aristotle's understanding of substance and nature to defend Boethius' definition of "person" and to distinguish its signification from that of "hypostasis," "subsistence," and "essence." Aquinas reasons: (1) "Person" signifies what is most perfect in all nature, namely, a subsistent individual of a rational nature. (2) Everything that is perfect must be attributed to God. (3) Ergo, God is personal. In fact, Aquinas contends that God is exactly three persons constituted by three really distinct relations subsisting in the divine nature: the Father (paternity), the Son (filiation), and the Holy Ghost (procession).

Summa Theologiae (1st Part, QQ. 29–30)

QUESTION 29: THE DIVINE PERSONS

FOUR ARTICLES

Having premised what have appeared necessary notions concerning the processions and the relations, we must now approach the subject of the persons.

First, we shall consider the persons absolutely, and then comparatively as regards each other. We must consider the persons absolutely first in common; and then singly.

The general consideration of the persons seemingly involves four points: (1) The signification of this word "person"; (2) the number of the persons; (3) what is involved in the number of persons, or is opposed thereto, as diversity, and similitude, and the like, and (4) what belongs to our knowledge of the persons.

Four subjects of inquiry are contained in the first point:

1. The definition of "person."
2. The comparison of person to essence, subsistence, and hypostasis.
3. Whether the name of person is becoming to God?
4. What does it signify in Him?

The definition of "person"

Objection 1: It would seem that the definition of person given by Boethius (*De Duab. Nat.*) is insufficient—that is, "a person is an individual substance of a rational nature." For nothing singular can be subject to definition. But "person" signifies something singular. Therefore person is improperly defined.

Objection 2: Further, substance as placed above in the definition of person, is either first substance, or second substance. If it is the former, the word "individual" is superfluous, because first substance is individual substance; if it stands for second substance, the word "individual" is false, for there is contradiction of terms; since second substances are the "genera" or "species." Therefore this definition is incorrect.

Objection 3: Further, an intentional term must not be included in the definition of a thing. For to define a man as "a species of animal" would not be a correct definition; since man is the name of a thing, and "species" is a name of an intention. Therefore, since person is the name of a thing (for it signifies a substance of a rational nature), the

---

Source: Reproduced from Benziger Bros. 1947 edition translated by Fathers of the English Dominican Province (public domain) http://www.ccel.org/a/aquinas/summa/cache/summa.html3

word "individual" which is an intentional name comes improperly into the definition.

Objection 4: Further, "Nature is the principle of motion and rest, in those things in which it is essentially, and not accidentally," as Aristotle says (*Phys.* ii). But person exists in things immovable, as in God, and in the angels. Therefore the word "nature" ought not to enter into the definition of person, but the word should rather be "essence."

Objection 5: Further, the separated soul is an individual substance of the rational nature; but it is not a person. Therefore person is not properly defined as above.

I answer that, Although the universal and particular exist in every genus, nevertheless, in a certain special way, the individual belongs to the genus of substance. For substance is individualized by itself; whereas the accidents are individualized by the subject, which is the substance; since this particular whiteness is called "this," because it exists in this particular subject. And so it is reasonable that the individuals of the genus substance should have a special name of their own; for they are called "hypostases," or first substances.

Further still, in a more special and perfect way, the particular and the individual are found in the rational substances which have dominion over their own actions; and which are not only made to act, like others; but which can act of themselves; for actions belong to singulars. Therefore also the individuals of the rational nature have a special name even among other substances; and this name is "person."

Thus the term "individual substance" is placed in the definition of person, as signifying the singular in the genus of substance; and the term "rational nature" is added, as signifying the singular in rational substances.

Reply to Objection 1: Although this or that singular may not be definable, yet what belongs to the general idea of singularity can be defined; and so the Philosopher* (*De Praedic., cap. De substantia*) gives a definition of first substance; and in this way Boethius defines person.

Reply to Objection 2: In the opinion of some, the term "substance" in the definition of person stands for first substance, which is the hypostasis; nor is the term "individual" superfluously added, forasmuch as by the name of hypostasis or first substance the idea of universality and of part is excluded. For we do not say that man in general is an hypostasis, nor that the hand is since it is only a part. But where "individual" is added, the idea of assumptibility is excluded from person; for the human nature in Christ is not a person, since it is assumed by a greater—that is, by the Word of God. It is, however, better to say that substance is here taken in a general sense, as divided into first and second, and when "individual" is added, it is restricted to first substance.

Reply to Objection 3: Substantial differences being unknown to us, or at least unnamed by us, it is sometimes necessary to use accidental differences in the place of substantial; as, for example, we may say that fire is a simple, hot, and dry body: for proper accidents are the effects of substantial forms, and make them known. Likewise, terms expressive of intention can be used in defining realities if used to signify things which are unnamed. And so the term "individual" is placed in the definition of person to signify the mode of subsistence which belongs to particular substances.

Reply to Objection 4: According to the Philosopher (*Metaph.* v, 5), the word "nature" was first used to signify the generation of living things, which is called nativity. And because this kind of generation comes from an intrinsic principle, this term is extended to signify the intrinsic principle of any kind of movement. In this sense he defines "nature" (*Phys.* ii, 3). And since this kind of principle is either formal or material, both matter and

*Aristotle.

form are commonly called nature. And as the essence of anything is completed by the form; so the essence of anything, signified by the definition, is commonly called nature. And here nature is taken in that sense. Hence Boethius says (*De Duab. Nat.*) that, "nature is the specific difference giving its form to each thing," for the specific difference completes the definition, and is derived from the special form of a thing. So in the definition of "person," which means the singular in a determined "genus," it is more correct to use the term "nature" than "essence," because the latter is taken from being, which is most common.

Reply to Objection 5: The soul is a part of the human species; and so, although it may exist in a separate state, yet since it ever retains its nature of unibility, it cannot be called an individual substance, which is the hypostasis or first substance, as neither can the hand nor any other part of man; thus neither the definition nor the name of person belongs to it.

Whether "person" is the same as hypostasis, subsistence, and essence?

Objection 1: It would seem that "person" is the same as "hypostasis," "subsistence," and "essence." For Boethius says (*De Duab. Nat.*) that "the Greeks called the individual substance of the rational nature by the name hypostasis." But this with us signifies "person." Therefore "person" is altogether the same as "hypostasis."

Objection 2: Further, as we say there are three persons in God, so we say there are three subsistences in God; which implies that "person" and "subsistence" have the same meaning. Therefore "person" and "subsistence" mean the same.

Objection 3: Further, Boethius says (*Com. Praed.*) that the Greek {ουσία}, which means essence, signifies a being composed of matter and form. Now that which is composed of matter and form is the individual substance called "hypostasis" and "person." Therefore all the aforesaid names seem to have the same meaning.

Objection 4: On the contrary, Boethius says (*De Duab. Nat.*) that genera and species only subsist; whereas individuals are not only subsistent, but also substand. But subsistences are so called from subsisting, as substance or hypostasis is so called from substanding. Therefore, since genera and species are not hypostases or persons, these are not the same as subsistences.

Objection 5: Further, Boethius says (*Com. Praed.*) that matter is called hypostasis, and form is called {οὐσιώσις}—that is, subsistence. But neither form nor matter can be called person. Therefore person differs from the others.

I answer that, According to the Philosopher (*Metaph.* v), substance is twofold. In one sense it means the quiddity of a thing, signified by its definition, and thus we say that the definition means the substance of a thing; in which sense substance is called by the Greeks {ουσία}, what we may call "essence." In another sense substance means a subject or "suppositum," which subsists in the genus of substance. To this, taken in a general sense, can be applied a name expressive of an intention; and thus it is called "suppositum." It is also called by three names signifying a reality—that is, "a thing of nature," "subsistence," and "hypostasis," according to a threefold consideration of the substance thus named. For, as it exists in itself and not in another, it is called "subsistence"; as we say that those things subsist which exist in themselves, and not in another. As it underlies some common nature, it is called "a thing of nature"; as, for instance, this particular man is a human natural thing. As it underlies the accidents, it is called "hypostasis," or "substance." What these three names signify in common to the whole genus of substances, this name "person" signifies in the genus of rational substances.

Reply to Objection 1: Among the Greeks the term "hypostasis," taken in the strict interpretation of the word, signifies any individual of the genus substance; but in the usual way of speaking, it means the individual of the rational nature, by reason of the excellence of that nature.

Reply to Objection 2: As we say "three persons" plurally in God, and "three subsistences," so the Greeks say "three hypostases." But because the word "substance," which, properly speaking, corresponds in meaning to "hypostasis," is used among us in an equivocal sense, since it sometimes means essence, and sometimes means hypostasis, in order to avoid any occasion of error, it was thought preferable to use "subsistence" for hypostasis, rather than "substance."

Reply to Objection 3: Strictly speaking, the essence is what is expressed by the definition. Now, the definition comprises the principles of the species, but not the individual principles. Hence in things composed of matter and form, the essence signifies not only the form, nor only the matter, but what is composed of matter and the common form, as the principles of the species. But what is composed of this matter and this form has the nature of hypostasis and person. For soul, flesh, and bone belong to the nature of man; whereas this soul, this flesh and this bone belong to the nature of this man. Therefore hypostasis and person add the individual principles to the idea of essence; nor are these identified with the essence in things composed of matter and form, as we said above when treating of divine simplicity.

Reply to Objection 4: Boethius says that genera and species subsist, inasmuch as it belongs to some individual things to subsist, from the fact that they belong to genera and species comprised in the predicament of substance, but not because the species and genera themselves subsist; except in the opinion of Plato, who asserted that the species of things subsisted separately from singular things. To substand, however, belongs to the same individual things in relation to the accidents, which are outside the essence of genera and species.

Reply to Objection 5: The individual composed of matter and form substands in relation to accident from the very nature of matter. Hence Boethius says (*De Trin.*): "A simple form cannot be a subject." Its self-subsistence is derived from the nature of its form, which does not supervene to the things subsisting, but gives actual existence to the matter and makes it subsist as an individual. On this account, therefore, he ascribes hypostasis to matter, and {οὐσιώσις}, or subsistence, to the form, because the matter is the principle of substanding, and form is the principle of subsisting.

WHETHER THE WORD "PERSON" SHOULD BE SAID OF GOD?

Objection 1: It would seem that the name "person" should not be said of God. For Dionysius says (*Div. Nom.*): "No one should ever dare to say or think anything of the supersubstantial and hidden Divinity, beyond what has been divinely expressed to us by the oracles." But the name "person" is not expressed to us in the Old or New Testament. Therefore "person" is not to be applied to God.

Objection 2: Further, Boethius says (*De Duab. Nat.*): "The word person seems to be taken from those persons who represented men in comedies and tragedies. For person comes from sounding through [*personando*], since a greater volume of sound is produced through the cavity in the mask. These "persons" or masks the Greeks called {πρόσωπα}, as they were placed on the face and covered the features before the eyes." This, however, can apply to God only in a metaphorical sense. Therefore the word "person" is only applied to God metaphorically.

Objection 3: Further, every person is a hypostasis. But the word "hypostasis" does not apply to God, since, as Boethius says (*De Duab. Nat.*), it signifies what is the subject of accidents, which do not exist in God. Jerome also says (*Ep. ad Damas.*) that, "in this word hypostasis, poison lurks in honey." Therefore the word "person" should not be said of God.

Objection 4: Further, if a definition is denied of anything, the thing defined is also denied of it. But the definition of "person," as given above, does not apply to God. Both because reason implies a discursive knowledge, which does not apply to God, as we proved above; and thus God cannot be said to have "a rational nature." And also because God cannot be called an individual substance, since the principle of individuation is matter; while God is immaterial: nor is He the subject of accidents, so as to be called a substance. Therefore the word "person" ought not to be attributed to God.

On the contrary, In the Creed of Athanasius we say: "One is the person of the Father, another of the Son, another of the Holy Ghost."

I answer that, "Person" signifies what is most perfect in all nature—that is, a subsistent individual of a rational nature. Hence, since everything that is perfect must be attributed to God, forasmuch as His essence contains every perfection, this name "person" is fittingly applied to God; not, however, as it is applied to creatures, but in a more excellent way; as other names also, which, while giving them to creatures, we attribute to God; as we showed above when treating of the names of God.

Reply to Objection 1: Although the word "person" is not found applied to God in Scripture, either in the Old or New Testament, nevertheless what the word signifies is found to be affirmed of God in many places of Scripture; as that He is the supreme self-subsisting being, and the most perfectly intelligent being. If we could speak of God only in the very terms themselves of Scripture, it would follow that no one could speak about God in any but the original language of the Old or New Testament. The urgency of confuting heretics made it necessary to find new words to express the ancient faith about God. Nor is such a kind of novelty to be shunned; since it is by no means profane, for it does not lead us astray from the sense of Scripture. The Apostle warns us to avoid "profane novelties of words" (1 *Tim.* 6:20).

Reply to Objection 2: Although this name "person" may not belong to God as regards the origin of the term, nevertheless it excellently belongs to God in its objective meaning. For as famous men were represented in comedies and tragedies, the name "person" was given to signify those who held high dignity. Hence, those who held high rank in the Church came to be called "persons." Thence by some the definition of person is given as "hypostasis distinct by reason of dignity." And because subsistence in a rational nature is of high dignity, therefore every individual of the rational nature is called a "person." Now the dignity of the divine nature excels every other dignity; and thus the name "person" pre-eminently belongs to God.

Reply to Objection 3: The word "hypostasis" does not apply to God as regards its source of origin, since He does not underlie accidents; but it applies to Him in its objective sense, for it is imposed to signify the subsistence. Jerome said that "poison lurks in this word," forasmuch as before it was fully understood by the Latins, the heretics used this term to deceive the simple, to make people profess many essences as they profess several hypostases, inasmuch as the word "substance," which corresponds to hypostasis in Greek, is commonly taken amongst us to mean essence.

Reply to Objection 4: It may be said that God has a rational "nature," if reason be taken to mean, not discursive thought, but in a general sense, an intelligent nature. But God cannot be called an "individual" in the sense that His individuality comes from matter; but only in the sense which implies incommunicability. "Substance" can be applied to God in the sense of signifying self-subsistence. There are some, however, who say that the definition of Boethius, quoted above, is not a definition of person in the sense we use when speaking of persons in God. Therefore Richard of St. Victor amends this definition by adding that

"Person" in God is "the incommunicable existence of the divine nature."

Whether this word "person" signifies relation?

Objection 1: It would seem that this word "person," as applied to God, does not signify relation, but substance. For Augustine says (*De Trin.* vii, 6): "When we speak of the person of the Father, we mean nothing else but the substance of the Father, for person is said in regard to Himself, and not in regard to the Son."

Objection 2: Further, the interrogation "What?" refers to essence. But, as Augustine says: "When we say there are three who bear witness in heaven, the Father, the Word, and the Holy Ghost, and it is asked, Three what? the answer is, Three persons." Therefore person signifies essence.

Objection 3: According to the Philosopher (*Metaph.* iv), the meaning of a word is its definition. But the definition of "person" is this: "The individual substance of the rational nature," as above stated. Therefore "person" signifies substance.

Objection 4: Further, person in men and angels does not signify relation, but something absolute. Therefore, if in God it signified relation, it would bear an equivocal meaning in God, in man, and in angels.

On the contrary, Boethius says (*De Trin.*) that "every word that refers to the persons signifies relation." But no word belongs to person more strictly than the very word "person" itself. Therefore this word "person" signifies relation.

I answer that, A difficulty arises concerning the meaning of this word "person" in God, from the fact that it is predicated plurally of the Three in contrast to the nature of the names belonging to the essence; nor does it in itself refer to another, as do the words which express relation.

Hence some have thought that this word "person" of itself expresses absolutely the divine essence; as this name "God" and this word "Wise"; but that to meet heretical attack, it was ordained by conciliar decree that it was to be taken in a relative sense, and especially in the plural, or with the addition of a distinguishing adjective; as when we say, "Three persons," or, "one is the person of the Father, another of the Son," etc. Used, however, in the singular, it may be either absolute or relative. But this does not seem to be a satisfactory explanation; for, if this word "person," by force of its own signification, expresses the divine essence only, it follows that forasmuch as we speak of "three persons," so far from the heretics being silenced, they had still more reason to argue. Seeing this, others maintained that this word "person" in God signifies both the essence and the relation. Some of these said that it signifies directly the essence, and relation indirectly, forasmuch as "person" means as it were "by itself one" [*per se una*]; and unity belongs to the essence. And what is "by itself" implies relation indirectly; for the Father is understood to exist "by Himself," as relatively distinct from the Son. Others, however, said, on the contrary, that it signifies relation directly; and essence indirectly; forasmuch as in the definition of "person" the term nature is mentioned indirectly; and these come nearer to the truth.

To determine the question, we must consider that something may be included in the meaning of a less common term, which is not included in the more common term; as "rational" is included in the meaning of "man," and not in the meaning of "animal." So that it is one thing to ask the meaning of the word animal, and another to ask its meaning when the animal in question is man. Also, it is one thing to ask the meaning of this word "person" in general; and another to ask the meaning of "person" as applied to God. For "person" in general signifies the individual substance of a rational figure. The individual in itself is undivided, but is distinct from others. Therefore "person" in any nature signifies what is distinct in that nature: thus in human nature it signifies this flesh, these bones, and this soul, which are the individuating principles of a man, and which, though not belonging to "person" in general, nevertheless do belong to the meaning of a particular human person.

Now distinction in God is only by relation of origin, as stated above, while relation in God is not as an accident in a subject, but is the divine essence itself; and so it is subsistent, for the divine essence subsists. Therefore, as the Godhead is God so the divine paternity is God the Father, Who is a divine person. Therefore a divine person signifies a relation as subsisting. And this is to signify relation by way of substance, and such a relation is a hypostasis subsisting in the divine nature, although in truth that which subsists in the divine nature is the divine nature itself. Thus it is true to say that the name "person" signifies relation directly, and the essence indirectly; not, however, the relation as such, but as expressed by way of a hypostasis. So likewise it signifies directly the essence, and indirectly the relation, inasmuch as the essence is the same as the hypostasis: while in God the hypostasis is expressed as distinct by the relation: and thus relation, as such, enters into the notion of the person indirectly. Thus we can say that this signification of the word "person" was not clearly perceived before it was attacked by heretics. Hence, this word "person" was used just as any other absolute term. But afterwards it was applied to express relation, as it lent itself to that signification, so that this word "person" means relation not only by use and custom, according to the first opinion, but also by force of its own proper signification.

Reply to Objection 1: This word "person" is said in respect to itself, not to another; forasmuch as it signifies relation not as such, but by way of a substance—which is a hypostasis. In that sense Augustine says that it signifies the essence, inasmuch as in God essence is the same as the hypostasis, because in God what He is, and whereby He is are the same.

Reply to Objection 2: The term "what" refers sometimes to the nature expressed by the definition, as when we ask; What is man? and we answer: A mortal rational animal. Sometimes it refers to the "suppositum," as when we ask, What swims in the sea? and answer, A fish. So to those who ask, Three what? we answer, Three persons.

Reply to Objection 3: In God the individual—i.e. distinct and incommunicable substance—includes the idea of relation, as above explained.

Reply to Objection 4: The different sense of the less common term does not produce equivocation in the more common. Although a horse and an ass have their own proper definitions, nevertheless they agree univocally in animal, because the common definition of animal applies to both. So it does not follow that, although relation is contained in the signification of divine person, but not in that of an angelic or of a human person, the word "person" is used in an equivocal sense. Though neither is it applied univocally, since nothing can be said univocally of God and creatures.

QUESTION 30: THE PLURALITY OF PERSONS IN GOD

FOUR ARTICLES

We are now led to consider the plurality of the persons: about which there are four points of inquiry:

1. Whether there are several persons in God?
2. How many are they?
3. What the numeral terms signify in God?
4. The community of the term "person."

Whether there are several persons in God?

Objection 1: It would seem that there are not several persons in God. For person is "the individual substance of a rational nature." If then there are several persons in God, there must be several substances; which appears to be heretical.

Objection 2: Further, Plurality of absolute properties does not make a distinction of persons, either in God, or in ourselves. Much less therefore is this effected by a plurality of relations. But in God there is no plurality but of relations. Therefore there cannot be several persons in God.

Objection 3: Further, Boethius says of God (*De Trin.* i), that "this is truly one which has no number." But plurality implies number. Therefore there are not several persons in God.

Objection 4: Further, where number is, there is whole and part. Thus, if in God there exist a number of persons, there must be whole and part in God; which is inconsistent with the divine simplicity.

On the contrary, Athanasius says: "One is the person of the Father, another of the Son, another of the Holy Ghost." Therefore the Father, and the Son, and the Holy Ghost are several persons.

I answer that, It follows from what precedes that there are several persons in God. For it was shown above (Q29, A4) that this word "person" signifies in God a relation as subsisting in the divine nature. It was also established that there are several real relations in God; and hence it follows that there are also several realities subsistent in the divine nature; which means that there are several persons in God.

Reply to Objection 1: The definition of "person" includes "substance," not as meaning the essence, but the "suppositum" which is made clear by the addition of the term "individual." To signify the substance thus understood, the Greeks use the name "hypostasis." So, as we say, "Three persons," they say "Three hypostases." We are not, however, accustomed to say Three substances, lest we be understood to mean three essences or natures, by reason of the equivocal signification of the term.

Reply to Objection 2: The absolute properties in God, such as goodness and wisdom, are not mutually opposed; and hence, neither are they really distinguished from each other. Therefore, although they subsist, nevertheless they are not several subsistent realities—that is, several persons. But the absolute properties in creatures do not subsist, although they are really distinguished from each other, as whiteness and sweetness; on the other hand, the relative properties in God subsist, and are really distinguished from each other. Hence there is the plurality of persons in God.

Reply to Objection 3: The supreme unity and simplicity of God exclude every kind of plurality of absolute things, but not plurality of relations. Because relations are predicated relatively, and thus the relations do not import composition in that of which they are predicated, as Boethius teaches in the same book.

Reply to Objection 4: Number is twofold, simple or absolute, as two and three and four; and number as existing in things numbered, as two men and two horses. So, if number in God is taken absolutely or abstractedly, there is nothing to prevent whole and part from being in Him, and thus number in Him is only in our way of understanding; forasmuch as number regarded apart from things numbered exists only in the intellect. But if number be taken as it is in the things numbered, in that sense as existing in creatures, one is part of two, and two of three, as one man is part of two men, and two of three; but this does not apply to God, because the Father is of the same magnitude as the whole Trinity, as we shall show further on.

Whether there are more than three persons in God?

Objection 1: It would seem that there are more than three persons in God. For the plurality of persons in God arises from the plurality of the relative properties as stated above. But there are four relations in God as stated above, paternity, filiation, common spiration, and procession. Therefore there are four persons in God.

Objection 2: The nature of God does not differ from His will more than from His intellect. But in God, one person proceeds from the will, as love; and another proceeds from His nature, as Son. Therefore another proceeds from His intellect, as Word, besides the one Who proceeds from His nature, as Son; thus again it follows that there are not only three persons in God.

Objection 3: Further, the more perfect a creature is, the more interior operations it has; as a man has understanding and will beyond other animals. But God infinitely excels every creature. Therefore in God not only is there a person proceeding from the will, and another from the intellect, but also in an infinite number of ways. Therefore there are an infinite number of persons in God.

Objection 4: Further, it is from the infinite goodness of the Father that He communicates Himself infinitely in the production of a divine person. But also in the Holy Ghost is infinite goodness. Therefore the Holy Ghost produces a divine person; and that person another; and so to infinity.

Objection 5: Further, everything within a determinate number is measured, for number is a measure. But the divine persons are immense, as we say in the Creed of Athanasius: "The Father is immense, the Son is immense, the Holy Ghost is immense." Therefore the persons are not contained within the number three.

On the contrary, It is said: "There are three who bear witness in heaven, the father, the Word, and the Holy Ghost" (1 *Jn.* 5:7). To those who ask, "Three what?" we answer, with Augustine (*De Trin.* vii, 4), "Three persons." Therefore there are but three persons in God.

I answer that, As was explained above, there can be only three persons in God. For it was shown above that the several persons are the several subsisting relations really distinct from each other. But a real distinction between the divine relations can come only from relative opposition. Therefore two opposite relations must needs refer to two persons: and if any relations are not opposite they must needs belong to the same person. Since then paternity and filiation are opposite relations, they belong necessarily to two persons. Therefore the subsisting paternity is the person of the Father; and the subsisting filiation is the person of the Son. The other two relations are not opposed to each other; therefore these two cannot belong to one person: hence either one of them must belong to both of the aforesaid persons; or one must belong to one person, and the other to the other. Now, procession cannot belong to the Father and the Son, or to either of them; for thus it would follows that the procession of the intellect, which in God is generation, wherefrom paternity and filiation are derived, would issue from the procession of love, whence spiration and procession are derived, if the person generating and the person generated proceeded from the person spirating; and this is against what was laid down above. We must frequently admit that spiration belongs to the person of the Father, and to the person of the Son, forasmuch as it has no relative opposition either to paternity or to filiation; and consequently that procession belongs to the other person who is called the person of the Holy Ghost, who proceeds by way of love, as above explained. Therefore only three persons exist in God, the Father, the Son, and the Holy Ghost.

Reply to Objection 1: Although there are four relations in God, one of them, spiration, is not separated from the person of the Father and of the Son, but belongs to both; thus, although it is a relation, it is not called a property, because it does not belong to only one person; nor is it a personal relation—i.e. constituting a person. The three relations—paternity, filiation, and procession—are called personal properties, constituting as it were the persons; for paternity is the person of the Father, filiation is the person of the Son, procession is the person of the Holy Ghost proceeding.

Reply to Objection 2: That which proceeds by way of intelligence, as word, proceeds according to similitude, as also that which proceeds by way of nature; thus, as above explained, the procession of the divine Word is the very same as generation by way of nature. But love, as such, does not proceed as the similitude of that whence it proceeds; although in God love is co-essential as being divine; and therefore the procession of love is not called generation in God.

Reply to Objection 3: As man is more perfect than other animals, he has more intrinsic operations than other animals, because his perfection is something composite. Hence the angels, who are more perfect and more simple, have fewer intrinsic operations than man, for they have no imagination, or feeling, or the like. In God there exists only one real operation—that is, His essence. How there are in Him two processions was above explained.

Reply to Objection 4: This argument would prove if the Holy Ghost possessed another goodness apart from the goodness of the Father; for then if the Father produced a divine person by His goodness, the Holy Ghost also would do so. But the Father and the Holy Ghost have one and the same goodness. Nor is there any distinction between them except by the personal relations. So goodness belongs to the Holy Ghost, as derived from another; and it belongs to the Father, as the principle of its communication to another. The opposition of relation does not allow the relation of the Holy Ghost to be joined with the relation of principle of another divine person; because He Himself proceeds from the other persons who are in God.

Reply to Objection 5: A determinate number, if taken as a simple number, existing in the mind only, is measured by one. But when we speak of a number of things as applied to the persons in God, the notion of measure has no place, because the magnitude of the three persons is the same, and the same is not measured by the same.

Whether the numeral terms denote anything real in God?

Objection 1: It would seem that the numeral terms denote something real in God. For the divine unity is the divine essence. But every number is unity repeated. Therefore every numeral term in God signifies the essence; and therefore it denotes something real in God.

Objection 2: Further, whatever is said of God and of creatures belongs to God in a more eminent manner than to creatures. But the numeral terms denote something real in creatures; therefore much more so in God.

Objection 3: Further, if the numeral terms do not denote anything real in God, and are introduced simply in a negative and removing sense, as plurality is employed to remove unity and unity to remove plurality; it follows that a vicious circle results, confusing the mind and obscuring the truth; and this ought not to be. Therefore it must be said that the numeral terms denote something real in God.

On the contrary, Hilary says (*De Trin.* iv): "If we admit companionship"—that is, plurality—"we exclude the idea of oneness and of solitude;" and Ambrose says (*De Fide* i): "When we say one God, unity excludes plurality of gods, and does not imply quantity in God." Hence we see that these terms are applied to God in order to remove something; and not to denote anything positive.

I answer that, The Master* (*Sent.* i, D, 24) considers that the numeral terms do not denote

*Peter Lombard.

anything positive in God, but have only a negative meaning. Others, however, assert the contrary.

In order to resolve this point, we may observe that all plurality is a consequence of division. Now division is twofold; one is material, and is division of the continuous; from this results number, which is a species of quantity. Number in this sense is found only in material things which have quantity. The other kind of division is called formal, and is effected by opposite or diverse forms; and this kind of division results in a multitude, which does not belong to a genus, but is transcendental in the sense in which being is divided by one and by many. This kind of multitude is found only in immaterial things.

Some, considering only that multitude which is a species of discrete quantity, and seeing that such kind of quantity has no place in God, asserted that the numeral terms do not denote anything real in God, but remove something from Him. Others, considering the same kind of multitude, said that as knowledge exists in God according to the strict sense of the word, but not in the sense of its genus (as in God there is no such thing as a quality), so number exists in God in the proper sense of number, but not in the sense of its genus, which is quantity.

But we say that numeral terms predicated of God are not derived from number, a species of quantity, for in that sense they could bear only a metaphorical sense in God, like other corporeal properties, such as length, breadth, and the like; but that they are taken from multitude in a transcendent sense. Now multitude so understood has relation to the many of which it is predicated, as "one" convertible with "being" is related to being; which kind of oneness does not add anything to being, except a negation of division, as we saw when treating of the divine unity; for "one" signifies undivided being. So, of whatever we say "one," we imply its undivided reality: thus, for instance, "one" applied to man signifies the undivided nature or substance of a man. In the same way, when we speak of many things, multitude in this latter sense points to those things as being each undivided in itself.

But number, if taken as a species of quantity, denotes an accident added to being; as also does "one" which is the principle of that number. Therefore the numeral terms in God signify the things of which they are said, and beyond this they add negation only, as stated (*Sent.* i, D, 24); in which respect the Master was right (*Sent.* i, D, 24). So when we say, the essence is one, the term "one" signifies the essence undivided; and when we say the person is one, it signifies the person undivided; and when we say the persons are many, we signify those persons, and their individual undividedness; for it is of the very nature of multitude that it should be composed of units.

Reply to Objection 1: One, as it is a transcendental, is wider and more general than substance and relation. And so likewise is multitude; hence in God it may mean both substance and relation, according to the context. Still, the very signification of such names adds a negation of division, beyond substance and relation; as was explained above.

Reply to Objection 2: Multitude, which denotes something real in creatures, is a species of quantity, and cannot be used when speaking of God: unlike transcendental multitude, which adds only indivision to those of which it is predicated. Such a kind of multitude is applicable to God.

Reply to Objection 3: "One" does not exclude multitude, but division, which logically precedes one or multitude. Multitude does not remove unity, but division from each of the individuals which compose the multitude. This was explained when we treated of the divine unity.

It must be observed, nevertheless, that the opposite arguments do not sufficiently prove the point advanced. Although the idea of solitude is excluded by plurality, and the plurality of gods by unity, it does not follow that these terms express this signification alone. For blackness is excluded by whiteness; nevertheless, the term whiteness does not signify the mere exclusion of blackness.

Whether this term "person" can be common to the three persons?

Objection 1: It would seem that this term "person" cannot be common to the three persons. For nothing is common to the three persons but the essence. But this term "person" does not signify the essence directly. Therefore it is not common to all three.

Objection 2: Further, the common is the opposite of the incommunicable. But the very meaning of person is that it is incommunicable; as appears from the definition given by Richard of St. Victor (Q29, A3, ad 4). Therefore this term "person" is not common to all the three persons.

Objection 3: Further, if the name "person" is common to the three, it is common either really, or logically. But it is not so really; otherwise the three persons would be one person; nor again is it so logically; otherwise person would be a universal. But in God there is neither universal nor particular, neither genus nor species, as we proved above. Therefore this term "person" is not common to the three.

On the contrary, Augustine says (*De Trin.* vii, 4) that when we ask, "Three what?" we say, "Three persons," because what a person is, is common to them.

I answer that, The very mode of expression itself shows that this term "person" is common to the three when we say "three persons"; for when we say "three men" we show that "man" is common to the three. Now it is clear that this is not community of a real thing, as if one essence were common to the three; otherwise there would be only one person of the three, as also one essence.

What is meant by such a community has been variously determined by those who have examined the subject. Some have called it a community of exclusion, forasmuch as the definition of "person" contains the word "incommunicable." Others thought it to be a community of intention, as the definition of person contains the word "individual"; as we say that to be a "species" is common to horse and ox. Both of these explanations, however, are excluded by the fact that "person" is neither a name of exclusion nor of intention, but the name of a reality. We must therefore resolve that even in human affairs this name "person" is common by a community of idea, not as genus or species, but as a vague individual thing. The names of genera and species, as man or animal, are given to signify the common natures themselves, but not the intentions of those common natures, signified by the terms "genus" or "species." The vague individual thing, as "some man," signifies the common nature with the determinate mode of existence of singular things—that is, something self-subsisting, as distinct from others. But the name of a designated singular thing signifies that which distinguishes the determinate thing; as the name Socrates signifies this flesh and this bone. But there is this difference—that the term "some man" signifies the nature, or the individual on the part of its nature, with the mode of existence of singular things; while this name "person" is not given to signify the individual on the part of the nature, but the subsistent reality in that nature. Now this is common in idea to the divine persons, that each of them subsists distinctly from the others in the divine nature. Thus this name "person" is common in idea to the three divine persons.

Reply to Objection 1: This argument is founded on a real community.

Reply to Objection 2: Although person is incommunicable, yet the mode itself of incommunicable existence can be common to many.

Reply to Objection 3: Although this community is logical and not real, yet it does not follow that in God there is universal or particular, or genus, or species; both because neither in human affairs is the community of person the same as community of genus or species; and because the divine persons have one being; whereas genus and species and every other universal are predicated of many which differ in being.

DISCUSSION QUESTIONS

1. Explain the five objections to Boethius' definition of "person."
2. How does Aquinas reply to the objection that "person" is not a term used in the Bible, and so should not be applied to God?
3. How does Aquinas reply to the objection that "person" (*persona* in Latin) derives from the Greek word for a dramatic mask (πρόσωπον), and so can only apply to God metaphorically?
4. According to Aquinas, how does "person" express relation?
5. Which does Aquinas think has more intrinsic operations, human beings or other animals? Human beings or angels? Angels or God? What reasons does Aquinas give for his claims? Are they persuasive?

Chapter 9

JOHN DUNS SCOTUS

Born around 1266 in the Scottish village of Duns, a few miles from the English border, Scotus earned the nickname "the subtle doctor" for his intricately nuanced philosophy. He entered the Franciscan order and was ordained at Northampton in 1291. Founder and leader of the Scotist School, he studied at Oxford and Paris, and possibly Cambridge, and became a master at Paris in 1305. He may have taught briefly at Cologne as well, where he died in 1308 and was buried in the monastery of the Minorites.

Most medieval philosophers hold that the persons of the Trinity are constituted by relations. While not rejecting this view, Scotus proposes a viable alternative. He suggests that the divine persons are constituted by something absolute. The selection below, "Are the Persons Constituted in Personal Being through Relations of Origin?" contains one of Scotus' presentations of that suggestion.

Ordinatio (I, d. 26, q. un.)

ARE THE PERSONS OF THE TRINITY CONSTITUTED IN PERSONAL BEING THROUGH RELATIONS OF ORIGIN?

An Untraditional View?

A third view maintains,[1] in contrast, that the Divine Persons are absolute. That this might not strike us as novel and foreign [to our tradition], I will adduce what's said by a certain Doctor of the past,[2] who distinguishes two ways in which something is said substantially. For he says: "As Richard of St. Victor says, there are two ways in which something is said substantially: (1) when it indicates a substance according to its common nature. It's in this way that "human being" is said substantially. (2) When it indicates a substance as a certain suppossit, for instance, "a certain human being." Speaking of the substance in the first way (that is, as equivalent to the quiddity) is saying *what* [sort of thing it is]. Speaking of the substance in the second way is saying some *one*.[3]

Accordingly, he says further that "the noun 'substance' or 'essence' (or 'quiddity') is said substantially because it indicates the common nature. In contrast, the noun 'person' is said substantially because it indicates a certain and distinct supposit. After all, the common nature is not multiplied—nor is it related. For this reason, what expresses a substance according to its common nature is said toward itself[4] so that it cannot in any way be said relationally. On the other hand, a supposit (or hypostasis) is of a nature to be multiplied and to be on a par with another, and therefore to be related. There is no reason why something said substantially in this way cannot be said relationally, in virtue of a relation added to it. This is what Richard of St. Victor means."

Moreover, that same Doctor, in the question "Do Proper Characteristics Distinguish the Persons?" answers that "they do not insofar as they are dispositions, but they do insofar as they are origins." This passage (although presumably he himself would not take it in this way) can be construed as follows: Origins distinguish the Persons not formally, but source-wise, so to speak, just as among creatures change—and especially if it were in the thing effecting the change and not the thing changed—would distinguish the terms of the change not in a formal way, but in an effective one. This belongs to the genus of efficient cause. For instance, even if human nature were found in a single human being and it could not be multiplied except through generation, it could be said that generation multiplies human beings—not *formally* (as if human beings could be formally distinguished by generations as such), but *effectively*, so to speak, because generation belongs to the genus of efficient cause. Likewise, we could say in the matter under discussion that the divine nature is shared among the supposits only by their origin, and so by their origin the Persons in that na-

---

ture are distinguished source-wise, in tracing back to that source that distinguishes them not formally, but in a way corresponding to what distinguishes effectively in the case of creatures.[5]

Therefore, in keeping with this line of thought, one might hold that absolute realities distinguish the Divine Persons and constitute them in personal being, and that the Persons who have issued forth are distinguished by their origins not formally, but source-wise, so to speak. However, it's not the case that these Person-constituters are absolute in the first way, but in the second, because even if there were not formally relations [among the Persons], the things they constitute would still be relatable. This is a view one might maintain.

PROOFS

Besides the four lines of argument treated in the section "Arguments Against the Second View,"[6] some further, persuasive arguments establish the resolution of this position.

First, primary substance is substance preeminently, according to the Philosopher in the *Categories,* and this is not characterized by imperfection. Therefore, it appears that one might in this way posit in the Godhead a primary substance (that is, a Person), to which subsisting (that is, existing through itself) preeminently belongs. But a relation does not appear capable of formally constituting anything subsistent and, therefore, not any primary substance.

Confirmation of this argument: A secondary substance expresses the whole essence of the primary substance. Therefore, in the primary substance there is no accompanying quiddity distinct from that of the secondary substance. Therefore, the quiddity of a relation, which is distinct from that of the essence, does not belong to the nature of the primary substance.

A further confirming argument: In the case of what is relative in the Godhead, if we must posit not just the quiddity, for instance, not just fatherhood but *this* fatherhood, and this qua unsharable, and if we must maintain that all these things belong to it insofar as it is relative and not insofar as it is formally what is towards itself—why can't it in like manner have unsharability not through what is formally relative, but in what is toward itself?

Finally, this argument is confirmed powerfully, it appears: Although among creatures it is an imperfection to be limited to a single subsistent or to a single most perfect being that is in no way determinable or contractible and cannot be a part of anything; even so, it is not an imperfection that the nature itself could have an ultimate being in keeping with which it is not naturally apt to be contracted by anything else (this, after all, we grant of substances but deny of accidents, due to their imperfection). Therefore, it appears that the divine nature, insofar as it is towards itself, will have from itself ultimate actual being and ultimate unity apart from limitation to the single being of a subsistent.

We might, then, offer an example. Suppose that, first, the intellectual soul completed or constituted the heart in the being of a supposit; and next, the heart thus enlivened by the soul could produce the hand in the being of the supposit. Any distinct things in the nature of the enlivened being would be distinct only through their origins, and yet formally they would be absolute things, one of which is produced by the other. Moreover, in them there would really be the relations of producer and produced; for positing absolute things that could be related clearly preserves relations better and not worse than not positing some such absolute things would.

Response in opposition to what was said about primary substance in this Question: In this case, a relation does have the power of constituting a primary substance or a supposit of secondary substance. A confirming argument: What are separated in the case of lower things are united in the case of higher things. Accordingly, even though subsisting and being towards each belongs to something different in the case of creatures, these can belong to God or the divine persons in virtue of the same thing.

Counterargument to this response: What power do you mean, I ask? The power of an efficient cause? or of a formal cause? If you mean the power of an efficient cause, it will, so to speak, cause in the Godhead an absolute reality that formally constitutes in it a primary substance. In that case, the point at issue—that a primary substance is constituted by an absolute reality—is granted. And once we are furnished with this [point], one further—an impossibility—is added: that a relation would be able to cause that absolute Person.

Suppose you mean the power to cause in the second way, formally. Since no form has the power of constituting anything formally unless it is the sort of thing that is naturally apt to be something through this sort of form (for instance, whiteness does not have the power of constituting anything except what's white and what is included in what's white), it follows that a relation, which is essentially a disposition towards another, does not have the power of constituting anything towards itself. The confirming argument appears to be ineffectual for the following reason. The infinity of the divine essence issues in so great a union in God, one that includes in itself in a unific way every absolute perfection and even every reality compossible with it. However, the proper characteristic [of each person] is not formally infinite, and so it need not be that every reality be united in it (and especially not that which appears to be formally incompatible with it or impossible to be included in it) as if it expressed formally a greater perfection than the divine essence, or no less a perfection.

WHAT JUDGMENT SHOULD WE PASS ON THE THIRD VIEW?

Suppose one objects against this view that it is incompatible with the faith on the grounds that the Savior, expressing the entire truth of the faith, named three Persons, Father, Son, and Holy Spirit (at the conclusion of Matthew), and St. John says "There are three that bear witness in heaven: the Father, the Word, and the Holy Spirit" (1 John 5). Furthermore, the saints who take up this issue later, grounding themselves in these words of Scripture, always appear to say explicitly that the Persons are distinguished formally only by relations, as the arguments for the second view concluded.

Here one might respond that the Savior did in fact teach of three Persons, and that they are relative by these relations, and that one Person takes its essence from another Person—and that the third view does not deny this. "The Savior did not say that the Divine Persons are constituted by something absolute, and so they are not constituted in this way" is not a valid inference (since the topic from authority does not hold negatively),[7] just as "I speak with the bishop, and the official, and the archdeacon; therefore, they are distinguished in personal being through these relations" is not a valid inference. Perhaps the Savior, seeing that we are unable to conceive the proper characteristic absolute realities that formally constitute the Divine Persons in personal being, if it turns out there are any such realities, wanted to express them to us in names we would find more understandable. After all, we can in a way conceive these relations of origin on the basis of relations of origin among creatures.

We might perhaps impute yet a different reason to the Savior: This way, more of the truth of the faith is expressed simultaneously than would be otherwise. Here is the reason. Suppose that there are absolute Persons, that they are constituted by absolute proper characteristics a, b, and c, and that these can be named by names. If the Savior had expressed those names, he would not thereby have expressed the origin of one Person from another; he would have expressed precisely their distinction. In contrast, by expressing the Persons by relative names, he thereby expressed both—their distinction as well as their origin.

At any rate, it appears that Scripture can show that absolute names can name and express the Divine Persons. For instance, Proverbs 30, where, after posing many questions about God, Solomon asks: "What is his name, and what is the name of his Son, if you know?" If the primary name of his Son is "Son" (as it must be if filiation were to constitute him in being), that question is obviously no question at all, because every question supposes something certain and asks about something uncertain (see the conclusion of *Metaphysics* VII). So, that would be no question, because he would suppose and ask about the very same thing: He supposes that he is the Son, and he asks what his name is. Likewise, by the nature of the relation he supposes that to which he is relative to be the Father and asks his name. One might reply to him: You are asking the name of the Father and of the Son, and you are speaking their primary names!

It appears, then, that one can make this reply: Suppose that the New Testament plainly means that the Persons are relative, and that this fact is part of the substance of the faith. Even so, it nowhere makes plain that relations are the primary forms constituting and distinguishing the Persons in the first place. Moreover, the Church has not made this clear either: It is not made clear in the Apostle's Creed, in the Nicene Creed, or in the Ecumenical Council under Innocent III (with regard to this article "On the Trinity," it is found in the *Librum Extra,* "The Most High Trinity and the Catholic Faith," "*Firmiter*"), nor in the Ecumenical Council of Lyons under Gregory X (with regard to this subject "On the Trinity," it is found in the *Librum Extra,* "The Most High Trinity and the Catholic Faith," "*Fideli,*" and is today in *Decretals* VI), nor in any other council, so that what is handed down in some authentic Scripture might now be plainly apparent.

Therefore, if Christ did not teach, and the Church did not make clear, that the Persons are distinguished in the first place by relations, then it does not seem right to assert that this is part of the faith, because it does not seem reverent to say that the Divine Persons are only subsistent relations if that's not true. But if it is true, it still isn't handed down as certain truth, and it does not seem to be without its risks to assert that we ought to maintain this as a certain truth. And while it is true that the Persons are distinguished by relations (and persevering in this general claim, the saints have struggled over how the distinction among the Persons is compatible with the unity of the divine essence), there is still no need to deny that some "prior" distinction can be posited—a distinction that also allows the distinction [by relations]. The result is that each approach maintains this affirmative truth: the Divine Persons are distinguished by relations. However, one approach would say that a real distinction "precedes" this relational one. Moreover, there is no need to restrict an article of faith handed down in a general form to one specific understanding of it, as if the general understanding could not be true except in the specific one. For instance, there is no need to restrict the article of faith "The Word of God became a human being" to one determinate way of understanding it, one that is not made plain in scripture or by the Church, so that it could be true only if that way of understanding it were true. After all, that is to reduce an article of faith to an uncertainty, if anything is uncertain that is not handed down as an article of faith; for what cannot be held without some uncertain element appears to be uncertain.

If one were to hold this third view, one would say that the absolute reality constituting and distinguishing the person is not a toward itself reality the way essential characteristics are toward themselves, but the personal reality is toward itself in the second way, on the distinction drawn by the professor found at the beginning of the discussion of the third view.[8]

NOTES

1. Earlier in this Question Scotus raises the possibility that the Persons of the Trinity are not constituted by anything; rather, each Person is distinguished from the others in and of itself. After refuting this thesis, Scotus turns to the question of what it is that does constitute and distinguish the Persons. After discussing the thesis that subsistent relations constitute them—the dominant position in Scotus's time—he raises this third possibility: The Persons are constituted by something absolute and not relative.
2. Scotus is referring to Bonaventure (1221–1274). However, he is not attributing this third view to Bonaventure, who held instead the dominant position that the Persons are constituted by relations. Scotus is simply using what Bonaventure says at *In I Sent.* d.25 a.1 q.1 to help make his case for the third view. In the Middle Ages, proponents of the third view included William of Auvergne (d. 1249) and Robert Grosseteste (d. 1253). What Scotus writes elsewhere in the *Ordinatio* (I, d. 28) shows that he knew Bonaventure did not hold this third view.
3. Scotus follows Aristotle in dividing created being into various categories. The most fundamental of the categories is substance. Things in the other categories (called "accidents") are naturally apt to be in a substance and to depend on it for their existence (a contemporary philosopher might say they are apt to be "properties" of substances), while substances are not naturally apt to be in anything. Primary substances are individuals, while a common nature, the nature in itself, can be in a plurality of primary substances (as well as in concepts). For instance, Socrates is a primary substance, while *human being* is a common nature. Although primary substances are not naturally apt to depend on anything else for their existence, one primary substance—Jesus Christ—is united to and depends on the Divine Word, the second Person of the Trinity. Jesus, considered apart from his connection to the Divine Word, is therefore a primary substance that is not a supposit. Supposits are not simply naturally apt to be independent; they are in fact independent.
4. "Toward itself" (*ad se*) is simply the opposite of "relationally" (*ad aliud*).
5. Scotus is arguing that even if the Persons are constituted by something absolute, as long as they are on a par with each other (as they are, since they are all supposits that share the same Divine Essence) they can bear relations to each other. It's important for Scotus to establish this, since in the Christian tradition the Persons are described relationally. Scotus suggests that the Persons bear relations of origin to each other: The Father "originates" the Son, and the Father and Son "originate" the Holy Spirit. However, on this view, these relations do not *constitute* the Persons. The constitution of each Person is logically prior to their being related.
6. See the Vatican edition of the *Ordinatio,* paragraphs 32ff.
7. A topic is a self-evident statement called a "maximal proposition" and its differentiae. Ancient and medieval logicians used them to discover arguments. One example of the topic from authority is "Experts should be believed in their field of expertise."
8. In other words, it is toward itself in the way a primary substance is, not in the way a common nature is.

DISCUSSION QUESTIONS

1. Scotus proposes the view that the Persons are distinguished from each other by something absolute and something relative, but in different ways. Explain these different ways.
2. What does Scotus mean when he describes the divine Persons as constituted by something absolute?
3. Scotus raises a challenge to those philosophers who hold that relations constitute the Persons. What reply does he anticipate them offering, and how does he assess their reply?
4. If the Christian Scriptures never teach that the Persons are constituted by something absolute but always describe them relationally, then shouldn't a Christian infer that the Persons are constituted by relations? How does Scotus answer this question?

Chapter 10

RENÉ DESCARTES

René Descartes (1591–1650) was born in La Haye, France. He studied law at Poitiers, graduating in 1616. He then travelled to Holland, Germany, and Bavaria, where his ambition to reconstruct the whole of philosophy anew was born. Descartes was a mathematician and scientist who made mathematical reasoning the paradigm for his new system of knowledge. His habit was to stay in bed meditating until noon. But in 1649 Queen Christina of Sweden invited him to Stockholm to tutor her in philosophy. Forced to rise at five in the morning for the tutorials, Descartes contracted pneumonia and died in February 1650.

In this selection, Descartes describes his dualistic conception of a human person as a machine made of earth—the body—and a rational soul. God places the principal seat of this rational soul in the brain. Descartes explains how stimulation of the tiny fibers in the nerves connected to the brain produce sensations of pain, pleasure, heat, cold and the like in the soul, which resides immobile in the same location. The machine's heart and arteries, which push the animal spirits into the cavities of the brain, Descartes likens to the bellows of a church organ. He describes how objects imprint ideas through vision into the brain in a similarly mechanistic way. Descartes diagrams the locations of both the precise gland in the head, where the seat of the imagination and the common sense are, as well as the internal part of the brain, which is the seat of memory. He concludes that explaining all bodily functions requires no appeal to any vegetative or sensitive soul (cf. Aristotle), but only the clock-like movements of the material body's blood and spirits being agitated by the heat of the fire burning in its heart.

Treatise on Man

These men will be composed, as we are, of a soul and a body.[1] First I must describe the body on its own; then the soul, again on its own; and finally I must show how these two natures would have to be joined and united in order to constitute men who resemble us.

I suppose the body to be nothing but a statue or machine made of earth,[2] which God forms with the explicit intention of making it as much as possible like us. Thus God not only gives it externally the colours and shapes of all the parts of our bodies, but also places inside it all the parts required to make it walk, eat, breathe, and indeed to imitate all those of our functions which can be imagined to proceed from matter and to depend solely on the disposition of our organs.

We see clocks, artificial fountains, mills, and other such machines which, although only man-made, have the power to move of their own accord in many different ways. But I am supposing this machine to be made by the hands of God, and so I think you may reasonably think it capable of a greater variety of movements than I could possibly imagine in it, and of exhibiting more artistry than I could possibly ascribe to it.

Now I shall not pause to describe the bones, nerves, muscles, veins, arteries, stomach, liver, spleen, heart, brain, or any of the various other parts from which this machine must be composed. For I am supposing that they are entirely like the parts of our own bodies which have the same names, and I assume that if you do not already have sufficient first-hand knowledge of them, you can get a learned anatomist to show them to you—at any rate, those which are large enough to be seen with the naked eye. As for the parts which are too small to be seen, I can inform you about them more easily and clearly by speaking of the movements which depend on them. Thus I need only give an orderly account of these movements in order to tell you which of our functions they represent . . .[3]

The parts of the blood which penetrate as far as the brain serve not only to nourish and sustain its substance, but also and primarily to produce in it a certain very fine[4] wind, or rather a very lively and pure flame, which is called the *animal spirits.* For it must be noted that the arteries which carry blood to the brain from the heart, after dividing into countless tiny branches which make up the minute tissues that are stretched like tapestries at the bottom of the cavities of the brain, come together again around a certain little *gland*[5] situated near the middle of the substance of the brain, right at the entrance to its cavities. The arteries in this region have a great many little holes through which the finer parts of the blood can flow into this gland . . . These parts of the blood, without any preparation or alteration except for their separation from the coarser parts and their retention

---

Source: René Descartes, excerpt from *Treatise on Man* in *The Philosophical Writings of Descartes,* J. Cottingham et al. tr., Cambridge University Press (1985): 99–108. Reprinted with the permission of Cambridge University Press. Line numbers have been deleted.

of the extreme rapidity which the heat of the heart has given them, cease to have the form of blood, and are called the 'animal spirits'.

Now in the same proportion as the animal spirits enter the cavities of the brain, they pass from there into the pores of its substance, and from these pores into the nerves. And depending on the varying amounts which enter (or merely tend to enter) some nerves more than others, the spirits have the power to change the shape of the muscles in which the nerves are embedded, and by this means to move all the limbs. Similarly you may have observed in the grottos and fountains in the royal gardens that the mere force with which the water is driven as it emerges from its source is sufficient to move various machines, and even to make them play certain instruments or utter certain words depending on the various arrangements of the pipes through which the water is conducted.

Indeed, one may compare the nerves of the machine I am describing with the pipes in the works of these fountains, its muscles and tendons with the various devices and springs which serve to set them in motion, its animal spirits with the water which drives them, the heart with the source of the water, and the cavities of the brain with the storage tanks. Moreover, breathing and other such activities which are normal and natural to this machine, and which depend on the flow of the spirits, are like the movements of a clock or mill, which the normal flow of water can render continuous. External objects, which by their mere presence stimulate its sense organs and thereby cause them to move in many different ways depending on how the parts of its brain are disposed, are like visitors who enter the grottos of these fountains and unwittingly cause the movements which take place before their eyes. For they cannot enter without stepping on certain tiles which are so arranged that if, for example, they approach a Diana who is bathing they will cause her to hide in the reeds, and if they move forward to pursue her they will cause a Neptune to advance and threaten them with his trident; or if they go in another direction they will cause a sea-monster to emerge and spew water onto their faces; or other such things according to the whim of the engineers who made the fountains. And finally, when a *rational soul* is present in this machine it will have its principal seat in the brain, and reside there like the fountain-keeper who must be stationed at the tanks to which the fountain's pipes return if he wants to produce, or prevent, or change their movements in some way . . .[6]

Next, to understand how the external objects which strike the sense organs can prompt this machine to move its limbs in numerous different ways, you should consider that the tiny fibres (which, as I have already told you, come from the innermost region of its brain and compose the marrow of the nerves) are so arranged in each part of the machine that serves as the organ of some sense that they can easily be moved by the objects of that sense. And when they are moved, with however little force, they simultaneously pull the parts of the brain from which they come, and thereby open the entrances to certain pores in the internal surface of the brain. Through these pores the animal spirits in the cavities of the brain immediately begin to make their way into the nerves and so to the muscles which serve to cause movements in the machine quite similar to those we are naturally prompted to make when our senses are affected in the same way.

Thus, for example [in Fig. 1], if fire A is close to foot B, the tiny parts of this fire (which, as you know, move about very rapidly) have the power also to move the area of skin which they touch. In this way they pull the tiny fibre *cc* which you see attached to it, and simultaneously open the entrance to the pore *de*, located opposite the point where this fibre terminates—just as when you pull one end of a string, you cause a bell hanging at the other end to ring at the same time.

When the entrance to the pore or small tube *de* is opened in this way, the animal spirits from cavity *F* enter and are carried through it—some to muscles which serve to pull the foot away from

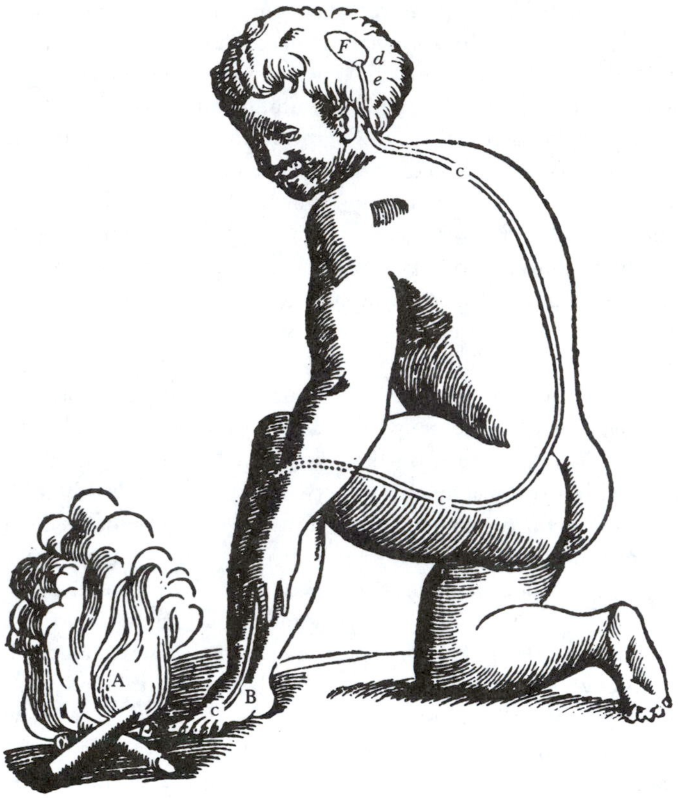

Fig. 1

the fire, some to muscles which turn the eyes and head to look at it, and some to muscles which make the hands move and the whole body turn in order to protect it . . .

Now I maintain that when God unites a rational soul to this machine (in a way that I intend to explain later) he will place its principal seat in the brain, and will make its nature such that the soul will have different sensations corresponding to the different ways in which the entrances to the pores in the internal surface of the brain are opened by means of the nerves.

Suppose, firstly, that the tiny fibres which make up the marrow of the nerves are pulled with such force that they are broken and separated from the part of the body to which they are joined, with the result that the structure of the whole machine becomes somehow less perfect. Being pulled in this way, the fibres cause a movement in the brain which gives occasion for the soul (whose place of residence must remain constant) to have the sensation of *pain.*

Now suppose the fibres are pulled with a force almost as great as the one just mentioned, but without their being broken or separated from the parts to which they are attached. Then they will cause a movement in the brain which, testifying to the good condition of the other parts of the body, will give the soul occasion to feel a certain bodily pleasure which we call '*titillation*'. This, as you see, is very close to pain in respect of its cause but quite opposite in its effect.

Again, if many of these tiny fibres are pulled equally and all together, they will make the soul perceive that the surface of the body touching the limb where they terminate is *smooth;* and if the fibres are pulled unequally they will make the soul feel the surface to be uneven and *rough.*

And if the fibres are disturbed only slightly and separately from one another, as they constantly are by the heat which the heart transmits to the other parts of the body, the soul will have no more sensation of this than of any other normal function of the body. But if this stimulation is increased or decreased by some unusual cause, its increase will make the soul have a sensation of *heat,* and its decrease a sensation of *cold.* Finally, according to the various other ways in which they are stimulated, the fibres will cause the soul to perceive all the other qualities belonging to touch in general, such as *moisture, dryness, weight* and the like.

It must be observed, however, that despite the extreme thinness and mobility of these fibres, they are not thin and mobile enough to transmit to the brain all the more subtle motions that take place in nature. In fact the slightest motions they transmit are ones involving the coarser parts of terrestrial bodies. And even among these bodies there may be some whose parts, although rather coarse, can slide against the fibres so gently that they compress them or cut right through them without their action passing to the brain. In just the same way there are certain drugs which have the power to numb or even destroy the parts of the body to which they are applied without causing us to have any sensation of them at all . . .[7]

It is time for me to begin to explain how the animal spirits make their way through the cavities and pores of the brain of this machine, and which of the machine's functions depend on these spirits.

If you have ever had the curiosity to examine the organs in our churches, you know how the bellows push the air into certain receptacles' (which are called, presumably for this reason, wind-chests). And you know how the air passes from there into one or other of the pipes, depending on the different ways in which the organist moves his fingers on the keyboard. You can think of our machine's heart and arteries, which push the animal spirits into the cavities of its brain, as being like the bellows of an organ, which push air into the wind-chests; and you can think of external objects, which stimulate certain nerves and cause spirits contained in the cavities to pass into some of the pores, as being like the fingers of the organist, which press certain keys and cause the air to pass from the wind-chests into certain pipes. Now the harmony of an organ does not depend on the externally visible arrangement of the pipes or on the shape of the wind-chests or other parts. It depends solely on three factors: the air which comes from the bellows, the pipes which make the sound, and the distribution of the air in the pipes. In just the same way, I would point out, the functions we are concerned with here do not depend at all on the external shape of the visible parts which anatomists distinguish in the substance of the brain, or on the shape of the brain's cavities, but solely on three factors: the spirits which come from the heart, the pores of the brain through which they pass, and the way in which the spirits are distributed in these pores. Thus my sole task here is to give an orderly account of the most important features of these three factors . . .[8]

Now, the substance of the brain being soft and pliant, its cavities would be very narrow and almost all closed (as they appear in the brain of a corpse) if no spirits entered them. But the source which produces these spirits is usually so abundant that they enter these cavities in sufficient quantity to have the force to push out against the surrounding matter and make it expand, thus tightening all the tiny nerve-fibres which come from it (in the way that a moderate wind can inflate the sails of a ship and tighten all the ropes to which the sails are attached.) It follows that at such times the machine is disposed to respond to all the actions of the spirits, and hence it represents the body of a man who is *awake.* Or at least the spirits have enough force to push against some parts of the surrounding matter in this way, and so make it tight, while the other parts remain free and relaxed (as happens in parts of a sail when the wind is a little too weak to fill it). At such times the machine represents the body of a man who is *asleep* and who has *various dreams* as he sleeps . . .

But before I speak in greater detail about *sleep* and *dreams,* I must have you consider the most noteworthy events that take place in the brain during the time of waking: namely, how ideas of objects are formed in the place assigned to the *imagination* and to the *'common' sense,* how the ideas are retained in the *memory,* and how they cause *movement in all the parts of the body* . . .

In order . . . to see clearly how ideas are formed of the objects which strike the senses, observe in this diagram [Fig. 2] the tiny fibres 12, 34, 56, and the like, which make up the optic nerve and stretch from the back of the eye at 1, 3, 5 to the internal surface of the brain at 2, 4, 6. Now assume that these fibres are so arranged that if the rays coming, for example, from point A of the object happen to press upon the back of the eye at point 1, they pull the whole of fibre 12 and enlarge the opening of the tiny tube marked 2. In the same way, the rays which come from point B enlarge the opening of the tiny tube 4, and likewise for the others. We have already described how, depending on the different ways in which the points 1, 3, 5 are pressed by these rays, a figure is traced on the back of the eye corresponding to that of the object ABC. Similarly, it is obvious that, depending on the different ways in which the tiny tubes 2, 4, 6 are opened by the fibres 12, 34, 56, etc., a corresponding figure must also be traced on the internal surface of the brain.

Suppose next that the spirits which tend to enter each of the tiny tubes 2, 4, 6, and the like, do not come indifferently from all points on the surface of gland H, but only from certain of these points: those coming from point *a* on this surface, for example, tend to enter tube 2, those from points *b* and *c* tend to enter tubes 4 and 6, and likewise for the others. As a result, at the same instant that the openings to these tubes expand, the spirits begin to leave the corresponding points on the gland more freely and more rapidly than they did previously. Thus, just as a figure corresponding to that of the object ABC is traced on the internal surface of the brain according to the different ways in which tubes 2, 4, 6 are opened, likewise that figure is traced on the surface of the gland according to the ways in which the spirits leave from points *a, b, c.*

And note that by 'figures' I mean not only things which somehow represent the position of the edges and surfaces of objects, but also anything which, as I said above, can give the soul occasion to perceive movement, size, distance, colours, sounds, smells and other such qualities. And I also include anything that can make the

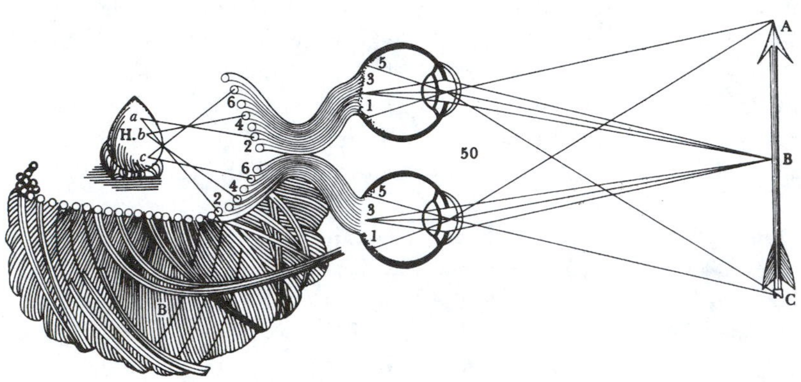

Fig. 2

soul feel pleasure, pain, hunger, thirst, joy, sadness and other such passions. For it is easy to understand that tube 2, for example, may be opened in different ways—in one way by the action which I said causes sensory perception of the colour red, or of tickling, and in another way by the action which I said causes sensory perception of the colour white, or of pain; and the spirits which leave from point *a* will tend to move towards this tube in a different manner according to differences in its manner of opening, and likewise for the others.

Now among these figures, it is not those imprinted on the external sense organs, or on the internal surface of the brain, which should be taken to be ideas—but only those which are traced in the spirits on the surface of the gland H (*where the seat of the imagination and the 'common' sense is located*)[9] That is to say, it is only the latter figures which should be taken to be the forms or images which the rational soul united to this machine will consider directly when it imagines some object or perceives it by the senses.

And note that I say 'imagines or perceives by the senses'. For I wish to apply the term 'idea' generally to all the impressions which the spirits can receive as they leave gland H. These are to be attributed to the 'common' sense when they depend on the presence of objects; but they may also proceed from many other causes (as I shall explain later), and they should then be attributed to the imagination.

Here I could add something about how the traces of these ideas pass through the arteries to the heart, and thus radiate through all the blood; and about how certain actions of a mother may sometimes even cause such traces to be imprinted on the limbs of the child being formed in her womb. But I shall content myself with telling you more about how the traces are imprinted on the internal part of the brain [marked B on Fig. 2] which is the seat of the *memory*.

To this end, suppose that after the spirits leaving gland H have received the impression of some idea, they pass through tubes 2, 4, 6, and the like, into the pores or gaps lying between the tiny fibres which make up part B of the brain. And suppose that the spirits are strong enough to enlarge these gaps somewhat, and to bend and arrange in various ways any fibres they encounter, according to the various ways in which the spirits are moving and the different openings of the tubes into which they pass. Thus they also trace figures in these gaps, which correspond to those of the objects. At first they do this less easily and perfectly than they do on gland H, but gradually they do it better and better, as their action becomes stronger and lasts longer, or is repeated more often. That is why these figures are no longer so easily erased, and why they are preserved in such a way that the ideas which were previously on the gland can be formed again long afterwards without requiring the presence of the objects to which they correspond. And this is what *memory* consists in . . .[10]

But before going on to describe the rational soul, I should like you once again to give a little thought to everything I have said about this machine. Consider, in the first place, that I have supposed in it only organs and mechanisms of such a type that you may well believe very similar ones to be present both in us and in many animals which lack reason as well. Regarding those which can be seen clearly with the naked eye, the anatomists have already observed them all. And as for what I have said about the way in which the arteries carry the spirits into the head, and about the difference between the internal surface of the brain and its central substance, the anatomists will, if they simply make closer observations, be able to see sufficient indications of this to allay any doubts about these matters too. Nor will they be able to have doubts about the tiny doors or valves which I have placed in the nerves where they enter each muscle, if they take care to note that nature generally has formed such valves at all the places in our bodies where some matter regularly goes in and may tend to come out, as at the entrances to the heart, gall-bladder, throat, and large intestine, and at the main divisions of all the veins. Again, regarding the brain, they will not be able to imagine anything more plausible than that it is composed of many tiny fibres variously interlaced; for, in view of the fact that every type of skin and flesh appears to be similarly composed of many fibres or threads, and that the same thing is observed in all plants, such fibrous composition is apparently a common property of all bodies that can grow and be nourished by the union and joining together of the minute parts of other bodies. Finally, as for the rest of the things I have assumed which cannot be perceived by any sense, they are all so simple and commonplace, and also so few in number, that if you compare them with the diverse composition and marvellous artistry which is evident in the structure of the visible organs, you will have more reason to think I have omitted many that are in us than to think I have introduced any that are not. And, knowing that nature always acts by the simplest and easiest means, you will perhaps conclude that it is possible to find some which are more similar to the ones she in fact uses than to those proposed here.

I should like you to consider, after this, all the functions I have ascribed to this machine—such as the digestion of food, the beating of the heart and arteries, the nourishment and growth of the limbs, respiration, waking and sleeping, the reception by the external sense organs of light, sounds, smells, tastes, heat and other such qualities, the imprinting of the ideas of these qualities in the organ of the 'common' sense and the imagination, the retention or stamping of these ideas in the memory, the internal movements of the appetites and passions, and finally the external movements of all the limbs (movements which are so appropriate not only to the actions of objects presented to the senses, but also to the passions and the impressions found in the memory, that they imitate perfectly the movements of a real man). I should like you to consider that these functions follow from the mere arrangement of the machine's organs every bit as naturally as the movements of a clock or other automaton follow from the arrangement of its counterweights and wheels. In order to explain these functions, then, it is not necessary to conceive of this machine as having any vegetative or sensitive soul or other principle of movement and life, apart from its blood and its spirits, which are agitated by the heat of the fire burning continuously in its heart—a fire which has the same nature as all the fires that occur in inanimate bodies.

NOTES

1. By 'these men', Descartes means the fictional men he introduced in an earlier (lost) part of the work. Their description is intended to cast light on the nature of real men in the same way that the description of a 'new world' in *The World,* ch. 6, is intended to cast light on the real world. See also *Discourse,* part 5.
2. By 'earth' Descartes means the third 'element', which he had discussed in *The World,* ch. 5.
3. There follows a description of digestion, the formation and circulation of the blood, the action of the heart, and respiration. Cf. *Discourse,* part 5, and *Passions,* Part 1, art. 3–10, and *Description of the Human Body.* For an English version of material omitted here and below, see *Descartes: Treatise on Man,* tr. T. S. Hall (Cambridge: Harvard U.P., 1972).
4. Fr. *subtil,* by which Descartes means 'composed of very small, fast-moving particles'.
5. The pineal gland, which Descartes later identifies as the seat of the imagination and the 'common' sense. See also *Passions,* where the gland is identified as the seat of the soul.
6. There follows a description of the way in which the animal spirits bring about muscular movements, breathing, swallowing, etc. See *Passions,* Part 1.
7. There follows an account of the other external senses (taste, smell, hearing and sight) and of internal sensations (hunger, thirst, joy and sadness). For Descartes' theory of vision, see *Optics,* for the other external senses, see *Principles,* Part 4, art. 192–4 and for the internal sensations, see *Passions, passim.*

8. There follows a description of the animal spirits and how their state is affected by digestion, respiration, and other bodily functions; of the pores of the brain; and of the movement of the spirits through the pores.
9. See note 5, p. 74.
10. There follows an account of the way in which the animal spirits form ideas on the surface of the pineal gland, and produce bodily movements like those of real men, despite the absence of any soul. See *Passions,* Part 1, art. 13–16, 21–4.

DISCUSSION QUESTIONS

1. Explain Descartes' analogy of the pipes in the works of fountains in the royal gardens with the nerves, muscles, and tendons of the human "machine" body.
2. Which three factors does Descartes say determine how the perception of external objects, digestion, respiration, and other bodily functions work?
3. Explain how Descartes uses the simile of wind inflating the sails of a ship to illustrate how the actions of the spirits cause a man to be awake or asleep.
4. Descartes thinks that "nature always acts by the simplest and easiest means." What does he mean by this? Do you agree? Explain.

Chapter 11

THOMAS HOBBES

Thomas Hobbes (1588–1679), born the second son of a wayward country vicar in Malmesbury, Wiltshire, was a precocious scholar of Greek and Latin, a scientist of optics, and a mathematician. As a philosopher, Hobbes was the founding father of modern metaphysical materialism. He wrote the Third Set of Objections to Descartes' Meditations. *Hobbes is also arguably the founding father of modern political philosophy.*

This selection is from Hobbes' masterpiece published in 1651. He defines a natural *person as he whose words or actions are considered as his own. He defines an* artificial *person as he whose words or actions are considered as representing the words or actions of another man, or of any other thing to which they are attributed. Hobbes explains that to personate is to* act, or represent *oneself or another. The* author *is the "owner" of the words and actions of the* actor, *who is an example of an artificial person. This sense of "author" derives from the Latin term* dominus, *meaning the one who has dominion, i.e., the right of possession. "Authority" thus means the right to perform any act. Hobbes denies that inanimate things can be authors. He thinks that God may be personated (by Moses, by Jesus, or by the Holy Ghost). Children, fools, and madmen who lack the use of reason may be personated by guardians, but can be no authors of any of their actions. Moreover, Hobbes argues that a multitude of men are made one person when every member of that multitude consents to be represented by one individual. It is the unity of the* representer, *not the unity of those represented, that makes the person one, according to Hobbes. Finally, he distinguishes between the author simply so called, who owns the action of another simply, and the author who owns an action or covenant of another conditionally.*

Leviathan (1st Part)

CHAPTER XVI

OF PERSONS, AUTHORS, *AND THINGS PERSONATED*

A person is he *whose words or actions are considered either as his own, or as representing the words or actions of another man, or of any other thing in whom they are attributed, whether truly or by fiction.*

When they are considered as his own, then is he called a *natural person:* and when they are considered as representing the words and actions of another, then is he a *feigned* or *artificial person.*

The word Person is Latin, instead whereof the Greeks have *prosopon,* which signifies the *face,* as *persona* in Latin signifies the *disguise* or *outward appearance* of a man, counterfeited on the stage, and sometimes more particularly that part of it which disguiseth the face (as a mask or vizard); and from the stage hath been translated to any representer of speech and action, as well in tribunals as theatres. So that a *person* is the same that an *actor* is, both on the stage and in common conversation; and to *personate* is to *act,* or *represent,* himself or another; and he that acteth another is said to bear his person, or act in his name (in which sense *Cicero* useth it where he says *Unus sustineo tres personas: mei, adversarii, et judicis,* I bear three persons: my own, my adversary's, and the judge's),[1] and is called in divers occasions diversly (as a *representer,* or *representative,* a *lieutenant,* a *vicar,* an *attorney,* a *deputy,* a *procurator,* an *actor,* and the like).

Of persons artificial, some have their words and actions *owned* by those whom they represent. And then the person is the *actor,* and he that owneth his words and actions is the AUTHOR, in which case the actor acteth by authority.[2] For that which in speaking of goods and possessions is called an *owner* (and in Latin *dominus,* in Greek *kurios*), speaking of actions is called author. And as the right of possession is called dominion, so the right of doing any action is called AUTHORITY. So that by authority is always understood a right of doing any act; and *done by authority,* done by commission or licence from him whose right it is.

From hence it followeth that when the actor maketh a covenant by authority, he bindeth thereby the author, no less than if he had made it himself, and no less subjecteth him to all the consequences of the same. And therefore all that hath been said formerly (*chap.* 14) of the nature of covenants between man and man in their natural capacity is true also when they are made by their actors, representers, or procurators, that have authority from them so far forth as is in their commission, but no farther.

And therefore, he that maketh a covenant with the actor, or representer, not knowing the

---

Source: Thomas Hobbes, *Leviathan,* First Part: Of Man, Chapter 16: Of Persons, Authors, and Things Personated. Edwin Curley ed., Hackett Publishing (1994): 101–105. Paragraph numbers and marginal notations have been deleted.

authority he hath, doth it at his own peril. For no man is obliged by a covenant whereof he is not author, nor consequently by a covenant made against or beside the authority he gave.

When the actor doth anything against the law of nature by command of the author, if he be obliged by former covenant to obey him, not he, but the author breaketh the law of nature; for though the action be against the law of nature, yet it is not his; but contrarily, to refuse to do it is against the law of nature that forbiddeth breach of covenant.[3]

And he that maketh a covenant with the author by mediation of the actor, not knowing what authority he hath, but only takes his word, in case such authority be not made manifest unto him upon demand, is no longer obliged; for the covenant made with the author is not valid without his counter-assurance. But if he that so covenanteth knew beforehand he was to expect no other assurance[4] than the actor's word, then is the covenant valid, because the actor in this case maketh himself the author. And therefore, as when the authority is evident the covenant obligeth the author, not the actor, so when the authority is feigned it obligeth the actor only, there being no author but himself.

There are few things that are incapable of being represented by fiction.[5] Inanimate things (as a church, an hospital, a bridge) may be personated by a rector, master, or overseer. But things inanimate cannot be authors, nor therefore give authority to their actors; yet the actors may have authority to procure their maintenance given them by those that are owners or governors of those things. And therefore, such things cannot be personated before there be some state of civil government.

Likewise, children, fools, and madmen that have no use of reason may be personated by guardians or curators, but can be no authors (during that time) of any action done by them, longer than (when they shall recover the use of reason) they shall judge the same reasonable. Yet during the folly, he that hath right of governing them may give authority to the guardian. But this again has no place but in a state civil, because before such estate, there is no dominion of persons.

An idol, or mere figment of the brain, may be personated (as were the gods of the heathen, which by such officers as the state appointed were personated, and held possessions, and other goods, and rights, which men from time to time dedicated and consecrated unto them). But idols cannot be authors; for an idol is nothing. The authority proceeded from the state; and therefore, before introduction of civil government the gods of the heathen could not be personated.

The true God may be personated. As he was, first by *Moses,* who governed the Israelites (that were not his, but God's people) not in his own name (with *hoc dicit Moses* [thus says Moses]), but in God's name (with *hoc dicit Dominus* [thus says the Lord]). Secondly, by the Son of man, his own Son, our blessed Saviour *Jesus Christ,* that came to reduce the Jews, and induce all nations into the kingdom of his father, not as of himself, but as sent from his father. And thirdly, by the Holy Ghost, or Comforter, speaking and working in the Apostles; which Holy Ghost was a Comforter that came not of himself, but was sent and proceeded from them both.[6]

A multitude of men are made *one* person, when they are by one man, or one person, represented so that it be done with the consent of every one of that multitude in particular.[7] For it is the *unity* of the representer, not the *unity* of the represented, that maketh the person *one.* And it is the representer that beareth the person, and but one person,[8] and *unity* cannot otherwise be understood in multitude.

And because the multitude naturally is not *one,* but *many,* they cannot be understood for one, but many, authors of everything their representative saith or doth in their name, every man giving their common representer authority from himself in particular, and owning all the actions the representer doth, in case they give him authority without stint; otherwise, when they limit him in what, and how far, he shall represent them, none of them owneth more than they gave him commission to act.[9]

And if the representative consist of many men, the voice of the greater number must be considered as the voice of them all. For if the lesser number pronounce (for example) in the affirmative, and the greater in the negative, there will be negatives more than enough to destroy the affirmatives; and thereby the excess of negatives, standing uncontradicted, are the only voice the representative hath.[10]

And a representative of even number, especially when the number is not great, whereby the contradictory voices are oftentimes equal, is therefore oftentimes mute and incapable of action. Yet in some cases contradictory voices equal in number may determine a question (as, in condemning or absolving, equality of votes, even in that they condemn not, do absolve; but not on the contrary condemn, in that they absolve not). For when a cause is heard, not to condemn is to absolve; but on the contrary, to say that not absolving is condemning, is not true. The like it is in a deliberation of executing presently, or deferring till another time; for when the voices are equal, the not decreeing execution is a decree of dilation.

Or if the number be odd, as three (or more) men (or assemblies) whereof every one has, by a negative voice, authority to take away the effect of all the affirmative voices of the rest, this number is no representative; because, by the diversity of opinions and interests of men, it becomes oftentimes, and in cases of the greatest consequence, a mute person, and unapt, as for many things else, so for the government of a multitude, especially in time of war.

Of authors there be two sorts. The first simply so called, which I have before defined to be him that owneth the action of another simply. The second is he that owneth an action or covenant of another conditionally (that is to say, he undertaketh to do it, if the other doth it not at, or before, a certain time). And these authors conditional are generally called SURETIES (in Latin *fidejussores* and *sponsores;* and particularly for debt, *praedes;* and for appearance before a judge or magistrate, *vades*).

NOTES

1. *De oratore,* II, 102; cf. in the Appendix, OL III, 533–36.
2. OL: "The words and deeds of those who represent are sometimes acknowledged as their own by whom they represent; and then the one who represents is called the actor, and the one who is represented is called the author, as the one by whose authority the actor acts."
3. OL: "not the actor's but the author's; because the actor would have violated the law if he had not done it, since he had covenanted to do it."
4. OL: "was not expecting any other assurance."
5. OL: "of which there cannot be a person. For although a person is by nature something which understands, still, that whose person is borne is not always necessarily so."
6. OL: "Also, the person of the true God is borne and has been borne. For he created the world in his own person; and in redeeming the human race, Jesus Christ bore the person of God; and in sanctifying the elect, the Holy Ghost bore the person of the same God. This we are taught in the catechism authorized by the state, viz., *to believe in God the father, who created me and the whole world; and in God the Son, who redeemed me and the whole human race; and in the Holy Ghost, who sanctified me and all the elect people of God.*" The revision stems from concerns about the orthodoxy of the English version. Cf. the Appendix, OL III, 563 & xlii, 3. In the large-paper copy the English concludes: "proceeded from them both on the day of Pentecost." Bramhall complained that Hobbes' interpretation of the trinity implied that there was a time when there was no trinity, and hence that its three persons were not coeternal (*Catching of Leviathan,* p. 474). Hobbes claimed not to see why (EW IV, 317), though it seems a clear implication of the large-paper version of this passage.

   In EW IV, 316, Hobbes defends his explanation of the doctrine of the trinity as an attempt to meet the objection of "Lucian and heathen scoffers" who say it involves a contradiction to hold that God is one and three. His account of the trinity shows it not to be contradictory. But then he abandons the account, claiming to have discovered his error independently of Bramhall. So it seems that he leaves Lucian unanswered.

7. OL: "it is represented by one who has authority from each one."
8. Not in OL.
9. OL: "But the authority given is limited; each one is the author of only those actions which are contained in the commission."
10. OL: "the negative voices exceeding the affirmative, as [the excess] is not contradicted by [the affirmatives], it is the voice of the person, i.e., of all. For otherwise, the person would be mute, which is contrary to nature."

DISCUSSION QUESTIONS

1. Hobbes claims that "a person is he whose words or actions are considered either as his own, or as representing the words or actions of another man . . ." On this definition, can nonhuman animals or computers count as persons?
2. Discuss what makes something a person, an author, and a thing personated. Provide examples of each. How should idols (figments of the brain) be categorized?
3. If a being simulated human behavior so well that all who observed it believed it to be a human being but it was later discovered to be a sophisticated electronic inanimate robot, would Hobbes consider it to be a person? Would you? Explain.

Chapter 12

JOHN LOCKE

John Locke was born at Wrington, a village in Somerset, in 1632. He was a student for decades at Christ Church, Oxford before finally graduating as bachelor of medicine in 1674. His career benefited greatly from the patronage of Lord Ashley, Earl of Shaftesbury. Robert Boyle, the leading scientist in England, influenced his thought as well. Locke became arguably the most influential English philosopher as the founder of British empiricism and liberal democracy. He died in 1704.

Locke defines a "person" as a thinking intelligent being, that has reason and reflection, and can consider itself as itself, the same thinking thing in different times and places, which it does only by that consciousness which is inseparable from thinking. He argues that a succession of different substances, separated by fits of forgetfulness, remains the same person as long as the same consciousness can extend to actions past or to come in one continued life. A severed hand, for example, is a lost chunk of substance, not a lost bit of one's personal self. Locke remarks that Cartesian dualists will not admit that one immaterial spirit makes the same person in different human bodies, for fear of granting that nonhuman animals are also thinking things. Locke thinks that if the same consciousness can be transferred from one thinking substance to another, then it will be possible that two thinking substances may make but one person. Locke contends that continuity of memory and identity of consciousness determine sameness of person. If the soul of a prince were to enter the body of a cobbler, he would be the same person *as the prince, but Locke doubts he would be the same* man *as the prince. He holds that unless we understand personal identity to be nothing but consciousness, we are involved in great absurdities. He admits that it is more probable that his own consciousness is connected to, and the affection of, one individual immaterial substance. Locke concludes that "person" is a forensic term that belongs only to intelligent agents capable of law, happiness, and misery.*

An Essay Concerning Human Understanding (Book II, Ch. 27, §§9–27)

Personal identity. This being premised to find wherein *personal identity* consists, we must consider what *person* stands for; which, I think, is a thinking intelligent being, that has reason and reflection, and can consider itself as itself, the same thinking thing in different times and places; which it does only by that consciousness, which is inseparable from thinking, and as it seems to me essential to it: it being impossible for anyone to perceive, without perceiving, that he does perceive. When we see, hear, smell, taste, feel, meditate, or will anything, we know that we do so. Thus it is always as to our present sensations and perceptions: and by this everyone is to himself, that which he calls *self:* it not being considered in this case, whether the same *self* be continued in the same, or divers substances. For since consciousness always accompanies thinking, and 'tis that, that makes everyone to be, what he calls *self;* and thereby distinguishes himself from all other thinking things, in this alone consists *personal identity, i.e.* the sameness of a rational being: and as far as this consciousness can be extended backwards to any past action or thought, so far reaches the identity of that *person;* it is the same *self* now it was then; and 'tis by the same *self* with this present one that now reflects on it, that that action was done.

Consciousness makes personal identity. But it is farther inquired whether it be the same identical substance. This few would think they had reason to doubt of, if these perceptions, with their consciousness, always remained present in the mind, whereby the same thinking thing would be always consciously present, and, as would be thought, evidently the same to itself. But that which seems to make the difficulty is this, that the consciousness, being interrupted always by forgetfulness, there being no moment of our lives wherein we have the whole train of all our past actions before our eyes in one view: but even the best memories losing the sight of one part whilst they are viewing another; and we sometimes, and that the greatest part of our lives, not reflecting on our past selves, being intent on our present thoughts, and in sound sleep, having no thoughts at all, or at least none with that consciousness, which remarks our waking thoughts. I say, in all these cases, our consciousness being interrupted, and we losing the sight of our past *selves,* doubts are raised whether

Source: John Locke, *An Essay Concerning Human Understanding,* Book II, Chapter 27, §§ 9–27. K. P. Winkler ed., Hackett Publishing (1996): 138–149. Selections by and abridgment Paragraph numbers have been deleted.

we are the same thinking thing; *i.e.* the same substance or no. Which however reasonable, or unreasonable concerns not *personal identity* at all. The question being what makes the same *person,* and not whether it be the same identical substance, which always thinks in the same *person,* which in this case matters not at all. Different substances, by the same consciousness (where they do partake in it) being united into one person; as well by different bodies, by the same life are united into one animal, whose *identity* is preserved, in that change of substances, by the unity of one continued life. For it being the same consciousness that makes a man be himself to himself, *personal identity* depends on that only, whether it be annexed only to one individual substance, or can be continued in a succession of several substances. For as far as any intelligent being can repeat the *idea* of any past action with the same consciousness it had of it at first, and with the same consciousness it has of any present action; so far it is the same *personal self.* For it is by the consciousness it has of its present thoughts and actions, that is is *self* to it*self* now, and so will be the same *self* as far as the same consciousness can extend to actions past or to come; and would be by distance of time, or change of substance, no more two *persons* than a man be two men, by wearing other clothes today than he did yesterday, with a long or short sleep in between: the same consciousness uniting those distant actions into the same *person,* whatever substances contributed to their production.

Personal identity in change of substances. That this is so, we have some kind of evidence in our very bodies, all whose particles, whilst vitally united to this same thinking conscious self, so that we feel when they are touched, and are affected by, and conscious of good or harm that happens to them, are a part of our *selves; i.e.* of our thinking conscious *self.* Thus the limbs of his body is to everyone a part of *himself:* he sympathizes and is concerned for them. Cut off an hand, and thereby separate it from that consciousness, we had of its heat, cold, and other affections; and it is then no longer a part of that which is *himself,* any more than the remotest part of matter. Thus we see the *substance,* whereof *personal self* consisted at one time, may be varied at another, without the change of personal *identity:* there being no question about the same person, though the limbs, which but now were a part of it, be cut off.

Whether in the change of thinking substances. But the question is, whether if the same substance, which thinks, be changed, it can be the same person, or remaining the same, it can be different persons.

And to this I answer first, this can be no question at all to those, who place thought in a purely material, animal, constitution, void of an immaterial substance. For, whether their supposition be true or no, 'tis plain they conceive personal identity preserved in something else than identity of substance; as animal identity is preserved in identity of life, not of substance. And therefore those, who place thinking in an immaterial substance only, before they can come to deal with these men, must show why personal identity cannot be preserved in the change of immaterial substances, or variety of particular immaterial substances, as well as animal identity is preserved in the change of material substances, or variety of particular bodies; unless they will say, 'tis one immaterial spirit, that makes the same life in brutes; as it is one immaterial spirit that makes the same person in men, which the *Cartesians* at least will not admit, for fear of making brutes thinking things too.[1]

But next, as to the first part of the question, whether if the same thinking substance (supposing immaterial substances only to think) be changed, it can be the same person. I answer, that cannot be resolved, but by those, who know what kind of substances they are, that do think; and whether the consciousness of past actions can be transferred from one thinking substance to another. I grant, were the same consciousness the same individual action, it could not: but it being but a present representation of a past action, why it may not be possible, that that may be represented to the mind to have been, which really never was, will remain to be shown. And therefore how far the consciousness of past actions is annexed to any individual agent, so that another cannot possibly have it, will be hard for us to determine, till we know what kind of action it is, that cannot be done with a reflex act of perception accompanying it, and how performed by thinking substances, who cannot think without being conscious of it. But that which we call the *same consciousness,* not being the same individual act, why one intellectual substance may not have represented to it, as done by itself, what it never did, and was perhaps done by some other agent, why I say such a representation may not possibly be without reality of matter of fact, as well as several representations in dreams are, which yet, whilst dreaming, we take for true, will be difficult to conclude from the nature of things. And that it never is so, will by us, till we have clearer views of the nature of thinking substances, be best resolved into the goodness of God, who as far as the happiness or misery of any of his sensible creatures is concerned in it, will not by a fatal error of theirs transfer from one to another, that consciousness, which draws reward or punishment with it. How far this may be an argument against those who would place thinking in a system of fleeting animal spirits, I leave to be considered. But yet to return to the question before us, it must be allowed, that if the same consciousness (which, as has been shown, is quite a different thing from the same numerical figure or motion in body) can be transferred from one thinking substance to another, it will be possible, that two thinking substances may make but one person. For the same consciousness being preserved, whether in the same or different substances, the personal identity is preserved.

As to the second part of the question, whether the same immaterial substance remaining, there may be two distinct persons; which question seems to me to be built on this, whether the same immaterial being, being conscious of the actions of its past duration, may be wholly stripped of all the consciousness of its past existence, and lose it beyond the power of ever retrieving it again: and so as it were beginning a new account from a new period, have a consciousness that cannot reach beyond this new state. All those who hold pre-existence, are evidently of this mind, since they allow the soul to have no remaining consciousness of what it did in that pre-existent state, either wholly separate from body, or informing any other body; and if they should not, 'tis plain experience would be against them. So that personal identity reaching no farther than consciousness reaches, a pre-existent spirit not having continued so many ages in a state of silence, must needs make different persons. Suppose a Christian *Platonist* or *Pythagorean,* should upon God's having ended all his works of creation the seventh day, think his soul has existed ever since; and should imagine it has revolved in several human bodies, as I once met with one, who was persuaded his had been the soul of *Socrates* (how reasonably I will not dispute. This I know, that in the post he filled, which was no inconsiderable one, he passed for a very rational man, and the press has shown, that he wanted not parts or learning) would anyone say, that he, being not conscious of any of *Socrates's* actions or thoughts, could be the same person with *Socrates?*[2] Let anyone reflect upon himself, and conclude, that he has in himself an immaterial spirit, which is that which thinks in him, and in the constant change of his body keeps him the same; and is that which he calls himself: let him also suppose it to be the same soul, that was in *Nestor* or *Thersites,* at the siege of *Troy,* (for souls being, as far as we know anything of them in their nature, indifferent to any parcel of matter, the supposition has no apparent absurdity in it) which it may have been, as well as it is now, the soul of any other man: but he, now having no consciousness of any of the actions either of *Nestor* or *Thersites,* does, or can he, conceive himself the same person with either of them? Can he be concerned in either of their actions? Attribute them to himself, or think them his own more than the actions of any other man, that ever existed? So that this consciousness not reaching to any of the actions of either of those men, he is no more one *self* with either of them, than if the soul or immaterial spirit, that now informs him, had been created, and began to exist, when it began to inform his present body, though it were never so true, that the same spirit that informed *Nestor*'s or *Thersites*'s body, were numerically the same that now informs his. For this would no more make him the same person with *Nestor,* than if some of the particles of matter, that were once a part of *Nestor,* were now a part of this man, the same immaterial substance without the same consciousness, no more making the same person by being united to any body, than the same particle of matter without consciousness united to any body, makes the same person. But let him once find himself conscious of any of the actions of *Nestor,* he then finds himself the same person with *Nestor.*

And thus we may be able without any difficulty to conceive, the same person at the Resurrection, though in a body not exactly in make or parts the same which he had here, the same consciousness going along with the soul that inhabits it.[3] But yet the soul alone in the change of bodies, would scarce to anyone, but to him that makes the soul the *man,* be enough to make the same *man.* For should the soul of a prince, carrying with it the consciousness of the prince's past life, enter and inform the body of a cobbler as soon as deserted by his own soul, everyone sees, he would be the same person with the prince, accountable only for the prince's actions: but who would say it was the same man? The body too goes to the making the man, and would, I guess, to everybody determine the man in this case, wherein the soul, with all its princely thoughts about it, would not make another man: but he would be the same cobbler to everyone besides himself. I know that in the ordinary way of speaking, the same person, and the same man, stand for one and the same thing. And indeed everyone will always have a liberty to speak, as he pleases, and to apply what articulate sounds to what *ideas* he thinks fit, and change them as often as he pleases. But yet when we will inquire, what makes the same *spirit, man,* or *person,* we must fix the *ideas of spirit, man,* or *person,* in our minds; and having resolved with ourselves what we mean by them, it will not be hard to determine, in either of them, or the like, when it is the *same,* and when not.

Consciousness makes the same person. But though the same immaterial substance, or soul does not alone, wherever it be, and in whatsoever state, make the same man; yet 'tis plain consciousness, as far as ever it can be extended, should it be to ages past, unites existences, and actions, very remote in time, into the same person, as well as it does the existence and actions of the immediately preceding moment: so that whatever has the consciousness of present and past actions, is the same person to whom they both belong. Had I the same consciousness, that I saw the Ark and *Noah*'s flood, as that I saw an overflowing of the *Thames* last winter, or as that I write now, I could no more doubt that I, that write this now, that saw the *Thames* overflowed last winter, and that viewed the flood at the general deluge, was the same *self,* place that *self* in whatever substance you please, than that I that write this am the same *myself* now whilst I write (whether I consist of all the same substance, material or immaterial, or no) that I was yesterday. For as to this point of being the same *self,* it matters not whether this present *self* be made up of the same or other substances, I being as much concerned, and as justly accountable for any action was done a thousand years since, appropriated to me now by this self-consciousness, as I am, for what I did the last moment.

Self depends on consciousness. Self is that conscious thinking thing, (whatever substance made up of whether spiritual, or material, simple, or compounded, it matters not) which is sensible, or conscious of pleasure and pain, capable of happiness or misery, and so is concerned for it*self,* as far as that consciousness extends. Thus everyone finds, that whilst comprehended under that consciousness, the little finger is as much a part of it*self,* as what is most so. Upon separation of this little finger, should this consciousness go along with the little finger, and leave the rest of the body, 'tis evident the little finger would be the *person,* the *same person;* and *self* then would have nothing to do with the rest of the body. As in this case it is the consciousness that goes along with the substance, when one part is separate from another, which makes the same *person,* and constitutes this inseparable *self:* so it is in reference to substances remote in time. That with which the *consciousness* of this present thinking thing can join itself, makes the same *person,* and is one *self* with it, and with nothing else; and so attributes to it*self,* and owns all the actions of that thing, as its own, as far as that consciousness reaches, and no farther; as everyone who reflects will perceive.

Object of reward and punishment. In this *personal identity* is founded all the right and justice of reward and punishment; happiness and misery, being that, for which everyone is concerned for *himself,* not mattering what becomes of any substance, not joined to, or affected with that consciousness. For as it is evident in the instance I gave but now, if the consciousness went along with the little finger, when it was cut off, that would be the same *self* which was concerned for the whole body yesterday, as making a part of it*self,* whose actions then it cannot but admit as its own now. Though if the same body should still live, and immediately from the separation of the little finger have its own peculiar consciousness, whereof the little finger knew nothing, it would not at all be concerned for it, as a part of it*self,* or could own any of its actions, or have any of them imputed to him.

This may show us wherein *personal identity* consists, not in the identity of substance, but, as I have said, in the identity of *consciousness,* wherein, if *Socrates* and the present Mayor of *Quinborough* agree, they are the same person: if the same *Socrates* waking and sleeping do not partake of the same *consciousness, Socrates* waking and sleeping is not the same person. And to punish *Socrates* waking, for what sleeping *Socrates* thought, and waking *Socrates* was never conscious of, would be no more of right, than to punish one twin for what his brother-twin did, whereof he knew nothing, because their outsides were so alike, that they could not be distinguished; for such twins have been seen.

But yet possibly it will still be objected, suppose I wholly lose the memory of some parts of my life, beyond a possibility of retrieving them, so that perhaps I shall never be conscious of them again; yet am I not the same person, that did those actions, had those thoughts, that I was once conscious of, though I have now forgot them? To which I answer, that we must here take notice what the word *I* is applied to, which in this case is the man only. And the same man being presumed to be the same person, *I* is easily here supposed to stand also for the same person. But if it be possible for the same man to have distinct incommunicable consciousnesses at different times, it is past doubt the same man would at different times make different persons; which, we see, is the sense of mankind in the solemnest declaration of their opinions, human laws not punishing the *madman* for the *sober man's* actions, nor the *sober man* for what the *madman* did, thereby making them two persons; which is somewhat explained by our way of speaking in *English,* when we say such an one *is not himself,* or is *besides himself;* in which phrases it is insinuated, as if those who now, or, at least, first used them, thought, that *self* was changed, the *self*same person was no longer in that man.

Difference between identity of man and person. But yet 'tis hard to conceive, that *Socrates* the same individual man should be two persons. To help us a little in this, we must consider what is meant by *Socrates,* or the same individual *man.*

First, it must be either the same individual, immaterial, thinking substance; in short, the same numerical soul, and nothing else.

Secondly, or the same animal, without regard to an immaterial soul.

Thirdly, or the same immaterial spirit united to the same animal.

Now take which of these suppositions you please, it is impossible to make personal identity to consist in anything but consciousness; or reach any farther than that does.

For by the first of them, it must be allowed possible that a man born of different women, and in distant times, may be the same man. A way of speaking, which whoever admits, must allow it possible, for the same man to be two distinct persons, as any two that have lived in different ages without the knowledge of one another's thoughts.

By the second and third, *Socrates* in this life, and after it, cannot be the same man any way, but by the same consciousness; and so making *human identity* to consist in the same thing wherein we place *personal identity,* there will be no difficulty to allow the same man to be the same person. But then they who place *human identity* in consciousness only, and not in something else, must consider how they will make the infant *Socrates* the same man with *Socrates* after the Resurrection. But whatsoever to some men makes a *man,* and consequently the same individual man, wherein perhaps few are agreed, personal identity can by us be placed in nothing but consciousness (which is that alone which makes what we call *self*) without involving us in great absurdities.

But is not a man drunk and sober the same person, why else is he punished for the fact he commits when drunk, though he be never afterwards conscious of it? Just as much the same person, as a man that walks, and does other things in his sleep, is the same person, and is answerable for any mischief he shall do in it. Human laws punish both with a justice suitable to their way of knowledge: because in these cases, they cannot distinguish certainly what is real, what counterfeit; and so the ignorance in drunkenness or sleep is not admitted as a plea. For though punishment be annexed to personality, and personality to consciousness, and the drunkard perhaps be not conscious of what he did; yet human judicatures justly punish him; because the fact is proved against him, but want of consciousness cannot be proved for him. But in the great day, wherein the secrets of all hearts shall be laid open, it may be reasonable to think, no one shall be made to answer for what he knows nothing of; but shall receive his doom, his conscience accusing or excusing him.

Consciousness alone makes self. Nothing but consciousness can unite remote existences into the same person, the identity of substance will not do it. For whatever substance there is, however framed, without consciousness, there is no person: and a carcass may be a person, as well as any sort of substance be so without consciousness.

Could we suppose two distinct incommunicable consciousnesses acting the same body, the one constantly by day, the other by night; and on the other side the same consciousness acting by intervals two distinct bodies: I ask in the first case, whether the *day* and the *night-man* would not be two as distinct persons, as *Socrates* and *Plato;* and whether in the second case, there would not be one person in two distinct bodies, as much as one man is the same in two distinct clothings. Nor is it at all material to say, that this same, and this distinct *consciousness* in the cases above-mentioned, is owing to the same and distinct immaterial substances, bringing it with them to those bodies, which whether true or no, alters not the case: since 'tis evident the *personal identity* would equally be determined by consciousness, whether that consciousness were annexed to some individual immaterial substance or no. For granting that the thinking substance in man must be necessarily supposed immaterial, 'tis evident, that immaterial thinking thing may sometimes part with its past consciousness, and be restored to it again, as appears in the forgetfulness men often have of their past actions, and the mind many times recovers the memory of a past consciousness, which it had lost for twenty years together. Make these intervals of memory and forgetfulness to take their turns regularly by day and night, and you have two persons with the same immaterial spirit, as much as in the former instance two persons with the same body. So that *self* is not determined by identity or diversity of substance, which it cannot be sure of, but only by identity of consciousness.

Indeed it may conceive the substance whereof it is now made up, to have existed formerly, united in the same conscious being: but consciousness removed, that substance is no more it*self,* or makes no more a part of it, than any other substance, as is evident in the instance, we have already given, of a limb cut off, of whose heat, or cold, or other affections, having no longer any consciousness, it is no more of a man's self than any other matter of the universe. In like manner it will be in reference to any immaterial substance, which is void of that consciousness whereby I am my*self* to my*self:* if there be any part of its existence, which I cannot upon recollection join with that present consciousness, whereby I am now my*self,* it is in that part of its existence no more my*self,* than any other immaterial being. For whatsoever any substance has thought or done, which I cannot recollect, and by my consciousness make my own thought and action, it will no more belong to me, whether a part of me thought or did it, than if it had been thought or done by any other immaterial being anywhere existing.

I agree the more probable opinion is, that this consciousness is annexed to, and the affection of one individual immaterial substance.

But let men according to their divers hypotheses resolve of that as they please. This every intelligent being, sensible of happiness or misery, must grant, that there is something that is *himself,* that he concerned for, and would have happy; that this *self* has existed in a continued duration more than one instant, and therefore 'tis possible may exist, as it has done, months and years to come, without any certain bounds to be set to its duration; and may be the same *self,* by the same consciousness, continued on for the future. And thus, by this consciousness, he finds himself to be the *same self* which did such or such an action some years since, by which he comes to be happy or miserable now. In all which account of *self,* the same numerical substance is not considered, as making the same *self:* but the same continued consciousness, in which several substances may have been united, and again separated from it, which, whilst they continued in a vital union with that, wherein this consciousness then resided, made a part of that same *self.* Thus any part of our bodies vitally united to that, which is conscious in us, makes a part of our *selves:* but upon separation from the vital union, by which that consciousness is communicated, that, which a moment since was part of our *selves,* is now no more so, than a part of another man's *self* is part of me; and 'tis not impossible, but in a little time may become a real part of another person. And so we have the same numerical substance become a part of two different persons; and the same person preserved under the change of various substances. Could we suppose any spirit wholly stripped of all its memory or consciousness of past actions, as we find our minds always are of a great part of ours, and sometimes of them all, the union or separation of such a spiritual substance would make no variation of personal identity, any more than that of any particle of matter does. Any substance vitally united to the present thinking being, is part of that very *same self* which now is: anything united to it by a consciousness of former actions makes also a part of the *same self,* which is the same both then and now.

Person a forensic term. Person, as I take it, is the name for this *self.* Wherever a man finds, what he calls *himself,* there I think another may say is the same *person.* It is a forensic term appropriating actions and their merit; and so belongs only to intelligent agents capable of a law, and happiness and misery. This personality extends it*self* beyond present existence to what is past, only by consciousness, whereby it becomes concerned and accountable, owns and imputes to it*self* past actions, just upon the same ground, and for the same reason, that it does the present. All which is founded in a concern for happiness the unavoidable concomitant of consciousness, that which is conscious of pleasure and pain, desiring, that that *self,* that is conscious, should be happy. And therefore whatever past actions it cannot reconcile or appropriate to that present *self* by consciousness, it can be no more concerned in, than if they had never been done: and to receive pleasure or pain; *i.e.* reward or punishment, on the account of any such action, is all one, as to be made happy or miserable in its first being, without any demerit at all. For supposing a man punished now, for what he had done in another life, whereof he could be made to have no consciousness at all, what difference is there between that punishment, and being created miserable? And therefore conformable to this, the apostle tells us, that at the great day, when everyone shall *receive according to his doings, the secrets of all hearts shall be laid open.*[4] The sentence shall be justified by the consciousness all persons shall have, that they *themselves* in what bodies soever they appear, or what substances soever that consciousness adheres to, are the *same,* that committed those actions, and deserve that punishment for them.

I am apt enough to think I have in treating of this subject made some suppositions that will look strange to some readers, and possibly they are so in themselves. But yet I think, they are such, as are pardonable in this ignorance we are in of the nature of that thinking thing, that is in us, and which we look on as our*selves.* Did we know what it was, or how it was tied to a certain system of fleeting animal spirits; or whether it could, or could not perform its operations of thinking and memory out of a body organized as ours is; and whether it has pleased God, that no one such spirit shall ever be united to any but one such body, upon the right constitution of whose organs its memory should depend, we might see the absurdity of some of those suppositions I have made. But taking, as we ordinarily now do, (in the dark concerning these matters) the soul of a man, for an immaterial substance, independent from matter, and indifferent alike to it all, there can from the nature of things, be no absurdity at all, to suppose, that the same soul may, at different times be united to different bodies, and with them make up, for that time, one man; as well as we suppose part of a sheep's body yesterday should be a part of a man's body tomorrow, and in that union make a vital part of *Melibœus* as well as it did of his ram.

NOTES

1. The Cartesians are the followers of René Descartes (1596–1650). They believed that animals are mere mechanisms or machines, incapable of thought and feeling.
2. Christian Platonists sought to combine the philosophy of Plato (428–347 B.C.) with Christian doctrine; Pythagoreans were followers of Pythagoras (c. 570–c. 495 B.C.). Both Christian Platonists and Pythagoreans were reputed to believe in the reincarnation or transmigration of souls.
3. The Resurrection is the raising of the dead.
4. *receive according to . . . doings,* 2 Corinthians 5:10; *the secrets . . . shall be . . . open,* 1 Corinthians 14:25.

DISCUSSION QUESTIONS

1. What is personal identity, according to Locke? What does it consist in, and why?
2. Why does Locke think that interruptions of our consciousness (e.g., forgetting our past actions) do not concern personal identity?
3. Do you agree with Locke that your severed hand is no longer a part of you "any more than the remotest part of matter"? Explain.
4. Recall the prince and the cobbler example. Is the cobbler a prince after the prince's soul is transplanted into him? What is Locke illustrating with this thought-experiment?
5. According to Locke, is there a difference between *consciousness* and *self?*
6. What does Locke mean when he calls "person" a forensic term?
7. Imagine a woman so afflicted by Alzheimer's disease that she cannot remember any of her past actions or experiences. Would Locke consider her a person with an *identity?*

Chapter 13

J. O. DE LA METTRIE

Born in the town of Saint Malo, Julien Offray de la Mettrie (1709–1751) was a French physician and philosopher. The provocative book this selection is taken from was published in 1747. Opposition to his views was so harsh that he was compelled to leave France for Berlin, where he was protected by his patron Frederick the Great. In L'Art de jouir *(1751) he propounds purely hedonistic ethics. He died in the house of Milord Tirconnel, minister plenipotentiary of France, whose life he had saved.*

He rejects the view he calls materialism, which he attributes to Locke, according to which matter can think. He also rejects spiritualism, which he attributes to Descartes and Malebranche, according to which a person is composed of a mental substance and a physical substance, the body. Only the experience of physicians who have observed the internal organs of the body guides de la Mettrie's view of human nature. A human being, he argues, is a machine which winds itself up with food. The characters, temperaments, and mental conditions of people differ as their bodily humors and organs differ. The brains of certain mammals, on the other hand, are similar to human brains. He claims that Nature created all creatures to be happy. The existence of a supreme being de la Mettrie believes is a probable theoretic truth with little practical value.

Man a Machine

A wise man should do more than study nature and truth; he should dare state the truth for the benefit of the few who are willing and able to think. As for the rest, who are the willing slaves of prejudice, they can no more attain truth than frogs can fly.

I reduce to two the systems of philosophers on the subject of man's soul. The first and older system is materialism; the second is spiritualism.

The metaphysicians who hinted that matter may well be endowed with the faculty of thought did not perhaps reason too badly. Why? Because they had the very real advantage in this case of not expressing their true meaning. For to ask whether matter can think, without considering it otherwise than it itself, is like asking whether matter can tell time. It may be foreseen that we shall avoid this reef on which Locke had the bad luck to founder.

The Leibnitzians with their monads set up an unintelligible hypothesis. They rather spiritualized matter than materialized the soul. How can we define a being whose nature is absolutely unknown to us?

Descartes and all the Cartesians, among whom the followers of Malebranche have long been numbered, made the same mistake. They recognized two distinct substances in man, as if they had seen them, and actually counted them. . . .

Experience and observation should here be our only guides. They are to be found throughout the records of physicians who were philosophers, and not in the works of philosophers who were not physicians. The former have traveled through and illuminated the labyrinth of man; they alone have exposed for us those vital elements hidden beneath the skin, which hides from us so many wonderful things. They alone, tranquilly contemplating our soul, have surprised it, a thousand times, both in its wretchedness and its glory, and have no more despised it in the first state, than admired it in the second. Once again we see that only physicians have the right to speak on this subject. What could the others, especially the theologians, have to tell us? Is it not ridiculous to hear them shamelessly dogmatize on a subject which lies completely out of their province and from which on the contrary they have been completely turned aside by obscure studies that have led them to a thousand prejudiced opinions, in a word, to fanaticism, which only increases their ignorance of the mechanism of the body?

But even though we have chosen the best guides, we shall still find many thorns and obstructions in our path.

Man is such a complicated machine that it is impossible to form a clear idea of it beforehand, and hence impossible to define it. For this reason, all the investigations which the greatest philosophers have conducted *a priori,* that is to say, by attempting in a way to use the wings of the spirit, have been fruitless. Thus it is only *a posteriori* or by seeking to discover the soul through the organs of the body, so to speak, that we can reach the high-

Source: J. O. de la Mettrie (1747), excerpt from *Man a Machine,* selection from *The Portable Enlightenment Reader,* Isaac Kramnick, ed., Penguin Books (1995): 202–209. Public domain.

est probability concerning man's own nature, even though one can not discover with certainty what that nature is.

Let us lean then on the staff of experience and pay no attention to the history of all idle philosophical theories. To be blind and to think that we can do without this staff is the worst kind of blindness. How truly a modern writer has said that through vanity alone do we fail to draw from secondary causes the same conclusions as from primary causes! We even should admire all these fine geniuses in their most useless works, Descartes, Malebranche, Leibnitz, Wolff, and the rest, but what profit, I ask, has anyone gained from their profound meditations, and from all their works? Let us start afresh then and discover not what has been thought, but what must be thought for the sake of repose in life.

There are as many different minds, characters, and customs, as there are different temperaments. Even Galen knew this truth, which Descartes carried so far as to claim that medicine alone could change minds and morals, along with bodies. It is true that melancholy, bile, phlegm, blood, etc., and the nature, abundance and diverse combinations of these humors, make one man different from another.

In disease the soul is sometimes hidden, showing no sign of life; sometimes it is so inflamed by fury that it seems to be doubled; sometimes imbecility vanishes and convalescence turns a fool into a wit. Sometimes the greatest genius becomes imbecile and no longer recognizable. Farewell then to all that fine knowledge, acquired at so high a price, and with so much trouble! Here is a paralytic, who asks if his leg is in bed with him; there is a soldier, who thinks he still has the arm which has been cut off. The memory of his old sensations, and of the place to which they were referred by his soul, is the cause of his illusion and kind of delirium. The mere mention of the member which he has lost is enough to make him remember and feel all its motions; and this produces an indefinable and inexpressible kind of imaginary suffering.

This man cries like a child at death's approach, while this other jests. What was needed to change the bravery of Caius Julius, Seneca or Petronius into faintheartedness or cowardice? An obstruction in the spleen, in the liver, an impediment in the portal vein. Why? Because the imagination is obstructed along with the viscera, and this gives rise to all those strange phenomena of hysteria and hypochondria.

What could I add to what has been told of those who imagine themselves transformed into wolf-men, cocks or vampires, or those who think that the dead suck their blood? Why should I stop to speak of those who imagine that their noses or some other members are made of glass and who must be advised to sleep on straw to keep from breaking them, so that they may recover the use of their flesh-and-blood organs by setting the straw afire and scaring them—a fright that has sometimes cured paralysis? I must not tarry over facts that are common knowledge.

Nor shall I dwell at length on the effects of sleep. Take this tired soldier. He snores in a trench, to the sound of a hundred cannon. His soul hears nothing; his sleep is perfect apoplexy. A bomb is about to wipe him out. He will feel the shock less perhaps than an insect under his foot.

On the other hand, this man who is devoured by jealousy, hatred, avarice, or ambition, can never find any rest. The most peaceful spot, the coolest and most calming drinks, all have no effect on a man whose heart is a prey to the torment of passion.

The soul and the body fall asleep together. As the pulse gradually slows down, a sweet feeling of peace and quiet spreads throughout the whole machine. The soul feels itself gently sinking along with the eyelids and relaxing along with the fibers of the brain; thus little by little it becomes as if paralyzed along with all the muscles of the body. These can no longer sustain the weight of the head, and the soul can no longer bear the burden of thought; in sleep it is as if it did not exist.

Is the pulse too quick? the soul cannot sleep. Is the soul too agitated? the pulse cannot be quieted: the blood gallops through the veins with an audible murmur. Such are the two interacting causes of insomnia. A simple fright in our dreams makes the heart beat twice as fast and snatches us from needed or delightful repose, as a sharp pain or dire necessity would do. Lastly, just as the cessation of the functions of the soul induces sleep, the mind, even when we are awake (or in this case half awake), takes very frequent short naps, or day dreams, which show that the soul does not always wait for the body to sleep. For if the soul is not fast asleep, it surely is almost so, since it cannot point out a single object to which it has paid attention, among the countless confused ideas which, like so many clouds, so to speak, fill the atmosphere of our brains. . . .

The human body is a machine which winds itself up, the living image of perpetual motion. Food nourishes the movements which fever excites. Without food, the soul pines away, goes mad, and dies exhausted. It is a candle whose light flares up the moment before it goes out. But nourish the body, pour into its veins invigorating juices and strong liquors; then the soul, taking on their strength, arms itself with a proud courage, and the soldier whom water would have made flee, now made bold, runs joyously to death to the sound of drums. Thus a warming drink excites the blood which a cold drink would have calmed.

What power there is in a meal! Joy is born again in a sad heart; it infects the souls of table-companions, who burst into the friendly songs in which the French excel. The melancholy man alone is dejected, and the studious man is likewise out of place. . . .

In general, the form and structure of the brains of quadrupeds are almost the same as in man; the same shape, the same arrangement everywhere, but with this essential difference, that of all the animals man has the largest brain, and, in proportion to its mass, the brain with the most convolutions. Then comes the monkey, the beaver, the elephant, the dog, the fox, the cat, etc., animals which are the most like man; for among them, too, the same progressive analogy can be seen in relation to the *corpus callosum,* in which Lancisi established the seat of the soul—anticipating the late M. de la Peyronie, who illustrated the theory with a great many experiments.

After all the quadrupeds, birds have the most brains. Fish have large heads, but these are void of sense, like the heads of many men. Fish have no *corpus callosum,* and very little brain, while insects entirely lack brain. . . .

The imbecile may not lack brain, as commonly observed, but its consistency will be faulty, for instance, in being too soft. The same thing is true of the insane; the defects of their brains do not always escape our investigation; but if the causes of imbecility, insanity, etc., are not perceptible, how can we hope to discover the causes of the diversity of minds in general? They would escape the eyes of a lynx and an Argus. A mere nothing, a tiny fiber, something that the most delicate dissection cannot discover, would have made two idiots of Erasmus and Fontenelle, and Fontenelle himself makes this observation in one of his best dialogues. . . .

From animals to man, the transition is not violent, as good philosophers will admit. What was man before the invention of words and the knowledge of tongues? An animal of his species, who, with much less native instinct than the others, whose king he then considered himself to be, could not be distinguished from the ape and from the rest, except as the ape itself differs from the other animals; which means, by a face giving promise of more intelligence. Reduced to the bare "intuitive knowledge" of the Leibnitzians he saw only shapes and colors, without being able to distinguish between them; the same, old as young, child at all ages, he stammers out his feelings and needs, like a dog who asks for food when he is hungry or, tired of sleeping, wants to be let out.

Words, languages, laws, sciences, and the fine arts, have come, and by them our rough diamond of a mind has been polished. Man has been trained in the same way as animals; he has become an author, as they become beasts of burden. A geometrician has learned to perform the most difficult demonstrations and calculations, as a monkey has learned to take off or put on his little hat to mount his tame dog. All this has been done through signs, every species has learned what it could understand, and in this way men have acquired "symbolic knowledge," still so called by our German philosophers. . . .

All this knowledge, which blows up the balloon-like brains of our proud pedants, is therefore but a huge mass of words and figures, which form in the brain all the marks by which we distinguish and recall objects. All our ideas are awakened in the same way that a gardener who knows plants recalls, at the sight of them, all the stages of their growth. These words and the objects designated by them are so connected in the brain that it is comparatively rare to imagine a thing without the name or sign that is attached to it.

I always use the word "imagine," because I think that everything is imagined and that all the faculties of the soul can be correctly reduced to pure imagination, which gives form to them all. Thus judgment, reason and memory, are in no wise absolute parts of the soul, but real modifications of the kind of medullary screen upon which images of the objects painted in the eye are reflected as by a magic lantern.

But if such is the marvelous and incomprehensible result of the structure of the brain, if everything is perceived and explained by imagination, why should we divide the sensitive principle which thinks in man? Is not this clearly an inconsistency on the part of those who uphold the simplicity of the mind? For a thing that can be divided can no longer without absurdity be regarded as indivisible. This is where we come to through the abuse of language and those fine words "spirituality," "immateriality," etc., used haphazardly and not understood even by the most intelligent. . . .

We were not originally made to be learned; we have become so perhaps by a sort of abuse of our organic faculties, and at the expense of the State, which nourishes a host of loafers whom vanity has adorned with the name of "philosophers." Nature created us all solely to be happy—yes, all, from the crawling worm to the eagle that soars out of sight in the clouds. That is why she has given all animals some share of natural law, a share of greater or less delicacy according to the needs of each animal's organs when in good condition.

Now how shall we define natural law? It is a feeling which teaches us what we should not do, because we would not wish it to be done to us. Would I dare add to this common idea, that this feeling seems to me but a kind of fear or dread, as salutary to the race as to the individual? For perhaps we respect the purses and lives of others only to save our own possessions, our honor, and our own lives; like those "Ixions of Christianity" who love God and embrace so many fantastic virtues, merely because of their fear of hell.

You see that natural law is nothing but an intimate feeling which belongs also to the imagination like all other feelings, thought included. Consequently it evidently does not presuppose education, revelation or legislator, unless we confuse it with civil laws, in the ridiculous fashion of the theologians.

The arms of fanaticism may destroy those who maintain these truths, but they will never destroy the truths themselves.

Not that I call in question the existence of a supreme being; on the contrary it seems to me that the greatest degree of probability is in favor of this belief. But since the existence of this being does not prove that one form of worship is more necessary than any other, it is a theoretic truth with very little practical value. Therefore, since we may say, after such long experience, that religion does not imply exact honesty, we are authorized by the same reasons to think that atheism does not exclude it.

Furthermore, who knows whether the reason for man's existence is not simply the fact that he exists? Perhaps he was thrown by chance on some spot of the earth's surface, nobody knows how or why, but simply that he must live and die, like mushrooms that appear from one day to the next, or like the flowers which border ditches and cover walls. . . .

Let us conclude boldly then that man is a machine, and that in the whole universe there is but a single substance with various modifications. This is no hypothesis set up by dint of proposals and assumptions. It is not the work of prejudice, nor even of my reason alone; I would have disdained a guide which I believe so untrustworthy, had not my senses held the torch, so to speak, and induced me to follow reason by lighting the way. Experience has thus spoken to me in behalf of reason; and in this way I have combined the two.

But it must have been noticed that I have not allowed myself even the most forceful and immediately deduced reasoning, except as it followed a multitude of observations which no scholar will contest; and furthermore, I recognize only scientists as judges of the conclusions which I draw, and I hereby challenge every prejudiced man who is not an anatomist, or acquainted with the only philosophy which is to the purpose, that of the human body. Against such a strong and solid oak, what could the weak reeds of theology, metaphysics and scholasticism, avail; childish weapons, like our foils, which may well afford the pleasure of fencing, but can never wound an adversary. Need I say that I refer to the hollow and trivial notions, to the trite and pitiable arguments that will be urged, as long as the shadow of prejudice or superstition remains on earth, for the supposed incompatibility of two substances which meet and interact unceasingly? Such is my system, or rather the truth, unless I am very much mistaken. It is short and simple. Dispute it now who will.

DISCUSSION QUESTIONS

1. How might Richard Taylor reply to de la Mettrie's statement that asking whether matter can think is like asking whether matter can tell time?
2. What does de la Mettrie think about theologians and philosophers and their metaphysics and scholasticism? Do you agree? Explain.
3. How does de la Mettrie try to support his position with the examples of the person with a paralyzed leg, the amputee soldier, and those deluded into believing they are vampires?
4. What does de la Mettrie think the nature of sleep reveals about the soul and the body?
5. How does de la Mettrie rank, in decreasing size, the human brain and the brains of other animals?
6. What is de la Mettrie's account of imagination? Is it persuasive?
7. How does he define natural law?
8. How are human beings like mushrooms or flowers which border ditches, according to de la Mettrie?

Chapter 14

G. W. LEIBNIZ

Born in Leipzig, Gottfried Wilhelm von Leibniz (1646–1716) was a German jurist, historian, philosopher, mathematician, logician, librarian, and engineer. Though a Lutheran, one of his lifelong aims was reunification of the Christian churches. Another was to collate all human knowledge. He corresponded with over 600 scholars in Europe. He was perhaps best known for inventing the differential and integral calculus (independently of Sir Isaac Newton).

This selection is from his dialogue between Philalethes *(the spokesman for John Locke the empiricist and author of* An Essay Concerning Human Understanding*) and* Theophilus *(the spokesman for Leibniz the rationalist). Leibniz explains that Aristotle and Locke think the human soul in itself is completely blank like a writing tablet on which nothing yet has been written. Leibniz, in contrast, sees his own philosophy as closer to Plato's. He agrees with most of the ancients that every soul is always united with a body, and that no soul is ever entirely without one. He holds that souls change in states from more to less sensible, more to less perfect, and vice versa. Rational souls always preserve the* persona *which they have been given in the city of God; they retain their memories so that they may be more susceptible of punishments and rewards. Leibniz denies transmigration of the soul. Instead, he believes that the soul's body over time is reshaped, infolded, unfolded, and flows. Memory must connect the different* personae *which are made by the same soul to constitute sufficient moral identity in a single person. Thus Leibniz argues that identity of substance is not sufficient for identity of person. The souls of nonhuman animals are* imperishable *(incessant), whereas the souls of human beings are* immortal. *The souls of beasts and human souls preserve physical identity, but human souls retain a* moral *identity and personality. Theophilus (Leibniz) argues as follows: (1) If the immediate inner experience, e.g., a present memory of what I was thinking five seconds ago, is not certain, then we cannot be sure of any truth of fact. (2) But it is false that we cannot be sure of any truth of fact. (3) Therefore, the immediate inner experience is infallible. Nature establishes a pre-existing harmony of perfect correspondence between all mental events in the soul and all physical events in the body.*

New Essays on the Human Understanding

PREFACE

. . . I agree with most of the ancients that every Spirit, every soul, every created simple substance is always united with a body and that no soul is ever entirely without one. I have *a priori* reasons for this doctrine, but it will be found to have the further merit of solving all the philosophical difficulties about the state of souls, their perpetual preservation, their immortality, and their mode of operation. Their changes of state never are and never were anything but changes from more to less sensible, from more perfect to less perfect, or the reverse, so that their past and future states are just as explicable as their present one. Even the slightest reflection shows that this is reasonable, and that a leap from one state to an infinitely different one cannot be natural. I am surprised that the Schoolmen—unreasonably abandoning nature—deliberately plunged into the greatest difficulties and provided free-thinkers with apparent cause for triumph. The latters' arguments are pulled down all at once by my account of things, in which there is no more difficulty in conceiving the preservation of the soul (or rather, on my view, of the animal) than in conceiving the transformation of a caterpillar into a butterfly, or the preservation of thought during sleep—to which Jesus Christ has sublimely compared death. I have also said already that no sleep could last for ever; and in the case of rational souls it will be of even briefer duration or almost none at all. These souls are destined always to preserve the *persona*[1] which they have been given in the city of God, and hence to retain their memories, so that they may be more susceptible of punishments and rewards. I further add that in general no disruption of its visible organs can reduce an animal to total confusion, or destroy all the organs and deprive the soul of its entire organic body and of the ineradicable vestiges of its previous traces. But people's readiness to abandon the ancient doctrine of the rarefied bodies annexed to angels (which was confused with the corporeality of the angels themselves), the inclusion among created things of alleged separate intelligences (and notably the ones which in Aristotle's doctrine make the heavens revolve), and lastly the misconception to which some have been subject, that preservation of the souls of beasts would lead one to metempsychosis and to their transmigration from body to body—the perplexity that people have been in through not knowing what they should do about all this has resulted, in my opinion, in their overlooking the natural way to explain the preservation of the soul.

Source: G.W. Leibniz, excerpts from *New Essays on the Human Understanding,* P. Remnant and J. Bennett tr., Cambridge University Press (1981): Preface (Akademie) 58–59 and Book II, ch. 27 (Akademie): 232–247. Reprinted with the permission of Cambridge University Press. Line references have been deleted.

BOOK II, CHAPTER 27

THEO. If plants and brutes have no souls, then their identity is only apparent, but if they do have souls their identity is strictly genuine, although their organic bodies do not retain such an identity.

PHIL. He that shall place the identity of man in any thing else, but in one fitly organized body taken in any one instant, and from thence continued under one organization of life in several successively fleeting particles of matter, united to it, will find it hard, to make an embryo, one of years, mad, and sober, the same man, without its following from this supposition that it is 'possible for Seth, Ishmael, Socrates, Pilate, St. Augustine to be the same man. This would agree yet worse with the notions of those philosophers, who allow of transmigration, and are of opinion that the souls of men may, for their miscarriages, be detruded into the bodies of beasts. . . . But yet I think no body, could he be sure that the soul of Heliogabalus were in a hog, would yet say that hog were a man, and the same man as Heliogabalus.'

THEO. We have here both a question about the name and a question about the thing. As regards the thing, a single individual substance can retain its identity only by preservation of the same soul, for the body is in continual flux and the soul does not reside in certain atoms which are reserved for it or in some little indestructible bone, like the *luz** of the rabbins. However, there is no transmigration in which the soul entirely abandons its body and passes into another. Even in death it always retains an organic body, part of its former one, although what it retains is always subject to wasting away insensibly and to restoring itself, and even at a given time to undergoing a great change. Thus, instead of transmigration of the soul there is reshaping, infolding, unfolding, and flowing, in the soul's body. M. van Helmont the younger believed that souls pass from body to body, but always within the same species. This implies that there will always be the same number of souls of a given species—the same number of men or of wolves, so that if the wolves have been reduced or wiped out in England they must have correspondingly increased elsewhere. Certain meditations published in France seemed to take the same view.

If transmigration is not taken strictly, i.e. if anyone thought that souls remain in the same rarefied bodies and only change their coarse bodies, that would be possible, even to the extent of the same soul's passing into a body of another species in the Brahmin or Pythagorean manner. But not everything which is possible is therefore in conformity with the order of things. If such a transformation did occur, however, and assuming in accordance with rabbinical doctrine that Cain, Ham and Ishmael had the same soul, the question of whether they ought to be called the same man is merely a question of a name. I have noticed that the distinguished author whose opinions you have supported recognizes this and sets it forth very clearly (in the final paragraph of this chapter). There would be identity of substance but, if there were no connection by way of memory between the different *personae*[2] which were made by the same soul, there would not be enough moral identity to say that this was a single person. And if God wished a human soul to pass into the body of a hog and to forget the man and perform no rational acts, it would not constitute a man. But if while in the body of the beast it had the thoughts of a man, and even of the man whom it had animated before the change, like the golden ass of Apuleius, perhaps no one would object to saying that the same Lucius, who had come to Thessaly to see his friends, remained inside the skin of the ass where Photis had inadvertently put him, and wandered from master to master until by eating the roses he was restored to his natural shape.

PHIL. § **8.** I think I may be confident, that whoever of us should see a creature of his own shape and make, though it gave no more appearance of[3] reason all its life, than a cat or a parrot, would call

*In a rabbinic tradition, the bone from which the body is resurrected. [Ed.]

him still a man; or whoever should hear[4] a parrot discourse, reason, and philosophize, would call or think it nothing but a parrot; and say, the first of these animals was a dull irrational man, and the second a very intelligent rational parrot.

THEO. I agree more with the second point than with the first, although something needs to be said about that too. Few theologians would be bold enough to decide straight away and without qualification to baptize an animal of human shape, lacking the appearance of reason, which[5] had been found as an infant in the woods. A priest of the Roman Church might say conditionally If you are a man I baptize you. For it would not be known whether it belonged to the human race and whether there was a rational soul in it; it might be an orang-outang—a monkey closely resembling a man in external features—like the one Tulp speaks of having seen, and the one whose anatomy has been published by a learned physician. It is certain, I admit, that a man can become as stupid as an orang-outang; but the inner being of the rational soul would remain despite the suspending of the exercise of reason, as I have already explained. So that is the essential point, and it cannot be settled by appearances. As to the second case, there is no obstacle to there being rational animals of some other species than ours, like the poet's birds who had their kingdom in the sun, where a parrot who had gone there from this world after his death saved the life of a traveller who had been kind to him on earth. However if, as happens in fairy-land and in Mother Goose, a parrot were the transformed daughter of a king and revealed itself as such by speaking, no doubt the father and mother would caress it as their daughter and would believe that they had her back though concealed in that alien form. Still, I would not quarrel with someone who said that in the Golden Ass there is still the same self or individual (because of the same immaterial spirit), as well as the same Lucius or person (because of his awareness of this *I*), but that it is no longer a man. Indeed it does seem that we have to add something about the shape and constitution of the body to the definition of man, when he is said to be a rational animal; otherwise, according to my views, Spirits would also be men.

PHIL. § **9.** The word *person* stands for a thinking intelligent being, that has reason and reflection, and can consider it self as it self, the same thinking thing in different times and places; which it does only by the sense that it has of its own actions.[6] And this knowledge[7] always accompanies our present sensations and perceptions—when they are sufficiently distinct, as I have remarked more than once already—and by this every one is to himself, that which he calls *self:* it not being considered in this case, whether the same self be continued in the same, or divers substances. For since consciousness[8] always accompanies thinking, and 'tis that, that makes every one to be, what he calls *self;* and thereby distinguishes himself from all other thinking things, in this alone consists personal identity, i.e. what makes a rational being always the same: and as far as this consciousness can be extended backwards to any past action or thought, so far reaches the identity of that person; it is the same self now as it was then.

THEO. I also hold this opinion that consciousness or the sense of *I* proves moral or personal identity. And that is how I distinguish the *incessancy* of a beast's soul from the *immortality* of the soul of a man: both of them preserve *real, physical identity;* but it is consonant with the rules of divine providence that in man's case the soul should also retain a moral identity which is apparent to us ourselves, so as to constitute the same person, which is therefore sensitive to punishments and rewards. You seem to hold, sir, that this apparent identity could be preserved in the absence of any real identity. Perhaps that could happen through God's absolute power; but I should have thought that, according to the order of things, an identity which is apparent to the person concerned—one who senses himself to be the same—presupposes a real identity obtaining through each immediate temporal transition accompanied by reflection, or by the sense of *I;* because an intimate and immediate perception cannot be mistaken in the natural course of things. If a man could be a mere machine and still possess consciousness, I would have to agree with you, sir; but I hold that that state of affairs is not possible—at least not naturally. I would not wish to deny, either, that personal identity and even the self persist in us, and that I am that *I* who was in the cradle, merely on the grounds that I can no longer remember anything that I did at that time. To discover one's own moral identity unaided, it is sufficient that between one state and a neighbouring (or just a nearby) one there be a mediating bond of consciousness, even if this has a jump or forgotten interval mixed into it. Thus, if an illness had interrupted the continuity of my bond of consciousness, so that I did not know how I had arrived at my present state even though I could remember things further back, the testimony of others could fill in the gap in my recollection. I could even be punished on this testimony if I had done some deliberate wrong during an interval which this illness had made me forget a short time later. And if I forgot my whole past, and[9] needed to have myself taught all over again, even my name and how to read and write, I could still learn from others about my life during my preceding state; and, similarly, I would have retained[10] my rights without having to be divided into two persons and made to inherit from myself. All this is enough to maintain the moral identity which makes the same person. It is true that if the others conspired to deceive me (just as I might deceive myself by some vision or dream or illness, thinking that what I had dreamed had really happened to me), then the appearance would be false; but sometimes we can be morally certain of the truth on the credit of others' reports. And in relation to God, whose social bond with us is the cardinal point of morality, error cannot occur. As regards self, it will be as well to distinguish it from the appearance of self and from consciousness. The self makes real physical identity, and the appearance of self, when accompanied by truth, adds to it personal identity. So, not wishing to say that personal identity extends no further than memory, still less would I say that the 'self', or physical identity, depends upon it. The existence of real personal identity is proved with as much certainty as any matter of fact can be, by present and immediate reflection; it is proved conclusively enough for ordinary purposes by memories across intervals[11] and by the concurring testimony of other people. Even if God were to change the real identity in some extraordinary manner, the personal identity would remain, provided that the man preserved the appearances of identity—the inner ones (i.e. the ones belonging to consciousness) as well as outer ones such as those consisting in what appears to other people. Thus, consciousness is not the only means of establishing personal identity, and its deficiencies may be made up by other people's accounts or even by other indications. But difficulties arise when there is a conflict between these various appearances. Consciousness may stay silent, as in loss of memory; but if it spoke out plainly in opposition to the other appearances, we would be at a loss to decide and would sometimes be suspended between two possibilities: that the memory is mistaken or that outer appearances are deceptive.

PHIL. § **11.** It will be said that the limbs of each man's body are parts of himself; and that therefore, since his body is in constant flux, the man cannot remain the same.

THEO. I would rather say that the *I* and the *he* are without parts, since we say, quite correctly, that he continues to exist as really the same substance, the same physical *I;* but we cannot say—with complete fidelity to the truth of things—that the same whole continues to exist if a part of it is lost. And what has bodily parts cannot avoid losing some of them at every moment.

PHIL. § **13.** The consciousness of one's past actions could not be transferred from one thinking substance to another—and our having a sense of ourselves as the same would render it certain that the same substance remained[12]—if the same consciousness were the same individual action, that is, if there were no difference between the action of reflecting and the action on which one reflected in being aware of it.[13] But it being but a present representation of a past action, why it may not be possible, that that may be represented to the mind to have been, which really never was, will remain to be shown.

THEO. We can be deceived by a memory across an interval—one often experiences this and one can conceive of a natural cause of such an error. But a present or immediate memory, the memory of what was taking place immediately before—or in other words, the consciousness or reflection which accompanies inner activity—cannot naturally deceive us. If it could, we would not even be certain that we are thinking about such and such a thing; for this too sc. ['I think . . .' as well as 'I remember . . .'] is silently said only about past actions, not about the very action of saying it. But if the immediate inner experience is not certain, we cannot be sure of any truth of fact. I have already said that there can be an intelligible reason for the element of error in perceptions which are mediate and outer, but with regard to immediate inner ones such a reason could not be found except by having recourse to God's omnipotence.

PHIL. § **14.** As to the question, whether the same immaterial substance remaining, there may be two distinct persons; which question seems to me to be built on this, whether, the same immaterial being may be stripped of all sense[14] of its past existence, and lose it beyond the power of ever retrieving again: and so as it were beginning a new account from a new period, have a consciousness that cannot reach beyond this new state. All those who hold pre-existence of souls are evidently of this mind. I once met with one, who was persuaded his had been the soul of Socrates (I know, that in the post he filled, which was no inconsiderable one, he passed for a very rational man, and his published works have shown, that he wanted not parts or learning). Souls being, as far as we know any thing of them in their nature, indifferent to any parcel of matter, the supposition of a single soul's passing from one body to another has no apparent absurdity in it. But he, now having no sense of anything at all that Nestor or Socrates ever did or thought,[15] does, or can he, conceive himself the same person with either of them? Can he be concerned in either of their actions? Attribute them to himself, or think them his own more than the actions of any other man, that already existed? He is no more one person[16] with either of them, than if the soul which is now in him, had been created when it began to inform his present body. This would no more make him the same person with Nestor, than if some of the particles of matter, that were once a part of Nestor, were now a part of this man, the same immaterial substance without the same consciousness, no more making the same person by being united to any body, than the same particles of matter united to any body without a common consciousness can make[17] the same person.

THEO. An immaterial being or spirit cannot be stripped of all perception of its past existence. It retains impressions of everything which has previously happened to it, and it even has presentiments of everything which will happen to it; but these states of mind[18] are mostly too minute to be distinguishable and for one to be aware of them, although they may perhaps grow some day. It is this continuity and interconnection[19] of perceptions which make someone really the same individual; but our awarenesses—i.e. when we are aware of past states of mind[20]—prove a moral identity as well, and make the real identity appear. The pre-existence of souls does not appear to us through our perceptions. But if it really were the case, it could some day make itself known. So it is unreasonable to suppose that memory should be lost beyond any possibility of recovery, since insensible perceptions, whose usefulness I have shown in so many other important connections, serve a purpose here too—preserving the seeds of memory. The late Mr Henry More, the Anglican theologian was convinced of the pre-existence of the soul and wrote in support of it. The late

M. van Helmont the younger went further, as I have just said, and believed in the transmigration of souls, although always between bodies of the same species, so that in his opinion human souls always animate men. He believed, like certain rabbins, that the soul of Adam passed into the Messiah as the new Adam. For all I know he may, clever man though he was, have believed himself to be one of the ancients. I have explained earlier [p. 99] a way in which the migration of souls is possible (though it does not appear likely), namely that souls might, while retaining rarefied bodies, pass suddenly into other coarse bodies. If migration really did occur—at least, if it occurred in that manner—then the same individual would exist throughout, in Nestor, in Socrates and in some modern; and it[21] could even let its identity be known to someone who penetrated deeply enough into its nature, by means of the impressions or records of all that Nestor or Socrates had done, which remained in it and could be read there by a sufficiently acute mind. Yet if the modern man had no way, inner or outer, of knowing what he has been, it would from a moral point of view be as though he had never been it. But it appears that nothing in the world lacks significance—moral significance, indeed—since God reigns over the world and his government is perfect. On my hypotheses souls are not indifferent to any parcel of matter, as it seems to you that they are; on the contrary they inherently express those portions with which they are and must be united in an orderly way. So if they passed into a new coarse or sensible body, they would still retain the expression of everything of which they had had any perception in the old one; and indeed the new body would have to feel the effects of it, so that there will always be real marks of the continuance of the individual. But whatever our past state may have been, we cannot always be aware of the effect which it leaves behind. The able author of the *Essay on Understanding,* whose views you had adopted, remarks (xxvii.27) that his suppositions or fictions about the migration of souls—considered as being possible—rest partly on the fact that the mind is commonly regarded not merely as independent of matter but also as indifferent to every kind of matter. But I hope, sir, that what I have said to you on this topic, in one place and another, will clear up this uncertainty and will give a better grasp of what can naturally happen. It shows in what way the actions of an ancient would belong to a modern who possessed the same soul, even though he was unaware of them. But if it did come to be known, that would imply personal identity in addition. What makes the same human individual is not a parcel of matter which passes from one body to another, nor is it what we call *I;* rather, it is the soul.

PHIL. § **16.** However, it is true that I am as much concerned, and as justly accountable for any action was done a thousand years since, appropriated to me now by this self-consciousness[22] which I now have, as having been done by myself[23] as I am, for what I did the last moment.

THEO. This belief that we have done something can deceive us if the action was long ago. People have mistaken their dreams for reality, and have come to believe their own stories by constantly repeating them. Such a false belief can cause perplexity, but it cannot make one liable to punishment if there are no other beliefs which confirm it. On the other hand, one can be accountable for what one has done, even if one has forgotten it, provided that there is independent confirmation of the action.

PHIL. § **17.** Every one finds daily that whilst comprehended under that consciousness, the little finger is as much a part of it self (of him)[24] as what is most so.

THEO. I have said (§ 11) why I would not wish to maintain that my finger is part of *me;* but it is true that it belongs to me and is a part of my body.

PHIL. Those who hold a different view will say: Upon separation of this little finger, should this consciousness go along with the little finger, and leave the rest of the body, 'tis evident the little finger would be the person, the same person; and self then would have nothing to do with the rest of the body.

THEO. Nature does not permit these fictions, which are eliminated by the system of harmony, i.e. of the perfect correspondence between soul and body.

PHIL. § **18.** It seems, though, that if the same body should still live, and have its own peculiar consciousness, whereof the little finger knew nothing—and if, nevertheless, the soul was in the finger—the finger could not acknowledge any of the actions of the rest of the body, nor could one impute them to it.

THEO. Nor would the soul which was in the finger belong to this body. I admit that if God brought it about that consciousness were transferred to other souls, the latter would have to be treated according to moral notions as though they were the same. But this would disrupt the order of things for no reason, and would divorce what can come before our awareness from the truth—the truth which is preserved by insensible perceptions. That would not be reasonable, since perceptions which are at present insensible may grow some day: nothing is useless, and eternity provides great scope for change.

PHIL. § **20.** Human laws do not punish the mad man for the sober man's actions, nor the sober man for what the mad man did, and so they make them two persons. Thus we say such an one is *besides himself.*

THEO. The laws threaten punishment and promise reward in order to discourage evil actions and encourage good ones. But a madman may be in a condition where threats and promises barely influence him, since his reason is no longer in command; and so the severity of the penalty should be relaxed in proportion to his incapacity. On the other hand, we want the criminal to have a sense of the effects of the evil he has done, in order to increase people's fear of committing crimes; but since the madman is not sufficiently sensitive, we are content to postpone for some time carrying out the sentence by which we punish him for what he did while in his right mind. Thus what laws and judges do in these cases is not the result of their supposing that two persons are involved.

PHIL. § **22.** Indeed, those whose views I am presenting to you have raised this objection against themselves: if a man who is drunk and who then becomes sober is not the same person, he ought not to be punished for what he did while drunk, since he no longer has any sense of it. To this it is replied that he is just as much the same person, as a man that walks, and does other things in his sleep, is the same person, and is answerable for any mischief he shall do in it.

THEO. There is a great deal of difference between the actions of a drunk man and of a true and acknowledged sleepwalker. We punish drunkards because they could stay sober and may even retain some memory of the punishment while they are drunk. But a sleepwalker is less able to abstain from his nocturnal walk and from what he does during it. Still, if it were true that a good birching on the spot would make him stay in bed, we would have the right to carry it out—and we would carry it out, too, although this would be a remedy rather than a punishment. Indeed, this remedy is reported to have been effective.

PHIL. Human laws punish both with a justice suitable to men's way of knowledge of things: because in these sorts of cases, they cannot distinguish certainly what is real, what counterfeit; and so the ignorance in drunkenness or sleep is not admitted as a plea. The fact is proved against him, but want of consciousness cannot be proved for him.

THEO. The real question is not so much that as what to do when it has been well established—as it can be—that the drunkard or the sleepwalker really was beside himself. In that case the sleepwalker can only be regarded as victim of a mania; but since drunkenness is voluntary and sickness is not, we punish the one rather than the other.

PHIL. But in the great and fearful day of judgment, wherein the secrets of all hearts shall be laid open, we are entitled[25] to think, no one shall be made to answer for what he knows nothing of; but shall receive his doom, his conscience accusing or excusing him.

THEO. I doubt that man's memory will have to be raised up on the day of judgment so that he can remember everything which he had forgotten, and that the knowledge of others, and especially of that just Judge who is never deceived, will not suffice. One could invent the fiction, not much in accord with the truth but at least possible, that a man on the day of judgment believed himself to have been wicked and that this also appeared true to all the other created spirits who were in a position to offer a judgment on the matter, even though it was not the truth. Dare one say that the supreme and just Judge, who alone knew differently, could damn this person and judge contrary to his knowledge? Yet this seems to follow from the notion of moral person which you offer. It may be said that if God judges contrary to appearances, he will not be sufficiently glorified and will bring distress to others; but it can be replied that he is himself his own unique and supreme law, and that in this case the others should conclude that they were mistaken.

PHIL. § **23.** If we could suppose either that two distinct incommunicable consciousnesses might act alternately in the same body, the one constantly by day, the other by night; or that the same consciousness might act by intervals in two distinct bodies; I ask in the first case, whether the *day* and the *night*-man, if I may express myself in this way,[26] would not be two as distinct persons, as Socrates and Plato; and whether in the second case, there would not be one person in two distinct bodies? It is not relevant that this single consciousness which affects two different bodies, and these consciousnesses which affect the same body at different times, belong in the one case to the same immaterial substance, and in the other to two distinct immaterial substances, which introduce those different consciousnesses into those bodies; since the personal identity would equally be determined by the consciousness, whether that consciousness were annexed to some individual immaterial substance or no. Furthermore, that immaterial thinking thing may sometimes lose sight of its past consciousness, and recall it again.[27] Make these intervals of memory and forgetfulness to take their turns regularly by day and night, and you have two persons with the same immaterial spirit. So that *self* is not determined by identity or diversity of substance, which one cannot be sure of, but only by identity of consciousness.

THEO. I acknowledge that if all the appearances of one mind were transferred to another, or if God brought about an exchange between two minds by giving to one the visible body of the other and its appearances and states of consciousness, then personal identity would not be tied to the identity of substance but rather would go with the constant appearances, which are what human morality must give heed to. But these appearances would not consist merely in states of consciousness: God would have to exchange not only the states of awareness or consciousness of the individuals concerned, but also the appearances which were presented to others; otherwise what the others had to say would conflict with the consciousnesses of the individuals themselves, which would disturb the moral order. Still, it must be granted to me that the divorce between the insensible and sensible realms, i.e. between the insensible perceptions which remained in the same substances and the states of awareness which were exchanged, would be a miracle—like supposing God to create a vacuum. For I have already explained why this is not in conformity with the natural order. Here is something we could much more fittingly suppose: in another region of the universe or at some other time there may be a sphere in no way sensibly different from this sphere of earth on which we live, and inhabited by men each of whom differs sensibly in no way from his counterpart among us. Thus at one time there will be more than a hundred million pairs of similar persons, i.e. pairs of persons with the same appearances and states of consciousness. God could transfer the minds, by themselves or with their bodies, from one sphere to the other without their being aware of it; but whether they are transferred or left where they are, what would your authorities say about their persons or selves? Given that the states of consciousness and the inner and outer appearances of the men on these two spheres cannot yield a distinction between them, are they two persons or are they one and the same? It is true that they could be told apart by God, and by minds which were capable of grasping the intervals between the spheres and their outer relations of space and time, and even the inner constitutions, of which the men on the two spheres would be insensible. But since according to your theories consciousness[28] alone distinguishes persons, with no need for us to be concerned about the real identity or diversity of substance or even about what would appear to other people, what is to prevent us from saying that these two persons who are at the same time in these two similar but inexpressibly distant spheres, are one and the same person? Yet that would be a manifest absurdity. I will add that if we are speaking of what can naturally occur, the two similar spheres and the two similar souls on them could remain similar only for a time. Since they would be numerically different, there would have to be a difference at least in their insensible constitutions, and the latter must unfold in the fullness of time.

PHIL. **§ 26.** Supposing a man punished now, for what he had done in another life, whereof he could be made to have no consciousness at all, what difference is there between such treatment and the treatment he would get in being created miserable?[29]

THEO. Platonists, Origenists, certain Hebrews and other defenders of the pre-existence of souls have believed that the souls of this world were put into imperfect bodies to make them suffer for crimes committed in a former world. But the fact is that if one does not know the truth of the matter, and will never find it out either by recalling it through memory or from traces or from what other people know, it cannot be called punishment according to the ordinary way of thinking. If we are to speak quite generally of punishment, however, there are grounds for questioning whether it is absolutely necessary that those who suffer should themselves eventually learn why, and whether it would not quite often be sufficient that those punishments should afford, to other and better informed Spirits, matter for glorifying divine justice. Still, it is more likely, at least in general, that the sufferers will learn why they suffer.

PHIL. **§ § 28–9.**[30] Perhaps, all things considered, you can agree with my author when he concludes his chapter on identity by saying that the question of whether the same man remains is a question of name, depending on whether by a man we understand just a rational spirit, or just a body of the form we call human, or, finally, a spirit united with such a body. On the first account, the spirit which is separated (from the coarse body at least) will still be a man; on the second, an orang-outang which was exactly like us apart from reason would be a man, and if a man were deprived of his rational soul and given the soul of a beast he would remain the same man. On the third account both must remain, still united to one another: the same spirit, and the same body too in part—or at least its equivalent as regards sensible bodily form. Thus one could remain the same being physically and morally, that is the same substance and the same person, without remaining a man, if we follow the third account in regarding this shape as essential to the identity of the man.

THEO. I admit that there is a question of name involved here. And the third account is like the same animal being at one time a caterpillar or silk-worm and at another a butterfly; or, as some have imagined, the angels of this world having been men in a former world. But we have met to discuss more important matters than the signification of words. I have shown you the basis of true physical identity, and have shown that it does not clash with moral identity or with memory either. And I have also shown that although they sc. moral identity and memory[31] cannot always indicate a person's physical identity either to the person in question or to his acquaintances, they never run counter to physical identity and are never totally divorced from it. Finally, I have shown that there are always created spirits who know or can know the truth of the matter, and that there is reason to think that things which make no difference from the point of view of the persons themselves will do so only temporarily.

NOTES

1. '*personnage*': a standard word for a character in a play, one of the *dramatis personae.*
2. *personnages;* see note 1.
3. Locke: had no more. Coste's change.
4. Locke: a cat or. Coste's omission.
5. Or who: the French leaves the question open.
6. Locke: only by consciousness. Coste's change.
7. Locke: consciousness. Coste's change.
8. *conscience* (consciousness, *consciosité*).
9. Replacing *je serais* by *et fusse* from an earlier version.
10. Or: and learn about how I had retained. Or: just as I have retained.
11. *par nôtre souvenir d'intervalle.*
12. Added by Leibniz.
13. Added by Leibniz.
14. Locke: consciousness. Coste: *sentiment,* with *ou conscience* in the margin.
15. Locke: no consciousness of any of the actions either of Nestor or Thersites. Coste's changes, except for Leibniz's Socrates.
16. Locke: self. Coste's change.
17. Locke: particle of matter without consciousness united to any body, makes. Coste's change.
18. *sentiments.*
19. *liaison.*
20. *sentiments.*
21. Or 'he', and so throughout the rest of the sentence.
22. Leibniz and Coste use *conscience* and the English word.
23. Added by Coste.
24. Added by Leibniz.
25. Locke: it may be reasonable. Coste's change.
26. Added by Coste.
27. Locke: part with its past consciousness, and be restored to it again. Coste's change.
28. Taking *conscienciosité* to be a slip for *consciosité.*
29. Locke: between that punishment, and being created miserable? Coste's change.
30. This paragraph is very loosely based upon Locke.
31. Taking '*elles*' to be a slip for '*ils*'.

DISCUSSION QUESTIONS

1. What does the identity of a human individual consist in, according to Leibniz?
2. How long can a conscious being sleep, according to Leibniz? How long can a rational soul? Do you agree? Explain.
3. Does Leibniz think a man can become as stupid as an orangutan? In such a case, does he think that the man loses his rational soul? Explain.
4. Explain Leibniz's distinction between imperishable souls and immortal souls.
5. Theophilus insists that the existence of real personal identity is proved with as much certainty as any matter of fact can be, by present and immediate reflection. Are you convinced by his (*modus tollens*) argument that immediate inner experience is infallible? How might someone (e.g., Hume) argue against it?
6. Theophilus says that an immaterial spirit cannot be stripped of all perception of its past existence. It retains impressions of everything which has happened to it, and it even has presentiments of everything which *will* happen to it. How plausible is this view? Explain.
7. Theophilus thinks his finger is not a part of him, rather it *belongs* to him. Is this the best way to describe the relation between your finger and yourself?

Chapter 15

DAVID HUME

Born in Edinburgh, Scotland in 1711, David Hume died in 1776. He was a philosopher, historian, pen-pal of Montesquieu, and friend of Jean-Jacques Rousseau, with whom he also quarreled. Hume's monumental Treatise *was published in 1739 when he was only twenty-eight years old.*

Here we read that philosophers like Leibniz imagine that every moment we are intimately conscious of what we call our perfectly identical, simple self. Yet Hume insists that ideas arise from impressions. He reasons as follows: (1) If any impression gives rise to the idea of self, then that impression must continue invariably the same, through the whole course of our lives, since self is supposed to exist that way. (2) But there is no impression that is constant and invariable; pain and pleasure, grief and joy, passions and sensations all succeed each other—they never all exist simultaneously. (3) Hence, there is no impression that gives rise to an idea of self. (4) Therefore, the self is merely a fictional notion. Hume likens the mind to a kind of theater where several perceptions successively appear, pass, and mingle in an infinite variety of postures and situations. There is properly no simplicity *in it at one time, nor* identity *in different times. We have no notion of the place (the stage) where these scenes are represented, nor of the materials of which it is composed. Identity is merely a quality which we attribute to the succession of relations which we call a single object. Hume also compares the soul to a republic in which the members produce, and are incessantly replaced by, other members. Just as the same individual republic may change both its members and its laws and constitutions, Hume contends that the same person may vary his character, disposition, impressions, and ideas without losing his identity. Memory does not so much produce as* discover *personal identity by showing us the relation of cause and effect among our different perceptions.*

A Treatise of Human Nature (Book I, Part 4)

SECTION VI OF PERSONAL IDENTITY

There are some philosophers who imagine we are every moment intimately conscious of what we call our *self;* that we feel its existence and its continuance in existence; and are certain, beyond the evidence of a demonstration, both of its perfect identity and simplicity. The strongest sensation, the most violent passion, say they, instead of distracting us from this view, only fix it the more intensely, and make us consider their influence on *self* either by their pain or pleasure. To attempt a further proof of this were to weaken its evidence; since no proof can be derived from any fact of which we are so intimately conscious; nor is there anything of which we can be certain if we doubt of this.

Unluckily all these positive assertions are contrary to that very experience which is pleaded for them; nor have we any idea of *self,* after the manner it is here explained. For, from what impression could this idea be derived? This question it is impossible to answer without a manifest contradiction and absurdity; and yet it is a question which must necessarily be answered, if we would have the idea of self pass for clear and intelligible. It must be some one impression that gives rise to every real idea. But self or person is not any one impression, but that to which our several impressions and ideas are supposed to have a reference. If any impression gives rise to the idea of self, that impression must continue invariably the same, through the whole course of our lives; since self is supposed to exist after that manner. But there is no impression constant and invariable. Pain and pleasure, grief and joy, passions and sensations succeed each other, and never all exist at the same time. It cannot therefore be from any of these impressions, or from any other, that the idea of self is derived; and consequently there is no such idea.

But further, what must become of all our particular perceptions upon this hypothesis? All these are different, and distinguishable, and separable from each other, and may be separately considered, and may exist separately, and have no need of anything to support their existence. After what manner therefore do they belong to self, and how are they connected with it? For my part, when I enter most intimately into what I call *myself,* I always stumble on some particular perception or other, of heat or cold, light or shade, love or hatred, pain or pleasure. I never can catch *myself* at any time without a perception, and never can observe anything but the perception. When my perceptions are removed for any time, as by sound sleep, so long am I insensible of *myself,* and may truly be said not to exist. And were all my perceptions removed by death, and could I neither think, nor feel, nor see, nor love, nor hate, after the

---

Source: David Hume (1739), *A Treatise of Human Nature,* Everyman (1911). Public domain.

dissolution of my body, I should be entirely annihilated, nor do I conceive what is further requisite to make me a perfect nonentity. If any one, upon serious and unprejudiced reflection, thinks he has a different notion of *himself,* I must confess I can reason no longer with him. All I can allow him is, that he may be in the right as well as I, and that we are essentially different in this particular. He may, perhaps, perceive something simple and continued, which he calls *himself;* though I am certain there is no such principle in me.

But setting aside some metaphysicians of this kind, I may venture to affirm of the rest of mankind, that they are nothing but a bundle or collection of different perceptions, which succeed each other with an inconceivable rapidity, and are in a perpetual flux and movement. Our eyes cannot turn in their sockets without varying our perceptions. Our thought is still more variable than our sight; and all our other senses and faculties contribute to this change; nor is there any single power of the soul, which remains unalterably the same, perhaps for one moment. The mind is a kind of theatre, where several perceptions successively make their appearance; pass, repass, glide away, and mingle in an infinite variety of postures and situations. There is properly no *simplicity* in it at one time, nor *identity* in different, whatever natural propension we may have to imagine that simplicity and identity. The comparison of the theatre must not mislead us. They are the successive perceptions only, that constitute the mind; nor have we the most distant notion of the place where these scenes are represented, or of the materials of which it is composed.

What then gives us so great a propension to ascribe an identity to these successive perceptions, and to suppose ourselves possessed of an invariable and uninterrupted existence through the whole course of our lives? In order to answer this question we must distinguish betwixt personal identity, as it regards our thought or imagination, and as it regards our passions or the concern we take in ourselves. The first is our present subject; and to explain it perfectly we must take the matter pretty deep, and account for that identity, which we attribute to plants and animals; there being a great analogy betwixt it and the identity of a self or person.

We have a distinct idea of an object that remains invariable and uninterrupted through a supposed variation of time; and this idea we call that of *identity* or *sameness.* We have also a distinct idea of several different objects existing in succession, and connected together by a close relation; and this to an accurate view affords as perfect a notion of *diversity* as if there was no manner of relation among the objects. But though these two ideas of identity, and a succession of related objects, be in themselves perfectly distinct, and even contrary, yet it is certain that, in our common way of thinking, they are generally confounded with each other. That action of the imagination, by which we consider the uninterrupted and invariable object, and that by which we reflect on the succession of related objects, are almost the same to the feeling; nor is there much more effort of thought required in the latter case than in the former. The relation facilitates the transition of the mind from one object to another, and renders its passage as smooth as if it contemplated one continued object. This resemblance is the cause of the confusion and mistake, and makes us substitute the notion of identity, instead of that of related objects. However at one instant we may consider the related succession as variable or interrupted, we are sure the next to ascribe to it a perfect identity, and regard it as invariable and uninterrupted. Our propensity to this mistake is so great from the resemblance above mentioned, that we fall into it before we are aware; and though we incessantly correct ourselves by reflection, and return to a more accurate method of thinking, yet we cannot long sustain our philosophy, or take off this bias from the imagination. Our last resource is to yield to it, and boldly assert that these different related objects are in effect the same, however interrupted and variable. In order to justify to ourselves this absurdity, we often feign some new and unintelligible principle, that connects the objects together, and prevents their interruption or variation. Thus we feign the continued existence of the perceptions of our senses, to remove the interruption; and run into the notion of a *soul,* and *self,* and *substance,* to disguise the variation. But, we may further observe, that where we do not give rise to such a fiction, our propension to confound identity with relation is so great, that we are apt to imagine something unknown and mysterious,[1] connecting the parts, beside their relation; and this I take to be the case with regard to the identity we ascribe to plants and vegetables. And even when this does not take place, we still feel a propensity to confound these ideas, though we are not able fully to satisfy ourselves in that particular, nor find anything invariable and uninterrupted to justify our notion of identity.

Thus the controversy concerning identity is not merely a dispute of words. For when we attribute identity, in an improper sense, to variable or interrupted objects, our mistake is not confined to the expression, but is commonly attended with a fiction, either of something invariable and uninterrupted, or of something mysterious and inexplicable, or at least with a propensity to such fictions. What will suffice to prove this hypothesis to the satisfaction of every fair inquirer, is to show, from daily experience and observation, that the objects which are variable or interrupted, and yet are supposed to continue the same, are such only as consist of a succession of parts, connected together by resemblance, contiguity, or causation. For as such a succession answers evidently to our notion of diversity, it can only be by mistake we ascribe to it an identity; and as the relation of parts, which leads us into this mistake, is really nothing but a quality, which produces an association of ideas, and an easy transition of the imagination from one to another, it can only be from the resemblance, which this act of the mind bears to that by which we contemplate one continued object, that the error arises. Our chief business, then, must be to prove, that all objects, to which we ascribe identity, without observing their invariableness and uninterruptedness, are such as consist of a succession of related objects.

In order to this, suppose any mass of matter, of which the parts are contiguous and connected, to be placed before us; it is plain we must attribute a perfect identity to this mass, provided all the parts continue uninterruptedly and invariably the same, whatever motion or change of place we may observe either in the whole or in any of the parts. But supposing some very *small* or *inconsiderable* part to be added to the mass, or subtracted from it; though this absolutely destroys the identity of the whole, strictly speaking, yet as we seldom think so accurately, we scruple not to pronounce a mass of matter the same, where we find so trivial an alteration. The passage of the thought from the object before the change to the object after it, is so smooth and easy, that we scarce perceive the transition, and are apt to imagine, that it is nothing but a continued survey of the same object.

There is a very remarkable circumstance that attends this experiment; which is, that though the change of any considerable part in a mass of matter destroys the identity of the whole, yet we must measure the greatness of the part, not absolutely, but by its *proportion* to the whole. The addition or diminution of a mountain would not be sufficient to produce a diversity in a planet; though the change of a very few inches would be able to destroy the identity of some bodies. It will be impossible to account for this, but by reflecting that objects operate upon the mind, and break or interrupt the continuity of its actions, not according to their real greatness, but according to their proportion to each other; and therefore, since this interruption makes an object cease to appear the same, it must be the uninterrupted progress of the thought which constitutes the imperfect identity.

This may be confirmed by another phenomenon. A change in any considerable part of a body destroys its identity; but it is remarkable, that where the change is produced *gradually* and *insensibly,* we are less apt to ascribe to it the same effect. The reason can plainly be no other, than that the mind, in following the successive changes of the body, feels an easy passage from the surveying its condition in one moment, to the viewing of it in another, and in no particular time perceives any interruption in its actions. From which continued perception, it ascribes a continued existence and identity to the object.

But whatever precaution we may use in introducing the changes gradually, and making them proportionable to the whole, it is certain, that where the changes are at last observed to become considerable, we make a scruple of ascribing identity to such different objects. There is, however, another artifice, by which we may induce the imagination to advance a step further; and that is, by producing a reference of the parts to each other, and a combination to come *common end* or purpose. A ship, of which a considerable part has been changed by frequent reparations, is still considered as the same; nor does the difference of the materials hinder us from ascribing an identity to it. The common end, in which the parts conspire, is the same under all their variations, and affords an easy transition of the imagination from one situation of the body to another.

But this is still more remarkable, when we add a *sympathy* of parts to their *common end,* and suppose that they bear to each other the reciprocal relation of cause and effect in all their actions and operations. This is the case with all animals and vegetables; where not only the several parts have a reference to some general purpose, but also a mutual dependence on, and connection with, each other. The effect of so strong a relation is, that though every one must allow, that in a very few years both vegetables and animals endure a *total* change, yet we still attribute identity to them, while their form, size, and substance, are entirely altered. An oak that grows from a small plant to a large tree is still the same oak, though there be not one particle of matter or figure of its parts the same. An infant becomes a man, and is sometimes fat, sometimes lean, without any change in his identity.

We may also consider the two following phenomena, which are remarkable in their kind. The first is, that though we commonly be able to distinguish pretty exactly betwixt numerical and specific identity, yet it sometimes happens that we confound them, and in our thinking and reasoning employ the one for the other. Thus, a man who hears a noise that is frequently interrupted and renewed, says it is still the same noise, though it is evident the sounds have only a specific identity or resemblance, and there is nothing numerically the same but the cause which produced them. In like manner it may be said, without breach of the propriety of language, that such a church, which was formerly of brick, fell to ruin, and that the parish rebuilt the same church of freestone, and according to modern architecture. Here neither the form nor materials are the same, nor is there anything common to the two objects but their relation to the inhabitants of the parish; and yet this alone is sufficient to make us denominate them the same. But we must observe, that in these cases the first object is in a manner annihilated before the second comes into existence; by which means, we are never presented, in any one point of time, with the idea of difference and multiplicity; and for that reason are less scrupulous in calling them the same.

Secondly, we may remark, that though, in a succession of related objects, it be in a manner requisite that the change of parts be not sudden nor entire, in order to preserve the identity, yet where the objects are in their nature changeable and inconstant, we admit of a more sudden transition than would otherwise be consistent with that relation. Thus, as the nature of a river consists in the motion and change of parts, though in less than four-and-twenty hours these be totally altered, this hinders not the river from continuing the same during several ages. What is natural and essential to anything is, in a manner, expected; and what is expected makes less impression, and appears of less moment than what is unusual and extraordinary. A considerable change of the former kind seems really less to the imagination than the most trivial alteration of the latter; and by breaking less the continuity of the thought, has less influence in destroying the identity.

We now proceed to explain the nature of *personal identity,* which has become so great a question in philosophy, especially of late years, in England, where all the abstruser sciences are studied with a peculiar ardour and application. And here it is evident the same method of reasoning must be continued which has so successfully explained the identity of plants, and animals, and ships, and houses, and of all compounded and changeable productions either of art or nature. The identity which we ascribe to the mind of man is only a fictitious one, and of a like kind with that which we ascribe to vegetable and animal bodies. It cannot therefore have a different origin, but must proceed from a like operation of the imagination upon like objects.

But lest this argument should not convince the reader, though in my opinion perfectly decisive, let him weigh the following reasoning, which is still closer and more immediate. It is evident that the identity which we attribute to the human mind, however perfect we may imagine it to be, is not able to run the several different perceptions into one, and make them lose their characters of distinction and difference, which are essential to them. It is still true that every distinct perception which enters into the composition of the mind, is a distinct existence, and is different, and distinguishable, and separable from every other perception, either contemporary or successive. But as, notwithstanding this distinction and separability, we suppose the whole train of perceptions to be united by identity, a question naturally arises concerning this relation of identity, whether it be something that really binds our several perceptions together, or only associates their ideas in the imagination; that is, in other words, whether, in pronouncing concerning the identity of a person, we observe some real bond among his perceptions, or only feel one among the ideas we form of them. This question we might easily decide, if we would recollect what has been already proved at large, that the understanding never observes any real connection among objects, and that even the union of cause and effect, when strictly examined, resolves itself into a customary association of ideas. For from thence it evidently follows, that identity is nothing really belonging to these different perceptions, and uniting them together, but is merely a quality which we attribute to them, because of the union of their ideas in the imagination when we reflect upon them. Now, the only qualities which can give ideas a union in the imagination, are these three relations above mentioned. These are the uniting principles in the ideal world, and without them every distinct object is separable by the mind, and may be separately considered, and appears not to have any more connection with any other object than if disjoined by the greatest difference and remoteness. It is therefore on some of these three relations of resemblance, contiguity, and causation, that identity depends; and as the very essence of these relations consists in their producing an easy transition of ideas, it follows that our notions of personal identity proceed entirely from the smooth and uninterrupted progress of the thought along a train of connected ideas, according to the principles above explained.

The only question, therefore, which remains is, by what relations this uninterrupted progress of our thought is produced, when we consider the successive existence of a mind or thinking person. And here it is evident we must confine ourselves to resemblance and causation, and must drop contiguity, which has little or no influence in the present case.

To begin with *resemblance;* suppose we could see clearly into the breast of another, and observe that succession of perceptions which constitutes his mind or thinking principle, and suppose that he always preserves the memory of a considerable part of past perceptions, it is evident that nothing could more contribute to the bestowing a relation on this succession amidst all its variations. For what is the memory but a faculty, by which we raise up the images of past perceptions? And as an image necessarily resembles its object, must not the frequent placing of these resembling perceptions in the chain of thought, convey the imagination more easily from one link to another, and make the whole seem like the continuance of one object? In this particular, then, the memory not only discovers the identity, but also contributes to its production, by producing the relation of resemblance among the perceptions. The case is the same, whether we consider ourselves or others.

As to *causation;* we may observe that the true idea of the human mind, is to consider it as a system of different perceptions or different existences, which are linked together by the relation of cause and effect, and mutually produce, destroy, influence, and modify each other. Our impressions give rise to their correspondent ideas; and these ideas, in their turn, produce other impressions. One thought chases another, and draws after it a third, by which it is expelled in its turn. In this respect, I cannot compare the soul more properly to anything than to a republic or commonwealth, in which the several members are united by the reciprocal ties of government and subordination, and give rise to other persons who propagate the same republic in the incessant changes of its parts. And as the same individual republic may not only change its members, but also its laws and constitutions; in like manner the same person may vary his character and disposition, as well as his impressions and ideas, without losing his identity. Whatever changes he endures, his several parts are still connected by the relation of causation. And in this view our identity with regard to the passions serves to corroborate that with regard to the imagination, by the making our distant perceptions influence each other, and by giving us a present concern for our past or future pains or pleasures.

As memory alone acquaints us with the continuance and extent of this succession of perceptions, it is to be considered, upon that account chiefly, as the source of personal identity. Had we no memory, we never should have any notion of causation, nor consequently of that chain of causes and effects, which constitute our self or person. But having once acquired this notion of causation from the memory, we can extend the same chain of causes, and consequently the identity of our persons beyond our memory, and can comprehend times, and circumstances, and actions, which we have entirely forgot, but suppose in general to have existed. For how few of our past actions are there, of which we have any memory? Who can tell me, for instance, what were his thoughts and actions on the first of January 1715, the eleventh of March 1719, and the third of August 1733? Or will he affirm, because he has entirely forgot the incidents of these days, that the present self is not the same person with the self of that time; and by that means overturn all the most established notions of personal identity? In this view, therefore, memory does not so much *produce* as *discover* personal identity, by showing us the relation of cause and effect among our different perceptions. It will be incumbent on those who affirm that memory produces entirely our personal identity, to give a reason why we can thus extend our identity beyond our memory.

The whole of this doctrine leads us to a conclusion, which is of great importance in the present affair, viz. that all the nice and subtile questions concerning personal identity can never possibly be decided, and are to be regarded rather as grammatical than as philosophical difficulties. Identity depends on the relations of ideas; and these relations produce identity, by means of that easy transition they occasion. But as the relations, and the easiness of the transition may diminish by insensible degrees, we have no just standard by which we can decide any dispute concerning the time when they acquire or lose a title to the name of identity. All the disputes concerning the identity of connected objects are merely verbal, except so far as the relation of parts gives rise to some fiction or imaginary principle of union, as we have already observed.

What I have said concerning the first origin and uncertainty of our notion of identity, as applied to the human mind, may be extended with little or no variation to that of *simplicity*. An object, whose different coexistent parts are bound together by a close relation, operates upon the imagination after much the same manner as one perfectly simple and indivisible, and requires not a much greater stretch of thought in order to its conception. From this similarity of operation we attribute a simplicity to it, and feign a principle of union as the support of this simplicity, and the centre of all the different parts and qualities of the object.

Thus we have finished our examination of the several systems of philosophy, both of the intellectual and moral world; and, in our miscellaneous way of reasoning, have been led into several topics, which will either illustrate and confirm some preceding part of this discourse, or prepare the way for our following opinions. It is now time to return to a more close examination of our subject, and to proceed in the accurate anatomy of human nature, having fully explained the nature of our judgment and understanding.

NOTES

1. If the reader is desirous to see how a great genius may be influenced by these seemingly trivial principles of the imagination, as well as the mere vulgar, let him read my Lord Shaftesbury's reasonings concerning the uniting principle of the universe, and the identity of plants and animals. See his *Moralists,* or *Philosophical Rhapsody.*

DISCUSSION QUESTIONS

1. What three types of relations does Hume say connect the succession of parts that a plant or an animal consists in?
2. Why does Hume think the identity that we ascribe to the mind of man is only a fictitious one?
3. Why does Hume think that a ship whose parts have been changed and so is composed of different materials at different times is still considered the same ship? Why does Hume think that a small tree that grows into a large oak, despite having no material parts in common, does not change identity? Is he right?
4. Hume thinks that the personal identity of a human being (an infant becoming a fat, then a lean man) is of a like kind with the identity we ascribe to vegetable and animal bodies. Do you agree? Explain.
5. How does Hume reach the conclusion that questions concerning personal identity are grammatical, not philosophical, difficulties?

Chapter 16

IMMANUEL KANT

Immanuel Kant (1724–1804) lived and died in Königsberg, Prussia (now Kaliningrad, Russia)—a town he never strayed more than 30 miles from for his entire life. Kant criticized Locke for "sensualizing concepts" and Leibniz for "intellectualizing appearances." Hume he credited with awakening him from his "dogmatic slumber."

In the first selection, taken from the monumentally influential first Critique (first published in 1781), Kant presents the third paralogism of reason: (1) That which is conscious of the numerical identity of itself at different times is a person. *(2) The soul is conscious of itself in this way. (3) Therefore, the soul is a person. He argues that the personality of our own soul has to be regarded as a completely identical proposition of self-consciousness in time, and so is valid a* priori. *Other people, however, perceive us as external objects represented in time. Kant admits that the identity of the consciousness of himself at different times is only a formal condition of his thoughts and their coherence, and in no way proves the numerical identity of his subject. He thinks that from our own consciousness, we cannot determine whether, as souls, we are permanent. The "I" we encounter in our soul is a mere thought, and so it may be in flux like other thoughts that the "I" links together.*

In the second reading Kant distinguishes three predispositions of a human being—animality (as a living being), humanity (as a living and rational *being), and personality (as a rational and* responsible *being). Animality mechanically drives us to self-preservation, propagation of the species, and social community with other human beings. Humanity inclines us to judge our happiness in comparison with others and to gain worth in their opinion. Kant describes personality itself as the idea of the moral law alone, together with the respect that is inseparable from it.*

The third selection elaborates on Kant's idea of a person as the subject of morally practical reason. A person is a subject whose actions can be imputed *to him. Moral personality, according to Kant, is the freedom of a rational being under moral laws. Whereas a thing is any object of free choice that lacks freedom, a person has the freedom to* subject himself *to laws. A human being insofar as he is a* phenomenon *is a rational animal in the sensible world, whereas a human being insofar as he is a* noumenon *is an end in itself that possesses dignity and demands respect from all other rational beings.*

Critique of Pure Reason

THIRD PARALOGISM OF PERSONALITY.

What is conscious of the numerical identity of its Self in different times, is to that extent a **person.**

Now the soul is etc.

Thus it is a person.

CRITICISM OF THE THIRD PARALOGISM OF TRANSCENDENTAL PSYCHOLOGY.

If I want to cognize through experience the numerical identity of an external object, then I will attend to what is persisting in its appearance, to which, as subject, everything else relates as a determination, and I will notice the identity of the former in the time in which the latter changes. But now I am an object of inner sense and all time is merely the form of inner sense. Consequently, I relate each and every one of my successive determinations to the numerically identical Self in all time, i.e., in the form of the inner intuition of my self. On this basis the personality of the soul must be regarded not as inferred but rather as a completely identical proposition of self-consciousness in time, and that is also the cause of its being valid *a priori*. For it really says no more than that in the whole time in which I am conscious of myself, I am conscious of this time as belonging to the unity of my Self, and it is all the same whether I say that this whole time is in Me, as an individual unity, or that I am to be found with numerical identity, in all of this time.

The identity of person is therefore inevitably to be encountered in my own consciousness. But if I consider myself from the standpoint of another (as an object of his outer intuition), then it is this external observer who originally considers **me** as **in time;** for in apperception **time** is properly represented only **in me.** Thus from the I that accompanies—and indeed with complete identity—all representations at every time in **my** consciousness, although he admits this I, he will still not infer the objective persistence of my Self. For just as the time in which the observer posits me is not the time that is encountered in my sensibility but that which is encountered in his own, so the identity that is necessarily combined with my consciousness is not therefore combined with his consciousness, i.e., with the outer intuition of my subject.

The identity of the consciousness of Myself in different times is therefore only a formal condition of my thoughts and their connection, but it does not prove at all the numerical identity of my subject, in which—despite the logical identity of the I—a change can go on that does not allow it

---

Source: From the Cambridge Edition of the Works of Immanuel Kant (1998): 422–425. *Critique of Pure Reason,* Translated by Paul Guyer and Allen Wood (1998). Reprinted with the permission of Cambridge University Press.

to keep its identity; and this even though all the while the identical-sounding "I" is assigned to it, which in every other state, even in the replacement of the subject, still keeps in view the thought of the previous subject, and thus could also pass it along to the following one.*

Even if the saying of some ancient schools, that everything is **transitory** and nothing in the world is **persisting** and abiding, cannot hold as soon as one assumes substances, it is still not refuted through the unity of self-consciousness. For we cannot judge even from our own consciousness whether as soul we are persisting or not, because we ascribe to our identical Self only that of which we are conscious; and so we must necessarily judge that we are the very same in the whole of the time of which we are conscious. But from the standpoint of someone else we cannot declare this to be valid because, since in the soul we encounter no persisting appearance other than the representation "I," which accompanies and connects all of them, we can never make out whether this I (a mere thought) does not flow as well as all the other thoughts that are linked to one another through it.

It is remarkable, however, that personality, and its presupposition, persistence, hence the substantiality of the soul, must be proved only now for the first time. For if we could presuppose these, then what would of course follow is not the continuous duration of consciousness, but rather the possibility of a continuing consciousness in an abiding subject, which is already sufficient for personality, since that does not cease at once just because its effect is perhaps interrupted for a time. This persistence, however, is not given to us through anything prior to the numerical identity of our Self, which we conclude from identical apperception, but rather is concluded for the first time from it (and, if things went rightly, we would have to conclude from this first of all the concept of substance, which is usable only empirically). Now since this identity of person in no way follows from the identity of the I in the consciousness of all the time in which I cognize myself, even the substantiality of the soul cannot be grounded on it above.

Meanwhile, the concept of personality, just like the concepts of substance and of the simple, can remain (insofar as it is merely transcendental, i.e., a unity of the subject which is otherwise unknown to us, but in whose determinations there is a thoroughgoing connection of apperception), and to this extent this concept is also necessary and sufficient for practical use; but we can never boast of it as an extension of our self-knowledge through pure reason, which dazzles us with the uninterrupted continuous duration of the subject drawn from the mere concept of the identical self, since this concept merely revolves in a circle around itself and brings us no farther in regard to even one single question about synthetic cognition. What matter is, as a thing in itself (transcendental object), is of course entirely unknown to us; nevertheless its persistence will be observed as appearance as long as it is represented to us as something external. But since I want to observe the mere I through the change in all my representations, I have once again no correlate other than Myself for my comparisons with the general conditions of my consciousness; I can therefore give nothing but tautological answers to all questions, because I substitute my concept and its unity for the properties pertaining to my self as an object, and thus merely presuppose what one demanded to know.

---

*An elastic ball that strikes another one in a straight line communicates to the latter its whole motion, hence its whole state (if one looks only at their positions in space). Now assuming substances, on the analogy with such bodies, in which representations, together with consciousness of them, flow from one to another, a whole series of these substances may be thought, of which the first would communicate its state, together with its consciousness, to the second, which would communicate its own state, together with that of the previous substance, to a third substance, and this in turn would share the states of all previous ones, together with their consciousness and its own. The last substance would thus be conscious of all the states of all the previously altered substances as its own states, because these states would have been carried over to it, together with the consciousness of them; and in spite of this it would not have been the very same person in all these states.

Religion within the Boundaries of Mere Reason

I. CONCERNING THE ORIGINAL PREDISPOSITION TO GOOD IN HUMAN NATURE

We may justifiably bring this predisposition, with reference to its end, under three headings, as elements of the determination of the human being:

1. The predisposition to the *animality* of the human being, as a *living being;*
2. To the *humanity* in him, as a living and at the same time *rational* being;
3. To his *personality,* as a rational and at the same time *responsible* being.*

1. The predisposition to animality in the human being may be brought under the general title of physical or merely *mechanical* self-love, i.e. a love for which reason is not required. It is threefold: *first,* for self-preservation; *second,* for the propagation of the species, through the sexual drive, and for the preservation of the offspring thereby begotten through breeding; *third,* for community with other human beings, i.e. the social drive.—On these three can be grafted all sorts of vices (which, however, do not of themselves issue from this predisposition as a root). They can be named vices of the *savagery* of nature, and, at their greatest deviation from the natural ends, are

*We cannot consider this predisposition as already included in the concept of the preceding one, but must necessarily treat it as a special predisposition. For from the fact that a being has reason does not at all follow that, simply by virtue of representing its maxims as suited to universal legislation, this reason contains a faculty of determining the power of choice unconditionally, and hence to be "practical" on its own; at least, not so far as we can see. The most rational being of this world might still need certain incentives, coming to him from the objects of inclination, to determine his power of choice. He might apply the most rational reflection to these objects—about what concerns their greatest sum as well as the means for attaining the goal determined through them—without thereby even suspecting the possibility of such a thing as the absolutely imperative moral law which announces to be itself an incentive, and, indeed, the highest incentive. Were this law not given to us from within, no amount of subtle reasoning on our part would produce it or win our power of choice over to it. Yet this law is the only law that makes us conscious of the independence of our power of choice from determination by all other incentives (of our freedom) and thereby also of the accountability of all our actions.

Source: Religion within the Boundaries of Mere Reason, George Di Giovanni tr., The Cambridge Edition of the Works of Immanuel Kant: *Religion and Rational Theology* (1996): 74–76. Reprinted with the permission of Cambridge University Press.

called the *bestial vices of gluttony, lust and wild lawlessness* (in relation to other human beings).

2. The predispositions to humanity can be brought under the general title of a self-love which is physical and yet *involves comparison* (for which reason is required); that is, only in comparison with others does one judge oneself happy or unhappy. Out of this self-love originates the inclination *to gain worth in the opinion of others,* originally, of course, merely *equal worth:* not allowing anyone superiority over oneself, bound up with the constant anxiety that others might be striving for ascendancy; but from this arises gradually an unjust desire to acquire superiority for oneself over others.—Upon this, namely, upon *jealousy* and *rivalry,* can be grafted the greatest vices of secret or open hostility to all whom we consider alien to us. These vices, however, do not really issue from nature as their root but are rather inclinations, in the face of the anxious endeavor of others to attain a hateful superiority over us, to procure it for ourselves over them for the sake of security, as preventive measure; for nature itself wanted to use the idea of such a competitiveness (which in itself does not exclude reciprocal love) as only an incentive to culture. Hence the vices that are grafted upon this inclination can also be named vices of *culture,* and in their extreme degree of malignancy (where they are simply the idea of a maximum of evil that surpasses humanity), e.g. in *envy, ingratitude, joy in others' misfortunes,* etc., they are called *diabolical vices.*

3. The predisposition to personality is the susceptibility to respect for the moral law *as of itself a sufficient incentive to the power of choice.* This susceptibility to simple respect for the moral law within us would thus be the moral feeling, which by itself does not yet constitute an end of the natural predisposition but only insofar as it is an incentive of the power of choice. But now this is possible only because the free power of choice incorporates moral feeling into its maxim: so a power of choice so constituted is a good character, and this character, as in general every character of the free power of choice, is something that can only be acquired; yet, for its possibility there must be present in our nature a predisposition onto which nothing evil can be grafted. The idea of the moral law alone, together with the respect that is inseparable from it, cannot be properly called a *predisposition to personality;* it is personality itself (the idea of humanity considered wholly intellectually). The subjective ground, however, of our incorporating this incentive into our maxims seems to be an addition to personality, and hence seems to deserve the name of a predisposition on behalf of it.

If we consider the three predispositions just named according to the conditions of their possibility, we find that the *first* does not have reason at its root at all; that the *second* is rooted in a reason which is indeed practical, but only as subservient to other incentives; and that the *third* alone is rooted in reason practical of itself, i.e. in reason legislating unconditionally. All these predispositions in the human being are not only (negatively) *good* (they do not resist the moral law) but they are also predispositions *to the good* (they demand compliance with it). They are *original,* for they belong to the possibility of human nature. The human being can indeed use the first two inappropriately, but cannot eradicate either of the two. By the predispositions of a being we understand the constituent parts required for it as well as the forms of their combination that make for such a being. They are *original* if they belong with necessity to the possibility of this being, but *contingent* if the being in question is possible in itself also without them. It should be noted, finally, that there is no question here of other predispositions except those that relate immediately to the faculty of desire and the exercise of the power of choice.

The Doctrine of Virtue

An action is called a *deed* in so far as it comes under obligatory laws and hence in so far as it is referred to the freedom of the agent's power of choice. The agent is considered the *author* of the effects of his deed, and these, along with the action itself, can be *imputed* to him if, before he acts, he knows the law by virtue of which they come under an obligation.

A *person* is a subject whose actions can be *imputed* to him. *Moral* personality is thus the freedom of a rational being under moral laws. (Psychological personality is merely the power to become conscious of one's self-identity at different times and under the different conditions of one's existence.) From this it follows that a person is subject to no other laws than those which he (either alone or at least along with others) gives himself.

A *thing* is something that is not susceptible of imputation. Thus any object of free choice which itself lacks freedom is called a thing (*res corporalis*).

III. ON SERVILITY

§ 11.

Man in the system of nature (*homo phaenomenon, animal rationale*) is a being of slight importance and shares with the rest of the animals, as offspring of the earth, a common value (*pretium vulgare*). Although man has, in his reason, something more than they and can set his own ends, even this gives him only an *extrinsic* value in terms of his usefulness (*pretium usus*). This extrinsic value is the value of one man above another—that is, his *price* as a ware that can be exchanged for these other animals, as things. But, so considered, man still has a lower value than the universal medium of exchange, money, the value of which can therefore be called preeminent (*pretium eminens*).

But man regarded as a *person*—that is, as the subject of morally practical reason—is exalted above any price; for as such (*homo noumenon*) he is not to be valued as a mere means to the ends of others or even to his own ends, but as an end in himself. He possesses, in other words, a *dignity* (an absolute inner worth) by which he exacts *respect* for himself from all other rational beings in the world: he can measure himself with every other being of this kind and value himself on a footing of equality with them.

Humanity in his own person is the object of respect, and he can demand this respect from every other man; but he must, also, do nothing by which he would forfeit this respect. Hence he can and should value himself by a low as well as by a high standard, depending on whether he views himself as a being of the sensible world (in terms of his animal nature) or as an intelligible being (in terms of his moral disposition).—When, as he must do, he regards himself not merely as a person as such but also as a man—that is, as a person who

---

Source: From Immanuel Kant, *Introduction to the Metaphysics of Morals,* Mary J. Gregor translation, *The Doctrine of Virtue,* University of Pennsylvania Press, Philadelphia (1964): pp. 22, 92–93, 99, 103–105.

has duties laid upon him by his own reason—his insignificance as a *natural man* cannot detract from his consciousness of his dignity as a *moral man,* and he should not disavow his moral self-esteem regarding the latter: he should seek his end, which is in itself a duty, not abjectly, not in a *servile spirit* (*animo servili*) as if he were seeking a favour, not disavowing his dignity, but always with consciousness of his sublime moral disposition (which is already contained in the concept of virtue). And this *self-esteem* is a duty of man to himself.

The consciousness and feeling of one's insignificant moral worth in *comparison* with the *law* is *humility* (*humilitas moralis*). To be convinced of the greatness of one's moral worth, but only for want of comparing it with the law, can be called *moral arrogance* (*arrogantia moralis*).—The disavowal of all claim to any moral worth in oneself, in the belief that one will thus acquire a borrowed worth, is morally *false humility* (*humilitas spuria*).

Humility in *comparing oneself with other men* (and indeed with any finite being, even a seraph) is no duty; rather, the man who tries to equal or surpass others in humility, believing that in this way he will also acquire a greater inner worth, is guilty of *pride* (*ambitio*), which is directly contrary to his duty to others. But deliberately to set aside one's own moral worth merely as a means to acquiring the favour of another, no matter who he may be (hypocrisy and flattery) . . . is false (lying) humility, which is contrary to duty to oneself since it is an abasement of one's personality.

True humility follows inevitably from our sincere and strict comparison of ourselves with the moral law (its holiness and strictness). But along with it comes exaltation and the highest self-esteem, as the feeling of our inner worth (*valor*), when we realize that we are capable of this inner legislation, and the (natural) man feels himself compelled to reverence the (moral) man in his own person. By virtue of this worth we are not for sale at any price (*pretium*) and possess an inalienable dignity (*dignitas interna*) which instills in us reverence (*reverentia*) for ourselves.

§ 12.

This duty to ourselves regarding the dignity of humanity within us can be recognized, more or less, in the following examples.

Be no man's lackey.—Do not let others tread with impunity on your right.—Contract no debt for which you cannot give full security.—Do not accept favours you could do without, and do not be a parasite or a flatterer or (what really differs from these only in degree) a beggar. Be thrifty, then, so that you will not become destitute.—Complaining and whining—even a mere cry in bodily pain—is unworthy of you, especially if you know you have deserved the pain; thus a criminal's death may be ennobled (its disgrace averted) by the resoluteness with which he dies.—Kneeling down or prostrating oneself on the ground, even as an outward sign of veneration for holy things, is contrary to the dignity of humanity, as is invoking these in the presence of images; for you then humble yourself, not before an *Ideal* presented by your own reason, but before an *idol* of your own making.

Casuistical Questions

May not man's feeling for his sublime destiny, *i.e.* his *elation of spirit* (*elatio animi*) or esteem for himself, come so close to *self-conceit* (*arrogantia*)—the very opposite of true *humility* (*humilitas moralis*)—that it is inadvisable to cultivate self-esteem even when we compare ourselves with other men, and not only when we compare ourselves with the law? Or is it not more likely that this kind of self-abnegation, confirming others' opinion of us, would encourage them to despise our person and so constitute a violation of our duty (of reverence) to ourselves? In any case, bowing and scraping before a man seems beneath man's dignity.

Preferential tributes of respect in words and manners even to those who have no authority in the State—reverences, obeisances (compliments) and courtly phrases marking with the utmost precision every distinction in status (something altogether different from courtesy, which must also be reciprocal)—the *Du, Er, Ihr* and *Sie,* or *Ew. Wohledeln, Hochedeln, Hochedelgeborenen, Wohlgeborenen* (*ohe, iam satis est!**) as forms of address, a pedantry in which the Germans seem to outdo any other people in the world (except possibly the Indian castes): does not all this prove that there is a widespread propensity to servility in men? (*Hae nugae in seria ducunt.*†) But one who makes himself a worm cannot complain if people step on him.

CHAPTER II. SECTION 1. ON MAN'S DUTY TO HIMSELF AS HIS OWN INNATE JUDGE

§ 13.

Every concept of duty contains objective necessitation by the law (as a moral imperative limiting our freedom) and belongs to practical reason, which gives the rule. But the inner *imputation* of a deed, as a case that comes under the law (*in meritum aut demeritum*), belongs to the *power of judgment* (*iudicium*), which, as the subjective principle imputing an action, judges with legal effect whether an action considered as a deed (an action coming under a law) took place or not. On this there follows the verdict of *reason* (the sentence), which (as condemnation or acquittal) joins with the action its legal effect. All of this takes place before a *tribunal* (*coram iudicio*), which, as a moral person giving effect to the law, is called a *court of justice* (*forum*).—Consciousness of an *inner court* in man ("before which his thoughts accuse or excuse one another") is *conscience.*

Every man has a conscience and finds himself watched, threatened, and, in general, kept in an attitude of respect (of esteem coupled with fear) by an inner judge; and this power watching over the law in him is not something that he himself (arbitrarily) *makes,* but something incorporated in his being. It follows him like his shadow when he plans to escape. He can indeed numb himself or put himself to sleep by pleasures and distractions, but he cannot avoid coming to himself or waking up from time to time; and when he does, he hears at once its fearful voice. He can at most, in the extremity of corruption, induce himself to pay no more attention to it, but he still cannot help *hearing* it.

Now this inherent intellectual and (since it is the thought of duty) moral disposition called *conscience* has something peculiar about it: although its business is an affair of man with himself, man yet sees himself necessitated by his reason to carry it on as if at the bidding of *another person.* For this action is the bringing of a *case* (*causa*) before a court; and to think of the man *accused by* his conscience as *one and the same person* with the judge is an absurd way of representing a court of justice, since then the prosecutor would always lose.—Hence for every duty man's conscience will have to conceive someone *other* than himself (*i.e.* other than man as such) as the judge of his actions; otherwise it would be in contradiction with itself. This other may be a [438] real person or a merely ideal person which reason itself produces.*

*"enough already!" [Ed.]

†"These trifles lead into serious matters." [Ed.]

*The man who accuses and judges himself in conscience must think of himself as a twofold personage, a doubled self who, on the one hand, has to stand in fear and trembling at the bar of the tribunal which is yet entrusted to him, but who, on the other hand, must himself administer the office of judge which he holds by inborn authority. And this requires clarification, if reason is not to fall into self-contradiction.—I, the prosecutor and yet the accused as well, am the same *man* (*numero idem*). But man as the subject of the moral legislation which proceeds from the concept of freedom and in which he is subject to a law that he himself gives (*homo noumenon*) is to be considered different (*specie diversus*) from man as a member the sensible world who is endowed with reason. But it is only from the viewpoint of practical knowledge that he is to be regarded in this way, since there is no theoretical knowledge of the causal relation of the intelligible to the sensible; and this specific difference is that of the human faculties (the higher and the lower) which characterize man.

Such an ideal person (the authorized judge of conscience) must be a scrutinizer of hearts, since the court of justice is set up *within* man. But at the same time he must *impose all obligation:* since conscience is the inner judge of all free actions, he must be, or must be conceived as, a person in relation to whom all our duties are to be regarded as also his commands.—Now since such a moral being must also have all power (in heaven and on earth) in order to be able to give his law its due effect (a function essential to the office of judge), and since such an omnipotent moral being is called God, conscience must be conceived as a subjective principle of responsibility before God for our deeds. In fact the latter concept will always be contained (even if only in an obscure way) in the moral self-awareness of conscience.

DISCUSSION QUESTIONS

1. Explain Kant's example of "elastic motion." How does this example relate to his conception of the soul? Is the soul a permanent, everlasting entity, according to Kant?
2. If the soul is what makes someone a "person," what does Kant think the soul consists in materially? How is the soul observed?
3. Which bestial vices can be grafted onto the mechanical self-love of animality?
4. Which vices can be grafted onto the inclinations of humanity?
5. Do you agree with Kant that the first two predispositions can be used inappropriately but not eradicated?
6. When, according to Kant, do we feel humility?

Chapter 17

SØREN KIERKEGAARD

Søren Aabye Kierkegaard (1813–1855) was born the youngest of seven children of a somber, dominating father in Copenhagen, Denmark. Raised in a strict form of Christianity that emphasized the sufferings of Christ, Kierkegaard became a prolific writer and influential existentialist theologian. His books were published under various pseudonyms. In 1840 he broke off his engagement to Regine Olsen because he believed his personal mission from God to be a writer precluded marriage.

In this reading from his work published in 1849, Kierkegaard holds that a human being is spirit, the self, a relation that relates itself to itself. He argues that to despair over oneself, in despair to will to be rid of oneself, is the formula for all despair. In contrast, to will to be the self that a person is in truth is the very opposite of despair. He reasons that if there were nothing eternal in a person, he could not despair at all. And if despair could consume and extinguish a person's self, then there would be no despair at all. But eternity forces despair upon us. To be a self, Kierkegaard believes, is the greatest, infinite concession given to a human being, but it is also eternity's claim upon him. Despair is a sickness of the spirit, and whereas the common view is that despair is rare, Kierkegaard thinks that it is universal. Moreover, an even more horrible expression of this despair is that it can hide unknown in the very heart of a happy person. Most people, he holds, live without ever becoming conscious of being destined as spirit. Kierkegaard believes that only that person's life is wasted who lived without becoming eternally conscious as spirit that there is a God and that his self exists before this God.

The Sickness unto Death

A

DESPAIR IS THE SICKNESS UNTO DEATH

A.

Despair is a sickness of the spirit, of the self, and accordingly can take three forms: In despair not to be conscious of having a self (not despair in the strict sense); in despair not to will to be oneself; in despair to will to be oneself

A human being is spirit. But what is spirit? Spirit is the self. But what is the self? The self is a relation that relates itself to itself or is the relation's relating itself to itself in the relation; the self is not the relation but is the relation's relating itself to itself. A human being is a synthesis of the infinite and the finite, of the temporal and the eternal, of freedom and necessity, in short, a synthesis. A synthesis is a relation between two. Considered in this way, a human being is still not a self.

In the relation between two, the relation is the third as a negative unity, and the two relate to the relation and in the relation to the relation; thus under the qualification of the psychical the relation between the psychical and the physical is a relation. If, however, the relation relates itself to itself, this relation is the positive third, and this is the self.

Such a relation that relates itself to itself, a self, must either have established itself or have been established by another.

If the relation that relates itself to itself has been established by another, then the relation is indeed the third, but this relation, the third, is yet again a relation and relates itself to that which established the entire relation.

The human self is such a derived, established relation, a relation that relates itself to itself and in relating itself to itself relates itself to another. This is why there can be two forms of despair in the strict sense. If a human self had itself established itself, then there could be only one form: not to will to be oneself, to will to do away with oneself, but there could not be the form: in despair to will to be oneself. This second formulation is specifically the expression for the complete dependence of the relation (of the self), the expression for the inability of the self to arrive at or to be in equilibrium and rest by itself, but only, in relating itself to itself, by relating itself to that which has established the entire relation. Yes, this second form of despair (in despair to will to be oneself) is so far from designating merely a distinctive kind of despair that, on the contrary, all despair ultimately can be traced back to and be resolved in it. If the despairing person is aware of his despair, as he thinks he is, and does not speak meaninglessly of it as of something that is happening to him (somewhat as one suffering from dizziness speaks in nervous delusion of a weight on his head or of something that has fallen down on him, etc., a weight and a pressure that nevertheless are not

---

Source: Søren Kierkegaard, *The Sickness Unto Death,* H. V. Hong and E. H. Hong tr., Princeton, Princeton University Press (1980): 13–28. Reprinted by permission of Princeton University Press. Line references have been deleted.

something external but a reverse reflection of the internal) and now with all his power seeks to break the despair by himself and by himself alone—he is still in despair and with all his presumed effort only works himself all the deeper into deeper despair. The misrelation of despair is not a simple misrelation but a misrelation in a relation that relates itself to itself and has been established by another, so that the misrelation in that relation which is for itself [*for sig*] also reflects itself infinitely in the relation to the power that established it.

The formula that describes the state of the self when despair is completely rooted out is this: in relating itself to itself and in willing to be itself, the self rests transparently in the power that established it.

B.

The possibility and the actuality of despair

Is despair an excellence or a defect? Purely dialectically, it is both. If only the abstract idea of despair is considered, without any thought of someone in despair, it must be regarded as a surpassing excellence. The possibility of this sickness is man's superiority over the animal, and this superiority distinguishes him in quite another way than does his erect walk, for it indicates infinite erectness or sublimity, that he is spirit. The possibility of this sickness is man's superiority over the animal; to be aware of this sickness is the Christian's superiority over the natural man; to be cured of this sickness is the Christian's blessedness.

Consequently, to be able to despair is an infinite advantage, and yet to be in despair is not only the worst misfortune and misery—no, it is ruination. Generally this is not the case with the relation between possibility and actuality. If it is an excellence to be able to be this or that, then it is an even greater excellence to be that; in other words, to be is like an ascent when compared with being able to be. With respect to despair, however, to be is like a descent when compared with being able to be; the descent is as infinitely low as the excellence of possibility is high. Consequently, in relation to despair, not to be in despair is the ascending scale. But here again this category is equivocal. Not to be in despair is not the same as not being lame, blind, etc. If not being in despair signifies neither more nor less than not being in despair, then it means precisely to be in despair. Not to be in despair must signify the destroyed possibility of being able to be in despair; if a person is truly not to be in despair, he must at every moment destroy the possibility. This is generally not the case in the relation between actuality and possibility. Admittedly, thinkers say that actuality is annihilated possibility, but that is not entirely true; it is the consummated, the active possibility. Here, on the contrary, the actuality (not to be in despair) is the impotent, destroyed possibility, which is why it is also a negation; although actuality in relation to possibility is usually a corroboration, here it is a denial.

Despair is the misrelation in the relation of a synthesis that relates itself to itself. But the synthesis is not the misrelation; it is merely the possibility, or in the synthesis lies the possibility of the misrelation. If the synthesis were the misrelation, then despair would not exist at all, then despair would be something that lies in human nature as such. That is, it would not be despair; it would be something that happens to a man, something he suffers, like a disease to which he succumbs, or like death, which is everyone's fate. No, no, despairing lies in man himself. If he were not a synthesis, he could not despair at all; nor could he despair if the synthesis in its original state from the hand of God were not in the proper relationship.

Where, then, does the despair come from? From the relation in which the synthesis relates itself to itself, inasmuch as God, who constituted man a relation, releases it from his hand, as it were—that is, inasmuch as the relation relates itself to itself. And because the relation is spirit, is the self, upon it rests the responsibility for all despair at every moment of its existence, however much the despairing person speaks of his despair as a misfortune and however ingeniously he deceives himself and others, confusing it with that previously mentioned case of dizziness, with which despair, although qualitatively different, has much in common, since dizziness corresponds, in the category of the psychical, to what despair is in the category of the spirit, and it lends itself to numerous analogies to despair.

Once the misrelation, despair, has come about, does it continue as a matter of course? No, it does not continue as a matter of course; if the misrelation continues, it is not attributable to the misrelation but to the relation that relates itself to itself. That is, every time the misrelation manifests itself and every moment it exists, it must be traced back to the relation. For example, we say that someone catches a sickness, perhaps through carelessness. The sickness sets in and from then on is in force and is an *actuality* whose origin recedes more and more into the *past*. It would be both cruel and inhuman to go on saying, "You, the sick person, are in the process of catching the sickness right now." That would be the same as perpetually wanting to dissolve the actuality of the sickness into its possibility. It is true that he was responsible for catching the sickness, but he did that only once; the continuation of the sickness is a simple result of his catching it that one time, and its progress cannot be traced at every moment to him as the cause; he brought it upon himself, but it cannot be said that he *is bringing* it upon himself. To despair, however, is a different matter. Every actual moment of despair is traceable to possibility; every moment he is in despair he *is bringing* it upon himself. It is always the present tense; in relation to the actuality there is no pastness of the past: in every actual moment of despair the person in despair bears all the past as a present in possibility. The reason for this is that to despair is a qualification of spirit and relates to the eternal in man. But he cannot rid himself of the eternal—no, never in all eternity. He cannot throw it away once and for all, nothing is more impossible; at any moment that he does not have it, he must have thrown it or is throwing it away—but it comes again, that is, every moment he is in despair he is bringing his despair upon himself. For despair is not attributable to the misrelation but to the relation that relates itself to itself. A person cannot rid himself of the relation to himself any more than he can rid himself of his self, which, after all, is one and the same thing, since the self is the relation to oneself.

C.

Despair is "The Sickness unto Death"

This concept, the sickness unto death, must, however, be understood in a particular way. Literally it means a sickness of which the end and the result are death. Therefore we use the expression "fatal sickness" as synonymous with the sickness unto death. In that sense, despair cannot be called the sickness unto death. Christianly understood, death itself is a passing into life. Thus, from a Christian point of view, no earthly, physical sickness is the sickness unto death, for death is indeed the end of the sickness, but death is not the end. If there is to be any question of a sickness unto death in the strictest sense, it must be a sickness of which the end is death and death is the end. This is precisely what despair is.

But in another sense despair is even more definitely the sickness unto death. Literally speaking, there is not the slightest possibility that anyone will die from this sickness or that it will end in physical death. On the contrary, the torment of despair is precisely this inability to die. Thus it has more in common with the situation of a mortally ill person when he lies struggling with death and yet cannot die. Thus to be sick *unto* death is to be unable to die, yet not as if there were hope of life; no, the hopelessness is that there is not even the ultimate hope, death. When death is the greatest danger, we hope for life; but when we learn to know the even greater danger, we hope for death. When the danger is so great that death becomes the hope, then despair is the hopelessness of not even being able to die.

It is in this last sense that despair is the sickness unto death, this tormenting contradiction, this sickness of the self, perpetually to be dying, to die and yet not die, to die death. For to die signifies that it is all over, but to die death means to experience dying, and if this is experienced for one single moment, one thereby experiences it forever. If a person were to die of despair as one dies of a sickness, then the eternal in him, the self, must be able to die in the same sense as the body dies of sickness. But this is impossible; the dying of despair continually converts itself into a living. The person in despair cannot die; "no more than the dagger can slaughter thoughts" can despair consume the eternal, the self at the root of despair, whose worm does not die and whose fire is not quenched. Nevertheless, despair is veritably a self-consuming, but an impotent self-consuming that cannot do what it wants to do. What it wants to do is to consume itself, something it cannot do, and this impotence is a new form of self-consuming, in which despair is once again unable to do what it wants to do, to consume itself; this is an intensification, or the law of intensification. This is the provocativeness or the cold fire in despair, this gnawing that burrows deeper and deeper in impotent self-consuming. The inability of despair to consume him is so remote from being any kind of comfort to the person in despair that it is the very opposite. This comfort is precisely the torment, is precisely what keeps the gnawing alive and keeps life in the gnawing, for it is precisely over this that he despairs (not as having despaired): that he cannot consume himself, cannot get rid of himself, cannot reduce himself to nothing. This is the formula for despair raised to a higher power, the rising fever in this sickness of the self.

An individual in despair despairs over *something.* So it seems for a moment, but only for a moment; in the same moment the true despair or despair in its true form shows itself. In despairing over *something,* he really despaired over *himself,* and now he wants to be rid of himself. For example, when the ambitious man whose slogan is "Either Caesar or nothing" does not get to be Caesar, he despairs over it. But this also means something else: precisely because he did not get to be Caesar, he now cannot bear to be himself. Consequently he does not despair because he did not get to be Caesar but despairs over himself because he did not get to be Caesar. This self, which, if it had become Caesar, would have been in seventh heaven (a state, incidentally, that in another sense is just as despairing), this self is now utterly intolerable to him. In a deeper sense, it is not his failure to become Caesar that is intolerable, but it is this self that did not become Caesar that is intolerable; or, to put it even more accurately, what is intolerable to him is that he cannot get rid of himself. If he had become Caesar, he would despairingly get rid of himself, but he did not become Caesar and cannot despairingly get rid of himself. Essentially, he is just as despairing, for he does not have his self, is not himself. He would not have become himself by becoming Caesar but would have been rid of himself, and by not becoming Caesar he despairs over not being able to get rid of himself. Thus it is superficial for someone (who probably has never seen anyone in despair, not even himself) to say of a person in despair: He is consuming himself. But this is precisely what he in his despair [wants] and this is precisely what he to his torment cannot do, since the despair has inflamed something that cannot burn or be burned up in the self.

Consequently, to despair over something is still not despair proper. It is the beginning, or, as the physician says of an illness, it has not yet declared itself. The next is declared despair, to despair over oneself. A young girl despairs of love, that is, she despairs over the loss of her beloved, over his death or his unfaithfulness to her. This is not declared despair; no, she despairs over herself. This self of hers, which she would have been rid of or would have lost in the most blissful manner had it become "his" beloved, this self becomes a torment to her if it has to be a self without "him." This self, which would have become her treasure (although, in another sense, it would have been just as despairing), has now become to her an abominable void since "he" died, or it has become to her a nauseating reminder that she has been deceived. Just try it, say to such a girl, "You are consuming yourself," and you will hear her answer, "Oh, but the torment is simply that I cannot do that."

To despair over oneself, in despair to will to be rid of oneself—this is the formula for all despair. Therefore the other form of despair, in despair to will to be oneself, can be traced back to the first, in despair not to will to be oneself, just as we previously resolved the form, in despair not to will to be oneself, into the form, in despair to will to be oneself (see A). A person in despair despairingly wills to be himself. But if he despairingly wills to be himself, he certainly does not want to be rid of himself. Well, so it seems, but upon closer examination it is clear that the contradiction is the same. The self that he despairingly wants to be is a self that he is not (for to will to be the self that he is in truth is the very opposite of despair), that is, he wants to tear his self away from the power that established it. In spite of all his despair, however, he cannot manage to do it; in spite of all his despairing efforts, that power is the stronger and forces him to be the self he does not want to be. But this is his way of willing to get rid of himself, to rid himself of the self that he is in order to be the self that he has dreamed up. He would be in seventh heaven to be the self he wants to be (although in another sense he would be just as despairing), but to be forced to be the self he does not want to be, that is his torment—that he cannot get rid of himself.

Socrates demonstrated the immortality of the soul from the fact that sickness of the soul (sin) does not consume it as sickness of the body consumes the body. Thus, the eternal in a person can be demonstrated by the fact that despair cannot consume his self, that precisely this is the torment of contradiction in despair. If there were nothing eternal in a man, he could not despair at all; if despair could consume his self, then there would be no despair at all.

Such is the nature of despair, this sickness of the self, this sickness unto death. The despairing person is mortally ill. In a completely different sense than is the case with any illness, this sickness has attacked the most vital organs, and yet he cannot die. Death is not the end of the sickness, but death is incessantly the end. To be saved from this sickness by death is an impossibility, because the sickness and its torment—and the death—are precisely this inability to die.

This is the state in despair. No matter how much the despairing person avoids it, no matter how successfully he has completely lost himself (especially the case in the form of despair that is ignorance of being in despair) and lost himself in such a manner that the loss is not at all detectable—eternity nevertheless will make it manifest that his condition was despair and will nail him to himself so that his torment will still be that he cannot rid himself of his self, and it will become obvious that he was just imagining that he had succeeded in doing so. Eternity is obliged to do this, because to have a self, to be a self, is the greatest concession, an infinite concession, given to man, but it is also eternity's claim upon him.

B

THE UNIVERSALITY OF THIS SICKNESS (DESPAIR)

Just as a physician might say that there very likely is not one single living human being who is completely healthy, so anyone who really knows mankind might say that there is not one single living human being who does not despair a little, who does not secretly harbor an unrest, an inner strife, a disharmony, an anxiety about an unknown something or a something he does not even dare to try to know, an anxiety about some possibility in existence or an anxiety about himself, so that, just as the physician speaks of going around with an illness in the body, he walks around with a sickness, carries around a sickness of the spirit that signals its presence at rare intervals in and through an anxiety he cannot explain. In any case, no human being ever lived and no one lives outside of Christendom who has not despaired, and no one in Christendom if he is not a true Christian, and insofar as he is not wholly that, he still is to some extent in despair.

No doubt this observation will strike many people as a paradox, an overstatement, and also a somber and depressing point of view. But it is none of these things. It is not somber, for, on the contrary, it tries to shed light on what generally is left somewhat obscure; it is not depressing but instead is elevating, inasmuch as it views every human being under the destiny of the highest claim upon him, to be spirit; nor is it a paradox but, on the contrary, a consistently developed basic view, and therefore neither is it an overstatement.

However, the customary view of despair does not go beyond appearances, and thus it is a superficial view, that is, no view at all. It assumes that every man must himself know best whether he is in despair or not. Anyone who says he is in despair is regarded as being in despair, and anyone who thinks he is not is therefore regarded as not. As a result, the phenomenon of despair is infrequent rather than quite common. That one is in despair is not a rarity; no, it is rare, very rare, that one is in truth not in despair.

The common view has a very poor understanding of despair. Among other things, it completely overlooks (to name only this, which, properly understood, places thousands and thousands and millions in the category of despair), it completely overlooks that not being in despair, not being conscious of being in despair, is precisely a form of despair. In a much deeper sense, the position of the common view in interpreting despair is like that of the common view in determining whether a person is sick—in a much deeper sense, for the common view understands far less well what spirit is (and lacking this understanding, one cannot understand despair, either) than it understands sickness and health. As a rule, a person is considered to be healthy when he himself does not say that he is sick, not to mention when he himself says that he is well. But the physician has a different view of sickness. Why? Because the physician has a defined and developed conception of what it is to be healthy and ascertains a man's condition accordingly. The physician knows that just as there is merely imaginary sickness there is also merely imaginary health, and in the latter case he first takes measures to disclose the sickness. Generally speaking, the physician, precisely because he is a physician (well informed), does not have complete confidence in what a person says about his condition. If everyone's statement about his condition, that he is healthy or sick, were completely reliable, to be a physician would be a delusion. A physician's task is not only to prescribe remedies but also, first and foremost, to identify the sickness, and consequently his first task is to ascertain whether the supposedly sick person is actually sick or whether the supposedly healthy person is perhaps actually sick. Such is also the relation of the physician of the soul to despair. He knows what despair is; he recognizes it and therefore is satisfied neither with a person's declaration that he is not in despair nor with his declaration that he is. It must be pointed out that in a certain sense it is not even always the case that those who say they despair are in despair. Despair can be affected, and as a qualification of the spirit it may also be mistaken for and confused with all sorts of transitory states, such as dejection, inner conflict, which pass without developing into despair. But the physician of the soul properly regards these also as forms of despair; he sees very well that they are affectation. Yet this very affectation is despair: he sees very well that this dejection etc. are not of great significance, but precisely this—that it has and acquires no great significance—is despair.

The common view also overlooks that despair is dialectically different from what is usually termed a sickness, because it is a sickness of the spirit. Properly understood, this dialectic again brings thousands under the definition of despair. If at a given time a physician has made sure that someone is well, and that person later becomes ill, then the physician may legitimately say that this person at one time was healthy but now is sick. Not so with despair. As soon as despair becomes apparent, it is manifest that the individual was in despair. Hence, at no moment is it possible to decide anything about a person who has not been saved by having been in despair, for whenever that which triggers his despair occurs, it is immediately apparent that he has been in despair his whole life. On the other hand, when someone gets a fever, it can by no means be said that it is now apparent that he has had a fever all his life. Despair is a qualification of the spirit, is related to the eternal, and thus has something of the eternal in its dialectic.

Despair is not only dialectically different from a sickness, but all its symptoms are also dialectical, and therefore the superficial view is very easily deceived in determining whether or not despair is present. Not to be in despair can in fact signify precisely to be in despair, and it can signify having been rescued from being in despair. A sense of security and tranquillity can signify being in despair; precisely this sense of security and tranquillity can be the despair, and yet it can signify having conquered despair and having won peace. Not being in despair is not similar to not being sick, for not being sick cannot be the same as being sick, whereas not being in despair can be the very same as being in despair. It is not with despair as with a sickness, where feeling indisposed is the sickness. By no means. Here again the indisposition is dialectical. Never to have sensed this indisposition is precisely to be in despair.

This means and has its basis in the fact that the condition of man, regarded as spirit (and if there is to be any question of despair, man must be regarded as defined by spirit), is always critical. We speak of a crisis in relation to sickness but not in relation to health. Why not? Because physical health is an immediate qualification that first becomes dialectical in the condition of sickness, in which the question of a crisis arises. Spiritually, or when man is regarded as spirit, both health and sickness are critical; there is no immediate health of the spirit.

As soon as man ceases to be regarded as defined by spirit (and in that case there can be no mention of despair, either) but only as psychical-physical synthesis, health is an immediate qualification, and mental or physical sickness is the only dialectical qualification. But to be unaware of being defined as spirit is precisely what despair is. Even that which, humanly speaking, is utterly beautiful and lovable—a womanly youthfulness that is perfect peace and harmony and joy—is nevertheless despair. To be sure, it is happiness, but happiness is not a qualification of spirit, and deep, deep within the most secret hiding place of happiness there dwells also anxiety, which is despair; it very much wishes to be allowed to remain there, because for despair the most cherished and desirable place to live is in the heart of happiness. Despite its illusory security and tranquillity, all immediacy is anxiety and thus, quite consistently, is most anxious about nothing. The most gruesome description of something most terrible does not make immediacy as anxious as a subtle, almost carelessly, and yet deliberately and calculatingly dropped allusion to some indefinite something—in fact, immediacy is made most anxious by a subtle implication that it knows very well what is being talked about. Immediacy probably does not know it, but reflection never snares so unfailingly as when it fashions its snare out of nothing, and reflection is never so much itself as when it is—nothing. It requires extraordinary reflection, or, more correctly, it requires great faith to be able to endure reflection upon nothing—that is, infinite reflection. Consequently, even that which is utterly beautiful and lovable, womanly youthfulness, is still despair, is happiness. For that reason, it is impossible to slip through life on this immediacy. And if this happiness does succeed in slipping through, well, it is of little use, for it is despair. Precisely because the sickness of despair is totally dialectical, it is the worst misfortune never to have had that sickness: it is a true godsend to get it, even if it is the most dangerous of illnesses, if one does not want to be cured of it. Generally it is regarded as fortunate to be cured of a sickness; the sickness itself is the misfortune.

Therefore, the common view that despair is a rarity is entirely wrong; on the contrary, it is universal. The common view, which assumes that everyone who does not think or feel he is in despair is not or that only he who says he is in despair is, is totally false. On the contrary, the person who without affectation says that he is in despair is still a little closer, is dialectically closer, to being cured than all those who are not regarded as such and who do not regard themselves as being in despair. The physician of souls will certainly agree with me that, on the whole, most men live without ever becoming conscious of being destined as spirit—hence all the so-called security, contentment with life, etc., which is simply despair. On the other hand, those who say they are in despair are usually either those who have so deep a nature that they are bound to become conscious as spirit or those whom bitter experiences and dreadful decisions have assisted in becoming conscious as spirit: it is either the one or the other; the person who is really devoid of despair is very rare indeed.

There is so much talk about human distress and wretchedness—I try to understand it and have also had some intimate acquaintance with it—there is so much talk about wasting a life, but only that person's life was wasted who went on living so deceived by life's joys or its sorrows that he never became decisively and eternally conscious as spirit, as self, or, what amounts to the same thing, never became aware and in the deepest sense never gained the impression that there is a God and that "he," he himself, his self, exists before this God—an infinite benefaction that is never gained except through despair. What wretchedness that so many go on living this way, cheated of this most blessed of thoughts! What wretchedness that we are engrossed in or encourage the human throng to be engrossed in everything else, using them to supply the energy for the drama of life but never reminding them of this blessedness. What wretchedness that they are lumped together and deceived instead of being split apart so that each individual may gain the highest, the only thing worth living for and enough to live in for an eternity. I think that I could weep an eternity over the existence of such wretchedness! And to me an even more horrible expression of this most terrible sickness and misery is that it is hidden—not only that the person suffering from it may wish to hide it and may succeed, not only that it can so live in a man that no one, no one detects it, no, but also that it can be so hidden in a man that he himself is not aware of it! And when the hourglass has run out, the hourglass of temporality, when the noise of secular life has grown silent and its restless or ineffectual activism has come to an end, when everything around you is still, as it is in eternity, then—whether you were man or woman, rich or poor, dependent or independent, fortunate or unfortunate, whether you ranked with royalty and wore a glittering crown or in humble obscurity bore the toil and heat of the day, whether your name will be remembered as long as the world stands and consequently as long as it stood or you are nameless and run nameless in the innumerable multitude, whether the magnificence encompassing you surpassed all human description or the most severe and ignominious human judgment befell you—eternity asks you and every individual in these millions and millions about only one thing: whether you have lived in despair or not, whether you have despaired in such a way that you did not realize that you were in despair, or in such a way that you covertly carried this sickness inside of you as your gnawing secret, as a fruit of sinful love under your heart, or in such a way that you, a terror to others, raged in despair. And if so, if you have lived in despair, then, regardless of whatever else you won or lost, everything is lost for you, eternity does not acknowledge you, it never knew you—or, still more terrible, it knows you as you are known and it binds you to yourself in despair.

DISCUSSION QUESTIONS

1. Explain how Kierkegaard believes despair can exist "deep, deep within the most secret hiding place of happiness." Do you agree?
2. Do you agree with Kierkegaard that "no human being ever lived and no one lives outside of Christendom who has not despaired"? Explain.
3. How does Kierkegaard use the analogy of a physician diagnosing a sickness to support his claim that a person can be wrong about whether or not he is in despair?
4. Which view is more intuitive, the common view or Kierkegaard's view of despair? Which view is ultimately more compelling? Explain.

Chapter 18

AUGUSTE COMTE

Auguste Comte (1798–1857) was an influential French philosopher of the positivist school. Denied university appointments, Comte lectured to private audiences. He claimed to have pioneered sociology as the positive study of social structures and development. Comte's main philosophical work, Cours de philosophie positive, *in six volumes, was published between 1830 and 1842.*

In this brief selection Comte criticizes preceding metaphysicians for subordinating the affections and passions to intellect and self-consciousness. They made the intellect supreme in order to radically separate human beings from other animals and to preserve the unity of what they called the "I" and the unity of the soul. Comte argues that human nature is multiple, not single. Due to their more isolated lives, the sense of personality of the "superior" animals is more pronounced than it is in human beings. He argues that if intelligence (practical reason) is the aptitude to modify conduct in conformity to changing circumstances, then both humans and animals must have it, only in different degrees of development. Intelligence in no way conflicts with instinct; humans have as many or more instincts than brute animals. Gall's two doctrines, (1) that the fundamental affective and intellectual dispositions are innate, and (2) that there are many distinct and independent faculties, Comte calls indisputable philosophical principles. He defends human liberty from the theory of causal necessity by holding that phenomena become susceptible of modification in proportion to their complexity, and that the phenomena of life and acts of the mind are exceedingly complex.

The Positive Philosophy

As to the doctrine, the first glance shows a radical fault in it, common to all sects,—a false estimate of the general relations between the affective and the intellectual faculties. However various may be the theories about the preponderance of the latter, all metaphysicians assert that preponderance by making these faculties their starting-point. The intellect is almost exclusively the subject of their speculations, and the affections have been almost entirely neglected; and, moreover, always subordinated to the understanding. Now, such a conception represents precisely the reverse of the reality, not only for animals, but also for Man: for daily experience shows that the affections, the propensities, the passions, are the great springs of human life; and that, so far from resulting from intelligence, their spontaneous and independent impulse is indispensable to the first awakening and continuous development of the various intellectual faculties, by assigning to them a permanent end, without which—to say nothing of the vagueness of their general direction—they would remain dormant in the majority of men. It is even but too certain that the least noble and most animal propensities are habitually the most energetic, and therefore the most influential. The whole of human nature is thus very unfaithfully represented by these futile systems, which, if noticing the affective faculties at all, have vaguely connected them with one single principle, sympathy, and, above all, self-consciousness, always supposed to be directed by the intellect. Thus it is that, contrary to evidence, Man has been represented as essentially a reasoning being, continually carrying on, unconsciously, a multitude of imperceptible calculations, with scarcely any spontaneity of action, from infancy upward. This false conception has doubtless been supported by a consideration worthy of all respect,—that it is by the intellect that Man is modified and improved; but science requires, before all things, the reality of any views, independently of their desirableness; and it is always this reality which is the basis of genuine utility. Without denying the secondary influence of such a view, we can show that two purely philosophical causes, quite unconnected with any idea of application, and inherent in the nature of the method, have led the metaphysicians of all sects to this hypothesis of the supremacy of the intellect. The first is the radical separation which it was thought necessary to make between brutes and man, and which would have been affected at once by the admission of the preponderance of the affective over the intellectual faculties; and the second was the necessity that the metaphysicians found themselves under, of preserving the unity of what they called the *I,* that it might correspond with the unity of the *soul,* in obedience to the requisitions of the theological philosophy, of which metaphysics is, as we must ever bear in mind, the final transformation. But the positive philosophers, who approach the questions with

---

Source: Public domain. Translation by Harriet Martineau. Reprinted from *The Postive Philosophy of Auguste Comte,* New York: William Gowans (1868) pp. 384–389. Annotations have been deleted.

the simple aim of ascertaining the true state of things, and reproducing it with all possible accuracy in their theories, have perceived that, according to universal experience, human nature is so far from being single that it is eminently multiple; that is, usually induced in various directions by distinct and independent powers, among which equilibrium is established with extreme difficulty when, as usually happens in civilized life, no one of them is, in itself, sufficiently marked to acquire spontaneously any considerable preponderance over the rest. Thus, the famous theory of the *I* is essentially without a scientific object, since it is destined to represent a purely fictitious state. There is, in this direction, as I have already pointed out, no other real subject of positive investigation than the study of equilibrium of the various animal functions,—both of irritability and of sensibility,—which marks the normal state, in which each of them, duly moderated, is regularly and permanently associated with the whole of the others, according to the laws of sympathy, and yet more of synergy. The very abstract and indirect notion of the *I* proceeds from the continuous sense of such a harmony; that is, from the universal accordance of the entire organism. Psychologists have attempted in vain to make out of this idea, or rather sense, an attribute of humanity exclusively. "It is evidently a necessary result of all animal life; and therefore it must belong to all animals, whether they are able to discourse upon it or not. No doubt a cat, or any other vertebrated animal, without knowing how to say "I," is not in the habit of taking itself for another. Moreover, it is probable that among the superior animals the sense of personality is still more marked than in Man, on account of their more isolated life; though if we descended too far in the zoological scale we should reach organisms in which the continuous degradation of the nervous system attenuates this compound sense, together with the various simple feelings on which it depends.

It must not be overlooked that though the psychologists have agreed in neglecting the intellectual and moral faculties of brutes, which have been happily left to the naturalists, they have occasioned great mischief by their obscure and indefinite distinction between intelligence and instinct, thus setting up a division between human and animal nature which has had too much effect even upon zoologists to this day. The only meaning that can be attributed to the word *instinct,* is any spontaneous impulse in a determinate direction, independently of any foreign influence. In this primitive sense, the term evidently applies to the proper and direct activity of any faculty whatever, intellectual as well as affective; and it therefore does not conflict with the term *intelligence* in any way, as we so often see when we speak of those who, without any education, manifest a marked talent for music, painting, mathematics, etc. In this way there is instinct, or rather, there are instincts in Man, as much or more than in brutes. If, on the other hand, we describe *intelligence* as the aptitude to modify conduct in conformity to the circumstances of each case,—which, in fact, is the main practical attribute of *reason,* in its proper sense,—it is more evident than before that there is no other essential difference between humanity and animality than that of the degree of development admitted by a faculty which is, by its nature, common to all animal life, and without which it could not even be conceived to exist. Thus the famous scholastic definition of Man as a *reasonable animal* offers a real no-meaning, since no animal, especially in the higher parts of the zoological scale, could live without being to a certain extent reasonable, in proportion to the complexity of its organism. Though the moral nature of animals has been but little and very imperfectly explored, we can yet perceive, without possibility of mistake, among those that live with us and that are familiar with us,—judging of them by the same means of observation that we should employ about men whose language and ways were previously unknown to us,—that they not only apply their intelligence to the satisfaction of their organic wants, much as men do, aiding themselves also with some sort of language; but that they are, in like manner, susceptible of a kind of wants more disinterested, inasmuch as they consist in a need to exercise their faculties for the mere pleasure of the exercise. It is the same thing that leads children or savages to invent new sports, and that renders them, at the same time, liable to *ennui*. That state, erroneously set up as a special privilege of human nature, is sometimes sufficiently marked, in the case of certain animals, to urge them to suicide, when captivity has become intolerable. An attentive examination of the facts therefore discredits the perversion of the word *instinct* when it is used to signify the fatality under which animals are impelled to the mechanical performance of *acts* uniformly determinate, without any possible modification from corresponding circumstances, and neither requiring nor allowing any education properly so called. This gratuitous supposition is evidently a remnant of the automatic hypothesis of Descartes. Leroy has demonstrated that among mammifers and birds this ideal fixity in the construction of habitations, in the seeking of food by hunting, in the mode of migration, etc., exist only in the eyes of closet-naturalists or inattentive observers.

After thus much notice of the radical vice of all psychological systems, it would be departing from the object of this work to show how the intellectual faculties themselves have been misconceived. It is enough to refer to the refutation by which Gall and Spurzheim have introduced their labors: and I would particularly point out the philosophical demonstration by which they have exhibited the conclusion that sensation, memory, imagination, and even judgment—all the scholastic faculties, in short—are not, in fact, fundamental and abstract faculties, but only different degrees or consecutive modes of the same phenomenon, proper to each of the true elementary phrenological functions, and necessarily variable in different cases, with a proportionate activity. One virtue of this admirable analysis is that it deprives the various metaphysical theories of their one remaining credit—their mutual criticism, which is here effected, once for all, with more efficacy than by any one of the mutually opposing schools.

Again, it would be departing from the object of this portion of our work to judge of the doctrines of the schools by their results. What these have been we shall see in the next book; the deplorable influence on the political and social condition of two generations of the doctrines of the French school, as presented by Helvetius, and of the German psychology, with the ungovernable *I* for its subject; and the impotence of the Scotch school, through the vagueness of what is called its doctrines, and their want of mutual connection. Dismissing all these for the present, we must examine the great attempt of Gall, in order to see what is wanting in phrenological philosophy to form it into the scientific constitution which is proper to it, and from which it is necessarily still more remote than organic, and even animal physiology.

Two philosophical principles, now admitted to be indisputable, serve as the immovable basis of Gall's doctrine as a whole: viz., the innateness of the fundamental dispositions, affective and intellectual, and the plurality of the distinct and independent faculties; though real acts usually require their more or less complex concurrence. Within the limits of the human race, all cases of marked talents or character prove the first; and the second is proved by the diversity of such marked cases, and by most pathological states—especially by those in which the nervous system is directly affected. A comparative observation of the higher animals would dispel all doubt, if any existed in either case. These two principles—aspects of a single fundamental conception—are but the scientific expression of the results of experience, in all times and places, as to the intellectual and moral nature of Man—an indispensable symptom of truth, with regard to all parent ideas, which must always be connected with the spontaneous indications of popular reason, as we have seen in preceding cases in natural philosophy. Thus, besides all guidance from analogy, after the study of animal life, we derive confirmation from all the methods of investigation that physiology admits; from direct observation, experiment, pathological analysis, the comparative method, and popular good sense—all of which converge toward the establishment of this double principle. Such a collection of proofs secures the stability of this much of phrenological doctrine, whatever transformations other parts may have to undergo. In the anatomical view, this physiological conception corresponds with the division of the brain into a certain number of partial organs, symmetrical like those of the animal life, and, though more contiguous and mutually resembling than in any other system, and therefore more adapted both for sympathy and synergy, still distinct and mutually independent, as we were already aware was the case with the ganglions appropriate to the external senses. In brief, the brain is no longer an organ, but an apparatus of organs, more complex in proportion to the degree of animality. The proper object of phrenological physiology thence consists in determining the cerebral organ appropriate to each clearly-marked, simple disposition, affective or intellectual; or, reciprocally, which is more difficult, what function is fulfilled by any portion of the mass of the brain which exhibits the anatomical conditions of a distinct organ. The two processes are directed to develop the agreement between physiological and anatomical analysis which constitutes the true science of living beings. Unfortunately, our means are yet further from answering our aims than in the two preceding divisions of the science.

The scientific principle involved in the phrenological view is that the functions, affective and intellectual, are more elevated, more human, if you will, and at the same time less energetic, in proportion to the exclusiveness with which they belong to the higher part of the zoological series, their positions being in portions of the brain more and more restricted in extent, and further removed from its immediate origin,—according to the anatomical decision that the skull is simply a prolongation of the vertebral column, which is the primitive centre of the nervous system. Thus, the least developed and anterior part of the brain is appropriated to the characteristic faculties of humanity; and the most voluminous and hindmost part to those which constitute the basis of the whole of the animal kingdom. Here we have a new and confirmatory instance of the rule which we have had to follow in every science; that it is necessary to proceed from the most general to the more special attributes, in the order of their diminishing generality. We shall meet with it again in the one science which remains for us to review; and its constant presence; through the whole range, points it out as the first law of the dogmatic procedure of the positive spirit.

A full contemplation of Gall's doctrine convinces us of its faithful representation of the intellectual and moral nature of Man and animals. All the psychological sects have misconceived or ignored the pre-eminence of the affective faculties, plainly manifest as it is in all the moral phenomena of brutes, and even of Man; but we find this fact placed on a scientific basis by the discovery that the affective organs occupy all the hinder and middle portions of the cerebral apparatus, while the intellectual occupy only the front portion, which, in extreme cases, is not more than a fourth, or even a sixth part of the whole. The difference between Gall and his predecessors was not in the separation of the two kinds of faculties, but that they assigned the brain to the intellectual faculties alone, regarding it as a single organ, and distributing the passions among the organs pertaining to the vegetative life,—the heart, the liver, etc. Bichat supported this view by the argument of the sympathies of those organs, under the excitement of the respective passions; but the variableness of the seat of sympathy, according to native susceptibility or to accident, is a sufficient answer to such a plea, and teaches us simply the importance of considering the influence exercised by the state of the brain upon the nerves which supply the apparatus of the organic life.

Next comes the subdivision established by Gall and Spurzheim in each of these two orders. The affective faculties are divided into the propensities, and the affections or sentiments: the first residing in the hindmost and lowest part of the brain; and the other class in the middle portion. The intellectual faculties are divided into the various perceptive faculties, which together constitute the range of observation: and the small number of reflective faculties, the highest of all, constituting the power of combination, by comparison and co-ordination. The upper part of the frontal region is the seat of these last, which are the chief characteristic attribute of human nature. There is a certain deficiency of precision in this description; but, besides that we may expect improving knowledge to clear it up, we shall find, on close examination, that the inconvenience lies more in the language than in the idea. The only language we have is derived from a philosophical period when all moral and even intellectual ideas were shrouded in a mysterious metaphysical unity, which allows us now no adequate choice of terms.

Taking the ordinary terms in their literal sense, we should misconceive the fundamental distinction between the intellectual faculties and the others. When the former are very marked, they unquestionably produce real inclinations or propensities, which are distinguished from the inferior passions only by their smaller energy. Nor can we deny that their action occasions true emotions or sentiments, more rare, more pure, more sublime than any other, and, though less vivid than others, capable of moving to tears; as is testified by so many instances of the rapture excited by the discovery of truth, in the most eminent thinkers that have done honor to their race—as Archimedes, Descartes, Kepler, Newton, etc. Would any thoughtful student take occasion, by such approximations, to deny all real distinction between the intellectual and affective faculties? The wiser conclusion to be drawn from the case is that we must reform our philosophical language, to raise it, by rigorous precision, to the dignity of scientific language. We may say as much about the subdivision of the affective faculties into propensities and sentiments, the distinction being, though less marked, by no means less real. Apart from all useless discussion of nomenclature, we may say that the real difference has not been clearly seized. In a scientific view, it would suffice to say that the first and fundamental class relates to the individual alone, or, at most, to the family, regarded successively in its principal needs of preservation,—such as reproduction, the rearing of young, the mode of alimentation, of habitation, etc. Whereas, the second more special class supposes the existence of some social relations, either among individuals of a different species, or especially between individuals of the same species, apart from sex, and determines the character which the tendencies of the animal must impress on each of these relations, whether transient or permanent. If we keep this distinctive character of the two classes in view, it will matter little what terms we use to indicate them, when once they shall have acquired a sufficient fixedness, through rational use.

These are the great philosophical results of Gall's doctrine, regarded, as I have now presented it, apart from all vain attempts to localize in a special manner the cerebral or phrenological functions. I shall have to show how such an attempt was imposed upon Gall by the necessities of his glorious mission: but notwithstanding this unfortunate necessity, the doctrine embodies already a real knowledge of human and brute nature very far superior to all that had ever been offered before.

Among the innumerable objections which have been aimed at this fine doctrine,—considered always as a whole, the only one which merits discussion here is the supposed necessity of human actions. This objection is not only of high importance in itself, but it casts new light back upon the spirit of the theory; and we must briefly examine it from the point of view of positive philosophy.

When objectors confound the subjection of events to invariable laws with their necessary exemption from modification, they lose sight of the fact that phenomena become susceptible of modification in proportion to their complexity. The only irresistible action that we know of is that of weight, which takes place under the most general and simple of all natural laws. But the phenomena of life and acts of the mind are so highly complex as to admit of modification beyond all estimate; and in the intermediate regions, phenomena are under control precisely in the order of their complexity. Gall and Spurzheim have shown how human action depends on the combined operation of several faculties; how exercise develops them; how inactivity wastes them; and how the intellectual faculties, adapted to modify the general conduct of the animal according to the variable exigencies of his situation, may overrule the practical influence of all his other faculties. It is only in mania, when disease interferes with the natural action of the faculties, that fatality, or what is popularly called irresponsibility, exists. It is therefore a great mistake to accuse cerebral physiology of disowning the influence of education or legislation, because it fixes the limits of their power. It denies the possibility, asserted by the ideology of the French school, of converting by suitable arrangements, all men into so many Socrateses, Homers, or Archimedeses; and it denies the ungovernable energy of the *I,* asserted by the German school; but it does not therefore affect Man's reasonable liberty, or interfere with his improvement by the aid of a wise education. It is evident indeed that improvement by education supposes the existence of requisite predispositions: and that each of them is subject to determinate laws, without which they could not be systematically influenced; so that it is, after all, cerebral physiology that is in possession of the philosophical problem of education. Furthermore, this physiology shows us that men are commonly of an average constitution; that is, that, apart from a very few exceptional organizations, every one possesses in a moderate degree all the propensities, all the sentiments, and all the elementary aptitudes, without any one faculty being remarkably preponderant. The widest field is thus open for education, in modifying in almost any direction organisms so flexible, though the degree of their development may remain of that average amount which consists very well with social harmony; as we shall have occasion to see hereafter.

DISCUSSION QUESTIONS

1. Comte says that even without knowing how to say "I," a cat does not take itself for another. Do you agree with him that all animals share self-awareness with human beings?
2. Is Comte correct that physiology shows us that human beings are commonly of an average constitution? Do you agree with him that, apart from a very few exceptions, "everyone possesses in a moderate degree all the propensities, all the sentiments, and all the elementary aptitudes, without any one faculty being remarkably preponderant"? Explain.
3. What does Comte mean by "the phrenological view"?

Chapter 19

F. W. NIETZSCHE

Friedrich Wilhelm Nietzsche (1844–1900) was born in Röchen, the son of a Lutheran pastor. Fritz was educated at Pforta, the most famous classical boarding school in Germany, and at the Universities of Bonn and Leipzig. An outstandingly brilliant student, at 24 he was appointed professor of Classics at the University of Basel. He battled headaches, eye pains, stomach pains, vomiting, and debility most of his life. Delusions of grandeur consumed his mind for months when, in January 1889, seeing a cab-driver beating his horse, Nietzsche tearfully flung his arms around the horse's neck and collapsed. He awoke insane. Cerebral syphilis may have caused his stroke in 1898. He was one of the greatest prose stylists of modern times. The incendiary, radical ideas in his many books have influenced many subsequent philosophers.

In these brief selections, Nietzsche judges the personal relationship of a thinker to his problems to be superior to the detached, "selfless" approach to philosophy. To question the value of morality is his own personal torment. He contrasts the scholar's impersonal drive to knowledge with every great philosophy, which has been a personal confession of its author. He raises questions of conscience for the intellect that claims "I think" as an immediate certainty. A thought comes when "it" wants, he observes, not when "I" want. Willing is no unity, but a complex of feeling and thinking and the affect of command. Nietzsche contends that personality is very rarely expressed in a work or act because its production requires unusually low impressionability.

The Gay Science

345

Morality as a problem. –

The lack of personality always takes its revenge: A weakened, thin, extinguished personality that denies itself is no longer fit for anything good—least of all for philosophy. "Selflessness" has no value either in heaven or on earth. All great problems demand *great love,* and of that only strong, round, secure spirits who have a firm grip on themselves are capable. It makes the most telling difference whether a thinker has a personal relationship to his problems and finds in them his destiny, his distress, and his greatest happiness, or an "impersonal" one, meaning that he can do no better than to touch them and grasp them with the antennae of cold, curious thought. In the latter case nothing will come of it; that much one can promise in advance, for even if great problems should allow themselves to be *grasped* by them they would not permit frogs and weaklings to *hold on* to them; such has been their taste from time immemorial—a taste, incidentally, that they share with all redoubtable females.

Why is it then that I have never yet encountered anybody, not even in books, who approached morality in this personal way and who knew morality as a problem, and this problem as his own personal distress, torment, voluptuousness, and passion? It is evident that up to now morality was no problem at all but, on the contrary, precisely that on which after all mistrust, discord, and contradiction one could agree—the hallowed place of peace where our thinkers took a rest even from themselves, took a deep breath, and felt revived. I see nobody who ventured a *critique* of moral valuations; I miss even the slightest attempts of scientific curiosity, of the refined, experimental imagination of psychologists and historians that readily anticipates a problem and catches it in flight without quite knowing what it has caught. I have scarcely detected a few meager preliminary efforts to explore the *history of the origins* of these feelings and valuations (which is something quite different from a critique and again different from a history of ethical systems). In one particular case I have done everything to encourage a sympathy and talent for this kind of history—in vain, as it seems to me today.

These historians of morality (mostly Englishmen) do not amount to much. Usually they themselves are still quite unsuspectingly obedient to one particular morality and, without knowing it, serve that as shield-bearers and followers—for example, by sharing that popular superstition of Christian Europe which people keep mouthing so guilelessly to this day, that what is characteristic of moral actions is selflessness, self-sacrifice, or sympathy and pity. Their usual mistaken premise is that they affirm some consensus of the nations, at least of tame nations, concerning certain principles of morals, and then they infer from this that

---

Source: From *The Gay Science,* §345, 283–285 by Friedrich Nietzche, translated by Walter Kaufmann,

these principles must be unconditionally binding also for you and me; or, conversely, they see the truth that among different nations moral valuations are *necessarily* different and then infer from this that *no* morality is at all binding. Both procedures are equally childish.

The mistake made by the more refined among them is that they uncover and criticize the perhaps foolish opinions of a people about their morality, or of humanity about all human morality—opinions about its origin, religious sanction, the superstition of free will and things of that sort—and then suppose that they have criticized the morality itself. But the value of a command "thou shalt" is still fundamentally different from and independent of such opinions about it and the weeds of error that may have overgrown it—just as certainly as the value of a medication for a sick person is completely independent of whether he thinks about medicine scientifically or the way old women do. Even if a morality has grown out of an error, the realization of this fact would not as much as touch the problem of its value.

Thus nobody up to now has examined the *value* of that most famous of all medicines which is called morality; and the first step would be—for once to *question* it. Well then, precisely this is our task.—

Beyond Good and Evil

6

It has gradually become clear to me what every great philosophy has hitherto been: a confession on the part of its author and a kind of involuntary and unconscious memoir; moreover, that the moral (or immoral) intentions in every philosophy have every time constituted the real germ of life out of which the entire plant has grown. To explain how a philosopher's most remote metaphysical assertions have actually been arrived at, it is always well (and wise) to ask oneself first: what morality does this (does *he*—) aim at? I accordingly do not believe a 'drive to knowledge' to be the father of philosophy, but that another drive has, here as elsewhere, only employed knowledge (and false knowledge!) as a tool. But anyone who looks at the basic drives of mankind to see to what extent they may in precisely this connection have come into play as *inspirational* spirits (or demons and kobolds—) will discover that they have all at some time or other practised philosophy —and that each one of them would be only too glad to present *itself* as the ultimate goal of existence and as the legitimate *master* of all the other drives. For every drive is tyrannical: and it is as *such* that it tries to philosophize.—In the case of scholars, to be sure, in the case of really scientific men, things may be different—'better', if you will—there may really exist something like a drive to knowledge there, some little independent clockwork which, when wound up, works bravely on *without* any of the scholar's other drives playing any essential part. The scholar's real 'interests' therefore generally lie in quite another direction, perhaps in his family or in making money or in politics; it is, indeed, almost a matter of indifference whether his little machine is set up in this region of science or that, whether the 'promising' young worker makes himself into a good philologist or a specialist in fungus or a chemist—he is not *characterized* by becoming this or that. In the philosopher, on the contrary, there is nothing whatever impersonal; and, above all, his morality bears decided and decisive testimony to *who he is*—that is to say, to the order of rank the innermost drives of his nature stand in relative to one another.

★

16

There are still harmless self-observers who believe 'immediate certainties' exist, for example 'I think' or, as was Schopenhauer's superstition, 'I will': as though knowledge here got hold of its object pure and naked, as 'thing in itself', and no falsification occurred either on the side of the subject or on that of the object. But I shall reiterate a hundred times that 'immediate certainty', like 'absolute knowledge' and 'thing in itself', contains a *contradictio in adjecto:*[1] we really ought to get free

---

Source: From *Beyond Good and Evil,* Part 1 §6, §16–§19, Part 2 §41, Part 3 §54, Part 6 §207 pp. 37–38, 45–49, 70, 80–81, 133–135 in R.J. Hollingdale tr., M. Tanner intro. (Penguin Classics: April 2003) ISBN 0-14-044923-X.

from the seduction of words! Let the people believe that knowledge is total knowledge, but the philosopher must say to himself: when I analyse the event expressed in the sentence 'I think', I acquire a series of rash assertions which are difficult, perhaps impossible, to prove—for example, that it is *I* who think, that it has to be something at all which thinks, that thinking is an activity and operation on the part of an entity thought of as a cause, that an 'I' exists, finally that what is designated by 'thinking' has already been determined—that I *know* what thinking is. For if I had not already decided that matter within myself, by what standard could I determine that what is happening is not perhaps 'willing' or 'feeling'? Enough: this 'I think' presupposes that I *compare* my present state with other known states of myself in order to determine what it is: on account of this retrospective connection with other 'knowledge' at any rate it possesses no immediate certainty for me.—In place of that 'immediate certainty' in which the people may believe in the present case, the philosopher acquires in this way a series of metaphysical questions, true questions of conscience for the intellect, namely: 'Whence do I take the concept thinking? Why do I believe in cause and effect? What gives me the right to speak of an "I", and even of an "I" as cause, and finally of an "I" as cause of thought?' Whoever feels able to answer these metaphysical questions straight away with an appeal to a sort of *intuitive* knowledge, as he does who says: 'I think, and know that this at least is true, actual and certain'—will find a philosopher today ready with a smile and two question-marks. 'My dear sir,' the philosopher will perhaps give him to understand, 'it is improbable you are not mistaken: but why do you want the truth at all?'—

17

As for the superstitions of the logicians, I shall never tire of underlining a concise little fact which these superstitious people are loath to admit—namely, that a thought comes when 'it' wants, not when 'I' want; so that it is a *falsification* of the facts to say: the subject 'I' is the condition of the predicate 'think'. *It* thinks: but that this 'it' is precisely that famous old 'I' is, to put it mildly, only an assumption, an assertion, above all not an 'immediate certainty'. For even with this 'it thinks' one has already gone too far: this 'it' already contains an *interpretation* of the event and does not belong to the event itself. The inference here is in accordance with the habit of grammar: 'thinking is an activity, to every activity pertains one who acts, consequently—'. It was more or less in accordance with the same scheme that the older atomism sought, in addition to the 'force' which acts, that little lump of matter in which it resides, out of which it acts, the atom; more rigorous minds at last learned to get along without this 'residuum of earth', and perhaps we and the logicians as well will one day accustom ourselves to getting along without that little 'it' (which is what the honest old 'I' has evaporated into).

18

It is certainly not the least charm of a theory that it is refutable: it is with precisely this charm that it entices subtler minds. It seems that the hundred times refuted theory of 'free will' owes its continued existence to this charm alone—: again and again there comes along someone who feels he is strong enough to refute it.

19

Philosophers are given to speaking of the will as if it were the best-known thing in the world; Schopenhauer, indeed, would have us understand that the will alone is truly known to us, known completely, known without deduction or addition. But it seems to me that in this case too Schopenhauer has done only what philosophers in general are given to doing: that he has taken up a *popular prejudice* and exaggerated it. Willing seems to me to be above all something *complicated,* something that is a unity only as a word—and it is precisely in this *one* word that the popular prejudice resides which has overborne the always inadequate caution of the philosophers. Let us therefore be more cautious for once, let us be 'unphilosophical'—let us say: in all willing there is, first of all, a plurality of sensations, namely the sensation of the condition we *leave,* the sensation of the condition towards which we *go,* the sensation of this 'leaving' and 'going' itself, and then also an accompanying muscular sensation which, even without our putting 'arms and legs' in motion, comes into play through a kind of habit as soon as we 'will'. As feelings, and indeed many varieties of feeling, can therefore be recognized as an ingredient of will, so, in the second place, can thinking: in every act of will there is a commanding thought—and do not imagine that this thought can be separated from the 'willing', as though will would then remain over! Thirdly, will is not only a complex of feeling and thinking, but above all an *affect:* and in fact the affect of command. What is called 'freedom of will' is essentially the affect of superiority over him who must obey: 'I am free, "he" must obey'—this consciousness adheres to every will, as does that tense attention, that straight look which fixes itself exclusively on *one* thing, that unconditional evaluation 'this and nothing else is necessary now', that inner certainty that one will be obeyed, and whatever else pertains to the state of him who gives commands. A man who *wills*—commands something in himself which obeys or which he believes obeys. But now observe the strangest thing of all about the will—about this so complex thing for which people have only *one* word: inasmuch as in the given circumstances we at the same time command *and* obey, and as the side which obeys know the sensations of constraint, compulsion, pressure, resistance, motion which usually begin immediately after the act of will; inasmuch as, on the other hand, we are in the habit of disregarding and deceiving ourselves over this duality by means of the synthetic concept 'I'; so a whole chain of erroneous conclusions and consequently of false evaluations of the will itself has become attached to the will as such—so that he who wills believes wholeheartedly that willing *suffices* for action. Because in the great majority of cases willing takes place only where the effect of the command, that is to say obedience, that is to say the action, was to be *expected,* the *appearance* has translated itself into the sensation, as if there were here a *necessity of effect.* Enough: he who wills believes with a tolerable degree of certainty that will and action are somehow one—he attributes the success, the carrying out of the willing, to the will itself, and thereby enjoys an increase of that sensation of power which all success brings with it. 'Freedom of will'—is the expression for that complex condition of pleasure of the person who wills, who commands and at the same time identifies himself with the executor of the command—who as such also enjoys the triumph over resistances involved but who thinks it was his will itself which overcame these resistances. He who wills adds in this way the sensations of pleasure of the successful executive agents, the serviceable 'under-wills' or under-souls—for our body is only a social structure composed of many souls—to his sensations of pleasure as commander. *L'effet, c'est moi:*[2] what happens here is what happens in every well-constructed and happy commonwealth: the ruling class identifies itself with the successes of the commonwealth. In all willing it is absolutely a question of commanding and obeying, on the basis, as I have said already, of a social structure composed of many 'souls': on which account a philosopher should claim the right to include willing as such within the field of morality: that is, of morality understood as the theory of the relations of dominance under which the phenomenon 'life' arises.—

41

One must test oneself to see whether one is destined for independence and command; and one must do so at the proper time. One should not avoid one's tests, although they are perhaps the most dangerous game one could play and are in the end tests which are taken before ourselves and before no other judge. Not to cleave to another person, though he be the one you love most—every person is a prison, also a nook and corner. Not to cleave to a fatherland, though it be the most suffering and in need of help—it is already easier to sever your heart from a victorious fatherland. Not to cleave to a feeling of pity, though it be for higher men into whose rare torment and helplessness chance allowed us to look. Not to cleave to a science, though it lures one with the most precious discoveries seemingly reserved precisely for *us.* Not to cleave to one's own detachment, to that voluptuous remoteness and strangeness of the bird which flies higher and higher so as to see more and more beneath it—the danger which threatens the flier. Not to cleave to our own virtues and become as a whole the victim of some part of us, of our 'hospitality' for example, which is the danger of dangers for rich and noble souls who expend themselves prodigally, almost indifferently, and take the virtue of liberality to the point where it becomes a vice. One must know how *to conserve oneself:* the sternest test of independence.

★

54

What, at bottom, is the whole of modern philosophy doing? Since Descartes—and indeed rather in spite of him than on the basis of his precedent—all philosophers have been making an *attentat*[3] on the ancient soul concept under the cloak of a critique of the subject-and-predicate concept—that is to say, an *attentat* on the fundamental presupposition of Christian doctrine. Modern philosophy, as an epistemological scepticism, is, covertly or openly, *anti-Christian:* although, to speak to more refined ears, by no means anti-religious. For in the past one believed in 'the soul' as one believed in grammar and the grammatical subject: one said 'I' is the condition, 'think' is the predicate and conditioned—thinking is an activity to which a subject *must* be thought of as cause. Then one tried with admirable artfulness and tenacity to fathom whether one could not get out of this net—whether the reverse was not perhaps true: 'think' the condition, 'I' conditioned; 'I' thus being only a synthesis *produced* by thinking. *Kant* wanted fundamentally to prove that, starting from the subject, the subject could not be proved—nor could the object: the possibility of an *apparent existence* of the subject, that is to say of 'the soul', may not always have been remote from him, that idea which, as the philosophy of the Vedanta, has exerted immense influence on earth before.

★

207

However gratefully one may go to welcome an *objective* spirit—and who has not been sick to death of everything subjective and its accursed ipsissimosity!—in the end one has to learn to be cautious with one's gratitude too and put a stop to the exaggerated way in which the depersonalization of the spirit is today celebrated as redemption and transfiguration, as if it were the end in itself: as is usually the case within the pessimist school, which also has good reason to accord the highest honours to 'disinterested knowledge'. The objective man who no longer scolds or curses as the pessimist does, the *ideal* scholar in whom the scientific instinct, after thousandfold total and partial failure, for once comes to full bloom, is certainly one of the most precious instruments there are: but he belongs in the hand of one who is mightier. He is only an instrument, let us say a *mirror*—he is not an 'end in himself'. And the objective man is in fact a mirror: accustomed to submitting to whatever wants to be known, lacking any other pleasure than that provided by knowledge, by 'mirroring'—he waits until something comes along and then gently spreads himself out, so that not even the lightest footsteps and the fluttering of ghostly beings shall be lost on his surface and skin. Whatever still remains to him of his 'own person' seems to him accidental, often capricious, more often disturbing: so completely has he become a passage and reflection of forms and events not his own. He finds it an effort to think about 'himself', and not infrequently he thinks about himself mistakenly; he can easily confuse himself with another, he fails to understand his own needs and is in this respect alone unsubtle and negligent. Perhaps he is troubled by his health or by the pettiness and stuffiness of his wife and friends, or by a lack of companions and company—yes, he forces himself to reflect on his troubles: but in vain! Already his thoughts are roaming, off to a *more general* case, and tomorrow he will know as little how to help himself as he did yesterday. He no longer knows how to take himself seriously, nor does he have the time for it: he is cheerful, *not* because he has no troubles but because he has no fingers and facility for dealing with *his troubles.* His habitual going out to welcome everything and every experience, the sunny and ingenuous hospitality with which he accepts all he encounters, his inconsiderate benevolence, his perilous unconcernedness over Yes and No: alas, how often he has to suffer for these his virtues!—and as a human being in general he can all too easily become the *caput mortuum*[4] of these virtues. If love and hatred are demanded of him, I mean love and hatred as God, woman and animal understand them —: he will do what he can and give what he can. But one ought not to be surprised if it is not very much—if he proves spurious, brittle, questionable and soft. His love and his hatred are artificial and more of a *tour de force,* a piece of vanity and exaggeration. For he is genuine only when he can be objective: only in his cheerful totalism can he remain 'nature' and 'natural'. His mirroring soul, for ever polishing itself, no longer knows how to affirm or how to deny; he does not command, neither does he destroy. '*Je ne méprise presque rien*'[5]—he says with Leibniz: one should not overlook or underestimate the *presque!* Nor is he an exemplar; he neither leads nor follows; he sets himself altogether too far off to have any reason to take sides between good and evil. When he was for so long confused with the *philosopher,* with the Caesarian cultivator and *Gewaltmensch*[6] of culture, he was done much too great honour and what is essential in him was overlooked—he is an instrument, something of a slave, if certainly the sublimest kind of slave, but in himself he is nothing—*presque rien!* The objective man is an instrument, a precious, easily damaged and tarnished measuring instrument and reflecting apparatus which ought to be respected and taken good care of; but he is not an end, a termination and ascent, a complementary man in whom the *rest* of existence is justified, a conclusion—and even less a beginning, a begetting and first cause, something solid, powerful and based firmly on itself that wants to be master: but rather only a delicate, empty, elegant, flexible mould which has first to wait for some content so as 'to form' itself by it—as a rule a man without content, a 'selfless' man. Consequently nothing for women either, *in parenthesis.*—

The Will to Power

886 (SPRING–FALL 1887)

The order of rank of human values.—

a. One should not evaluate a man according to individual works. *Epidermal actions.* Nothing is rarer than a personal action. A class, a rank, a race, an environment, an accident—anything is more likely to be expressed in a work or act than is a "personality" [*eine "Person"*].

b. One should not assume in any case that many men are "personalities." And then some are *several* personalities, most are *none.* Wherever the average qualities preponderate, on which the preservation of a type depends, being a personality would be a waste, a luxury, it would be senseless to demand a "personality." They are bearers, tools of transmission.

c. The "personality," a relatively *isolated* fact; considering the far greater importance of continuation and averageness, almost something *anti-natural.* For the production of a personality one needs early isolation, a compulsion to an existence of defense and combat, something like an incarceration, a greater power of self-definition; and above all a much lower impressionability than that of the average man, whose humanity is contagious.

First question concerning order of rank: how solitary or how gregarious one is. (In the latter case, one's value resides in the qualities that secure the survival of one's herd, one's type; in the former, in that which distinguishes, isolates, defends one, and makes one's solitariness possible.)

Consequence: one should not evaluate the solitary type from the viewpoint of the gregarious, nor the gregarious from the viewpoint of the solitary.

Viewed from a height, both are necessary; their antagonism is also necessary—and nothing should be banished more thoroughly than the "desirability" that some third thing might evolve out of the two ("virtue" as hermaphroditism). That is as little "desirable" as the approximation and reconciliation of the sexes. To evolve further that which is typical, to make the gulf wider and wider—

Concept of degeneration in both cases: when the herd starts to acquire the qualities of the solitary, and the latter the qualities of the herd—in short, when they approximate each other. This concept of degeneration has nothing to do with moral evaluation.

NOTES

1. "a contradiction in terms" [Ed.]
2. "The effect, it is me." It is a parody of Louis XIV's saying, "L'etat, c'est moi": "The state, it is me." [Ed.]
3. "attempt." [Ed.]
4. "dead head." [Ed.]
5. "I despise nearly (presque) nothing." [Ed.]
6. "brutal person." [Ed.]

DISCUSSION QUESTIONS

1. Why does Nietzsche think historians of morality employ childish procedures?
2. Explain what Nietzsche means by saying that every drive is tyrannical. Do you agree?
3. How does Nietzsche understand "freedom of will"? What does he mean by saying that "our body is only a social structure composed of many souls"?
4. Why might Nietzsche think that every person is a prison, a nook and corner?
5. How does incarceration help to produce personality?

Chapter 20

SIMONE WEIL

Weil (1909–1943) was born in her parents' apartment on the Rue de Strasbourg in Paris. Raised in an agnostic Jewish family by a father who was a physician and a germ-phobic mother, Weil avoided most forms of physical contact throughout her life. By her early teens Weil had learned ancient Greek and several modern languages. Called "the Red virgin" because of her radical opinions and support of the Bolsheviks, Weil distinguished herself academically. She alternated teaching philosophy with periods working in fields and factories with manual laborers, whose company she preferred to her faculty colleagues. Weil shared her salary with the unemployed. In the 1930s, possibly due to malnutrition, she had mystical experiences. Starvation hastened her death. Her posthumous works have been published in sixteen volumes.

In this essay, Weil criticizes the philosophy of personalism, the (originally Roman) notion of natural rights, and the party politics of democracy. She argues that what is sacred in every human being is not his person or his personality, but rather his heart's unwavering expectation, from infancy to death, despite all experience of crimes committed, suffered, and witnessed, that good and not evil will be done to him. The supernatural good is the only source of the sacred, Weil insists, and she locates the sacred in the impersonal and anonymous divine realm where truth, beauty, justice, compassion, and perfection dwell. Our personality, in contrast, is the part of us which belongs to error and sin. Weil contends that a collectivity of people must dissolve into separate persons before, through solitude, silence, and warmth, the impersonal can be reached by the practice of a rare form of attention. She defends the ideas of justice and love expressed by Antigone and Jesus Christ.

I. Human Personality

1943*

'You do not interest me.' No man can say these words to another without committing a cruelty and offending against justice.

'Your person[1] does not interest me.' These words can be used in an affectionate conversation between close friends, without jarring upon even the tenderest nerve of their friendship.

In the same way, one can say without degrading oneself, 'My person does not count', but not 'I do not count'.

This proves that something is amiss with the vocabulary of the modern trend of thought known as Personalism. And in this domain, where there is a grave error of vocabulary it is almost certainly the sign of a grave error of thought.

There is something sacred in every man, but it is not his person. Nor yet is it the human personality. It is this man; no more and no less.

I see a passer-by in the street. He has long arms, blue eyes, and a mind whose thoughts I do not know, but perhaps they are commonplace.

It is neither his person, nor the human personality in him, which is sacred to me. It is he. The whole of him. The arms, the eyes, the thoughts, everything. Not without infinite scruple would I touch anything of this.

If it were the human personality in him that was sacred to me, I could easily put out his eyes. As a blind man he would be exactly as much a human personality as before. I should not have touched the person in him at all. I should have destroyed nothing but his eyes.

It is impossible to define what is meant by respect for human personality. It is not just that it cannot be defined in words. That can be said of many perfectly clear ideas. But this one cannot be conceived either; it cannot be defined nor isolated by the silent operation of the mind.

To set up as a standard of public morality a notion which can neither be defined nor conceived is to open the door to every kind of tyranny.

The notion of rights, which was launched into the world in 1789, has proved unable, because of its intrinsic inadequacy, to fulfil the role assigned to it.

To combine two inadequate notions, by talking about the rights of human personality, will not bring us any further.

What is it, exactly, that prevents me from putting that man's eyes out if I am allowed to do so and if it takes my fancy?

Although it is the whole of him that is sacred to me, he is not sacred in all respects and from

*This essay appeared in *La Table Ronde* (December 1950) with the title 'La Personnalité humaine, le juste et l'injuste', and in *Écrits de Londres* with the title 'La Personne et le sacré'.

Source: Simone Weil, "Human Personality," Richard Rees tr., Selected Essays 1934–1943. London: Oxford University Press (1962): 9–34. Reproduced by permission of PFD on behalf of the Estate of Richard Rees.

every point of view. He is not sacred in as much as he happens to have long arms, blue eyes, or possibly commonplace thoughts. Nor as a duke, if he is one; nor as a dustman, if that is what he is. Nothing of all this would stay my hand.

What would stay it is the knowledge that if someone were to put out his eyes, his soul would be lacerated by the thought that harm was being done to him.

At the bottom of the heart of every human being, from earliest infancy until the tomb, there is something that goes on indomitably expecting, in the teeth of all experience of crimes committed, suffered, and witnessed, that good and not evil will be done to him. It is this above all that is sacred in every human being.

The good is the only source of the sacred. There is nothing sacred except the good and what pertains to it.

This profound and childlike and unchanging expectation of good in the heart is not what is involved when we agitate for our rights. The motive which prompts a little boy to watch jealously to see if his brother has a slightly larger piece of cake arises from a much more superficial level of the soul. The word justice means two very different things according to whether it refers to the one or the other level. It is only the former one that matters.

Every time that there arises from the depths of a human heart the childish cry which Christ himself could not restrain, 'Why am I being hurt?', then there is certainly injustice. For if, as often happens, it is only the result of a misunderstanding, then the injustice consists in the inadequacy of the explanation.

Those people who inflict the blows which provoke this cry are prompted by different motives according to temperament or occasion. There are some people who get a positive pleasure from the cry; and many others simply do not hear it. For it is a silent cry, which sounds only in the secret heart.

These two states of mind are closer than they appear to be. The second is only a weaker mode of the first; its deafness is complacently cultivated because it is agreeable and it offers a positive satisfaction of its own. There are no other restraints upon our will than material necessity and the existence of other human beings around us. Any imaginary extension of these limits is seductive, so there is a seduction in whatever helps us to forget the reality of the obstacles. That is why upheavals like war and civil war are so intoxicating; they empty human lives of their reality and seem to turn people into puppets. That is also why slavery is so pleasant to the masters.

In those who have suffered too many blows, in slaves for example, that place in the heart from which the infliction of evil evokes a cry of surprise may seem to be dead. But it is never quite dead; it is simply unable to cry out any more. It has sunk into a state of dumb and ceaseless lamentation.

And even in those who still have the power to cry out, the cry hardly ever expresses itself, either inwardly or outwardly, in coherent language. Usually, the words through which it seeks expression are quite irrelevant.

That is all the more inevitable because those who most often have occasion to feel that evil is being done to them are those who are least trained in the art of speech. Nothing, for example, is more frightful than to see some poor wretch in the police court stammering before a magistrate who keeps up an elegant flow of witticisms.

Apart from the intelligence, the only human faculty which has an interest in public freedom of expression is that point in the heart which cries out against evil. But as it cannot express itself, freedom is of little use to it. What is first needed is a system of public education capable of providing it, so far as possible, with means of expression; and next, a régime in which the public freedom of expression is characterized not so much by freedom as by an attentive silence in which this faint and inept cry can make itself heard; and finally, institutions are needed of a sort which will, so far as possible, put power into the hands of men who are able and anxious to hear and understand it.

Clearly, a political party busily seeking, or maintaining itself in, power can discern nothing in these cries except a noise. Its reaction will be different according to whether the noise interferes with or contributes to that of its own propaganda. But it can never be capable of the tender and sensitive attention which is needed to understand its meaning.

The same is true to a lesser degree of organizations contaminated by party influences; in other words, when public life is dominated by a party system, it is true of all organizations, including, for example, trade unions and even churches.

Naturally, too, parties and similar organizations are equally insensitive to intellectual scruples.

So when freedom of expression means in fact no more than freedom of propaganda for organizations of this kind, there is in fact no free expression for the only parts of the human soul that deserve it. Or if there is any, it is infinitesimal; hardly more than in a totalitarian system.

And this is how it is in a democracy where the party system controls the distribution of power; which is what we call democracy in France, for up to now we have known no other. We must therefore invent something different.

Applying the same criterion in the same way to any public institution we can reach equally obvious conclusions.

It is not the person which provides this criterion. When the infliction of evil provokes a cry of sorrowful surprise from the depth of the soul, it is not a personal thing. Injury to the personality and its desires is not sufficient to evoke it, but only and always the sense of contact with injustice through pain. It is always, in the last of men as in Christ himself, an impersonal protest.

There are also many cries of personal protest, but they are unimportant; you may provoke as many of them as you wish without violating anything sacred.

* * *

So far from its being his person, what is sacred in a human being is the impersonal in him.

Everything which is impersonal in man is sacred, and nothing else.

In our days, when writers and scientists have so oddly usurped the place of priests, the public acknowledges, with a totally unjustified docility, that the artistic and scientific faculties are sacred. This is generally held to be self-evident, though it is very far from being so. If any reason is felt to be called for, people allege that the free play of these faculties is one of the highest manifestations of the human personality.

Often it is, indeed, no more than that. In which case it is easy to see how much it is worth and what can be expected from it.

One of its results is the sort of attitude which is summed up in Blake's horrible saying: 'Sooner murder an infant in its cradle than nurse unacted desires',[2] or the attitude which breeds the idea of the 'gratuitous act.' Another result is a science in which every possible standard, criterion, and value is recognized except truth.

Gregorian chant, Romanesque architecture, the *Iliad,* the invention of geometry were not, for the people through whom they were brought into being and made available to us, occasions for the manifestation of personality.

When science, art, literature, and philosophy are simply the manifestation of personality they are on a level where glorious and dazzling achievements are possible, which can make a man's name live for thousands of years. But above this level, far above, separated by an abyss, is the level where the highest things are achieved. These things are essentially anonymous.

It is pure chance whether the names of those who reach this level are preserved or lost; even when they are remembered they have become anonymous. Their personality has vanished.

Truth and beauty dwell on this level of the impersonal and the anonymous. This is the realm of the sacred; on the other level nothing is sacred, except in the sense that we might say this of a touch of colour in a picture if it represented the Eucharist.

What is sacred in science is truth; what is sacred in art is beauty. Truth and beauty are impersonal. All this is too obvious.

If a child is doing a sum and does it wrong, the mistake bears the stamp of his personality. If he does the sum exactly right, his personality does not enter into it at all.

Perfection is impersonal. Our personality is the part of us which belongs to error and sin. The whole effort of the mystic has always been to become such that there is no part left in his soul to say 'I'.

But the part of the soul which says 'We' is infinitely more dangerous still.

* * *

Impersonality is only reached by the practice of a form of attention which is rare in itself and impossible except in solitude; and not only physical but mental solitude. This is never achieved by a man who thinks of himself as a member of a collectivity, as part of something which says 'We'.

Men as parts of a collectivity are debarred from even the lower forms of the impersonal. A group of human beings cannot even add two and two. Working out a sum takes place in a mind temporarily oblivious of the existence of any other minds.

Although the personal and the impersonal are opposed, there is a way from the one to the other. But there is no way from the collective to the impersonal. A collectivity must dissolve into separate persons before the impersonal can be reached.

This is the only sense in which the person has more of the sacred than the collectivity.

The collectivity is not only alien to the sacred, but it deludes us with a false imitation of it.

Idolatry is the name of the error which attributes a sacred character to the collectivity; and it is the commonest of crimes, at all times, at all places. The man for whom the development of personality is all that counts has totally lost all sense of the sacred; and it is hard to know which of these errors is the worst. They are often found combined, in various proportions, in the same mind. But the second error is much less powerful and enduring than the first.

Spiritually, the struggle between Germany and France in 1940 was in the main not a struggle between barbarism and civilization or between evil and good, but between the first of these two errors and the second. The victory of the former is not surprising; it is by nature the stronger.

There is nothing scandalous in the subordination of the person to the collectivity; it is a mechanical fact of the same order as the inferiority of a gram to a kilogram on the scales. The person is in fact always subordinate to the collectivity, even in its so-called free expression.

For example, it is precisely those artists and writers who are most inclined to think of their art as the manifestation of their personality who are in fact the most in bondage to public taste. Hugo had no difficulty in reconciling the cult of the self with his role of 'resounding echo'; and examples like Wilde, Gide, and the Surrealists are even more obvious. Scientists of the same class are equally enslaved by fashion, which rules over science even more despotically than over the shape of hats. For these men the collective opinion of specialists is practically a dictatorship.

The person, being subordinate to the collective both in fact and by the nature of things, enjoys no natural rights which can be appealed to on its behalf.

It is said, quite correctly, that in antiquity there existed no notion of respect for the person. The ancients thought far too clearly to entertain such a confused idea.

The human being can only escape from the collective by raising himself above the personal and entering into the impersonal. The moment he does this, there is something in him, a small portion of his soul, upon which nothing of the collective can get a hold. If he can root himself in the impersonal good so as to be able to draw energy from it, then he is in a condition, whenever he feels the obligation to do so, to bring to bear without any outside help, against any collectivity, a small but real force.

There are occasions when an almost infinitesimal force can be decisive. A collectivity is much stronger than a single man; but every collectivity depends for its existence upon operations, of which simple addition is the elementary example, which can only be performed by a mind in a state of solitude.

This dependence suggests a method of giving the impersonal a hold on the collective, if only we could find out how to use it.

Every man who has once touched the level of the impersonal is charged with a responsibility towards all human beings: to safeguard, not their persons, but whatever frail potentialities are hidden within them for passing over to the impersonal.

It is primarily to these men that the appeal to respect the sacredness of the human being should be addressed. For such an appeal can have no reality unless it is addressed to someone capable of understanding it.

It is useless to explain to a collectivity that there is something in each of the units composing it which it ought not to violate. To begin with, a collectivity is not someone, except by a fiction; it has only an abstract existence and can only be spoken to fictitiously. And, moreover, if it were someone it would be someone who was not disposed to respect anything except himself.

Further, the chief danger does not lie in the collectivity's tendency to circumscribe the person, but in the person's tendency to immolate himself in the collective. Or perhaps the first danger is only a superficial and deceptive aspect of the second.

Just as it is useless to tell the collectivity that the person is sacred, it is also useless to tell the person so. The person cannot believe it. It does not feel sacred. The reason that prevents the person from feeling sacred is that actually it is not.

If there are some people who feel differently, who feel something sacred in their own persons and believe they can generalize and attribute it to every person, they are under a double illusion.

What they feel is not the authentic sense of the sacred but its false imitation engendered by the collective; and if they feel it in respect of their own person it is because it participates in collective prestige through the social consideration bestowed upon it.

So they are mistaken in thinking they can generalize from their own case. Their motive is generous, but it cannot have enough force to make them really see the mass of people as anything but mere anonymous human matter. But it is hard for them to find this out, because they have no contact with the mass of people.

The person in man is a thing in distress; it feels cold and is always looking for a warm shelter.

But those in whom it is, in fact or in expectation, warmly wrapped in social consideration are unaware of this.

That is why it was not in popular circles that the philosophy of personalism originated and developed, but among writers, for whom it is part of their profession to have or hope to acquire a name and a reputation.

Relations between the collectivity and the person should be arranged with the sole purpose of removing whatever is detrimental to the growth and mysterious germination of the impersonal element in the soul.

This means, on the one hand, that for every person there should be enough room, enough freedom to plan the use of one's time, the opportunity to reach ever higher levels of attention, some solitude, some silence. At the same time the person needs warmth, lest it be driven by distress to submerge itself in the collective.

* * *

If this is the good, then modern societies, even democratic ones, seem to go about as far as it is possible to go in the direction of evil. In particular, a modern factory reaches perhaps almost the limit of horror. Everybody in it is constantly harassed and kept on edge by the interference of extraneous wills while the soul is left in cold and desolate misery. What man needs is silence and warmth; what he is given is an icy pandemonium.

Physical labour may be painful, but it is not degrading as such. It is not art; it is not science; it is something else, possessing an exactly equal value with art and science, for it provides an equal opportunity to reach the impersonal stage of attention.

To take a youth who has a vocation for this kind of work and employ him at a conveyor-belt or as a piece-work machinist is no less a crime than to put out the eyes of the young Watteau and make him turn a grindstone. But the painter's vocation can be discerned and the other cannot.

Exactly to the same extent as art and science, though in a different way, physical labour is a certain contact with the reality, the truth, and the beauty of this universe and with the eternal wisdom which is the order in it.

For this reason it is sacrilege to degrade labour in exactly the same sense that it is sacrilege to trample upon the Eucharist.

If the workers felt this, if they felt that by being the victim they are in a certain sense the accomplice of sacrilege, their resistance would have a very different force from what is provided by the consideration of personal rights. It would not be an economic demand but an impulse from the depth of their being, fierce and desperate like that of a young girl who is being forced into a brothel; and at the same time it would be a cry of hope from the depth of their heart.

This feeling, which surely enough exists in them, is so inarticulate as to be indiscernible even to themselves; and it is not the professionals of speech who can express it for them.

Usually, when addressing them on their conditions, the selected topic is wages; and for men burdened with a fatigue that makes any effort of attention painful it is a relief to contemplate the unproblematic clarity of figures.

In this way, they forget that the subject of the bargain, which they complain they are being forced to sell cheap and for less than the just price, is nothing other than their soul.

Suppose the devil were bargaining for the soul of some poor wretch and someone, moved by pity, should step in and say to the devil: 'It is a shame for you to bid so low; the commodity is worth at least twice as much.'

Such is the sinister farce which has been played by the working-class movement, its trade unions, its political parties, its leftist intellectuals.

This bargaining spirit was already implicit in the notion of rights which the men of 1789 so unwisely made the keynote of their deliberate challenge to the world. By so doing, they ensured its inefficacy in advance.

* * *

The notion of rights is linked with the notion of sharing out, of exchange, of measured quantity. It has a commercial flavour, essentially evocative of legal claims and arguments. Rights are always asserted in a tone of contention; and when this tone is adopted, it must rely upon force in the background, or else it will be laughed at.

There are a number of other notions, all in the same category, which are themselves entirely alien to the supernatural but nevertheless a little superior to brute force. All of them relate to the behaviour of the collective animal, to use Plato's language, while it still exhibits a few traces of the training imposed on it by the supernatural working of grace. If they are not continually revived by a renewal of this working, if they are merely survivals of it, they become necessarily subject to the animal's caprice.

To this category belong the notion of rights, and of personality, and of democracy. As Bernanos had the courage to point out, democracy offers no defence against dictatorship. By the nature of things, the person is subdued to the collectivity, and rights are dependent upon force. The lies and misconceptions which obscure this truth are extremely dangerous because they prevent us from appealing to the only thing which is immune to force and can preserve us from it: namely, that other force which is the radiance of the spirit. It is only in plants, by virtue of the sun's energy caught up by the green leaves and operating in the sap, that inert matter can find its way upward against the law of gravity. A plant deprived of light is gradually but inexorably overcome by gravity and death.

Among the lies in question is the eighteenth-century materialists' notion of natural right. We do not owe this to Rousseau, whose lucid and powerful spirit was of genuinely Christian inspiration, but to Diderot and the Encyclopedists.

It was from Rome that we inherited the notion of rights, and like everything that comes from ancient Rome, who is the woman full of the names of blasphemy in the Apocalypse, it is pagan and unbaptizable. The Romans, like Hitler, understood that power is not fully efficacious unless clothed in a few ideas, and to this end they made use of the idea of rights, which is admirably suited to it. Modern Germany has been accused of flouting the idea; but she invoked it *ad nauseam* in her role of deprived, proletarian nation. It is true, of course, that she allows only one right to her victims: obedience. Ancient Rome did the same.

It is singularly monstrous that ancient Rome should be praised for having bequeathed to us the notion of rights. If we examine Roman law in its cradle, to see what species it belongs to, we discover that property was defined by the *jus utendi et abutendi*.[3] And in fact the things which the property owner had the right to use or abuse at will were for the most part human beings.

The Greeks had no conception of rights. They had no words to express it. They were content with the name of justice.

It is extraordinary that Antigone's unwritten law should have been confused with the idea of natural right. In Creon's eyes there was absolutely nothing that was natural in Antigone's behaviour. He thought she was mad.

And we should be the last people to disagree with him; we who at this moment are thinking, talking, and behaving exactly as he did. One has only to consult the text.

Antigone says to Creon: 'It was not Zeus who published that edict; it was not Justice, companion of the gods in the other world, who set such laws among men.'[4] Creon tries to convince her that his orders were just; he accuses her of having outraged one of her brothers by honouring the other, so that the same honour has been paid to the impious and the loyal, to the one who died in the attempt to destroy his own country and the one who died defending it.

She answers: 'Nevertheless the other world demands equal laws.' To which he sensibly objects: 'There can be no equal sharing between a brave man and a traitor', and she has only the absurd reply: 'Who knows whether this holds in the other world?'

Creon's comment is perfectly reasonable: 'A foe is never a friend, not even in death.' And the little simpleton can only reply: 'I was born to share, not hate, but love.'

To which Creon, ever more reasonable: 'Pass, then, to the other world, and if thou must love, love those who dwell there.'

And, truly, this was the right place for her. For the unwritten law which this little girl obeyed had nothing whatsoever in common with rights, or with the natural; it was the same love, extreme and absurd, which led Christ to the Cross.

It was Justice, companion of the gods in the other world, who dictated this surfeit of love, and not any right at all. Rights have no direct connexion with love.

Just as the notion of rights is alien to the Greek mind, so also it is alien to the Christian inspiration whenever it is pure and uncontaminated by the Roman, Hebraic, or Aristotelian heritage. One cannot imagine St. Francis of Assisi talking about rights.

If you say to someone who has ears to hear: 'What you are doing to me is not just', you may touch and awaken at its source the spirit of attention and love. But it is not the same with words like 'I have the right . . .' or 'you have no right to . . .' They evoke a latent war and awaken the spirit of contention. To place the notion of rights at the centre of social conflicts is to inhibit any possible impulse of charity on both sides.

Relying almost exclusively on this notion, it becomes impossible to keep one's eyes on the real problem. If someone tries to browbeat a farmer to sell his eggs at a moderate price, the farmer can say: 'I have the right to keep my eggs if I don't get a good enough price.' But if a young girl is being forced into a brothel she will not talk about her rights. In such a situation the word would sound ludicrously inadequate.

Thus it is that the social drama, which corresponds to the latter situation, is falsely assimilated, by the use of the word 'rights', to the former one.

Thanks to this word, what should have been a cry of protest from the depth of the heart has been turned into a shrill nagging of claims and counter-claims, which is both impure and unpractical.

* * *

The notion of rights, by its very mediocrity, leads on naturally to that of the person, for rights are related to personal things. They are on that level.

It is much worse still if the word 'personal' is added to the word 'rights', thus implying the rights of the personality to what is called full expression. In that case the tone that colours the cry of the oppressed would be even meaner than bargaining. It would be the tone of envy.

For the full expression of personality depends upon its being inflated by social prestige; it is a social privilege. No one mentions this to the masses when haranguing them about personal rights. They are told the opposite; and their minds have not enough analytic power to perceive this truth clearly for themselves. But they feel it; their everyday experience makes them certain of it.

However, this is not a reason for them to reject the slogan. To the dimmed understanding of our age there seems nothing odd in claiming an equal share of privilege for everybody—an equal share in things whose essence is privilege. The claim is both absurd and base; absurd because privilege is, by definition, inequality; and base because it is not worth claiming.

But the category of men who formulate claims, and everything else, the men who have the monopoly of language, is a category of privileged people. They are not the ones to say that privilege is unworthy to be desired. They don't think so and, in any case, it would be indecent for them to say it.

Many indispensable truths, which could save men, go unspoken for reasons of this kind; those who could utter them cannot formulate them and those who could formulate them cannot utter them. If politics were taken seriously, finding a remedy for this would be one of its more urgent problems.

In an unstable society the privileged have a bad conscience. Some of them hide it behind a defiant air and say to the masses: 'It is quite appropriate that I should possess privileges which you are denied.' Others benevolently profess: 'I claim for all of you an equal share in the privileges I enjoy.'

The first attitude is odious. The second is silly, and also too easy.

Both of them equally encourage the people down the road of evil, away from their true and unique good, which they do not possess, but to which, in a sense, they are so close. They are far closer than those who bestow pity on them to an authentic good, which could be a source of beauty and truth and joy and fulfilment. But since they have not reached it and do not know how to, this good might as well be infinitely far away. Those who speak for the people and to them are incapable of understanding either their distress or what an overflowing good is almost within their reach. And, for the people, it is indispensable to be understood.

Affliction is by its nature inarticulate. The afflicted silently beseech to be given the words to express themselves. There are times when they are given none; but there are also times when they are given words, but ill-chosen ones, because those who choose them know nothing of the affliction they would interpret.

Usually, they are far removed from it by the circumstances of their life; but even if they are in close contact with it or have recently experienced it themselves, they are still remote from it because they put it at a distance at the first possible moment.

Thought revolts from contemplating affliction, to the same degree that living flesh recoils from death. A stag advancing voluntarily step by step to offer itself to the teeth of a pack of hounds is about as probable as an act of attention directed towards a real affliction, which is close at hand, on the part of a mind which is free to avoid it.

But that which is indispensable to the good and is impossible naturally is always possible supernaturally.

* * *

Supernatural good is not a sort of supplement to natural good, as we are told, with support from Aristotle, for our greater comfort. It would be nice if this were true, but it is not. In all the crucial problems of human existence the only choice is between supernatural good on the one hand and evil on the other.

To put into the mouth of the afflicted words from the vocabulary of middle values, such as democracy, rights, personality, is to offer them something which can bring them no good and will inevitably do them much harm.

These notions do not dwell in heaven; they hang in the middle air, and for this very reason they cannot root themselves in earth.

It is the light falling continually from heaven which alone gives a tree the energy to send powerful roots deep into the earth. The tree is really rooted in the sky.

It is only what comes from heaven that can make a real impress on the earth.

In order to provide an armour for the afflicted, one must put into their mouths only those words whose rightful abode is in heaven, beyond heaven, in the other world. There is no fear of its being impossible. Affliction disposes the soul to welcome and avidly drink in everything which comes from there. For these products it is not consumers but producers who are in short supply.

The test for suitable words is easily recognized and applied. The afflicted are overwhelmed with evil and starving for good. The only words suitable for them are those which express nothing but good, in its pure state. It is easy to discriminate. Words which can be associated with something signifying an evil are alien to pure good. We are criticizing a man when we say: 'He puts his person forward'; therefore the person is alien to good. We can speak of an abuse of democracy; therefore democracy is alien to good. To possess a right implies the possibility of making good or bad use of it; therefore rights are alien to good. On the other hand, it is always and everywhere good to fulfil an obligation. Truth, beauty, justice, compassion are always and everywhere good.

For the aspirations of the afflicted, if we wish to be sure of using the right words, all that is necessary is to confine ourselves to those words and phrases which always, everywhere, in all circumstances express only the good.

This is one of the only two services which can be rendered to the afflicted with words. The other is to find the words which express the truth of their affliction, the words which can give resonance, through the crust of external circumstances, to the cry which is always inaudible: 'Why am I being hurt?'

For this, they cannot count upon men of talent, personality, celebrity, or even genius in the sense in which the word is usually employed, which assimilates it to talent. They can count only upon men of the very highest genius: the poet of the *Iliad,* Aeschylus, Sophocles, Shakespeare as he was when he wrote *Lear,* or Racine when he wrote *Phèdre.* There are not very many of them.

But there are many human beings only poorly or moderately endowed by nature, who seem infinitely inferior not merely to Homer, Aeschylus, Sophocles, Shakespeare, and Racine but also to Virgil, Corneille, and Hugo, but who nevertheless inhabit the realm of impersonal good where the latter poets never set foot.

A village idiot in the literal sense of the word, if he really loves truth, is infinitely superior to Aristotle in his thought, even though he never utters anything but inarticulate murmurs. He is infinitely closer to Plato than Aristotle ever was. He has genius, while only the word talent applies to Aristotle. If a fairy offered to change his destiny for one resembling Aristotle's he would be wise to refuse unhesitatingly. But he does not know this. And nobody tells him. Everybody tells him the contrary. But he must be told. Idiots, men without talent, men whose talent is average or only a little more, must be encouraged if they possess genius. We need not be afraid of making them proud, because love of truth is always accompanied by humility. Real genius is nothing else but the supernatural virtue of humility in the domain of thought.

What is needed is to cherish the growth of genius, with a warm and tender respect, and not, as the men of 1789 proposed, to encourage the flowering of talents. For it is only heroes of real purity, the saints and geniuses, who can help the afflicted. But the help is obstructed by a screen which is formed between the two by the men of talent, intelligence, energy, character, or strong personality. The screen must not be damaged, but put aside as gently and imperceptibly as possible. The far more dangerous screen of the collective must be broken by abolishing every part of our institutions and customs which harbours the party spirit in any form whatsoever. Neither a personality nor a party is ever responsive either to truth or to affliction.

* * *

There is a natural alliance between truth and affliction, because both of them are mute suppliants, eternally condemned to stand speechless in our presence.

Just as a vagrant accused of stealing a carrot from a field stands before a comfortably seated judge who keeps up an elegant flow of queries, comments, and witticisms while the accused is unable to stammer a word, so truth stands before an intelligence which is concerned with the elegant manipulation of opinions.

It is always language that formulates opinions, even when there are no words spoken. The natural faculty called intelligence is concerned with opinion and language. Language expresses relations; but it expresses only a few, because its operation needs time. When it is confused and vague, without precision or order, when the speaker or listener is deficient in the power of holding a thought in his mind, then language is empty or almost empty of any real relational content. When it is perfectly clear, precise, rigorous, ordered, when it is addressed to a mind which is capable of keeping a thought present while it adds another to it and of keeping them both present while it adds a third, and so on, then in such a case language can hold a fairly rich content of relations. But like all wealth, this relative wealth is abject poverty compared with the perfection which alone is desirable.

At the very best, a mind enclosed in language is in prison. It is limited to the number of relations which words can make simultaneously present to it; and remains in ignorance of thoughts which involve the combination of a greater number. These thoughts are outside language, they are unformulable, although they are perfectly rigorous and clear and although every one of the relations they involve is capable of precise expression in words. So the mind moves in a closed space of partial truth, which may be larger or smaller, without ever being able so much as to glance at what is outside.

If a captive mind is unaware of being in prison, it is living in error. If it has recognized the fact, even for the tenth of a second, and then quickly forgotten it in order to avoid suffering, it is living in falsehood. Men of the most brilliant intelligence can be born, live, and die in error and falsehood. In them, intelligence is neither a good, nor even an asset. The difference between more or less intelligent men is like the difference between criminals condemned to life imprisonment in smaller or larger cells. The intelligent man who is proud of his intelligence is like a condemned man who is proud of his large cell.

A man whose mind feels that it is captive would prefer to blind himself to the fact. But if he hates falsehood, he will not do so; and in that case he will have to suffer a lot. He will beat his head against the wall until he faints. He will come to again and look with terror at the wall, until one day he begins afresh to beat his head against it; and once again he will faint. And so on endlessly and without hope. One day he will wake up on the other side of the wall.

Perhaps he is still in a prison, although a larger one. No matter. He has found the key; he knows the secret which breaks down every wall. He has passed beyond what men call intelligence, into the beginning of wisdom.

The mind which is enclosed within language can possess only opinions. The mind which has learned to grasp thoughts which are inexpressible because of the number of relations they combine, although they are more rigorous and clearer than anything that can be expressed in the most precise language, such a mind has reached the point where it already dwells in truth. It possesses certainty and unclouded faith. And it matters little whether its original intelligence was great or small, whether its prison cell was narrow or wide. All that matters is that it has come to the end of its intelligence, such as it was, and has passed beyond it. A village idiot is as close to truth as a child prodigy. The one and the other are separated from it only by a wall. But the only way into truth is through one's own annihilation; through dwelling a long time in a state of extreme and total humiliation.

It is the same barrier which keeps us from understanding affliction. Just as truth is a different thing from opinion, so affliction is a different thing from suffering. Affliction is a device for pulverizing the soul; the man who falls into it is like a workman who gets caught up in a machine. He is no longer a man but a torn and bloody rag on the teeth of a cog-wheel.

The degree and type of suffering which constitutes affliction in the strict sense of the word varies greatly with different people. It depends chiefly upon the amount of vitality they start with and upon their attitude towards suffering.

Human thought is unable to acknowledge the reality of affliction. To acknowledge the reality of affliction means saying to oneself: 'I may lose at any moment, through the play of circumstances over which I have no control, anything whatsoever that I possess, including those things which are so intimately mine that I consider them as being myself. There is nothing that I might not lose. It could happen at any moment that what I am might be abolished and replaced by anything whatsoever of the filthiest and most contemptible sort.'

To be aware of this in the depth of one's soul is to experience non-being. It is the state of extreme and total humiliation which is also the condition for passing over into truth. It is a death of the soul. This is why the naked spectacle of affliction makes the soul shudder as the flesh shudders at the proximity of death.

We think piously of the dead when we evoke them in memory, or when we walk among graves, or when we see them decently laid out on a bed. But the sight of corpses lying about as on a battlefield can sometimes be both sinister and grotesque. It arouses horror. At the stark sight of death, the flesh recoils.

When affliction is seen vaguely from a distance, either physical or mental, so that it can be confused with simple suffering, it inspires in generous souls a tender feeling of pity. But if by chance it is suddenly revealed to them in all its nakedness as a corrosive force, a mutilation or leprosy of the soul, then people shiver and recoil. The afflicted themselves feel the same shock of horror at their own condition.

To listen to someone is to put oneself in his place while he is speaking. To put oneself in the place of someone whose soul is corroded by affliction, or in near danger of it, is to annihilate oneself. It is more difficult than suicide would be for a happy child. Therefore the afflicted are not listened to. They are like someone whose tongue has been cut out and who occasionally forgets the fact. When they move their lips no ear perceives any sound. And they themselves soon sink into impotence in the use of language, because of the certainty of not being heard.

That is why there is no hope for the vagrant as he stands before the magistrate. Even if, through his stammerings, he should utter a cry to pierce the soul, neither the magistrate nor the public will hear it. His cry is mute. And the afflicted are nearly always equally deaf to one another; and each of them, constrained by the general indifference, strives by means of self-delusion or forgetfulness to become deaf to his own self.

Only by the supernatural working of grace can a soul pass through its own annihilation to the place where alone it can get the sort of attention which can attend to truth and to affliction. It is the same attention which listens to both of them. The name of this intense, pure, disinterested, gratuitous, generous attention is love.

Because affliction and truth need the same kind of attention before they can be heard, the spirit of justice and the spirit of truth are one. The spirit of justice and truth is nothing else but a certain kind of attention, which is pure love.

Thanks to an eternal and providential decree, everything produced by a man in every sphere, when he is ruled by the spirit of justice and truth, is endowed with the radiance of beauty.

Beauty is the supreme mystery of this world. It is a gleam which attracts the attention and yet does nothing to sustain it. Beauty always promises, but never gives anything; it stimulates hunger but has no nourishment for the part of the soul which looks in this world for sustenance. It feeds only the part of the soul that gazes. While exciting desire, it makes clear that there is nothing in it to be desired, because the one thing we want is that it should not change. If one does not seek means to evade the exquisite anguish it inflicts, then desire is gradually transformed into love; and one begins to acquire the faculty of pure and disinterested attention.

In proportion to the hideousness of affliction is the supreme beauty of its true representation. Even in recent times one can point to *Phèdre, L'École des femmes, Lear,* and the poems of Villon; but far better examples are the plays of Aeschylus and Sophocles, and far better still, the *Iliad,* the book of Job and certain folk poems; and far beyond these again are the accounts of the Passion in the Gospels. The radiance of beauty illumines affliction with the light of the spirit of justice and love, which is the only light by which human thought can confront affliction and report the truth of it.

And it sometimes happens that a fragment of inexpressible truth is reflected in words which, although they cannot hold the truth that inspired them, have nevertheless so perfect a formal correspondence with it that every mind seeking that truth finds support in them. Whenever this happens a gleam of beauty illumines the words.

Everything which originates from pure love is lit with the radiance of beauty.

Beauty can be perceived, though very dimly and mixed with many false substitutes, within the cell where all human thought is at first imprisoned. And upon her rest all the hopes of truth and justice, with tongue cut out. She, too, has no language; she does not speak; she says nothing. But she has a voice to cry out. She cries out and points to truth and justice who are dumb, like a dog who barks to bring people to his master lying unconscious in the snow.

Justice, truth, and beauty are sisters and comrades. With three such beautiful words we have no need to look for any others.

⋆ ⋆ ⋆

Justice consists in seeing that no harm is done to men. Whenever a man cries inwardly: 'Why am

I being hurt?' harm is being done to him. He is often mistaken when he tries to define the harm, and why and by whom it is being inflicted on him. But the cry itself is infallible.

The other cry, which we hear so often: 'Why has somebody else got more than I have?', refers to rights. We must learn to distinguish between the two cries and to do all that is possible, as gently as possible, to hush the second one, with the help of a code of justice, regular tribunals, and the police. Minds capable of solving problems of this kind can be formed in a law school.

But the cry 'Why am I being hurt?' raises quite different problems, for which the spirit of truth, justice, and love is indispensable.

In every soul the cry to be delivered from evil is incessant. The Lord's Prayer addresses it to God. But God has power to deliver from evil only the eternal part of the soul of those who have made real and direct contact with him. The rest of the soul, and the entire soul of whoever has not received the grace of real and direct contact with God, is at the mercy of men's caprice and the hazards of circumstance.

Therefore it is for men to see that men are preserved from harm.

When harm is done to a man, real evil enters into him; not merely pain and suffering, but the actual horror of evil. Just as men have the power of transmitting good to one another, so they have the power to transmit evil. One may transmit evil to a human being by flattering him or giving him comforts and pleasures; but most often men transmit evil to other men by doing them harm.

Nevertheless, eternal wisdom does not abandon the soul entirely to the mercy of chance and men's caprice. The harm inflicted on a man by a wound from outside sharpens his thirst for the good and thus there automatically arises the possibility of a cure. If the wound is deep, the thirst is for good in its purest form. The part of the soul which cries 'Why am I being hurt?' is on the deepest level and even in the most corrupt of men it remains from earliest infancy perfectly intact and totally innocent.

To maintain justice and preserve men from all harm means first of all to prevent harm being done to them. For those to whom harm has been done, it means to efface the material consequences by putting them in a place where the wound, if it is not too deep, may be cured naturally by a spell of well-being. But for those in whom the wound is a laceration of the soul it means further, and above all, to offer them good in its purest form to assuage their thirst.

Sometimes it may be necessary to inflict harm in order to stimulate this thirst before assuaging it, and that is what punishment is for. Men who are so estranged from the good that they seek to spread evil everywhere can only be re-integrated with the good by having harm inflicted upon them. This must be done until the completely innocent part of their soul awakens with the surprised cry 'Why am I being hurt?' The innocent part of the criminal's soul must then be fed to make it grow until it becomes able to judge and condemn his past crimes and at last, by the help of grace, to forgive them. With this the punishment is completed; the criminal has been reintegrated with the good and should be publicly and solemnly reintegrated with society.

That is what punishment is. Even capital punishment, although it excludes reintegration with society in the literal sense, should be the same thing. Punishment is solely a method of procuring pure good for men who do not desire it. The art of punishing is the art of awakening in a criminal, by pain or even death, the desire for pure good.

* * *

But we have lost all idea of what punishment is. We are not aware that its purpose is to procure good for a man. For us it stops short with the infliction of harm. That is why there is one, and only one, thing in modern society more hideous than crime—namely, repressive justice.

To make the idea of repressive justice the main motive of war or revolt is inconceivably dangerous. It is necessary to use fear as a deterrent against the criminal activity of cowards; but that repressive justice, as we ignorantly conceive it today, should be made the motive of heroes is appalling.

All talk of chastisement, punishment, retribution, or punitive justice nowadays always refers solely to the basest kind of revenge.

The treasure of suffering and violent death, which Christ chose for himself and which he so often offers to those he loves, means so little to us that we throw it to those whom we least esteem, knowing that they will make nothing of it and having no intention of helping them to discover its value.

For criminals, true punishment; for those whom affliction has bitten deep into the soul, such help as may bring them to quench their thirst at the supernatural springs; for everyone else, some well-being, a great deal of beauty, and protection from those who would harm him; in every sphere, a strict curb upon the chatter of lies, propaganda, and opinion, and the encouragement of a silence in which truth can germinate and grow; this is what is due to men.

To ensure that they get it, we can only count upon those who have passed beyond a certain barrier, and it may be objected that they are too few in number. Probably there are not many of them, but they are no object for statistics, because most of them are hidden. Pure good from heaven only reaches the earth in imperceptible quantities, whether in the individual soul or in society. The grain of mustard seed is 'the least of all seeds'. Persephone ate only one grain of the pomegranate. A pearl buried deep in a field is not visible; neither is the yeast in dough.

But just as the catalysts or bacteria, such as yeast, operate by their mere presence in chemical reactions, so in human affairs the invisible seed of pure good is decisive when it is put in the right place.

How is it to be put there?

Much could be done by those whose function it is to advise the public what to praise, what to admire, what to hope and strive and seek for. It would be a great advance if even a few of these makers of opinion were to resolve in their hearts to eschew absolutely and without exception everything that is not pure good, perfection, truth, justice, love.

It would be an even greater advance if the majority of those who possess today some fragments of spiritual authority were aware of their obligation never to hold up for human aspiration anything but the real good in its perfect purity.

* * *

By the power of words we always mean their power of illusion and error. But, thanks to a providential arrangement, there are certain words which possess, in themselves, when properly used, a virtue which illumines and lifts up towards the good. These are the words which refer to an absolute perfection which we cannot conceive. Since the proper use of these words involves not trying to make them fit any conception, it is in the words themselves, as words, that the power to enlighten and draw upward resides. What they express is beyond our conception.

God and *truth* are such words; also *justice, love,* and *good*.

It is dangerous to use words of this kind. They are like an ordeal. To use them legitimately one must avoid referring them to anything humanly conceivable and at the same time one must associate with them ideas and actions which are derived solely and directly from the light which they shed. Otherwise, everyone quickly recognizes them for lies.

They are uncomfortable companions. Words like *right, democracy* and *person* are more accommodating and are therefore naturally preferred by even the best intentioned of those who assume public functions. Public functions have no other meaning except the possibility of doing good to men, and those who assume them with good intentions do in fact want to procure good for their contemporaries; but they usually make the mistake of thinking they can begin by getting it at bargain prices.

Words of the middle region, such as *right, democracy, person,* are valid in their own region, which is that of ordinary institutions. But for the sustaining inspiration of which all institutions are, as it were, the projection, a different language is needed.

The subordination of the person to the collectivity is in the nature of things, like the inferiority of a gram to a kilogram on the scales. But there can be a scales on which the gram outweighs the kilogram. It is only necessary for one arm to be more than a thousand times as long as the other. The law of equilibrium easily overcomes an inequality of weight. But the lesser will never outweigh the greater unless the relation between them is regulated by the law of equilibrium.

In the same way, there is no guarantee for democracy, or for the protection of the person against the collectivity, without a disposition of public life relating it to the higher good which is impersonal and unrelated to any political form.

It is true that the word person is often applied to God. But in the passage where Christ offers God himself as an example to men of the perfection which they are told to achieve, he uses not only the image of a person but also, above all, that of an impersonal order: 'That ye may be like the children of your Father which is in heaven; for he maketh his sun to rise on the evil and on the good, and sendeth rain on the just and on the unjust.'

Justice, truth, and beauty are the image in our world of this impersonal and divine order of the universe. Nothing inferior to them is worthy to be the inspiration of men who accept the fact of death.

Above those institutions which are concerned with protecting rights and persons and democratic freedoms, others must be invented for the purpose of exposing and abolishing everything in contemporary life which buries the soul under injustice, lies, and ugliness.

They must be invented, for they are unknown, and it is impossible to doubt that they are indispensable.

NOTES

1. The implications of the French *personne* cannot be conveyed completely by a single word in English. What Simone Weil meant by 'person' in this context will become clearer as the essay proceeds, as also will the pejorative sense in which she uses the word 'personality'.
2. It seems possible that Simone Weil took Blake to mean: *If you desire to murder an infant you should do so,* instead of: *If you stifle your desires, you are doing something similar to murdering an infant.* But her point does not depend upon this illustration.
3. "right of use and abuse." [Ed.]
4. We have translated the author's own versions of the Greek.

DISCUSSION QUESTIONS

1. When does Weil think science, art, literature, and philosophy are simply the manifestation of personality?
2. What does Weil mean by "idolatry" and by "pure love"?
3. Explain the contrast Weil makes between the modern factory and physical labor.
4. How does Weil contrast geniuses with talents like Aristotle?
5. Why does Weil think that a soul can attend to affliction only by the supernatural working of grace?
6. Do you agree with Weil that punishment is solely a method of procuring good for people who do not desire it?

Chapter 21

JEAN-PAUL SARTRE

Sartre was born in Paris in 1905. Though intelligent, eloquent, and witty, he was also mentally undisciplined and disorganized. He studied philosophy and psychology at the prestigious École Normale Supérieure. When faced with conscription into the French military in 1928, he signed a petition against military training. That same year he scored last in his class of 50 on his agrégation (exit exam) at the Sorbonne, but his intimate association with Simone de Beauvoir helped him to finish first (she was second) the next year. During World War II Sartre was conscripted into military service. In 1940 he began writing his major work Being and Nothingness *while prisoner in a German stalag. In 1964 Sartre won the Nobel Prize for literature, but refused to accept the award on "political" grounds. He protested the war in Vietnam. Heavy smoking and drinking and the use of amphetamines when writing led to his death in 1980.*

This essay is an excerpt from a lecture Sartre gave in 1946. Sartre argues that the essence of an artifact like a paper-cutter exists in the mind of the maker of the paper-cutter before the object itself is made and exists. In contrast, Sartre believes that if God does not exist, then in the human being, existence precedes essence. This "subjectivity" means that there is no objective human nature, since a person is what he makes himself. Moreover, in inventing our image, we simultaneously uphold that image for all of humanity. Sartre reasons that determinism is false, persons are condemned to be free, and we are responsible for all our choices, passions, interpretations, and actions. Since we are nothing else than our plan, we are nothing other than the ensemble of our acts in this life.

Existentialism

What is meant by the term *existentialism?*

Most people who use the word would be rather embarrassed if they had to explain it, since, now that the word is all the rage, even the work of a musician or painter is being called existentialist. A gossip columnist in *Clartés* signs himself *The Existentialist,* so that by this time the word has been so stretched and has taken on so broad a meaning, that it no longer means anything at all. It seems that for want of an advance-guard doctrine analogous to surrealism, the kind of people who are eager for scandal and flurry turn to this philosophy which in other respects does not at all serve their purposes in this sphere.

Actually, it is the least scandalous, the most austere of doctrines. It is intended strictly for specialists and philosophers. Yet it can be defined easily. What complicates matters is that there are two kinds of existentialist; first, those who are Christian, among whom I would include Jaspers and Gabriel Marcel, both Catholic; and on the other hand the atheistic existentialists, among whom I class Heidegger, and then the French existentialists and myself. What they have in common is that they think that existence precedes essence, or, if you prefer, that subjectivity must be the starting point.

Just what does that mean? Let us consider some object that is manufactured, for example, a book or a paper-cutter: here is an object which has been made by an artisan whose inspiration came from a concept. He referred to the concept of what a paper-cutter is and likewise to a known method of production, which is part of the concept, something which is, by and large, a routine. Thus, the paper-cutter is at once an object produced in a certain way and, on the other hand, one having a specific use; and one can not postulate a man who produces a paper-cutter but does not know what it is used for. Therefore, let us say that, for the paper-cutter, essence—that is, the ensemble of both the production routines and the properties which enable it to be both produced and defined—precedes existence. Thus, the presence of the paper-cutter or book in front of me is determined. Therefore, we have here a technical view of the world whereby it can be said that production precedes existence.

When we conceive God as the Creator, He is generally thought of as a superior sort of artisan. Whatever doctrine we may be considering, whether one like that of Descartes or that of Leibnitz, we always grant that will more or less follows understanding or, at the very least, accompanies it, and that when God creates He knows exactly what He is creating. Thus, the concept of man in the mind of God is comparable to the concept of paper-cutter in the mind of the manufacturer, and, following certain techniques and a conception, God produces man, just as the artisan, following a

---

Source: Jean-Paul Sartre, "Existentialism," Bernard Frechtman tr., *Existentialism and Human Emotions.* Kensington Books (Philosophical Library, Carol Publishing Group). (1957): 12–35.

definition and a technique, makes a paper-cutter. Thus, the individual man is the realization of a certain concept in the divine intelligence.

In the eighteenth century, the atheism of the *philosophes* discarded the idea of God, but not so much for the notion that essence precedes existence. To a certain extent, this idea is found everywhere; we find it in Diderot, in Voltaire, and even in Kant. Man has a human nature; this human nature, which is the concept of the human, is found in all men, which means that each man is a particular example of a universal concept, man. In Kant, the result of this universality is that the wild-man, the natural man, as well as the bourgeois, are circumscribed by the same definition and have the same basic qualities. Thus, here too the essence of man precedes the historical existence that we find in nature.

Atheistic existentialism, which I represent, is more coherent. It states that if God does not exist, there is at least one being in whom existence precedes essence, a being who exists before he can be defined by any concept, and that this being is man, or, as Heidegger says, human reality. What is meant here by saying that existence precedes essence? It means that, first of all, man exists, turns up, appears on the scene, and, only afterwards, defines himself. If man, as the existentialist conceives him, is indefinable, it is because at first he is nothing. Only afterward will he be something, and he himself will have made what he will be. Thus, there is no human nature, since there is no God to conceive it. Not only is man what he conceives himself to be, but he is also only what he wills himself to be after this thrust toward existence.

Man is nothing else but what he makes of himself. Such is the first principle of existentialism. It is also what is called subjectivity, the name we are labeled with when charges are brought against us. But what do we mean by this, if not that man has a greater dignity than a stone or table? For we mean that man first exists, that is, that man first of all is the being who hurls himself toward a future and who is conscious of imagining himself as being in the future. Man is at the start a plan which is aware of itself, rather than a patch of moss, a piece of garbage, or a cauliflower; nothing exists prior to this plan; there is nothing in heaven; man will be what he will have planned to be. Not what he will want to be. Because by the word "will" we generally mean a conscious decision, which is subsequent to what we have already made of ourselves. I may want to belong to a political party, write a book, get married; but all that is only a manifestation of an earlier, more spontaneous choice that is called "will." But if existence really does precede essence, man is responsible for what he is. Thus, existentialism's first move is to make every man aware of what he is and to make the full responsibility of his existence rest on him. And when we say that a man is responsible for himself, we do not only mean that he is responsible for his own individuality, but that he is responsible for all men.

The word subjectivism has two meanings, and our opponents play on the two. Subjectivism means, on the one hand, that an individual chooses and makes himself; and, on the other, that it is impossible for man to transcend human subjectivity. The second of these is the essential meaning of existentialism. When we say that man chooses his own self, we mean that every one of us does likewise; but we also mean by that that in making this choice he also chooses all men. In fact, in creating the man that we want to be, there is not a single one of our acts which does not at the same time create an image of man as we think he ought to be. To choose to be this or that is to affirm at the same time the value of what we choose, because we can never choose evil. We always choose the good, and nothing can be good for us without being good for all.

If, on the other hand, existence precedes essence, and if we grant that we exist and fashion our image at one and the same time, the image is valid for everybody and for our whole age. Thus, our responsibility is much greater than we might have supposed, because it involves all mankind. If I am a workingman and choose to join a Christian trade-union rather than be a communist, and if by being a member I want to show that the best thing for man is resignation, that the kingdom of man is not of this world, I am not only involving my own case—I want to be resigned for everyone. As a result, my action has involved all humanity. To take a more individual matter, if I want to marry, to have children; even if this marriage depends solely on my own circumstances or passion or wish, I am involving all humanity in monogamy and not merely myself. Therefore, I am responsible for myself and for everyone else. I am creating a certain image of man of my own choosing. In choosing myself, I choose man.

This helps us understand what the actual content is of such rather grandiloquent words as anguish, forlornness, despair. As you will see, it's all quite simple.

First, what is meant by anguish? The existentialists say at once that man is anguish. What that means is this: the man who involves himself and who realizes that he is not only the person he chooses to be, but also a lawmaker who is, at the same time, choosing all mankind as well as himself, cannot help escape the feeling of his total and deep responsibility. Of course, there are many people who are not anxious; but we claim that they are hiding their anxiety, that they are fleeing from it. Certainly, many people believe that when they do something, they themselves are the only ones involved, and when someone says to them, "What if everyone acted that way?" they shrug their shoulders and answer, "Everyone doesn't act that way." But really, one should always ask himself, "What would happen if everybody looked at things that way?" There is no escaping this disturbing thought except by a kind of double-dealing. A man who lies and makes excuses for himself by saying "not everybody does that," is someone with an uneasy conscience, because the act of lying implies that a universal value is conferred upon the lie.

Anguish is evident even when it conceals itself. This is the anguish that Kierkegaard called the anguish of Abraham. You know the story: an angel has ordered Abraham to sacrifice his son; if it really were an angel who has come and said, "You are Abraham, you shall sacrifice your son," everything would be all right. But everyone might first wonder, "Is it really an angel, and am I really Abraham? What proof do I have?"

There was a madwoman who had hallucinations; someone used to speak to her on the telephone and give her orders. Her doctor asked her, "Who is it who talks to you?" She answered, "He says it's God." What proof did she really have that it was God? If an angel comes to me, what proof is there that it's an angel? And if I hear voices, what proof is there that they come from heaven and not from hell, or from the subconscious, or a pathological condition? What proves that they are addressed to me? What proof is there that I have been appointed to impose my choice and my conception of man on humanity? I'll never find any proof or sign to convince me of that. If a voice addresses me, it is always for me to decide that this is the angel's voice; if I consider that such an act is a good one, it is I who will choose to say that it is good rather than bad.

Now, I'm not being singled out as an Abraham, and yet at every moment I'm obliged to perform exemplary acts. For every man, everything happens as if all mankind had its eyes fixed on him and were guiding itself by what he does. And every man ought to say to himself, "Am I really the kind of man who has the right to act in such a way that humanity might guide itself by my actions?" And if he does not say that to himself, he is masking his anguish.

There is no question here of the kind of anguish which would lead to quietism, to inaction. It is a matter of a simple sort of anguish that anybody who has had responsibilities is familiar with. For example, when a military officer takes the responsibility for an attack and sends a certain number of men to death, he chooses to do so, and in the main he alone makes the choice. Doubtless, orders come from above, but they are too broad; he interprets them, and on this interpretation depend the lives of ten or fourteen or twenty men. In making a decision he cannot help having a certain anguish. All leaders know this anguish. That doesn't keep them from acting; on the contrary, it is the very condition of their action. For it implies that they envisage a number of possibilities, and when they choose one, they realize that it has value only because it is chosen. We shall see that this kind of anguish, which is the kind that existentialism describes, is explained, in addition, by a direct responsibility to the other men whom it involves. It is not a curtain separating us from action, but is part of action itself.

When we speak of forlornness, a term Heidegger was fond of, we mean only that God does not exist and that we have to face all the consequences of this. The existentialist is strongly opposed to a certain kind of secular ethics which would like to abolish God with the least possible expense. About 1880, some French teachers tried to set up a secular ethics which went something like this: God is a useless and costly hypothesis; we are discarding it; but, meanwhile, in order for there to be an ethics, a society, a civilization, it is essential that certain values be taken seriously and that they be considered as having an *a priori* existence. It must be obligatory, *a priori,* to be honest, not to lie, not to beat your wife, to have children, etc., etc. So we're going to try a little device which will make it possible to show that values exist all the same, inscribed in a heaven of ideas, though otherwise God does not exist. In other words—and this, I believe, is the tendency of everything called reformism in France—nothing will be changed if God does not exist. We shall find ourselves with the same norms of honesty, progress, and humanism, and we shall have made of God an outdated hypothesis which will peacefully die off by itself.

The existentialist, on the contrary, thinks it very distressing that God does not exist, because all possibility of finding values in a heaven of ideas disappears along with Him; there can no longer be an *a priori* Good, since there is no infinite and perfect consciousness to think it. Nowhere is it written that the Good exists, that we must be honest, that we must not lie; because the fact is we are on a plane where there are only men. Dostoievsky said, "If God didn't exist, everything would be possible." That is the very starting point of existentialism. Indeed, everything is permissible if God does not exist, and as a result man is forlorn, because neither within him nor without does he find anything to cling to. He can't start making excuses for himself.

If existence really does precede essence, there is no explaining things away by reference to a fixed and given human nature. In other words, there is no determinism, man is free, man is freedom. On the other hand, if God does not exist, we find no values or commands to turn to which legitimize our conduct. So, in the bright realm of values, we have no excuse behind us, nor justification before us. We are alone, with no excuses.

That is the idea I shall try to convey when I say that man is condemned to be free. Condemned, because he did not create himself, yet, in other respects is free; because, once thrown into the world, he is responsible for everything he does. The existentialist does not believe in the power of passion. He will never agree that a sweeping passion is a ravaging torrent which fatally leads a man to certain acts and is therefore an excuse. He thinks that man is responsible for his passion.

The existentialist does not think that man is going to help himself by finding in the world some omen by which to orient himself. Because he thinks that man will interpret the omen to suit himself. Therefore, he thinks that man, with no support and no aid, is condemned every moment to invent man. Ponge, in a very fine article, has said, "Man is the future of man." That's exactly it. But if it is taken to mean that this future is recorded in heaven, that God sees it, then it is false, because it would really no longer be a future. If it is taken to mean that, whatever a man may be, there is a future to be forged, a virgin future before him, then this remark is sound. But then we are forlorn.

To give you an example which will enable you to understand forlornness better, I shall cite the case of one of my students who came to see me under the following circumstances: his father was on bad terms with his mother, and, moreover, was inclined to be a collaborationist; his older brother had been killed in the German offensive of 1940, and the young man, with somewhat immature but generous feelings, wanted to avenge him. His mother lived alone with him, very much upset by the half-treason of her husband and the death of her older son; the boy was her only consolation.

The boy was faced with the choice of leaving for England and joining the Free French Forces—that is, leaving his mother behind—or remaining with his mother and helping her to carry on. He was fully aware that the woman lived only for him and that his going-off—and perhaps his death—would plunge her into despair. He was also aware that every act that he did for his mother's sake was a sure thing, in the sense that it was helping her to carry on, whereas every effort he made toward going off and fighting was an uncertain move which might run aground and prove completely useless; for example, on his way to England he might, while passing through Spain, be detained indefinitely in a Spanish camp; he might reach England or Algiers and be stuck in an office at a desk job. As a result, he was faced with two very different kinds of action: one, concrete, immediate, but concerning only one individual; the other concerned an incomparably vaster group, a national collectivity, but for that very reason was dubious, and might be interrupted en route. And, at the same time, he was wavering between two kinds of ethics. On the one hand, an ethics of sympathy, of personal devotion; on the other, a broader ethics, but one whose efficacy was more dubious. He had to choose between the two.

Who could help him choose? Christian doctrine? No. Christian doctrine says, "Be charitable, love your neighbor, take the more rugged path, etc., etc." But which is the more rugged path? Whom should he love as a brother? The fighting man or his mother? Which does the greater good, the vague act of fighting in a group, or the concrete one of helping a particular human being to go on living? Who can decide *a priori?* Nobody. No book of ethics can tell him. The Kantian ethic says, "Never treat any person as a means, but as an end." Very well, if I stay with my mother, I'll treat her as an end and not as a means; but by virtue of this very fact, I'm running the risk of treating the people around me who are fighting, as means; and, conversely, if I go to join those who are fighting, I'll be treating them as an end, and, by doing that, I run the risk of treating my mother as a means.

If values are vague, and if they are always too broad for the concrete and specific case that we are considering, the only thing left for us is to trust our instincts. That's what this young man tried to do; and when I saw him, he said, "In the end, feeling is what counts. I ought to choose whichever pushes me in one direction. If I feel that I love my mother enough to sacrifice everything else for her—my desire for vengeance, for action, for adventure—then I'll stay with her. If, on the contrary, I feel that my love for my mother isn't enough, I'll leave."

But how is the value of a feeling determined? What gives his feeling for his mother value? Precisely the fact that he remained with her. I may say that I like so-and-so well enough to sacrifice a certain amount of money for him, but I may say so only if I've done it. I may say "I love my mother well enough to remain with her" if I have remained with her. The only way to determine the value of this affection is, precisely, to perform an act which confirms and defines it. But, since I require this affection to justify my act, I find myself caught in a vicious circle.

On the other hand, Gide has well said that a mock feeling and a true feeling are almost indistinguishable; to decide that I love my mother and will remain with her, or to remain with her by putting on an act, amount somewhat to the same thing. In other words, the feeling is formed by the acts one performs; so, I cannot refer to it in order to act upon it. Which means that I can neither seek within myself the true condition which will impel me to act, nor apply to a system of ethics for concepts which will permit me to act. You will say, "At least, he did go to a teacher for advice." But if you seek advice from a priest, for example, you have chosen this priest; you already knew, more or less, just about what advice he was going to give you. In other words, choosing your adviser is involving yourself. The proof of this is that if you are a Christian, you will say, "Consult a priest." But some priests are collaborating, some are just marking time, some are resisting. Which to choose? If the young man chooses a priest who is resisting or collaborating, he has already decided on the kind of advice he's going to get. Therefore, in coming to see me he knew the answer I was going to give him, and I had only one answer to give: "You're free, choose, that is, invent." No general ethics can show you what is to be done; there are no omens in the world. The Catholics will reply, "But there are." Granted—but, in any case, I myself choose the meaning they have.

When I was a prisoner, I knew a rather remarkable young man who was a Jesuit. He had entered the Jesuit order in the following way: he had had a number of very bad breaks; in childhood, his father died, leaving him in poverty, and he was a scholarship student at a religious institution where he was constantly made to feel that he was being kept out of charity; then, he failed to get any of the honors and distinctions that children like; later on, at about eighteen, he bungled a love affair; finally, at twenty-two, he failed in military training, a childish enough matter, but it was the last straw.

This young fellow might well have felt that he had botched everything. It was a sign of something, but of what? He might have taken refuge in bitterness or despair. But he very wisely looked upon all this as a sign that he was not made for secular triumphs, and that only the triumphs of religion, holiness, and faith were open to him. He saw the hand of God in all this, and so he entered the order. Who can help seeing that he alone decided what the sign meant?

Some other interpretation might have been drawn from this series of setbacks; for example, that he might have done better to turn carpenter or revolutionist. Therefore, he is fully responsible for the interpretation. Forlornness implies that we ourselves choose our being. Forlornness and anguish go together.

As for despair, the term has a very simple meaning. It means that we shall confine ourselves to reckoning only with what depends upon our will, or on the ensemble of probabilities which make our action possible. When we want something, we always have to reckon with probabilities. I may be counting on the arrival of a friend. The friend is coming by rail or street-car; this supposes that the train will arrive on schedule, or that the street-car will not jump the track. I am left in the realm of possibility; but possibilities are to be reckoned with only to the point where my action comports with the ensemble of these possibilities, and no further. The moment the possibilities I am considering are not rigorously involved by my action, I ought to disengage myself from them, because no God, no scheme, can adapt the world and its possibilities to my will. When Descartes said, "Conquer yourself rather than the world," he meant essentially the same thing.

The Marxists to whom I have spoken reply, "You can rely on the support of others in your action, which obviously has certain limits because you're not going to live forever. That means: rely on both what others are doing elsewhere to help you, in China, in Russia, and what they will do later on, after your death, to carry on the action and lead it to its fulfillment, which will be the revolution. You even *have* to rely upon that, otherwise you're immoral." I reply at once that I will always rely on fellow-fighters insofar as these comrades are involved with me in a common struggle, in the unity of a party or a group in which I can more or less make my weight felt; that is, one whose ranks I am in as a fighter and whose movements I am aware of at every moment. In such a situation, relying on the unity and will of the party is exactly like counting on the fact that the train will arrive on time or that the car won't jump the track. But, given that man is free and that there is no human nature for me to depend on, I cannot count on men whom I do not know by relying on human goodness or man's concern for the good of society. I don't know what will become of the Russian revolution; I may make an example of it to the extent that at the present time it is apparent that the proletariat plays a part in Russia that it plays in no other nation. But I can't swear that this will inevitably lead to a triumph of the proletariat. I've got to limit myself to what I see.

Given that men are free and that tomorrow they will freely decide what man will be, I cannot be sure that, after my death, fellow-fighters will carry on my work to bring it to its maximum perfection. Tomorrow, after my death, some men may decide to set up Fascism, and the others may be cowardly and muddled enough to let them do it. Fascism will then be the human reality, so much the worse for us.

Actually, things will be as man will have decided they are to be. Does that mean that I should abandon myself to quietism? No. First, I should involve myself; then, act on the old saw, "Nothing ventured, nothing gained." Nor does it mean that I shouldn't belong to a party, but rather that I shall have no illusions and shall do what I can. For example, suppose I ask myself, "Will socialization, as such, ever come about?" I know nothing about it. All I know is that I'm going to do everything in my power to bring it about. Beyond that, I can't count on anything. Quietism is the attitude of people who say, "Let others do what I can't do." The doctrine I am presenting is the very opposite of quietism, since it declares, "There is no reality except in action." Moreover, it goes further, since it adds, "Man is nothing else than his plan; he exists only to the extent that he fulfills himself; he is therefore nothing else than the ensemble of his acts, nothing else than his life."

According to this, we can understand why our doctrine horrifies certain people. Because often the only way they can bear their wretchedness is to think, "Circumstances have been against me. What I've been and done doesn't show my true worth. To be sure, I've had no great love, no great friendship, but that's because I haven't met a man or woman who was worthy. The books I've written haven't been very good because I haven't had the proper leisure. I haven't had children to devote myself to because I didn't find a man with whom I could have spent my life. So there remains within me, unused and quite viable, a host of propensities, inclinations, possibilities, that one wouldn't guess from the mere series of things I've done."

Now, for the existentialist there is really no love other than one which manifests itself in a person's being in love. There is no genius other than one which is expressed in works of art; the genius of Proust is the sum of Proust's works; the genius of Racine is his series of tragedies. Outside of that, there is nothing. Why say that Racine could have written another tragedy, when he didn't write it? A man is involved in life, leaves his impress on it, and outside of that there is nothing. To be sure, this may seem a harsh thought to someone whose life hasn't been a success. But, on the other hand, it prompts people to understand that reality alone is what counts, that dreams, expectations, and hopes warrant no more than to define a man as a disappointed dream, as miscarried hopes, as vain expectations. In other words, to define him negatively and not positively. However, when we say, "You are nothing else than your life," that does not imply that the artist will be judged solely on the basis of his works of art; a thousand other things will contribute toward summing him up. What we mean is that a man is nothing else than a series of undertakings, that he is the sum, the organization, the ensemble of the relationships which make up these undertakings.

When all is said and done, what we are accused of, at bottom, is not our pessimism, but an optimistic toughness. If people throw up to us our works of fiction in which we write about people who are soft, weak, cowardly, and sometimes even downright bad, it's not because these people are soft, weak, cowardly, or bad; because if we were to say, as Zola did, that they are that way because of heredity, the workings of environment, society, because of biological or psychological determinism, people would be reassured. They would say, "Well, that's what we're like, no one can do anything about it." But when the existentialist writes about a coward, he says that this coward is responsible for his cowardice. He's not like that because he has a cowardly heart or lung or brain; he's not like that on account of his physiological make-up; but he's like that because he has made himself a coward by his acts. There's no such thing as a cowardly constitution; there are nervous constitutions; there is poor blood, as the common people say, or strong constitutions. But the man whose blood is poor is not a coward on that account, for what makes cowardice is the act of renouncing or yielding. A constitution is not an act; the coward is defined on the basis of the acts he performs. People feel, in a vague sort of way, that this coward we're talking about is guilty of being a coward, and the thought frightens them. What people would like is that a coward or a hero be born that way.

One of the complaints most frequently made about *The Ways of Freedom** can be summed up as follows: "After all, these people are so spineless, how are you going to make heroes out of them?" This objection almost makes me laugh, for it assumes that people are born heroes. That's what people really want to think. If you're born cowardly, you may set your mind perfectly at rest; there's nothing you can do about it; you'll be cowardly all your life, whatever you may do. If you're born a hero, you may set your mind just as much at rest; you'll be a hero all your life; you'll drink like a hero and eat like a hero. What the existentialist says is that the coward makes himself cowardly, that the hero makes himself heroic. There's always a possibility for the coward not to be cowardly any more and for the hero to stop being heroic. What counts is total involvement; some one particular action or set of circumstances is not total involvement.

**Les Chemins de la Liberté,* M. Sartre's projected trilogy of novels, two of which, *L'Age de Raison* (*The Age of Reason*) and *Le Sursis* (*The Reprieve*) have already appeared—Translator's note.

DISCUSSION QUESTIONS

1. Explain what Sartre means by "anguish." Do you feel a total and deep responsibility about the choices in your life?
2. Why does Sartre think it is very distressing if God does not exist? Explain what he means by "forlornness." Is Sartre's idea of forlornness similar to Kierkegaard's notion of despair? Explain.
3. Why does Sartre think an individual is responsible for acts he performs out of passion? Do you agree? Explain.
4. Describe the dilemma of Sartre's student who had to choose between caring for his mother and leaving her behind to go to England to join the Free French Forces and avenge the death of his brother by the Germans in 1940. What would you do in such a situation? How does Sartre use this case to support the idea of existence preceding essence?
5. What does Sartre say about asking people for advice? How does he use this example to argue that we are fully responsible for how we choose to interpret signs?
6. Does Sartre think that existentialism leads to quietism? Do you agree with his reasoning? Explain.
7. Do you agree with Sartre that cowards and heroes are made, not born? Does heredity have any effect on a person's behavior? Discuss.

Chapter 22

P. F. STRAWSON

Peter Frederick Strawson was born in London in 1919 and was educated at Christ College Oxford. In 1968 he was named Waynflete Professor of Metaphysical Philosophy at Oxford. His first book, Introduction to Logical Theory *(1952), studies the relationship between formal logic and the logical features of ordinary language. His* The Bounds of Sense *(1966) is an extended commentary on the critical philosophy of Kant. His* Analysis and Metaphysics: An Introduction to Philosophy *(1992) demonstrates the analytical method of philosophical problem solving.*

This selection is taken from Strawson's second book (1959). Here he argues for the primitiveness of the concept of a person. What he means is that the concept of a person is logically prior to the concept of a pure individual consciousness or ego. He conceives of a person as a type of entity for which two kinds of predicates equally apply. States of consciousness are described by one type of predicate, corporeal (material) characteristics by the other. The latter he calls Material-predicates or "M-predicates"; examples include "weighs 140 lbs.," "is in the drawing room." The former he calls Personal-predicates or "P-predicates," and these include ascriptions like "is smiling," "is in pain," "believes in God," "is depressed." The primitiveness of its concept rules out thinking of a person as a secondary kind of entity composed of a particular consciousness and a particular human body. Strawson further contends that in order to have the concept of a person, one must be both a self-ascriber and an other-ascriber of P-predicates, and one must see every other as a self-ascriber too. In this light, some familiar difficulties in the philosophy of mind are overcome by avoiding both scepticism and behaviorism. He suggests that a condition for the existence of the concept of an individual person is that we only sometimes say of a group of human beings that its members think and act "as one."

Individuals: An Essay in Descriptive Metaphysics

What we have to acknowledge, in order to begin to free ourselves from these difficulties, is the primitiveness of the concept of a person. What I mean by the concept of a person is the concept of a type of entity such that *both* predicates ascribing states of consciousness *and* predicates ascribing corporeal characteristics, a physical situation &c. are equally applicable to a single individual of that single type. What I mean by saying that this concept is primitive can be put in a number of ways. One way is to return to those two questions I asked earlier: viz. (1) why are states of consciousness ascribed to anything at all? and (2) why are they ascribed to the very same thing as certain corporeal characteristics, a certain physical situation &c.? I remarked at the beginning that it was not to be supposed that the answers to these questions were independent of each other. Now I shall say that they are connected in this way: that a necessary condition of states of consciousness being ascribed at all is that they should be ascribed to the *very same things* as certain corporeal characteristics, a certain physical situation &c. That is to say, states of consciousness could not be ascribed at all, *unless* they were ascribed to persons, in the sense I have claimed for this word. We are tempted to think of a person as a sort of compound of two kinds of subjects: a subject of experiences (a pure consciousness, an ego) on the one hand, and a subject of corporeal attributes on the other. Many questions arise when we think in this way. But, in particular, when we ask ourselves how we come to frame, to get a use for, the concept of this compound of two subjects, the picture—if we are honest and careful—is apt to change from the picture of two subjects to the picture of one subject and one non-subject. For it becomes impossible to see how we could come by the idea of different, distinguishable, identifiable subjects of experiences—different consciousnesses—*if this idea is thought of as logically primitive,* as a logical ingredient in the compound-idea of a person, the latter being composed of two subjects. For there could never be any question of assigning an experience, as such, to any subject other than oneself; and therefore never any question of assigning it to oneself either, never any question of ascribing it to a subject at all. So the concept of the pure individual consciousness—the pure ego—is a concept that cannot exist; or, at least, cannot exist as a primary concept in terms of which the concept of a person can be explained or analysed. It can exist only, if at all, as a secondary, non-primitive

Source: P. F. Strawson, excerpt from *Individuals: An Essay in Descriptive Metaphysics.* London: Methuen (1959): 97–113. Reprinted with permission of Routledge.

concept, which itself is to be explained, analysed, in terms of the concept of a person. It was the entity corresponding to this illusory primary concept of the pure consciousness, the ego-substance, for which Hume was seeking, or ironically pretending to seek, when he looked into himself, and complained that he could never discover himself without a perception and could never discover anything but the perception. More seriously—and this time there was no irony, but a confusion, a Nemesis of confusion for Hume—it was this entity of which Hume vainly sought for the principle of unity, confessing himself perplexed and defeated; sought vainly because there is no principle of unity where there is no principle of differentiation. It was this, too, to which Kant, more perspicacious here than Hume, accorded a purely formal ('analytic') unity: the unity of the 'I think' that accompanies all my perceptions and therefore might just as well accompany none. Finally it is this, perhaps, of which Wittgenstein spoke, when he said of the subject, first that there is no such thing, and then that it is not a part of the world, but its limit.

So, then, the word 'I' never refers to this, the pure subject. But this does not mean, as the no-ownership theorist must think, that 'I' in some cases does not refer at all. It refers; because I am a person among others; and the predicates which would, *per impossible* belong to the pure subject if it could be referred to, belong properly to the person to which 'I' does refer.

The concept of a person is logically prior to that of an individual consciousness. The concept of a person is not to be analysed as that of an animated body or of an embodied anima. This is not to say that the concept of a pure individual consciousness might not have a logically secondary existence, if one thinks, or finds, it desirable. We speak of a dead person—a body—and in the same secondary way we might at least think of a disembodied person. A person is not an embodied ego, but an ego might be a disembodied person, retaining the logical benefit of individuality from having been a person.

[5] It is important to realize the full extent of the acknowledgement one is making in acknowledging the logical primitiveness of the concept of a person. Let me rehearse briefly the stages of the argument. There would be no question of ascribing one's own states of consciousness, or experiences, to anything, unless one also ascribed, or were ready and able to ascribe, states of consciousness, or experiences, to other individual entities of the same logical type as that thing to which one ascribes one's own states of consciousness. The condition of reckoning oneself as a subject of such predicates is that one should also reckon others as subjects of such predicates. The condition, in turn, of this being possible, is that one should be able to distinguish from one another, to pick out or identify, different subjects of such predicates, i.e. different individuals of the type concerned. The condition, in turn, of this being possible is that the individuals concerned, including oneself, should be of a certain unique type: of a type, namely, such that to each individual of that type there must be ascribed, or ascribable, *both* states of consciousness *and* corporeal characteristics. But this characterization of the type is still very opaque and does not at all clearly bring out what is involved. To bring this out, I must make a rough division, into two, of the kinds of predicates properly applied to individuals of this type. The first kind of predicate consists of those which are also properly applied to material bodies to which we would not dream of applying predicates ascribing states of consciousness. I will call this first kind M-predicates: and they include things like 'weighs 10 stone', 'is in the drawing-room' and so on. The second kind consists of all the other predicates we apply to persons. These I shall call P-predicates. P-predicates, of course, will be very various. They will include things like 'is smiling', 'is going for a walk', as well as things like 'is in pain', 'is thinking hard', 'believes in God' and so on.

So far I have said that the concept of a person is to be understood as the concept of a type of entity such that *both* predicates ascribing states of consciousness *and* predicates ascribing corporeal characteristics, a physical situation &c. are equally applicable to an individual entity of that type. All I have said about the meaning of saying that this concept is primitive is that it is not to be analysed in a certain way or ways. We are not, for example, to think of it as a secondary kind of entity in relation to two primary kinds, viz. a particular consciousness and a particular human body. I implied also that the Cartesian error is just a special case of the more general error, present in a different form in theories of the no-ownership type, of thinking of the designations, or apparent designations, of persons as *not* denoting precisely the same thing or entity for all kinds of predicate ascribed to the entity designated. That is, if we are to avoid the general form of this error, we must *not* think of 'I' or 'Smith' as suffering from type-ambiguity. Indeed, if we want to locate type-ambiguity somewhere, we would do better to locate it in certain predicates like 'is in the drawing-room' 'was hit by a stone' &c., and say they mean one thing when applied to material objects and another when applied to persons.

This is all I have so far said or implied about the meaning of saying that the concept of a person is primitive. What has to be brought out further is what the implications of saying this are as regards the logical character of those predicates with which we ascribe states of consciousness. For this purpose we may well consider P-predicates in general. For though not all P-predicates are what we should call 'predicates ascribing states of consciousness' (e.g. 'going for a walk' is not), they may be said to have this in common, that they imply the possession of consciousness on the part of that to which they are ascribed.

What then are the consequences of the view as regards the character of P-predicates? I think they are these. Clearly there is no sense in talking of identifiable individuals of a special type, a type, namely, such that they possess both M-predicates and P-predicates, unless there is in principle some way of telling, with regard to any individual of that type, and any P-predicate, whether that individual possesses that P-predicate. And, in the case of at least some P-predicates, the ways of telling must constitute in some sense logically adequate kinds of criteria for the ascription of the P-predicate. For suppose in no case did these ways of telling constitute logically adequate kinds of criteria. Then we should have to think of the relation between the ways of telling and what the P-predicate ascribes, or a part of what it ascribes, always in the following way: we should have to think of the ways of telling as *signs* of the presence, in the individual concerned, of this different thing, viz. the state of consciousness. But then we could only know that the way of telling was a sign of the presence of the different thing ascribed by the P-predicate, by the observation of correlations between the two. But this observation we could each make only in one case, viz. our own. And now we are back in the position of the defender of Cartesianism, who thought our way with it was too short. For what, now, does 'our own case' mean? There is no sense in the idea of ascribing states of consciousness to oneself, or at all, unless the ascriber already knows how to ascribe at least some states of consciousness to others. So he cannot argue in general 'from his own case' to conclusions about how to do this; for unless he already knows how to do this, he has no conception of *his own case,* or any *case,* i.e. any subject of experiences. Instead, he just has evidence that pain &c. may be expected when a certain body is affected in certain ways and not when others are. If he speculated to the contrary, his speculations would be immediately falsified.

The conclusion here is not, of course, new. What I have said is that one ascribes P-predicates to others on the strength of observation of their behaviour; and that the behaviour-criteria one goes on are not just signs of the presence of what is meant by the P-predicate, but are criteria of a logically adequate kind for the ascription of the P-predicate. On behalf of this conclusion, however, I am claiming that it follows from a consideration of the conditions necessary for any ascription of states of consciousness to anything. The point is not that we must accept this conclusion in order to avoid scepticism, but that we must accept it in order to explain the existence of the conceptual scheme in terms of which the sceptical problem is stated. But once the conclusion is accepted, the sceptical problem does not arise. So with many sceptical problems: their statement involves the pretended acceptance of a conceptual scheme and at the same time the silent repudiation of one of the conditions of its existence. That is why they are, in the terms in which they are stated, insoluble.

But this is only one half of the picture about P-predicates. For of course it is true of some important classes of P-predicates, that when one ascribes them to *oneself,* one does not do so on the strength of observation of those behaviour criteria on the strength of which one ascribes them to others. This is not true of all P-predicates. It is not, in general, true of those which carry assessments of character or capability: these, when self-ascribed, are in general ascribed on the same kind of basis as that on which they are ascribed to others. Even of those P-predicates of which it is true that one does not generally ascribe them to oneself on the basis of the criteria on the strength of which one ascribes them to others, there are many of which it is also true that their ascription is liable to correction by the self-ascriber on this basis. But there remain many cases in which one has an entirely adequate basis for ascribing a P-predicate to oneself, and yet in which this basis is quite distinct from those on which one ascribes the predicate to another. Thus one says, reporting a present state of mind or feeling: 'I feel tired, am depressed, am in pain'. How can this fact be reconciled with the doctrine that the criteria on the strength of which one ascribes P-predicates to others are criteria of a logically adequate kind for this ascription?

The apparent difficulty of bringing about this reconciliation may tempt us in many directions. It may tempt us, for example, to deny that these self-ascriptions are really ascriptive at all, to *assimilate* first-person ascriptions of states of consciousness to those other forms of behaviour which constitute criteria on the basis of which one person ascribes P-predicates to another. This device seems to avoid the difficulty; it is not, in all cases, entirely inappropriate. But it obscures the facts; and is needless. It is merely a sophisticated form of failure to recognize the special character of P-predicates, or, rather, of a crucial class of P-predicates. For just as there is not in general one primary process of learning, or teaching oneself, an inner private meaning for predicates of this class, then another process of learning to apply such predicates to others on the strength of a correlation, noted in one's own case, with certain forms of behaviour, so—and equally—there is not in general one primary process of learning to apply such predicates to others on the strength of behaviour criteria, and then another process of acquiring the secondary technique of exhibiting a new form of behaviour, viz. first-person P-utterances. Both these pictures are refusals to acknowledge the unique logical character of the predicates concerned. Suppose we write 'Px' as the general form of propositional function of such a predicate. Then, according to the first picture, the expression which primarily replaces 'x' in this form is 'I', the first person singular pronoun: its uses with other replacements are secondary, derivative and shaky. According to the second picture, on the other hand, the primary replacements of 'x' in this form are 'he', 'that person', &c., and its use with 'I' is secondary, peculiar, not a true ascriptive use. But it is essential to the character of these predicates that they have both first- and third-person ascriptive uses, that they are both self-ascribable otherwise than on the basis of observation of the behaviour of the subject of them, and other-ascribable on the basis of behaviour criteria. To learn their use is to learn both aspects of their use. In order to *have* this type of concept, one must be both a self-ascriber and an other-ascriber of such predicates, and must see every other as a self-ascriber. In order to *understand* this type of concept, one must acknowledge that there is a kind of predicate which is unambiguously and adequately ascribable *both* on the basis of observation of the subject of the predicate *and* not on this basis, i.e. independently of observation of the subject: the second case is the case where the ascriber is also the subject. If there were no concepts answering to the characterization I have just given, we should indeed have no philosophical problem about the soul; but equally we should not have our concept of a person.

To put the point—with a certain unavoidable crudity—in terms of one particular concept of this class, say, that of depression. We speak of behaving in a depressed way (of depressed behaviour) and we also speak of feeling depressed (of a feeling of depression). One is inclined to argue that feelings can be felt but not observed, and behaviour can be observed but not felt, and that therefore there must be room here to drive in a logical wedge. But the concept of depression spans the place where one wants to drive it in. We might say: in order for there to be such a concept as that of X's depression, the depression which X has, the concept must cover both what is felt, but not observed, by X, and what may be observed, but not felt, by others than X (for all values of X). But it is perhaps better to say: X's depression *is* something, one and the same thing, which is felt, but not observed, by X, and observed, but not felt, by others than X. (Of course, what can be observed can also be faked or disguised.) To refuse to accept this is to refuse to accept the *structure* of the language in which we talk about depression. That is, in a sense, all right. One might give up talking or devise, perhaps, a different structure in terms of which to soliloquize. What is not all right is simultaneously to pretend to accept that structure and to refuse to accept it; i.e. to couch one's rejection in the language of that structure.

It is in this light that we must see some of the familiar philosophical difficulties in the topic of the mind. For some of them spring from just such a failure to admit, or fully to appreciate, the character which I have been claiming for at least some P-predicates. It is not seen that these predicates could not have either aspect of their use, the self-ascriptive or the non-self-ascriptive, without having the other aspect. Instead, one aspect of their use is taken as self-sufficient, which it could not be, and then the other aspect appears as problematical. So we oscillate between philosophical scepticism and philosophical behaviourism. When we take the self-ascriptive aspect of the use of some P-predicates, say 'depressed', as primary, then a logical gap seems to open between the criteria on the strength of which we say that another is depressed, and the actual state of being depressed. What we do not realize is that if this logical gap is allowed to open, then it swallows not only his depression, but our depression as well. For if the logical gap exists, then depressed behaviour, however much there is of it, is no more than a sign of depression. But it can only become a sign of depression because of an observed correlation between it and depression. But whose depression? Only mine, one is tempted to say. But if *only* mine, then *not* mine at all. The sceptical position customarily represents the crossing of the logical gap as at best a shaky inference. But the point is that not even the syntax of the premises of the inference exists, if the gap exists.

If, on the other hand, we take the other-ascriptive uses of these predicates as primary or self-sufficient, we may come to think that all there is in the meaning of these predicates, as predicates, is the criteria on the strength of which we ascribe them to others. Does this not follow from the denial of the logical gap? It does not follow. To think that it does is to forget the self-ascriptive use of these predicates, to forget that we have to do with a class of predicates to the meaning of which it is essential that they should be both self-ascribable and other-ascribable to the same individual, where self-ascriptions are not made on the observational basis on which other-ascriptions are made, but on another basis. It is not that these predicates have two kinds of meaning. Rather, it is essential to the single kind of meaning that they do have, that both ways of ascribing them should be perfectly in order.

If one is playing a game of cards, the distinctive markings of a certain card constitute a logically adequate criterion for calling it, say, the Queen of Hearts; but, in calling it this, in the context of the game, one is ascribing to it properties over and above the possession of these markings. The predicate gets its meaning from the whole structure of the game. So with the language in which we ascribe P-predicates. To say that the criteria on the strength of which we ascribe P-predicates to others are of a logically adequate kind for this ascription, is not to say that all there is to the ascriptive meaning of these predicates is these criteria. To say this is to forget that they are P-predicates, to forget the rest of the language-structure to which they belong.

[6] Now our perplexities may take a different form, the form of the question: 'But how can one ascribe to oneself, not on the basis of observation, the very same thing that others may have, on the basis of observation, reasons of a logically adequate kind for ascribing to one?' This question may be absorbed in a wider one, which might be phrased: 'How are P-predicates possible?' or: 'How is the concept of a person possible?' This is the question by which we replace those two earlier questions, viz.: 'Why are states of consciousness ascribed at all, ascribed to anything?' and 'Why are they ascribed to the very same thing as certain corporeal characteristics &c.?' For the answer to these two initial questions is to be found nowhere else but in the admission of the primitiveness of the concept of a person, and hence of the unique character of P-predicates. So residual perplexities have to frame themselves in this new way. For when we have acknowledged the primitiveness of the concept of a person, and, with it, the unique character of P-predicates, we may still want to ask what it is in the natural facts that makes it intelligible that we should have this concept, and to ask this in the hope of a nontrivial answer, i.e. in the hope of an answer which does not *merely* say: 'Well, there are people in the world'. I do not pretend to be able to satisfy this demand at all fully. But I may mention two very different things which might count as beginnings or fragments of an answer.

First, I think a beginning can be made by moving a certain class of P-predicates to a central position in the picture. They are predicates, roughly, which involve doing something, which clearly imply intention or a state of mind or at least consciousness in general, and which indicate a characteristic pattern, or range of patterns, of bodily movement, while not indicating at all precisely any very definite sensation or experience. I mean such things as 'going for a walk', 'coiling a rope', 'playing ball', 'writing a letter'. Such predicates have the interesting characteristic of many P-predicates, that one does not, in general, ascribe them to oneself on the strength of observation, whereas one does ascribe them to others on the strength of observation. But, in the case of these predicates, one feels minimal reluctance to concede that what is ascribed in these two different ways is the same. This is because of the marked dominance of a fairly definite pattern of bodily movement in what they ascribe, and the marked absence of any distinctive experience. They release us from the idea that the only things we can know about without observation or inference, or both, are private experiences; we can know, without telling by either of these means, about the present and future movements of a body. Yet bodily movements are certainly also things we can know about by observation and inference. Among the things that we observe, as opposed to the things we know about without observation, are the movements of bodies similar to that about which we have knowledge not based on observation. It is important that we should understand such movements, for they bear on and condition our own; and in fact we understand them, we interpret them, only by seeing them as elements in just such plans or schemes of action as those of which we know the present course and future development without observation of the relevant present movements. But this is to say that we see such movements as *actions,* that we interpret them in terms of intention, that we see them as movements of individuals of a type to which also belongs that individual whose present and future movements we know about without observation; it is to say that we see others as self-ascribers, not on the basis of observation, of what we ascribe to them on this basis.

These remarks are not intended to suggest how the 'problem of other minds' could be solved, or our beliefs about others given a general philosophical 'justification'. I have already argued that such a 'solution' or 'justification' is impossible, that the demand for it cannot be coherently stated. Nor are these remarks intended as *a priori* genetic psychology. They are simply intended to help to make it seem intelligible to us, at this stage in the history of the philosophy of this subject, that we have the conceptual scheme we have. What I am suggesting is that it is easier to understand how we can see each other, and ourselves, as persons, if we think first of the fact that we act, and act on each other, and act in accordance with a common human nature. Now 'to see each other as persons' is a lot of things, but not a lot of separate and unconnected things. The class of P-predicates that I have moved into the centre of the picture are not unconnectedly there, detached from others irrelevant to them. On the contrary, they are inextricably bound up with the others, interwoven with them. The topic of the mind does not divide into unconnected subjects.

I spoke just now of a common human nature. But there is also a sense in which a condition of the existence of the conceptual scheme we have is that human nature should not be common—should not be, that is, a community nature. Philosophers used to discuss the question of whether there was, or could be, such a thing as a 'group mind'. For some the idea had a peculiar fascination, while to others it seemed utterly absurd and nonsensical and at the same time, curiously enough, pernicious. It is easy to see why these last found it pernicious: they found something horrible in the thought that people should cease to have to individual persons the kind of attitudes that they did have, and instead have attitudes in some way analogous towards groups; and that they might cease to decide individual courses of action for themselves and instead merely participate in corporate activities. But their finding it pernicious showed that they understood the idea they claimed to be absurd only too well. The fact that we find it natural to individuate as persons the members of a certain class of moving natural objects does not mean that such a conceptual scheme is inevitable for any class of beings not utterly unlike ourselves. A technique similar to that which I used in the last chapter to decide whether there was a place in the restricted auditory world for the concept of the self, is available to determine whether we might not construct the idea of a special kind of social world in which the concept of an individual person is replaced by that of a group. Think, to begin with, of certain aspects of actual human existence. Think, for example, of two groups of human beings engaged in some competitive, but corporate activity, such as battle, for which they have been exceedingly well trained. We may even suppose that orders are superfluous, though information is passed. It is easy to suppose that, while absorbed in such activity, the members of the groups make no references to individual persons at all, have no use for personal names or pronouns. They do, however, refer to the groups and apply to them predicates analogous to those predicates ascribing purposive activity which we normally apply to individual persons. They may *in fact* use in such circumstances the plural forms 'we' and 'they'; but these are not genuine plurals, they are plurals without a singular, such as occur in sentences like: 'We have taken the citadel', 'We have lost the game'. They may also refer to elements in the group, to members of the group, but exclusively in terms which get their sense from the parts played by these elements in the corporate activity. Thus we sometimes refer to what are in fact persons as 'stroke' or 'square-leg'.

When we think of such cases, we see that we ourselves, over a part of our social lives—not, happily, a very large part—do work with a set of ideas from which that of the individual person is excluded, in which its place is taken by that of the group. But might we not think of communities or groups such that this part of the lives of their members was the dominant part—or was not merely a part, but the whole? It sometimes happens, with groups of human beings, that, as *we* say, their members think, feel and act 'as one'. I suggest it is a condition for the existence of the concept of an individual person, that this should happen only sometimes.

It is quite useless to say, at this point: 'But all the same, even if it happened all the time, every member of the group would *have* an individual consciousness, would embody an individual subject of experience.' For, once more, there is no sense in speaking of the individual consciousness just as such, of the individual subject of experience just as such; there is no way of identifying such pure entities. It is true, of course, that, in suggesting the fantasy of total absorption in the group, I took our concept of an individual person as a starting point. It is this fact which makes the useless reaction a natural one. But suppose someone seriously advanced the following 'hypothesis': that each part of the human body, each organ and each member, had an individual consciousness, was a separate centre of experiences. The 'hypothesis' would be useless in the same way as the above remark, only more obviously so. Let us now suppose that there is a class of moving natural objects, divided into groups, each group exhibiting the same characteristic pattern of activity. Within each group there are certain differentiations of appearance accompanying differentiations of function, and in particular there is one member of each group with a distinctive appearance. Cannot one imagine different sets of observations which might lead us in the one case to think of the particular member as the spokesman of the group, as its mouthpiece; and in the other case to think of him as its mouth, to think of the group as a single *scattered* body? The important point is that as soon as we adopt the latter way of thinking, then we abandon the former; we are no longer influenced by the human analogy in its first form, but only in its second; we are no longer tempted to say: Perhaps the members have consciousness. It is helpful here to remember the startling ambiguity of the phrase, 'a body and its members'.

[7] Earlier, when I was discussing the concept of a pure individual consciousness, I said that though it could not exist as a primary concept to be used in the explanation of the concept of a person (so that there is no mind–body problem, as traditionally conceived), yet it might have a logically secondary existence. Thus, from within our actual conceptual scheme, each of us can quite intelligibly conceive of his or her individual survival of bodily death. The effort of imagination is not even great. One has simply to think of oneself as having thoughts and memories as at present, visual and auditory experiences largely as at present, even, perhaps—though this involves certain complications—some quasi-tactual and organic sensations as at present, whilst *(a)* having no perceptions of a body related to one's experience as one's own body is, and *(b)* having no power of initiating changes in the physical condition of the world, such as one at present does with one's hands, shoulders, feet and vocal chords. Condition *(a)* must be expanded by adding that no one else exhibits reactions indicating that he perceives a body at the point which one's body would be occupying if one were seeing and hearing in an embodied state from the point from which one is seeing and hearing in a disembodied state. One could, of course, imagine condition *(a)* being fulfilled, in both its parts, without condition *(b)* being fulfilled. This would be a rather vulgar fancy, in the class of the table-tapping spirits with

familiar voices. But suppose we take disembodiment strictly in the sense that we imagine both *(a)* and *(b)* fulfilled. Then two consequences follow, one of which is commonly noted, the other of which is perhaps insufficiently attended to. The first is that the strictly disembodied individual is strictly solitary, and it must remain for him indeed an utterly empty, though not meaningless, speculation, as to whether there are any other members of his class. The other, and less commonly noticed point, is that in order to retain his idea of himself as an individual, he must always think of himself as *dis*-embodied, as a *former* person. That is to say, he must contrive still to have the idea of himself as a member of a class or type of entities with whom, however, he is now debarred from entering into any of those transactions the past fact of which was the condition of his having any idea of himself at all. Since then he has, as it were, no personal life of his own to lead, he must live much in the memories of the personal life he did lead; or he might, when this living in the past loses its appeal, achieve some kind of attenuated vicarious personal existence by taking a certain kind of interest in the human affairs of which he is a mute and invisible witness—much like that kind of spectator at a play who says to himself: 'That's what I should have done (or said)' or 'If I were he, I should . . .'. In proportion as the memories fade, and this vicarious living palls, to that degree his concept of himself as an individual becomes attenuated. At the limit of attenuation there is, *from the point of view of his survival as an individual,* no difference between the continuance of experience and its cessation. Disembodied survival, on such terms as these, may well seem unattractive. No doubt it is for this reason that the orthodox have wisely insisted on the resurrection of the body.

DISCUSSION QUESTIONS

1. What does Strawson say is a necessary condition of states of consciousness being ascribed at all to an individual?
2. Explain the point about which Kant was more perspicacious than Hume, according to Strawson.
3. Explain why Strawson thinks the word "I" never refers to the pure, conscious subject.
4. What are Strawson's reasons for thinking that a person is not an embodied ego, but an ego might be a disembodied person? Are you persuaded by his reasons? Explain.
5. Why does Strawson believe that skeptical problems, in the terms in which they are stated, are insoluble? Do you agree?
6. Explain the comparison of calling a card the Queen of Hearts and ascribing it certain properties in a structured game with the language-structure in which we ascribe P-predicates.
7. Describe Strawson's remarks on individual survival of bodily death. Do you agree with him that such a disembodied condition seems unattractive? Explain.

Chapter 23

C. D. BROAD

Charlie Dunbar Broad (1887–1971) was born in Harlesden, Middlesex, England. He was Knightbridge Professor of Moral Philosophy at Cambridge University from 1933 to 1953. Broad also had a strong interest in parapsychology, and was president of the Society for Psychical Research. He wrote out every lecture he delivered, reading aloud each sentence verbatim twice.

In this essay, Broad conceives of a personal God as either a God that is a person or a God that is a whole composed of nothing but interrelated persons. However, he doesn't know if we can define what a person is. A sane grown man is an example of a person; a chair, a dog, a cat, and a very young human baby are examples of non-persons. Broad identifies four necessary and jointly sufficient conditions of a person: (1) it thinks, feels, wills, etc; (2) its various contemporary states together make up a single total state of mind; (3) its successive total states are so many different stages in the history of a single mind; (4) it knows immediately, in part at least, that it is a mind. Broad thinks that the more fully one's mental states are unified, the more personal one is, and the more fully and immediately one recognizes this unity it possesses, the more personal one is. Broad distinguishes three senses of God. In the popular sense, God is a being much more powerful and much wiser than the strongest and wisest of human beings. In the theological sense, God need not be one person but could be three, is perfectly wise, omnipotent, morally perfect, unique, and is not identified with the universe (which is existentially dependent on God). In the philosophical sense, God is the universe as a whole, the Absolute (according to Hegel), or Nature (according to Spinoza). Broad sees three ways of justifying belief in god: (1) claiming to have direct knowledge of it, (2) claiming to be able to prove it, or (3) appealing to the authority of others. In reply to (1), Broad doesn't think it is possible to test the alleged supersensible perception which some people claim to have of God. As for (2), Broad explains why he is not alone in thinking that the ontological, the cosmological, and the design arguments for God's existence are all fallacious. In response to (3), Broad denies that there are any expert authorities on God's existence. So while there are grave difficulties in the notion of a God in the theological sense, Broad admits that his objections do not preclude the view that many very powerful deities collaborated in creating the universe, but either no longer exist or ceased to be involved with the world after its creation.

The Validity of Belief in a Personal God

In order to discuss the question whether there is any ground for believing in the existence of a personal God it is necessary to begin by defining our terms. For the word 'personal' and the word 'God' are both highly ambiguous. I will begin with the word 'personal'.

The natural interpretation of the phrase 'a personal God' would be 'a God who is a person'. But, if this were the only meaning that could be attached to the phrase, we should have to say that orthodox Christians deny the existence of a personal God. For the Christian God is the Trinity; and the Trinity is not a person, though its members are persons. Now it would be extremely inconvenient to define the phrase 'personal God' in such a way that we should have to hold that all orthodox Christians deny the existence of a personal God. And, as we have seen, this inconvenient result would follow if we defined a 'personal God' to mean 'a God who is a person'. We must therefore adopt a somewhat wider definition of 'personal'. Now we notice that, whilst the Trinity is denied to be a person, it is asserted to be a complex unity composed of three intimately related constituents, each of which is a person. And I think that we should deny that a man believed in a personal God unless he believed that God either is a person or is a complex whole composed of nothing but interrelated persons. I therefore suggest that the phrase 'a personal God' means 'a God which either is a person or is a whole composed of nothing but interrelated persons'. This definition is certainly wide enough, whilst the first suggested definition was certainly too narrow. It might perhaps be objected that the proposed definition is now too wide. Would any and every God which is composed of nothing but interrelated persons be counted as a personal God? Or must the relations be of a specially intimate kind before we can apply the adjective 'personal' to a whole composed of nothing but persons? It is admitted that, according to the Christian doctrine of the Trinity, the relations between the constituent persons are extremely intimate; so much so that there is a constant danger of making statements about the Trinity which are true only of its constituents, and of making statements about its constituents which are true only of the Trinity as a whole. But I think that this question really arises rather under the definition of 'God' than under the definition of 'personal'. It is quite certain that we should not apply the name 'God' to any and every whole composed of interrelated persons; we should apply this name only if the relations were peculiarly intimate. I shall assume, therefore, that any whole composed of nothing but persons may be

Source: C. D. Broad, "The Validity of Belief in a Personal God," *Religion, Philosophy and Psychical Research*. New York: Humanities Press (1969): 159–174. Reprinted with permission of Routledge.

called 'personal' provided that the relations between the constituent persons are intimate enough for this whole to be called a 'God'.

We have not, however, finished with the definition of the adjective 'personal'. We have said that 'a personal God' means 'a God which either is a person or is a whole composed of nothing but interrelated persons'. But what do we mean by a 'person'? I do not know that we can define the term; but, by considering examples of what we should call 'persons' and by contrasting them with examples of what we should refuse to call 'persons', we can see pretty well what is involved in being a person. We call a sane grown man a 'person'. We refuse to call any inanimate object, such as a chair, a 'person'. We also refuse to call a cat or a dog or a horse a 'person', though we admit that they have feelings, impulses, instincts, habits, etc. And I think that it would be felt to be a strained and metaphorical use of language to call a very young baby a 'person'. If we reflect on these examples I think we shall see that we apply the name 'person' literally to a substance if, and only if, it fulfils the following conditions: (1) It must think, feel, will, etc. (2) Its various contemporary states must have that peculiar kind of unity which we express by saying that they 'together make up a single total state of mind'. (3) Its successive total states must have that peculiar kind of unity with each other which we express by saying that they are 'so many different stages in the history of a single mind'. (4) These two kinds of unity must be recognized by itself, and not only by some external observer, i.e. it must not only be in fact a mind, but must also know that it is a mind. And this knowledge must be, in part at least, immediate and not merely inferential; though its knowledge of many details about itself may, of course, be inferential and not immediate. It may be the case that every substance which has the kind and degree of internal unity necessary for *being* a mind also *knows* immediately that it is a mind. Still, it is one thing to *have* this kind and degree of unity, and it is another thing to *know* immediately that one has it; and it seems logically possible that the former might happen without the latter. In that case we should not, I think, refer to this mind as a 'person'. It is therefore necessary explicitly to introduce this fourth condition.

If we accept this as an adequate description of 'being a person' there are certain further remarks to be made.

(1) There are, presumably, different degrees of personality. These differences may arise in two different ways, which must be distinguished in theory even if in fact they be causally connected so that variations in one respect causally determine variations in the other respect. *(a)* A mind will be more fully personal the more completely its contemporary states are united with each other to form a single total state, and the more completely its successive total states are united with each other to form the history of a single mind. In every human mind there are conflicting desires, inconsistent beliefs, and contemporary mental processes which have very little connexion with each other. And the history of every human mind is broken by gaps of dreamless sleep, fainting fits, drunkenness, and so on. *(b)* A mind will be more fully personal the more fully and immediately it recognizes such unity as it in fact possesses. We have all forgotten a great many states which have in fact been experienced by us, and we cannot recall them at will. And, on the other hand, we are liable to 'remember' events that never happened, and to believe falsely that they formed parts of our mental history. Now, since these defects are present in different degrees in different human minds, though they are present in some degree in all human minds, we can form the conception of a mind which is much more completely a person than any human being is; just as we can form the conception of a perfect gas or a frictionless fluid from our experiences of more or less imperfect gases and more or less viscous fluids. An ideal person would be a mind which is as fully unified as possible; which has no inconsistent beliefs, or conflicting desires, or mutually indifferent mental processes; which never sleeps or faints; and so on. And it must be as fully and

immediately aware of this unity as possible. It must not forget anything that has belonged to it, though it is not necessary to suppose that it is always actually remembering everything that has ever happened to it. It is enough to suppose that it could remember any of these events whenever it wanted to. There seems to be no logical objection to the concept of an ideal person, if this be all that is meant by the phrase.

(2) There are certain judgments which we make only about persons, and certain emotions which we feel only towards what we take to be persons. We should not literally ascribe moral goodness or badness to anything which we did not believe to be a person. No one seriously talks of a virtuous baby, or regards a cat as being morally responsible for its actions. And no one can strictly feel the emotions of love or gratitude to anything which he does not at the time regard as a person. It is true, I think, that a man may quite literally love his cat or dog, though he would admit, if questioned, that it is not a person. But an intelligent domestic animal probably has, in fact, the rudiments of personality, and, whether it has or not, its master almost certainly treats it in practice as a person whatever his theoretical beliefs on the subject may be. Again, it is certainly possible to feel emotions which are analogous to love and to gratitude towards certain wholes composed of interrelated persons, though we should admit that these wholes are not themselves persons. E.g. there is an emotion which we call 'love' for a public school, a college, or a country. And there is an emotion which we call 'gratitude' towards these institutions for the benefits which we believe them to have bestowed on us. But, in the first place, it is plain that we tend in practice to personify such a group of persons, although we know that it is not really a person. We tend, e.g. to substitute for Trinity College, which is a Society and not a person, a kind of idealized man who combines all the best qualities of all the nicest Trinity men that we have known. And, if we literally love certain actual Trinity men, we shall tend to feel an analogous emotion at the thought of this idealized Trinity man who represents Trinity College to us. Moreover, I think it is plain that, although some of the emotions which we feel towards certain groups of interrelated persons are *analogous* to love and to gratitude, they are not strictly the *same* emotions as love and gratitude. Love, in the strict sense, can be felt only towards something which we believe to be capable of loving us in return; it is always accompanied by a desire to be loved in return, and in the absence of such a response it tends at length to fade away. But we know perfectly well that a college or a public school cannot literally love us, though some of its members may do so. Yet this does not prevent us from feeling for it the emotion which I have described. Hence this emotion cannot be the same as love, in the strict sense. I conclude, then, that we cannot strictly love anything unless we believe it to be a person at the time when we are feeling the emotion.

I have now, I hope, made clear what is meant by 'being a person', and have stated some important additional facts about this characteristic. The next point to be considered is what is meant by being a 'God'. I think it is quite certain that the word 'God' is extremely ambiguous, and that it has commonly been used in at least three different, though connected, senses. I distinguish these as the popular sense, the theological sense, and the philosophical sense. In the popular sense of the word 'God' a God is *ipso facto* a person. This person is supposed to be analogous to a human being, but to be much more powerful. It is supposed to be able to do things of a different kind from those which human beings can do, and I think that it is generally conceived as not subject to death and as exercising an important influence on the weal or woe of human beings. This is all that is involved in the notion of a God in the popular sense. It is not supposed to be necessarily unique; it is not supposed to be infinitely powerful or perfectly wise, but merely to be a great deal more powerful and a great deal wiser than any living human being. And it is not supposed of necessity to have created men or to have created the material world, nor is the continued existence of nature and of men supposed necessarily to be dependent on the continued support of a God in this sense. Lastly, a God, in the popular sense, need not be morally superior to the best human beings, though he must be wiser than the wisest and stronger than the strongest human beings. Jehovah and Apollo are Gods in the popular sense; but Jehovah inculcated a high moral tone by precept rather than by example; and Apollo, in view of his relations with Cassandra and with Hyacinthus, might have had difficulty in obtaining the College testimonial for deacon's orders, which has never been held to require a superhuman level of moral achievement.

The word 'God', in the theological sense, has in one respect a wider meaning, and in other respects a narrower meaning, than the same word when used in the popular sense. A God, in the theological sense, need not be a person. According to orthodox Christian theology nothing can strictly be called 'God' except the Trinity as a whole. And the Trinity is certainly not a person. It is true that the Athanasian Creed says that the Father is God, and the Son is God, and the Holy Ghost is God; but it immediately adds that nevertheless there are not three Gods, but one God. If these statements are to be rendered consistent it is plain that the word 'God' must be used in different senses in the two. Nor is there the least difficulty in seeing what these senses are. The creed means that there is only one being that can with strict theological correctness be called 'God', viz. the Trinity as a whole. But each of the three persons can be called 'God' in a looser sense, because they are divine persons and essential constituents of the Trinity, which is God in the strict sense. Thus we might say loosely: 'The King is the sovereign of England, and the House of Lords is the sovereign of England, and the House of Commons is the sovereign of England.' But we should immediately add, in order to ward off possible errors, 'Of course, strictly speaking, there is only one sovereign of England, viz. the whole composed of King, Lords, and Commons in their proper constitutional relations to each other'. In the popular sense of 'God' each person of the Trinity is a God, and the Trinity as a whole is not a God; but, in the theological sense of the word, the persons are not Gods, whilst the whole composed of them is a God, and is the only God that there is.

The theological sense of the word 'God' is thus wider than the popular sense, in so far as the former can be applied either to a person or to certain wholes composed of interrelated persons, whilst the latter can be applied only to a person. In all other respects, however, the theological conception of God is narrower and more rigid than the popular conception. (1) Theologians push all the attributes of God to extremes. A God, in the theological sense, must be not merely very wise and very strong; he must be perfectly wise, and capable of doing anything which does not involve some internal logical inconsistency. (2) It is an essential part of the theological conception of God that he shall be morally perfect. (3) It is also part of the theological conception of God that he shall be unique. By this I mean that theologians are not content to hold that there happens to be only one thing answering to the definition of 'God', just as there happens to be only one thing answering to the description of 'the brother of Romulus'. They hold that, from the nature of the case, there *could* only be one God, just as, from the nature of the case, there *could* only be one individual answering to the description 'the most virtuous undergraduate in Trinity'. I think that this is one reason why theologians refuse to call the persons of the Trinity 'Gods', and confine the name 'God' to the Trinity as a whole. For, in all other respects but uniqueness, the persons of the Trinity would seem to be 'Gods' in the strict theological sense. (4) Finally, it is, I think, part of the theological conception of God that he cannot be identified with the universe. There has to be some asymmetrical relation between God and the rest of the universe, so that there is a sense in which we can say that the latter is existentially dependent on the former whilst the former is not existentially dependent on the latter.

I will make a few explanatory comments on the theological conception of God before passing to the philosophical conception. (1) I do not know how far the statements of theologians about the omniscience, omnipotence, and moral perfection of God are to be taken literally. It may be that this pushing of God's attributes to extremes is only intended as a compliment; and that when God is said to be perfectly wise, and good, and powerful, these phrases are to be regarded as analogous to 'Your Serene Transparency' when applied to German princes or 'His Most Religious Majesty' when applied to Charles II. Persons who used the latter phrases plainly did not intend to deny that German princes are opaque to light, or that Charles II was sometimes inclined to be a little careless about the higher spiritual values. And it may be that theologians do not intend their statements about God's attributes to be interpreted too literally. On that hypothesis the theological conception of God may not really differ so much from the popular conception as it seems to do. (2) We must clearly understand that not any and every group of interrelated persons would be regarded as a God even in the theological sense. It is necessary that the persons should be of a certain kind, and that their relations should have a certain high degree of intimacy. I think that the component persons must be such that each would be a God in the popular sense. And I think that the relations must be so intimate that none of the persons could exist apart from each other and outside the whole which they together form. We can see the necessity of both these conditions by taking cases where one is fulfilled and the other fails. The society of Olympus was a whole composed of interrelated persons, each of which was a God in the popular sense. But no one ever thought of regarding this whole as a God. And the reason is that the relations were not intimate enough. Zeus could have existed without Hera, and Hera could have existed without Zeus. Again, on Dr. McTaggart's view, the universe is a whole composed of persons so intimately related that none could have existed without the rest and apart from this whole. But no one would call the universe, as conceived by McTaggart, a 'God'. For its components are ourselves and other persons like us. And we are not Gods.

I pass now to the philosophic sense of the word 'God'. This is very much wider than either the theological or the popular sense of the word. A 'God', in the philosophical sense, need not be a person or a whole composed of nothing but interrelated persons. It therefore need not be wise or good, for these epithets apply only to persons. The name 'God' has been applied by certain philosophers to the Universe as a whole. Thus Hegel calls the Absolute 'God', and Spinoza talks of 'God or Nature' as synonymous terms like Augustus and Octavius. I think, however, that even in philosophy the name 'God' would be applied to the Universe only on the supposition that the Universe has a much more intimate internal unity than it appears to have at first sight, and that this unity is of a special kind. I think that all philosophers who have asserted the existence of God have held one of three views about the internal structure of the Universe: (1) That there is a certain *part* of the Universe which is not existentially dependent on anything else, and that all the rest of the Universe is existentially dependent on this part of it. This substance is then called 'God', whatever its other characteristics may be. This is the doctrine which is known as *Deism*. It is held by those philosophers who talk of God as 'the great First Cause'. (2) That there are certain characteristics of the Universe from which all its other characteristics necessarily follow. In that case the name 'God' will often be applied by philosophers to the Universe in virtue of its having this peculiar internal structure. Thus Spinoza distinguishes between Natura Naturans and Natura Naturata. Natura Naturans is the Universe, regarded as having certain fundamental characteristics from which all the rest follow. And Natura Naturata is the Universe, regarded as having all the characteristics which follow from these fundamental ones and as having no others. The Universe in its completeness is thus Natura Naturans and Natura Naturata; and Spinoza calls it 'God' in virtue of its having this kind of internal structure. This doctrine is one form of *Pantheism.* (3) That many of the features which seem to characterize the Universe or parts of it do not really belong to it, but are distorted and partly illusory appearances of characteristics which really do belong to it; in particular, that the Universe is in reality purely mental (i.e. that it is a mind or a society of minds), and that matter, space, and motion are distorted appearances of this mind and its states or of these minds and their mutual relations. The name 'God' is then often applied by philosophers to the Universe as it really is on this view, as distinct from the Universe as it appears to be. This, I suppose, is why Hegel called the Universe 'God'.

I think we may say that no philosopher asserts the existence of God unless he holds one of these three views about the nature of the Universe. On the other hand, many philosophers who do hold one of these three views would refuse to assert the existence of God, on the ground that the word has much more definite implications in theology and in ordinary life and that the use of it in the philosophic sense is misleading. E.g., the Universe, as Dr. McTaggart believed it to be, is a God in the third philosophic sense of the term. But McTaggart always refused to call it 'God' and blamed Hegel for doing so, on the ground that the phrase 'The Absolute' completely conveys his meaning whilst the word 'God' inevitably has associations and arouses emotions which are not justified by what he believed to be the facts. Here I agree with him. I think that we ought to confine the word 'God' to the theological and the popular senses of it; and that, unless we have reason to believe in the existence of a God or Gods in one of these senses, we ought not to say that we believe in the existence of God at all. Now, in these senses of the word, a God is necessarily a personal God. It is either a divine person, or it is a whole composed of nothing but divine persons so intimately related that none of them could exist apart from the rest and outside this whole. And I have defined what I mean by a 'person' and what I mean by 'divine'. The question then is: What reason, if any, have we to believe in the existence of divine persons? For it is plain that we can have no reason to believe in wholes composed of nothing but divine persons related in certain ways unless we have reason to believe in divine persons. And we might have reason to believe in the existence of divine persons whilst we had no means of deciding whether there was one or a dozen, and no means of deciding whether they stood in such and such relations to each other or not.

A man who believes in the existence of a divine person might try to justify his belief in one of three ways: (1) He might claim to know directly that such a being exists; or (2) he might claim to be able to prove the existence of such a being, or to make it very probable, by argument; or (3) he might believe it on the authority of others. I will consider these three alleged grounds in turn.

(1) A claim to direct knowledge of God's existence might take two different forms: *(a)* A man might find the proposition 'God exists' self-evident, as most men find the proposition $2 + 2 = 4$. Or *(b)* he might claim to know that God exists because he has in some supersensible way perceived God; just as most people claim to know that their chairs and tables exist because they have perceived these objects with their senses. It is quite certain that most people who believe in the existence of God do not pretend that their belief can be justified in either of these ways. Very few people would claim that they find the proposition that God exists self-evident; and still fewer people would claim to have themselves perceived God. But such claims have been made; and there is no way of positively refuting them. But there are reasons which ought to make the claimants themselves extremely doubtful, and which ought to

make us still more doubtful, about accepting their claims at their face value. It is notorious that propositions may seem self-evident although they are not true. For propositions which are inconsistent with each other, and which therefore cannot both be true, have seemed to be self-evident to different people. During the war it seemed self-evident to most Englishmen that Germans are morally inferior to the English; and it seemed equally self-evident to most Germans that Englishmen are morally inferior to Germans. One of these propositions must have been false, and probably both of them were. It may be said that in this case both parties were blinded by patriotic emotion; but it might equally be suggested that those persons who find the existence of God self-evident are blinded by religious emotion. If it appears self-evident to some people that there is a perfectly wise, good, and powerful being, it appears equally self-evident to many other people that the existence of such a being is inconsistent with the amount and kind of evil which exists in the world. Lastly, we know what sort of propositions have appeared to be self-evident to nearly everyone and have never been in any danger of being refuted. They are always propositions which assert that one quality is necessarily accompanied by a certain other quality; they are never propositions which assert that there exists an object which has such and such qualities. Now the proposition that God exists is of the latter kind, and not of the former; it is therefore most unlikely that it is really self-evident in the sense which it is self-evident that $2 + 2 = 4$.

Let us now consider the claim to know directly that God exists because one has perceived him in some supersensible way. Perception may roughly be defined as being in direct cognitive contact with an existent something which manifests certain qualities to the percipient, and is instinctively regarded by him as a part or an appearance of a more extended and more enduring object which has certain other qualities that are not manifested to the percipient at the moment. E.g., when I say that I see a penny, I am in direct cognitive contact with something which manifests the qualities of brownness and approximately circular shape; and I instinctively regard this as a part or an appearance of something which is permanent, which has an inside as well as an outside, and which has qualities like hardness and coldness that are not at present being manifested to me. If this belief be mistaken, I am not perceiving what would commonly be called a 'penny'. Now it is notorious that in ordinary sense-perception we are often deluded and sometimes wildly deluded. A simple example is mistaking a mere mirror-image for a physical object, and a still more striking example is perceiving snakes or pink rats when one is suffering from *delirium tremens.* It is quite certain, then, that there are delusive sense-perceptions. Now, in the case of sense-perception there are several tests which we can use to tell whether a perception is delusive or not. We can check one sense by another, e.g., sight by touch. We can appeal to the testimony of others and find out whether they see anything that corresponds to what we see. Finally, we can make inferences from what we think we perceive, and find whether they are verified. We can say: 'If there are really rats running about my bed my dog will be excited, bread and cheese will disappear, and so on.' And then we can see whether anything of the kind happens. Now it does not seem to be possible to test the alleged supersensible perception which some people claim to have of God by any of these means. Very few people have had the experiences at all; they are very difficult to describe, and therefore to compare; and it is very hard to point to any verifiable consequences which would follow if, and only if, these perceptions were not delusive. And, so far as I can see, nothing comparable to supporting the testimony of one sense by that of another is here possible. This does not, of course, prove that such supersensible perceptions *are* delusive; but it does show that we have no means of telling whether they are or are not. And, as we already know that many perceptions are delusive, this is a serious matter. As Hobbes says: 'When a man tells me that God spoke to him in a dream, all that I can be sure of is that he dreamed that God spoke to him.'

Even if we waive this objection, and take at their face value the statements of people who say that they have perceived God, they give no support whatever to the existence of a single perfectly wise, good, and powerful being, on whom all the rest of the Universe depends. They would tend rather to support the view that there is a bewildering variety of Gods in the popular sense, many of whom possess the oddest personal peculiarities.

(2) I pass now to arguments for the existence of God. These may be divided into deductive and inductive arguments. There are two of the former. One professes to prove from the definition of God that such a being must exist. This argument, if it were valid, would have the advantage of proving the existence of an unique individual possessed of all possible perfections, i.e. of God, in the theological sense. But it is universally admitted by philosophers and theologians that the argument is logically fallacious. It is called the Ontological Argument.

The second deductive argument starts from the premiss that no thing or event in nature exists of intrinsic necessity. Such necessity as we find within nature is purely relative and hypothetical. We can say that, given A, B necessarily follows. But we cannot say that A's existence or B's existence is intrinsically necessary if A and B be things or events in nature. It is then argued that, since nature as a whole has this contingent character, its existence must depend on something else whose existence is intrinsically necessary. This something is called 'God'. The argument is known as the Cosmological Argument. It is not so obviously fallacious as the Ontological Argument, and it has been accepted by some very able theologians and philosophers, such as St. Thomas Aquinas and Locke. Nevertheless, I agree with Kant and Hume that it is fallacious. Fortunately it is not necessary for me to prove this here, because the argument is irrelevant for our present purpose. For it is certain that, even if it be valid, it has no tendency to prove the existence of a *personal* God. At best it would prove the existence of God only in one of the three philosophical senses of that term, and not in the theological or the popular sense.

We may therefore dismiss the deductive arguments and consider the inductive ones. These start with certain admitted facts about nature and man, and argue back to the existence of God as the hypothesis which best explains these facts. Of course, the conclusions of such arguments could never be more than highly probable. But I do not think that this is a serious objection. We could quite reasonably say that the existence of God was 'proved' if it could be rendered as probable as the existence of Julius Caesar. Such arguments may be classified according to their premisses. *(a)* They may start from certain facts about inorganic nature and living organisms. *(b)* They may start from the fact that nature contains minds which are capable of distinguishing good and evil and of guiding their actions by ideals. *(c)* They may start from the fact that certain minds have, in addition, specifically religious emotions and other experiences. A complete inductive argument would presumably use all these facts as premisses.

(a) The first set of facts forms the basis of the famous Design Argument. This has been so thoroughly discussed by Hume in his *Dialogues on Natural Religion* that there is little left to say about it. I will content myself with the following remarks: (i) We must distinguish between the adaptation of inorganic nature to life in general, and the peculiarities of organisms as such. Let us begin with the former. It is certain that the condition of inorganic nature on the earth is, and has long been, extremely well adapted to the existence and growth of living organisms. So far as we know, the conditions under which organisms can exist are very peculiar, so that it is antecedently improbable that they should be fulfilled. Hence it is argued that they must have been deliberately brought about by a mind which wanted organisms to exist and flourish. This, I think, is a fallacious argument. It seems certain that the fulfilment of these conditions is really very local and temporary. They are probably not fulfilled now in the greater part of

the Universe; they certainly were not fulfilled formerly on the earth, and they almost certainly will cease to be fulfilled there in the distant future. Now it is not antecedently improbable that even very peculiar conditions shall be fulfilled for a comparatively short time in a comparatively small region of a universe which is indefinitely extended in both Space and Time.

(ii) The position about organisms themselves is as follows. An organism is an extremely intricate system which appears, even to the most superficial view, to be extraordinarily well adapted to preserve itself in face of varying conditions and to produce things like itself. And the more minutely we examine it the more accurately true do we find this to be. Now the only other things that we know of which have the least analogy to this are artificial machines. We know that these have been designed by minds, and we have not the least reason to think that they could have existed unless there had been minds which designed them and arranged their parts in such a way as to carry out these designs. Of course organisms are now produced by other organisms, just as typewriters are produced by other machines. But in the history of any artificial machine we eventually come back to a mind which had designs and arranged matter in such a way as to carry them out. We may assume, by analogy, that if we went far enough back in the history of organisms we should come on a mind which designed them and arranged matter accordingly. This mind was certainly not human, and it must certainly have been of superhuman wisdom and power to produce such results. It may therefore fairly be called 'God'.

I may say at once that I consider this to be an extremely strong argument if we grant two assumptions which are commonly made. The first is that organisms originated from inorganic matter. The second is that an organism really is nothing but a complicated machine, i.e. that its characteristic behaviour is wholly due to the peculiar arrangement of its parts, and is not due to entirely new properties of matter which first appear at the organic level. If we reject either of these assumptions the argument loses much of its force. If there have always been organisms of some kind, and no organism has ever originated from inorganic matter, there is no need to postulate a designing mind even though organisms be nothing but machines. And if organisms be not merely machines, there is no need to postulate a designing mind even though organisms did originate out of inorganic matter. Now, I do not see the least reason to believe that the characteristic behaviour of organisms can be wholly explained by the peculiar arrangement of their parts and the laws and properties of inorganic matter. Hence the argument for the existence of a designing mind from the peculiarities of organisms does not convince me, though I think it ought to have great weight with a purely mechanistic biologist.

(iii) Even if we accept the argument it will not prove the existence of God, in the theological sense. In the first place, it would prove only that a designing mind *had* existed in the past, not that it *does* exist now. It is quite compatible with this argument that God should have died long ago, or that he should have turned his attention to other parts of the Universe. Again, so far from proving the existence of a being on whom the rest of the Universe is existentially dependent, it negatives this supposition. It proves the existence of a superhuman workman faced with material whose properties he has to recognize and make use of, and not of a creative being. Thirdly, there is nothing in the facts to suggest that there is only one such being. And lastly, there is nothing to suggest that he is morally perfect. We must grant him superhuman skill and power, but the actual state of the world forces us to limit either his power or his goodness, or his wisdom, or all three. So, at the very best, the argument would prove only that at some time in the remote past there had been one or more Gods in the popular sense of the word.

(b) I will now consider the argument for the existence of God from the existence of minds like ours which can look before and after, make judgments of good and evil, and guide their conduct by them. It may be admitted that we cannot con-

ceive of any natural process by which minds could have arisen spontaneously from mere matter. So it has been suggested that we must postulate the existence of God to account for the facts. But, in the first place, there is no reason to accept the alleged facts; and secondly, the hypothesis of a God would provide no explanation of them. (i) It is quite possible that there have always been minds, and that no mind has ever originated from anything but another mind by a natural process. In that case the hypothesis of God is needless for the present purpose. (ii) If we make the hypothesis we have explained absolutely nothing. We are still obliged to suppose that there have always been minds, though not always non-divine minds. And the production of non-divine minds from mere matter remains just as unintelligible whether we say that it happens spontaneously or that it is miraculously accomplished by God.

The fact is that the Argument from Design and the argument which I have just been discussing illustrate an important general principle. If you start with a sufficiently narrow and inadequate view of nature you will have to postulate a God to get you out of the difficulties in which it lands you. E.g., if you insist that living organisms are mere machines, you have to postulate God to construct them out of unorganized matter. And if you insist that nature is fundamentally material and that mind is a kind of afterthought, you have to postulate God to account for the origin of mind, though, as I have pointed out, the hypothesis does not here really help you. But why should you start with these narrow and inadequate views of nature? They have no trace of self-evidence and they conflict with the observable facts in every direction. And, unless you make this mistake at the outset, I do not think you will be able to find any inductive proof of the existence of God.

(c) Finally, I come to the argument for the existence of God which is based on the occurrence of specifically mystical and religious experiences. I am prepared to admit that such experiences occur among people of different races and social traditions, and that they have occurred at all periods of history. I am prepared to admit that, although the experiences have differed considerably at different times and places, and although the interpretations which have been put on them have differed still more, there are probably certain characteristics which are common to all of them and which suffice to distinguish them from all other kinds of experience. In view of this I think it more likely than not that in religious and mystical experience men come into contact with some Reality or some aspect of Reality which they do not come into contact with in any other way.

But I do not think that there is any good reason to suppose that this Reality which manifests itself to certain men in religious and mystical experiences is personal. I think that we are inclined to believe this because we are most familiar with the religious experiences of Western Europeans and of Jews, most of whom have put this interpretation upon them. We do not know, or we forget, that the mystics and religious teachers of the Far East on the whole definitely reject this interpretation. And we are inclined to forget that certain Europeans, such as Plotinus and Spinoza, who have had these experiences also reject this interpretation of them.

I think on the whole, then, that there is no inductive argument which makes it at all highly probable that there is a personal God.

(3) It only remains to consider whether it is reasonable to believe in the existence of a personal God on the authority of other men. We all believe many propositions on authority, and in many cases it would be most irrational not to do so. It is rational to believe a proposition on authority if one of two conditions is fulfilled. (i) If experts agree that it can be proved, but the argument is too difficult or unfamiliar for me to follow it myself. (ii) If persons whom I know to be competent and trustworthy tell me that they have perceived certain things which I have not perceived myself. I accept many propositions in mathematics on the authority of Professor Hardy, who tells me that they can be proved; and I accept many propositions in physics on the authority of

Professor Rutherford, whom I know to be a trustworthy person and a highly skilled experimenter and observer. But neither of these conditions is fulfilled in the case of the proposition that there exists a personal God. There is no consensus of experts about the alleged proofs, and I can see for myself that these arguments are fallacious. And I have tried to show that the claims of certain persons to have perceived God in some supersensible way are to be regarded with grave suspicion even if we accept their *bona fides.* Hence it would be irrational for me to believe in the existence of a personal God on the authority of others.

To conclude. Whether there be in fact a personal God or not, it seems to me that we have no good reason to believe in the existence of such a being. I think that there are such grave difficulties in the notion of a God in the theological sense that there are strong reasons against believing that such a being exists. These objections do not apply to the notion of Gods in the popular sense. For all I can see there may be dozens of such Gods; and the only reason *against* being a polytheist is that there is no reason *for* being one.

DISCUSSION QUESTIONS

1. Broad thinks it is logically possible to *be* a mind without immediately *knowing* oneself to be a mind. Do you agree? Explain.
2. Are you persuaded by Broad that there are different degrees of personality? Explain.
3. Describe the attributes of what Broad calls "an ideal person."
4. What is Broad's view of intelligent domestic animals? How do their owners treat them, according to Broad? Is he right?
5. Broad claims that love, in the strict sense, can be felt only towards something (namely, a person) which we believe to be capable of loving us in return. Do you agree? Explain.
6. Explain why Broad thinks that the society of Olympian gods cannot constitute a God in the theological sense.
7. If the Cosmological Argument were valid, why does Broad think it would still fail to prove the existence of a *personal* God?
8. Does Broad think there is any inductive proof of the existence of God? Explain.
9. Explain why Broad thinks it would be irrational for him to believe in the existence of a personal God on the authority of others. Do you agree?

Chapter 24

RICHARD TAYLOR

Taylor (1919–2003), who studied with Roderick Chisholm at Brown University, taught mostly at Brown, Columbia University, and the University of Rochester, from which he retired in 1985. He served as a commissioned officer on a submarine in World War II and became a pacifist late in life. His books include the popular and provocative Metaphysics *(1963, 4th ed. 1992),* Action and Purpose *(1966),* Good and Evil *(1970),* Freedom, Anarchy and the Law *(1973),* The Joys of Beekeeping *(1974),* Having Love Affairs *(1982),* Virtue Ethics *(1991), and* Restoring Pride: The Lost Virtue of Our Age *(1996).*

In this 1969 essay, Taylor argues for two claims—first, that there is no personal self because a particular person or self is the same thing as his body, and second, that this position is in keeping with the view of Gotama Buddha that there is no self. To say that "I have a body" does not mean that I am one thing and my body is another, according to Taylor. Rather, it is similar to saying that a table has four legs and a top. Wouldn't it be odd to say of a person's body *that it is politically liberal? Taylor replies that when we see a man tilling a field or reading an instruction book, it would be incongruous to say that his body is tilling, and it would be absurd to say that his mind is reading instructions. Rather, it is a palpable, living human body that does these things. One mistake is to say that a person "has" a sensation or thought, instead of simply saying that he senses or thinks. A second mistake is to assume that living human beings, which are bodies, cannot think because things like bricks, which are also bodies, cannot think. Taylor instead infers that some physical objects, namely, human beings, do think.*

The Anattā Doctrine and Personal Identity

Descartes saw that he could not identify himself with his body. He therefore vacillated between identifying himself with his mind, and with an awkward amalgam of his mind and his body. Gotama Buddha more profoundly argued that one could not identify himself with his mind either, nor, indeed, with anything at all. This is his doctrine of *anattā,* that there is no self. He evidently considered rejection of belief in the self as essential to blessedness, as Lucretius similarly abominated belief in life after death, for similar reasons.

It is essential to note, however, that the self whose existence the Buddha denied was an inner enduring self, having an identity through time and presumably being, therefore, capable of an existence independent of the body and the world, even after death. Thus:

> If there really existed the Self, there would be also something which belonged to the Self. As, however, in truth and reality, neither the Self, nor anything belonging to the Self, can be found, is it not therefore really an utter fool's doctrine to say: 'This is the world, this am I; after death I shall be permanent, persisting, and eternal'?[1]

And all speculations on the self—whether or not it is the self that perceives the self, whether or not the self is permanent, or subject to change—he dismissed as "mere views, a thicket of views, a puppet-show of views, a toil of views, a snare of views" through which no man will ever be "freed from rebirth, from decay, and from death, from sorrow, pain, grief and despair"—in short, from suffering[2]

Without considering the ethical and religious implications of this teaching, I wish in an indirect way to defend the claim itself, that there is no personal self. My approach will be indirect, in the sense that I shall maintain that a particular person or self is one and the same thing as his body.

This will, moreover, be quite in keeping with the claim of the Buddha, for in one place he said:

> It would be better for the unlearned worlding to regard this body, built up of the four elements, as his Self, rather than the mind. For it is evident that this body may last for a year, for two years, for three, four, five, or ten years, or even for a hundred years or more; but that which is called thought, or mind, or consciousness, continuously, during day and night, arises as one thing, and passes away as another thing.[3]

Now one should not, of course, on the basis of such passages as this, represent it as the teaching of ancient Buddhism that the self and the body are one, for it was clearly the doctrine of Gotama that there simply *is* no self. The difference between these two claims is, however, only one of emphasis; for, given that there are such things as living human bodies, i.e., living men, which the Buddha hardly denied, then the two claims are logically

Source: Richard Taylor, "The Anattā Doctrine and Personal Identity," *Philosophy East and West* 19, no. 4 (Oct. 1969): 359–366. Reprinted with permission of University of Hawai'i Press.

equivalent. For, given this uncontroversial presupposition, it is one and the same thing to say (a) there is no self, and (b) the self and the body are one and the same or, perhaps better, there is no personal self other than just the body.

I shall, in pursuing this theme, address myself to the question, What is a person? And I shall maintain that any given person, such as oneself, is identical with, or is one and the same thing as, that palpable physical object he refers to as his body; in short, that no philosophical reason can be given for believing in any inner "self" or person other than this. One argument often put forth for denying this claim, namely, that a man retains his identity through time, while his body does not, will be briefly discussed at the end.

Now this claim, that there is no inner self, or, as I prefer to express it, that the only thing a man can claim as himself is his body, is a purely negative one, and cannot therefore be proved by any philosophical discourse. All I can do, therefore, is to show that it is consistent with common sense, not inconsistent with anything that is known to be true, and that the typical philosophical arguments that are often given against it are inconclusive and, usually, question-begging.

WHAT IS A PERSON?

Now this question can, of course, be answered in a silly and superficial way, by saying that any given person is simply identical with himself. This, however, only calls attention to the identity of the ordinary concept of a person and the philosophical concept of the self, for it is just conceptually true that every person is a "self" and vice versa. And it is just for this reason that we are entitled to ask, What is a person? rather than the seemingly more esoteric question, What is the self?

But it is, of course, possible to suggest answers that are not merely analytic. One might say, for instance, that a given person, such as oneself, is (a) a particular body; for instance, that I am, or that I am identical with, or that I am one and the same thing as, that palpable physical object which I refer to as "my body." Or one might say that a given person, such as oneself, is (b) a particular mind; for instance, that I am identical with that thinking thing I refer to as "my mind." Or again, it might be claimed that a given person, such as oneself, is (c) an amalgam of these two; for instance, that I am identical with that composite of things I refer to as "my body" and "my mind." Or finally, it can be argued that a person is none of these things, but rather that a given person, such as oneself, is (d) something "primitive"; for example, that I am identical with something which is neither a body nor a mind, but something (namely, a given person, myself) which *has* both physical and mental properties.

This last answer is, I believe, esoteric. There is, in any case, no need to examine independently any of the last three answers if the first answer will do.

PERSONS AND BODIES

Apart from certain religious presuppositions, which I shall leave aside, there appear to be two kinds of consideration, and only two, which have led philosophers to doubt that persons are simply identical with those physical objects we see about us all the time and which we refer to as living human beings, or simply as men. The first is linguistic, and the second metaphysical.

LINGUISTIC CONSIDERATIONS

The grammatical forms we use to refer to our bodies and their parts appear to suggest a distinction between ourselves and our bodies. Thus, everyone can say truly "I am a person, and I have a body," though there seem to be no contexts in which one could say "I am a body, and I have a person." Again, it is usual for one to refer to his bodily parts, and even to the totality of these, by means of a first person possessive pronoun. For example, I can speak of my hands and feet, my heart, my brain, and even my body, which seems to suggest a relationship between myself and my body which is perhaps something like ownership or possession but not, apparently, identity.

Reply

Such purely linguistic considerations as these are highly superficial and prove nothing. In fact, if one compares them with the manner in which we commonly speak of other ordinary physical objects, they appear perfectly consistent with the supposition that there is no self in any absolute sense, but only bodily constituents related to each other and functioning in such a way as to constitute a human being. The Buddha has, with familiar analogies, made this point:

> Just as that what we designate by the name of 'chariot,' has no existence apart from axle, wheels, shaft, carriage, and so forth; or, as the word 'house' is merely a convenient designation for various materials put together after a certain fashion so as to enclose a portion of space, and there is no separate house-entity in existence:—in exactly the same way, that which we call a 'being,' or an 'individual,' or a 'person,' or by the name 'I', is nothing but a changing combination of physical and psychical phenomena, and has no real existence in itself.[4]

And I would express what I take to be the same point as follows.

Every man can truly say, "I have a body." But in the same way one can say of any physical object whatever that it has a body. Thus, I can say of my car that it has a body, or of a table that it has four legs and a top—and this might be *all* it has. This hardly suggests that the car or table is one thing and its body another. Similarly, I can say that I have (say) a heart, legs, arms, brain, and so on, but no special relationship is here connoted by "have." Such a statement only means, or certainly may only mean, that I consist of a heart, legs, brain, and so on, along with other physical parts, all related to each other and functioning in a manner necessary to constitute a living human being or, which is the same thing, a person.

METAPHYSICAL CONSIDERATIONS

If one ventures any true description of something, A, and likewise any true description of something, B, then one is entitled to affirm that these are alternative descriptions of the same thing—or in other words, that A and B are one and the same thing—if and only if the description rendered of A, whatever it might be, can now be applied to B without ceasing to be true; and, of course, vice versa. Thus, if one were to describe a given man A as the father of numerous children, and a given man B as the junior senator from New York, then one would be entitled to affirm that A and B are one and the same man only if one could likewise say that A is the junior senator from New York and B the father of numerous children. And in case *every* descriptive statement true of A turns out to be true of B as well, and vice versa, then it follows that A and B are the same man; or in other words, that these are all just alternative ways of describing one particular man.

Now philosophers have been apt in pointing out the incongruity of certain descriptive locutions which, it would seem, would not be incongruous if men thought of themselves and their bodies as identical things. A person can sometimes truly say of himself, for example, that he loves his country, is subject to quick changes of mood, admires Plato's theory of forms, is politically liberal, and things of that sort. It would seem utterly incongruous, however, to assert such things of any body whatsoever, and hence of one's own body; to assert, for example, that his *body* is politically liberal. There should not be such incongruity, however, if persons and their bodies are identical. For if I am one and the same thing as my body, then it must follow that if I, for example, admire Plato, then that physical object I refer to as "my body" must admire Plato too, this body referred to in the second statement and this self or "I" referred to in the first being one and the same thing, namely, that person I call "myself." But since this consequence seems absurd, we seem obliged to reject the antecedent from which it is derived; namely, that I and my body are one and the same thing.

CAN MATTER THINK?

There have in the history of thought been many ways of expressing essentially this same metaphysical point, all of which are capsulated in the dictum that "matter cannot think." Thus, it has been claimed that *ideas* can exist only in a mind, not in a body. Or again, it is thought obvious that matter cannot experience *self-awareness;* but since persons are undoubtedly sometimes aware of themselves, it follows again that persons are not bodies. Or again, it is said that sensations and feelings are not material states or processes. One could never say that *sensations* or *feelings* are transpiring in a test tube, for example, because the only kind of process that can occur there is a physical process. Persons, however, do have sensations and feelings, and are therefore quite unlike the matter that can exist in a test tube. Or again, there are certain uniquely mental things—*mental images,* for instance—which can by no means be described in terms of the concepts we apply to bodies. One can neither say, for example, that such images are soluble in alcohol, nor that they are not. Persons, however, can possess such things as mental images, so it would seem that persons must themselves be nonphysical things; and so on.

It is fairly clear that all of these and similar familiar remarks are but more or less crude ways of saying that matter cannot think, construing thinking sufficiently broadly to include feeling, sensing, imagining, and so on. And this dictum, that matter cannot think, is itself a crude, epigrammatic way of expressing the previous metaphysical point, to the effect that there are many descriptive predications which are applicable to persons but not to their bodies. What we have here are certain descriptions which, it is claimed, "make sense" when applied to persons, but "make no sense" when applied to any body whatsoever, and hence make no sense when applied to one's own body.

Reply

In order to overturn this line of thought we have to get a fresh orientation on the thing, and this I propose to do as follows.

When one sees a man—sees a man tilling a field, for instance, or assembling an engine—what one sees is a person. One can point to that man and say, for instance, that he, that person, is tilling, tinkering, or whatnot. It would be incongruous to say that his visible *body* is tilling or tinkering, unless this were understood as a funny way of saying that the man himself, the person pointed to, is tilling or tinkering; for this latter is the truth of the matter. One might say of the man assembling the engine, for instance, that he is reading the instructions, inferring the proper position of this part or that, getting things wrong sometimes, perhaps, and right other times, adjusting this or that, contemplating the result, checking against diagrams, and so on. It would be quite strange to say that his body was doing these things. It would be incongruous, indeed, absurd, to set all these activities down to his mind; to say that his mind is reading instructions, adjusting this and that, and so on. It would be downright primitive to attempt distributing these various tasks between two things—to say, for example, that his mind makes the appropriate inferences, that his body then makes the needed adjustments, that his mind then contemplates the result, his body moving parts this way and that, and so on—as though the work of assembling the engine were somehow divided between them.

Clearly, we are talking about one and the same being when we say all of these things. And the being we are describing is a certain man, whom we see and point to. And that man, thus described, is a person; for nothing except a person could be so described.

The next thing to observe, then, is that this man, whom we see and point to, and who is one and the same thing as the person we are describing, is a visible, palpable, physical object. What else, indeed, *could* one see and point to? And from this it surely does follow that the person we are describing, the man who is assembling the engine, is a visible, palpable object, a living human body or, in short, a body.

TWO COMMON MISTAKES

Why, then, do such commonsense observations as these fail to satisfy so many philosophers? The explanation is mainly found, I think, in two common mistakes. The first is to treat certain psychological states and activities as things rather than as states and activities, and the second is to suppose that the human body, being a body, can have only those capacities that are discoverable in lifeless things. I shall consider these in turn.

The First Mistake

Instead of saying, for example, that a given person, such as oneself, "has" an image, sensation, or thought, one can simply say that he imagines, senses, or thinks. For instance, instead of saying that I "have" a mental image of my birthplace, I can surely say, conveying exactly the same claim, that I *imagine* my birthplace. The former inept but common expression implies the existence of a thing called an image. It is true that no such thing can be a physical thing, but it should not therefore be supposed that it must be a nonphysical thing. One can say, rather, that there is no such thing to begin with; that there is only a person *imagining* something. This implies only the existence of that person, that is, a certain man, or living human being, and, perhaps (though not necessarily), the thing imagined. There is no reason why that person may not be the very man one points to when one points to him. Indeed, it must be, for otherwise we could not point and say truly that he, the person so indicated, is imagining his birthplace.

This same observation can be applied, I think, to every other philosophical locution that is brought forth as implying a distinction between persons and their bodies—such as "idea," "sensation," "thought," and so on. At least, I have discovered none which cannot be so dealt with.

The Second Mistake

It seems quite obviously gratuitous to assume that the living human beings we see (which are bodies) can have no capacities not exemplified in inanimate things, and to rest this assumption on nothing more than the fact that things of either kind are bodies. One might as well claim that inanimate things, like bricks and stones, *can* think, resting this on the fact that, like men, they are bodies. If one gravely asserts that matter cannot think, and then quite validly infers from this that persons, who think, are not bodies, we can surely reply that since those living human beings we see around us all the time *do* think—or at least, that there is every reason to believe they do, and no reason to doubt it—then the proper inference should be that some physical objects, namely, those very men we see, do think. And the same, of course, applies to every other capacity which is alleged to be a unique capacity of a person: the capacity to reason, daydream, plan for the future, and so on.

PERSONAL IDENTITY THROUGH TIME

Are there, then, any special problems arising from the identity of a given person through time which cast doubt on the foregoing suggestions? I cannot attempt discussion of all such alleged problems, but one or two samples will, I believe, typify them all. And it can be seen, I think, that they simply beg the question.

Thus, it might be asked, what if two persons changed bodies—perhaps gradually, bit by bit, over a long period? Or what if they merely exchanged brains? Or suppose you and I were physically conditioned, perhaps unbeknown to us, in such a way that I (note) "woke up" with all your memories and you with all mine. Which would be you, and which me? What if, for example, I were forced to decide which of these bodies should suffer pain and death, the other to be set free—which, out of self-interest, would I designate for each fate?

Now it should be obvious that in all such questions it is simply presupposed that a person is something distinct from his body, such that the question can, it is thought, be seriously asked, Which person goes with which body?

To see the absurdity of these questions and others like them, let us consider two nonhuman things, such as two automobiles, yours and mine, and fabricate similar "problems." Thus, what if the two cars changed bodies, perhaps gradually, bit by bit, over a long period? Which would be yours, and which mine? Or what if we merely exchanged their engines? Or suppose my car were made to look just like yours, and yours like mine. Suppose further that each was physically conditioned, perhaps unbeknown to us, in such a way that there was every reason to believe that what I supposed was my car had the history which was uniquely that of your car, and vice versa. Which would be which? What if I were forced to decide which of the two cars should be wrecked, and which overhauled? Which, out of self-interest, would I designate for each fate?

Now to affirm an analogy here is, of course, to presuppose that persons are, like cars, identical with their bodies. But to deny the analogy is equally to presuppose that they are not. So, just as this alleged analogy does not *show* that persons are bodies—which it was not intended to show—the denial that the two cases are analogous does not prove any distinction between persons and their bodies. It merely presupposes that distinction.

I do affirm, however, that no absurdity whatever can be derived from giving the same kinds of answers to both sets of questions. If my car were made to look like yours, I might think it was yours—but I would be wrong. If it were conditioned to appear to have had the history yours had, I might think it was yours—but I would be wrong. If all the parts of these objects were gradually exchanged, there would be a point at which each would be about half yours, half mine. If the engines were switched, the exact truth would be that my car had your engine, or that your engine had my car. And, I submit, exactly the same kinds of answer can be given, with no absurdity whatever, to the similar questions about persons and their bodies. What any man would *think* or *say* under such fanciful circumstances is not in every case easy to see, but what the truth of the matter would be to someone not misled and knowing the facts, knowing just what has happened with respect to the two men involved, is not so recondite.

NOTES

1. *The Word of the Buddha,* ed. Nyanatiloka (Colombo: Word of the Buddha Publishing Committee, 1952), p. 34.
2. *Ibid.,* p. 34.
3. *Ibid.,* p. 40.
4. *Ibid.,* p. 11.

DISCUSSION QUESTIONS

1. On the basis of what Taylor quotes, how similar is the Buddha's view of what human beings are to Taylor's?
2. Can matter think? Explain your view.
3. Taylor says that if he and another person switched brains, then that would present no more difficult a problem for their personal identities than if his car and the other person's car switched engines. Do you agree with this? Explain.
4. In Leibniz's dialogue, Theophilus says that his finger is not a part of him, it *belongs* to him. How would Taylor respond to this?

Chapter 25

HARRY G. FRANKFURT

Since receiving his Ph.D. from Johns Hopkins in 1954, Frankfurt has been on the philosophy faculty at Ohio State University, SUNY Binghamton, Rockefeller University, and Yale University. He is currently Professor Emeritus at Princeton University. His books include Demons, Dreamers, and Madmen: The Defense of Reason in Descartes' Metaphysics *(1968),* The Importance of What We Care About *(1988), and* The Reasons of Love *(2003).*

In this widely influential essay, Frankfurt begins with Strawson's concept of a person. Frankfurt holds that nonhuman animals have only first-order desires (e.g., wanting to eat, sleep, walk), whereas only humans also have second-order desires (e.g., wanting to have different preferences than they do). If an agent A *wants his desire* X *to effectively motivate his actions, that is, to be his will, then* A *has a second-order volition. Frankfurt argues that persons are agents with second-order volitions. He defines* wantons *as agents who may or may not have second-order desires, but lack second-order volitions. Wantons are not concerned with the desirability of their desires. All nonhuman animals and all very young children Frankfurt considers wantons. Perhaps some adult human addicts are also wantons. Frankfurt sees the concept of a person as the concept of a type of entity for whom the freedom of its will may be a problem.*

Freedom of the Will and the Concept of a Person

What philosophers have lately come to accept as analysis of the concept of a person is not actually analysis of *that* concept at all. Strawson, whose usage represents the current standard, identifies the concept of a person as "the concept of a type of entity such that *both* predicates ascribing states of consciousness *and* predicates ascribing corporeal characteristics . . . are equally applicable to a single individual of that single type."[1] But there are many entities besides persons that have both mental and physical properties. As it happens—though it seems extraordinary that this should be so—there is no common English word for the type of entity Strawson has in mind, a type that includes not only human beings but animals of various lesser species as well. Still, this hardly justifies the misappropriation of a valuable philosophical term.

Whether the members of some animal species are persons is surely not to be settled merely by determining whether it is correct to apply to them, in addition to predicates ascribing corporeal characteristics, predicates that ascribe states of consciousness. It does violence to our language to endorse the application of the term 'person' to those numerous creatures which do have both psychological and material properties but which are manifestly not persons in any normal sense of the word. This misuse of language is doubtless innocent of any theoretical error. But although the offense is "merely verbal," it does significant harm. For it gratuitously diminishes our philosophical vocabulary, and it increases the likelihood that we will overlook the important area of inquiry with which the term 'person' is most naturally associated. It might have been expected that no problem would be of more central and persistent concern to philosophers than that of understanding what we ourselves essentially are. Yet this problem is so generally neglected that it has been possible to make off with its very name almost without being noticed and, evidently, without evoking any widespread feeling of loss.

There is a sense in which the word 'person' is merely the singular form of 'people' and in which both terms connote no more than membership in a certain biological species. In those senses of the word which are of greater philosophical interest, however, the criteria for being a person do not serve primarily to distinguish the members of our own species from the members of other species. Rather, they are designed to capture those attributes which are the subject of our most humane concern with ourselves and the source of what we regard as most important and most problematical

Source: Harry G. Frankfurt, "Freedom of the Will and the Concept of a Person." *The Journal of Philosophy,* 68: (1): 5–20 January 14, 1971. Reprinted with the permission of *The Journal of Philosophy* and the author.

in our lives. Now these attributes would be of equal significance to us even if they were not in fact peculiar and common to the members of our own species. What interests us most in the human condition would not interest us less if it were also a feature of the condition of other creatures as well.

Our concept of ourselves as persons is not to be understood, therefore, as a concept of attributes that are necessarily species-specific. It is conceptually possible that members of novel or even of familiar nonhuman species should be persons; and it is also conceptually possible that some members of the human species are not persons. We do in fact assume, on the other hand, that no member of another species is a person. Accordingly, there is a presumption that what is essential to persons is a set of characteristics that we generally suppose—whether rightly or wrongly—to be uniquely human.

It is my view that one essential difference between persons and other creatures is to be found in the structure of a person's will. Human beings are not alone in having desires and motives, or in making choices. They share these things with the members of certain other species, some of whom even appear to engage in deliberation and to make decisions based upon prior thought. It seems to be peculiarly characteristic of humans, however, that they are able to form what I shall call "second-order desires" or "desires of the second order."

Besides wanting and choosing and being moved *to do* this or that, men may also want to have (or not to have) certain desires and motives. They are capable of wanting to be different, in their preferences and purposes, from what they are. Many animals appear to have the capacity for what I shall call "first-order desires" or "desires of the first order," which are simply desires to do or not to do one thing or another. No animal other than man, however, appears to have the capacity for reflective self-evaluation that is manifested in the formation of second-order desires.[2]

1

The concept designated by the verb 'to want' is extraordinarily elusive. A statement of the form "*A* wants to *X*"—taken by itself, apart from a context that serves to amplify or to specify its meaning—conveys remarkably little information. Such a statement may be consistent, for example, with each of the following statements: (a) the prospect of doing *X* elicits no sensation or introspectible emotional response in *A;* (b) *A* is unaware that he wants to *X;* (c) *A* believes that he does not want to *X;* (d) *A* wants to refrain from *X*-ing; (e) *A* wants to *Y* and believes that it is impossible for him both to *Y* and to *X;* (f) *A* does not "really" want to *X;* (g) *A* would rather die than *X;* and so on. It is therefore hardly sufficient to formulate the distinction between first-order and second-order desires, as I have done, by suggesting merely that someone has a first-order desire when he wants to do or not to do such-and-such, and that he has a second-order desire when he wants to have or not to have a certain desire of the first order.

As I shall understand them, statements of the form "*A* wants to *X*" cover a rather broad range of possibilities.[3] They may be true even when statements like (a) through (g) are true: when *A* is unaware of any feelings concerning *X*-ing, when he is unaware that he wants to *X,* when he deceives himself about what he wants and believes falsely that he does not want to *X,* when he also has other desires that conflict with his desire to *X,* or when he is ambivalent. The desires in question may be conscious or unconscious, they need not be univocal, and *A* may be mistaken about them. There is a further source of uncertainty with regard to statements that identify someone's desires, however, and here it is important for my purposes to be less permissive.

Consider first those statements of the form "*A* wants to *X*" which identify first-order desires—that is, statements in which the term 'to *X*' refers to an action. A statement of this kind does not, by itself, indicate the relative strength of *A*'s desire to *X*. It does not make it clear whether this desire is at all likely to play a decisive role in what *A* actually does or tries to do. For it may correctly be said that *A* wants to *X* even when his desire to *X* is only one among his desires and when it is far from being paramount among them. Thus, it may be true that *A* wants to *X* when he strongly prefers to do something else instead; and it may be true that he wants to *X* despite the fact that, when he acts, it is not the desire to *X* that motivates him to do what he does. On the other hand, someone who states that *A* wants to *X* may mean to convey that it is this desire that is motivating or moving *A* to do what he is actually doing or that *A* will in fact be moved by this desire (unless he changes his mind) when he acts.

It is only when it is used in the second of these ways that, given the special usage of 'will' that I propose to adopt, the statement identifies *A*'s will. To identify an agent's will is either to identify the desire (or desires) by which he is motivated in some action he performs or to identify the desire (or desires) by which he will or would be motivated when or if he acts. An agent's will, then, is identical with one or more of his first-order desires. But the notion of the will, as I am employing it, is not coextensive with the notion of first-order desires. It is not the notion of something that merely inclines an agent in some degree to act in a certain way. Rather, it is the notion of an *effective* desire—one that moves (or will or would move) a person all the way to action. Thus the notion of the will is not coextensive with the notion of what an agent intends to do. For even though someone may have a settled intention to do *X*, he may nonetheless do something else instead of doing *X* because, despite his intention, his desire to do *X* proves to be weaker or less effective than some conflicting desire.

Now consider those statements of the form "*A* wants to *X*" which identify second-order desires—that is, statements in which the term 'to *X*' refers to a desire of the first order. There are also two kinds of situation in which it may be true that *A* wants to want to *X*. In the first place, it might be true of *A* that he wants to have a desire to *X* despite the fact that he has a univocal desire, altogether free of conflict and ambivalence, to refrain from *X*-ing. Someone might want to have a certain desire, in other words, but univocally want that desire to be unsatisfied.

Suppose that a physician engaged in psychotherapy with narcotics addicts believes that his ability to help his patients would be enhanced if he understood better what it is like for them to desire the drug to which they are addicted. Suppose that he is led in this way to want to have a desire for the drug. If it is a genuine desire that he wants, then what he wants is not merely to feel the sensations that addicts characteristically feel when they are gripped by their desires for the drug. What the physician wants, insofar as he wants to have a desire, is to be inclined or moved to some extent to take the drug.

It is entirely possible, however, that, although he wants to be moved by a desire to take the drug, he does not want this desire to be effective. He may not want it to move him all the way to action. He need not be interested in finding out what it is like to take the drug. And insofar as he now wants only to *want* to take it, and not to *take* it, there is nothing in what he now wants that would be satisfied by the drug itself. He may now have, in fact, an altogether univocal desire *not* to take the drug; and he may prudently arrange to make it impossible for him to satisfy the desire he would have if his desire to want the drug should in time be satisfied.

It would thus be incorrect to infer, from the fact that the physician now wants to desire to take the drug, that he already does desire to take it. His second-order desire to be moved to take the drug does not entail that he has a first-order desire to take it. If the drug were now to be administered to him, this might satisfy no desire that is implicit in his desire to want to take it. While he wants to want to take the drug, he may have *no* desire to take it; it may be that *all* he wants is to taste the desire for it. That is, his desire to have a certain desire that he does not have may not be a desire that his will should be at all different than it is.

Someone who wants only in this truncated way to want to *X* stands at the margin of preciosity, and the fact that he wants to want to *X* is not pertinent to the identification of his will. There is, however, a second kind of situation that may be described by '*A* wants to want to *X*'; and when the statement is used to describe a situation of this second kind, then it does pertain to what *A* wants his will to be. In such cases the statement means that *A* wants the desire to *X* to be the desire that moves him effectively to act. It is not merely that he wants the desire to *X* to be among the desires by which, to one degree or another, he is moved or inclined to act. He wants this desire to be effective—that is, to provide the motive in what he actually does. Now when the statement that *A* wants to want to *X* is used in this way, it does entail that *A* already has a desire to *X*. It could not be true both that *A* wants the desire to *X* to move him into action and that he does not want to *X*. It is only if he does want to *X* that he can coherently want the desire to *X* not merely to be one of his desires but, more decisively, to be his will.[4]

Suppose a man wants to be motivated in what he does by the desire to concentrate on his work. It is necessarily true, if this supposition is correct, that he already wants to concentrate on his work. This desire is now among his desires. But the question of whether or not his second-order desire is fulfilled does not turn merely on whether the desire he wants is one of his desires. It turns on whether this desire is, as he wants it to be, his effective desire or will. If, when the chips are down, it is his desire to concentrate on his work that moves him to do what he does, then what he wants at that time is indeed (in the relevant sense) what he wants to want. If it is some other desire that actually moves him when he acts, on the other hand, then what he wants at that time is not (in the relevant sense) what he wants to want. This will be so despite the fact that the desire to concentrate on his work continues to be among his desires.

II

Someone has a desire of the second order either when he wants simply to have a certain desire or when he wants a certain desire to be his will. In situations of the latter kind, I shall call his second-order desires "second-order volitions" or "volitions of the second order." Now it is having second-order volitions, and not having second-order desires generally, that I regard as essential to being a person. It is logically possible, however unlikely, that there should be an agent with second-order desires but with no volitions of the second order. Such a creature, in my view, would not be a person. I shall use the term 'wanton' to refer to agents who have first-order desires but who are not persons because, whether or not they have desires of the second order, they have no second-order volitions.[5]

The essential characteristic of a wanton is that he does not care about his will. His desires move him to do certain things, without its being true of him either that he wants to be moved by those desires or that he prefers to be moved by other desires. The class of wantons includes all nonhuman animals that have desires and all very young children. Perhaps it also includes some adult human beings as well. In any case, adult humans may be more or less wanton; they may act wantonly, in response to first-order desires concerning which they have no volitions of the second order, more or less frequently.

The fact that a wanton has no second-order volitions does not mean that each of his first-order desires is translated heedlessly and at once into action. He may have no opportunity to act in accordance with some of his desires. Moreover, the translation of his desires into action may be delayed or precluded either by conflicting desires of the first order or by the intervention of deliberation. For a wanton may possess and employ rational faculties of a high order. Nothing in the concept of a wanton implies that he cannot reason or that he cannot deliberate concerning how to do what he wants to do. What distinguishes the rational wanton from other rational agents is that he is not concerned with the desirability of his desires themselves. He ignores the question of what his will is to be. Not only does he pursue whatever course of action he is most strongly inclined to pursue, but he does not care which of his inclinations is the strongest.

Thus a rational creature, who reflects upon the suitability to his desires of one course of action or another, may nonetheless be a wanton. In maintaining that the essence of being a person lies not in reason but in will, I am far from suggesting that a creature without reason may be a person. For it is only in virtue of his rational capacities that a person is capable of becoming critically aware of his own will and of forming volitions of the second order. The structure of a person's will presupposes, accordingly, that he is a rational being.

The distinction between a person and a wanton may be illustrated by the difference between two narcotics addicts. Let us suppose that the physiological condition accounting for the addiction is the same in both men, and that both succumb inevitably to their periodic desires for the drug to which they are addicted. One of the addicts hates his addiction and always struggles desperately, although to no avail, against its thrust. He tries everything that he thinks might enable him to overcome his desires for the drug. But these desires are too powerful for him to withstand, and invariably, in the end, they conquer him. He is an unwilling addict, helplessly violated by his own desires.

The unwilling addict has conflicting first-order desires: he wants to take the drug, and he also wants to refrain from taking it. In addition to these first-order desires, however, he has a volition of the second order. He is not a neutral with regard to the conflict between his desire to take the drug and his desire to refrain from taking it. It is the latter desire, and not the former, that he wants to constitute his will; it is the latter desire, rather than the former, that he wants to be effective and to provide the purpose that he will seek to realize in what he actually does.

The other addict is a wanton. His actions reflect the economy of his first-order desires, without his being concerned whether the desires that move him to act are desires by which he wants to be moved to act. If he encounters problems in obtaining the drug or in administering it to himself, his responses to his urges to take it may involve deliberation. But it never occurs to him to consider whether he wants the relations among his desires to result in his having the will he has. The wanton addict may be an animal, and thus incapable of being concerned about his will. In any event he is, in respect of his wanton lack of concern, no different from an animal.

The second of these addicts may suffer a first-order conflict similar to the first-order conflict suffered by the first. Whether he is human or not, the wanton may (perhaps due to conditioning) both want to take the drug and want to refrain from taking it. Unlike the unwilling addict, however, he does not prefer that one of his conflicting desires should be paramount over the other; he does not prefer that one first-order desire rather than the other should constitute his will. It would be misleading to say that he is neutral as to the conflict between his desires, since this would suggest that he regards them as equally acceptable. Since he has no identity apart from his first-order desires, it is true neither that he prefers one to the other nor that he prefers not to take sides.

It makes a difference to the unwilling addict, who is a person, which of his conflicting first-order desires wins out. Both desires are his, to be sure; and whether he finally takes the drug or finally succeeds in refraining from taking it, he acts to satisfy what is in a literal sense his own desire. In either case he does something he himself wants to do, and he does it not because of some external influence whose aim happens to coincide with his own but because of his desire to do it. The unwilling addict identifies himself, however, through the formation of a second-order volition, with one rather than with the other of his conflicting first-order desires. He makes one of them more truly his own and, in so doing, he withdraws himself from the other. It is in virtue of this identification and withdrawal, accomplished through the formation of a second-order volition, that the unwilling addict may meaningfully make the analytically puzzling statements that the force moving him to take the drug is a force other than his own, and that it is not of his own free will but rather against his will that this force moves him to take it.

The wanton addict cannot or does not care which of his conflicting first-order desires wins out. His lack of concern is not due to his inability to find a convincing basis for preference. It is due either to his lack of the capacity for reflection or to his mindless indifference to the enterprise of evaluating his own desires and motives.[6] There is only one issue in the struggle to which his first-order conflict may lead: whether the one or the other of his conflicting desires is the stronger. Since he is moved by both desires, he will not be altogether satisfied by what he does no matter which of them is effective. But it makes no difference *to him* whether his craving or his aversion gets the upper hand. He has no stake in the conflict between them and so, unlike the unwilling addict, he can neither win nor lose the struggle in which he is engaged. When a *person* acts, the desire by which he is moved is either the will he wants or a will he wants to be without. When a *wanton* acts, it is neither.

III

There is a very close relationship between the capacity for forming second-order volitions and another capacity that is essential to persons—one that has often been considered a distinguishing mark of the human condition. It is only because a person has volitions of the second order that he is capable both of enjoying and of lacking freedom of the will. The concept of a person is not only, then, the concept of a type of entity that has both first-order desires and volitions of the second order. It can also be construed as the concept of a type of entity for whom the freedom of its will may be a problem. This concept excludes all wantons, both infrahuman and human, since they fail to satisfy an essential condition for the enjoyment of freedom of the will. And it excludes those suprahuman beings, if any, whose wills are necessarily free.

Just what kind of freedom is the freedom of the will? This question calls for an identification of the special area of human experience to which the concept of freedom of the will, as distinct from the concepts of other sorts of freedom, is particularly germane. In dealing with it, my aim will be primarily to locate the problem with which a person is most immediately concerned when he is concerned with the freedom of his will.

According to one familiar philosophical tradition, being free is fundamentally a matter of doing what one wants to do. Now the notion of an agent who does what he wants to do is by no means an altogether clear one: both the doing and the wanting, and the appropriate relation between them as well, require elucidation. But although its focus needs to be sharpened and its formulation refined, I believe that this notion does capture at least part of what is implicit in the idea of an agent who *acts* freely. It misses entirely, however, the peculiar content of the quite different idea of an agent whose *will* is free.

We do not suppose that animals enjoy freedom of the will, although we recognize that an animal may be free to run in whatever direction it wants. Thus, having the freedom to do what one wants to do is not a sufficient condition of having a free will. It is not a necessary condition either. For to deprive someone of his freedom of action is not necessarily to undermine the freedom of his will. When an agent is aware that there are certain things he is not free to do, this doubtless affects his desires and limits the range of choices he can make. But suppose that someone, without being aware of it, has in fact lost or been deprived of his freedom of action. Even though he is no longer free to do what he wants to do, his will may remain as free as it was before. Despite the fact that he is not free to translate his desires into actions or to act according to the determinations of his will, he may still form those desires and make those determinations as freely as if his freedom of action had not been impaired.

When we ask whether a person's will is free we are not asking whether he is in a position to translate his first-order desires into actions. That is the question of whether he is free to do as he pleases. The question of the freedom of his will does not concern the relation between what he does and what he wants to do. Rather, it concerns his desires themselves. But what question about them is it?

It seems to me both natural and useful to construe the question of whether a person's will is free in close analogy to the question of whether an agent enjoys freedom of action. Now freedom of action is (roughly, at least) the freedom to do what one wants to do. Analogously, then, the statement that a person enjoys freedom of the will means (also roughly) that he is free to want what he wants to want. More precisely, it means that he is free to will what he wants to will, or to have the will he wants to have. Just as the question about the freedom of an agent's action has to do with whether it is the action he wants to perform, so the question about the freedom of his will has to do with whether it is the will he wants to have.

It is in securing the conformity of his will to his second-order volitions, then, that a person exercises freedom of the will. And it is in the discrepancy between his will and his second-order volitions, or in his awareness that their coincidence is not his own doing but only a happy chance, that a person who does not have his freedom feels its lack. The unwilling addict's will is not free. This is shown by the fact that it is not the will he wants. It is also true, though in a different way, that the will of the wanton addict is not free. The wanton addict neither has the will he wants nor has a will that differs from the will he wants. Since he has no volitions of the second order, the freedom of his will cannot be a problem for him. He lacks it, so to speak, by default.

People are generally far more complicated than my sketchy account of the structure of a person's will may suggest. There is as much opportunity for ambivalence, conflict, and self-deception with regard to desires of the second order, for example, as there is with regard to first-order desires. If there is an unresolved conflict among someone's second-order desires, then he is in danger of having no second-order volition; for unless this conflict is resolved, he has no preference concerning which of his first-order desires is to be his will. This condition, if it is so severe that it prevents him from identifying himself in a sufficiently decisive way with *any* of his conflicting first-order desires, destroys him as a person. For it either tends to paralyze his will and to keep him from acting at all, or it tends to remove him from his will so that his will operates without his participation. In both cases he becomes, like the unwilling addict though in a different way, a helpless bystander to the forces that move him.

Another complexity is that a person may have, especially if his second-order desires are in conflict, desires and volitions of a higher order than the second. There is no theoretical limit to the length of the series of desires of higher and higher orders; nothing except common sense and, perhaps, a saving fatigue prevents an individual from obsessively refusing to identify himself with any of his desires until he forms a desire of the next higher order. The tendency to generate such a series of acts of forming desires, which would be a case of humanization run wild, also leads toward the destruction of a person.

It is possible, however, to terminate such a series of acts without cutting it off arbitrarily. When a person identifies himself *decisively* with one of his first-order desires, this commitment "resounds" throughout the potentially endless array of higher orders. Consider a person who, without reservation or conflict, wants to be motivated by the desire to concentrate on his work. The fact that his second-order volition to be moved by this desire is a decisive one means that there is no room for questions concerning the pertinence of desires or volitions of higher orders. Suppose the person is asked whether he wants to want to want to concentrate on his work. He can properly insist that this question concerning a third-order desire does not arise. It would be a mistake to claim that, because he has not considered whether he wants the second-order volition he has formed, he is indifferent to the question of whether it is with this volition or with some other that he wants his will to accord. The decisiveness of the commitment he has made means that he has decided that no further question about his second-order volition, at any higher order, remains to be asked. It is relatively unimportant whether we explain this by saying that this commitment implicitly generates an endless series of confirming desires of higher orders, or by saying that the commitment is tantamount to a dissolution of the pointedness of all questions concerning higher orders of desire.

Examples such as the one concerning the unwilling addict may suggest that volitions of the second order, or of higher orders, must be formed deliberately and that a person characteristically struggles to ensure that they are satisfied. But the conformity of a person's will to his higher-order volitions may be far more thoughtless and spontaneous than this. Some people are naturally moved by kindness when they want to be kind, and by nastiness when they want to be nasty, without any explicit forethought and without any need for energetic self-control. Others are moved by nastiness when they want to be kind and by kindness when they intend to be nasty, equally without forethought and without active resistance to these violations of their higher-order desires. The enjoyment of freedom comes easily to some. Others must struggle to achieve it.

IV

My theory concerning the freedom of the will accounts easily for our disinclination to allow that this freedom is enjoyed by the members of any species inferior to our own. It also satisfies another condition that must be met by any such theory, by making it apparent why the freedom of the will should be regarded as desirable. The enjoyment of a free will means the satisfaction of certain desires—desires of the second or of higher orders—whereas its absence means their frustration. The satisfactions at stake are those which accrue to a person of whom it may be said that his will is his own. The corresponding frustrations are those suffered by a person of whom it may be said that he is estranged from himself, or that he finds himself a helpless or a passive bystander to the forces that move him.

A person who is free to do what he wants to do may yet not be in a position to have the will he wants. Suppose, however, that he enjoys both freedom of action and freedom of the will. Then he is not only free to do what he wants to do; he is also free to want what he wants to want. It seems to me that he has, in that case, all the freedom it is possible to desire or to conceive. There are other good things in life, and he may not possess some of them. But there is nothing in the way of freedom that he lacks.

It is far from clear that certain other theories of the freedom of the will meet these elementary but essential conditions: that it be understandable why we desire this freedom and why we refuse to ascribe it to animals. Consider, for example, Roderick Chisholm's quaint version of the doctrine that human freedom entails an absence of causal determination.[7] Whenever a person performs a free action, according to Chisholm, it's a miracle.

The motion of a person's hand, when the person moves it, is the outcome of a series of physical causes; but some event in this series, "and presumably one of those that took place within the brain, was caused by the agent and not by any other events" (18). A free agent has, therefore, "a prerogative which some would attribute only to God: each of us, when we act, is a prime mover unmoved" (23).

This account fails to provide any basis for doubting that animals of subhuman species enjoy the freedom it defines. Chisholm says nothing that makes it seem less likely that a rabbit performs a miracle when it moves its leg than that a man does so when he moves his hand. But why, in any case, should anyone *care* whether he can interrupt the natural order of causes in the way Chisholm describes? Chisholm offers no reason for believing that there is a discernible difference between the experience of a man who miraculously initiates a series of causes when he moves his hand and a man who moves his hand without any such breach of the normal causal sequence. There appears to be no concrete basis for preferring to be involved in the one state of affairs rather than in the other.[8]

It is generally supposed that, in addition to satisfying the two conditions I have mentioned, a satisfactory theory of the freedom of the will necessarily provides an analysis of one of the conditions of moral responsibility. The most common recent approach to the problem of understanding the freedom of the will has been, indeed, to inquire what is entailed by the assumption that someone is morally responsible for what he has done. In my view, however, the relation between moral responsibility and the freedom of the will has been very widely misunderstood. It is not true that a person is morally responsible for what he has done only if his will was free when he did it. He may be morally responsible for having done it even though his will was not free at all.

A person's will is free only if he is free to have the will he wants. This means that, with regard to any of his first-order desires, he is free either to make that desire his will or to make some other first-order order desire his will instead. Whatever his will, then, the will of the person whose will is free could have been otherwise; he could have done otherwise than to constitute his will as he did. It is a vexed question just how 'he could have done otherwise' is to be understood in contexts such as this one. But although this question is important to the theory of freedom, it has no bearing on the theory of moral responsibility. For the assumption that a person is morally responsible for what he has done does not entail that the person was in a position to have whatever will he wanted.

This assumption *does* entail that the person did what he did freely, or that he did it of his own free will. It is a mistake, however, to believe that someone acts freely only when he is free to do whatever he wants or that he acts of his own free will only if his will is free. Suppose that a person has done what he wanted to do, that he did it because he wanted to do it, and that the will by which he was moved when he did it was his will because it was the will he wanted. Then he did it freely and of his own free will. Even supposing that he could have done otherwise, he would not have done otherwise; and even supposing that he could have had a different will, he would not have wanted his will to differ from what it was. Moreover, since the will that moved him when he acted was his will because he wanted it to be, he cannot claim that his will was forced upon him or that he was a passive bystander to its constitution. Under these conditions, it is quite irrelevant to the evaluation of his moral responsibility to inquire whether the alternatives that he opted against were actually available to him.[9]

In illustration, consider a third kind of addict. Suppose that his addiction has the same physiological basis and the same irresistible thrust as the addictions of the unwilling and wanton addicts, but that he is altogether delighted with his condition. He is a willing addict, who would not have things any other way. If the grip of his addiction should somehow weaken, he would do whatever he could to reinstate it; if his desire for the drug should begin to fade, he would take steps to renew its intensity.

The willing addict's will is not free, for his desire to take the drug will be effective regardless of whether or not he wants this desire to constitute his will. But when he takes the drug, he takes it freely and of his own free will. I am inclined to understand his situation as involving the overdetermination of his first-order desire to take the drug. This desire is his effective desire because he is physiologically addicted. But it is his effective desire also because he wants it to be. His will is outside his control, but, by his second-order desire that his desire for the drug should be effective, he has made this will his own. Given that it is therefore not only because of his addiction that his desire for the drug is effective, he may be morally responsible for taking the drug.

My conception of the freedom of the will appears to be neutral with regard to the problem of determinism. It seems conceivable that it should be causally determined that a person is free to want what he wants to want. If this is conceivable, then it might be causally determined that a person enjoys a free will. There is no more than an innocuous appearance of paradox in the proposition that it is determined, ineluctably and by forces beyond their control, that certain people have free wills and that others do not. There is no incoherence in the proposition that some agency other than a person's own is responsible (even *morally* responsible) for the fact that he enjoys or fails to enjoy freedom of the will. It is possible that a person should be morally responsible for what he does of his own free will and that some other person should also be morally responsible for his having done it.[10]

On the other hand, it seems conceivable that it should come about by chance that a person is free to have the will he wants. If this is conceivable, then it might be a matter of chance that certain people enjoy freedom of the will and that certain others do not. Perhaps it is also conceivable, as a number of philosophers believe, for states of affairs to come about in a way other than by chance or as the outcome of a sequence of natural causes. If it is indeed conceivable for the relevant states of affairs to come about in some third way, then it is also possible that a person should in that third way come to enjoy the freedom of the will.

NOTES

1. P. F. Strawson, *Individuals* (London: Methuen, 1959), pp. 179–180 this volume. Ayer's usage of 'person' is similar: "it is characteristic of persons in this sense that besides having various physical properties . . . they are also credited with various forms of consciousness" [A. J. Ayer, *The Concept of a Person* (New York: St. Martin's, 1963), p. 82]. What concerns Strawson and Ayer is the problem of understanding the relation between mind and body, rather than the quite different problem of understanding what it is to be a creature that not only has a mind and a body but is also a person.
2. For the sake of simplicity, I shall deal only with what someone wants or desires, neglecting related phenomena such as choices and decisions. I propose to use the verbs 'to want' and 'to desire' interchangeably, although they are by no means perfect synonyms. My motive in forsaking the established nuances of these words arises from the fact that the verb 'to want', which suits my purposes better so far as its meaning is concerned, does not lend itself so readily to the formation of nouns as does the verb 'to desire'. It is perhaps acceptable, albeit graceless, to speak in the plural of someone's "wants." But to speak in the singular of someone's "want" would be an abomination.
3. What I say in this paragraph applies not only to cases in which 'to *X*' refers to a possible action or inaction. It also applies to cases in which 'to *X*' refers to a first-order desire and in which the statement that '*A* wants to *X*' is therefore a shortened version of a statement—"*A* wants to want to *X*"—that identifies a desire of the second order.

4. It is not so clear that the entailment relation described here holds in certain kinds of cases, which I think may fairly be regarded as nonstandard, where the essential difference between the standard and the nonstandard cases lies in the kind of description by which the first-order desire in question is identified. Thus, suppose that *A* admires *B* so fulsomely that, even though he does not know what *B* wants to do, he wants to be effectively moved by whatever desire effectively moves *B;* without knowing what *B*'s will is, in other words, *A* wants his own will to be the same. It certainly does not follow that *A* already has, among his desires, a desire like the one that constitutes *B*'s will. I shall not pursue here the questions of whether there are genuine counterexamples to the claim made in the text or of how, if there are, that claim should be altered.

5. Creatures with second-order desires but no second-order volitions differ significantly from brute animals, and, for some purposes, it would be desirable to regard them as persons. My usage, which withholds the designation 'person' from them, is thus somewhat arbitrary. I adopt it largely because it facilitates the formulation of some of the points I wish to make. Hereafter, whenever I consider statements of the form "*A* wants to want to *X*," I shall have in mind statements identifying second-order volitions and not statements identifying second-order desires that are not second-order volitions.

6. In speaking of the evaluation of his own desires and motives as being characteristic of a person, I do not mean to suggest that a person's second-order volitions necessarily manifest a *moral* stance on his part toward his first-order desires. It may not be from the point of view of morality that the person evaluates his first-order desires. Moreover, a person may be capricious and irresponsible in forming his second-order volitions and give no serious consideration to what is at stake. Second-order volitions express evaluations only in the sense that they are preferences. There is no essential restriction on the kind of basis, if any, upon which they are formed.

7. "Freedom and Action," in K. Lehrer, ed., *Freedom and Determinism* (New York: Random House, 1966), pp. 11–44.

8. I am not suggesting that the alleged difference between these two states of affairs is unverifiable. On the contrary, physiologists might well be able to show that Chisholm's conditions for a free action are not satisfied, by establishing that there is no relevant brain event for which a sufficient physical cause cannot be found.

9. For another discussion of the considerations that cast doubt on the principle that a person is morally responsible for what he has done only if he could have done otherwise, see my "Alternate Possibilities and Moral Responsibility," this JOURNAL, LXVI, 23 (Dec. 4, 1969): 829–839.

10. There is a difference between being *fully* responsible and being *solely* responsible. Suppose that the willing addict has been made an addict by the deliberate and calculated work of another. Then it may be that both the addict and this other person are fully responsible for the addict's taking the drug, while neither of them is solely responsible for it. That there is a distinction between full moral responsibility and sole moral responsibility is apparent in the following example. A certain light can be turned on or off by flicking either of two switches, and each of these switches is simultaneously flicked to the "on" position by a different person, neither of whom is aware of the other. Neither person is solely responsible for the light's going on, nor do they share the responsibility in the sense that each is partially responsible; rather, each of them is fully responsible.

DISCUSSION QUESTIONS

1. Frankfurt admits it is possible that some nonhumans are persons, and that some humans are nonpersons. Do you agree? Explain.
2. Frankfurt says that we generally presume, rightly or wrongly, that what is essential to persons is uniquely human. Is he correct? If we are wrong to presume this, would this undermine the rest of Frankfurt's essay? Explain.
3. Are there beings whose wills are necessarily free? Explain.
4. Explain why Frankfurt rejects Chisholm's view of human freedom as inadequate. Do you agree?

Chapter 26

MARY ANNE WARREN

Warren received her Ph.D. from the University of California, Berkeley in 1975. She is currently Professor of Philosophy at San Francisco State University. Her books include The Nature of Woman: An Encyclopedia and Guide to the Literature *(1980),* Gendercide: The Implications of Sex Selection *(1985), and* Moral Status: Obligations to Persons and Other Living Things *(1997).*

"Why fetuses are not persons and may be aborted" would be a good title for this selection from her influential 1973 paper which has been reprinted more than 50 times. Warren argues that the traits central to the concept of a person (understood as a full-fledged member of the moral community) are consciousness, the capacity to reason, self-motivated activity, the capacity to communicate, and self-awareness. A fetus is not a person, she argues, because it obviously satisfies none of these conditions. She infers that a fetus is not the sort of entity to which it is proper to ascribe full moral rights. Even if some entity is a potential *person with some prima facie right to life, such a right could not possibly outweigh the right of a woman to an abortion, according to Warren, since the rights of any actual person invariably outweigh those of any potential person.*

On the Moral and Legal Status of Abortion

We will be concerned with both the moral status of abortion, which for our purposes we may define as the act which a woman performs in voluntarily terminating, or allowing another person to terminate, her pregnancy, and the legal status which is appropriate for this act. I will argue that, while it is not possible to produce a satisfactory defense of a woman's right to obtain an abortion without showing that a fetus is not a human being, in the morally relevant sense of that term, we ought not to conclude that the difficulties involved in determining whether or not a fetus is human make it impossible to produce any satisfactory solution to the problem of the moral status of abortion. For it is possible to show that, on the basis of intuitions which we may expect even the opponents of abortion to share, a fetus is not a person, and hence not the sort of entity to which it is proper to ascribe full moral rights.

[. . .] The appeal to the right to control one's body, which is generally construed as a property right, is at best a rather feeble argument for the permissibility of abortion. Mere ownership does not give me the right to kill innocent people whom I find on my property, and indeed I am apt to be held responsible if such people injure themselves while on my property. It is equally unclear that I have any moral right to expel an innocent person from my property when I know that doing so will result in his death.

Furthermore, it is probably inappropriate to describe a woman's body as her property, since it seems natural to hold that a person is something distinct from her property, but not from her body. Even those who would object to the identification of a person with his body, or with the conjunction of his body and his mind, must admit that it would be very odd to describe, say, breaking a leg, as damaging one's property, and much more appropriate to describe it as injuring one*self.* Thus it is probably a mistake to argue that the right to obtain an abortion is in any way derived from the right to own and regulate property.

But however we wish to construe the right to abortion, we cannot hope to convince those who consider abortion a form of murder of the existence of any such right unless we are able to produce a clear and convincing refutation of the traditional antiabortion argument, and this has not, to my knowledge, been done. With respect to the two most vital issues which that argument involves, i.e., the humanity of the fetus and its implication for the moral status of abortion, confusion has prevailed on both sides of the dispute.

Thus, both proabortionists and antiabortionists have tended to abstract the question of whether

---

Source: Mary Anne Warren, excerpt from "On the Moral and Legal Status of Abortion." Copyright © 1973. *The Monist: An International Quarterly Journal of General Philosophical Inquiry,* 57, no. 1 (Jan. 1973): 43–61. Peru, Illinois, U.S.A. 61354. Reprinted by permission.

abortion is wrong to that of whether it is wrong to destroy a fetus, just as though the rights of another person were not necessarily involved. This mistaken abstraction has led to the almost universal assumption that if a fetus is a human being, with a right to life, then it follows immediately that abortion is wrong (except perhaps when necessary to save the woman's life), and that it ought to be prohibited. It has also been generally assumed that unless the question about the status of the fetus is answered, the moral status of abortion cannot possibly be determined.

[. . .] John Noonan is correct in saying that "the fundamental question in the long history of abortion is, How do you determine the humanity of a being?"[1] He summarizes his own antiabortion argument, which is a version of the official position of the Catholic Church, as follows:

> . . . it is wrong to kill humans, however poor, weak, defenseless, and lacking in opportunity to develop their potential they may be. It is therefore morally wrong to kill Biafrans. Similarly, it is morally wrong to kill embryos.[2]

Noonan bases his claim that fetuses are human upon what he calls the theologians' criterion of humanity: that whoever is conceived of human beings is human. But although he argues at length for the appropriateness of this criterion, he never questions the assumption that if a fetus is human then abortion is wrong for exactly the same reason that murder is wrong. [. . .]

[. . .] I will propose an answer to this question, namely, that a fetus cannot be considered a member of the moral community, the set of beings with full and equal moral rights, for the simple reason that it is not a person, and that it is personhood, and not genetic humanity, i.e., humanity as defined by Noonan, which is the basis for membership in this community. I will argue that a fetus, whatever its stage of development, satisfies none of the basic criteria of personhood, and is not even enough *like* a person to be accorded even some of the same rights on the basis of this resemblance. Nor, as we will see, is a fetus's *potential* personhood a threat to the morality of abortion, since, whatever the rights of potential people may be, they are invariably overridden in any conflict with the moral rights of actual people. [. . .]

The question which we must answer in order to produce a satisfactory solution to the problem of the moral status of abortion is this: How are we to define the moral community, the set of beings with full and equal moral rights, such that we can decide whether a human fetus is a member of this community or not? What sort of entity, exactly, has the inalienable rights to life, liberty, and the pursuit of happiness? Jefferson attributed these rights to all *men,* and it may or may not be fair to suggest that he intended to attribute them *only* to men. Perhaps he ought to have attributed them to all human beings. If so, then we arrive, first, at Noonan's problem of defining what makes a being human, and, second, at the equally vital question which Noonan does not consider, namely, What reason is there for identifying the moral community with the set of all human beings, in whatever way we have chosen to define that term?

1. ON THE DEFINITION OF 'HUMAN'

One reason why this vital second question is so frequently overlooked in the debate over the moral status of abortion is that the term 'human' has two distinct, but not often distinguished, senses. This fact results in a slide of meaning, which serves to conceal the fallaciousness of the traditional argument that since (1) it is wrong to kill innocent human beings, and (2) fetuses are innocent human beings, then (3) it is wrong to kill fetuses. For if 'human' is used in the same sense in both (1) and (2) then, whichever of the two senses is meant, one of these premises is question-begging. And if it is used in two different senses then of course the conclusion doesn't follow.

Thus, (1) is a self-evident moral truth,[3] and avoids begging the question about abortion, only if 'human being' is used to mean something like "a full-fledged member of the moral community." (It may or may not also be meant to refer exclusively to members of the species *Homo sapiens.*) We may call this the *moral* sense of 'human'. It is not to be confused with what we will call the *genetic* sense, i.e., the sense in which *any* member of the species is a human being, and no member of any other species could be. If (1) is acceptable only if the moral sense is intended, (2) is non-question-begging only if what is intended is the genetic sense.

In "Deciding Who is Human," Noonan argues for the classification of fetuses with human beings by pointing to the presence of the full genetic code, and the potential capacity for rational thought [p. 135]. It is clear that what he needs to show, for his version of the traditional argument to be valid, is that fetuses are human in the moral sense, the sense in which it is analytically true that all human beings have full moral rights. But, in the absence of any argument showing that whatever is genetically human is also morally human, and he gives none, nothing more than genetic humanity can be demonstrated by the presence of the human genetic code. And, as we will see, the *potential* capacity for rational thought can at most show that an entity has the potential for *becoming* human in the moral sense. . . .

2. DEFINING THE MORAL COMMUNITY

Can it be established that genetic humanity is sufficient for moral humanity? I think that there are very good reasons for not defining the moral community in this way. I would like to suggest an alternative way of defining the moral community, which I will argue for only to the extent of explaining why it is, or should be, self-evident. The suggestion is simply that the moral community consists of all and only *people,* rather than all and only human beings;[4] and probably the best way of demonstrating its self-evidence is by considering the concept of personhood, to see what sorts of entity are and are not persons, and what the decision that a being is or is not a person implies about its moral rights.

What characteristics entitle an entity to be considered a person? This is obviously not the place to attempt a complete analysis of the concept of personhood, but we do not need such a fully adequate analysis just to determine whether and why a fetus is or isn't a person. All we need is a rough and approximate list of the most basic criteria of personhood, and some idea of which, or how many, of these an entity must satisfy in order to properly be considered a person.

In searching for such criteria, it is useful to look beyond the set of people with whom we are acquainted, and ask how we would decide whether a totally alien being was a person or not. (For we have no right to assume that genetic humanity is necessary for personhood.) Imagine a space traveler who lands on an unknown planet and encounters a race of beings utterly unlike any he has ever seen or heard of. If he wants to be sure of behaving morally toward these beings, he has to somehow decide whether they are people, and hence have full moral rights, or whether they are the sort of thing which he need not feel guilty about treating as, for example, a source of food.

How should he go about making this decision? If he has some anthropological background, he might look for such things as religion, art, and the manufacturing of tools, weapons, or shelters, since these factors have been used to distinguish our human from our prehuman ancestors, in what seems to be closer to the moral than the genetic sense of 'human'. And no doubt he would be right to consider the presence of such factors as good evidence that the alien beings were people, and morally human. It would, however, be overly anthropocentric of him to take the absence of these things as adequate evidence that they were not, since we can imagine people who have progressed beyond, or evolved without ever developing, these cultural characteristics.

I suggest that the traits which are most central to the concept of personhood, or humanity in the moral sense, are, very roughly, the following:

1. consciousness (of objects and events external and/or internal to the being), and in particular the capacity to feel pain;
2. reasoning (the *developed* capacity to solve new and relatively complex problems);
3. self-motivated activity (activity which is relatively independent of either genetic or direct external control);
4. the capacity to communicate, by whatever means, messages of an indefinite variety of types, that is, not just with an indefinite number of possible contents, but on indefinitely many possible topics;
5. the presence of self-concepts, and self-awareness, either individual or racial, or both.

Admittedly, there are apt to be a great many problems involved in formulating precise definitions of these criteria, let alone in developing universally valid behavioral criteria for deciding when they apply. But I will assume that both we and our explorer know approximately what (1)–(5) mean, and that he is also able to determine whether or not they apply. How, then, should he use his findings to decide whether or not the alien beings are people? We needn't suppose that an entity must have *all* of these attributes to be properly considered a person; (1) and (2) alone may well be sufficient for personhood, and quite probably (1)–(3) are sufficient. Neither do we need to insist that any one of these criteria is *necessary* for personhood, although once again (1) and (2) look like fairly good candidates for necessary conditions, as does (3), if 'activity' is construed so as to include the activity of reasoning.

All we need to claim, to demonstrate that a fetus is not a person, is that any being which satisfies *none* of (1)–(5) is certainly not a person. I consider this claim to be so obvious that I think anyone who denied it, and claimed that a being which satisfied none of (1)–(5) was a person all the same, would thereby demonstrate that he had no notion at all of what a person is—perhaps because he had confused the concept of a person with that of genetic humanity. If the opponents of abortion were to deny the appropriateness of these five criteria, I do not know what further arguments would convince them. We would probably have to admit that our conceptual schemes were indeed irreconcilably different, and that our dispute could not be settled objectively.

I do not expect this to happen, however, since I think that the concept of a person is one which is very nearly universal (to people), and that it is common to both proabortionists and antiabortionists, even though neither group has fully realized the relevance of this concept to the resolution of their dispute. Furthermore, I think that on reflection even the antiabortionists ought to agree not only that (1)–(5) are central to the concept of personhood, but also that it is a part of this concept that all and only people have full moral rights. The concept of a person is in part a moral concept; once we have admitted that x is a person we have recognized, even if we have not agreed to respect, x's right to be treated as a member of the moral community. It is true that the claim that x is a *human being* is more commonly voiced as part of an appeal to treat x decently than is the claim that x is a person, but this is either because 'human being' is here used in the sense which implies personhood, or because the genetic and moral senses of 'human' have been confused.

Now if (1)–(5) are indeed the primary criteria of personhood, then it is clear that genetic humanity is neither necessary nor sufficient for establishing that an entity is a person. Some human beings are not people, and there may well be people who are not human beings. A man or woman whose consciousness has been permanently obliterated but who remains alive is a human being which is no longer a person; defective human beings, with no appreciable mental capacity, are not and presumably never will be people; and a fetus is a human being which is not yet a person, and which therefore cannot coherently be said to have full moral rights. Citizens of the next century should be prepared to recognize highly advanced, self-aware robots or computers, should such be developed, and intelligent inhabitants of other worlds, should such be found, as people in the fullest sense, and to respect their moral rights. But to ascribe full moral rights to an entity which is not a person is as absurd as to ascribe moral obligations and responsibilities to such an entity.

3. FETAL DEVELOPMENT AND THE RIGHT TO LIFE

Two problems arise in the application of these suggestions for the definition of the moral community to the determination of the precise moral status of a human fetus. Given that the paradigm example of a person is a normal adult human being, then (1) How like this paradigm, in particular how far advanced since conception, does a human being need to be before it begins to have a right to life by virtue, not of being fully a person as of yet, but of being *like* a person? and (2) To what extent, if any, does the fact that a fetus has the *potential* for becoming a person endow it with some of the same rights? Each of these questions requires some comment.

In answering the first question, we need not attempt a detailed consideration of the moral rights of organisms which are not developed enough, aware enough, intelligent enough, etc., to be considered people, but which resemble people in some respects. It does seem reasonable to suggest that the more like a person, in the relevant respects, a being is, the stronger is the case for regarding it as having a right to life, and indeed the stronger its right to life is. Thus we ought to take seriously the suggestion that, insofar as "the human individual develops biologically in a continuous fashion . . . the rights of a human person might develop in the same way."[5] But we must keep in mind that the attributes which are relevant in determining whether or not an entity is enough like a person to be regarded as having some of the same moral rights are no different from those which are relevant to determining whether or not it is fully a person—i.e., are no different from (1)–(5)—and that being genetically human, or having recognizably human facial and other physical features, or detectable brain activity, or the capacity to survive outside the uterus, are simply not among these relevant attributes.

Thus it is clear that even though a seven- or eight-month fetus has features which make it apt to arouse in us almost the same powerful protective instinct as is commonly aroused by a small infant, nevertheless it is not significantly more personlike than is a very small embryo. It is *somewhat* more personlike; it can apparently feel and respond to pain, and it may even have a rudimentary form of consciousness, insofar as its brain is quite active. Nevertheless, it seems safe to say that it is not fully conscious, in the way that an infant of a few months is, and that it cannot reason, or communicate messages of indefinitely many sorts, does not engage in self-motivated activity, and has no self-awareness. Thus, in the *relevant* respects, a fetus, even a fully developed one, is considerably less personlike than is the average mature mammal, indeed the average fish. And I think that a rational person must conclude that if the right to life of a fetus is to be based upon its resemblance to a person, then it cannot be said to have any more right to life than, let us say, a newborn guppy (which also seems to be capable of feeling pain), and that a right of that magnitude could never override a woman's right to obtain an abortion, at any stage of her pregnancy.

There may, of course, be other arguments in favor of placing legal limits upon the stage of pregnancy in which an abortion may be performed. Given the relative safety of the new techniques of artificially inducing labor during the third trimester, the danger to the woman's life or health is no longer such an argument. Neither is the fact that people tend to respond to the thought of abortion in the later stages of pregnancy with emotional repulsion, since mere emotional responses cannot take the place of moral reasoning in determining what ought to be permitted. Nor, finally, is the frequently heard argument that legalizing abortion, especially late in the pregnancy, may erode the level of respect for human life, leading, perhaps, to an increase in unjustified euthanasia and other crimes. For this threat, if it is a threat, can be better met by educating people to the kinds of moral distinctions which we are making here than by limiting access to abortion (which limitation may, in its disregard for the rights of women, be just as damaging to the level of respect for human rights).

Thus, since the fact that even a fully developed fetus is not personlike enough to have any significant right to life on the basis of its personlikeness shows that no legal restrictions upon the stage of pregnancy in which an abortion may be performed can be justified on the grounds that we should protect the rights of the older fetus; and since there is no other apparent justification for such restrictions, we may conclude that they are entirely unjustified. Whether or not it would be *indecent* (whatever that means) for a woman in her seventh month to obtain an abortion just to avoid having to postpone a trip to Europe, it would not, in itself, be *immoral,* and therefore it ought to be permitted.

4. POTENTIAL PERSONHOOD AND THE RIGHT TO LIFE

We have seen that a fetus does not resemble a person in any way which can support the claim that it has even some of the same rights. But what about its *potential,* the fact that if nurtured and allowed to develop naturally it will very probably become a person? Doesn't that alone give it at least some right to life? It is hard to deny that the fact that an entity is a potential person is a strong prima facie reason for not destroying it; but we need not conclude from this that a potential person has a right to life, by virtue of that potential. It may be that our feeling that it is better, other things being equal, not to destroy a potential person is better explained by the fact that potential people are still (felt to be) an invaluable resource, not to be lightly squandered. Surely, if every speck of dust were a potential person, we would be much less apt to conclude that every potential person has a right to become actual.

Still, we do not need to insist that a potential person has no right to life whatever. There may well be something immoral, and not just imprudent, about wantonly destroying potential people, when doing so isn't necessary to protect anyone's rights. But even if a potential person does have some prima facie right to life, such a right could not possibly outweigh the right of a woman to obtain an abortion, since the rights of any actual person invariably outweigh those of any potential person, whenever the two conflict. Since this may not be immediately obvious in the case of a human fetus, let us look at another case.

Suppose that our space explorer falls into the hands of an alien culture, whose scientists decide to create a few hundred thousand or more human beings, by breaking his body into its component cells, and using these to create fully developed human beings, with, of course, his genetic code. We may imagine that each of these newly created men will have all of the original man's abilities, skills, knowledge, and so on, and also have an individual self-concept, in short that each of them will be a bona fide (though hardly unique) person. Imagine that the whole project will take only seconds, and that its chances of success are extremely high, and that our explorer knows all of this, and also knows that these people will be treated fairly. I maintain that in such a situation he would have every right to escape if he could, and thus to deprive all of these potential people of their potential lives; for his right to life outweighs all of theirs together, in spite of the fact that they are all genetically human, all innocent, and all have a very high probability of becoming people very soon, if only he refrains from acting.

Indeed, I think he would have a right to escape even if it were not his life which the alien scientists planned to take, but only a year of his freedom, or, indeed, only a day. Nor would he be obligated to stay if he had gotten captured (thus bringing all these people-potentials into existence) because of his own carelessness, or even if he had done so deliberately, knowing the consequences. Regardless of how he got captured, he is not morally obligated to remain in captivity for *any* period of time for the sake of permitting any number of potential people to come into actuality, so great is the margin by which one actual person's right to liberty outweighs whatever right to life even a hundred thousand potential people have. And it seems reasonable to conclude that the rights of a woman will outweigh by a similar margin whatever right to life a fetus may have by virtue of its potential personhood.

Thus, neither a fetus's resemblance to a person, nor its potential for becoming a person provides any basis whatever for the claim that it has any significant right to life. Consequently, a woman's right to protect her health, happiness, freedom, and even her life,[6] by terminating an unwanted pregnancy, will always override whatever right to life it may be appropriate to ascribe to a fetus, even a fully developed one. And thus, in the absence of any overwhelming social need for every possible child, the laws which restrict the right to obtain an abortion, or limit the period of pregnancy during which an abortion may be performed, are a wholly unjustified violation of a woman's most basic moral and constitutional rights.

NOTES

1. John Noonan, "Abortion and the Catholic Church: A Summary History," *Natural Law Forum,* 12 (1967), 125.
2. John Noonan, "Deciding Who is Human," *Natural Law Forum,* 13 (1968), 134.
3. Of course, the principle that it is (always) wrong to kill innocent human beings is in need of many other modifications, e.g., that it may be permissible to do so to save a greater number of other innocent human beings, but we may safely ignore these complications here.
4. From here on, we will use 'human' to mean genetically human, since the moral sense seems closely connected to, and perhaps derived from, the assumption that genetic humanity is sufficient for membership in the moral community.
5. Thomas L. Hayes, "A Biological View," *Commonweal,* 85 (March 17, 1967), 677–78; quoted by Daniel Callahan, in *Abortion, Law, Choice, and Morality* (London: Macmillan & Co., 1970).
6. That is, insofar as the death rate, for the woman, is higher for childbirth than for early abortion.

DISCUSSION QUESTIONS

1. Explain why Warren believes that even a fully developed fetus is not personlike enough to have any significant right to life. Do you agree? Explain.
2. Warren imagines a space traveler visiting an unknown planet and encountering a race of beings utterly unlike any ever encountered. If *you* were this space traveler, how would *you* determine whether these beings had moral rights you ought to respect?
3. Recall the science fiction television series *Star Trek, Star Trek: Next Generation,* and *Star Trek: Voyager.* How did the crews of the Federation starships decide whether the beings they encountered deserved moral respect? Would Warren approve or disapprove of their methods? Explain.
4. Warren describes a situation in which the scientists of an alien culture decide to create thousands of human beings by taking them from the genes of a captured space explorer. The process will take only seconds, and the clones will be treated fairly. Do you agree with Warren that the explorer has every right to escape if he can and thereby deprive all of these potential people of their potential lives? Explain.

Chapter 27

DANIEL C. DENNETT

Born in Boston in 1942, Dennett earned his D.Phil. at Oxford University in 1965 where he studied with Gilbert Ryle. Dennett is a sailor, sculptor, and the author of many books, including Elbow Room *(1984),* The Intentional Stance *(1987),* Consciousness Explained *(1991), and* Darwin's Dangerous Idea *(1995). He is currently Austin B. Fletcher Professor of Philosophy and Director of the Center for Cognitive Studies at Tufts University.*

In this 1976 essay, Dennett asserts that one's dignity does not depend on one's parents being human, since we can contemplate inhabitants of other planets who are nonhuman persons. Moreover, he thinks that human infants, the mentally defective, and human beings declared insane by licensed psychiatrists, are human nonpersons. Dennett thinks the notion of a metaphysical person (an intelligent, conscious, feeling agent) and the notion of a moral person (an accountable agent with rights and responsibilities) are not separate concepts, but two different and unstable resting points on the same continuum. He arrives at this judgment by considering six themes as necessary conditions of moral personhood: (1) rationality, (2) intentionality, (3) a certain attitude being taken toward it, (4) reciprocity, (5) verbal communication, (6) a special consciousness. Dennett contends that themes (1), (2), and (3) are mutually interdependent, and are a necessary but not sufficient condition for (4); (4) is a necessary but not sufficient condition for (5); (5) is the necessary condition for (6); (6) is a necessary condition of moral personhood. Yet these six necessary conditions together are not a sufficient condition of moral personhood, Dennett concludes, because the concept of a person is a normative ideal which entities can only aspire to approximate.

Conditions of Personhood

I am a person, and so are you. That much is beyond doubt. I am a human being, and *probably* you are too. If you take offense at the "probably" you stand accused of a sort of racism, for what is important about us is not that we are of the same biological species, but that we are both persons, and I have not cast doubt on that. One's dignity does not depend on one's parentage even to the extent of having been born of woman or born at all. We normally ignore this and treat humanity as the deciding mark of personhood, no doubt because the terms are locally coextensive or almost coextensive. At this time and place human beings are the only persons we recognize, and we recognize almost all human beings as persons, but on the one hand we can easily contemplate the existence of biologically very different persons—inhabiting other planets, perhaps—and on the other hand we recognize conditions that exempt human beings from personhood, or at least some very important elements of personhood. For instance, infant human beings, mentally defective human beings, and human beings declared insane by licensed psychiatrists are denied personhood, or at any rate crucial elements of personhood.

One might well hope that such an important concept, applied and denied so confidently, would have clearly formulatable necessary and sufficient conditions for ascription, but if it does, we have not yet discovered them. In the end there may be none to discover. In the end we may come to realize that the concept of a person is incoherent and obsolete. Skinner, for one, has suggested this, but the doctrine has not caught on, no doubt in part because it is difficult or even impossible to conceive of what it would be like if we abandoned the concept of a person. The idea that we might cease to view others and *ourselves* as persons (if it does not mean merely that we might annihilate ourselves, and hence cease to view anything as anything) is arguably self-contradictory.[1] So quite aside from whatever might be right or wrong in Skinner's grounds for his claim, it is hard to see how it could win out in contest with such an intuitively invulnerable notion. If then the concept of a person is in some way an ineliminable part of our conceptual scheme, it might still be in rather worse shape than we would like. It might turn out, for instance, that the concept of a person is only a free-floating honorific that we are all happy to apply to ourselves, and to others as the spirit moves us, guided by our emotions, aesthetic sensibilities, considerations of policy, and the like—just as those who are *chic* are all and only those who can get themselves considered *chic* by others who consider themselves *chic*. Being a person is certainly *something* like that, and if it were no more, we would have to reconsider if we could the importance with which we now endow the concept.

Supposing there *is* something more to being a person, the searcher for necessary and sufficient conditions may still have difficulties if there is

Source: Daniel C. Dennett, "Conditions of Personhood." *The Identities of Persons,* Amélie O. Rorty ed., Berkeley: University of California Press (1976): 175–196. Reprinted with the generous permission of the author.

more than one concept of a person, and there are grounds for suspecting this. Roughly, there seem to be two notions intertwined here, which we may call the moral notion and the metaphysical notion. Locke says that "person"

> is a forensic term, appropriating actions and their merit; and so belongs only to intelligent agents, capable of a law, and happiness, and misery. This personality extends itself beyond present existence to what is past, only by consciousness—whereby it becomes concerned and accountable. (*Essays,* Book II, Chap. XXVII)

Does the metaphysical notion—roughly, the notion of an intelligent, conscious, feeling agent—*coincide* with the moral notion—roughly, the notion of an agent who is accountable, who has both rights and responsibilities? Or is it merely that being a person in the metaphysical sense is a necessary but not sufficient condition of being a person in the moral sense? Is being an entity to which states of consciousness or self-consciousness are ascribed *the same* as being an end-in-oneself, or is it merely one precondition? In Rawls's theory of justice, should the derivation from the original position be viewed as a demonstration of how metaphysical persons *can become* moral persons, or should it be viewed as a demonstration of why metaphysical persons *must be* moral persons?[2] In less technical surroundings the distinction stands out as clearly: when we declare a man insane we cease treating him as accountable, and we deny him most rights, but still our interactions with him are virtually indistinguishable from normal personal interactions unless he is very far gone in madness indeed. In one sense of "person," it seems, we continue to treat and view him as a person. I claimed at the outset that it was indubitable that you and I are persons. I could not plausibly hope—let alone aver—that all readers of this essay will be legally sane and morally accountable. What—if anything—was beyond all doubt may only have been that anything properly addressed by the opening sentence's personal pronouns, "you" and "I," was a person in the metaphysical sense. If that was all that was beyond doubt, then the metaphysical notion and the moral notion must be distinct. Still, even if we suppose there are these distinct notions, there seems every reason to believe that metaphysical personhood is a necessary condition of moral personhood.[3]

What I wish to do now is consider six familiar themes, each a claim to identify a necessary condition of personhood, and each, I think, a correct claim on some interpretation. What will be at issue here is first, how (on my interpretation) they are dependent on each other; second, why they are necessary conditions of moral personhood, and third, why it is so hard to say whether they are jointly sufficient conditions for moral personhood. The *first* and most obvious theme is that persons are *rational beings.* It figures, for example, in the ethical theories of Kant and Rawls, and in the "metaphysical" theories of Aristotle and Hintikka.[4] The *second* theme is that persons are beings to which states of consciousness are attributed, or to which psychological or mental or *Intentional predicates,* are ascribed. Thus Strawson identifies the concept of a person as "the concept of a type of entity such that *both* predicates ascribing states of consciousness *and* predicates ascribing corporeal characteristics" are applicable.[5] The *third* theme is that whether something counts as a person depends in some way on an *attitude taken* toward it, a *stance adopted* with respect to it. This theme suggests that it is not the case that once we have established the objective fact that something is a person we treat him or her or it a certain way, but that our treating him or her or it in this certain way is somehow and to some extent constitutive of its being a person. Variations on this theme have been expressed by MacKay, Strawson, Amelie Rorty, Putnam, Sellars, Flew, Thomas Nagel, Dwight Van de Vate, and myself.[6] The *fourth* theme is that the object toward which this personal stance is taken must be capable of *reciprocating* in some way. Very different versions of this are expressed or hinted at by Rawls, MacKay, Strawson, Grice, and others. This reciprocity has sometimes been rather uninformatively expressed by the slogan: to be a person is to treat others as persons, and with this expression has often gone the claim that treating another as a person is treating him morally—perhaps obeying the Golden Rule, but this conflates different sorts of reciprocity. As Nagel says, "extremely hostile behavior toward another is compatible with treating him as a person" (p. 134), and as Van de Vate observes, one of the differences between some forms of manslaughter and murder is that the murderer treats the victim as a person.

The *fifth* theme is that persons must be capable of *verbal communication*. This condition handily excuses nonhuman animals from full personhood and the attendant moral responsibility, and seems at least implicit in all social contract theories of ethics. It is also a theme that has been stressed or presupposed by many writers in philosophy of mind, including myself, where the moral dimension of personhood has not been at issue. The *sixth* theme is that persons are distinguishable from other entities by being *conscious* in some special way: there is a way in which *we* are conscious in which no other species is conscious. Sometimes this is identified as *self*-consciousness of one sort or another. Three philosophers who claim—in very different ways—that a special sort of consciousness is a precondition of being a moral agent are Anscombe, in *Intention,* Sartre, in *The Transcendence of the Ego,* and Harry Frankfurt, in his recent paper, "Freedom of the Will and the Concept of a Person."[7]

I will argue that the order in which I have given these six themes is—with one proviso—the order of their dependence. The proviso is that the first three are mutually interdependent; being rational is being Intentional is being the object of a certain stance. These three together are a necessary but not sufficient condition for exhibiting the form of reciprocity that is in turn a necessary but not sufficient condition for having the capacity for verbal communication, which is the necessary[8] condition for having a special sort of consciousness, which is, as Anscombe and Frankfurt in their different ways claim,[9] a necessary condition of moral personhood.

I have previously exploited the first three themes, rationality, Intentionality and stance, to define not persons, but the much wider class of what I call *Intentional systems,* and since I intend to build on that notion, a brief résumé is in order. An Intentional system is a system whose behavior can be (at least sometimes) explained and predicted by relying on ascriptions to the system of *beliefs* and *desires* (and other Intentionally characterized features—what I will call *Intentions* here, meaning to include hopes, fears, intentions, perceptions, expectations, etc.). There may *in every case* be other ways of predicting and explaining the behavior of an Intentional system—for instance, mechanistic or physical ways—but the Intentional stance may be the handiest or most effective or in any case *a* successful stance to adopt, which suffices for the object to be an Intentional system. So defined, Intentional systems are obviously not all persons. We ascribe beliefs and desires to dogs and fish and thereby predict their behavior, and we can even use the procedure to predict the behavior of some machines. For instance, it is a good, indeed the only good, strategy to adopt against a good chess-playing computer. By *assuming* the computer has certain beliefs (or information) and desires (or preference functions) dealing with the chess game in progress, I can calculate—under auspicious circumstances—the computer's most likely next move, *provided I assume the computer deals rationally with these beliefs and desires.* The computer is an Intentional system in these instances not because it has any particular intrinsic features, and not because it really and truly has beliefs and desires (whatever that would be), but just because it succumbs to a certain *stance* adopted toward it, namely the Intentional stance, the stance that proceeds by ascribing Intentional predicates under the usual constraints to the computer, the stance that proceeds by considering the computer as a rational practical reasoner.

It is important to recognize how bland this definition of *Intentional system* is, and how correspondingly large the class of Intentional systems can be. If, for instance, I predict that a particular plant—say a potted ivy—will grow around a corner and up into the light because it "seeks" the light and "wants" to get out of the shade it now finds itself in, and "expects" or "hopes" there is light around the corner, I have adopted the Intentional stance toward the plant, and lo and behold, within very narrow limits it works. Since it works, some plants are very low-grade Intentional systems.

The actual utility of adopting the Intentional stance toward plants was brought home to me talking with loggers in the Maine woods. These men invariably call a tree not "it" but "he," and will say of a young spruce "he wants to spread his limbs, but don't let him; then he'll have to stretch up to get his light" or "pines don't like to get their feet wet the way cedars do." You can "trick" an apple tree into "thinking it's spring" by building a small fire under its branches in the late fall; it will blossom. This way of talking is not just picturesque and is not really superstitious at all; it is simply an efficient way of making sense of, controlling, predicting, and explaining the behavior of these plants in a way that nicely circumvents one's ignorance of the controlling mechanisms. More sophisticated biologists may choose to speak of information transmission from the tree's periphery to other locations in the tree. This is less picturesque, but still Intentional. Complete abstention from Intentional talk about trees can become almost as heroic, cumbersome, and pointless as the parallel strict behaviorist taboo when speaking of rats and pigeons. And even when Intentional glosses on (e.g.) tree-activities are of vanishingly small heuristic value, it seems to me wiser to grant that such a tree is a very degenerate, uninteresting, negligible Intentional system than to attempt to draw a line above which Intentional interpretations are "objectively true."

It is obvious, then, that being an Intentional system is not sufficient condition for being a person, but is surely a necessary condition. Nothing to which we could not successfully adopt the Intentional stance, with its presupposition of rationality, could count as a person. Can we then define persons as a subclass of Intentional systems? At first glance it might seem profitable to suppose that persons are just that subclass of Intentional systems that *really* have beliefs, desires, and so forth, and are not merely *supposed* to have them for the sake of a short-cut prediction. But efforts to say what counts as really having a belief (so that no dog or tree or computer could qualify) all seem to end by putting conditions on genuine belief that (1) are too strong for our intuitions, and (2) allude to distinct conditions of personhood farther down my list. For instance, one might claim that genuine beliefs are necessarily *verbally expressible* by the believer,[10] or the believer must be *conscious* that he has them, but people seem to have many beliefs that they cannot put into words, and many that they are unaware of having—and in any case I hope to show that the capacity for verbal expression, and the capacity for consciousness, find different *loci* in the set of necessary conditions of personhood.

Better progress can be made, I think, if we turn to our fourth theme, reciprocity, to see what kind of definition it could receive in terms of Intentional systems. The theme suggests that a person must be able to reciprocate the stance, which suggests that an Intentional system that itself adopted the Intentional stance toward other objects would meet the test. Let us define a *second-order Intentional system* as one to which we ascribe not only simple beliefs, desires and other Intentions, but beliefs, desires, and other Intentions *about* beliefs, desires, and other Intentions. An Intentional system *S* would be a second-order Intentional system if among the ascriptions we make to it are such as *S believes that T desires that p, S hopes that T fears that q,* and reflexive cases like *S believes that S desires that p.* (The importance of the reflexive cases will loom large, not surprisingly, when we turn to those who interpret our sixth condition as *self*-consciousness. It may seem to some that the reflexive cases make all Intentional systems automatically second-order systems, and even *n*-order systems, on the grounds that believing that *p* implies believing that you believe that *p* and so forth, but this is a fundamental mistake; the iteration of beliefs and other Intentions is never redundant, and hence while some iterations are normal [are to be expected] they are never trivial or automatic.)

Now are human beings the only second-order Intentional systems so far as we know? I take this to be an empirical question. We ascribe beliefs and desires to dogs, cats, lions, birds, and dolphins, for example, and thereby often predict their behavior—when all goes well—but it is hard to think of a case where an animal's behavior was so sophisticated that we would need to ascribe second-order Intentions to it in order to predict or explain its behavior. Of course if some version of mechanistic physicalism is true (as I believe), we will never *need* absolutely to ascribe any Intentions to anything, but supposing that for heuristic and pragmatic reasons we were to ascribe Intentions to animals, would we ever feel the pragmatic tug to ascribe second-order Intentions to them? Psychologists have often appealed to a principle known as Lloyd Morgan's Canon of Parsimony, which can be viewed as a special case of Occam's Razor; it is the principle that one should attribute to an organism as little intelligence or consciousness or rationality or mind as will suffice to account for its behavior. This principle can be, and has been interpreted as demanding nothing short of radical behaviorism[11] but I think this is a mistake, and we can interpret it as the principle requiring us when we adopt the Intentional stance toward a thing to ascribe the simplest, least sophisticated, lowest-order beliefs, desires, and so on, that will account for the behavior. Then we will grant, for instance, that Fido *wants* his supper, and *believes* his master will give him his supper if he begs in front of his master, but we need not ascribe to Fido the further *belief* that his begging induces a *belief* in his master that he, Fido, *wants* his supper. Similarly, my *expectation* when I put a dime in the candy machine does not hinge on a further *belief* that inserting the coin induces the machine to *believe* I *want* some candy. That is, while Fido's begging looks very much like true second-order interacting (with Fido treating his master as an Intentional system), if we suppose that to Fido his master is just a supper machine activated by begging, we will have just as good a predictive ascription, more modest but still, of course, Intentional.

Are dogs, then, or chimps or other "higher" animals, incapable of rising to the level of second-order Intentional systems, and if so why? I used to think the answer was Yes, and I thought the reason was that nonhuman animals lack language, and that language was needed to represent second-order Intentions. In other words, I thought condition four might rest on condition five. I was tempted by the hypothesis that animals cannot, for instance, have second-order beliefs, beliefs about beliefs, for the same reason they cannot have beliefs about Friday, or poetry. Some beliefs can only be acquired, and hence represented, via language.[12] But if it is true that some beliefs cannot be acquired without language, it is false that all second-order beliefs are among them, and it is false that non-humans cannot be second-order Intentional systems. Once I began asking people for examples of non-human second-order Intentional systems, I found some very plausible cases. Consider this from Peter Ashley (in a letter):

> One evening I was sitting in a chair at my home, the *only* chair my dog is allowed to sleep in. The dog was lying in front of me, whimpering. She was getting nowhere in her trying to "convince" me to give up the chair to her. Her next move is the most interesting, nay, the *only* interesting part of the story. She stood up, and went to the front door where I could still easily see her. She scratched the door, giving me the impression that she had given up trying to get the chair and had decided to go out. However as soon as I reached the door to let her out, she ran back across the room and climbed into her chair, the chair she had "forced" me to leave.

Here it seems we must ascribe to the dog the *intention* that her master *believe* she *wants* to go out—not just a second-order, but a third-order Intention. The key to the example, what makes it an example of a higher-order Intentional system at work, is that the belief she intends to induce in her master is false. If we want to discover further examples of animals behaving as second-order Intentional systems it will help to think of cases of deception, where the animal, believing *p,* tries to get another Intentional system to believe *not-p.* Where an animal is trying to induce behavior in another which *true* beliefs about the other's environment would not induce, we cannot "divide through" and get an explanation that cites only first-level Intentions. We can make this point more general before explaining why it is so: where *x* is attempting to induce behavior in *y* which is inappropriate to *y*'s *true* environment and needs but appropriate to *y*'s *perceived* or *believed* environment and needs, we are forced to ascribe second-order Intentions to *x*. Once in this form the point emerges as a familiar one, often exploited by critics of behaviorism: one can be a behaviorist in explaining and controlling the behavior of laboratory animals only so long as he can rely on there being no serious dislocation between the actual environment of the experiment and the environment perceived by the animals. A tactic for embarrassing behaviorists in the laboratory is to set up experiments that deceive the subjects: if the deception succeeds their behavior is predictable from their false *beliefs* about the environment, not from the actual environment. Now a first-order Intentional system is a behaviorist; it ascribes no Intentions to anything. So if we are to have good evidence that some system *S* is *not* a behaviorist—is a second-order Intentional system—it will only be in those cases where behaviorist theories are inadequate to the data, only in those cases where behaviorism would not explain system *S*'s success in manipulating another system's behavior.

This suggests that Ashley's example is not so convincing after all, that it can be defeated by supposing his dog is a behaviorist of sorts. She need not believe that scratching on the door will induce Ashley to believe she wants to go out; she may simply believe, as a good behaviorist, that she has conditioned Ashley to go to the door when she scratches. So she applies the usual stimulus, gets the usual response, and that's that. Ashley's case succumbs if this is a *standard* way his dog has of getting the door opened, as it probably is, for then the more modest hypothesis is that the dog believes her master is conditioned to go to the door when she scratches. Had the dog done something *novel* to deceive her master (like running to the window and looking out, growling suspiciously) then we would have to grant that rising from the chair was no mere conditioned response in Ashley, and could not be "viewed" as such by his dog, but then, such virtuosity in a dog would be highly implausible.

Yet what is the difference between the implausible case and the well-attested cases where a low-nesting bird will feign a broken wing to lure a predator away from the nest? The effect achieved is novel, in the sense that the bird in all likelihood has not repeatedly conditioned the predators in the neighborhood with this stimulus, so we seem constrained to explain the ploy as a bit of genuine deception, where the bird *intends* to induce a false *belief* in the predator. Forced to this interpretation of the behavior, we would be mightily impressed with the bird's ingenuity were it not for the fact that we know such behavior is "merely instinctual." But why does it disparage this trick to call it merely instinctual? To claim it is instinctual is to claim that all birds of the species do it; they do it even when circumstances aren't entirely appropriate; they do it when there are better reasons for staying on the nest; the behavior pattern is rigid, a tropism of sorts, and presumably the controls are genetically wired in, not learned or invented.

We must be careful not to carry this disparagement too far; it is not that the bird does this trick "unthinkingly," for while it is no doubt true that she does not in any sense run through an argument or scheme in her head ("Let's see, if I were to flap my wing as if it were broken, the fox would think . . ."), a man might do something of similar subtlety, and of genuine intelligence, novelty, and appropriateness, and not run through the "conscious thoughts" either. *Thinking the thoughts,* however that is characterized, is not what makes truly intelligent behavior intelligent. Anscombe says at one point "If [such an expression of reasoning] were supposed to describe actual mental processes, it would in general be quite absurd. The interest of the account is that it described an order which is there whenever actions are done with intentions."[13] But the "order is there" in the case of the bird as well as the man. That is, when we ask why birds evolved with this tropism we explain it by noting the utility of having a means of *deceiving* predators, or inducing false beliefs in them; what must be explained is the provenance of the bird's second-order Intentions. I would be the last to deny or dismiss the vast difference between instinctual or tropistic behavior and the more versatile, intelligent behavior of humans and others, but what I want to insist on here is that if one is prepared to adopt the Intentional stance without qualms as a tool in predicting and explaining behavior, the bird is as much a second-order Intentional system as any man. Since this is so, we should be particularly suspicious of the argument I was tempted to use, viz., that *representations* of second order Intentions would depend somehow on language.[14] For it is far from clear that all or even any of the beliefs and other Intentions of an Intentional system need be *represented* "within" the system in any way for us to get a purchase on predicting its behavior by *ascribing* such Intentions to it.[15] The situation we elucidate by citing the bird's desire to induce a false belief in the predator seems to have no room or need for a representation of this sophisticated Intention in any entity's "thoughts" or "mind," for neither the bird nor evolutionary history nor Mother Nature need think these thoughts for our explanation to be warranted.

Reciprocity, then, provided we understand by it merely the capacity in Intentional systems to exhibit higher-order Intentions, while it depends on the first three conditions, is independent of the fifth and sixth. Whether this notion does justice to the reciprocity discussed by other writers will begin to come clear only when we see how it meshes with the last two conditions. For the fifth condition, the capacity for verbal communication, we turn to Grice's theory of meaning. Grice attempts to define what he calls nonnatural meaning, an utterer's meaning something by uttering something, in terms of the *intentions* of the utterer. His initial definition is as follows:[16]

> "U meant something by uttering *x*" is true if, for some audience A, U uttered x intending
>
> (1) A to produce a particular response *r*.
>
> (2) A to think (recognize) that U intends (1).
>
> (3) A to fulfill (1) on the basis of his fulfillment of (2).

Notice that intention (2) ascribes to U not only a second- but a third-order Intention: U must *intend* that A *recognize* that U *intends* that A produce *r*. It matters not at all that Grice has been forced by a series of counterexamples to move from this initial definition to much more complicated versions, for they all reproduce the third-order Intention of (2). Two points of great importance to us emerge from Grice's analysis of nonnatural meaning. First, since nonnatural meaning, meaning something by saying something, must be a feature of any true verbal communication, and since it depends on third-order Intentions on the part of the utterer, we have our case that condition five rests on condition four and not vice versa. Second, Grice shows us that mere *second*-order Intentions are not enough to provide genuine reciprocity; for that, *third*-order Intentions are needed. Grice introduces condition (2) in order to exclude such cases as this: I leave the china my daughter has broken lying around for my wife to see. This is not a case of meaning something by doing what I do intending what I intend, for though I am attempting thereby to induce my wife to believe something about our daughter (a second-order Intention on my part), success does not depend on her recognizing this intention of mine, or recognizing my intervention or existence at all. There has been no real *encounter,* to use Erving Goffman's apt term, between us, no *mutual recognition.* There must be an encounter between utterer and audience for utterer to mean anything, but encounters can occur in the absence of nonnatural meaning (witness Ashley's dog), and ploys that depend on third-order Intentions need not involve encounters (e.g., *A* can intend that *B* believe that *C* desires that *p*). So third-order Intentions are a necessary but not sufficient condition for encounters which are a necessary but not sufficient condition for instances of nonnatural meaning, that is, instances of verbal communication.

It is no accident that Grice's cases of nonnatural meaning fall into a class whose other members are cases of deception or manipulation. Consider, for instance, Searle's ingenious counterexample to one of Grice's formulations: the American caught behind enemy lines in World War II Italy who attempts to deceive his Italian captors into concluding he is a German officer by saying the one sentence of German he knows: "*Kennst du das Land, wo die Zitronen blühen?*"[17] As Grice points out, these cases share with cases of nonnatural meaning a reliance on or exploitation of the rationality of the victim. In these cases success hinges on inducing the victim to embark on a chain of reasoning to which one contributes premises directly or indirectly. In deception the premises are disbelieved by the supplier; in normal communication they are believed. Communication, in Gricean guise, appears to be a sort of collaborative manipulation of audience by utterer; it depends, not only on the rationality of the audience who must sort out the utterer's intentions, but on the audience's *trust* in the utterer. Communication, as a sort of manipulation, would not work, given the requisite rationality of the audience, unless the audience's trust in the utterer were *well-grounded* or reasonable. Thus the *norm* for utterance is sincerity; were utterances not normally trustworthy, they would fail of their purpose.[18]

Lying, as a form of deception, can only work against a background of truth-telling, but other forms of deception do not depend on the trust of the victim. In these cases success depends on the victim being *quite* smart, but not quite smart enough. Stupid poker players are the bane of clever poker players, for they fail to see the bluffs and ruses being offered them. Such sophisticated deceptions need not depend on direct encounters. There is a book on how to detect fake antiques (which is also, inevitably, a book on how to *make* fake antiques) which offers this sly advice to those who want to fool the "expert" buyer: once you have completed your table or whatever (having utilized all the usual means of simulating age and wear) take a modern electric drill and drill a hole right through the piece in some conspicuous but perplexing place. The would-be buyer will argue: no one would drill such a disfiguring hole without a reason (it can't be supposed to look "authentic" in any way) so it must have served a purpose, which means this table must have been in use in someone's home; since it was in use in someone's home, it was not made expressly for sale in this antique shop . . . therefore it is authentic. Even if this "conclusion" left room for lingering doubts, the buyer will be so pre-occupied dreaming up uses for that hole it will be months before the doubts can surface.

What is important about these cases of deception is the fact that just as in the case of the feigning bird, success does not depend on the victim's *consciously entertaining* these chains of reasoning. It does not matter if the buyer just notices the hole and "gets a hunch" the piece is genuine. He *might* later accept the reasoning offered as his "rationale" for finding the piece genuine, but he might deny it, and in denying it, he might be deceiving himself, even though the *thoughts* never went through his head. The chain of reasoning explains why the hole works as it does (if it does), but as Anscombe says, it need not "describe actual mental processes," if we suppose actual mental processes are conscious processes or events. The same, of course, is true of Gricean communications; neither the utterer nor the audience need consciously entertain the complicated Intentions he outlines, and what is a bit surprising is that no one has ever used this fact as an objection to Grice. Grice's conditions for meaning have been often criticized for falling short of being sufficient, but there seems to be an argument not yet used to show they are not even necessary. Certainly few people ever consciously framed those ingenious intentions before Grice pointed them out, and yet people had been communicating for years. Before Grice, were one asked: "Did you intend your audience to recognize your intention to provoke that response in him?" one would most likely have retorted: "I intended nothing so devious. I simply intended to inform him that I wouldn't be home for supper" (or whatever). So it seems that if these complicated intentions underlay our communicating all along, they must have been unconscious intentions. Indeed, a perfectly natural way of responding to Grice's papers is to remark that *one was not aware* of doing these things when one communicated. Now Anscombe has held, very powerfully, that such a response establishes that the action under that description was not intentional.[19] Since one is not *aware* of these intentions in speaking, one cannot be speaking *with* these intentions.

Why has no one used this argument against Grice's theory? Because, I submit, it is just too plain that Grice is on to something, that Grice is giving us necessary conditions for nonnatural meaning. His analysis illuminates so many questions. Do we communicate with computers in Fortran? Fortran seems to be a language; it has a grammar, a vocabulary, a semantics. The transactions in Fortran between man and machine are often viewed as cases of *man communicating with machine,* but such transactions are pale copies of human verbal communication precisely because the Gricean conditions for nonnatural meaning have been bypassed. There is no room for them to apply. Achieving one's ends in transmitting a bit of Fortran to the machine does not hinge on getting the machine to recognize one's intentions. This does not mean that all communications with computers in the future will have this shortcoming (or strength, depending on your purposes), but just that we do not now communicate, in the strong (Gricean) sense, with computers.[20]

If we are not about to abandon the Gricean model, yet are aware of no such intentions in our normal conversation, we shall just have to drive these intentions underground, and call them unconscious or preconscious intentions. They are intentions that exhibit "an order which is there" when people communicate, intentions of which we are not normally aware, and intentions which are a precondition of verbal communication.[21]

We have come this far without having to invoke any sort of consciousness at all, so if there is a dependence between consciousness or self-consciousness and our other conditions, it will have to be consciousness depending on the others. But to show this I must first show how the first five conditions by themselves might play a role in ethics, as suggested by Rawls's theory of justice. Central to Rawls's theory is his setting up of an idealized situation, the "original position," inhabited by idealized persons, and deriving from this idealization the first principles of justice that generate and illuminate the rest of his theory. What I am concerned with now is neither the content of these principles nor the validity of their derivation, but the nature of Rawls's tactic. Rawls supposes that a group of idealized persons, defined by him as rational, self-interested entities, make calculations under certain constraints about the likely and possible interactive effects of their individual and antagonistic interests (which will require them to frame higher-order Intentions, for example, beliefs about the desires of others, beliefs about the beliefs of others about their own desires, and so forth). Rawls claims these calculations have an optimal "solution" that it would be reasonable for each self-interested person to adopt as an alternative to a Hobbesian state of nature. The solution is to agree with his fellows to abide by the principles of justice Rawls adumbrates. What sort of a proof of principles of justice would this be? Adopting these principles of justice can be viewed, Rawls claims, as the solution to the "highest order game" or "bargaining problem." It is analogous to derivations of game theory, and to proofs in Hintikka's epistemic logic,[22] and to a "demonstration" that the chess-playing computer will make a certain move because it is the most rational move given its information about the game. All depend on the assumption of ideally rational calculators and hence their outcomes are intrinsically normative. Thus I see the derivations from Rawls's original position as continuous with the deductions and extrapolations encountered in more simple uses of the Intentional stance to understand and control the behavior of simpler entities. Just as truth and consistency are norms for belief,[23] and sincerity is the norm for utterance, so, if Rawls is right, justice as he defines it is the norm for interpersonal interactions. But then, just as part of our warrant for considering an entity to have any beliefs or other Intentions is our ability to construe the entity as *rational,* so our grounds for considering an entity a person include our ability to view him as abiding by the principles of justice. A way of capturing the peculiar status of the concept of a person as I think it is exploited here would be to say that while Rawls does not at all intend to argue that justice is the inevitable result of *human* interaction, he does argue in effect that it is the inevitable result of *personal* interaction. That is, the concept of a person is itself inescapably normative or idealized; to the extent that justice does not reveal itself in the dealings and interactions of creatures, to that extent they are not persons. And once again we can see that there is "an order which is there" in a just society that is independent of any actual episodes of conscious thought. The existence of just practices and the "acknowledgment" implicit in them does not depend on anyone ever consciously or deliberately going through the calculations of the idealized original position, consciously arriving at the reciprocal agreements, consciously adopting a stance toward others.

> To recognize another as a person one must respond to him and act towards him in certain ways; and these ways are intimately connected with the various prima facie duties. Acknowledging these duties in some degree, and so having the elements of morality, is not a matter of choice or of intuiting moral qualities or a matter of the expression of feelings or attitudes . . . it is simply the pursuance of one of the forms of conduct in which the recognition of others as persons is manifested.[24]

The importance of Rawls's attempt to derive principles of justice from the "original position" is, of course, that while the outcome is recognizable as a *moral* norm, it is not *derived as* a moral norm. Morality is not presupposed of the parties in the original position. But this means that the derivation of the norm does not in itself give us any answer to the questions of when and why we have the right to hold persons *morally* responsible for deviations from that norm. Here Anscombe provides help and at the same time introduces our sixth condition. *If I am to be held responsible for an action* (a bit of behavior of mine under a particular description), I must have been *aware* of that action under that description.[25] Why? Because only if I was aware of the action can I *say* what I was about, and participate from a privileged position in the question-and-answer game of giving reasons for my actions. (If I am not in a privileged position to answer questions about the reasons for my actions, there is no special reason to ask *me.*) And what is so important about being able to participate in this game is that only those capable of participating in reason-giving can be argued into, or argued out of, courses of action or attitudes, and if one is incapable of "listening to reason" in some matter, one cannot be held responsible for it. The capacities for verbal communication and for awareness of one's actions are thus essential in one who is going to be amenable to argument or persuasion, and such persuasion, such reciprocal adjustment of interests achieved by mutual exploitation of rationality, is a feature of the optimal mode of personal interaction.

This capacity for participation in mutual persuasion provides the foundation for yet another condition of personhood recently exposed by Harry Frankfurt.[26] Frankfurt claims that persons are the subclass of Intentional systems capable of what he calls *second-order volitions.* Now at first this looks just like the class of second-order Intentional systems, but it is not, as we shall see.

> Besides wanting and choosing and being moved *to do* this or that, men may also want to have (or not to have) certain desires and motives. They are capable of wanting to be different, in their preferences and purposes, from what they are.. . . No animal other than man, however, appears to have the capacity for reflective self-evaluation that is manifested in the formation of second-order desires. (p. 208 this volume)

Frankfurt points out that there are cases in which a person might be said to want to have a particular desire even though he would not want that desire to be effective for him, to be "his will." (One might, for instance, want to desire heroin just to know what it felt like to desire heroin, without at all wanting this desire to become one's effective desire.) In more serious cases one wants to have a desire one currently does not have, and wants this desire to become one's will. These cases Frankfurt calls second-order volitions, and it is having these, he claims, that is "essential to being a person" (p. 210 this volume). His argument for this claim, which I will not try to do justice to here, proceeds from an analysis of the distinction between having freedom of action and having freedom of the will. One has freedom of the will, on his analysis, only when one can have the will one wants, when one's second-order volitions can be satisfied. Persons do not always have free will, and under some circumstances can be responsible for actions done in the absence of freedom of the will, but a person always must be an "entity for whom the freedom of its will may be a problem" (p. 212 this volume)— that is, one capable of framing second-order volitions, satisfiable or not. Frankfurt introduces the marvelous term "wanton" for those "who have first-order desires but . . . no second-order volitions." (Second-order volitions for Frankfurt are all, of course, *reflexive* second-order desires.) He claims that our intuitions support the opinion that all nonhuman animals, as well as small children and some mentally defective people, are wantons, and I for one can think of no plausible counterexamples. Indeed, it seems a strength of his theory, as he claims, that human beings—the only persons we recognize—are distinguished from animals in this regard. But what should be so special about second-order volitions? Why are they, among higher-order Intentions, the peculiar province of persons? Because, I believe, the "reflective self-evaluation" Frankfurt speaks of is, and must be, genuine self-consciousness, which is achieved only by adopting toward *oneself* the stance not simply of communicator but of Anscombian reason-asker and persuader. As Frankfurt points out, second-order desires are an empty notion unless one can *act* on them, and acting on a second-order desire must be logically distinct from acting on its first-order component. Acting on a second-order desire, doing something to bring it about that one acquires a first-order desire, is acting upon oneself just as one would act upon another person: one *schools* oneself, one offers oneself persuasions, arguments, threats, bribes, in the hopes of inducing oneself to acquire the first-order desire.[27] One's stance toward oneself *and access to oneself* in these cases is essentially the same as one's stance toward and access to another. One must *ask oneself* what one's desires, motives, reasons really are, and only if one can say, can become aware of one's desires, can one be in a position to induce oneself to change.[28] Only here, I think, is it the case that the "order which is there" cannot be there unless it is there in episodes of conscious thought, in a dialogue with oneself.[29]

Now, finally, why are we not in a position to claim that these necessary conditions of moral personhood are also sufficient? Simply because the concept of a person is, I have tried to show, inescapably normative. Human beings or other entities can only aspire to being approximations of the ideal, and there can be no way to set a "passing grade" that is not arbitrary. Were the six conditions (strictly interpreted) considered sufficient they would not ensure that any actual entity was a person, for nothing would ever fulfill them. The moral notion of a person and the metaphysical notion of a person are not separate and distinct concepts but just two different and unstable resting points on the same continuum. This relativity infects the satisfaction of conditions of personhood at every level. There is no objectively satisfiable sufficient condition for an entity's *really* having beliefs, and as we uncover apparent irrationality under an Intentional interpretation of an entity, our grounds for ascribing any beliefs at all wanes, especially when we have (what we always *can* have in principle) a non-Intentional, mechanistic account of the entity. In just the same way our assumption that an entity is a person is shaken precisely in those cases where it matters: when wrong has been done and the question of responsibility arises. For in these cases the grounds for saying that the person is culpable (the evidence that he did wrong, was aware he was doing wrong, and did wrong of his own free will) are in themselves grounds for doubting that it is a person we are dealing with at all. And if it is asked what could *settle* our doubts, the answer is: nothing. When such problems arise we cannot even tell in our own cases if we are persons.

NOTES

1. See my "Mechanism and Responsibility," in T. Honderich, ed., *Essays on Freedom of Action* (London: Routledge & Kegan Paul, 1973).
2. In "Justice as Reciprocity," a revision of "Justice as Fairness" printed in S. Gorovitz, ed., *Utilitarianism* (Indianapolis: Bobbs Merrill, 1971), Rawls allows that the persons in the original position may include "nations, provinces, business firms, churches, teams, and so on. The principles of justice apply to conflicting claims made by persons of all these separate kinds. There is, perhaps, a certain logical priority to the case of human individuals" (p. 245). In *A Theory of Justice* (Cambridge, Mass.: Harvard University Press, 1971), he acknowledges that parties in the original position may include associations and other entities not human individuals (e.g., p. 146), and the apparent interchangeability of "parties in the original position" and "persons in the original position" suggests that Rawls is claiming that for some moral concept of a person, the moral person is *composed* of metaphysical persons who may or may not themselves be moral persons.
3. Setting aside Rawls's possible compound moral persons. For more on compound persons see Amelie Rorty, "Persons, Policies, and Bodies," *International Philosophical Quarterly,* Vol. XIII, no. 1 (March 1973).
4. J. Hintikka, *Knowledge and Belief* (Ithaca: Cornell University Press, 1962).
5. P. F. Strawson, *Individuals* (London: Methuen, 1959), pp. 178–180 this volume. It has often been pointed out that Strawson's definition is obviously much too broad, capturing all sentient, active creatures. See, e.g. H. Frankfurt, "Freedom of the will and the concept of a person," *Journal of Philosophy* (January 14, 1971) pp. 206–217 this volume. It can also be argued (and I would argue) that states of consciousness are only a proper subset of psychological or Intentionally characterized states, but I think it is clear that Strawson here means to cast his net wide enough to include psychological states generally.
6. D. M. MacKay, "The use of behavioral language to refer to mechanical processes," *British Journal of Philosophy of Science* (1962), pp. 89–103; P. F. Strawson, "Freedom and resentment," *Proceedings of the British Academy* (1962), reprinted in Strawson, ed., *Studies in the Philosophy of Thought and Action* (Oxford, 1968); A. Rorty, "Slaves and machines," *Analysis* (1962); H. Putnam, "Robots: machines or artificially created life?" *Journal of Philosophy* (November 12, 1964); W. Sellars, "Fatalism and determinism," in K. Lehrer, ed., *Freedom and Determinism* (New York: Random House, 1966); A. Flew, "A

Rational Animal," in J.R. Smythies, ed., *Brain and Mind* (London: Routledge & Kegan Paul, 1968); T. Nagel, "War and Massacre," *Philosophy and Public Affairs* (Winter 1972); D. Van de Vate, "The problem of robot consciousness," *Philosophy and Phenomenological Research* (December 1971); my "Intentional Systems," *Journal of Philosophy* (February 25, 1971).

7. H. Frankfurt, "Freedom of the will and the concept of a person," op. cit.
8. And sufficient, but I will not argue it here. I argue for this in *Content and Consciousness* (London: Routledge & Kegan Paul, 1969), and more recently and explicitly in my "Reply to Arbib and Gunderson," APA Eastern Division Meetings, December 29, 1972.
9. I will not discuss Sartre's claim here.
10. Cf. Bernard Williams, "Deciding to Believe," in H.E. Kiefer and M.K. Munitz, eds., *Language, Belief and Metaphysics* (New York: New York University Press, 1970).
11. E.g., B.F. Skinner, "Behaviorism at Fifty," in T.W. Wann, ed., *Behaviorism and Phenomenology* (Chicago: University of Chicago Press, 1964).
12. For illuminating suggestions on the relation of language to belief and rationality, see Ronald de Sousa, "How to give a piece of your mind; or, a logic of belief and assent," *Review of Metaphysics* (September 1971).
13. G.E.M. Anscombe, *Intention* (Oxford: Blackwell, 1957), p. 80.
14. Cf. Ronald de Sousa, "Self-Deception," *Inquiry,* 13 (1970), esp. p. 317.
15. I argue this in more detail in "Brain Writing and Mind Reading," in K. Gunderson, ed., *Language, Mind, and Knowledge* (Minneapolis: University of Minnesota Press, 1975), and in my "Reply to Arbib and Gunderson."
16. The key papers are "Meaning," *Philosophical Review* (July 1957), and "Utterer's meaning and intentions," *Philosophical Review* (April 1969). His initial formulation, developed in the first paper, is subjected to a series of revisions in the second paper, from which this formulation is drawn (p. 151).
17. John Searle, "What is a Speech Act?" in Max Black, ed., *Philosophy in America* (London: Allen & Unwin, 1965), discussed by Grice in "Utterer's Meaning and Intentions," p. 160. "Do you know the country where the lemon trees bloom?" refers to Italy. It is the first line of Goethe's poem "Mignon" in *Wilhelm Meister's Apprenticeship.* [Ed.]
18. Cf. "Intentional Systems," pp. 102–103.
19. G.E.M. Anscombe, *Intention,* p. 11.
20. It has been pointed out to me by Howard Friedman that many current Fortran compilers which "correct" operator input by inserting "plus" signs and parentheses, etc., to produce well-formed expressions arguably meet Grice's criteria, since within a very limited sphere, they diagnose the "utterer's" intentions and proceed on the basis of this diagnosis. But first it should be noted that the machines to date can diagnose only what might be called the operator's syntactical intentions, and second, these machines do not seem to meet Grice's subsequent and more elaborate definitions, not that I wish to claim that no computer could.
21. In fact, Grice is describing only a small portion of the order which is there as a precondition of normal personal interaction. An analysis of higher order Intentions on a broader front is to be found in the works of Erving Goffman, especially in *The Presentation of Self in Everyday Life* (Garden City: Doubleday, 1959).
22. See Hintikka, *Knowledge and Belief,* p. 38.
23. See Dennett, "Intentional Systems," pp. 102–103.
24. J. Rawls, "Justice as Reciprocity," p. 259.
25. I can be held responsible for events and states of affairs that I was not aware of and ought to have been aware of, but these are not intentional actions. In these cases I am responsible for these further matters in virtue of being responsible for the foreseeable consequences of actions—including acts of omission—that I was aware of.
26. H. Frankfurt, "Freedom of the will and the concept of a person." Frankfurt does not say whether he conceives his condition to be merely a necessary or also a sufficient condition of moral personhood.
27. It has been brought to my attention that dogs at stud will often engage in masturbation, in order, apparently, to *increase their desire* to copulate. What makes these cases negligible is that even supposing the dog can be said to act on a desire to strengthen a desire, the effect is achieved in a non-Intentional ("purely physiological") way; the dog does not appeal to or exploit his own rationality in achieving his end. (As if the only way a person could act on a second-order volition were by taking a pill or standing on his head, etc.).
28. Margaret Gilbert, in "Vices and self-knowledge," *Journal of Philosophy* (August 5, 1971), p. 452, examines the implications of the fact that "when, and only when, one believes that one has a given trait can one decide to change out of it."

29. Marx, in *The German Ideology,* says: "Language, like consciousness, only arises from the need, the necessity, of intercourse with other men.. . . Language is as old as consciousness, language is practical consciousness." And Nietzsche, in *The Joyful Wisdom,* says: "For we could in fact think, feel, will, and recollect, we could likewise 'act' in every sense of the term, and nevertheless nothing of it at all need necessarily 'come into consciousness' (as one says metaphorically; . . . . *What* then is *the purpose* of consciousness generally, when it is in the main *superfluous?*—Now it seems to me, if you will hear my answer and its perhaps extravagant supposition, that the subtlety and strength of consciousness are always in proportion to the *capacity for communication* of a man (or an animal), the capacity for communication in its turn being in proportion to the *necessity for communication.* . . . In short, the development of speech and the development of consciousness (not of reason, but of reason becoming self-conscious) go hand in hand."

DISCUSSION QUESTIONS

1. Explain what Dennett means when he describes a chess-playing computer as an Intentional system.
2. What utility does Dennett see in adopting the Intentional stance toward trees? Do you agree with him?
3. What examples of animals displaying second-order (and higher) Intention does Dennett offer? Were you persauded by these examples? Explain.
4. Explain the role of third-order Intentions in Grice's account of nonnatural meaning.
5. Why does Dennett think that lying, as a form of deception, can only work against a background of truth-telling?
6. Explain what the "original position" is in Rawls' theory of justice. Why does Dennett think that Rawls in effect argues that justice is the inevitable result of personal interaction?
7. How does Frankfurt's "reflective self-evaluation" figure into Dennett's analysis of personhood?

Chapter 28

RAYMOND M. SMULLYAN

Born in 1919 in Far Rockaway, Long Island, New York City, Ray Smullyan is a concert pianist, some time magician, well-known mathematician and logician, and author of puzzlebooks on logic and chess. He is the Oscar Ewing Professor Emeritus of Philosophy at Indiana University and Professor Emeritus of the City University of New York–Lehman College and Graduate Center.

This piece is a lively, free wheeling dialogue between God and a Mortal. Ideas explored in the discussion range from the connections between free will, moral responsibility, and sin, to happiness, eternal life, how the existence of God can be known, and the fall of Man. The Mortal learns that God is a utilitarian, and that what is wrong with sin is nothing other than the suffering it causes sentient beings. God is not a perceivable object, but a subject who neither punishes nor rewards. The conversation reveals God to be the Cosmic Process by which all sentient beings evolve, over countless life cycles, from sinners to perfected angels. And just as human beings can be viewed either as personal *(conscious beings who choose) or as* impersonal *(collections of atoms behaving according to strict physical laws), similarly God can be viewed either as personal (a conversational partner) or as impersonal (the scheme of things, the very process of enlightenment). Free will is not, as is commonly believed, an added* gift *God gave human creatures; the truth is that a conscious, sentient being without free will would be as impossible as a physical object that exerts no gravitational attraction. The dialogue ends with God urging the Mortal to recognize the conflict between right and wrong as the sickness of the human mind; so-called moral duties are actually living impulses.*

Is God a Taoist?

MORTAL: And therefore, O God, I pray thee, if thou hast one ounce of mercy for this thy suffering creature, absolve me of *having* to have free will.

GOD: You reject the greatest gift I have given thee?

MORTAL: How can you call that which was forced on me a gift? I have free will, but not of my own choice. I have never freely chosen to have free will. I have to have free will, whether I like it or not!

GOD: Why would you wish not to have free will?

MORTAL: Because free will means moral responsibility, and moral responsibility is more than I can bear!

GOD: Why do you find moral responsibility so unbearable?

MORTAL: Why? I honestly can't analyze why; all I know is that I do.

GOD: All right, in that case suppose I absolve you from all moral responsibility but leave you still with free will. Will this be satisfactory?

MORTAL *(after a pause)*: No, I am afraid not.

GOD: Ah, just as I thought! So moral responsibility is not the only aspect of free will to which you object. What else about free will is bothering you?

MORTAL: With free will I am capable of sinning, and I don't want to sin!

GOD: If you don't want to sin, then why do you?

MORTAL: Good God! I don't know why I sin, I just do! Evil temptations come along, and try as I can, I cannot resist them.

GOD: If it is really true that you cannot resist them, then you are not sinning of your own free will and hence (at least according to me) not sinning at all.

MORTAL: No, no! I keep feeling that if only I tried harder I could avoid sinning. I understand that the will is infinite. If one wholeheartedly wills not to sin, then one won't.

GOD: Well now, you should know. Do you try as hard as you can to avoid sinning or don't you?

MORTAL: I honestly don't know! At the time, I feel I am trying as hard as I can, but in retrospect, I am worried that maybe I didn't!

GOD: So in other words, you don't really know whether or not you have been sinning. So the possibility is open that you haven't been sinning at all!

MORTAL: Of course this possibility is open, but maybe I have been sinning, and this thought is what so frightens me!

GOD: Why does the thought of your sinning frighten you?

MORTAL: I don't know why! For one thing, you do have a reputation for meting out rather gruesome punishments in the afterlife!

Source: From *The Tao is Silent* by Raymond Smullyan. Copyright © 1977 by Raymond M. Smullyan. New York: Harper & Row: 321–341. Reprinted with the permission of HarperCollins Publishers Inc.

GOD: Oh, that's what's bothering you! Why didn't you say so in the first place instead of all this peripheral talk about free will and responsibility? Why didn't you simply request me not to punish you for any of your sins?

MORTAL: I think I am realistic enough to know that you would hardly grant such a request!

GOD: You don't say! *You* have a realistic knowledge of what requests I will grant, eh? Well, I'll tell you what I'm going to do! I will grant you a very, very special dispensation to sin as much as you like, and I give you my divine word of honor that I will never punish you for it in the least. Agreed?

MORTAL *(in great terror):* No, no, don't do that!

GOD: Why not? Don't you trust my divine word?

MORTAL: Of course I do! But don't you see, I don't want to sin! I have an utter abhorrence of sinning, quite apart from any punishments it may entail.

GOD: In that case, I'll go you one better. I'll remove your abhorrence of sinning. Here is a magic pill! Just swallow it, and you will lose all *abhorrence* of sinning. You will joyfully and merrily sin away, you will have no regrets, no abhorrence and I still promise you will never be punished by me, or yourself, or by any source whatever. You will be blissful for all eternity. So here is the pill!

MORTAL: No, no!

GOD: Are you not being irrational? I am even removing your abhorrence of sin, which is your last obstacle.

MORTAL: I still won't take it!

GOD: Why not?

MORTAL: I believe that the pill will indeed remove my future abhorrence for sin, but my present abhorrence is enough to prevent me from being willing to take it.

GOD: I command you to take it!

MORTAL: I refuse!

GOD: What, you refuse of your own free will?

MORTAL: Yes!

GOD: So it seems that your free will comes in pretty handy, doesn't it?

MORTAL: I don't understand!

GOD: Are you not glad now that you have the free will to refuse such a ghastly offer? How would you like it if I forced you to take this pill, whether you wanted it or not?

MORTAL: No, no! Please don't!

GOD: Of course I won't; I'm just trying to illustrate a point. All right, let me put it this way. Instead of forcing you to take the pill, suppose I grant your original prayer of removing your free will—but with the understanding that the moment you are no longer free, then you *will* take the pill.

MORTAL: Once my will is gone, how could I possibly choose to take the pill?

GOD: I did not say you would choose it; I merely said you would take it. You would act, let us say, according to purely deterministic laws which are such that you would as a matter of fact take it.

MORTAL: I still refuse.

GOD: So you refuse my offer to remove your free will. This is rather different from your original prayer, isn't it?

MORTAL: Now I see what you are up to. Your argument is ingenious, but I'm not sure it is really correct. There are some points we will have to go over again.

GOD: Certainly.

MORTAL: There are two things you said which seem contradictory to me. First you said that one cannot sin unless one does so of one's own free will. But then you said you would give me a pill which would deprive me of my own free will, and then I could sin as much as I liked. But if I no longer had free will, then, according to your first statement, how could I be capable of sinning?

GOD: You are confusing two separate parts of our conversation. I never said the pill would deprive you of your free will, but only that it would remove your abhorrence of sinning.

MORTAL: I'm afraid I'm a bit confused.

GOD: All right, then let us make a fresh start. Suppose I agree to remove your free will, but with the understanding that you will then commit an enormous number of acts which you now regard as sinful. Technically speaking, you will not then be sinning since you will not be doing these acts of your own free will. And these acts will carry no moral responsibility, nor moral culpability, nor any punishment whatsoever. Nevertheless, these acts will all be of the type which you presently regard as sinful; they will all have this quality which you presently feel as abhorrent, but your abhorrence will disappear; so you will not *then* feel abhorrence toward the acts.

MORTAL: No, but I have present abhorrence toward the acts, and this present abhorrence is sufficient to prevent me from accepting your proposal.

GOD: Hm! So let me get this absolutely straight. I take it you no longer wish me to remove your free will.

MORTAL *(reluctantly)*: No, I guess not.

GOD: All right, I agree not to. But I am still not exactly clear as to why you now no longer wish to be rid of your free will. Please tell me again.

MORTAL: Because, as you have told me, without free will I would sin even more than I do now.

GOD: But I have already told you that without free will you cannot sin.

MORTAL: But if I choose now to be rid of free will, then all my subsequent evil actions will be sins, not of the future, but of the present moment in which I choose not to have free will.

GOD: Sounds like you are pretty badly trapped, doesn't it?

MORTAL: Of course I am trapped! You have placed me in a hideous double bind! Now whatever I do is wrong. If I retain free will, I will continue to sin, and if I abandon free will (with your help, of course), I will now be sinning in so doing.

GOD: But by the same token, you place me in a double bind. I am willing to leave you free will or remove it as you choose, but neither alternative satisfies you. I wish to help you, but it seems I cannot.

MORTAL: True!

GOD: But since it is not my fault, why are you still angry with me?

MORTAL: For having placed me in such a horrible predicament in the first place!

GOD: But, according to you, there is nothing satisfactory I could have done.

MORTAL: You mean there is nothing satisfactory you can now do, but that does not mean that there is nothing you could have done.

GOD: Why? What could I have done?

MORTAL: Obviously you should never have given me free will in the first place. Now that you have given it to me, it is too late—anything I do will be bad. But you should never have given it to me in the first place.

GOD: Oh, that's it! Why would it have been better had I never given it to you?

MORTAL: Because then I never would have been capable of sinning at all.

GOD: Well, I'm always glad to learn from my mistakes.

MORTAL: What!

GOD: I know, that sounds sort of self-blasphemous, doesn't it? It almost involves a logical paradox! On the one hand, as you have been taught, it is morally wrong for any sentient being to claim that I am capable of making mistakes. On the other hand, I have the right to do anything. But I am also a sentient being. So the question is, Do I or do I not have the right to claim that I am capable of making mistakes?

MORTAL: That is a bad joke! One of your premises is simply false. I have not been taught that it is wrong for any sentient being to doubt your omniscience, but only for a mortal to doubt it. But since you are not mortal, then you are obviously free from this injunction.

GOD: Good, so you realize this on a rational level. Nevertheless, you did appear shocked when I said, "I am always glad to learn from my mistakes."

MORTAL: Of course I was shocked. I was shocked not by your self-blasphemy (as you jokingly called it), not by the fact that you had no right to say it, but just by the fact that you did say it, since I have been taught that as a matter of fact you don't make mistakes. So I was amazed that you claimed that it is possible for you to make mistakes.

GOD: I have not claimed that it is possible. All I am saying is that *if* I make mistakes, I will be happy to learn from them. But this says nothing about whether the *if* has or ever can be realized.

MORTAL: Let's please stop quibbling about this point. Do you or do you not admit it was a mistake to have given me free will?

GOD: Well now, this is precisely what I propose we should investigate. Let me review your present predicament. You don't want to have free will because with free will you can sin, and you don't want to sin. (Though I still find this puzzling; in a way you must want to sin, or else you wouldn't. But let this pass for now.) On the other hand, if you agreed to give up free will, then you would now be responsible for the acts of the future. Ergo, I should never have given you free will in the first place.

MORTAL: Exactly!

GOD: I understand exactly how you feel. Many mortals—even some theologians—have complained that I have been unfair in that it was I, not they, who decided that they should have free will, and then I hold *them* responsible for their actions. In other words, they feel that they are expected to live up to a contract with me which they never agreed to in the first place.

MORTAL: Exactly!

GOD: As I said, I understand the feeling perfectly. And I can appreciate the justice of the complaint. But the complaint arises only from an unrealistic understanding of the true issues involved. I am about to enlighten you as to what these are, and I think the results will surprise you! But instead of telling you outright, I shall continue to use the Socratic method.

To repeat, you regret that I ever gave you free will. I claim that when you see the true ramifications you will no longer have this regret. To prove my point, I'll tell you what I'm going to do. I am about to create a new universe—a new space-time continuum. In this new universe will be born a mortal just like you—for all practical purposes, we might say that you will be reborn. Now, I can give this new mortal—this new you—free will or not. What would you like me to do?

MORTAL *(in great relief):* Oh, please! Spare him from having to have free will!

GOD: All right, I'll do as you say. But you do realize that this new *you* without free will, will commit all sorts of horrible acts.

MORTAL: But they will not be sins since he will have no free will.

GOD: Whether you call them sins or not, the fact remains that they will be horrible acts in the sense that they will cause great pain to many sentient beings.

MORTAL *(after a pause):* Good God, you have trapped me again! Always the same game! If I now give you the go-ahead to create this new creature with no free will who will nevertheless commit atrocious acts, then true enough he will not be sinning, but I again will be the sinner to sanction this.

GOD: In that case, I'll go you one better! Here, I have already decided whether to create this new *you* with free will or not. Now, I am writing my decision on this piece of paper and I won't show it to you until later. But my decision is now made and is absolutely irrevocable. There is nothing you can possibly do to alter it; you have no responsibility in the matter. Now, what I wish to know is this: Which way do you hope I have decided? Remember now, the responsibility for the decision falls entirely on my shoulders, not yours. So you can tell me perfectly honestly and without any fear, which way do you hope I have decided?

MORTAL *(after a very long pause):* I hope you have decided to give him free will.

GOD: Most interesting! I have removed your last obstacle! If I do not give him free will, then no sin is to be imputed to anybody. So why do you hope I will give him free will?

MORTAL: Because sin or no sin, the important point is that if you do not give him free will, then (at least according to what you have said) he will go around hurting people, and I don't want to see people hurt.

GOD *(with an infinite sigh of relief):* At last! At last you see the real point!

MORTAL: What point is that?

GOD: That sinning is not the real issue! The important thing is that people as well as other sentient beings don't get hurt!

MORTAL: You sound like a utilitarian!

GOD: I am a utilitarian!

MORTAL: What!

GOD: Whats or no whats, I am a utilitarian. Not a unitarian, mind you, but a utilitarian.

MORTAL: I just can't believe it!

GOD: Yes, I know, your religious training has taught you otherwise. You have probably thought of me more like a Kantian than a utilitarian, but your training was simply wrong.

MORTAL: You leave me speechless!

GOD: I leave you speechless, do I! Well, that is perhaps not too bad a thing—you have a tendency to speak too much as it is. Seriously, though, why do you think I ever did give you free will in the first place?

MORTAL: Why did you? I never have thought much about why you did; all I have been arguing for is that you shouldn't have! But why did you? I guess all I can think of is the standard religious explanation: Without free will, one is not capable of meriting either salvation or damnation. So without free will, we could not earn the right to eternal life.

GOD: Most interesting! *I* have eternal life; do you think I have ever done anything to merit it?

MORTAL: Of course not! With you it is different. You are already so good and perfect (at least allegedly) that it is not necessary for you to merit eternal life.

GOD: Really now? That puts me in a rather enviable position, doesn't it?

MORTAL: I don't think I understand you.

GOD: Here I am eternally blissful without ever having to suffer or make sacrifices or struggle against evil temptations or anything like that. Without any of that type of "merit," I enjoy blissful eternal existence. By contrast, you poor mortals have to sweat and suffer and have all sorts of horrible conflicts about morality, and all for what? You don't even know whether I really exist or not, or if there really is any afterlife, or if there is, where you come into the picture. No matter how much you try to placate me by being "good," you never have any real assurance that your "best" is good enough for me, and hence you have no real security in obtaining salvation. Just think of it! I already *have* the equivalent of "salvation"—and have never had to go through this infinitely lugubrious process of earning it. Don't you ever envy me for this?

MORTAL: But it is blasphemous to envy you!

GOD: Oh come off it! You're not now talking to your Sunday school teacher, you are talking to *me.* Blasphemous or not, the important question is not whether you have the right to be envious of me but whether you are. Are you?

MORTAL: Of course I am!

GOD: Good! Under your present world view, you sure should be most envious of me. But I think with a more realistic world view, you no longer will be. So you really have swallowed the idea which has been taught you that your life on earth is like an examination period and that the purpose of providing you with free will is to test you, to see if you merit blissful eternal life. But what puzzles me is this: If you really believe I am as good and benevolent as I am cracked up to be, why should I require people to merit things like happiness and eternal life? Why should I not grant such things to everyone regardless of whether or not he deserves them?

MORTAL: But I have been taught that your sense of morality—your sense of justice—demands that goodness be rewarded with happiness and evil be punished with pain.

GOD: Then you have been taught wrong.

MORTAL: But the religious literature is so full of this idea! Take for example Jonathan Edwards's "Sinners in the Hands of an Angry God." How he describes you as holding your enemies like loathsome scorpions over the flaming pit of hell, preventing them from falling into the fate that they deserve only by dint of your mercy.

GOD: Fortunately, I have not been exposed to the tirades of Mr. Jonathan Edwards. Few sermons have ever been preached which are more misleading. The very title "Sinners in the Hands of an Angry God" tells its own tale. In the first place, I am never angry. In the second place, I do not think at all in terms of "sin." In the third place, I have no enemies.

MORTAL: By that do you mean that there are no people whom you hate, or that there are no people who hate you?

GOD: I meant the former although the latter also happens to be true.

MORTAL: Oh come now, I know people who have openly claimed to have hated you. At times *I* have hated you!

GOD: You mean you have hated your image of me. That is not the same thing as hating me as I really am.

MORTAL: Are you trying to say that it is not wrong to hate a false conception of you, but that it is wrong to hate you as you really are?

GOD: No, I am not saying that at all; I am saying something far more drastic! What I am saying has absolutely nothing to do with right or wrong. What I am saying is that one who knows me for what I really am would simply find it psychologically impossible to hate me.

MORTAL: Tell me, since we mortals seem to have such erroneous views about your real nature, why don't you enlighten us? Why don't you guide us the right way?

GOD: What makes you think I'm not?

MORTAL: I mean, why don't you appear to our very senses and simply tell us that we are wrong?

GOD: Are you really so naive as to believe that I am the sort of being which can *appear* to your senses? It would be more correct to say that I *am* your senses.

MORTAL *(astonished):* You are my senses?

GOD: Not quite, I am more than that. But it comes closer to the truth than the idea that I am perceivable by the senses. I am not an object; like you, I am a subject, and a subject can perceive, but cannot be perceived. You can no more see me than you can see your own thoughts. You can see an apple, but the event of your seeing an apple is itself not seeable. And I am far more like the seeing of an apple than the apple itself.

MORTAL: If I can't see you, how do I know you exist?

GOD: Good question! How in fact do you know I exist?

MORTAL: Well, I am talking to you, am I not?

GOD: How do you know you are talking to me? Suppose you told a psychiatrist, "Yesterday I talked to God." What do you think he would say?

MORTAL: That might depend on the psychiatrist. Since most of them are atheistic, I guess most would tell me I had simply been talking to myself.

GOD: And they would be right!

MORTAL: What? You mean you don't exist?

GOD: You have the strangest faculty of drawing false conclusions! Just because you are talking to yourself, it follows that *I* don't exist?

MORTAL: Well, if I think I am talking to you, but I am really talking to myself, in what sense do you exist?

GOD: Your question is based on two fallacies plus a confusion. The question of whether or not you are now talking to me and the question of whether or not I exist are totally separate. Even if you were not now talking to me (which obviously you are), it still would not mean that I don't exist.

MORTAL: Well, all right, of course! So instead of saying "if I am talking to myself, then you don't exist," I should rather have said, "if I am talking to myself, then I obviously am not talking to you."

GOD: A very different statement indeed, but still false.

MORTAL: Oh, come now, if I am only talking to myself, then how can I be talking to you?

GOD: Your use of the word "only" is quite misleading! I can suggest several logical possibilities under which your talking to yourself does not imply that you are not talking to me.

MORTAL: Suggest just one!

GOD: Well, obviously one such possibility is that you and I are identical.

MORTAL: Such a blasphemous thought—at least had *I* uttered it!

GOD: According to some religions, yes. According to others, it is the plain, simple, immediately perceived truth.

MORTAL: So the only way out of my dilemma is to believe that you and I are identical?

GOD: Not at all! This is only one way out. There are several others. For example, it may be that you are part of me, in which case you may be talking to that part of me which is you. Or I may be part of you, in which case you may be talking to that part of you which is me. Or again, you and I might partially overlap, in which case you may be talking to the intersection and hence talking both to you and to me. The only way your talking to yourself might seem to imply that you are not talking to me is if you and I were totally disjoint—and even then, you could conceivably be talking to both of us.

MORTAL: So you claim you do exist.

GOD: Not at all. Again you draw false conclusions! The question of my existence has not even come up. All I have said is that from the fact that you are talking to yourself one cannot possibly infer my nonexistence, let alone the weaker fact that you are not talking to me.

MORTAL: All right, I'll grant your point! But what I really want to know is *do* you exist?

GOD: What a strange question!

MORTAL: Why? Men have been asking it for countless millennia.

GOD: I know that! The question itself is not strange; what I mean is that it is a most strange question to ask of *me!*

MORTAL: Why?

GOD: Because I am the very one whose existence you doubt! I perfectly well understand your anxiety. You are worried that your present experience with me is a mere hallucination. But how can you possibly expect to obtain reliable information from a being about his very existence when you suspect the nonexistence of the very same being?

MORTAL: So you won't tell me whether or not you exist?

GOD: I am not being willful! I merely wish to point out that no answer I could give could possibly satisfy you. All right, suppose I said, "No, I don't exist." What would that prove? Absolutely nothing! Or if I said, "Yes, I exist." Would that convince you? Of course not!

MORTAL: Well, if you can't tell me whether or not you exist, then who possibly can?

GOD: That is something which no one can tell you. It is something which only you can find out for yourself.

MORTAL: How do I go about finding this out for myself?

GOD: That also no one can tell you. This is another thing you will have to find out for yourself.

MORTAL: So there is no way you can help me?

GOD: I didn't say that. I said there is no way I can tell you. But that doesn't mean there is no way I can help you.

MORTAL: In what manner then can you help me?

GOD: I suggest you leave that to me! We have gotten sidetracked as it is, and I would like to return to the question of what you believed my purpose to be in giving you free will. Your first idea of my giving you free will in order to test whether you merit salvation or not may appeal to many moralists, but the idea is quite hideous to me. You cannot think of any nicer reason—any more humane reason—why I gave you free will?

MORTAL: Well now, I once asked this question of an Orthodox rabbi. He told me that the way we are constituted, it is simply not possible for us to enjoy salvation unless we feel we have earned it. And to earn it, we of course need free will.

GOD: That explanation is indeed much nicer than your former but still is far from correct. According to Orthodox Judaism, I created angels, and they have no free will. They are in actual sight of me and are so completely attracted by goodness that they never have even the slightest temptation toward evil. They really have no choice in the matter. Yet they are eternally happy even though they have never earned it. So if your rabbi's explanation were correct, why wouldn't I have simply created only angels rather than mortals?

MORTAL: Beats me! Why didn't you?

GOD: Because the explanation is simply not correct. In the first place, I have never created any ready-made angels. All sentient beings ultimately approach the state which might be called "angelhood." But just as the race of human beings is in a certain stage of biologic evolution, so angels are simply the end result of a process of Cosmic Evolution. The only difference between the so-called *saint* and the so called *sinner* is that the former is vastly older than the latter. Unfortunately it takes countless life cycles to learn what is perhaps the most important fact of the universe—evil is simply painful. All the arguments of the moralists—all the alleged reasons why people *shouldn't* commit evil acts—simply pale into insignificance in light of the one basic truth that *evil is suffering.*

No, my dear friend, I am not a moralist. I am wholly a utilitarian. That I should have been conceived in the role of a moralist is one of the great tragedies of the human race. My role in the scheme of things (if one can use this misleading expression) is neither to punish nor reward, but to aid the process by which all sentient beings achieve ultimate perfection.

MORTAL: Why did you say your expression is misleading?

GOD: What I said was misleading in two respects. First of all it is inaccurate to speak of my role in the scheme of things. I *am* the scheme of things. Secondly, it is equally misleading to speak of my aiding the process of sentient beings attaining enlightenment. I *am* the process. The ancient Taoists were quite close when they said of me (whom they called "Tao") that I do not *do* things, yet through me all things get done. In more modern terms, I am not the cause of Cosmic Process, I am Cosmic Process itself. I think the most accurate and fruitful definition of me which man can frame—at least in his present state of evolution—is that I am the very process of enlightenment. Those who wish to think of the devil (although I wish they wouldn't!) might analogously define him as the unfortunate length of time the process takes. In this sense, the devil is necessary; the process simply does take an enormous length of time, and there is absolutely nothing I can do about it. But, I assure you, once the process is more correctly understood, the painful length of time will no longer be regarded as an essential limitation or an evil. It will be seen to be the very essence of the process itself. I know this is not completely consoling to you who are now in the finite sea of suffering, but the amazing thing is that once you grasp this fundamental attitude, your very finite suffering will begin to diminish—ultimately to the vanishing point.

MORTAL: I have been told this, and I tend to believe it. But suppose I personally succeed in seeing things through your eternal eyes. Then I will be happier, but don't I have a duty to others?

GOD *(laughing):* You remind me of the Mahayana Buddhists! Each one says, "I will not enter Nirvana until I first see that all other sentient beings do so." So each one waits for the other fellow to go first. No wonder it takes them so long! The Hinayana Buddhist errs in a different direction. He believes that no one can be of the slightest help to others in obtaining salvation; each one has to do it entirely by himself. And so each tries only for his own salvation. But this very detached attitude makes salvation impossible. The truth of the matter is that salvation is partly an individual and partly a social process. But it is a grave mistake to believe—as do many Mahayana Buddhists—that the attaining of enlightenment puts one out of commission, so to speak, for helping others. The best way of helping others is by first seeing the light oneself.

MORTAL: There is one thing about your self-description which is somewhat disturbing. You describe yourself essentially as a *process.* This puts you in such an impersonal light, and so many people have a need for a personal God.

GOD: So because they need a personal God, it follows that I am one?

MORTAL: Of course not. But to be acceptable to a mortal a religion must satisfy his needs.

GOD: I realize that. But the so-called "personality" of a being is really more in the eyes of the beholder than in the being itself. The controversies which have raged about whether I am a personal or an impersonal being are rather silly because neither side is right or wrong. From one point of view, I am personal, from another, I am not. It is the same with a human being. A creature from another planet may look at him purely impersonally as a mere collection of atomic particles behaving according to strictly prescribed physical laws. He may have no more feeling for the personality of a human than the average human has for an ant. Yet an ant has just as much individual personality as a human to beings like myself who really know the ant. To look at something impersonally is no more correct or incorrect than to look at it personally, but in general, the better you get to know something, the more personal it becomes. To illustrate my point, do you think of me as a personal or impersonal being?

MORTAL: Well, I'm talking to you, am I not?

GOD: Exactly! From that point of view, your attitude toward me might be described as a personal one. And yet, from another point of view—no less valid—I can also be looked at impersonally.

MORTAL: But if you are really such an abstract thing as a process, I don't see what sense it can make my talking to a mere "process."

GOD: I love the way you say "mere." You might just as well say that you are living in a "mere universe." Also, why must everything one does make sense? Does it make sense to talk to a tree?

MORTAL: Of course not!

GOD: And yet, many children and primitives do just that.

MORTAL: But I am neither a child nor a primitive.

GOD: I realize that, unfortunately.

MORTAL: Why unfortunately?

GOD: Because many children and primitives have a primal intuition which the likes of you have lost. Frankly, I think it would do you a lot of good to talk to a tree once in a while, even more good than talking to me! But we seem always to be getting sidetracked! For the last time, I would like us to try to come to an understanding about why I gave you free will.

MORTAL: I have been thinking about this all the while.

GOD: You mean you haven't been paying attention to our conversation?

MORTAL: Of course I have. But all the while, on another level, I have been thinking about it.

GOD: And have you come to any conclusion?

MORTAL: Well, you say the reason is not to test our worthiness. And you disclaimed the reason that we need to feel that we must merit things in order to enjoy them. And you claim to be a utilitarian. Most significant of all, you appeared so delighted when I came to the sudden realization that it is not sinning in itself which is bad but only the suffering which it causes.

GOD: Well of course! What else could conceivably be bad about sinning?

MORTAL: All right, you know that, and now I know that. But all my life I unfortunately have been under the influence of those moralists who hold sinning to be bad in itself. Anyway, putting all these pieces together, it occurs to me that the only reason you gave free will is because of your belief that with free will, people will tend to hurt each other—and themselves—less than without free will.

GOD: Bravo! That is by far the best reason you have yet given! I can assure you that had I *chosen* to give free will, that would have been my very reason for so choosing.

MORTAL: What! You mean to say you did not choose to give us free will?

GOD: My dear fellow, I could no more choose to give you free will than I could choose to make an equilateral triangle equiangular. I could choose to make or not to make an equilateral triangle in the first place, but having chosen to make one, I would then have no choice but to make it equiangular.

MORTAL: I thought you could do anything!

GOD: Only things which are logically possible. As St. Thomas said, "It is a sin to regard the fact that God cannot do the impossible, as a limitation on His powers." I agree, except that in place of his using the word *sin* I would use the term *error.*

MORTAL: Anyhow, I am still puzzled by your implication that you did not choose to give me free will.

GOD: Well, it is high time I inform you that the entire discussion—from the very beginning—has been based on one monstrous fallacy! We have been talking purely on a moral level—you originally complained that I gave you free will, and raised the whole question as to whether I should have. It never once occurred to you that I had absolutely no choice in the matter.

MORTAL: I am still in the dark!

GOD: Absolutely! Because you are only able to look at it through the eyes of a moralist. The more fundamental *metaphysical* aspects of the question you never even considered.

MORTAL: I still do not see what you are driving at.

GOD: Before you requested me to remove your free will, shouldn't your first question have been whether as a matter of fact you *do* have free will?

MORTAL: That I simply took for granted.

GOD: But why should you?

MORTAL: I don't know. Do I have free will?

GOD: Yes.

MORTAL: Then why did you say I shouldn't have taken it for granted?

GOD: Because you shouldn't. Just because something happens to be true, it does not follow that it should be taken for granted.

MORTAL: Anyway, it is reassuring to know that my natural intuition about having free will is correct. Sometimes I have been worried that determinists are correct.

GOD: They are correct.

MORTAL: Wait a minute now, do I have free will or don't I?

GOD: I already told you you do. But that does not mean that determinism is incorrect.

MORTAL: Well, are my acts determined by the laws of nature or aren't they?

GOD: The word *determined* here is subtly but powerfully misleading and has contributed so much to the confusions of the free will versus determinism controversies. Your acts are certainly in accordance with the laws of nature, but to say they are *determined* by the laws of nature creates a totally misleading psychological image which is that your will could somehow be in conflict with the laws of nature and that the latter is somehow more powerful than you, and could "determine" your acts whether you liked it or not. But it is simply impossible for your will to ever conflict with natural law. You and natural law are really one and the same.

MORTAL: What do you mean that I cannot conflict with nature? Suppose I were to become very stubborn, and I *determined* not to obey the laws of nature. What could stop me? If I became sufficiently stubborn, even you could not stop me!

GOD: You are absolutely right! *I* certainly could not stop you. Nothing could stop you. But there is no need to stop you, because you could not even start! As Goethe very beautifully expressed it, "In trying to oppose Nature, we are, in the very process of doing so, acting according to the laws of nature!" Don't you see that the so-called "laws of nature" are nothing more than a description of how in fact you and other beings *do* act? They are merely a description of how you act, not a prescription of how you should act, not a power or force which compels or determines your acts. To be valid a law of nature must take into account how in fact you do act, or, if you like, how you choose to act.

MORTAL: So you really claim that I am incapable of determining to act against natural law?

GOD: It is interesting that you have twice now used the phrase "determined to act" instead of "chosen to act." This identification is quite common. Often one uses the statement "I am determined to do this" synonomously with "I have chosen to do this." This very psychological identification should reveal that determinism and choice are much closer than they might appear. Of course, you might well say that the doctrine of free will says that it is *you* who are doing the determining, whereas the doctrine of determinism appears to say that your acts are determined by something apparently outside you. But the confusion is largely caused by your bifurcation of reality into the "you" and the "not you." Really now, just where do you leave off and the rest of the universe begin? Or where does the rest of the universe leave off and you begin? Once you can see the so-called "you" and the so-called "nature" as a continuous whole, then you can never again be bothered by such questions as whether it is you who are controlling nature or nature who is controlling you. Thus the muddle of free will versus determinism will vanish. If I may use a crude analogy, imagine two bodies moving toward each other by virtue of gravitational attraction. Each body, if sentient, might wonder whether it is he or the other fellow who is exerting the "force." In a way it is both, in a way it is neither. It is best to say that it is the configuration of the two which is crucial.

MORTAL: You said a short while ago that our whole discussion was based on a monstrous fallacy. You still have not told me what this fallacy is.

GOD: Why, the idea that I could possibly have created you without free will! You acted as if this were a genuine possibility, and wondered why I did not choose it! It never occurred to you that a sentient being without free will is no more conceivable than a physical object which exerts no gravitational attraction. (There is, incidentally, more analogy than you realize between a physical object exerting gravitational attraction and a sentient being exerting free will!) Can you honestly even imagine a conscious being without free will? What on earth could it be like? I think that one thing in your life that has so misled you is your having been told that I gave man the *gift* of free will. As if I first created man, and then as an afterthought endowed him with the extra property of free will. Maybe you think I have some sort of "paint brush" with which I daub some creatures with free will and not others. No, free will is not an "extra"; it is part and parcel of the very essence of consciousness. A conscious being without free will is simply a metaphysical absurdity.

MORTAL: Then why did you play along with me all this while discussing what I thought was a moral problem, when, as you say, my basic confusion was metaphysical?

GOD: Because I thought it would be good therapy for you to get some of this moral poison out of your system. Much of your metaphysical confusion was due to faulty moral notions, and so the latter had to be dealt with first.

And now we must part—at least until you need me again. I think our present union will do much to sustain you for a long while. But do remember what I told you about trees. Of course, you don't have to literally talk to them if doing so makes you feel silly. But there is so much you can learn from them, as well as from the rocks and streams and other aspects of nature. There is nothing like a naturalistic orientation to dispel all these morbid thoughts of "sin" and "free will" and "moral responsibility." At one stage of history, such notions were actually useful. I refer to the days when tyrants had unlimited power and nothing short of fears of hell could possibly restrain them. But mankind has grown up since then, and this gruesome way of thinking is no longer necessary.

It might be helpful to you to recall what I once said through the writings of the great Zen poet Seng-Ts'an:

> If you want to get the plain truth,
> Be not concerned with right and wrong.
> The conflict between right and wrong
> Is the sickness of the mind.

I can see by your expression that you are simultaneously soothed and terrified by these words! What are you afraid of? That if in your mind you abolish the distinction between right and wrong you are more likely to commit acts which are wrong? What makes you so sure that self-consciousness about right and wrong does not in fact lead to more wrong acts than right ones? Do you honestly believe that so-called amoral people, when it comes to action rather than theory, behave less ethically than moralists? Of course not! Even most moralists acknowledge the ethical superiority of the behavior of most of those who theoretically take an amoral position. They seem so surprised that without ethical *principles* these people behave so nicely! It never seems to occur to them that it is by virtue of the very lack of moral principles that their good behavior flows so freely! Do the words "The conflict between right and wrong is the sickness of the human mind" express an idea so different from the story of the Garden of Eden and the fall of Man due to Adam's eating of the fruit of knowledge? This knowledge, mind you, was of ethical principles, not ethical feelings—these Adam already had. There is much truth in this story, though I never commanded Adam not to eat the apple, I merely advised him not to. I told him it would not be good for him. If the damn fool had only listened to me, so much trouble could have been avoided! But no, he thought he knew everything! But I wish the theologians would finally learn that I am not punishing Adam and his descendants for the act, but rather that the fruit in question is poisonous in its own right and its effects, unfortunately, last countless generations.

And now really I must take leave. I do hope that our discussion will dispel some of your ethical morbidity and replace it by a more naturalistic orientation. Remember also the marvelous words I once uttered through the mouth of Lao-tse when I chided Confucius for his moralizing:

> All this talk of goodness and duty, these perpetual pin-pricks unnerve and irritate the hearer—You had best study how it is that Heaven and Earth maintain their eternal course, that the sun and moon maintain their light, the stars their seried ranks, the birds and beasts their flocks, the trees and shrubs their station. This you too should learn to guide your steps by Inward Power, to follow the course that the Way of Nature sets; and soon you will no longer need to go round laboriously advertising goodness and duty. . . . The swan does not need a daily bath in order to remain white.

MORTAL: You certainly seem partial to Eastern philosophy!

GOD: Oh, not at all! Some of my finest thoughts have bloomed in your native American soil. For example, I never expressed my notion of "duty" more eloquently than through the thoughts of Walt Whitman:

> I give nothing as duties,
> What others give as duties, I give as living impulses.

DISCUSSION QUESTIONS

1. Contrast the account of free will in this dialogue with Frankfurt's account of free will.
2. Contrast the view of God in this dialogue with Broad's account of God. Which is more appealing to you and why?
3. Why does the Mortal wish to be absolved of having free will?
4. Why does the Mortal fear sinning?
5. What does God mean by saying that there are no people whom God hates and there are no people who hate God?
6. What is the "one monstrous fallacy" that God says their entire discussion has been based on?

Chapter 29

I. A. MENKITI

Ifeanyi Anthony Menkiti was born in Onitsha, Nigeria. He received degrees from Pomona College, Columbia University, and New York University before his Ph.D. from Harvard in 1974. He has been teaching Medical Ethics, Philosophy of Law, Philosophy and Literature, and African Philosophy on the faculty at Wellesley College since 1973. In this essay first published in 1979, Menkiti contrasts the conception of a person in Western thought and traditional African thought. The Western view, he contends, employs a minimal definition by identifying some isolated, static quality, such as having a soul, rationality, will, or memory. The African definition is maximal and processual. Personhood is a matter of degree; it is something which adults can fall short of to a greater or lesser extent. This is because becoming a person requires a long period of time during which the slowly maturing individual grows into a full societal participant embodying the excellences of the community in which he has become gradually ever more strongly rooted. The newborn child is a nameless nonperson, an "it," just like the completely forgotten, long departed ancestral spirit. Menkiti argues that personhood, in the African view, is directly proportional to involvement in communal life and fulfillment of social obligations; loss of communal incorporation marks loss of personal identity.

Person and Community in African Traditional Thought

My aim in this paper is to articulate a certain conception of the person found in African traditional thought. I shall attempt to do this in an idiom, or language, familiar to modern philosophy. In this regard it is helpful to begin by pointing to a few significant contrasts between this African conception of the person and various other conceptions found in Western thought.

The first contrast worth noting is that whereas most Western views of man abstract this or that feature of the lone individual and then proceed to make it the defining or essential characteristic which entities aspiring to the description "man" must have, the African view of man denies that persons can be defined by focusing on this or that physical or psychological characteristic of the lone individual. Rather, man is defined by reference to the environing community. As John Mbiti notes, the African view of the person can be summed up in this statement: "I am because we are, and since we are, therefore I am."[1]

One obvious conclusion to be drawn from this dictum is that, as far as Africans are concerned, the reality of the communal world takes precedence over the reality of individual life histories, whatever these may be. And this primacy is meant to apply not only ontologically, but also in regard to epistemic accessibility. It is in rootedness in an ongoing human community that the individual comes to see himself as man, and it is by first knowing this community as a stubborn perduring fact of the psychophysical world that the individual also comes to know himself as a durable, more or less permanent, fact of this world. In the language of certain familiar Western disciplines, we could say that not only the biological set through which the individual is capable of identification by reference to a communal gene pool, but also the language which he speaks and which is no small factor in the constitution of his mental dispositions and attitudes, belong to this or that specific human group. What is more, the sense of self-identity which the individual comes to possess cannot be made sense of except by reference to these collective facts. And thus, just as the navel points men to umbilical linkage with generations preceding them, so also does language and its associated social rules point them to a mental commonwealth with others whose life histories encompass the past, present, and future.

A crucial distinction thus exists between the African view of man and the view of man found in Western thought: in the African view it is the community which defines the person as person, not some isolated static quality of rationality, will, or memory.

Source: I. A. Menkiti, 1979. "Person and Community in African Traditional Thought." *African Philosophy: An Introduction,* edited by Richard A. Wright. New York: University Press of America, 3rd ed. (1984): 171–181. Reprinted with the generous permission of the author.

This brings us to the second point of contrast between the two views of man, namely, the *processual* nature of being in African thought—the fact that persons become persons only after a process of incorporation. Without incorporation into this or that community, individuals are considered to be mere danglers to whom the description 'person' does not fully apply. For personhood is something which has to be achieved, and is not given simply because one is born of human seed. This is perhaps the burden of the distinction which Placide Tempels' native informants saw fit to emphasize to him—i.e. the distinction between a *muntu mutupu* (a man of middling importance) and *muntu mukulumpe* (a powerful man, a man with a great deal of force). Because the word "muntu" includes an idea of excellence, of plenitude of force at maturation, the expression 'ke muntu po', which translates as 'this is not a man',[2] may be used in reference to a human being. Thus, it is not enough to have before us the biological organism, with whatever rudimentary psychological characteristics are seen as attaching to it. We must also conceive of this organism as going through a long process of social and ritual transformation until it attains the full complement of excellencies seen as truly definitive of man. And during this long process of attainment, the community plays a vital role as catalyst and as prescriber of norms.

In light of the above observations I think it would be accurate to say that whereas Western conceptions of man go for what might be described as a minimal definition of the person—whoever has soul, or rationality, or will, or memory, is seen as entitled to the description 'person'—the African view reaches instead for what might be described as a maximal definition of the person. As far as African societies are concerned, personhood is something at which individuals could fail, at which they could be competent or ineffective, better or worse. Hence, the African emphasized the rituals of incorporation and the overarching necessity of learning the social rules by which the community lives, so that what was initially biologically given can come to attain social self-hood, i.e., become a person with all the inbuilt excellencies implied by the term.

That full personhood is not perceived as simply given at the very beginning of one's life, but is attained after one is well along in society, indicates straight away that the older an individual gets the more of a person he becomes. As an Igbo proverb has it, "What an old man sees sitting down, a young man cannot see standing up." The proverb applies, it must be added, not just to the incremental growth of wisdom as one ages; it also applies to the ingathering of the other excellencies considered to be definitive of full personhood. What we have here then is both a claim that a qualitative difference exists between old and young, and a claim that some sort of ontological progression exists between infancy and ripening old age. One does not just take on additional features, one also undergoes fundamental changes at the very core of one's being.

Now, admittedly, the whole idea of ontological progression is something in need of elaboration. Offhand it may not sit very well in the minds of those unaccustomed to the view of personhood being presented here. The temptation might be strong in some quarters to retort that either an entity is a person or it is not; that there can be no two ways about it. In response to this misgiving let me note that the notion of an acquisition of personhood is supported by the natural tendency in many languages, English included, of referring to children and new-borns as *it*. Consider this expression: "We rushed the child to the hospital but before we arrived *it* was dead." We would never say this of a grown person. Of course, with a child or new-born, reference could also be made by use of a personal pronoun, with the statement reading instead: "We rushed the child to the hospital but before we arrived he/she was dead." This personalizing option does not, however, defeat the point presently being made. For the important thing is that we have the choice of an *it* for referring to children and new-borns, whereas we have no such choice in referring to older persons.

The fact, then, that a flexibility of referential designation exists in regard to the earliest stages of human life, but not in regard to the more established later stages, is something well worth keeping in mind. What we have is not just a distinction of language but a distinction laden with ontological significance. In the particular context of Africa, anthropologists have long noted the relative absence of ritualized grief when the death of a young child occurs, whereas with the death of an older person, the burial ceremony becomes more elaborate and the grief more ritualized—indicating a significant difference in the conferral of ontological status.

Before moving away from the foregoing observations made in support of the notion of personhood as acquired, let me note, in addition, that in African societies the ultimate termination of personal existence is also marked by an 'it' designation; thus, the same depersonalized reference marking the beginning of personal existence also marks the end of that existence. After birth the individual goes through the different rites of incorporation, including those of initiation at puberty time, before becoming a full person in the eyes of the community. And then, of course, there is procreation, old age, death, and entry into the community of departed ancestral spirits—a community viewed as continuous with the community of living men and women, and with which it is conceived as being in constant interaction.

Following John Mbiti, we could call the inhabitants of the ancestral community by the name of the "living dead."[3] For the ancestral dead are not dead in the world of spirits, nor are they dead in the memory of living men and women who continue to remember them, and who incessantly ask their help through various acts of libation and sacrificial offering. At the stage of ancestral existence, the dead still retain their personhood and are, as a matter of fact, addressed by their various names very much as if they were still at center stage. Later, however, after several generations, the ancestors cease to be remembered by their personal names; from this moment on they slide into personal non-existence, and lose all that they once possessed by way of personal identity. This, for the traditional African world-view, is the termination of personal existence, with entities that were once fully human agents becoming once again mere *its,* ending their worldly sojourn as they had started out—as un-incorporated non-persons. Mbiti has described this terminal stage of a person's life as one of "collective immortality" (in contrast to the "personal immortality" that marks the stage of ancestral existence, a stage in which the departed are remembered by name by the living, and do genuinely form a community of their own).[4]

But the expression "collective immortality" is misleading and problematic. At the stage of total dis-incorporation marked by the term, the mere *its* that the dead have now become cannot form a collectivity of any kind; and, since by definition no one now remembers them, there is not much sense in saying of them that they are immortal either. They no longer have an adequate sense of self; and having lost their names, lose also the means by which they could be immortalized. Hence, it is better to refer to them by the term the *nameless dead,* rather than designate their stage of existence by such a term as "collective immortality," thereby opening up the possibility of describing them as "collective immortals," which certainly they are not. This emendation apart, however, Mbiti is quite right when he states that for African man no ontological progression is possible beyond the spirit world: "Beyond the state of the spirits, men cannot go or develop. This is the destiny of man as far as African ontology is concerned."[5]

The point can be made then, that a significant symmetry exists between the opening phase of an individual's quest for personhood and the terminal phase of that quest. Both are marked by an absence of incorporation and this absence is made abundantly evident by the related absence of collectively conferred names. Just as the child has no name when it tumbles out into the world to begin the journey towards selfhood, so likewise, at the very end, it will have no name again.

At both points it is considered quite appropriate to use an 'it' designation precisely because what we are dealing with are entities in regard to which there is a total absence of incorporation.

Finally, it is perhaps worth noting that this phenomenon of a depersonalized status at the two polarities of existence makes a great deal of sense given the absence of moral function. The child, we all know, is usually preoccupied with his physical needs; and younger persons, generally, are notoriously lacking in moral perception. Most often they have a tendency towards self-centeredness in action, a tendency to see the world exclusively through their own vantage point. This absence of moral function cannot but have an effect on the view of them as persons. Likewise for the completely departed ancestral spirits, who, at the terminal point of their personal existence, have now become mere *its,* their contact with the human community completely severed. The various societies found in traditional Africa routinely accept this fact that personhood is the sort of thing which has to be attained, and is attained in direct proportion as one participates in communal life through the discharge of the various obligations defined by one's stations. It is the carrying out of these obligations that transforms one from the it-status of early childhood, marked by an absence of moral function, into the person-status, of later years, marked by a widened maturity of ethical sense—an ethical maturity without which personhood is conceived as eluding one.

John Rawls, of the Western-born philosophers, comes closest to a recognition of this importance of ethical sense in the definition of personhood. In *A Theory of Justice* he makes explicit part of what is meant by the general ethical requirement of respect for persons, noting that those who are capable of a sense of justice are owed the duties of justice, with this capability construed in its sense of a potentiality which may or may not have been realized. He writes:

> Equal justice is owed to those who have the capacity to take part in and to act in accordance with the public understanding of the initial situation. One should observe that moral personality is here defined as a potentiality that is ordinarily realized in due course. It is this potentiality which brings the claims of justice into play. . . . The sufficient condition for equal justice [is] the capacity for moral personality.[6]

I take it that an important implication of this claim is that if an individual comes to deserve the duties of justice (and the confirmation therein implied of the individual's worth as a person) only through possession of a capacity for moral personality, then morality ought to be considered as essential to our sense of ourselves as persons. And indeed Rawls has argued in another context that a Kantian interpretation is possible in which the transgression of accepted moral rules gives rise not just to a feeling of guilt but to a feeling of shame—the point being that once morality is conceived as a fundamental part of what it means to be a person, then an agent is bound to feel himself incomplete in violating its rules, thus provoking in himself the feeling properly describable as shame, with its usual intimation of deformity and unwholeness.[7]

If it is generally conceded, then, that persons are the sort of entities that are owed the duties of justice, it must also be allowed that each time we find an ascription of any of the various rights implied by these duties of justice, the conclusion naturally follows that the possessor of the rights in question cannot be other than a person. That is so because the basis of such rights ascription has now been made dependent on a possession of a capacity for moral sense, a capacity, which though it need not be realized, is nonetheless made most evident by a concrete exercise of duties of justice towards others in the ongoing relationships of everyday life.

The foregoing interpretation would incidentally rule out, I believe, some dangerous tendencies currently fashionable in some philosophical circles of ascribing rights to animals.[8] The danger as I see it is that such an extension of moral language to the domain of animals is bound to undermine, sooner or later, the clearness of our conception of what it means to be a person. The practical consequences are also something for us to worry about. For if there is legitimacy in ascribing rights to animals then human beings could come to be compelled to share resources with them. In such a situation, for instance, the various governmental programs designed to eradicate poverty in the inner cities of the United States could conceivably come under fire from the United Animal Lovers of America, or some other such group, with the claim seriously being lodged that everything was being done for the poor, but not enough for the equally deserving cats and dogs. Minority persons might then find themselves the victims of a peculiar philosophy in which the constitutive elements in the definition of human personhood have become blurred through unwarranted extensions to non-human entities.

Before bringing to a close the various comments made so far, it might be helpful to focus on two issues discussed earlier, in an effort to forestall possible misunderstanding. One issue is the acquisition of personhood, since the possibility exists of confusing the African viewpoint with the viewpoint known in the West as Existentialist Philosophy. The other issue is the articulation of the specific sense in which the term 'community' has been used in these pages, so as to avoid possible misinterpretation.

To begin with the first, it must be emphasized that the African concept of man contrasts in significant measure with Existentialism (which on the face of things appears to be its most natural ally among the various Western philosophies of the person). Jean-Paul Sartre tells us that prior to the choice of his fundamental project an individual is "nothing [and] will not be anything until later, and then he will be what he makes himself."[9] Such a statement immediately evokes favorable comparisons between the African view of man and the Existentialist view, both views being regarded as adopting a notion of personhood, or self-hood, as something acquired.

But this, it must be warned, is a hasty conclusion to draw. For the Sartrean view that man is a *free unconditioned* being, a being not constrained by social or historical circumstances, flies in the face of African beliefs. Given its emphasis on individuals solely constituting themselves into the selves that they are to become, by dint of their private choices, such a view cannot but encourage eccentricity and individualism—traits which run counter to African ideals of what the human person is all about. Although in important ways existence does precede essence, it is not for the reasons that Sartre gives. We simply cannot postulate man's freedom and independence from all determining factors, including even reason, which is sometimes viewed by Sartre as unduly circumscribing the individual in his quest for a free and spontaneously authentic existence. As Professor William Abraham has pointed out in his book, *The Mind of Africa,* if possession of reason is part of our nature, then we cannot be enslaved by reason as Sartre sometimes seems to suggest; for no entity can be enslaved by its own nature.[10]

Nor is the above the only point at which Existentialist philosophy diverges from the African in the conception of man. Because of the controlling force of freedom, Sartre was led to postulate an equality of status between infant and child, on the one hand, and the grown adult, on the other. What all individuals have in common is that they choose; and choice is freedom, and freedom choice. As he puts it elsewhere, "Man does not exist in order to be free *subsequently;* there is no difference between the being of man and his *being free.*"[11] But this collapsing of the ontological distinction between young child and grown man is an illegitimate and absurd move. Even assuming that Sartrean freedom is a *sine qua non* of the metaphysics of persons, how can children with their quite obvious lack of intelligent appreciation of the circumstances of their lives and of the alternatives open to them, choose rationally? Is a choice undertaken in childish ignorance a choice that is truly free?

These misgivings are serious; and it is frankly quite difficult to understand what is meant by the type of freedom which Sartre insists both adults and children have in equal measure, as a result of which it is then argued that they, and they alone, can define for themselves the selves that they are to be, each in his own way. As Anthony Manser has put it, and I entirely agree, "It would seem that little remains of the freedom Sartre has been emphasizing. . .; it is hard to see how an infant can be aware of what he is doing, and if not then it is odd to call him responsible."[12]

In the light of the foregoing observations, I take it then that the African view of human personhood and the Existentialist view should not be conflated. Even though both views adopt a dynamic, non-static approach to the problem of definition of human self-hood, the underpinning metaphysical assumptions diverge significantly. Above all, whereas in the African understanding human community plays a crucial role in the individual's acquisition of full personhood, in the Sartrean existentialist view, the individual alone defines the self, or person, he is to become. Such collectivist insistences as we find in the African world-view are utterly lacking in the Existentialist tradition. And this difference in the two approaches is not accidental. Rather it arises because there is at bottom a fundamental disagreement as to what reality is all about.

Finally, let me try to clarify the sense in which the term 'community' has been used throughout this paper. Western writers have generally interpreted the term 'community' in such a way that it signifies nothing more than a mere collection of self-interested persons, each with his private set of preferences, but all of whom get together nonetheless because they realize, each to each, that in association they can accomplish things which they are not able to accomplish otherwise. In this primarily additive approach, whenever the term 'community' or 'society' is used, we are meant to think of the aggregated sum of individuals comprising it. And this is argued, not just as an ontological claim, but also as a methodological recommendation to the various social or humanistic disciplines interested in the investigation of the phenomenon of individuals in groups; hence the term 'Methodological Individualism' so much bandied around in the literature.

Now this understanding of human community, and of the approach to its study, is something completely at odds with the African view of community. When Mbiti says that the African says to himself, "I am because we are," the *we* referred to here is not an additive 'we' but a thoroughly fused collective 'we'. It is possible to distinguish three senses of human grouping, the first of which I shall call *collectivities* in the truest sense; the second of which might be called *constituted* human groups; and the third of which might be called *random* collections of individuals. The African understanding of human society adopts the usage in description number one above, whereas the Western understanding would fall closer to description number two; the difference between the two being that in what I have called 'collectivities in the truest sense' there is assumed to be an *organic* dimension to the relationship between the component individuals, whereas in the understanding of human society as something *constituted* what we have is a non-organic bringing together of atomic individuals into a unit more akin to an association than to a community. The difference between the two views of society is profound and can be represented diagrammatically thus:

AFRICAN

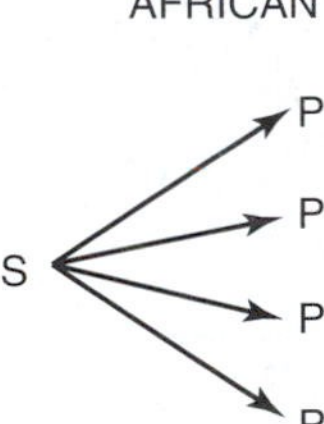

WESTERN

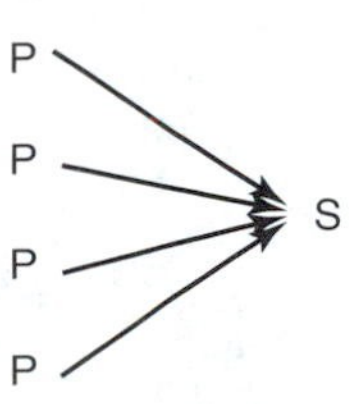

As can be seen from the diagram, whereas the African view asserts an ontological independence to human society, and moves from society to individuals, the Western view moves instead from individuals to society.

In looking at the distinction just noted, it becomes quite clear why African societies tend to be organized around the requirements of duty while Western societies tend to be organized around the postulation of individual rights. In the African understanding, priority is given to the duties which individuals owe to the collectivity, and their rights, whatever these may be, are seen as secondary to their exercise of their duties. In the West, on the other hand, we find a construal of things in which certain specified rights of individuals are seen as antecedent to the organization of society; with the function of government viewed, consequently, as being the protection and defense of these individual rights.

NOTES

1. John Mbiti, *African Religions and Philosophies* (New York: Doubleday and Company, 1970), p. 141.
2. Placide Tempels, *Bantu Philosophy* (Paris: Presence Africaine, 1959), p. 101.
3. Mbiti, *African Religions,* p. 32.
4. Ibid., p. 33.
5. Ibid., p. 34.
6. John Rawls, *A Theory of Justice* (Cambridge, Mass: Harvard University Press, 1971), pp. 505–506.
7. Ibid., p. 445.
8. See, for instance, Peter Singer, *Animal Liberation* (New York: Random House, 1975); as well as Tom Regan & Peter Singer eds., *Animal Rights and Human Obligations* (Englewood Cliffs, N. J.: Prentice Hall, 1976).
9. Jean-Paul Sartre, "Existentialism Is a Humanism" in Nino Languilli ed., *The Existentialist Tradition: Selected Writings,* trans. by Philip Mairet (New York: Doubleday-Anchor Books, 1971), p. 399; a close translation of p. 170 in this volume [Ed.].
10. William Abraham, *The Mind of Africa* (Chicago: The University of Chicago Press, 1962), pp. 20–21.
11. Jean-Paul Sartre, *Being and Nothingness: An essay on Phenomenological Ontology,* trans. with an introduction by Hazel E. Barnes (New York: The Philosophical Library, 1956), p. 25.
12. Anthony Manser, *Sartre: A Philosophical Study* (London: The University of London Press, 1966), p. 122.

DISCUSSION QUESTIONS

1. How is John Rawls' view in *A Theory of Justice* similar to Menkiti's emphasis on the ethical sense in the definition of personhood?
2. Explain why Menkiti believes that ascribing rights to nonhuman animals is dangerous for the conception of what it means to be a person. Do you share Menkiti's worry?
3. Menkiti describes why young children are not considered persons in African thought and how that is reflected in the linguistic practice of referring to a child as "it." Would he also consider it dangerous to ascribe rights to children given his reasons for denying rights and personhood to animals?
4. How does Menkiti contrast the African concept of person with Existentialism? Are his criticisms of Sartre persuasive?
5. Describe Menkiti's contrast between an organic collectivity and a constituted association interpretation of society.

Chapter 30

PETER A. FRENCH

Born in 1942 in Newburgh, New York, French received his Ph.D. in 1971 at the University of Miami, Coral Gables. He has authored or co-authored eighteen books, including Philosophers in Wonderland *(1975),* Ethics in Government *(Prentice Hall, 1982),* The Spectrum of Responsibility *(1991),* Cowboy Metaphysics: Ethics and Death in Westerns *(1997), and* The Virtues of Vengeance *(2001). In 2000 he became Lincoln Chair in Ethics and Professor of Philosophy at Arizona State University. French summers in the Colorado Rockies.*

His thesis in this 1979 essay is that corporations can be full-fledged moral persons with whatever privileges, rights, and duties are normally accorded to moral persons. French distinguishes four distinct notions of personhood: metaphysical, moral, legal, and sociological. Metaphysical persons are intelligent, rational agents. Moral persons are beings who are accountable. Legal persons are subjects of a right. Sociological persons are the offspring of certain social actions which the law recognizes de facto. *French approves of John Rawls' intuition that some associations of human beings should be treated as metaphysical persons capable of becoming moral persons. The Reality Theory recognizes corporations to be prelegal existing sociological persons, but French modifies such a theory so that it can identify a* de facto *metaphysical person, not just a sociological entity. He defines a moral person as a non-eliminatable subject of a responsibility ascription. Responsibility ascriptions focus on the subject's intentions. French contends that a Corporation's Internal Decision Structure is the device that allows us to describe it as acting with intentionality. Corporations, and not just people who work in them, have reasons for doing what they do. They have reasons because they have interests in doing those things that are likely to achieve their established corporate goals regardless of the transient self-interests of their biological human directors.*

The Corporation as a Moral Person

I

In one of his *New York Times* columns of not too long ago Tom Wicker's ire was aroused by a Gulf Oil Corporation advertisement that "pointed the finger of blame" for the energy crisis at all elements of our society (and supposedly away from the oil company). Wicker attacked Gulf Oil as the major, if not the sole, perpetrator of that crisis and virtually every other social ill, with the possible exception of venereal disease. It does not matter whether Wicker was serious or sarcastic in making his charges (I suspect he was in deadly earnest). I am interested in the sense ascriptions of moral responsibility make when their subjects are corporations. I hope to provide the foundation of a theory that allows treatment of corporations as members of the moral community, of equal standing with the traditionally acknowledged residents: biological human beings, and hence treats Wicker-type responsibility ascriptions as unexceptionable instances of a perfectly proper sort without having to paraphrase them. In short, corporations can be full-fledged moral persons and have whatever privileges, rights and duties as are, in the normal course of affairs, accorded to moral persons.

II

It is important to distinguish three quite different notions of what constitutes personhood that are entangled in our tradition: the metaphysical, moral and legal concepts. The entanglement is clearly evident in Locke's account of personal identity. He writes that the term "person" is "a *forensic* term, appropriating actions and their merit; and so belongs only to *intelligent agents,* capable of law, and happiness, and misery."[1] He goes on to say that by consciousness and memory persons are capable of extending themselves into the past and thereby become "concerned and *accountable.*"[2] Locke is historically correct in citing the law as a primary origin of the term "person." But he is incorrect in maintaining that its legal usage somehow entails its metaphysical sense, agency; and whether or not either sense, but especially the metaphysical, is interdependent on the moral sense, accountability, is surely controversial. Regarding the relationship between metaphysical and moral persons there are two distinct schools of thought. According to one, to be a metaphysical person is to be a moral one; to understand what it is to be accountable one must understand what it is to be an intelligent or a rational agent and vice-versa; while according to the

Source: Peter A. French, "The Corporation as a Moral Person." *American Philosophical Quarterly* 16, no. 3 (July 1979): 207–215. Reprinted with permission of *American Philosophical Quarterly*.

other, being an agent is a necessary but not sufficient condition of being a moral person. Locke holds the interdependence view with which I agree, but he roots both moral and metaphysical persons in the juristic person, which is, I think, wrongheaded. The preponderance of current thinking tends to some version of the necessary pre-condition view, but it does have the virtue of treating the legal person as something apart.

It is of note that many contemporary moral philosophers and economists both take a pre-condition view of the relationship between the metaphysical and moral person and also adopt a particular view of the legal personhood of corporations that effectually excludes corporations *per se* from the class of moral persons. Such philosophers and economists champion the least defensible of a number of possible interpretations of the juristic personhood of corporations, but their doing so allows them to systematically sidestep the question of whether corporations can meet the conditions of metaphysical personhood.[3]

III

John Rawls is, to some extent, guilty of fortifying what I hope to show is an indefensible interpretation of the legal concept and of thereby encouraging an anthropocentric bias that has led to the general belief that corporations just cannot be moral persons. As is well known, Rawls defends his two principles of justice by the use of a thought experiment that incorporates the essential characteristics of what he takes to be a pre-moral, though metaphysical population and then "derives" the moral guidelines for social institutions that they would accept. The persons (or parties) in the "original position" are described by Rawls as being mutually self-interested, rational, as having similar wants, needs, interests and capacities and as being, for all intents and purposes, equal in power (so that no one of them can dominate the others). Their choice of the principles of justice is, as Dennett has pointed out,[4] a rather dramatic rendering of one version of the compelling (though I think unnecessarily complex) philosophical thesis that only out of metaphysical persons can moral ones evolve.

But Rawls is remarkably ambiguous (and admittedly so) regarding who or what may qualify as a metaphysical person. He admits into the category, in one sentence, not only biological human beings but "nations, provinces, business firms, churches, teams, and so on,"[5] then, perhaps because he does not want to tackle the demonstration of the rationality, etc., of those institutions and organizations, or because he is a captive of the traditional prejudice in favor of biological persons, in the next sentence he withdraws entry. "There is, perhaps, a certain logical priority to the case of human individuals: it may be possible to analyze the actions of so-called artificial persons as logical constructions of the actions of human persons . . ."[6] "Perhaps" is, of course, a rather large hedge behind which to hide; but it is, I suppose, of some significance that in *A Theory of Justice* when he is listing the nature of the parties in the "original position" he adds "c. associations (states, churches, or other corporate bodies)."[7] He does not, unhappily, discuss this entry on his list anywhere else in the book. Rawls has hold, I think, of an important intuition: that some associations of human beings should be treated as metaphysical persons capable on his account of becoming moral persons, in and of themselves. He has, however, shrunk from the task of exploring the implications of that intuition and has instead retreated to the comfortable bulwarks of the anthropocentric bias.

IV

Many philosophers, including, I think, Rawls, have rather uncritically relied upon what they incorrectly perceive to be the most defensible juristic treatment of collectivities such as corporations as a paradigm for the treatment of corporations in their moral theories. The concept of corporate legal personhood under any of its popular interpretations is, I want to argue, virtually useless for moral purposes.

Following many writers on jurisprudence, a juristic person may be defined as any entity that is a subject of a right. There are good etymological grounds for such an inclusive neutral definition. The Latin "*persona*" originally referred to *dramatis personae,* and in Roman law the term was adopted to refer to anything that could act on either side of a legal dispute. [It was not until Boethius' definition of a person: "*Persona est naturae rationabilis individua substantia* (a person is the individual subsistence of a rational nature)" that metaphysical traits were ascribed to persons.] In effect, in Roman legal tradition persons are creations, artifacts, of the law itself, i.e., of the legislature that enacts the law, and are not considered to have or only have incidentally, existence of any kind outside of the legal sphere. The law, on the Roman interpretation, is systematically ignorant of the biological status of its subjects.

The Roman notion applied to corporations is popularly known as the Fiction Theory. Hallis characterizes that theory as maintaining that "the personality of a corporate body is a pure fiction and owes its existence to a creative act of the state."[8] Rawls' view of corporate persons could not, however, be motivated by adherence to the Fiction Theory for two reasons. The theory does not demand a dichotomy between real and artificial persons. All juristic persons, on the theory, are creations of the law. The theory does not view the law as recognizing or verifying some pre-legally existing persons; it argues that the law creates its own subjects. Secondly, the theory, in its pure form at least, does not regard any juristic persons as composites. All things which are legislatively created as subjects of rights are non-reducible or, if you will, primitive individual legal persons. (It is of some note that the Fiction Theory is enshrined in English law in regard to corporate bodies by no less an authority than Sir Edward Coke who wrote that corporations "rest only in intendment and consideration of the law."[9])

The Fiction Theory's major rival in American jurisprudence and the view that does seem to inform Rawls' account is what I shall call "the Legal Aggregate Theory of the Corporation." It holds that the names of corporate bodies are only umbrellas that cover (but do not shield) certain biological persons. The Aggregate Theory treats biological status as having legal priority and corporate existence as a contrivance for purposes of summary reference. (Generally, it may be worth mention, Aggregate Theorists tend to ignore employees and identify corporations with directors, executives and stockholders. The model on which they stake their claim is no doubt that of the primitive partnership.) I have shown elsewhere[10] that to treat a corporation as an aggregate for any purposes is to fail to recognize the key logical differences between corporations and mobs. The Aggregate Theory, then, despite the fact that it has been quite popular in legislatures, courtrooms, and on streetcorners simply ignores key logical, socio-economic and historical facts of corporate existence. [It might prove of some value in clarifying the dispute between Fiction and Aggregate theorists to mention a rather famous case in the English law. (The case is cited by Hallis.) It is that of *Continental Tyre and Rubber Co., Ltd.* vs *Daimler Co. Ltd.* Very sketchily, the Continental Tyre company was incorporated in England and carried on its business there. Its business was the selling of tires made in Germany, and all of its directors were German subjects in residence in Germany, and all but one of its shares were held by German subjects. The case arose during the First World War, and it turned on the issue of whether the company was an English subject by virtue of its being incorporated under the English law and independent of its directors and stockholders, and could hence bring suit in an English court against an English subject while a state of war existed. The majority opinion of The Court of Appeals (5–1) was that the corporation was an entity created by statute and hence was "a different person altogether from the subscribers to the memorandum or the shareholders on the register."[11] Hallis aptly summarizes the judgment of the court when he writes that "The Continental Tyre and Rubber Co., Ltd., was an English company with a personality at law distinct from the personalities of its members and could therefore sue in the English Courts as a British Subject."[12] The House of Lords, however, supporting the Aggregate Theory and no doubt motivated by the demands of the War, overturned the Court of Appeals. Lord Buckley wrote "The artificial legal entity has no independent power of motion. It is moved by the corporator. . . . He is German in fact although British in form."[13] This view has seen many incarnations since on both sides of the Atlantic. I take Rawls' burying of his intuition in the logical priority of human beings as a recent echoing of the words of Lord Parker who in the Continental Tyre case wrote for the majority in the House of Lords: ". . . the character in which the property is held and the character in which the capacity to act is enjoyed and acts are done are not *in pari materia*. The latter character is a quality of the company itself, and conditions its capacities and its acts and is attributable only to human beings . . ."][14]

In Germanic legal tradition resides the third major rival interpretation of corporate juristic personhood. Due primarily to the advocacy of Otto von Gierke, the so-called Reality Theory recognizes corporations to be pre-legal existing sociological persons. Underlying the theory is the view that law cannot create its subjects, it only determines which societal facts are in conformity with its requirements. At most, law endorses the pre-legal existence of persons for its own purposes. Gierke regards the corporation as an offspring of certain social actions having then a *de facto* personality, which the law only declares to be a juridical fact.[15] The Reality Theory's primary virtue is that it does not ignore the non-legal roots of the corporation while it, as does the Fiction Theory, acknowledges the non-identity of the corporation and the aggregate of its directors, stockholders, executives and employees. The primary difference between the Fiction and Reality Theories, that one treats the corporate person as *de jure* and the other as *de facto,* however, turns out to be of no real importance in regard to the issue of the moral personhood of a corporation. Admittedly the Reality Theory encapsulates a view at least superficially more amenable to arguing for discrete corporate moral personhood than does the Fiction Theory just because it does acknowledge *de facto* personhood, but theorists on both sides will admit that they are providing interpretations of only the formula "juristic person = the subject of rights," and as long as we stick to legal history, no interpretation of that formula need concern itself with metaphysical personhood or agency. The *de facto* personhood of the Reality Theory is that of a sociological entity only, of which no claim is or need be made regarding agency or rationality etc. One could, without contradiction, hold the Reality Theory and deny the metaphysical or moral personhood of corporations. What is needed is a Reality Theory that identifies a *de facto* metaphysical person not just a sociological entity.

Underlying all of these interpretations of corporate legal personhood is a distinction, embedded in the law itself, that renders them unhelpful for our purposes. Being a subject of rights is often contrasted in the law with being an "administrator of rights." Any number of entities and associations can and have been the subjects of legal rights. Legislatures have given rights to unborn human beings, they have reserved rights for human beings long after their death, and in some recent cases they have invested rights in generations of the future.[16] Of course such subjects of rights, though they are legal persons, cannot dispose of their rights, cannot administer them, because to administer a right one must be an agent, i.e., able to act in certain ways. It may be only an historical accident that most legal cases are cases in which "the subject of right *X*" and "the administrator of right *X*" are co-referential. It is nowhere required by law, under any of the three above theories or elsewhere, that it be so. Yet, it is possession of the attributes of an administrator of rights and not those of a subject of rights that are among the generally regarded conditions of moral personhood. It is a fundamental mistake to regard the fact of juristic corporate personhood as having settled the question of the moral personhood of a corporation one way or the other.

V

Two helpful lessons however, are learned from an investigation of the legal personhood of corporations: (1) biological existence is not essentially associated with the concept of a person (only the fallacious Aggregate Theory depends upon reduction to biological referents) and (2) a paradigm for the form of an inclusive neutral definition of a moral person is provided: "a subject of a right." I shall define a moral person as the referent of any proper name or description that can be a non-eliminatable subject of what I shall call (and presently discuss) a responsibility ascription of the second type. The non-eliminatable nature of the subject should be stressed because responsibility and other moral predicates are neutral as regards person and personsum predication.[17] Though we might say that The Ox-Bow mob should be held responsible for the death of three men, a mob is an example of what I have elsewhere called an aggregate collectivity with no identity over and above that of the sum of the identities of its component membership, and hence to use "The Ox-Bow mob" as the subject of such ascriptions is to make summary reference to each member of the mob. For that reason mobs do not qualify as metaphysical or moral persons.

VI

There are at least two significantly different types of responsibility ascriptions that should be distinguished in ordinary usage (not counting the laudatory recommendation, "He is a responsible lad.") The first-type pins responsibility on someone or something, the who-dun-it or what-dun-it sense. Austin has pointed out that it is usually used when an event or action is thought by the speaker to be untoward. (Perhaps we are more interested in the failures rather than the successes that punctuate our lives.)

The second-type of responsibility ascription, parasitic upon the first, involves the notion of accountability. "Having a responsibility" is interwoven with the notion "Having a liability to answer," and having such a liability or obligation seems to imply (as Anscombe has noted[18]) the existence of some sort of authority relationship either between people or between people and a deity or in some weaker versions between people and social norms. The kernel of insight that I find intuitively compelling, is that for someone to legitimately hold someone else responsible for some event there must exist or have existed a responsibility relationship between them such that in regard to the event in question the latter was answerable to the former. In other words, "X is responsible for y," as a second-type ascription, is properly uttered by someone Z if X in respect to y is or was accountable to Z. Responsibility relationships are created in a multitude of ways, e.g., through promises, contracts, compacts, hirings, assignments, appointments, by agreeing to enter a Rawlsian original position, etc. The right to hold responsible is often delegatable to third parties; though in the case of moral responsibility no delegation occurs because no person is excluded from the relationship: moral responsibility relationships hold reciprocally and without prior agreements among all moral persons. No special arrangement needs to be established between parties for anyone to hold someone morally responsible for his acts or, what amounts to the same thing, every person is a party to a responsibility relationship with all other persons as regards the doing or refraining from doing of certain acts: those that take descriptions that use moral notions.

Because our interest is in the criteria of moral personhood and not the content of morality we need not pursue this idea further. What I have maintained is that moral responsibility, although it is neither contractual nor optional, is not a class apart but an extension of ordinary, garden-variety, responsibility. What is needed in regard to the present subject then is an account of the requirements for entry into any responsibility relationship, and we have already seen that the notion of the juristic person does not provide a sufficient account. For example, the deceased in a probate case cannot be held responsible in the relevant way by anyone, even though the deceased is a juristic person, a subject of rights.

VII

A responsibility ascription of the second type amounts to the assertion of a conjunctive proposition, the first conjunct of which identifies the subject's actions with or as the cause of an event (usually an untoward one) and the second conjunct asserts that the action in question was intended by the subject or that the event was the direct result of an intentional act of the subject. In addition to what it asserts it implies that the subject is accountable to the speaker (in the case at hand) because of the subject's relationship to the speaker (who the speaker is or what the speaker is, a member of the "moral community," a surrogate for the aggregate). The primary focus of responsibility ascriptions of the second type is on the subject's intentions rather than, though not to the exclusion of, occasions. Austin wrote: "In considering responsibility, few things are considered more important than to establish whether a man *intended* to do A, or whether he did A intentionally."[19] To be the subject of a responsibility ascription of the second type, to be a party in responsibility relationships, hence to be a moral person, the subject must be at minimum, what I shall call a Davidsonian agent.[20] If corporations are moral persons, they will be non-eliminatable Davidsonian agents.

VIII

For a corporation to be treated as a Davidsonian agent it must be the case that some things that happen, some events, are describable in a way that makes certain sentences true, sentences that say that some of the things a corporation does were intended by the corporation itself. That is not accomplished if attributing intentions to a corporation is only a shorthand way of attributing intentions to the biological persons who comprise e.g. its board of directors. If that were to turn out to be the case then on metaphysical if not logical grounds there would be no way to distinguish between corporations and mobs. I shall argue, however, that a *C*orporation's *I*nternal *D*ecision Structure (its CID Structure) is the requisite redescription device that licenses the predication of corporate intentionality.

Intentionality, though a causal notion, is an intensional one and so it does not mark out a class of actions or events. Attributions of intentionality in regard to any event are referentially opaque with respect to other descriptions of that event, or, in other words, the fact that, given one description, an action was intentional does not entail that on every other description of the action it was intentional. A great deal depends upon what aspect of an event is being described. We can correctly say, e.g., "Hamlet intentionally kills the person hiding in Gertrude's room (one of Davidson's examples), but Hamlet does not intentionally kill Polonius," although "Polonius" and "the person hiding in Gertrude's room" are co-referential. The event may be properly described as "Hamlet killed Polonius" and also as "Hamlet intentionally killed the person hiding in Gertrude's room (behind the arras)," but not as "Hamlet intentionally killed

Polonius," for that was not Hamlet's intention. (He, in fact, thought he was killing the King.) The referential opacity of intentionality attributions, I shall presently argue, is congenial to the driving of a wedge between the descriptions of certain events as individual intentional actions and as corporate intentional actions.

Certain events, that is, actions, are describable as simply the bodily movements of human beings and sometimes those same events are redescribable in terms of their upshots, as bringing about something, e.g., (from Austin[21]) feeding penguins *by* throwing them peanuts ("by" is the most common way we connect different descriptions of the same event[22]) and sometimes those events can be redescribed as the effects of some prior cause; then they are described as done for reasons, done in order to bring about something, e.g., feeding the penguins peanuts in order to kill them. Usually what we single out as that prior cause is some desire or felt need combined with the belief that the object of the desire will be achieved by the action undertaken. (This, I think, is what Aristotle meant when he maintained that acting requires desire.) Saying "someone (*X*) did *y* intentionally" is to describe an event (*y*) as the upshot of *X*'s having had a reason for doing it which was the cause of his doing it.

It is obvious that a corporation's doing something involves or includes human beings doing things and that the human beings who occupy various positions in a corporation usually can be described as having reasons for *their* behavior. In virtue of those descriptions they may be properly held responsible for their behavior, *ceteris paribus*. What needs to be shown is that there is sense in saying that corporations and not just the people who work in them, have reasons for doing what they do. Typically, we will be told that it is the directors, or the managers, etc., that really have the corporate reasons and desires, etc., and that although corporate actions may not be reducible without remainder, corporate intentions are always reducible to human intentions.

IX

Every corporation has an internal decision structure. CID Structures have two elements of interest to us here: (1) an organizational or responsibility flow chart that delineates stations and levels within the corporate power structure and (2) corporate decision recognition rule(s) (usually embedded in something called "corporation policy"). The CID Structure is the personnel organization for the exercise of the corporation's power with respect to its ventures, and as such its primary function is to draw experience from various levels of the corporation into a decision-making and ratification process. When operative and properly activated, the CID Structure accomplishes a subordination and synthesis of the intentions and acts of various biological persons into a corporate decision. When viewed in another way, as already suggested, the CID Structure licenses the descriptive transformation of events, seen under another aspect as the acts of biological persons (those who occupy various stations on the organizational chart), to corporate acts by exposing the corporate character of those events. A functioning CID Structure *incorporates* acts of biological persons. For illustrative purposes, suppose we imagine that an event E has at least two aspects, that is, can be described in two non-identical ways. One of those aspects is "Executive *X*'s doing *y*" and one is "Corporation *C*'s doing *z*." The corporate act and the individual act may have different properties; indeed they have different causal ancestors though they are causally inseparable. (The causal inseparability of these acts I hope to show is a product of the CID Structure, *X*'s doing *y* is not the cause of *C*'s doing *z* nor is *C*'s doing *z* the cause of *X*'s doing *y* although if *X*'s doing *y* causes event *F* then *C*'s doing *z* causes *F* and *vice versa*.)

Although I doubt he is aware of the metaphysical reading that can be given to this process, J. K. Galbraith rather neatly captures what I have in mind when he writes in his recent popular book on the history of economics: "From [the] interpersonal exercise of power, the interaction . . . of the participants, comes the *personality* of the corporation."[23] I take Galbraith here to be quite literally correct, but it is important to spell out how a CID Structure works this "miracle."

In philosophy in recent years we have grown accustomed to the use of games as models for understanding institutional behavior. We all have some understanding of how rules in games make certain descriptions of events possible that would not be so if those rules were non-existent. The CID Structure of a corporation is a kind of constitutive rule (or rules) analogous to the game rules with which we are familiar. The organization chart of a corporation distinguishes "players" and clarifies their rank and the interwoven lines of responsibility within the corporation. An organizational chart tells us, for example, that anyone holding the title "Executive Vice President for Finance Administration" stands in a certain relationship to anyone holding the title "Director of Internal Audit" and to anyone holding the title "Treasurer," etc. In effect it expresses, or maps, the interdependent and dependent relationships, line and staff, that are involved in determinations of corporate decisions and actions. The organizational chart provides what might be called the grammar of corporate decision-making. What I shall call internal recognition rules provide its logic.

By "recognition rule(s)" I mean what Hart, in another context, calls "conclusive affirmative indication"[24] that a decision on an act has been made or performed for corporate reasons. Recognition rules are of two sorts. Partially embedded in the organizational chart are procedural recognitors: we see that decisions are to be reached collectively at certain levels and that they are to be ratified at higher levels (or at inner circles, if one prefers that Galbraithean model). A corporate decision is recognized internally, however, not only by the procedure of its making, but by the policy it instantiates. Hence every corporation creates an image (not to be confused with its public image) or a general policy, what G. C. Buzby of the Chilton Company has called the "basic belief of the corporation,"[25] that must inform its decisions for them to be properly described as being those of that corporation. "The moment policy is sidestepped or violated, it is no longer the policy of that company."[26]

Peter Drucker has seen the importance of the basic policy recognitors in the CID Structure (though he treats matters rather differently from the way I am recommending.) Drucker writes:

> Because the corporation is an institution it must have a basic policy. For it must subordinate individual ambitions and decisions to the *needs* of the corporation's welfare and survival. That means that it must have a set of principles and a rule of conduct which limit and direct individual actions and behavior. . .[27]

X

Suppose, for illustrative purposes, we activate a CID Structure in a corporation, Wicker's favorite, the Gulf Oil Corporation. Imagine that three executives *X*, *Y* and *Z* have the task of deciding whether or not Gulf Oil will join a world uranium cartel. *X*, *Y* and *Z* have before them an Everest of papers that have been prepared by lower echelon executives. Some of the papers will be purely factual reports, some will be contingency plans; some will be formulations of positions developed by various departments, some will outline financial considerations, some will be legal opinions and so on. In so far as these will all have been processed through Gulf's CID Structure system, the personal reasons, if any, individual executives may have had when writing their reports and recommendations in a specific way will have been diluted by the subordination of individual inputs to peer group input even before *X*, *Y* and *Z* review the matter. *X*, *Y* and *Z* take a vote. Their taking of a vote is authorized procedure in the Gulf CID Structure, which is to say that under these circumstances the vote of *X*, *Y* and *Z* can be redescribed as the corporation's making a decision: that is, the event "*XYZ* voting" may be redescribed to expose an aspect otherwise unrevealed, that is quite different from its other aspects e.g., from *X*'s voting in the affirmative. Redescriptive exposure of a procedurally corporate aspect of an event, however, is not to be confused with a description of an event that makes true a sentence that says that the corporation did something intentionally. But the CID Structure, as already suggested, also provides the grounds in its other type of recognitor for such an attribution of corporate intentionality. Simply, when the corporate act is consistent with, an instantiation or an implementation of established corporate policy, then it is proper to describe it as having been done for corporate reasons, as having been caused by a corporate desire coupled with a corporate belief and so, in other words, as corporate intentional.

An event may, under one of its aspects, be described as the conjunctive act "*X* did *a* (or as *X* intentionally did *a*) ε *Y* did *a* (or as *Y* intentionally did *a*) ε *Z* did *a* (or as *Z* intentionally did *a*)" (where *a* = voted in the affirmative on the question of Gulf Oil joining the cartel). Given the Gulf CID Structure, formulated in this instance as the conjunction of rules: when the occupants of positions *A*, *B* and *C* on the organizational chart unanimously vote to do something and if doing that something is consistent with, an instantiation or an implementation of general corporate policy and *ceteris paribus,* then the corporation has decided to do it for corporate reasons, the event is redescribable as "the Gulf Oil Corporation did *j* for corporate reasons *f*." (where *j* is "decided to join the cartel" and *f* is any reason (desire + belief) consistent with basic policy of Gulf Oil, e.g., increasing profits) or simply as "Gulf Oil Corporation intentionally did *j*." This is a rather technical way of saying that in these circumstances the executives voting is, given its CID Structure, also the corporation deciding to do something, and that regardless of the personal reasons the executives have for voting as they do and even if their reasons are inconsistent with established corporate policy or even if one of them has no reason at all for voting as he does, the corporation still has reasons for joining the cartel; that is, joining is consistent with the inviolate corporate general policies as encrusted in the precedent of previous corporate actions and its statements of purpose as recorded in its certificate of incorporation, annual reports, etc. The corporation's only method of achieving its desires or goals is the activation of the personnel who occupy its various positions. However, if *X* voted affirmatively purely for reasons of personal monetary gain (suppose he had been bribed to do so) that does not alter the fact that the corporate reason for joining the cartel was to minimize competition and hence pay higher dividends to its shareholders. Corporations have reasons because they have interests in doing those things that are likely to result in realization of their established corporate goals regardless of the transient self-interest of directors, managers, etc. If there is a difference between corporate goals and desires and those of human beings it is probably that the corporate ones are relatively stable and not very wide ranging, but that is only because corporations can do relatively fewer things than human beings, being confined in action predominately to a limited socio-economic sphere. The attribution of corporate intentionality is opaque with respect to other possible descriptions of the event in question. It is, of course, in a corporation's interest that its component membership view the corporate purposes as instrumental in the achievement of their own goals. (Financial reward is the most common way this is achieved.)

It will be objected that a corporation's policies reflect only the current goals of its directors. But that is certainly not logically necessary nor is it in practice true for most large corporations. Usually, of course, the original incorporators will have organized to further their individual interests and/or to meet goals which they shared. But even in infancy the melding of disparate interests and purposes gives rise to a corporate long range point of view that is distinct from the intents and purposes of the collection of incorporators viewed individually. Also, corporate basic purposes and policies, as already mentioned, tend to be relatively stable when compared to those of individuals and not couched in the kind of language that would be appropriate to individual purposes. Furthermore, as histories of corporations will show, when policies are amended or altered it is usually only peripheral issues that are involved. Radical policy alteration constitutes a new corporation, a point that is captured in the incorporation laws of such states as Delaware. ("Any power which is not enumerated in the charter and the general law or which cannot be inferred from these two sources is *ultra vires* of the corporation.") Obviously underlying the objection is an uneasiness about the fact that corporate intent is dependent upon policy and purpose that is but an artifact of the socio-psychology of a group of biological persons. Corporate intent seems somehow to be a tarnished illegitimate offspring of human intent. But this objection is another form of the anthropocentric bias. By concentrating on possible descriptions of events and by acknowledging only that the possibility of describing something as an agent depends upon whether or not it can be properly described as having done something (the description of some aspect of an event) for a reason, we avoid the temptation to look for extensional criteria that would necessitate reduction to human referents.

The CID Structure licenses redescriptions of events as corporate and attributions of corporate intentionality while it does not obscure the private acts of executives, directors etc. Although X voted to support the joining of the cartel because he was bribed to do so, X did not join the cartel, Gulf Oil Corporation joined the cartel. Consequently, we may say that X did something for which he should be held morally responsible, yet whether or not Gulf Oil Corporation should be held morally responsible for joining the cartel is a question that turns on issues that may be unrelated to X's having accepted a bribe.

Of course Gulf Oil Corporation cannot join the cartel unless X or somebody who occupies position A on the organizational chart votes in the affirmative. What that shows, however, is that corporations are collectivities. That should not, however, rule out the possibility of their having metaphysical status, as being Davidsonian agents, and being thereby full-fledged moral persons.

This much seems to me clear: we can describe many events in terms of certain physical movements of human beings and we also can sometimes describe those events as done for reasons by those human beings, but further we can sometimes describe those events as corporate and still further as done for corporate reasons that are qualitatively different from whatever personal reasons, if any, component members may have for doing what they do.

Corporate agency resides in the possibility of CID Structure licensed redescription of events as corporate intentional. That may still appear to be downright mysterious, although I do not think it is, for human agency as I have suggested, resides in the possibility of description as well.

Although further elaboration is needed, I hope I have said enough to make plausible the view that we have good reasons to acknowledge the non-eliminatable agency of corporations. I have maintained that Davidsonian agency is a necessary and sufficient condition of moral personhood. I cannot further argue that position here (I have done so elsewhere). On the basis of the foregoing analysis, however, I think that grounds have been provided for holding corporations *per se* to account for what they do, for treating them as metaphysical persons *qua* moral persons.[28]

NOTES

1. John Locke. *An Essay Concerning Human Understanding* (1960), Bk. II, Ch. XXVII. This volume, p. 88.
2. *Ibid.*
3. For a particularly flagrant example see: Michael Jensen and William Meckling, "Theory of the Firm: Managerial Behavior, Agency Costs and Ownership Structure," *Journal of Financial Economics,* vol. 3 (1976), pp. 305–360. On p. 311 they write, "The private corporation or firm is simply one form of legal fiction which serves as a nexus for contracting relationships . . ."
4. Daniel Dennett, "Conditions of Personhood" in *The Identities of Persons,* ed. by A. O. Rorty (Berkeley, 1976), pp. 382–403. This volume pp. 227–240.
5. John Rawls, "Justice as Reciprocity," in *John Stuart Mill, Utilitarianism,* ed. by Samuel Gorovitz (Indianapolis, 1971), pp. 244–245.
6. *Ibid.*
7. John Rawls, *A Theory of Justice* (Cambridge, 1971), p. 146.
8. Frederick Hallis, *Corporate Personality* (Oxford, 1930), p. xlii.
9. 10 *Co. Rep.* 253, see Hallis, p. xlii.
10. "Types of Collectivities and Blame," *The Personalist,* vol. 56 (1975), pp. 160–169, and in the first chapter of my *Foundations of Corporate Responsibility* (forthcoming).
11. "Continental Tyre and Rubber Co., Ltd. vs. Daimler Co., Ltd." (1915), K.B., p. 893.
12. Hallis, p. xlix.
13. "Continental Tyre and Rubber Co., Ltd. vs. Daimler Co., Ltd." (1915), K.B., p. 918.
14. (1916), 2 A.C., p. 340.
15. See in particular Otto von Gierke, *Die Genossenschoftstheorie* (Berlin, 1887).
16. And, of course, in earlier times animals have been given legal rights.
17. See Gerald Massey, "Tom, Dick, and Harry, and All The King's Men," *American Philosophical Quarterly,* vol. 13 (1976), pp. 89–108.
18. G. E. M. Anscombe, "Modern Moral Philosophy," *Philosophy,* vol. 33 (1958), pp. 1–19.
19. J. L. Austin, "Three Ways of Spilling Ink" in *Philosophical Papers* (Oxford, 1970), p. 273.
20. See for example Donald Davidson, "Agency," in *Agent, Action, and Reason,* ed. by Binkley, Bronaugh, and Marras (Toronto, 1971).
21. Austin, p. 275.
22. See Joel Feinberg, *Doing and Deserving* (Princeton, 1970), p. 134f.
23. John Kenneth Galbraith, *The Age of Uncertainty* (Boston, 1971), p. 261.
24. H. L. A. Hart, *The Concept of Law* (Oxford, 1961), Ch. VI.
25. G. C. Buzby, "Policies—A Guide to What A Company Stands For," *Management Record,* vol. 24 (1962), p. 5ff.
26. *Ibid.*
27. Peter Drucker, *Concept of Corporation* (New York, 1964/1972), pp. 36–37.
28. This paper owes much to discussions and comments made by J. L. Mackie, Donald Davidson and Howard K. Wettstein. An earlier version was read at a conference on "Ethics and Economics" at the University of Delaware. I also acknowledge the funding of the University of Minnesota Graduate School that supports the project of which this is a part.

DISCUSSION QUESTIONS

1. What two schools of thought on the relationship between metaphysical and moral persons does French describe?
2. Contrast the Fiction Theory with the Legal Aggregate Theory of the Corporation. What is the primary difference between them, according to French? Which do you think is more plausible and why?
3. What kinds of entities and associations does French mention as having been the subjects of legal rights?
4. Explain why French considers a mob to be neither a metaphysical nor a moral person. Are his reasons good?
5. What exactly does French mean when he describes corporations as "non-eliminatable Davidsonian agents"?

Chapter 31

CHARLES TAYLOR

Taylor (1931–) is a Canadian philosopher at McGill University who was educated at Oxford. In the 1965 federal election in Canada, Taylor lost to Prime Minister Pierre Trudeau. His many books include Hegel and Modern Society *(1979),* Human Agency and Language *(1985),* Sources of the Self *(1989),* Reconciling the Solitudes: Essays on Canadian Federalism and Nationalism *(1993), and* Multiculturalism: Examining the Politics of Recognition *(1994).*

In this essay, Taylor believes that to be a being who can be addressed and who can reply, that is, being a "respondent," is a necessary condition of being a person. He thinks it is clear that persons are a sub-class of agents; animals are in some sense agents, but not persons. Two doctrines of what it is to be a person are explained in detail. The scientific view, rooted in the 17th-century, epistemologically grounded notion of the subject, seeks to answer the question: How are we to explain human behavior? This view sees the person as an agent with the power to frame representations of things. This "representation" view identifies agency by means of a performance criterion: animals exhibit highly complex adaptive behavior. But then no distinction of nature between animals and machines is allowed on this unproblematic conception of the nature of agency. By contrast, the practical-moral view focuses on the nature of agency. This view seeks to answer the question: What is a good life? What is crucial about agents is that things matter to them, according to this "significance" view. Moral agency requires some kind of linguistic awareness of the distinction between things one just wants to do (e.g., the cat stalking the bird) and things that are worthy to be done (e.g., Taylor writing this essay). On the representation view, what makes an agent a person, a fully human respondent, is his strategic power to plan, which is superior to that of animals. In contrast, on the significance view, what distinguishes persons from other agents is not strategic power, but openness to peculiarly human standards, goals, and matters of significance. These peculiarly human motivations are reflexively constituted by our interpretations, and therefore are deeply embedded in culture. What is a matter of shame, guilt, dignity, and moral goodness notoriously varies from culture to culture. Taylor concludes that both these models of the person are current in modern Western culture, that most people operate with a combination of the two, and that these rival moral and spiritual outlooks clash.

The Concept of a Person

Where it is more than simply a synonym for 'human being', 'person' figures primarily in moral and legal discourse. A person is a being with a certain moral status, or a bearer of rights. But underlying the moral status, as its condition, are certain capacities. A person is a being who has a sense of self, has a notion of the future and the past, can hold values, make choices; in short, can adopt life-plans. At least, a person must be the kind of being who is in principle capable of all this, however damaged these capacities may be in practice.

Running through all this we can identify a necessary (but not sufficient) condition. A person must be a being with his/her own point of view on things. The life-plan, the choices, the sense of self must be attributable to him/her as in some sense their point of origin. A person is a being who can be addressed, and who can reply. Let us call a being of this kind a 'respondent'.

Any philosophical theory of the person must give some account of what it is to be a respondent. At the same time, it is clear that persons are a sub-class of agents. We do not accord personal status to animals, to whom we do however attribute actions in some sense. This poses a second question which any theory must answer: what is special about agents who are also persons?

With these questions in mind, I want to present, partly in summary, partly in reconstruction, two views of what it is to be a person, which I believe underpin a host of different positions and attitudes evident in modern culture. And clearly, our (perhaps implicit) notion of what it is to be a person will be determining for two orders of question: scientific ones: how are we to explain human behaviour? and practical-moral ones: what is a good/decent/acceptable form of life?

The first one is rooted in the seventeenth century, epistemologically-grounded notion of the subject. A person is a being with consciousness, where consciousness is seen as a power to frame representations of things. Persons have consciousness, and alone possess it, or at least they have it in a manner and to a degree that animals do not. This answers the second question. But it also answers the first, the question what makes a respondent. What makes it possible to attribute a point of view to persons is that they have a representation of things. They have the wherewithal to reply when addressed, because they respond out of their own representation of the world and their situation.

What this view takes as relatively unproblematic is the nature of agency. The important boundary is that between persons and other agents, the one marked by consciousness. The boundary between agents and mere things is not recognized as important at all, and is not seen as reflecting a qualitative distinction. This was so at the very beginning, where Descartes saw animals as complex

Source: Charles Taylor, "The Concept of a Person." *Social Theory as Practice,* The B. N. Ganguli Memorial Lectures 1981, Delhi: Oxford University Press (1983): 48–67. Reproduced by permission of Oxford University Press India, New Delhi.

machines; and it continues to be so today, where proponents of this first view tend to assume that some reductive account of living beings will be forthcoming. What makes out agents from other things tends to be identified by a performance criterion: animals somehow maintain and reproduce themselves through a wide variety of circumstances. They show highly complex adaptive behaviour. But understanding them in terms of performance allows for no distinction of nature between animals and machines which we have latterly designed to exhibit similarly complex adaptive behaviour.

We see this, for instance, with proponents of computer-based models of intelligence. They see no problem in offering these as explanations of animal performance. They only admit to puzzlement when it comes to relating consciousness to performance. We are conscious, but the machines which simulate our intelligent behaviour are not. But perhaps some day they might be? Speculation here is ragged and confused, the symptom of a big intellectual puzzle. By contrast, the reductive view of agency is subscribed to with serene confidence.

The second view I want to explore here does, by contrast, focus on the nature of agency. What is crucial about agents is that things matter to them. We thus cannot simply identify agents by a performance criterion, nor assimilate animals to machines.

To say things matter to agents is to say that we can attribute purposes, desires, aversions to them in a strong, original sense. There is, of course, a sense in which we can attribute purposes to a machine, and thus apply action terms to it. We say of a computing machine that it's, say, 'calculating the payroll'. But that is because it plays this purpose in our lives. It was designed by us, and is being used by us to do this. Outside of this designer's or user's context, the attribution could not be made. What identifies the action is what I want to call here a derivative purpose. The purpose is, in other words, user-relative. If tomorrow someone else makes it run through exactly the same programme, but with the goal of calculating *pi* to the nth place, then *that* will be what the machine is 'doing'.

By contrast, animals and human beings are subjects of original purpose. That the cat is stalking the bird is not a derivative, or observer-relative fact about it. Nor is it a derivative fact about me that I am trying to explain two doctrines of the person.

Now one of the crucial issues dividing the first and second concepts of the person is what to make of this difference between original and derived purpose. If you take it seriously, then you can no longer accept a performance criterion for agency, because some agent's performances can be matched derivatively on machines. For the first view, the difference has to be relegated to the status of mere appearance. Some things (animals, ourselves) look to us to have purposes in a stronger, more original sense than mere machines.

But the second view does take it seriously, and hence sees the agent/thing boundary as being an important and problematic one. And it offers therefore a different answer to the question, what makes a respondent? This is no longer seen in terms of consciousness, but rather in terms of mattering itself. An agent can be a respondent, because things matter to it in an original way. What it responds out of is the original significance of things for it.

But then we have a very different conception from the first. The answers to the two questions are related in a very different way. The basic condition for being a respondent, that one have an original point of view, is something all agents fulfil. Something else needs to be said in answer to the question, what distinguishes persons from other agents?

And the answer to neither question can be given just in terms of a notion of consciousness as the power to frame representations. The answer to the respondent question clearly cannot be given in these terms, because agents who have nothing like conciousness in the human sense have original purposes. Consciousness in the characteristically human form can be seen as what we attain when we come to formulate the significance of things for us. We then have an articulate view of our self and world. But things matter to us prior to this formulation. So original purpose can not be confused with consciousness.

But nor does the notion of consciousness as representation help us to understand the difference between persons and animals. This is so for two related reasons which it is worth exploring at some length.

The first is that, built into the notion of representation in this view is the idea that representations are of independent objects. I frame a representation of something which is there independently of my depicting it, and which stands as a standard for this depiction. But when we look at a certain range of formulations which are crucial to human consciousness, the articulation of our human feelings, we can see that this doesn't hold. Formulating how we feel, or coming to adopt a new formulation, can frequently change how we feel. When I come to see that my feeling of guilt was false, or my feeling of love self-deluded, the emotions themselves are different. The one I now experience as a compulsive malaise rather than a genuine recognition of wrong-doing, the other as a mere infatuation rather than a genuine bent of my life. It is rare that the emotion we experience can survive unchanged such a radical shift in interpretation.

We can understand this, if we examine more closely the range of human feelings like pride, shame, guilt, sense of worth, love, and so on. When we try to state what is particular to each one of these feelings, we find we can only do so if we describe the situation in which we feel them, and what we are inclined to do in it. Shame is what we feel in a situation of humiliating exposure, and we want to hide ourselves from this; fear, what we feel in a situation of danger, and we want to escape it; guilt, when we are aware of transgression; and so on.

One could say that there is a judgement integral to each one of these emotions: 'this is shameful' for shame; 'there is danger' for fear, etc. Not that to feel the emotion is to assent to the judgement. We can feel the emotion irrationally; and sometimes see that the judgement holds dispassionately. It is rather that feeling the emotion in question is just being struck by, moved by, the state of affairs the judgement describes. We can sometimes make the judgement without being moved (the case of dispassionate observation); or we can feel very moved to assent to the judgement, but see rationally that it does not hold (irrational emotion). But the inner connection of feeling and judgement is attested in the fact that we speak here of 'irrational' emotion; and that we define and distinguish the feelings by the type of situation.

It follows from this that I can describe my emotions by describing my situation, and very often must do so really to give the flavour of what I feel. But then I alter the description of my emotions in altering the description I accept of my situation. But to alter my situation-description will be to alter my feelings, if I am moved by my newly-perceived predicament. And even if I am not, the old emotion will now seem to me irrational, which itself constitutes a change in what I experience. So we can understand why in this domain, our formulations about ourselves can alter what they are about.

We could say that for these emotions, our understanding of them or the interpretations we accept, are constitutive of the emotion. The understanding helps shape the emotion. And that is why the latter cannot be considered a fully independent object, and the traditional theory of consciousness as representation does not apply here.

This might be understandable about the traditional theory if our formulations weren't representative at all, i.e., if there were no question of right and wrong here. It might be that thinking simply made it so, that how we sincerely describe our feelings just is how we feel, and that there is no point in distinguishing between the two. We might think that there are some domains of feeling where this is so. For instance, if on sincere introspection, I come up with the verdict that I like blueberries, there is no further room here for talk of error or delusion.

But this is emphatically not the case with the emotions I described above. Here we can and do delude ourselves, or imperfectly understand ourselves, and struggle for a better formulation. The peculiarity of these emotions is that it is at one and the same time the case that our formulations are constitutive of the emotion, *and* that these formulations can be right or wrong. They do in a sense thus offer representations, but not of an independent object. This is what makes the representative theory of consciousness inapplicable in this domain.

And so consciousness in this traditional sense does not seem to be the conception we need to capture the distinction between persons and other agents. The consciousness of persons, wherein they formulate their emotions, seems to be of another sort.

The second reason why representative consciousness cannot fill the bill here also comes to mind if we consider this range of human emotions. As long as we think of agents as the subjects of strategic action, then we might be inclined to think that the superiority of persons over animals lies in their ability to envisage a longer time scale, to understand more complex cause-effect relationships, and thus engage in calculations, and the like. These are all capacities to which the power to frame representations is essential. If we think merely in this strategic dimension, then we will tend to think that this representative power is the key to our evolution from animal to man.

But if we adopt the second view, and understand an agent essentially as a subject of significance, then what will appear evident is that there are matters of significance for human beings which are peculiarly human, and have no analogue with animals. These are just the ones I mentioned earlier, matters of pride, shame, moral goodness, evil, dignity, the sense of worth, the various human forms of love, and so on. If we look at goals like survival and reproduction, we can perhaps convince ourselves that the difference between men and animals lies in a strategic superiority of the former: we can pursue the same ends much more effectively than our dumb cousins. But when we consider these human emotions, we can see that the ends which make up a human life are *sui generis.* And then even the ends of survival and reproduction will appear in a new light. What it is to maintain and hand on a human form of life, i.e., a given culture, is also a peculiarly human affair.

These human matters are also connected with consciousness in some sense. One could indeed argue that no agent could be sensitive to them who was not capable of formulating them, or at least giving expression to them; and hence that the kind of consciousness which language brings is essential to them. We can perhaps see this if we take one example from the above list, being a moral agent. To be a moral agent is to be sensitive to certain standards. But 'sensitive' here must have a strong sense: not just that one's behaviour follows a certain standard, but also that one in some sense recognizes or acknowledges the standard.

Animals can follow standards in the weaker sense. My cat will not eat fishmeal below a certain quality. With knowledge of the standard I can predict his behaviour. But there need be no recognition here that he is following a standard. This kind of thing, however, would not be sufficient to attribute moral action to an agent. We could imagine some animal who was systematically beneficent in his behaviour; what he did always redounded to the good of man and beast. We still would not think of him as a moral agent, unless there were some recognition on his part that in acting this way he was following a higher standard. Morality requires some recognition that there are higher demands on one, and hence the recognition of some distinction between kinds of goal. This has nothing to do with the Kantian diremption between duty and inclination. Even the holy will, which gladly does the good, must have some sense that this is the good, and as such worthy to be done.

Moral agency, in other words, requires some kind of reflexive awareness of the standards one is living by (or failing to live by). And something analogous is true of the other human concerns I mentioned. And so some kind of consciousness is essential to them. I think we can say that being a linguistic animal is essential to one's having these concerns. Because it is impossible to see how one could make a distinction like the one above, between, e.g., things one just wants to do, and things that are worthy to be done, unless one was able to mark the distinction in some way: either by formulation in language, or at least by some expressive ceremonial which would acknowledge the higher demands.

And so when we ask what distinguishes persons from other agents, consciousness in some sense is unquestionably a part of the answer. But not consciousness understood as just representation. That can help explain some of the differences; for instance, the great superiority of man as strategic agent. But when we come to the peculiarly human concerns, the consciousness they presuppose can not be understood just as the power to frame representations of independent objects. Consciousness—perhaps we might better here say language—is as it were the medium within which they first arise as concerns for us. The medium here is in some way inseparable from the content; which is why as we saw above our self-understanding in this domain is constitutive of what we feel.

We should try to gather the threads together, and show how the two conceptions square off against each other. They both start off with our ordinary notion of a person, defined by certain capacities: a person is an agent who has a sense of self, of his/her own life, who can evaluate it, and make choices about it. This is the basis of the respect we owe persons. Even those who through some accident or misfortune are deprived of the ability to exercise these capacities are still understood as belonging to the species defined by this potentiality. The central importance of all this for our moral thinking is reflected in the fact that these capacities form an important part of what we should respect and nourish in human beings. To make someone less capable of understanding himself, evaluating and choosing is to deny totally the injunction that we should respect him as a person.

What we have in effect are two readings of what these capacities consist in. The first takes agency as unproblematic. An agent is a being who acts, hence who has certain goals and endeavours to fulfil them. But this range of features is identified by a performance criterion, so that no difference of principle is admitted between animals and, say, complex machines, which also adaptively react to their surroundings so as to attain certain ends (albeit in a derivative way).

Along with agency, its ends too are seen as unproblematic. What is striking about persons, therefore, is their ability to conceive different possibilities, to calculate how to get them, to choose between them, and thus to plan their lives. The striking superiority of man is in strategic power. The various capacities definitive of a person are understood in terms of this power to plan. Central to this is the power to represent things clearly. We can plan well when we can lay out the possibilities clearly, when we can calculate their value to us in terms of our goals, as well as the probabilities and cost of their attainment. Our choices can then be clear and conscious.

On this view, what is essential to the peculiarly human powers of evaluating and choosing is the clarity and complexity of the computation. Evaluation is assessment in the light of our goals, which are seen ultimately as given, or perhaps as given for one part, and for the rest as arbitrarily chosen. But in either case the evaluation process takes the goal as fixed. 'Reason is and ought to be, the slave of the passions'.* Choice is properly choice in the light of clear evaluation. To the human capacities thus conceived, the power of clear and distinct representation is obviously central.

* A famous quotation from David Hume. [Ed.]

So on one view, what makes an agent a person, a fully human respondent, is this power to plan. My interlocutor replies to me out of his/her power to make a life-plan and act on it. This is what I have to respect.

By contrast, the other view starts off quite differently. It raises the question of agency, and understands agents as in principle distinct from other things. Agents are beings for whom things matter, who are subjects of significance. This is what gives them a point of view on the world. But what distinguishes persons from other agents is not strategic power, i.e., the capacity to deal with the same matter of concern more effectively. Once one focuses on the significance of things for agents, then what springs to view is that persons have qualitatively different concerns.

In other terms, once one raises the question of agency, then that of the ends of agents comes into view. And what is clear is that there are some peculiarly human ends. Hence the important difference between men and animals cannot simply consist in strategic power; it is also a matter of our recognizing certain goals. Consciousness is indeed essential to us. But this can not be understood simply as the power to frame representations, but also as what enables us to be open to these human concerns. Our consciousness is somehow constitutive of these matters of significance, and does not just enable us to depict them.

This grounds a quite different reading of the essentially personal capacities. The essence of evaluation no longer consists in assessment in the light of fixed goals, but also and even more in the sensitivity to certain standards, those involved in the peculiarly human goals. The sense of self is the sense of where one stands in relation to these standards, and properly personal choice is one informed by these standards. The centre of gravity thus shifts in our interpretation of personal capacities. The centre is no longer the power to plan, but rather the openness to certain matters of significance. This is now what is essential to personal agency.

Naturally these conceptions ramify into very different views in both the sciences of man and the practical deliberations of how we ought to live. These are the two orders of questions I mentioned at the outset: how are we to explain human behaviour? and, what is a good life? We can for the sake of simplicity consider different doctrines in science and morals as consequences of these two underlying conceptions. But of course the motivation for our holding one or the other is more complex. We may be led to adopt one, because it relates to a certain approach to science, or goes with a certain style of moral deliberation, rather than adopting the approach or the style, because they are consequences of an already established core conception of the person.

In fact the order of motivation is mixed and varies from person to person. One can adopt a given core conception because its scientific ramifications strike him as valid, but only reluctantly accept what it entails about moral deliberation. Here it may rub against the grain of his intuitions, but because it seems true for what appear unanswerable reasons, he has no option but to endorse it. For another, it may be the moral consequences which make it plausible, and the scientific ones may be a matter of indifference. In fact, in talking about ramifications, I am also talking about possible motivations, although they may also be reluctant consequences of someone's vision of things.

In the remainder of my remarks, I would like to discuss the ramifications of these two conceptions, accounting for them for the sake of simplicity as motivations. I hope that this will make my rather abstract sketches somewhat fuller and more life-like, and that you might see these core conceptions actually at work in modern culture.

First, in the scientific domain. I am of course not natural between them; and so the question that strikes me here is, what makes the first—let us call it the representation conception—so popular in our culture? I think an important part of the answer can be found in the prestige of the natural science model, which I have been discussing—and arguing against—throughout these lectures. Perhaps one of the key theses of the seventeenth century revolution which inaugurates modern natural sciences is the eschewing of what one could call anthropocentric properties. Anthropocentric properties are properties of things, but which they only have in so far as they are objects of experience. This was crucially at stake in the seventeenth century distinction between primary and secondary properties. Secondary properties, like colour and felt heat, only applied to things insofar as they were being experienced. In a world without experiencing subjects, such properties could no longer be sensibly attributed to objects. They were therefore understood as merely subjective, as relative to us, not as absolute properties of things.

It was an important step in the development of modern natural science, when these properties were distinguished and set aside. This distinction was a polemical instrument in the struggle against the older conceptions of the universe as meaningful order. Such hypotheses, which explained features of the world in terms of their 'correspondences' against a background order of ideas, were condemned as mere projections. They concerned purely the significance of things for us, not the way things were.

This eschewal of anthropocentric properties was undoubtedly one of the bases of the spectacular progress of natural science during the last three centuries. And ever since, therefore, the idea has seemed attractive of somehow adapting this to the science of man. We can see here, I think, one of the sources of that basic feature of the representation conception, its assimilating agency to things; or put in another way, its understanding agency by a performance criterion.

We are motivated to distinguish animals from machines which imitate their adaptive performances, only if we take significance seriously, the fact that things matter to animals in an original way. But the significance of things is paradigmatically a range of anthropocentric properties (or in the case of other animals, properties which are relative to them; in any case, not absolute). So it can easily appear that a scientific approach to behaviour which incorporates this important founding step of natural science would be one which gave no weight to significance.

Of course, we can admit that the distinction is in some way important for us. Things feel different inside to a human being, and to an animal; and there probably is nothing comparable in a machine. But all this has to do with the way things appear. It thus has no weight when we come to identifying the explanatory factors of a science of behaviour. Just as, analogously, we can admit that it really does appear that the sun goes below the horizon, but this must just be ignored when we want to establish a scientific theory of the movement of earth and the heavenly bodies.

Now if we follow out what is involved in a significance-free account we shall come across themes that tend to recur in the modern sciences of man. We can see this if we return to my discussion above of our emotions, where I said that they incorporate in a sense a view of our situation. To experience an emotion is to be in a sense struck or moved by our situation being of a certain nature. Hence, I said, we can describe our emotions by describing our situation.

But this is only so because we describe our situation in its significance for us. We can usually understand how someone feels when he describes his predicament, because we share normally the same sense of significance. So someone says: 'imagine what I felt when he walked in just then and saw me. . .'; and we can quite easily do so, because we share just this sense of embarrassment. Of course, it is a commonplace that between different cultures the sense of significance can vary, and then we can be quite baffled. Nothing comes across of how people feel from the simple narrative of events, or only something confused and perplexing.

So situation-description is only self-description because the situation is grasped in its significance. And in fact, we have a host of terms which operate in tandem with our emotion terms and which designate different significances a situation can have; such as, 'humiliating', 'exciting', 'dismaying', 'exhilarating', 'intriguing', 'fascinating', 'frightening', 'provoking', 'awe-inspiring', 'joyful', and so on. We can often describe our predicament with one of these, or alternatively we can give a sense of it by saying what it inclines us to do. Certain standard emotion terms are linked, as we saw, to standard situation-descriptions, as well as responses we are inclined to make. So fear is experienced at something dangerous, and inclines us to flee; shame at what is shameful or humiliating, and inclines us to do away with this, or at least to hide it; and so on.

Now our ordinary description/explanation of action in terms of our emotions and other motives is based on our sense of significance. That is, it either invokes this directly by using terms like the above, or it assumes it as the background which makes predicament descriptions intelligible as accounts of what we feel or want to do. The actions we are inclined to take are identified by their purposes, and frequently these are only intelligible against the background of significance. For instance, we understand the inclination to hide what is humiliating, only through understanding the humiliation. Someone who had no grasp of a culture's sense of shame would never know what constituted a successful case of hiding, or cover-up. We wouldn't be able to explain to him even what people are inclined to do in humiliating predicaments in this culture, let alone why they want to do it.

What would it mean then to set about designing a significance-free account? Well, plainly what would remain basic is that people respond to certain situations, and perhaps also that they respond by trying to encompass certain ends. But if we had an account which really eschewed anthropocentric properties, and thus which didn't have to draw on our background sense of significance for its intelligibility, it would characterize situation and end in absolute terms. Now in one way this might seem relatively easy. Any situation bears a great number, an indefinite number of descriptions. The predicament that I find humiliating is also one that can be described in a host of other ways, including some which make no reference to any significance at all. But of course the claim involved in this redescription would be that none of the important explanatory factors are lost from sight. It is that the explanatory relationship between situation and response can be captured in an absolute description; or that, in other words, the features picked out in the significance description are not essential to the explanation, but just concern the way things appear to us in ordinary life.

This kind of ambition has underlain various influential schools in academic psychology. At its most reductive, where there was a suspicion even of goal-seeking behaviour, as somehow tinged with anthropocentrism, we had behaviourism. Everything was to be explained in terms of responses to stimuli. But these were to be characterized in the most rigorously significance-free terms, as 'colourless movement and mere receptor impulse', according to Hull. This school has passed its prime; the development of computing machines has shown how goal-behaviour can be accounted for in mechanistic terms, and so strategic action can now be allowed into the account. But the goal is to account for animate strategic action in the same terms as we explain the analogous behaviour of machines. And since for the latter case it is clear that the goal states have to be describable in absolute terms, this must also be true of the former, if the account is to succeed.

It seems to me then that this ambition to follow natural science, and avoid anthropocentric properties has been an important motivation of the representation view. It gives us an important reason to ignore significance, and to accept a performance criterion for agency, where what matters is the encompassing of certain, absolutely-identified ends. But the drive for absolute (i.e., non-anthropocentric) explanation can be seen not only in psychology. It is also at the origin of a reductive bent in social science. To see the connection here, we will have to follow the argument a little farther, and appreciate the limitations on this transposition into absolute terms.

These are evident when we return to what I called above the peculiarly human motivations, like shame, guilt, a sense of morality, and so on. Finding absolute descriptions which nevertheless capture the explanatory relevance of situation and goal is in principle impossible in this domain.

To see this, let us contrast one of these motives, shame, with one where the absolute transposition seems possible, say, physical fear. This latter is fear of physical danger, danger to life or limb. Now the significance of the situation here can perhaps be spelled out in medical terms: something in my predicament threatens to end my life in some particular way—say, I am likely to fall, and the impact would be lethal. Here we have a sense that we could describe the impending outcome in physiological terms, terms that made no reference to its importance to me, as we might describe the death of a sparrow, or any other process in nature.

And so we might think of a disengaged, absolute account that might be offered of my behaviour; where we would be told that this fall, and the resulting physiological changes occurring on impact, constituted a counter-goal for me; something I strove to avoid. And my behaviour could be explained strategically on this basis. Here we have an account of behaviour which we could imagine being matched on a machine. This too might become irreparably damaged on impact. And so we might design a machine to compute the likelihood of certain possible modes of destruction possible in its environment, and to take evasive action. What would be left out of account, of course, would be the subjective experience of the fear. This would survive in the account only as a direction of behaviour, a bent to avoidance. It would be a mere 'con-attitude' towards falling, and quite colourless. That is, the specific experienced difference between avoiding something out of fear, and avoiding it out of distaste, would fall away. This would be part of the subjective 'feel' of the lived experience which would be left outside the account. But we might nevertheless understand the claim here that all the really explanatory factors had been captured. We can presumably predict the behaviour of both machine and person, granted a knowledge of the situation described absolutely. What more could one want?

In fact, one might ask a lot more. But I do not want to argue this here. Let me concede the seeming success of the absolute transposition for this case of physical danger, in order to be able to show how impossible it is for shame. The corresponding task in this latter case would be to give an absolute account of a situation which was humiliating or shameful. This would be the analogue to the absolute description of danger above.

But this we cannot do. The reason lies in the reflexive nature of these motives, which I noted above. I can give sufficient conditions of a situation being dangerous in absolute terms, because there are no necessary conditions concerning its significance. The fall will be lethal, however I or mankind in general regard it. This is a hard, culture-resistant fact. But a situation is not humiliating independent of all significance conditions. For a situation to be humiliating or shameful, the agent has to be of the kind who is in principle sensitive to shame.

This can perhaps come clearer, if we reflect that shame involves some notion of standards. To feel shame is to sense that I fail on some standard. We can only get an adequate account of the shameful, if we can get clear on these standards. But built into the essence of these standards is that they are those of a being who is potentially sensitive to them. The subject of shame must be one who can be motivated by shame. It might appear that in certain cultures a sufficient condition of the shameful could be given in purely objective terms. For instance, defeat in battle might be shameful for the warrior. But what is forgotten here is that defeat is only shameful for the warrior, because he ought to have been so powerfully moved by the love of glory to have conquered, or at least to have died in the attempt. And the trudge back in the dust in chains is only humiliating because he is—or ought to be—a being who glories in power, in strutting over the earth as master.

We can see the essential place of significance conditions here, when we note that shamelessness is shameful. In other words, there are conditions of motivation for avoiding shame, viz., that one be sensitive to shame. The one who does not care, who runs away without a scruple, earns the deepest contempt.

It is these significance conditions that make it the case that we cannot attribute shame to animals, let alone to machines. And this makes the contrast with danger. Just because this can be defined absolutely, we have no difficulty in envisaging animals as standing in danger in exactly the same sense as we can; and the extension to machines does not seem a very great step.

We can thus distinguish between motives which *seem* potentially capable of a significance-free account, and those which definitely are not. I emphazise 'seem' because even for these, I have doubts on other grounds which I haven't time to go into here. But they contrast with the peculiarly human in that these plainly are irreducible. These are the ones where the significance itself is such that we cannot explain it without taking into account that it is significant for us. These are the ones therefore, where the variations occur between human cultures, i.e., between different ways of shaping and interpreting that significance. So that what is a matter of shame, of guilt, of dignity, of moral goodness, is notoriously different and often hard to understand from culture to culture, whereas the conditions of medical health are far more uniform. (But not totally, which is part of my reason for doubt above, and my unwillingness to concede even the case of physical danger to a reductive account.)

This distinction underlies the reductive bent we see in much modern social science, towards accounts of human behaviour and society which are grounded in goals of the first type. The contemporary fad for sociobiology provides a good example. To explain human practices and values in terms of the goals of survival and reproduction, is to account for things ultimately by explanatory factors which can be described in absolute terms. Survival, reproduction, these are conditions that can be predicated of animals as well, and could be extended analogously to machines, for that matter. The enterprise of giving a reductive account of culture in terms of these ends can thus appear as an answer to the demands of science, whereas anti-reductionist objections seem counsels of obscurity, or of despair of the scientific cause. The old requirement, that we eschew anthropocentric properties, is here working its way out, via the absolute transposition. The fact that it leads us into a blind alley in social science ought to make us reflect on the validity of this basic requirement, and hence of the natural science model. But that is a point I have sufficiently argued above.

But the point of link-up with my last lecture is that an absolute account would be a culture-free one, for reasons I have just touched on. It is the peculiarly human motivations which are reflexively constituted by our interpretations and therefore are deeply embedded in culture. The search for a 'materialist' account, as I interpret it here, is the search for an explanation in terms of ends which can be absolutely described. But this would not only meet the demands of 'science', it would at a stroke cut through the intractable difficulties of comparative social science. It would give us a truly neutral standpoint, from which we could survey all cultures without ethnocentricity. We have seen above that this is an illusion, but we can also appreciate how powerful an attraction it exercises in modern culture.

In the time remaining, I would like to make a few remarks about the ramifications of the two conceptions of a person for our views about moral deliberation. Here too, the first conception has its attractions. If we understand ourselves in terms of certain absolutely defined ends, then the proper form of deliberation is strategic thinking. And this conception sees the superiority of man over animal as lying in greater strategic capacity. Reason is and ought to be primarily instrumental.

The pattern is familiar enough, but its attractions are insufficiently understood. There is, of course, the sense of control. The subject according to the significance perspective is in a world of meanings that he imperfectly understands. His task is to interpret it better, in order to know who he is and what he ought to seek. But the subject according to the representation view already understands his ends. His world is one of potential means, which he understands with a view to control. He is in a crucial sense disengaged. To understand things in the absolute perspective is to understand them in abstraction from their significance for you. To be able to look on everything, world and society, in this perspective would be to neutralize its significance, and this would be a kind of freedom—the freedom of the self-defining subject, who determines his own purposes, or finds them in his own natural desires.

Now I believe that the attractions of this freedom come from more than the sense of control that accompany submitting nature and society to instrumental reason. They are also of spiritual origin, in a sense which is understandable from our Western religious tradition. In both its Greek and Christian roots (albeit a deviation in this latter stream), this has included an aspiration to rise above the merely human, to step outside the prison of the peculiarly human emotions, and to be free of the cares and the demands they make on us. This is of course an aspiration which also has analogous forms in Indian culture, and perhaps indeed, in all human cultures.

My claim is that the ideal of the modern free subject, capable of objectifying the world, and reasoning about it in a detached, instrumental way, is a novel variant of this very old aspiration to spiritual freedom. I want to say, that is, that the motive force that draws us to it is closely akin to the traditional drive to spiritual purity. This is, of course, highly paradoxical, since the modern ideal understands itself as naturalistic, and thus as quite antithetical to any religious outlook. But I believe that in this it is self-deluded. This is one place where Nietzsche had more insight than most modern philosophers; he saw the connection between the modern scientific ideal of austere truth and the spiritual traditions of self-denial that come to us from the ancients. From this point of view, it is not surprising to see a modern naturalist like Hobbes denouncing vain-glory with the vigour of an ancient moralist.

The analogy is that in both cases, we have a place to stand outside the context of human emotions in order to determine what is truly important. In one case, that of the tradition, this is seen as a larger order which is the locus of more than human significance; in the modern case, it is an order of nature which is meant to be understood free of any significance at all, merely naturalistically. And this is by no means a minor difference. That is not my claim. Rather it is that beyond this difference, something of the same aspiration is evident in both. And this is linked with my belief that the aspiration to spiritual freedom, to something more than the merely human, is much too fundamental a part of human life ever to be simply set aside. It goes on, only under different forms—and even in forms where it is essential not to appear as such; this is the paradox of modernity.

But whatever the motive, this first conception of the person grounds a certain view about moral deliberation. Our ends are seen as set by nature, and thus discoverable by objective scrutiny, or else as autonomously chosen; but in either case, as beyond the ambiguous field of interpretation of the peculiarly human significances. In the light of these ends, reason is and ought to be instrumental. Utilitarianism is a product of this modern conception with its stress on instrumental reasoning, on calculation, and on a naturalistically identified end, happiness (or on a neutral, interpretation-free account of human choice, in terms of preferences). The stress on freedom emerges in its rejection of paternalism. And in rationality it has a stern and austere ideal of disengaged, disciplined choice. This is by no means the only fruit of this modern conception, but it has been one of the most widespread and influential.

The alternative perspective, which I have called the significance view, has arisen in the last centuries as a reaction to the first. It objects to the first as a flight from the human, and sets up a completely different model of practical deliberation. Rather than side-stepping the peculiarly human emotions, and turning to instrumental reason, the main form this deliberation takes is a search for the true form of these emotions. Typical questions of this kind of thinking are of the form: what is really, i.e., properly shameful? What ought we to feel guilty about? In what does dignity consist? And so on.

This deliberation, of course, takes place in a modern context, i.e., one in which no larger order of more than human significance can be just assumed as an unargued context. And this gives it its tentative, exploratory nature. Those who hunger for certainty will only find it in the first perspective, where the ends of man are thought to be defined by a naturalistic science.

I believe that both these models of the person are current in modern Western culture, and that most people operate with a (perhaps inconsistent) combination of the two. It is on the level of theory that they are sorted out, and become exclusive alternatives. But this does not make them unimportant. Theoretical models with their inner coherence have a great impact on our thinking even where—perhaps especially where—they are not fully conscious or explicit. I hope I demonstrated something of this in the previous lectures concerning the baleful effects of the natural science model in social science. In this lecture, I have been trying to dig deeper, into some of the sources of that model. I have been looking for these in a conception of the person, which is also the background of modern views about practical deliberation. I have tried to contrast this with an alternative conception, which I believe is its chief rival in modern Western culture.

Some of my reasoning here has been perhaps too tenuous to be fully convincing. But I believe that a deeper examination must show that the struggle between rival approaches in the science of man, that we have been looking at here, is no mere question of the relative efficacy of different methodologies, but is rather one facet of a clash of moral and spiritual outlooks. And I believe that we can only make even the first halting steps towards resolving it, if we can give explicit recognition to this fact.

DISCUSSION QUESTIONS

1. What does Taylor mean by saying that "animals and human beings are subjects of original purpose"?
2. Why does Taylor think that on one view of what it is to be a person, being a linguistic animal is essential to having concerns about matters of pride, shame, evil, dignity, and love?
3. Explain Taylor's account of shame. Why is it important?
4. On what point does Taylor say that Nietzsche had more insight than most modern philosophers?

Chapter 32

ROLAND PUCCETTI

Roland Peter Puccetti was born in Oak Park, IIlinois in 1924. He earned his B.A. from the University of Illinois, an M.A. from the University of Toronto, and a doctorate from the Sorbonne, University of Paris. He taught at the American University of Beirut from 1954 to 1965, the University of Singapore from 1965 to 1971, and Dalhousie University in Halifax, Nova Scotia from 1971 until his death. His publications include works on the person and the mind and two fictional novels. In Brain and Mind *(1980) he argues that the mind is entirely dependent on the brain, and that there are two minds inside our heads, only one of which is able to talk and write.*

In this 1983 essay, Puccetti uses the view he ascribes to the ancient Roman poet and philosopher Lucretius to argue that the biological life of a human being begins well before, and tends to extend beyond, that human being's life as a person. The author holds that life cannot be withheld from a nonexistent subject. Fetuses and neonates (newborns) are potential persons, not actual persons. Apallic patients have had the seat of consciousness in their brains destroyed, so they are former persons whose organic existence is worth little.

The Life of a Person

When one reflects on the life of a person, it becomes immediately apparent that this can be done in two very different ways. One way is to look upon the person as a particular organism with a spatiotemporal history of its own; there the identity question is approached from the outside, so to speak, and differs not at all from questions about the identity of material objects through time. The other way is to look upon the person's life history as the total span of conscious experience that this person has had; here identity is approached from the inside, whether it be your own life you are reflecting on, or that of another person. It was Lucretius' contention, in Book III of *De Rerum Natura,* that since good or harm can accrue only to a subject of conscious experiences, the latter is the correct view and the former leads to superstition.

I am inclined to think Lucretius was right about this, that personal life is ineluctably shorter at both ends than the life of the organism which is the biological substrate of the person, because developmental processes at the beginning and degenerative processes at the end of organic life are insufficient to support conscious functions, and without these nothing done to the living tissue has personal value or disvalue. But to bring out the intuitive force of Lucretius' position, consider the following parable.

1. THE GENIE'S BARGAIN

Suppose that one day a genie appears before you and convincingly displays magical powers. Now he tells you that he will, if you want, expand your brain so that you will have an IQ of 400. This means that whatever you're interested in achieving will come within easy grasp, whether it be leadership of state, heading a conglomerate, outpainting Picasso or getting a Nobel Prize in medicine. However, he explains, there is one hitch. If you want him to do this for you, you will at the moment of brain expansion cease forever to have conscious experience. No one will know this, for he will program your brain to make all the correct responses to questions, etc. Nevertheless the great future achiever will be an automaton and no more. Would you accept this offer?

I have tried this out on several groups of students and it is amazing how uniform the reaction has been. A few say they would accept the bargain, but upon probing it turns out they have in mind an altruistic act that might lead to discovering a cure for cancer or building world government. They, as well as the majority who refused, all agreed that accepting would be tantamount to personal annihilation, at least in this world, and that one could indeed doubt that wholly unconscious

Source: Reprinted with kind permission from Springer Science and Business Media, Kluwer Academic Publishers, from W. B. Bondeson et al., eds. Dordrecht, Holland. *Abortion and the Status of the Fetus,* ©1983, pp. 169–182, "The Life of a Person" by Roland Puccetti.

achieving automata with their bodies would still be *them*. But if this is correct, and given that the one and same living organism persists from conscious to permanently unconscious activity, it appears bodily continuity through time is not a sufficient condition of personal identity, whereas continuity of consciousness is, and that without even a capacity for conscious experience there is no person any more.

Let us now apply the same lesson to the other end of the life spectrum. Suppose the genie tells you that you are the reincarnation of Napoleon Bonaparte, whose life you happen to admire greatly. You protest that this can't be, since you have no recollection of doing the things Napoleon did, or experiencing his triumphs and defeats. The genie replies that of course you do not because as a young man Napoleon accepted the genie's bargain and thus did all he is remembered for in the history books quite unconsciously. Just supposing you believed this, would you feel proud of Napoleon's deeds as if they had been yours? I think not, because without any sense of those deeds being included in your personal conscious history, they could just as well be the past deeds of anyone else around. Once again it is psychological continuity which underlies the strand of personal identity, and in its absence there is no clear notion of being one and the same person.

But if so, how vain it seems to extend personhood beyond the loss of a capacity for conscious experience, and equally so to thrust it back in time to a stage of organic life before that capacity existed. Yet, as we shall now see, this is exactly what many people tend to do.

2. POSSIBLE PERSONS

I begin with a notion Lucretius would certainly have found strange, namely that of *possible* persons. Here the reference is not to something so general as, say, persons who will live five generations from now, but to *specific* as yet unconceived humans. R. M. Hare [6], for example, asks whether a life-saving operation for an abnormal child might not be denied so that the parents, facing the burden of caring for such an offspring, will not be discouraged from having normal, healthy children later on. He invites us to imagine "the next child in the queue", whom he christens "Andrew", and asks if a full, constructive and probably happy life for this possible person is not a better moral outcome than sustaining the abnormal child and risking Andrew's future nonexistence. Hare grants that since Andrew is only a possible person he cannot be *deprived* of life, but suggests that he can be harmed by *withholding* life from him. And Derek Parfit [11], commenting on Hare's remarks, apparently concurs. He asks why, if it can be in a person's interest to have his life prolonged, it cannot be in his interest to have it started.

To this the Lucretian response would surely be that life cannot be *withheld* from a nonexistent subject any more than this nonexistent subject can be deprived of it. Similarly, a nonexistent subject cannot have his life *started* by anyone. To talk this way is to imagine there are ghostly persons somewhere just waiting to be given flesh and blood, but there are none. For suppose one agreed with Hare that it is unjust to withhold life from Andrew. In that case, how could one make restitution to him? Where would we go to find this possible person and give him, at last, the life he deserves? All one can do is imagine that the parents of the abnormal child, once it is gone, might conceive a healthy child two years down the road and, when it is born, baptize him "Andrew". It is only by retroactively predating this latter child's existence beyond the point of conception that we get the notion of him, quite illicitly, as a specific possible person awaiting conception. There are no such persons (except in the barren sense of a *logically* possible combination of genes occurring in the conceptus), and thus no harm can be done them.

3. POTENTIAL PERSONS

When I was writing on this topic many years ago [14], I used the term *potential* persons to refer to human children, for reasons I shall make clear later. However, I now find the term has been preempted in the literature to refer to fetuses, and shall follow that usage here. Fetuses have an advantage over possible persons in that they exist; the question is whether they are really the sorts of entities that qualify as having a right to life (assuming there are *any* such entities) by virtue of their potential for becoming human persons.

Michael Tooley [15] has argued strongly against the potentiality principle as follows. Most of us would agree that it is not morally wrong, or only slightly so, to destroy surplus newborn kittens. Now if a chemical were discovered that, when administered to newborn kittens, led to their developing into rational, language-using animals and hence candidate persons, would it become grossly immoral to continue destroying newborn kittens? If not, and if artificial vs. natural potentiality for becoming persons is not a morally relevant distinction, then naturally potential persons have no more right to life than such kittens would have.

What is it like to *be* a potential person, i.e., from the inside of that stage of life? None of us knows, not because we have forgotten what it is like, but because our conscious personal lives had not begun yet. I do not deny that it is possible a fetus has crude sensations of pressure, temperature, etc. But zygotes, morulae, blastocysts, embryos and even (in the technical sense) early 'fetuses' do not have the neural complexes necessary to sustain believably a conscious and therefore, by Lucretius' criterion, a personal life. If not, no *person* begins his or her personal life before late term in the intrauterine environment, and only barely then. Terminating a human life before that stage is not, therefore, killing an innocent *person*. It is destruction of at most the organic blueprint of a future person.

For suppose we had the means, technically, of saving life and promoting normal development of a spontaneously aborted fetus at *any* stage whatever. Would the zygote have *more* of life ahead than a near neonate? Biologically, yes. Does that mean more personal value accrues to the saved zygote than to the premature baby? Surely not, for if they both lived a normal human life span and had equal enjoyment of it, it matters not at all that the zygote's organic life was saved seven or so months earlier; that was time at which its personal life had not yet begun and nothing in the events of those months adds to that future person's enjoyment of life. If so, can any event detract from it?

Many would say yes, for abortion constitutes an abrupt cancellation of the promise of a future personal life. My point is that cancellation of a promise is not cancellation of the thing promised. Take a young couple who have two healthy, happy children. It may be that at the time of the second pregnancy they gave serious thought to terminating it as inopportune, but relented and now are glad they did, for he is a wonderful child who shows every sign of enjoying a long and prosperous life. The temptation is to say they are glad not only to have him as a son but glad they did not deprive *him* of his life. But on the Lucretian stance I am developing here, the latter source of self-contentment is confused. He did not exist as a *person* until shortly before his birth. Abortion of the fetus from which his personal life ensued would have prevented someone with his particular genetic throw of the dice from getting launched as a person, but could not have ended a personal life, for this had not yet begun. Blueprints and miniature models are not edifices. What is more, all those early formative experiences in his personal life, comparable to the architect's dabbling with the original design to secure improvements as it actually takes shape, are indispensable ingredients in the individuation of the growing structure of a conscious human, and none of those could have taken place before extra-uterine life, so the *particular person* he is would not have lost this actual life.

4. BEGINNING PERSONS

I will speak now of *beginning* persons, as a term to replace the pre-empted 'potential persons' I used to designate human neonates and infants more than a decade ago. The reason I did this was that I then wanted to reserve 'person' as co-extensive with *moral agent*. A moral agent, I said, is both moral subject and moral object, and while small human children are moral objects, as are other higher forms of animal life, by virtue of being able to suffer, they are not yet moral subjects but only potentially so. Adapting now to the terminological shift, I would say that potential persons, meaning fetuses before late term, are not even moral objects[1], whereas beginning persons are, just as they are potential moral subjects as well.

But Tooley [15] has questioned even this. He holds that it is only when an organism becomes *self-conscious* and has a concept of itself as a continuing subject of experiences that it qualifies as a person with a right to life. Such a view, if correct, could be used to justify infanticide as well as feticide, on grounds that without linguistic abilities normally not developed before the second or third year of life, human infants do not have a self-concept. However, Tooley recognizes that it is possible a nonverbal concept of self emerges as early as a month after birth, pushing back the 'cut-off point' between potential and actual personhood to the first few postnatal weeks; but then he worries that if there *is* such a nonverbal self-concept all kinds of infra-human species devoid of language functions might also qualify as persons whose right to life we humans routinely override.

Let us see what can be salvaged here. If it were true that without a verbal conceptual scheme no self-concept is possible, would this imply that beginning persons have no right to life (assuming, again, that any entity has this)? Consider, first, that there are some otherwise normal children who were raised in isolation by uncaring parents, cut off from human language, who if not rescued by age 10 or 12 are thereafter unable to learn language, even in an artificially enriched linguistic environment. Conversely, consider that some higher primate species who never develop symbolic language in natural conditions have been trained in similarly enriched environments to do so using plastic cutouts, computer consoles, and American Sign Language. If what Tooley suggested were true, it follows that the isolated, otherwise normal human 12-year-old unable to learn to talk has no right to life, while the chimp who can sign "You take out cabbage and give me monkey chow" is a person with a right to life! Yet what morally relevant difference is there between the isolated child and the run-of-the-mill infant toddler? The fact that the former is artificially speechless and the latter naturally so cannot serve to distinguish between them. And if not, the lack of a verbal self-concept in beginning persons cannot justify denying them whatever right to life anyone has.

5. ACTUAL PERSONS

Tooley's qualms about the person-status of languageless infra-human species can now be addressed. The only solid evidence for a nonverbal self-concept comes from Gordon Gallup's [4] studies of self-recognition in a reflecting surface by higher apes, something lower apes such as monkeys cannot learn to do. Yet monkeys rely on recognition of *other* monkeys' faces to establish their place in the troop's dominance hierarchy. How can this be? After all, brain-damaged humans who lose the ability to recognize faces not only cannot identify their own but cannot recognize those of close friends or loved ones. Apparently it is because chimpanzees and other higher apes have a self-concept to begin with that they quickly learn to recognize their own faces and bodies in a mirror. Lacking this, lower apes such as the monkey can identify and react to other monkey faces appropriately, but persist in seeing the reflected face and body as that of just another conspecific of similar age, sex and size. So if it were true that regarding oneself as a continuing subject of experiences is what qualifies an organism for personhood and the right to life, on present evidence only our closest phylogenetic relatives would make the grade.

But even this seems strained. According to many contemporary philosophers, the kind of rude nonvocal but still verbal abilities demonstrated by chimpanzees after arduous human training, plus the evidence for a nonverbal self-concept already in place in such species, is a far cry from what *actual* persons like you and me are able to do. For example, H. Frankfurt [3] has influentially espoused the view that a necessary condition of being a person is the capacity for having what he calls 'second-order volitions', i.e., the desire not to will what one wills and will something else instead. And this clearly requires a rich verbal conceptual scheme, for how else is one going to think the equivalent of, "I wish I were less ambitious"; or, "If only I could love her in return"? Beings that do not have this ability are simply characterized by Frankfurt as 'wantons', and include nonhuman animal species, mental defectives, and the small children I called beginning persons.

More than a decade ago, I would have welcomed Frankfurt's stipulation, because at that time I could not see how any entity could be a moral subject as well as a moral object, hence a moral agent and a full-blown person, without a complex verbal conceptual scheme. But since then I have come to distrust such maneuvers by philosophers, for the reason that they are dangerously exclusive. Who am I to say, for example, that someone with a lesion to Broca's area, a motor aphasic unable to think in propositional language anymore, is therefore a mere 'wanton', a nonperson without a right to life? Except in the narrow legal sense that such a human may not sign a contract or witness a will because of linguistic incompetence subsequent to the brain damage, I might indeed prefer to regard such a human as a person with a language defect, no more and no less than that. And in that case I would have to conclude that moral agents are just a subclass of persons.

Then what is a person? I have come to share the scepticism of D. C. Dennett [1] over ever being able to give an exhaustive list of the necessary and sufficient conditions of being a person; as he says, it might turn out that the concept of a person is only a free-floating honorific that we all happily apply to ourselves, and to others as the spirit moves us, rather as those who are *chic* are all and only those who can get themselves considered *chic* by others who consider themselves *chic.* In any case it is not my task here to say exactly what a person is, but only to argue that a person is more than a living human organism[2]; it is a conscious entity that builds a personal life from agency and experience, and until and only for so long as it has a capacity for conscious experience does the notion of a right to life, if there is such a thing, take hold.

6. FORMER PERSONS

Probably there has been no time before this when philosophers have been more conscious of the brain dependence of the human mind. Yet in spite of this, they sometimes talk of the brain as if it were a replaceable or substitutable organ a person has, on a par with the heart, a kidney, or the cornea of the eye. For example, John Perry [13] has suggested that some day it might be possible to make a duplicate 'rejuvenated' brain exactly like the original except for having healthy arteries, etc., which could then be used to replace the latter when it starts to wear out. If the copy were exact enough, he argues, all the individuating psychological characteristics of the person, including the long-term memories he has, would persist and exact similarity is as good as makes no matter to saying one and the same person has survived the operation. John Hick [7] has even extended this notion to the next world. He asks us to imagine that upon our earthly demise God will create a replica of each of us in a special Resurrection World, complete with an exactly similar brain containing the same memory traces, dispositions, etc., and holds that it would be unreasonable for these resurrectees not to regard themselves, and be regarded by others there, as continuants of the persons whose earthly pasts they recall as their own.

What such claims overlook is that for any future person to be me, any statement true of me now would have to be true of him as well, otherwise he is not me. Now it is true of me that I can really remember certain milestone events in my life, e.g., a delayed honeymoon on the island of Corfu. But the person with the duplicate of my brain came into existence as a subject of experiences only upon duplication, just as the replica of me in the Celestial City would come into existence upon my death, not before. But then neither the duplicatum nor the replicatum of me, given that the brain each has is what makes each a subject of experiences, could possibly have been a subject of experiences at the time of my honeymoon in Corfu, and so could not really remember the events there, but only seem to. If so, neither would be me and it would be vain for me to anticipate any experiences they are going to have as experiences I shall have. Duplication or replication of a brain cannot endow the resultant person with a retroactive personal history; not even God can change the past and tomorrow make true of it what was not true of it before. In sum, it is the spatiotemporal continuity of a particular living brain that is the anchor of personal identity through time.

If we have this straight, we may now ask when exactly does a person's life end and he or she become only a *former* person? At the beginning of this paper I suggested that on the Lucretian view personal life spans one's total conscious experience, and that this is necessarily shorter at both ends than the life of the organism supporting that conscious life. We have seen how this is probably so for the first several months of fetal development, but one might well wonder if it is true at the end of organic life in any more than a picayune sense. After all, if the organic basis for conscious life is the brain and total brain infarct subsequent to, say, cardiac standstill or lung failure causes the death of masses of central neurons by oxygen deprivation within, normally, a matter of minutes, organic death of the brain follows very quickly upon loss of consciousness. It is true that electrical activity can persist in the spinal cord for hours, and some somatic cells may take up to two days to die, such as those composing cartilage in the knee, but these lingering signs of life are no obstacle to a medical finding that the person has died.

Such is indeed normally the sequence of events, but not always. Consider the following case reported by Ingvar *et al.* [8].

Case 8. The patient (Th. Sv.) was a female who had been born in 1936. In July 1960, at the age of 24, she suffered severe eclampsia during pregnancy with serial epileptic attacks, followed by deep coma and transient respiratory and circulatory failure. In the acute phase, Babinski signs were present bilaterally and there was a transitory absence of pupillary, corneal and spinal reflexes. A left-sided carotid angiogram showed a slow passage of contrast medium and signs of brain edema. An EEG taken during the acute stage did not reveal any electrical cerebral activity. The EEG remained isoelectric for the rest of the survival time (seventeen years). After the first three to four months the patient's state became stable with complete absence of all higher functions.

Examination ten years after the initial anoxic episode showed the patient lying supine, motionless, and with closed eyes. Respiration was spontaneous, regular and slow with a tracheal cannula. The pulse was regular. The systolic blood pressure was 75–100 mm Hg. Severe flexion contractures had developed in all extremities. Stimulation with acoustic signals, touch or pain gave rise to primitive arousal reactions including eyeopening, rhythmic movements of the extremities, chewing and swallowing, and withdrawal reflexes. The corneal reflex was present on the left side. When testing was done on the right side, transient horizontal nystagmus movements were elicited. Pupillary reflexes were present and normal on both sides. On passive

> movements of the head, typical vestibulo-ocular reflexes were elicited. The spinal reflexes were symmetrical and hyperactive. Patellar clonus was present bilaterally. Divergent strabismus was found when the eyes were opened [by the examiner]. Measurement of the regional cerebral blood flow on the left side (ten years after the initial anoxic episode) showed a very low mean hemisphere flow of 9 ml/100 g/min. The distribution of the flow was also abnormal, high values being found over the brain stem. The patient's condition remained essentially unchanged for seven more years and she died seventeen years after the anoxic episode after repeated periods of pulmonary edema.
>
> Autopsy showed a highly atrophic brain weighing only 315 grams. The hemispheres were especially atrophied and they were in general transformed into thin-walled yellow-brown bags. The brain stem and cerebellum were sclerotic and shrunken. On the basal aspect some smaller parts of preserved cortex could be seen, mainly in the region of the unci. Microscopically the cerebral cortex was almost totally destroyed with some remnants of a thin gliotic molecular layer and underneath a microcystic spongy tissue with microphages containing iron pigment. The white matter was completely demyelinated and rebuilt into gliotic scar tissue, and there were also scattered macrophages containing iron pigment. The basal ganglia were severely destroyed, whereas less advanced destruction was found in the subfrontal basal cortex, the subcallosal gyrus, the unci, the thalamus and hypothalamus, and in the subocular and entorhinal areas. In the cerebellum the Purkinje cells had almost completely disappeared and were replaced by glial cells. The granular layer was partly destroyed. The cerebellar white matter was partly demyelinated. In the brain stem some neurons had disappeared and a diffuse gliosis was found. Several cranial nerve nuclei remained spared. The long sensory and motor tracts were completely demyelinated and gliotic, whereas transverse pontine tracts remained well myelinated ([8], pp. 196–198).

This clinical picture, confirmed by the autopsy findings, goes by various titles in the literature: cerebral as opposed to whole brain death; neocortical death without brain stem death; and more recently and appropriately, as 'the apallic syndrome', because the characteristic feature is selective destruction of the paleum, the cortical mantle of grey matter covering the cerebrum or telencephalon. As it happens, the neurons composing the paleum are the most vulnerable to oxygen deprivation during transient cardiac arrest or, as in the above case, asphyxiation. Whereas with whole brain death, therefore including the brain stem that mediates cardiopulmonary functions, the patient can be maintained on a respirator only up to a week in adults and two weeks in children before cardiac standstill, the apallic patient can breathe spontaneously and demonstrate cephalic reflexes, which are also brain stem mediated, for months and even years if fed intravenously and kept free of infection, thus allowing organic recovery after the top of the brain is gone.

I said 'organic recovery' is possible with destruction of the cerebral cortex; but on the Lucretian model *personal* life thereupon comes to an end, for with the paleum gone the very capacity for conscious experience goes as well. That such was indeed the case with this patient is obvious from the time of stabilization a few months after the anoxic episode: how else can one explain the persistently flat EEG, the inability to move even the eyes voluntarily, the reduction of cerebral blood flow to less than 20% of normal, and the spastic flexion of extremities? Thus 'the *patient*' was nonsentient and noncognitive for seventeen years, but the *person* was not, for she had died all that long ago, and what was left was a still breathing *former* person.

How can one be sure? Perhaps a homely analogy will help the medically uninitiated to understand this. Suppose we wanted to find out if anyone lives in an apparently abandoned house, on the top floor. But we dare not break into it to see, for legal and ethical reasons. So we stand outside, watching and listening. We can hear the furnace go on, but that could be due to an automatic thermostat. We also see the lights go on in the evening, but that could be the result of an automatic timer to thwart burglars. We dial the phone number and hear the instrument ringing, so the lines are still intact, but no one answers. We measure the heat flow from the furnace and find not enough is reaching that top floor to keep any occupants alive there in winter. Finally, we attach listening devices to the outer walls and videocameras to the windows, but absolutely no real activity is picked up. Surely at this juncture we would conclude it is pointless to go on fuelling the furnace and scrubbing the walls. Nobody is home upstairs.

Yet as things now stand, so long as the furnace goes on and the lights light up by themselves, we are supposed to be committed to heroic maintenance measures tying up scarce medical resources, even though there is *no one* being helped by these efforts. Lucretius would call this rank superstition and advise us to dispose of such former persons as reason dictates. After all, he would surely say, unconscious breathing and heart beating has no intrinsic value to a departed person; you could do no more harm to *that* individual, now dead, than you could do by opening a grave and stabbing a corpse. And I think he would be right.

No doubt this hard Lucretian line will appall many hearing it for the first time. I shall close by anticipating objections and trying to defuse them in advance.

7. OBJECTIONS AND REPLIES

OBJECTION: Current legislation in the United States, and apparently Canada is following suit [10], is in accord with the 1968 Harvard Statement, which allows a determination of death subsequent to the *whole* brain dying above level C_1, as evidenced by prolonged absence of cephalic reflexes and of spontaneous heart and lung activity. What you are suggesting is presently proscribed by law.

REPLY: Superstitious attitudes often get enshrined in law. Why not change the law? It's been done before.

OBJECTION: It is unconscionable to prepare a patient for burial who is not apneic.

REPLY: Spontaneous breathing is normally promissory of a return to conscious functions; with the apallic patient it is not. You can always stop the breathing.

OBJECTION: That's euthanasia, whether passive or active, and it's illegal.

REPLY: You're still confusing the patient with the person. If euthanasia means 'mercy killing', it has no application here. How can you be *merciful* to someone already long beyond any possible suffering?

OBJECTION: Nevertheless such actions would harden medical people. How do we know they won't just go through the wards disposing of helpless persons, such as mental defectives, the recoverably comatose, and the senile?

REPLY: It is not because the apallic patient is helpless that I am recommending disposal, but because he is a dead person. The categories you mention retain a capacity for conscious experience, even if diminished, and to dispose of them would be to deprive them of the rest of their personal lives. You can still harm such people.

OBJECTION: You take it for granted that the paleum is the seat of consciousness and a personal life. Yet Wilder Penfield [12], that great explorer of the cortex, believed to the end of his days that it was only a way-station and that the true site of personal being is central grey matter in the upper brain stem, which in the patient you referred to seems to have been well preserved. How can we be sure such patients are not secretly conscious?

REPLY: On this issue Penfield was wrong. Split-brain surgery for relief of epilepsy yields independent streams of consciousness in the disconnected hemispheres, yet the brain stem is untouched.

OBJECTION: Still, the autopsy showed a fairly well preserved hypothalamus and thalamus. Would this not indicate that the patient could feel thirst and pain?

REPLY: *Who,* exactly, would be feeling pain or thirst? Someone who cannot remember, dream, think, anticipate, or come into contact with reality? But even supposing our concept of a person could be reduced to sensory islands like these, what harm would accrue to such an individual if he or she were prevented from experiencing further thirst and pain? In my own case, were this my "personal" future, I would prefer to go without it; and so too, I think, would any rational person.

OBJECTION: The clinical picture included withdrawal reactions to noxious stimulation.

REPLY: Which can be mediated by spinal arc pathways alone, as has been shown by experiments with paraplegics [5].

OBJECTION: But if there's any uncertainty at all, why not give the patient the benefit of doubt? There have been misdiagnoses of even total brain death. It is always better to mistakenly assist a dead person than to mistakenly abandon someone who might otherwise survive.

REPLY: The only misdiagnoses of total brain death I have heard of involved reduced oxygen requirements due to hypothermia or barbiturate intoxication. But of course one must be cautious. Take six months, use four-vessel angiography, the bolus technique, measurement of regional cerebral blood flow, EEG, brain scan, everything. When there is no longer room for doubt, there is no longer reason for concern.

OBJECTION: Lucretius was an atheist. Why should a religious physician accept that personal annihilation is the result of the cessation of any particular bodily function?

REPLY: You could say the same for whole brain death. What matters is not whether the soul survives the body and goes on to another world, etc., but the point at which a person's life ends in *this* world.

OBJECTION: This is not so much an objection as a query. How is it that organic life can exceed conscious life so long, whereas a similar picture at the beginning of life is quickly fatal? I mean the anencephalic infant. Although the head is flattened, brain stem reflexes and spontaneous heart and lung activity are present, as in the apallic syndrome, yet the infant dies within weeks or at most a few months.

REPLY: There are anecdotal references to one case of anencephaly where the child, under the total care of the mother, survived beyond seventeen years [9]. Nature is cruel, and a fairly long organic human life can still preclude even beginning a personal life.

NOTES

1. However, Engelhardt [2], whose analysis is fully supported by my own, believes that there is sufficient evidence to indicate the aborted fetus feels pain ([2], p. 334). If so, it would be a moral object and I am wrong to think otherwise. Yet being a moral object is obviously not a sufficient condition of being a person, as Tooley's example [15] of surplus newborn kittens makes clear. The reason I hesitate to ascribe a 'right to life' unreservedly even to human beings is that I cannot see how this follows from being a person. My concern is to argue against those who hold that, assuming persons do have a right to life, the early fetus has one because it is already a person.
2. I cannot exactly say what love is, but I would argue confidently nonetheless that it is more than sexual desire. For example, it includes caring about the desired person's happiness and state of mind.

BIBLIOGRAPHY

1. Dennett, D. C.: 1978, 'Conditions of Personhood' in this volume pp. 227–240.
2. Engelhardt, Jr., H. T.: 1976, 'The Ontology of Abortion', in S. Gorowitz (ed.), *Moral Problems in Medicine,* Prentice-Hall, Inc., Englewood Cliffs, New Jersey, pp. 318–334.
3. Frankfurt, H.: 1971, 'Freedom of the Will and the Concept of the Person' in this volume pp. 207–217.

4. Gallup, G.: 1970, 'Chimpanzees: Self-Recognition', *Science* 167, 86–87.
5. Hardy, J. D.: 1953, 'Thresholds of Pain and Reflex Contractions as Related to Noxious Stimulation', *Journal of Applied Physiology* 5, 725–737.
6. Hare, R. M.: 1976, 'Survival of the Weakest', in S. Gorowitz (ed.), *Moral Problems in Medicine,* Prentice-Hall, Inc., Englewood Cliffs, New Jersey, pp. 364–369.
7. Hick, J.: 1976, *Death and the Eternal Life,* Collins, London, Chapter 14.
8. Ingvar, D. H. *et al.*: 1978, 'Survival After Severe Cerebral Anoxia with Destruction of the Cerebral Cortex: the Apallic Syndrome', in J. Korein (ed.), *Brain Death: Interrelated Medical and Social Issues, Annals of the New York Academy of Sciences* 315, 184–214.
9. Korein, J. (ed.): 1978, *Brain Death: Interrelated Medical and Social Issues. Annals of the New York Academy of Sciences* 315, 142 and 366.
10. Law Reform Commission of Canada: 1979, 'Criteria for the Determination of Death', *Working Paper* 23, 58–59.
11. Parfit, D.: 1976, 'Rights, Interests, and Possible People', in S. Gorowitz (ed.), *Moral Problems in Medicine,* Prentice-Hall, Inc., Englewood Cliffs, New Jersey, pp. 369–375.
12. Penfield, W.: 1975, *The Mystery of the Mind,* Princeton University Press, Princeton, New Jersey.
13. Perry, J.: 1978, *A Dialogue on Personal Identity and Immortality,* Hackett Publishing Company, Indianapolis.
14. Puccetti, R.: 1968, *Persons: A Study of Possible Moral Agents in the Universe,* Macmillan, London, Chapter 1.
15. Tooley, M.: 1976, 'Abortion and Infanticide', in S. Gorowitz (ed.), *Moral Problems in Medicine,* Prentice-Hall, Inc., Englewood Cliffs, New Jersey, pp. 297–317.

DISCUSSION QUESTIONS

1. Explain the contrast the author makes between personal life and (human) organic life. Which do you think is more valuable and why?
2. What is the genie's bargain? Would you accept it? Explain.
3. What does Puccetti mean by a "possible person"? What does he say Lucretius would think about possible persons? Do you agree? Explain.
4. Explain what *potential* (or *beginning*) persons are. Contrast them with *actual* persons and *former* persons.
5. Does Puccetti share Frankfurt's conception of a person or Dennett's? What are his reasons for this?
6. On Puccetti's Lucretian model, why is the functioning of the paleum, i.e., the part of the brain's cortex that covers the cerebrum, so important for the life of a person? Are his reasons persuasive? Explain.
7. If your grandmother had "the apallic syndrome" reported by Ingvar and quoted by Puccetti, would you want the attending physician to stop your grandmother's breathing? Would doing so be an act of euthanasia? Explain your reaction to Puccetti's view.
8. How does the apallic patient, according to the author, differ significantly from mental defectives, the recoverably comatose, and the senile? Does this difference morally justify treating these groups of human beings so differently?
9. How does Puccetti respond to the objection that since Lucretius was an atheist, a religious person need not accept that when the paleum permanently stops working, then the person is destroyed?

Chapter 33

DEREK PARFIT

Parfit was born in Chengtu, China in 1942. His leisure interest is architectural photography. He specializes in ethics, metaphysics, and philosophy of mind. He is a Senior Research Fellow of All Souls Oxford and a Fellow of the British Academy and the American Academy of Arts and Sciences.

In this excerpt from his only book (1984) Parfit describes a common science fiction scenario of a Teletransporter that makes an organic Replica of himself while at the same time damaging his heart. He argues that dying when he knows he will have a Replica to carry on his life after his death is not quite as bad as simply dying. Moreover, Parfit argues that being destroyed and replicated is about as good as ordinary survival. He contends that our chief concern is our numerical identity, but psychological changes matter too. To be a person, a being must be self-conscious, aware of its identity and its continued existence over time. Parfit reasons that since personal identity is a transitive relation, the criterion of identity is psychological continuity, i.e. overlapping chains of strong connectedness of memories of past experiences. He believes that division of his brain and transplantation of each half into the body of each of his triplet brothers is about as good as ordinary survival. For Parfit, the fact of personal identity just consists in the holding of psychological connectedness and/or psychological continuity, with the right kind of cause. He rejects the Non-Reductionist view that we are separately existing entities distinct from our brain and bodies and our experiences, and entities whose existence must be all-or-nothing.

Reasons and Persons

10

WHAT WE BELIEVE OURSELVES TO BE

I enter the Teletransporter. I have been to Mars before, but only by the old method, a space-ship journey taking several weeks. This machine will send me at the speed of light. I merely have to press the green button. Like others, I am nervous. Will it work? I remind myself what I have been told to expect. When I press the button, I shall lose consciousness, and then wake up at what seems a moment later. In fact I shall have been unconscious for about an hour. The Scanner here on Earth will destroy my brain and body, while recording the exact states of all of my cells. It will then transmit this information by radio. Travelling at the speed of light, the message will take three minutes to reach the Replicator on Mars. This will then create, out of new matter, a brain and body exactly like mine. It will be in this body that I shall wake up.

Though I believe that this is what will happen, I still hesitate. But then I remember seeing my wife grin when, at breakfast today, I revealed my nervousness. As she reminded me, she has been often teletransported, and there is nothing wrong with *her*, I press the button. As predicted, I lose and seem at once to regain consciousness, but in a different cubicle. Examining my new body, I find no change at all. Even the cut on my upper lip, from this morning's shave, is still there.

Several years pass, during which I am often Teletransported. I am now back in the cubicle, ready for another trip to Mars. But this time, when I press the green button, I do not lose consciousness. There is a whirring sound, then silence. I leave the cubicle, and say to the attendant: 'It's not working. What did I do wrong?'

'It's working', he replies, handing me a printed card. This reads: 'The New Scanner records your blueprint without destroying your brain and body. We hope that you will welcome the opportunities which this technical advance offers.'

The attendant tells me that I am one of the first people to use the New Scanner. He adds that, if I stay for an hour, I can use the Intercom to see and talk to myself on Mars.

'Wait a minute', I reply, 'If I'm here I can't *also* be on Mars'.

Someone politely coughs, a white-coated man who asks to speak to me in private. We go to his office, where he tells me to sit down, and pauses. Then he says: 'I'm afraid that we're having problems with the New Scanner. It records your blueprint just as accurately, as you will see when you talk to yourself on Mars. But it seems to be damaging the cardiac systems which it scans. Judging from the results so far, though you will be quite healthy on Mars, here on Earth you must expect cardiac failure within the next few days.'

The attendant later calls me to the Intercom. On the screen I see myself just as I do in the mirror every morning. But there are two differences. On the screen I am not left-right reversed. And, while I stand here speechless, I can see and hear myself, in the studio on Mars, starting to speak.

What can we learn from this imaginary story? Some believe that we can learn little. This would have been Wittgenstein's view.[1] And Quine writes: 'The method of science fiction has its uses

---

Source: Derek Parfit, excerpts from *Reasons and Persons.* Reprinted with the permission of Oxford University Press.

in philosophy, but. . . I wonder whether the limits of the method are properly heeded. To seek what is 'logically required' for sameness of person under unprecedented circumstances is to suggest that words have some logical force beyond what our past needs have invested them with.'[2]

This criticism might be justified if, when considering such imagined cases, we had no reactions. But these cases arouse in most of us strong beliefs. And these are beliefs, not about our words, but about ourselves. By considering these cases, we discover what we believe to be involved in our own continued existence, or what it is that makes us now and ourselves next year the same people. We discover our beliefs about the nature of personal identity over time. Though our beliefs are revealed most clearly when we consider imaginary cases, these beliefs also cover actual cases, and our own lives. In Part Three of this book I shall argue that some of these beliefs are false, then suggest how and why this matters.

75. Simple Teletransportation and the Branch-Line Case

At the beginning of my story, the Scanner destroys my brain and body. My blueprint is beamed to Mars, where another machine makes an organic *Replica* of me. My Replica thinks that he is me, and he seems to remember living my life up to the moment when I pressed the green button. In every other way, both physically and psychologically, we are exactly similar. If he returned to Earth, everyone would think that he was me.

Simple Teletransportation, as just described, is a common feature in science fiction. And it is believed, by some readers of this fiction, merely to be the fastest way of travelling. They believe that my Replica *would* be *me.* Other science fiction readers, and some of the characters in this fiction, take a different view. They believe that, when I press the green button, I die. My Replica is *someone else,* who has been made to be exactly like me.

This second view seems to be supported by the end of my story. The New Scanner does not destroy my brain and body. Besides gathering the information, it merely damages my heart. While I am in the cubicle, with the green button pressed, nothing seems to happen. I walk out, and learn that in a few days I shall die. I later talk, by two-way television, to my Replica on Mars. Let us continue the story. Since my Replica knows that I am about to die, he tries to console me with the same thoughts with which I recently tried to console a dying friend. It is sad to learn, on the receiving end, how unconsoling these thoughts are. My Replica then assures me that he will take up my life where I leave off. He loves my wife, and together they will care for my children. And he will finish the book that I am writing. Besides having all of my drafts, he has all of my intentions. I must admit that he can finish my book as well as I could. All these facts console me a little. Dying when I know that I shall have a Replica is not quite as bad as, simply, dying. Even so, I shall soon lose consciousness, forever.

In Simple Teletransportation, I am destroyed before I am Replicated. This makes it easier to believe that this *is* a way of travelling—that my Replica *is* me. At the end of my story, my life and that of my Replica overlap. Call this the *Branch-Line Case.* In this case, I cannot hope to travel on the *Main Line,* waking up on Mars with forty years of life ahead. I shall stay on the Branch-Line, here on Earth, which ends a few days later. Since I can talk to my Replica, it seems clear that he is *not* me. Though he is exactly like me, he is one person, and I am another. When I pinch myself, he feels nothing. When I have my heart attack, he will again feel nothing. And when I am dead he will live for another forty years.

If we believe that my Replica is not me, it is natural to assume that my prospect, on the Branch Line, is almost as bad as ordinary death. I shall deny this assumption. As I shall argue later, being destroyed and Replicated is about as good as ordinary survival. I can best defend this claim, and the wider view of which it is part, after discussing the past debate about personal identity.

76. Qualitative and Numerical Identity

There are two kinds of sameness, or identity. I and my Replica are *qualitatively identical,* or exactly alike. But we may not be *numerically identical,* or one and the same person. Similarly, two white billiard balls are not numerically but may be qualitatively identical. If I paint one of these balls red, it will cease to be qualitatively identical with itself as it was. But the red ball that I later see and the white ball that I painted red are numerically identical. They are one and the same ball.

We might say, of someone, 'After his accident, he is no longer the same person'. This is a claim about both kinds of identity. We claim that *he,* the same person, is *not* now the same person. This is not a contradiction. We merely mean that this person's character has changed. This numerically identical person is now qualitatively different.

When we are concerned about our future, it is our numerical identity that we are concerned about. I may believe that, after my marriage, I shall not be the same person. But this does not make marriage death. However much I change, I shall still be alive if there will be some person living who will *be* me.

Though our chief concern is our numerical identity, psychological changes matter. Indeed, on one view, certain kinds of qualitative change destroy numerical identity. If certain things happen to me, the truth might not be that I become a very different person. The truth might be that I cease to exist—that the resulting person is someone else.

77. The Physical Criterion of Personal Identity

There has been much debate about the nature both of persons and of personal identity over time. It will help to distinguish these questions:

1. What is the nature of a person?
2. What makes a person at two different times one and the same person? What is necessarily involved in the continued existence of each person over time?

The answer to (2) can take this form: '*X* today is one and the same person as *Y* at some past time *if and only if . . .*' Such an answer states the *necessary and sufficient conditions* for personal identity over time.

In answering (2) we shall also partly answer (1). The necessary features of our continued existence depend upon our nature. And the simplest answer to (1) is that, to be a person, a being must be self-conscious, aware of its identity and its continued existence over time.

We can also ask

3. What is in fact involved in the continued existence of each person over time?

Since our continued existence has features that are not necessary, the answer to (2) is only part of the answer to (3). For example, having the same heart and the same character are not necessary to our continued existence, but they are usually part of what this existence involves.

Many writers use the ambiguous phrase 'the criterion of identity over time'. Some mean by this 'our way of telling whether some present object is identical with some past object'. But I shall mean *what this identity necessarily involves, or consists in.*

In the case of most physical objects, on what I call the *standard view,* the criterion of identity over time is the spatio-temporal physical continuity of this object. This is something that we all understand, even if we fail to understand the description I shall now give. In the simplest case of physical continuity, like that of the Pyramids, an apparently static object continues to exist. In another simple case, like that of the Moon, an object moves in a regular way. Many objects move in less regular ways, but they still trace physically continuous spatio-temporal paths. Suppose that the billiard ball that I painted red is the same as the white ball with which last year I made a winning shot. On the standard view, this is true only if this ball traced such a continuous path. It must be true (1) that there is a line through space and time, starting where the white ball rested before I made my winning shot, and ending where the red ball now is, (2) that at every point on this line there was a billiard ball, and (3) that the existence of a ball at each point on this line was in part caused by the existence of a ball at the immediately preceding point.[3]

Some kinds of thing continue to exist even though their physical continuity involves great changes. A Camberwell Beauty is first an egg, then a caterpillar, then a chrysalis, then a butterfly. These are four stages in the physically continuous existence of a single organism. Other kinds of thing cannot survive such great changes. Suppose that an artist paints a self-portrait and then, by repainting, turns this into a portrait of his father. Even though these portraits are more similar than a caterpillar and a butterfly, they are not stages in the continued existence of a single painting. The self-portrait is a painting that the artist destroyed. In a general discussion of identity, we would need to explain why the requirement of physical continuity differs in such ways for different kinds of thing. But we can ignore this here.

Can there be gaps in the continued existence of a physical object? Suppose that I have the same gold watch that I was given as a boy even though, for a month, it lay disassembled on a watch-repairer's shelf. On one view, in the spatio-temporal path traced by this watch there was not at every point a watch, so my watch does not have a history of full physical continuity. But during the month when my watch was disassembled, and did not exist, all of its parts had histories of full continuity. On another view, even when it was disassembled, my watch existed.

Another complication again concerns the relation between a complex thing and the various parts of which it is composed. It is true of some of these things, though not true of all, that their continued existence need not involve the continued existence of their components. Suppose that a wooden ship is repaired from time to time while it is floating in harbour, and that after fifty years it contains none of the bits of wood out of which it was first built. It is still one and the same ship, because, as a ship, it has displayed throughout these fifty years full physical continuity. This is so despite the fact that it is now composed of quite different bits of wood. These bits of wood might be qualitatively identical to the original bits, but they are not one and the same bits. Something similar is partly true of a human body. With the exception of some brain cells, the cells in our bodies are replaced with new cells several times in our lives.

I have now described the physical continuity which, on the standard view, makes a physical object one and the same after many days or years. This enables me to state one of the rival views about personal identity. On this view, what makes me the same person over time is that I have the same brain and body. The criterion of my identity over time—or what this identity involves—is the physical continuity, over time, of my brain and body. I shall continue to exist if and only if this particular brain and body continue both to exist and to be the brain and body of a living person.

This is the simplest version of this view. There is a better version. This is

> *The Physical Criterion:* (1) What is necessary is not the continued existence of the whole body, but the continued existence of *enough* of the brain to be the brain of a living person. *X* today is one and the same person as *Y* at some past time if and only if (2) enough of Y's brain continued to exist, and is now X's brain, and (3) this physical continuity has not taken a 'branching' form. (4) Personal identity over time just consists in the holding of facts like (2) and (3).

(1) is clearly true in certain actual cases. Some people continue to exist even though they lose, or lose the use of, much of their bodies. (3) will be explained later.

Those who believe in the Physical Criterion would reject Teletransportation. They would believe this to be a way, not of travelling, but of dying. They would also reject, as inconceivable, reincarnation. They believe that someone cannot have a life after death, unless he lives this life in a resurrection of the very same, physically continuous body. This is why some Christians insist that they be buried. They believe that if, like Greek and Trojan heroes, they were burnt on funeral pyres, and their ashes scattered, not even God could bring them to life again. God could create only a Replica, someone else who was exactly like them. Other Christians believe that God could resurrect *them* if He reassembled their bodies out of the bits of matter that, when they were last alive, made up their bodies. This would be like the reassembly of my gold watch.[4]

78. The Psychological Criterion

Some people believe in a kind of psychological continuity that resembles physical continuity. This involves the continued existence of a purely mental *entity,* or thing—a soul, or spiritual substance. I shall return to this view. But I shall first explain another kind of psychological continuity. This is less like physical continuity, since it does not consist in the continued existence of some entity. But this other kind of psychological continuity involves only facts with which we are familiar.

What has been most discussed is the continuity of memory. This is because it is memory that makes most of us aware of our own continued existence over time. The exceptions are the people who are suffering from amnesia. Most amnesiacs lose only two sets of memories. They lose all of their memories of having particular past experiences—or, for short, their *experience memories.* They also lose some of their memories about facts, those that are about their own past lives. But they remember other facts, and they remember how to do different things, such as how to speak, or swim.

Locke suggested that experience-memory provides the criterion of personal identity.[5] Though this is not, on its own, a plausible view, I believe that it can be part of such a view. I shall therefore try to answer some of Locke's critics.

Locke claimed that someone cannot have committed some crime unless he now remembers doing so. We can understand a reluctance to punish people for crimes that they cannot remember. But, taken as a view about what is involved in a person's continued existence, Locke's claim is clearly false. If it was true, it would not be possible for someone to forget any of the things that he once did, or any of the experiences that he once had. But this *is* possible. I cannot now remember putting on my shirt this morning.

There are several ways to extend the experience-memory criterion so as to cover such cases. I shall appeal to the concept of an overlapping chain of experience-memories. Let us say that, between X today and Y twenty years ago, there are *direct memory connections* if X can now remember having some of the experiences that Y had twenty years ago. On Locke's view, only this makes X and Y one and the same person. But even if there are *no* such direct memory connections, there may be *continuity of memory* between X now and Y twenty years ago. This would be so if between X now and Y at that time there has been an overlapping chain of direct memories. In the case of most adults, there would be such a chain. In each day within the last twenty years, most of these people remembered some of their experiences on the previous day. On the revised version of Locke's view, some present person X is the same as some past person Y if there is between them continuity of memory.

This revision meets one objection to Locke's view. We should also revise the view so that it appeals to other facts. Besides direct memories, there are several other kinds of direct psychological connection. One such connection is that which holds between an intention and the later act in which this intention is carried out. Other such direct connections are those which hold when a belief, or a desire, or any other psychological feature, continues to be had.

I can now define two general relations:

> *Psychological connectedness* is the holding of particular direct psychological connections.
>
> *Psychological continuity* is the holding of overlapping chains of *strong* connectedness.

Of these two general relations, connectedness is more important both in theory and in practice. Connectedness can hold to any degree. Between X today and Y yesterday there might be several thousand direct psychological connections, or only a single connection. If there was only a single connection, X and Y would not be, on the revised Lockean View, the same person. For X and Y to be the same person, there must be over every day *enough* direct psychological connections. Since connectedness is a matter of degree, we cannot plausibly define precisely what counts as enough. But we can claim that there is enough connectedness if the number of direct connections, over any day, is *at least half* the number that hold, over every day, in the lives of nearly every actual person.[6] When there are enough direct connections, there is what I call *strong* connectedness.

Could this relation be the criterion of personal identity? A relation *F* is *transitive* if it is true that, if X is F-related to Y, and Y is F-related to *Z,* X and Z *must* be F-related. Personal identity is a transitive relation. If Bertie was one and the same person as the philosopher Russell, and Russell was one and the same person as the author of *Why I Am Not a Christion,* this author and Bertie must be one and the same person.

Strong connectedness is *not* a transitive relation. I am now strongly connected to myself yesterday, when I was strongly connected to myself two days ago, when I was strongly connected to myself three days ago, and so on. It does not follow that I am now strongly connected to myself twenty years ago. And this is not true. Between me now and myself twenty years ago there are many fewer than the number of direct psychological connections that hold over any day in the lives of nearly all adults. For example, while most adults have many memories of experiences that they had in the previous day, I have few memories of experiences that I had on any day twenty years ago.

By 'the criterion of personal identity over time' I mean what this identity *necessarily involves or consists in.* Because identity is a transitive relation, the criterion of identity must also be a transitive relation. Since strong connectedness is not transitive, it cannot be the criterion of identity. And I have just described a case in which this is clear. I am the same person as myself twenty years ago, though I am not now strongly connected to myself then.

Though a defender of Locke's view cannot appeal to psychological connectedness, he can appeal to psychological continuity, which *is* transitive. He can appeal to

> *The Psychological Criterion:* (1) There is *psychological continuity* if and only if there are overlapping chains of strong connectedness. X today is one and the same person as Y at some past time if and only if (2) X is psychologically continuous with Y, (3) this continuity has the right kind of cause, and (4) it has not taken a 'branching' form. (5) Personal identity over time just consists in the holding of facts like (2) to (4).

[. . .]

[. . .] Reductionists admit that there is a difference between numerical identity and exact similarity. In some cases, there would be a real difference between some person's being me, and his being someone else who is merely exactly like me. Many people assume that there must *always* be such a difference.

In the case of nations, or clubs, such an assumption is false. Two clubs could exist at the same time, and be, apart from their membership, exactly similar. If I am a member of one of these clubs, and you claim also to be a member, I might ask, 'Are you a member of the very same club of which I am a member? Or are you merely a member of the other club, that is exactly similar?' This is not an empty question, since it describes two different possibilities. But, though there are two possibilities in a case in which the two clubs co-exist, there may not be two such possibilities when we are discussing the relation between some presently existing club and some past club. There were not two possibilities in the case that I described in Section 79. In this case there was nothing that would justify either the claim that we have the very same club, or the claim that we have a new club that is merely exactly similar. In this case these would *not* be two different possibilities.

In the same way, there are some cases where there is a real difference between someone's being me, and his being someone else who is exactly like me. This may be so in the Branch-Line Case, the version of Teletransportation where the Scanner does not destroy my brain and body. In the Branch-Line Case, my life overlaps with the life of my Replica on Mars. Given this overlap, we may conclude that we are two different people—that we are qualitatively but not numerically identical. If I am the person on Earth, and my Replica on Mars now exists, it makes a difference whether some pain will be felt by me, or will instead be felt by my Replica. This is a real difference in what will happen.

If we return to Simple Teletransportation, where there is no overlap between my life and that of my Replica, things are different. We could say here that my Replica will be me, or we could instead say that he will merely be someone else who is exactly like me. But we should not regard these as competing hypotheses about what will happen. For these to be competing hypotheses, my continued existence must involve a *further fact*. If my continued existence merely involves physical and psychological continuity, we know just what happens in this case. There will be some future person who will be physically exactly like me, and who will be fully psychologically continuous with me. This psychological continuity will have a reliable cause, the transmission of my blueprint. But this continuity will not have its normal cause, since this future person will not be physically continuous with me. This is a full description of the facts. There is no further fact about which we are ignorant. If personal identity does not involve a further fact, we should not believe that there are here two different possibilities: that my Replica will be me, or that he will be someone else who is merely like me. What could make these different possibilities? In what could the difference consist?

[. . .] To simplify the case, I assume that I am one of three identical triplets. Consider

> *My Division*. My body is fatally injured, as are the brains of my two brothers. My brain is divided, and each half is successfully transplanted into the body of one of my brothers. Each of the resulting people believes that he is me, seems to remember living my life, has my character, and is in every other way psychologically continuous with me. And he has a body that is very like mine.

This case is likely to remain impossible. Though it is claimed that, in certain people, the two hemispheres may have the same full range of abilities, this claim might be false. I am here assuming that this claim is true when applied to me. I am also assuming that it would be possible to connect a transplanted half-brain with the nerves in its new body. And I am assuming that we could divide, not just the upper hemispheres, but also the lower brain. My first two assumptions may be able to be made true if there is enough progress in neurophysiology. But it seems likely that it would never be possible to divide the lower brain, in a way that did not impair its functioning.

Does it matter if, for this reason, this imagined case of complete division will always remain impossible? Given the aims of my discussion, this does not matter. This impossibility is merely technical. The one feature of the case that might be held to be *deeply* impossible—the division of a person's consciousness into two separate streams—is the feature that has actually happened. It would have been important if this had been impossible, since this might have supported some claim about what we really are. It might have supported the claim that we are indivisible Cartesian Egos. It therefore matters that the division of a person's consciousness is in fact possible. There seems to be no similar connection between a particular view about what we really are and the impossibility of dividing and successfully transplanting the two halves of the lower brain. This impossibility thus provides no ground for refusing to consider the imagined case in which we suppose that this can be done. And considering this case may help us to decide both what we believe ourselves to be, and what in fact we are. As

Einstein's example showed, it can be useful to consider impossible thought-experiments.

It may help to state, in advance, what I believe this case to show. It provides a further argument against the view that we are separately existing entities. But the main conclusion to be drawn is that *personal identity is not what matters.*

It is natural to believe that our identity is what matters. Reconsider the Branch-Line Case, where I have talked to my Replica on Mars, and am about to die. Suppose we believe that I and my Replica are different people. It is then natural to assume that my prospect is almost as bad as ordinary death. In a few days, there will be no one living who will be me. It is natural to assume that *this* is what matters. In discussing My Division, I shall start by making this assumption.

In this case, each half of my brain will be successfully transplanted into the very similar body of one of my two brothers. Both of the resulting people will be fully psychologically continuous with me, as I am now. What happens to me?

There are only four possibilities: (1) I do not survive; (2) I survive as one of the two people; (3) I survive as the other; (4) I survive as both.

The objection to (1) is this. I would survive if my brain was successfully transplanted. And people have in fact survived with half their brains destroyed. Given these facts, it seems clear that I would survive if half my brain was successfully transplanted, and the other half was destroyed. So how could I fail to survive if the other half was also successfully transplanted? How could a double success be a failure?

Consider the next two possibilities. Perhaps one success is the maximum score. Perhaps I shall be one of the two resulting people. The objection here is that, in this case, each half of my brain is exactly similar, and so, to start with, is each resulting person. Given these facts, how can I survive as only one of the two people? What can make me one of them rather than the other?

These three possibilities cannot be dismissed as incoherent. We can understand them. But, while we assume that identity is what matters, (1) is not plausible. My Division would not be as bad as death. Nor are (2) and (3) plausible. There remains the fourth possibility: that I survive as both of the resulting people.

[. . .]

90. What Matters When I Divide?

Some people would regard division as being as bad, or nearly as bad, as ordinary death. This reaction is irrational. We ought to regard division as being about as good as ordinary survival. As I have argued, the two 'products' of this operation would be two different people. Consider my relation to each of these people. Does this relation fail to contain some vital element that is contained in ordinary survival? It seems clear that it does not. I would survive if I stood in this very same relation to only one of the resulting people. It is a fact that someone can survive even if half his brain is destroyed. And on reflection it was clear that I would survive if my whole brain was successfully transplanted into my brother's body. It was therefore clear that I would survive if half my brain was destroyed, and the other half was successfully transplanted into my brother's body. In the case that we are now considering, my relation to each of the resulting people thus contains everything that would be needed for me to survive as that person. It cannot be the *nature* of my relation to each of the resulting people that, in this case, causes it to fail to be survival. Nothing is *missing.* What is wrong can only be the duplication.

Suppose that I accept this, but still regard division as being nearly as bad as death. My reaction is now indefensible. I am like someone who, when told of a drug that could double his years of life, regards the taking of this drug as death. The only difference in the case of division is that the extra years are to run concurrently. This is an interesting difference; but it cannot mean that there are *no* years to run. We might say: 'You will lose your identity. But there are different ways of doing this. Dying is one, dividing is another. To regard these as the same is to confuse two with zero. Double survival is not the same as ordinary survival. But this does not make it death. It is even less like death.'

The problem with double survival is that it does not fit the logic of identity. Like several Reductionists, I claim

> *Relation R* is what matters. R is psychological connectedness and/or psychological continuity, with the right kind of cause.[7]

I also claim

> In an account of what matters, the right kind of cause could be any cause.

Other Reductionists might require that R have a reliable cause, or have its normal cause. To postpone this disagreement, consider only cases where R would have its normal cause. In these cases, Reductionists would all accept the following claim. A future person will be me if he will be R-related to me as I am now, and no different person will be R-related to me. If there is no such different person, the fact that this future person will be me just consists in the fact that relation R holds between us. There is nothing more to personal identity than the holding of relation R. In nearly all of the actual cases, R takes a one-one form. It holds between one presently existing person and one future person. When R takes a one-one form, we can use the language of identity. We can claim that this future person will be this present person.

In the imagined case where I divide, R takes a branching form. But personal identity cannot take a branching form. I and the two resulting people cannot be one and the same person. Since I cannot be identical with two different people, and it would be arbitrary to call one of these people me, we can best describe the case by saying that neither will be me.

Which is the relation that is important? Is what matters personal identity, or relation R? In ordinary cases we need not decide which of these is what matters, since these relations coincide. In the case of My Division these relations do not coincide. We must therefore decide which of the two is what matters.

If we believe that we are separately existing entities, we could plausibly claim that identity is what matters. On this view, personal identity is a deep further fact. But we have sufficient evidence to reject this view. If we are Reductionists, we cannot plausibly claim that, of these two relations, it is identity that matters. On our view, the fact of personal identity just consists in the holding of relation R, when it takes a non-branching form. If personal identity just consists in this other relation, this other relation must be what matters.

It may be objected: 'You are wrong to claim that there is nothing more to identity than relation R. As you have said, personal identity has one extra feature, not contained in relation R. Personal identity consists in R holding *uniquely*—holding between one present person and *only one* future person. Since there is something more to personal identity than to relation R, we can rationally claim that, of the two, it is identity which is what matters.'

In answering this objection, it will help to use some abbreviations. Call personal identity *PI*. When some relation holds uniquely, or in a one-one form, call this fact *U*. The view that I accept can be stated with this formula:

$$PI = R + U.$$

Most of us are convinced that PI matters, or has value. Assume that R may also have value. There are then four possibilities:

(1) R without U has no value.
(2) U enhances the value of R, but R has value even without U.
(3) U makes no difference to the value of R.
(4) U reduces the value of R (but not enough to eliminate this value, since R + U = PI, which has value).

Can the presence or absence of U make a great difference to the value of R? As I shall argue, this is not plausible. If I will be R-related to some future person, the presence or absence of U makes no difference to the intrinsic nature of my relation to this person. And what matters most must be the intrinsic nature of this relation.

Since this is so, R without U would still have at least most of its value. Adding U makes R = PI. If adding U does not greatly increase the value of R, R must be what fundamentally matters, and PI mostly matters just because of the presence of R. If U makes no difference to the value of R, PI matters only because of the presence of R. Since U can be plausibly claimed to make a small difference, PI may, compared with R, have some extra value. But this value would be much less than the intrinsic value of R. The value of PI is much less than the value that R would have in the absence of PI, when U fails to hold.

If it was put forward on its own, it would be difficult to accept the view that personal identity is not what matters. But I believe that, when we consider the case of division, this difficulty disappears. When we see *why* neither resulting person will be me, I believe that, on reflection, we can also see that this does not matter, or matters only a little.

[. . .]

92. Wittgenstein and Buddha

Wittgenstein would have rejected the Reductionist View. He believed that our concepts depend on the holding of certain facts, and that we should not consider imaginary cases where these facts no longer hold. The arguments for the Reductionist View appeal to such cases.

This disagreement is only partial. Most people have beliefs about these imaginary cases. As I have argued, these beliefs imply that we are separately existing entities, distinct from our brains and bodies, and entities whose existence must be all-or-nothing. A Reductionist's main claim is that we should reject these beliefs. *Wittgenstein would have agreed.* Given this agreement about this claim, I need not discuss Wittgenstein's view, or some other similar views, such as that advanced by Wiggins.[8]

With two exceptions that I shall soon mention, I believe that I have now considered those views that, in this debate, need to be considered. I may be unaware of some other published view. And I have not considered views held in different ages, or civilizations. This fact suggests a disturbing possibility. I believe that my claims apply to all people, at all times. It would be disturbing to discover that they are merely part of one line of thought, in the culture of Modern Europe and America.

Fortunately, this is not true. I claim that, when we ask what persons are, and how they continue to exist, the fundamental question is a choice between two views. On one view, we are separately existing entities, distinct from our brain and bodies and our experiences, and entities whose existence must be all-or-nothing. The other view is the Reductionist View. And I claim that, of these, the second view is true. As Appendix J shows, *Buddha would have agreed.* The Reductionist View is not merely part of one cultural tradition. It may be, as I have claimed, the true view about all people at all times.

[. . .]

13

WHAT DOES MATTER

95. Liberation From the Self

THE truth is very different from what we are inclined to believe. Even if we are not aware of this, most of us are Non-Reductionists. If we considered my imagined cases, we would be strongly inclined to believe that our continued existence is a deep further fact, distinct from physical and psychological continuity, and a fact that must be all-or-nothing. This is not true.

Is the truth depressing? Some may find it so. But I find it liberating, and consoling. When I believed that my existence was such a further fact, I seemed imprisoned in myself. My life seemed like a glass tunnel, through which I was moving faster every year, and at the end of which there was darkness. When I changed my view, the walls of my glass tunnel disappeared. I now live in the open air. There is still a difference between my life and the lives of other people. But the difference is less. Other people are closer. I am less concerned about the rest of my own life, and more concerned about the lives of others.

When I believed the Non-Reductionist View, I also cared more about my inevitable death. After my death, there will no one living who will be me. I can now redescribe this fact. Though there will later be many experiences, none of these experiences will be connected to my present experiences by chains of such direct connections as those involved in experience-memory, or in the carrying out of an earlier intention. Some of these future experiences may be related to my present experiences in less direct ways. There will later be some memories about my life. And there may later be thoughts that are influenced by mine, or things done as the result of my advice. My death will break the more direct relations between my present experiences and future experiences, but it will not break various other relations. This is all there is to the fact that there will be no one living who will be me. Now that I have seen this, my death seems to me less bad.

Instead of saying, 'I shall be dead', I should say, 'There will be no future experiences that will be related, in certain ways, to these present experiences'. Because it reminds me what this fact involves, this redescription makes this fact less depressing. Suppose next that I must undergo some ordeal. Instead of saying, 'The person suffering will be me', I should say, 'There will be suffering that will be related, in certain ways, to these present experiences'. Once again, the redescribed fact seems to me less bad.

[. . .]

J Buddha's View

At the beginning of their conversation the king politely asks the monk his name, and receives the following reply: 'Sir, I am known as "Nagasena"; my fellows in the religious life address me as "Nagasena". Although my parents gave (me) the name "Nagasena". . . it is just an appellation, a form of speech, a description, a conventional usage. "Nagasena" is only a name, for no person is found here.[9]

> A sentient being does exist, you think, O Mara?
> You are misled by a false conception.
> This bundle of elements is void of Self,
> In it there is no sentient being,
> Just as a set of wooden parts,
> Receives the name of carriage,
> So do we give to elements,
> The name of fancied being.[10]

Buddha has spoken thus: 'O Brethren, actions do exist, and also their consequences, but the person that acts does not. There is no one to cast away this set of elements and no one to assume a new set of them. There exists no Individual, it is only a conventional name given to a set of elements.'[11]

Vasubandhu:. . .When Buddha says, 'I myself was this teacher Sunetra', he means that his past and his present belong to one and the same lineage of momentary existences; he does not mean that the former elements did not disappear. Just as when we say 'this same fire which has been seen consuming that thing has reached this object', the fire is not the same, but overlooking this difference we indirectly call fire the continuity of its moments.[12]

Vatsiputriya. If there is no Soul, who is it that remembers? *Vasubandhu:* What is the meaning of the word 'to remember'? *Vatsiputriya.* It means to grasp an object by memory. *Vasubandhu.* Is this 'grasping by memory' something different from memory? *Vatsiputriya.* It is an agent who acts through memory. *Vasubandhu.* The agency by which memory is produced we have just explained. The cause productive of a recollection is a suitable state of mind, nothing more. *Vatsiputriya.* But when we use the expression 'Caitra remembers', what does it mean? *Vasubandhu.* In the current of phenomena which is designated by the name *Caitra,* a recollection appears.[13]

The Buddhist term for an individual, a term which is intended to suggest the difference between the Buddhist view and other theories, is *santana,* i.e. a 'stream'.[14]

Vatsiputriya. What is an actual, and what a nominal existence? *Vasubandhu.* If something exists by itself (as a separate element) it has an actual existence. But if something represents a combination (of such elements) it is a nominal existence.[15]

> The mental and the material are really here,
> But here there is no human being to be found.
> For it is void and merely fashioned like a doll,
> Just suffering piled up like grass and sticks.[16]

NOTES

1. See, for example, *Zettel,* ed. by G. Anscombe and G. von Wright, and translated by G. Anscombe, Blackwell, 1967, Proposition 350: 'It is as if our concepts involve a scaffolding of facts . . . If you imagine certain facts otherwise . . . then you can no longer imagine the application of certain concepts.'
2. Quine (1), p. 490.
3. This states a necessary condition for the continued existence of a physical object. Saul Kripke has argued, in lectures, that this condition is not sufficient. Since I missed these lectures, I cannot discuss this argument.
4. On this view, it could be fatal to live in what has long been a densely populated area, such as London. It may here be true of many bits of matter that they were part of the bodies of many different people, when they were last alive. These people could not all be resurrected, since there would not be enough such matter to be reassembled. Some hold a version of this view which avoids this problem. They believe that a resurrected body needs to contain only one particle from the original body.
5. Locke, Chapter 27, Section 16.
6. This suggestion would need expanding, since there are many ways to count the number of direct connections. And some kinds of connection should be given more importance than others. As I suggest later, more weight should be given to those connections which are distinctive, or different in different people. (All English-speakers, for example, share many undistinctive memories of how to speak English.)
7. Other Reductionists with whom, on the whole, I agree include H. P. Grice (in Perry (1)), A. J. Ayer (see especially 'The Concept of a Person'), in Ayer (1), A. Quinton, J. L. Mackie, (in Mackie (4) and (5)), J. Perry, especially in 'The Importance of Being Identical', in Rorty, and in Perry (2), D. K. Lewis (in Rorty), and S. Shoemaker (in his *Personal Identity,* Blackwell, 1984).
8. In Wiggins (3). Sadly, Wiggins does not here continue his discussion of his imagined case of division in Wiggins (1).
9. From the *Milina Panha,* quoted in Collins, pp. 182–3.
10. *Cila Mara,* quoted in Th. Stcherbatsky, 'The Soul Theory of the Buddhists', *Bulletin de l'Academie des Sciences de Russie,* 1919, p. 839.
11. *Vasubandhu,* quoted in Stcherbatsky, *op. cit.,* p. 845.
12. Quoted in Stcherbatsky, *op. cit.,* p. 851.
13. *op. cit.,* p. 853.
14. See Collins, pp. 247–61.
15. T. Stcherbatsky, *The Central Conception of Buddhism,* Royal Asiatic Society, London, 1923, p. 26.
16. The *Visuddhimagga,* quoted in Collins, p. 133.

REFERENCES

Ayer (1): A. J., *The Concept of a Person and Other Essays,* London, Macmillan, 1964.

Collins: S., *Selfless Persons,* Cambridge University Press, 1982.

Locke: J., *Essay Concerning Human Understanding,* partly reprinted in Perry (1).

Mackie (4): J. L., *Problems from Locke,* Oxford, Clarendon Press, 1976.

Mackie (5): J. L., 'The Transcendental "I" ', in Van Straaten.

Perry (1): J., ed., *Personal Identity,* Berkeley, University of California Press, 1975.

Perry (2): J., *A Dialogue on Personal Identity and Immortality,* Indianapolis, Hackett, 1978.

Quine (1): W. V., reviewing Milton K. Munitz., ed., *Identity and Individuation,* in *The Journal of Philosophy,* 1972.

Quinton: A., 'The Soul', *The Journal of Philosophy,* 59, No. 15, July 1962, reprinted in Perry (1).

Rorty: A., ed., *The Identities of Persons,* Berkeley, University of California Press, 1976.

Van Straaten (2): *Philosophical Subjects, Essays Presented to P. F. Strawson,* Oxford, Clarendon Press, 1980.

Wiggins (1): D., *Identity and Spatio-Temporal Continuity,* Oxford, Basil Blackwell, 1967.

Wiggins (3): D., *Sameness and Substance,* Oxford, Basil Blackwell, 1980.

DISCUSSION QUESTIONS

1. According to Parfit, how do we discover our beliefs about the nature of personal identity over time from the case of simple Teletransportation?
2. Explain the Branch-Line case. What does Parfit think it shows?
3. Explain the difference between qualitative and numerical identity.
4. Explain what Parfit calls the standard view of the criterion of identity for physical objects.
5. Contrast the identity over time of a Camberwell Beauty with that of an artist repainting a self-portrait into a portrait of his father.
6. Explain the Physical Criterion and its implications for Teletransportation, reincarnation, and resurrection.
7. Explain the relations of psychological connectedness and psychological continuity.
8. Explain the Reductionist view and why Parfit accepts it. Why does his death seem less bad to him on this view?
9. Compare the depictions of Buddha's view of the self by Parfit and by Richard Taylor.

Chapter 34

MARY MIDGLEY

Born in 1919, Midgley had a middle class upbringing in the village of Greenford, London. Her father was a pacifist and the chaplain of King's College, Cambridge. Her classmates at Somerville College, Oxford included Iris Murdoch, Elizabeth Anscombe, and Philippa Foot. Midgley was Senior Lecturer in Philosophy at the University of Newcastle 1962–1980. Her books include Beast and Man: The Roots of Human Nature *(1978),* Animals and Why They Matter *(1983),* Wickedness: A Philosophical Essay *(1984),* Evolution as a Religion *(1985),* Can't We Make Moral Judgements? *(1991),* The Ethical Primate *(1994), and* Science and Poetry *(2001).*

Here she argues against the natural, but untrue view that "person" means human being. Nonhuman persons include the divine Trinity, corporate bodies created by the law, and, following zoologists, individual members of a colonial organism, like jellyfish or coral. The original meaning of persona *is "mask," and thus a character or personage acted, one who plays or performs any part, a character, relation or capacity in which one acts, a being having legal rights. Midgley contends that not all human beings need be persons. Historically, attempts to introduce fresh characters (e.g., ancient Roman slaves, American women before the 1890s) into the drama of our lives have irritated people. Life does not contain just one purpose or drama, she argues, but many interwoven ones, with different characters mattering in different ways. She rejects the belief that the social contract is the only drama in town. Kant's conception of a person as a rational being, capable of choice, endowed with dignity, and worthy of respect as an end in itself, according to Midgley, in spirit does not exclude intelligent aliens or disembodied spirits. She discards Kant's all-or-nothing dichotomy between* persons *and* things *and she criticizes his view that cruelty to animals is wrong if and only if it leads to cruelty to humans. Quarry that are hunted, bulls that are fought, and Moby Dick are characters playing parts in dramas, they are not extras. What makes creatures entitled to basic consideration, she argues, is not intellectual or linguistic capacity but emotional fellowship. While "intelligent" computers do not worry us with any moral claims, Midgley thinks, highly sensitive social beings like apes, dolphins, and whales, do. Consequently, the law must give weight to moral considerations for such nonhuman animals.*

Persons and Non-Persons

Is a dolphin a person?

This question came up during the trial of the two people who, in May 1977, set free two bottle-nosed dolphins used for experimental purposes by the University of Hawaii's Institute of Marine Biology. It is an interesting question for a number of reasons, and I want to devote most of this chapter to interpreting it and tracing its connection with several others which may already be of concern to us. I shall not go into the details of the actual case but shall rely on the very clear and thoughtful account which Gavin Daws gives in his paper '"Animal Liberation" as Crime', published in *Ethics and Animals,* edited by Harlan B. Miller and William H. Williams.

Kenneth Le Vasseur, the first of the two men to be tried, attempted through his counsel what is called a 'choice of evils' defence. In principle the law allows this in cases where an act, otherwise objectionable, is necessary to avoid a greater evil. For this defence to succeed, the act has to be (as far as the defendant knows) the only way of avoiding an imminent, and more serious, harm or evil to himself or to 'another'. Le Vasseur, who had been involved in the care of the dolphins, believed that their captivity, with the conditions then prevailing in it, actually endangered their lives.

> in his opening statement for the defence, [his counsel] spoke of the exceptional nature of dolphins as animals; bad and rapidly deteriorating physical conditions at the laboratory; a punishing regimen for the dolphins, involving overwork, reductions in their food rations, the total isolation they endured, deprived of the company of other dolphins, even of contact with humans in the tank, deprived of all toys which they had formerly enjoyed playing with—to the point where Puka, having refused to take part consistently in experimental sessions, developed self-destructive behaviours symptomatic of deep disturbance, and finally became lethargic—'comatose'. Le Vasseur, seeing this, fearing that death would be the outcome, and knowing that there was no law that he could turn to, believed himself authorized, in the interests of the dolphins' well-being, to release them. The release was not a theft in that Le Vasseur did not intend to gain anything for himself. It was intended to highlight conditions in the laboratory.

But was a dolphin 'another'? The judge thought not. He said that 'another' would have to be another person, and he defined dolphins as property, not as persons, as a matter of law. A dolphin could not be 'another person' under the penal code. The defence tried and failed to get the judge disqualified for prejudice. It then asked leave to go to Federal Court in order to claim that Thirteenth Amendment rights in respect of involuntary servitude might be extended to dolphins. This plea the judge rejected:

> Judge Doi said, 'We get to dolphins, we get to orang-utans, chimpanzees, dogs, cats. I don't know at what level you say intelligence is insufficient to have that animal or thing, or whatever you want to

Source: "Persons and Non-Persons." From *In Defense of Animals,* edited by Peter Singer. Blackwell Publishing (1985): 52–62. Reprinted with the permission of Blackwell Publishing Ltd.

> call it, a human being under the penal code. I'm saying that they're not under the penal code and that's my answer.

At this point—which determined the whole outcome of the trial—something seemed perfectly obvious to the judge about the meaning of the words 'other' and 'person'. What was it? And how obvious is it to everybody else? In the answer just given, he raises the possibility that it might be a matter of intelligence, but he rejects it. That consideration, he says, is not needed. The question is quite a simple one; no tests are called for. The word 'person' means a human being.

I think that this is a very natural view but not actually a true one, and the complications which we find when we look into the use of this very interesting word are instructive. In the first place, there are several well-established and venerable precedents for calling non-human beings 'persons'. One concerns the persons of the Trinity and, indeed, the personhood of God. Another is the case of 'legal persons'—corporate bodies such as cities or colleges, which count as persons for various purposes, such as suing and being sued. As Blackstone says, these 'corporations or bodies politic . . . are formed and created by human laws for the purposes of society and government', unlike 'natural persons', who can be created only by God. The law then can, if it chooses, create persons; it is not merely a passive recorder of their presence (as, indeed, Judge Doi implied in making his ruling a matter of law and not of fact). Thirdly, an instance that seems closer to the case of the dolphins, the word is used by zoologists to describe the individual members of a compound or colonial organism, such as a jellyfish or coral, each having (as the dictionary reasonably puts it) a 'more or less independent life'. (It is also interesting that 'personal identity' is commonly held to belong to continuity of consciousness rather than of bodily form in stories where the two diverge. Science fiction strongly supports this view, which was first mooted by John Locke in his *Essay Concerning Human Understanding.*)

There is nothing stretched or paradoxical about these uses, for the word does not in origin mean 'human being' or anything like it at all. It means 'a mask', and its basic general sense comes from the drama. The 'masks' in a play are the characters who appear in it. Thus, to quote the Oxford Dictionary again, after 'a mask', it means 'a character or personage acted, one who plays or performs any part, a character, relation or capacity in which one acts, a being having legal rights, a juridical person'. The last two meanings throw a clear light on the difference between this notion and that of being human. Not all human beings need be persons. The word *persona* in Latin does not apply to slaves, though it does apply to the state as a corporate person. Slaves have, so to speak, no speaking part in the drama; they do not figure in it; they are extras. There are some similar, and entertaining, examples about women. The following is taken from Susan Möller Okin's book *Women in Western Political Thought:*

> One case, brought before the US Supreme Court in the 1890s, concerned Virginia's exclusion of a woman from the practice of the law, although the pertinent statute was worded in terms of 'persons'. The Court argued that it was indeed up to the State's Supreme Court '*to determine whether the word "person" as used (in the Statute) is confined to males,* and whether women are admitted to practise law in that Commonwealth'. The issue of whether women must be understood as included by the word 'persons' continued even into the twentieth century. . . . In a Massachusetts case in 1931 . . . women were denied eligibility for jury service, although the statute stated that every 'person qualified to vote' was so eligible. The Massachusetts Supreme Court asserted; 'No intention to include women can be deduced from the omission of the word male.' (Emphasis added)

What is going on here? We shall not understand it, I think, unless we grasp how deeply drama is interwoven with our thinking, how intimately its categories shape our ideas. People who talk like this have a clear notion of the drama which they think is going on around them. They know who is supposed to count in it and who is not. Attempts to introduce fresh characters irritate them.

They are inclined to dismiss these attempts sharply as obviously absurd and paradoxical. The question of who is and who is not a person seems at this point a quite simple and clear-cut one. Bertie Wooster simply is not a character in Macbeth and that is the end of the matter. It is my main business here to point out that this attitude is too crude. The question is actually a very complex one, much more like 'Who is important?' than 'Who has got two legs?' If we asked 'Who is important?', we would know that we needed to ask further questions, beginning with 'Important for what?' Life does not contain just one purpose or one drama but many interwoven ones. Different characters matter in different ways. Beings figure in some dramas who are absent from others, and we all play different parts in different scripts. Even in ordinary human life it is fatal to ignore this. To insist on reducing all relationships to those prescribed by a single drama—for instance, the social contract—is disastrous. Intellectuals are prone to such errors and need to watch out for them. But when we come to harder cases, where the variation is greater—cases such as abortion, euthanasia or the treatment of other species—this sort of mistake is still more paralysing. That is why these cases are so helpful in illuminating the more central ones.

It is clear that, over women, those who limited the use of the concept 'person' felt this difficulty. They did not want to deny altogether that women were persons, since in the dramas of private life women figured prominently. Public life, however, was a different stage, whose rules and conventions excluded them (queens apart) as completely as elephants or angels. The fact that private life often impinges on public was an informal matter and could not affect this ruling. Similarly in Rome, it is clear that slaves actually played a considerable part in life. In Greek and Roman comedy ingenious slaves, both male and female, often figure as central characters, organizing the intrigue and supplying the brains which the hero and heroine themselves unfortunately lack. This, however, did not confer legal rights on them. The boundaries of particular situations and institutions served to compartmentalize thought and to stop people from raising questions about the rights and status of those who were, for central purposes, currently disregarded.

I think it will be helpful here to follow a little further the accepted lines of usage for the word 'person'. How complete is its link with the human bodily form? What about intelligent alien beings, for instance? Could we call them persons? If not, then contact with them—which is certainly conceivable—would surely require us to coin a new word to do the quite subtle moral job which is done at present by 'person'. The idea of a person in the almost technical sense required by morality today is the one worked out by Kant in his *Foundations of the Metaphysic of Morals.* It is the idea of a rational being, capable of choice and therefore endowed with dignity, worthy of respect, having rights; one that must be regarded always as an end in itself, not only as a means to the ends of others. Because this definition deals solely with rational qualities, it makes no mention of human form or human descent, and the spirit behind it would certainly not license us to exclude intelligent aliens any more than disembodied spirits. The moral implications of the word 'person' would therefore, on our current Kantian principles, surely still have to attach to whatever word we might coin to include aliens. (C. S. Lewis, describing a planet where there are three distinct rational species, has them use the word *hnau* for the condition which they all share, and this term is naturally central to the morality of all of them.)

Now, if intelligence is really so important to the issue, a certain vertigo descends when we ask, 'Where do we draw the line?' because intelligence is a matter of degree. Some inhabitants of our own planet, including whales and dolphins, have turned out to be a lot brighter than was once supposed. Quite how bright they are is not yet really clear. Indeed, it may never become so to us because of the difference in the kind of intelligence appropriate to beings with very different sorts of life. How can we deal with such a situation?

The first thing that is needed is undoubtedly to get away from the single, simple, black-and-white antithesis with which Kant started, that between persons and things. Most of Kant's argument is occupied with this, and while it remains the focus of his concern he does not need to make finer distinctions. *Things* can properly be used as means to human ends in a way in which *people* cannot. Things have no aims of their own; they are not subjects but objects. Thing-treatment given to people is exploitation and oppression. It is an outrage, because, as Kant exclaims, 'A man is not a thing.' Masters sell slaves; rulers deceive and manipulate their subjects; employers treat their secretaries as part of the wallpaper. By dwelling on the simple, stark contrast involved here, Kant was able to make some splendid moral points, which are still vital to us today, about the thorough-going respect which is due to every free and rational human being. But the harsh, bright light which he turned on these situations entirely obscured the intermediate cases. A mouse is not a thing either, before we even start to think about a dolphin.

I find it interesting that, just as the American courts could not quite bring themselves to say that women were not persons, so Kant cannot quite get around to saying what his theory certainly implies—that animals are things. He does say in his lecture on 'Duties Towards Animals and Spirits' that they 'are not self-conscious and are there merely as a means to an end', that end being ours. But he does not actually call them things, nor does he write off their interests. In fact, he emphatically condemns cruel and mean treatment of them. But, like many other humane people who have got stuck with an inadequate moral theory, he gives ingenious but unconvincing reasons for this. He says—and this has gone on being said ever since—that it is only because cruelty to animals may lead to cruelty to humans, or degrade us, or be a sign of a bad moral character, that we have to avoid it. This means that if we can show, for instance, that venting our ill-temper on the dog will prevent our doing it on our families and can produce certificates declaring that we are, in general, people of high moral character, not easily degraded, we can go ahead with a clear conscience. Dog-bashing, properly managed, could count as a legitimate form of therapy, along with gardening, pottery and raffiawork. In no case would the physical materials involved be directly considered because all equally would be only objects, not subjects. And there is nothing degrading about hitting an object.

In spite of the appalling cruelty which human beings show towards animals the world over, it does not seem likely that anyone regards them consistently in this light. Spasms of regard, tenderness, comradeship and even veneration, alternating with unthinking callousness, seem to make up the typical human attitude. Towards fellow human beings too a rather similar alternation is often found. So this cannot really be an attitude confined to things. Even cruelty itself, when it is deliberate, seems to require that its objects should not be mere physical objects but should be capable of responding as separate characters in the drama. More widely, the appeal of hunting, and also of sports such as bull-fighting, seems to depend on the sense of outwitting and defeating a conscious quarry or opponent, 'another' able to be one's opposite in the game or drama. The script distinctly requires non-human characters who can play their parts well or badly. Moby Dick is not an extra. And the degradingness of deliberate cruelty itself surely requires this other-regarding element. 'Another' is not always another human being.

The degradingness of cruelty is, of course, widely admitted, and Le Vasseur's counsel used this admission as the ground of an alternative defence. He drew attention to his client's 'status as a state employee, which conferred authority on him to act as he did in coming to the defense of "another", in this case the United States, whose social values were injured by what was being done to the dolphins'. This argument was rejected on the ground that, in the eyes of the law, cruelty to animals is merely a misdemeanour, whereas theft is a felony. Accordingly, the choice of evils could not properly be resolved in favour of theft, the more serious offence. It is interesting that this argument makes no objection to treating the United States as 'another' or 'another person'—it does not insist that a person simply means a human being—but rests instead on contending that this 'other' finds its values more seriously attacked by theft than by cruelty to dolphins.

This sort of argument is not easy to come to grips with even in the case of an ordinary individual person, still less in that of a nation. How serious an evil is cruelty? Once it is conceded that the victim's point of view does not count, that the injury is done only to the offender or some body of which he is part, we seem to be cut off from the key considerations of the argument and forced to conduct it in a strained manner, on grounds which are not really central. Is cruelty necessarily depraving? On this approach, that seems partly to be a factual question about how easily people are depraved and partly, perhaps, an aesthetic one about how far cruel acts are necessarily disgusting and repellent. These acts seem now to be assimilated to others which are repellent without being clearly immoral, such as eating the bodies of people whom one has not killed or watching atrocities over which one has no control. The topic becomes a neighbour of pornography rather than of abortion and euthanasia. (In the disputes about permissiveness in the 1960s, an overlap actually developed here at times, as when a London art gallery organized a happening in which some fish were to be electrocuted as part of the show, and efforts to ban this were attacked as censorious manifestations of aesthetic narrow-mindedness.)

Something seems to have gone wrong with the thinking here. The distinctive feature of acts censured on purely aesthetic grounds should surely be that their effects are confined to those who actually perform them. No other sentient being is harmed by them. That is why they pose problems for libertarians when bystanders object to them. But cruelty does not pose this kind of problem, since the presence of 'another' who is harmed is essential to it. In our case it is the dolphin, who does seem to be 'another'. Can we avoid thinking of it in this way? Can the central objection to cruelty really be something rather indirect, such as its being in bad taste?

The law seems to rule so here. And in doing this the law shows itself to be in a not uncommon difficulty, one that arises when public opinion is changing. Legal standards are not altogether independent of moral standards. They flow from them and crystallize in ways designed to express certain selected moral insights. When those insights change radically enough, the law changes. But there are often jolts and discrepancies here because the pace of change is different. New moral perceptions require the crystals to be broken up and reformed, and this process takes time. Changes of this kind have repeatedly altered the rules surrounding the central crux which concerns us here: the stark division of the world into persons and property. Changing attitudes to slavery are a central case, to which we will return. But it is worth noticing first that plain, factual discoveries too can make a difference. When our civilization formed the views on the species barrier which it still largely holds, all the most highly developed non-human animals were simply unknown. Legend apart, it was assumed that whales and dolphins were much like fish. The great apes were not even discovered until the eighteenth century, and real knowledge of their way of living has been acquired only within the last few decades. About better-known creatures too there was a very general ignorance and unthinking dismissal of available evidence; their sociality was not noticed or believed in. The central, official intellectual tradition of our culture never expected to be forced to refine its crude, extreme, unshaded dichotomy between man and beast. In spite of the efforts of many concerned thinkers, from Plutarch to Montaigne and from Blake to John Stuart Mill, it did not develop other categories. If alien beings landed tomorrow, lawyers, philosophers and social scientists would certainly have to do some very quick thinking. (I don't expect the aliens myself, but they are part of the imaginative furniture of our age, and it is legitimate to use them to rouse us from our dogmatic slumbers.) Science fiction, though sometimes helpful, has far too often side-tracked the problem by making its aliens just scientists with green antennae, beings whose 'intelligence' is of a kind to be accepted instantly at the Massachusetts Institute of Technology—only, of course, a little greater. Since neither dolphins nor gorillas write doctoral theses, this would still let us out as far as terrestrial non-human creatures were concerned. 'Persons' and their appropriate rights could still go on being defined in terms of this sort of intelligence, and we could quietly continue to poison the pigeons in the park any time that we felt like it.

The question is, why should this kind of intelligence be so important, and why should it determine the limits of our moral concern? It is often assumed that we can owe duties only to beings capable of speech. Why this should be assumed is not altogether clear. At a simple level Bentham surely got it right in his *Introduction to the Principles of Morals and Legislation:* 'The question is not . . . Can they *talk?* but, *Can they suffer?*' With chimps, gorillas and dolphins, however, there is now a further problem because people have been trying, apparently with some degree of success, to teach them certain kinds of speech. This project might have taught us a great deal about just what new categories we need in our attempt to classify beings more subtly. But unluckily it is now becoming obscured by furious opposition from people who still have just the two categories and who see the whole proceedings as an illicit attempt to smuggle contraband from one to the other. This reaction is extremely interesting. What is the threat? Articulate apes and cetaceans are scarcely likely to take over the Government. What might happen, however, is that it would become much harder to exclude them from moral consideration. In particular, their use as experimental subjects might begin to look very different. Can the frontier be defended by a resolute and unbreakable refusal to admit that these animals can talk?

It is understandable that people should have thought so, but this surely cannot really be the issue. What makes creatures our fellow beings, entitled to basic consideration, is surely not intellectual capacity but emotional fellowship. And if we ask what powers can justify a higher claim, bringing some creatures nearer to the degree of consideration which is due to humans, those that seem to be most relevant are sensibility, social and emotional complexity of the kind which is expressed by the formation of deep, subtle and lasting relationships. The gift of imitating certain intellectual skills which are important to humans is no doubt an indicator of this, but it cannot be central. We already know that both apes and dolphins have this kind of social and emotional complexity. If we ask what elements in 'persons' are central in entitling them to moral consideration, we can, I think, cast some light on the point by contrasting the claim of these sensitive social creatures with that of a computer, of the present generation, programmed in a manner which entitles it, according to current controversial usage, to be called 'intelligent'. That computer does not trouble our sleep with any moral claims, and would not do so however much more 'intelligent' it became, unless it eventually seemed to be conscious, sensitive and endowed with emotions. If it did, we should be facing the Frankenstein problem in a very acute form. (The extraordinary eagerness with which Frankenstein drove his researchers to this disastrous point is something which contemporary monster-makers might like to ponder.) But those who at present emphasize the intelligence of computers do not see any reason to call them persons or to allow for them as members of the moral community. Speech alone, then, would scarcely do this job for the apes. What is at issue is the already glaring fact, which speech would make it finally impossible to deny, that they are highly sensitive social beings.

These considerations are not, I think, ones confined to cranks or extremists. They seem fairly widespread today and probably occur at times to all of us, however uncertain we may be about what to do with them. If so, and if the law really allows them no possible weight, then we seem to have reached the point at which the law will have to be changed because it shocks morality. There is an obvious precedent, to which the dolphin liberators tried to appeal:

> When the dolphins were taken from the tanks, a message was left behind identifying the releasers as the 'Undersea Railroad', a reference to the Underground Railroad, the Abolitionists' slave-freeing network of pre-Civil War days. Along the Underground Railroad in the 1850s, it sometimes happened that juries refused to convict people charged with smuggling slaves to freedom. That was the kind of vindication Le Vasseur and Sipman were looking for . . . They did not consider themselves to be criminals. In fact they took the view that, if there was a crime, it was the crime of keeping dolphins—intelligent, highly aware creatures with no criminal record of their own—in solitary confinement, in small, concrete tanks, made to do repetitious experiments, for life.

If we go back to the alien beings for a moment and consider whether even the most intelligent of them would have the right to keep visiting human beings, however stupid, in these conditions, even those of us least partial to astronauts may begin to see the point which Le Vasseur and Sipman were making. It surely cannot be dismissed merely by entrenching the law around the definition of the word 'person'. We need new thinking, new concepts and new words, and we are not less capable of providing these than people were in the 1850s.

DISCUSSION QUESTIONS

1. Did Judge Doi think that dolphins, orangutans, or chimpanzees are persons? Do you agree with the judge's legal ruling on the Le Vasseur case about the endangered dolphins? Explain.
2. Does Midgley think a dolphin is a person? What are her reasons? Do you agree with her? Explain.
3. Why does Midgley think the degree of intelligence does not determine personhood?
4. Explain C. S. Lewis' concept of *hnau*. Do you find it useful? Explain.
5. What definition of personhood does Midgley propose?
6. What is Kant's view on what makes cruelty wrong, according to Midgley? Is Midgley being charitable to Kant? Explain.
7. How serious an evil does Midgley believe cruelty is? Do you agree with her?
8. What question asked by Bentham in his *Introduction to the Principles of Morals and Legislation* does Midgley say is right? Do you agree with her? Explain.
9. Is sentience by itself sufficient to make it wrong to be cruel to animals? Explain.
10. Could you feel emotional fellowship with a dolphin or a chimpanzee? With a horse or a dog? With a cow or a pig? How would your answers influence your treatment of these animals, including the food you choose to eat?

Chapter 35

GARY LEGENHAUSEN

Legenhausen is co-editor of Jihad and Shahadat: Struggle and Martyrdom in Islam *(1986). He was on the faculty at Texas Southern University when this 1986 essay was published. Here he examines four Christian arguments for and four Muslim arguments against the claim that God is a person. The arguments in favor appeal to (1) belief in the divinity of Jesus; (2) scriptural language, which presupposes a personal God; (3) revelation, which requires that God is viewed as a person; and (4) the view that worship and prayer are only appropriately directed toward a personal God. Criticisms of each of these four arguments are discussed.*

The first argument against the claim is that persons are created but God is not. The second argument is that persons are substances, but God is not a substance since (a) God does not belong to a category, (b) God is not limited by anything, (c) God is simple and so is not composed of genus and difference. This argument can be attacked by holding that God's substantiality is compatible with God's transcendence, or holding that God's personality is compatible with God's transcendence, and that not all persons are substances. The third argument is that God is the ultimate ground of reality, and so God cannot be individuated, whereas substances and persons are necessarily distinctly individuated. This reasoning can be countered with the analogy that the ocean is to its waves as God is to this world. The fourth argument against the claim that God is a person is that there are no disembodied minds, and God does not have a body, so God does not have a mind (as persons do). Pantheists, however, deny that God has no body. The doctrine of the immortality of the soul conflicts with the claim that there are no disembodied minds. The doctrine of God's omniscience seems to require that God has a mind.

Legenhausen concludes that neither set of arguments is conclusive. Instead of seeing the issue as a controversy between Christians and Muslims, he suggests that God is neither personal nor impersonal, but transpersonal or suprapersonal.

Is God A Person?

The most striking difference between Christian and Muslim theologies is that while, for Christians, God is a person, Muslims worship an impersonal deity. Despite the importance of this difference for a host of theological issues, it is a difference which has gone largely unnoticed by Christians and Muslims alike. Yet Christians everywhere will affirm that God is a person, while the average Muslim will readily deny this. Theism is often defined by philosophers of religion who work in the Christian tradition in such a manner as to require the belief that God is a person. Thus *The Encyclopedia of Philosophy* has it that, 'THEISM signifies belief in one God (*theos*) who is *(a)* personal, *(b)* worthy of adoration, and *(c)* separate from the world but *(d)* continuously active in it'[1] John H. Hick admits that, '*Theism* . . . is strictly belief in a deity, but is generally used to mean belief in a personal deity'[2] Richard Swinburne states that a theist is one who believes that there is a God who is a 'person without a body (i.e. a spirit) who is eternal, free, able to do anything, knows everything, is perfectly good, is the proper object of human worship and obedience, the creator and sustainer of the universe',[3] and J. L. Mackie, while arguing the case of atheism, endorses Swinburne's definition of theism.[4]

Both theists and atheists in the Christian tradition agree that theism commits one to the view that God is a person of some sort, but there is no corresponding unanimity among Muslim theologians and philosophers in the claim that God is not a person. There have been Muslim theologians who have held that God quite literally sits upon his throne in heaven. Nevertheless, within the fold of Islam (at least among theologians), belief in a personal God is a minority position. The theological and philosophical groundwork for the Muslim claim that God is not a person is found in both Sunni and Shi'ite sources; however, in this paper I will concentrate on Shi'ite views on this issue.

This paper consists of two parts in which some arguments for and against the view that God is a person are summarized, and the strengths and weaknesses of these arguments are evaluated. None of these arguments will be defended as conclusive. However, it is my hope that this exposition of both impersonal and personal views of the deity will provide a groundwork for future dialogue between Christians and Muslims.

Before the arguments are presented it may be useful to mention an important distinction, that is the distinction between the claim that:

(1) God is a person,

and the claim that

(2) God is personal.

Some who accept (2) would deny (1) on the grounds that, since there are three persons of God, God is not *a* person. The indefinite article is

Source: "Is God a Person?" *Religious Studies* 22 (1986): 307–323. Reprinted with the permission of Cambridge University Press.

taken by such theologians to indicate a singularity incompatible with the trinitarian doctrine. Also, (2) is sometimes understood in a weak sense, to mean merely that personal, rather than impersonal, pronouns are applicable to God, and that other predicates applicable to persons are attributable to God, e.g. he is all-knowing, all-wise, he is aware, he is all merciful. No one in the Judeo-Christian-Islamic tradition (sometimes called the Abrahamic tradition[5] would deny (2) in this weak sense. What is at issue is whether or not the metaphysical category of *person* is in some sense attributable to God. Both (1) and (2) will be understood to assert this stronger claim. The indefinite article in (1) will be taken to mean 'at least one', and (2) will be understood to be an assertion about the nature of God, and not merely as a claim about scriptural language.

I. ARGUMENTS FOR THE CLAIM THAT GOD IS A PERSON

Although the claim that God is a person is usually assumed rather than defended by argument, four major arguments may be constructed which seem to reflect Christian thinking on this topic. The first of these is an argument stemming from belief in the divinity of Jesus Christ. Secondly, one may argue that scriptural language presupposes a personal God. Thirdly, one might claim that an adequate account of revelation requires that God be viewed as a person. The fourth argument that may be advanced asserts that worship and prayer are only appropriately directed toward a personal God. These arguments will be presented in succession and evaluated.

The word 'person' derives from the Latin '*persona*' which was the term for the mask worn by actors in dramatic performances. The Greek equivalent was used in somewhat this sense by Clement of Alexandria (*c.* 150–215) who described Christ as the divine substance which assumed the human mask, τὸ ἀνθρώπου προσωπειον, *prosopon* being the mask worn by Greek actors. Thus, the concept of a *person* was associated with Christ from as early as the second century. It is one thing to claim that Christ is the *persona* of God, and quite another to assert that God himself is a person. This latter doctrine was explicitly formulated only in nineteenth- and twentieth-century theology.[6] The doctrine of the personal God was made popular in twentieth-century Christian theological circles due to the influence of the Jewish philosopher, Martin Buber (1878–1965), and the American personalist, Edgar Sheffield Brightman (1884–1953). The most extreme form of the doctrine was that advanced by Brightman who held that God is limited by conditions within his nature which are neither created nor approved by his will, and that God maintains a constant and growing control over these conditions. Brightman's teaching, that *person* is the ontological ultimate, has had a strong influence on theologians such as Maritain, Gilson, and Mounier. Not all of the theologians who have been influenced by the personalists have accepted the extreme views of Brightman. The view that God is a person has nevertheless become extremely widespread among contemporary Christian theologians. No standard definition of 'person' has been adopted since that of Boethius, according to which a person is an individual substance of rational nature. Among different philosophers and theologians, different aspects of personhood have been emphasized, e.g. mind, self-consciousness, will. The ascription of such attributes to persons is by no means inconsistent with the Boethian definition. Depending upon one's theory of what it means to have a rational nature, such attributes may even be implied by the Boethian definition.

In the Christian setting, the move from the recognition of the person of Christ to the view that God is a person can be established by the following syllogism:

(3) Jesus is a person.
(4) Jesus is God.
∴ (5) God is a person.

The validity of the above argument depends upon the assumption that the second premise is an identity claim, and this assumption might be challenged even by Christians. While there is no hesitation among Christians in their acceptance of (4), there is room for doubt regarding the following:

(6) God is Jesus.

The equivalence of (4) and (6) is needed for the derivation of (5), and it is not clear that all those who accept the doctrine of the trinity will accept this equivalence. According to one possible reading of trinitarian doctrine, God is one substance which is manifest in three persons.[7] Because Jesus is a member of the trinity, (4) is true. However, since the trinity includes persons other than Jesus, (6) is to be rejected.

On the other hand, the equivalence of (4) and (6) might be maintained by arguing that these statements assert the identity of the substance named by 'Jesus' with the substance named by 'God'. Since there is only one being which is named by the term 'God' and only one being named by 'Jesus', (4) is an identity claim.

Even if (4) is taken as an identity claim, the validity of the argument may be questioned. It is not clear that the following argument form is valid:

(7) Jesus is _____.
(8) Jesus is God.
∴ (9) God is _____.

Does this argument form enable us to infer the mortality of God from the mortality of Jesus? If it does, how is this to be reconciled with claims of the immortality of God? Perhaps it could be argued that human mortality is consistent with divine immortality, and that human weakness is compatible with divine omnipotence, etc. Thus, one might hold that since Jesus is mortal and is God, that God is mortal. God is mortal in one sense and in another sense God is not mortal. The term 'mortal' is equivocal here. In this way, any attempt to use the above argument form to derive a claim based on the limited nature of Jesus as a human being which was inconsistent with the divine attributes could be met with the charge of equivocation. (To be more precise, the charge would not be that the terms were completely equivocal, but that they were analogical. In any case, it is the denial of univocacy which is important here.) Whether or not this response would prove satisfactory, some such attempt should be made by the Christian to defend the above argument form, for it is important for the Christian to claim that by studying the character of Jesus, we learn about the nature of God. Thus, from the kindness of Jesus, we learn that God is kind. God reveals his kindness through Jesus. The problem is to find some way to determine which attributes of Jesus reveal to us something about the nature of God, and which attributes of Jesus pertain only to this person of God. If we charge that the mortality of Jesus is compatible with the immortality of God, how can we deny the possibility that the kindness of Jesus is compatible with divine malevolence? The question is merely academic with regard to kindness and malevolence, for we may claim to know, independently of Christ's revelation, that God is good. Consider the proposition under examination, that God is a person. Is *being a person* the kind of predicate whose true application to Jesus implies an analogical application to God, or should we claim that the fact that God is a person in his human manifestation is compatible with his existence as an impersonal deity?

Nothing will be won with the claim that only the *moral* attributes of Jesus may be applied to God, and that these are to be applied only by analogy. This tactic will not solve our problem, for all it does is to ensure that God has the moral perfections of Jesus in an infinite degree. But the question with which we are faced is not with respect to the goodness of God, but with respect to the metaphysical issue of whether or not God is a person. It is by no means obvious that the property of being a person is a perfection, and not an imperfection. One might argue that to be a person is to have a kind of perfection. To be a person is to be superior to the animals. To be a person is thus to have a kind of perfection, and so God has this kind of perfection in an infinite degree. This argument fails because it is disputable whether entities which are superior to persons should still be termed persons, even if it is granted that to be a person is to be superior to other earthly creatures. To be a mammal is to be superior to earthly creatures which are not mammals, but this does not mean that mammality is a perfection which may be ascribed to God by analogy.

Aquinas argues that personhood is a kind of perfection since *being a person* connotes dignity.[8] But the claim that God is a person cannot be supported merely by reference to the dignity of persons. The problem is that *dignity* may be separately ascribed to God without claiming that God is a person. The simple connotation of perfection does not entail that the term with such a connotation designates a perfection, for it is consistent that one of the attributes connoted by a term may be a perfection and another a limitation. For example, 'muscular' connotes *power,* yet we do not say that God is muscular, since this would not only imply that God has power, but that he is corporeal. So, even if it is granted that 'person' connotes dignity, which is a perfection, this by itself does not establish that *person* is a perfection.

Our conclusion must be that argument (3)–(5) is of questionable worth in the attempt to demonstrate that God is a person. Even those who accept the premisses of this argument may have doubts as to its validity. In any case, the argument calls for serious attention. Given the reading of (8) as an identity claim, it is difficult to see how the validity of the argument form (7)–(9) can be denied, but given the validity of this argument form, an account is needed by which the apparent incompatibility of human and divine attributes may be resolved.

The second argument which will be presented for the claim that God is a person does not depend upon the assumption of the divinity of Christ. The argument is that scriptural statements pertaining to God presuppose that he is a person. This position is succinctly stated by John H. Hick.

> The conviction that God is personal, *He* rather than *It,* has always been plainly implied both in the biblical writings and in later Jewish and Christian devotional and theological literature. In the Old Testament God speaks in personal terms (for example, 'I am the God of your father, the God of Abraham, the God of Isaac, and the God of Jacob') and the prophets and psalmists address him in personal terms (for example, 'Hear my cry, O God, listen to my prayer.'). In the New Testament the same conviction as to the personal character of God is embodied in the figure of fatherhood that was constantly used by Jesus as the most adequate earthly image with which to think of God.[9]

This argument is especially appealing to contemporary philosophers who are keenly sensitive to the presuppositions of linguistic usage. The kind of attributes which are ascribed to God in scripture are applicable only to persons, it is claimed, and thus God is viewed as a person by those who accept the truth of scripture.

The trouble with this line of argument is that it could also be used to support an anthropomorphic view of God which is clearly and explicitly rejected by the orthodox. Consider the following two arguments:

(10) All fathers are persons.
(11) God is a father.
∴ (12) God is a person.
(13) All fathers have bodies.
(14) God is a father.
∴ (15) God has a body.

Hick would endorse the first argument but not the second, yet the language of scripture is corporeal just as much as it is personal. Those who would argue that God is a person because of the nature of scriptural language must come up with some way of blocking the argument from scriptural language to anthropomorphism. This difficulty is exploited by Kai Nielson, who argues that unless scriptural language is understood rather literally, it is unintelligible, and that since religious people do not take religious claims literally, they do not really understand what they are talking about!

> It may well be that when the engine isn't idling, when people are praying or worshipping, their childhood pictorial images of God as a material being unwittingly reassert themselves and in that way 'loving' comes to have an application when applied to God. But to reflective religious consciousness, He is 'Pure Spirit', and 'disembodied mind', but then, given their use of 'God' as 'Pure Spirit', we cannot understand what it would be for such a being to act and thus to be loving, merciful or just, for these predicates apply to things that *a person does.* But we have no understanding of 'a person' without 'a body' and it is only persons that in the last analysis can act or do things. We have no understanding of 'disembodied action' or 'bodiless doing' and thus no understanding of 'a loving but bodiless being'.[10]

Those who would argue with Hick that God is a person because scriptural language seems to indicate this must block the sort of attack on theism advanced by Nielson. If it is claimed that religious language is not to be interpreted literally, and that argument (13)–(15) may thus be countered, then argument (10)–(12) can no longer be used to establish that God is a person. It will be claimed that the scriptural statement that God is our Father is symbolic, and so cannot be taken to imply that God has all of the attributes which could be applied to fathers outside the scriptural context. But once this is admitted one can no longer argue that our acceptance of scripture commits us to the view that God is a person.

By referring to Jewish as well as to Christian scriptures, Hick attempts to support the claim that the view that God is a person is implicit in Judaism, and is thus independent of the doctrine of the incarnation. However, the classical solution in Jewish theology to the problem of anthropomorphic scriptural statements, as enunciated by Moses Maimonides (1135–1204), would require not only a denial that God has a body, but a denial that God is a person as well. According to Maimonides God is absolutely transcendent and unknowable. There is not the faintest resemblance between him and his creatures. Maimonides explains that the anthropomorphic language of scripture is necessary for it is only by the use of such language that the masses of people would be able to believe that God exists. When we say that God is just, this does not mean that God has the same attribute which we ascribe to just persons, but that God is not unjust and that he is the cause of all justice.[11]

Interpretations of scriptural statements which avoid commitment to anthropomorphism were common among Jewish, Christian and Muslim theologians of the Middle Ages. This is not the place to examine the differences in the various positions which have been taken with regard to the interpretation of religious language. The point is simply that any account of religious language sufficiently subtle to provide a response to the charge of anthropomorphism will be sufficient to rebut the argument that the use of religious language commits us to the existence of a personal God.

The third argument which will be considered in support of the claim that God is a person makes reference to the phenomenon of revelation. Revelation, according to many contemporary theologians, is God's communication to man. Communication is the exchange of information from one person to another. So, if God communicates, he must be a person. The same objections which were brought against the second argument could be used to refute this one. Nevertheless, this argument deserves special attention because of the importance of the notion of revelation as God's communication for many contemporary theologians. We can pose the argument from revelation in the following way:

(16) Only persons communicate.
(17) Revelation is a kind of communication between God and man.
∴ (18) God is a person.

The validity of this argument is not in question. Those who accept God's revelation as a kind of communication yet deny that God is a person must reject (16). This is precisely the line taken by Muslim theologians. The problem is to explain how communication can take place when at least one of the parties communicating is not a person.

The entire tradition of Muslim theology begins with controversy concerning the nature of divine revelation, the speech of God. This is why the expression for theology in the Muslim world is *'ilm al kalam,'* whose literal translation is, 'the science of the speech'[12] Several key points in the theology of the late Shi'ite philosopher, Allamah Tabataba'i, may shed some light on our problem. Tabataba'i goes to some trouble to distance himself from those Muslim theologians who have held that because everything leads back to God, the entire universe is the speech of God. Tabataba'i rejects this view because it would mean that any claim that God communicates to his prophets would have to be interpreted as mere allegory. On the contrary, Tabataba'i maintains that God's speech is real communication. Divine revelation is real communication because it is directed to specific individuals, and because through revelation a message is conveyed. However, when it is said that God communicates his message to the prophets, this does not mean that he has thoughts which are conveyed from one person to another. Tabataba'i writes that God is too great to be said to have a 'self' or 'mind' with which he might have ideas. When God is said to communicate with a man, this means that he creates something which gives that man an inner knowledge of a message.

> . . . [I]t becomes clear that the laws which can guarantee the happiness of human society cannot be perceived by reason. Since according to the thesis of general guidance running throughout creation the existence of an awareness of these laws in the human species is necessary, there must be another power of apprehension within the human species which enables man to understand the real duties of life and which places this knowledge within the reach of everyone. This consciousness and power of perception, which is other than reason and sense, is called the prophetic consciousness, or the consciousness of revelation.[13]

Tabataba'i claims that although we use the term 'communication' to signify the exchange of ideas between human beings, the term can be used to describe revelation because the effect or function is the same, i.e. a message is obtained. In like manner, we use the term 'lamp' to describe an electric light, even though it has none of the elements of the lamps to which the term was first applied, simply because the function is the same. Thus, revelation may be considered in a real sense to be God's communication to man, although this communication does not originate from a mind or person.[14]

Whether or not we accept Tabataba'i's theology, he shows us that one may consistently hold that revelation is divine communication without committing oneself to the view that God is a person.

The final argument which will be considered in favour of the view that God is a person is that the personality of God is a condition for the appropriateness of worship and supplication. Karl Rahner, for example, uses a form of this argument against those who would claim that while God appears as a person to us, he is not intrinsically a person. Rahner argues that if we say that God is a person 'in relation to us', but not 'in his own self', he would not be able to 'enter into that personal relationship to us which we presuppose in our religious activity, in prayer, and in our turning to God in faith, hope and love'.[15] There is a danger of question-begging in this argument. One might say, 'In my religious life I assume that God has attribute *X*, hence to deny that God has attribute *X* is to undermine completely my religious experience'. This is unwarranted. As my views of God become less naive, the attitudes and assumptions which I bring to my religious practice may be expected to change, but this may be seen as a matter of growth, and not necessarily one of abnegation. While Rahner sees an 'empty nothingness' as the only alternative to a personal God, it should be clear that there are other possibilities.

The argument that prayer and worship presuppose a personal God is more cautiously articulated by Frederick Copleston.

> . . . [W]hen we say that God is personal, we really mean that He is not less than what we experience as personality, in the sense that the perfection of personality must be in Him in the only manner in which it can be in an infinite Being . . . That there is a positive content of some sort to our idea of divine personality is shown by the fact that the meaning in the statement 'God is super-personal' (i.e. more than that which we directly experience as personality) is different from the meaning in the statement 'God is not personal' (i.e. in any sense, just as a stone is not personal). If we had reason to believe that God were not personal, we should see the uselessness of worship and prayer; but the statement that God is personal suggests immediately that worship and prayer are in place, even though we have no adequate idea of what the divine personality is in itself.[16]

Although Copleston's argument is more sophisticated than Rahner's, it also rests on a false dichotomy. It claims that God is either a person, or is not a person in the way that a stone is not a person. A similar argument could be made for the claim that God is a fish. Either God is super-fish, i.e. more than that which we experience as fish, or he is not fish, i.e. just as a stone is not a fish. God is not a fish in any sense. He is not even a super-fish. But this is not because he is less than a fish, but because fishiness is a limitation by which God is unconstrained. Likewise, one might argue that God is not a person, not because he is, like a stone, less than a person, but because to be a person in any sense is to be limited. While worship and prayer would not be appropriately directed toward something which was not a person like a stone is not a person, i.e. not a person because less than a person, would it be inappropriate to direct our worship and prayer toward something which is not a person because it belongs to a higher category than that of persons?

This question is adroitly taken up by John Laird in his *Mind and Deity.*

> As Luther said in his *Great Catechism:* 'A God is that whereto we are to look for all good and to take refuge in all distress; so that to have a God is to trust and believe him from the whole heart.' Is it credible, we may ask, that such things should be believed of God if reality were impersonally constituted?
>
> I would suggest, although with great diffidence, that it is not incredible. If man's environment did perform and would continue to perform these services, hope and confidence as well as acquiescence might be directed towards it. The environment would be dependable and, in that sense, trustworthy. It might be reverenced, admired, extolled and even worshipped. Affection might be felt for it as well as trust. It might be loved unless, in the English way, we restrict the term 'love' to the sort of feeling that can only be felt for another person . . .
>
> . . . The objector says that reverence, affection and admiration, except of a tepid and watery kind, could not be felt for physical nature, unless by inadvertence or mere illusion. Suppose that this statement is substantially true. We have still to remember that a spiritual community, i.e. a spiritual unity that need not itself be a self or a person, may and does inspire such feelings. Consider the possibility that the Holy Spirit, understood impersonally, is the principle agent in the Christian life. Consider the possibility that human history, despite so much in the past and despite nearly all in the present, is the gradual achievement of a heavenly republic, and is not a passing episode on the surface of a precarious planet. Such theories are impersonal but theistic. What right has anyone to say that they are quite absurd?
>
> . . . There is no reason for assuming that the *im*personal must be *sub*-personal.[17]

In short, prayer and worship are not incompatible with belief in an impersonal deity, provided that the impersonal is not equated with that which is less than a person.

II. ARGUMENTS FOR THE CLAIM THAT GOD IS NOT A PERSON

Although the arguments for the negative position, that God is not a person, will be taken from Muslim theology, not all of these arguments will be unfamiliar to the student of Christian theology, since both Christians and Muslims used arguments similar to these during the middle ages. It has often been remarked that theology strives for a balance between the belief that God is immanent and the belief that he is transcendent. Muslim and Christian theologians differ on how to strike the balance. For the Christian, although God is transcendent, he became man, and can be understood through this incarnation; and although God is immanent, the primary manifestation of his presence in the world is through the divinity of Jesus.[18] Both the transcendence and the immanence of God are understood more radically than this in the Muslim view, according to which, because of God's transcendence, he cannot be called a person, not even analogically. In brief, the Muslim argument against the personality of God is that personality is a limiting factor and is therefore incompatible with the infinite nature of God. God transcends such concepts as 'spirit', 'soul', 'self', and 'person'.

The Muslim denial that God is a person is not, however, a denial that God is immanent, and where the immanency of God is emphasized in Muslim thought, it is done so in a way that is appropriate to an impersonal view of God. This point is recognized by Webb, who expresses his own reservations about whether Muslims should be said to worship a personal God on the grounds that:

> . . . Personality is not expressly reckoned among [God's] attributes and that, when the Moslem aspires after a more intimate kind of piety than his canonical scriptures suggest, he seems to pass at once to a pantheistic mysticism wherein the personal distinction between the devotee and his God tends to disappear altogether.[19]

Although the charge of pantheism has been vigorously denied by such an eminent Muslim scholar as Seyyed Hossein Nasr, the point that the object of worship and contemplation in Islamic mysticism is not experienced as a personal being stands.

> The central doctrine concerning the ultimate nature of reality has usually been called *wahdat al-wujud* or the (transcendent) unity of Being. This cardinal doctrine, which is not pantheism, not panentheism nor natural mysticism as Western orientalists have called it, . . . asserts that there cannot be two completely independent orders of reality or being which would be sheer polytheism or *shirk*. . . . Through that mystery that lies in the heart of creation itself, everything is, in essence, identified with God while God infinitely transcends everything. To understand this doctrine intellectually is to possess contemplative intelligence; to realize it fully is to be a saint who alone sees 'God everywhere'.[20]

There is reason to describe the God worshipped by the Muslims as an impersonal deity, whether the deity is considered to be immanent or transcendent. From a Muslim perspective, the position that God is a person may be attacked by showing that this is incompatible with the transcendent nature of God, or by showing that this is incompatible with God's all-pervasive immanence.

One of the earliest arguments in favour of God's extreme transcendence was made by the son-in-law of Muhammad, Ali.

> The first act of worshipping God is to know Him. The basis of knowledge of Him lies in (the acknowledgement of) His Unity. The support for (the acknowledgement of) His Unity is the denial of any comparison of Him, the High, (with man) in terms of stating that human qualities (*sifat*) subsist in Him. (This is) because of the testimony of reason that everyone in whom human qualities subsist is created (*mansu*). Whereas the testimony of reason (requires) that He, the High and Exalted, Who is the Creator (*sani*), is not created.[21]

The argument may be applied to the question of God's personality by means of the following syllogism:

(19) All persons are created.
(20) God is not created.
∴ (21) God is not a person.

The problem with this argument is that anyone who believes that God is a person will simply deny the major premiss. God is the exception.

Another argument from God's transcendence can be found in *Al-Kafi,* one of the earliest Shi'ite theological texts.[22] There the question is entertained as to whether or not it is proper to say that God is a thing. It is concluded that it *is* proper to say that God is a thing, because to say otherwise would be tantamount to the denial of his existence. But God is a thing unlike anything else, with neither matter nor form. Were it not for the fact that to deny that God is a thing would be to deny his existence, it would be said that God is not a thing. In this tradition, it has often been denied that any metaphysical categories can be applied to God. From this the following argument can be constructed:

(22) Substance is a category.
(23) God does not belong to a category.
∴ (24) God is not a substance.

The conclusion to this argument has been defended by the contemporary Muslim philosopher, Ayatollah Ja'fary.[23] Ja'fary argues that every substance belongs to a genus and has some property which differentiates it from other members of that genus. But whatever is composed of genus and difference is limited by these terms. Its existence is circumscribed. But God is completely unlimited; and thus he is not a substance.

The argument from the unlimitedness of God to the claim that God is not something which has a genus and species can also be found in Mulla Sadra (*c.* 1572–1641), whose influence on contemporary Muslim philosophy in Iran cannot be overestimated. Mulla Sadra describes God as the 'pure reality of being'.

> This Reality is not restricted by any definition, limitation, imperfection, contingent potentiality, or quiddity; nor is It mixed with any generality, whether of genus, species, or differentia, nor with any accident, whether specific or general. For Being is prior to all these descriptions that apply to quiddities, and That which has no quiddity other than Being is not bound by any generality or specificity.[24]
>
> . . . For if His Being had some limit or particularity in any respect, It would have to be limited and particularized by something other than Being; there would have to be something with power over Him limiting, specifying, and circumscribing Him. But that is impossible.[25]

According to this line of thought, God cannot be a substance because substances consist of genus and difference. That which consists of genus and difference is limited by the conditions indicated by the genus and difference, but God is not limited by anything. So God is not a substance.

The conclusion could also be supported by appeal to the simplicity of God. Whatever is composed of genus and difference is not simple; but God is simple, so he is not a substance.

None of these arguments is conclusive. One who affirms that God is a substance might deny (23) by arguing that mere inclusion in a category does not entail limitation of a sort incompatible with the perfection and infinity of God. Against Mulla Sadra, it could be argued that not every differentiating property is privative. To pursue such arguments would involve exploring some of the fundamental issues of metaphysics, such as the nature of substance and of property. Claims about the simplicity of God are obscure and difficult to reconcile with the multiplicity of God's attributes. This and related issues have occupied an important place in the history of Muslim theology. The defence of the claim that God is not a substance is no easy matter.

If it is agreed that God is not a substance, it is a short step to the denial that God is a person.

(25) All persons are substances.
(26) God is not a substance.
∴ (27) God is not a person.

Interestingly enough, this is an argument which has not escaped the notice of Christian theology. Aquinas admits that God is not an individual substance, or hypostasis, in the sense of being a support for accidents, although God is a substance in the sense of being something which subsists, i.e. which has a nature distinct from any other. Recall that Boethius defines 'person' as 'individual substance of rational nature'. Thus,

Aquinas' admission that there is a sense in which God is not a substance threatens the claim that God is a person. Commenting on the Boethian definition, Aquinas also notes that God is not rational in the sense of being the subject of discursive thought. Aquinas concludes:

> There are some, however, who say that the definition of Boethius, quoted above (A.1), is not a definition of person in the sense we use when speaking of persons in God. Therefore Richard of St. Victor amends this definition by adding that Person in God is 'the incommunicable existence of the divine nature.'[26]

To accept Richard of St Victor's definition of 'person' is to give up the view that God is personal! Even those who believe in an impersonal deity may affirm the claim that the existence of the divine nature is not shared by any other entity.

One might deny that God is a substance and yet maintain that God is a person, by rejecting (25). This seems to be the line taken by certain recent Christian theologians. The Ritschlian school and H. R. Mackintosh have questioned the adequacy of the category of substance in terms of which the Nicene and Chalcedonian affirmations of the full humanity and real deity of Christ have been made. They claim that substance is a Hellenistic concept, not a Biblical one, and that it is static while Biblical concepts such as purpose and action are dynamic.[27] Although an attack on (25) might be mounted in this way, it is not clear how successful it would be at refuting the argument that God is not a person. Arguments that God is not a substance are not based on the stasis of substance, but on its complexity and limitedness. These features would not be eliminated by replacing substance by a more dynamic category. Unless it can be shown that persons need be neither complex nor limited, the claim that God is personal will be inconsistent with the claims that God is simple and absolute.

In summary, the arguments for the view that God is not a person which are based on God's transcendence may be attacked in two ways: *(a)* by claiming that God's substantiality is not incompatible with his transcendence, and *(b)* by claiming that his personality is not incompatible with his transcendence, and that not all persons are substances. The pursuit of either of these tactics would involve grappling with extremely difficult issues in metaphysics and theology. However, these difficulties await defenders of the above arguments, as well as their detractors.

The Muslim conception of God may be described as an impersonal one, not only in virtue of Islam's emphasis on the transcendence of God in Islam, but also in virtue of the Islamic conception of divine immanence. God's immanence is such that he is present in all things in a way which seems incompatible with his belonging to the category of substance or of person. One of the essential components of a relation between persons is the distinctness of the persons involved in the relation. The radical immanence of the God of Islam may be incompatible with the distinctness required of entities which take part in a personal relationship. There is a long tradition of Muslim theologians and philosophers who, like Mulla Sadra, hold that God is pure existence, the ultimate ground of all reality.[28] This ultimate ground cannot be individuated, as substances and persons must be, for according to the doctrine of God's immanence, God is undifferentiated. It is because God is undifferentiated and because he is not a distinct individual that he pervades all that exists, just as a universal pervades everything which exemplifies that universal. God's immanence has been portrayed by means of the image of the ocean and its waves:

> . . . [T]here is nothing other than God Almighty; whatever is, is He. The manifestation is not only His; it is also He. There is no exact image that can be evoked in this respect; the object that casts a shadow together with the shadow itself is imprecise and defective. A preferable image would be the ocean and its waves. The wave has no separate existence with respect to the ocean; it is the ocean, although one cannot say the converse, that the ocean is its waves. Waves come into existence only

> through the motion of the ocean. When we consider the matter rationally, it appears to us that both the ocean and the waves exist, the latter being an accident with respect to the former. But the truth of the matter is that there is nothing but ocean; the wave is also the ocean. This world is also like a wave with respect to God[29]

The conception of God's immanence presented above is admittedly obscure, and for this reason is not particularly useful to the defender of the claim that God is not a person. The personalist may simply deny that God is immanent in the extreme sense described here. While the Islamic conception of divine immanence may not be an appropriate *basis* for a defence of the impersonal view of God, one cannot properly understand that view without understanding the Islamic doctrine of immanence. The doctrine of God's immanence is no less important or central to Islamic theology than the experience of God as immanent is central to Islamic mysticism. In a frequently cited verse of the Qur'an (50:16) it is stated that God is nearer to man than his jugular vein.

The final argument against the view that God is a person which will be considered here is one which is not explicitly formulated in Islamic theology. Many western philosophers since Descartes have taken *mind* to be essential to personhood. Any argument that God does not have a mind would thus undermine the claim that God is a person. Here is one such argument.

(28) God does not have a body.
(29) There are no disembodied minds.
∴ (30) God does not have a mind.

The more controversial of the premises in this argument is (29). The belief that there are no disembodied minds is a commonplace of contemporary materialism. There is wide agreement among philosophers that Cartesian dualism founders on its inability to explain psycho-physical interaction. Idealistic monism is not taken seriously. The only plausible solution to the 'mind-body problem' seems to be to treat the mind as in some sense dependent upon the body, specifically on the brain. It is because the brain has the physical structure that it does that we are able to think. This claim draws support from the fact that those species of animals with more highly developed brains, also have more mental prowess than others. Exactly how minds and brains, or mental states and brain states, are to be correlated is a matter of great controversy among physicalists. What is agreed upon by all, however, is that brain activity is a prerequisite for mental activity.

Persons persuaded by the arguments of the physicalists that mind is dependent upon body might be tempted by atheism. Such persons might reason that since mind is dependent on body, God, who is a mind without a body, cannot exist. But given the impersonalist view of God, it is possible to draw a different conclusion, namely that God exists but does not have a mind.

The claim that God does not have a mind, and the premise (29) on which it rests, *viz.,* that there are no disembodied minds, might be thought to be contrary to religious belief. The doctrine of the immortality of the soul seems to require that human minds do not depend upon brains for their continued existence, and the doctrine of God's omniscience seems to require that God has a mind. But religious doctrines do not need to be understood in such a way as to require belief in disembodied minds, as the following considerations show.

First, with regard to God's knowledge, Mulla Sadra, for example, certainly does not understand this as implying that mind is ascribable to God.

> . . . His Knowledge of all existent things is Simple Knowledge, and . . . their presence in Him is Simple in its essential Reality. For all things in Him are included in His knowledge in a higher and more perfect way, since 'knowledge' is (only) an expression for Being, on the condition that It be unmixed with matter.[30]

On this account, at least, there is nothing mental about God's knowledge. Divine awareness and consciousness may each be understood as expressions of pure existence.

The contention that there are no human disembodied minds is more troublesome than the claim that God does not have a mind. Mulla Sadra, in accordance with Muslim theological tradition, is careful to distinguish the soul from the self-conscious psyche. The psyche is not immortal. The soul, on the other hand, is not only immortal, but has existed prior to the existence of the body. This doctrine is difficult, but it clearly implies that the soul is not mental, is not a mind, but is rather an immaterial aspect of the person.

Although (29) is the more controversial of the premises in the argument above, some might dispute (28). A pantheist, for example, might claim that the material world is the body of God, and that this world forms the material substrate for the mind of God. This is implausible. The organization of the material world as a whole does not appear to have a structure analogous to that of an organic brain, or even of a computer, in virtue of which one could be warranted in claiming that the material world could serve as the material support of the mind of God.

Of course, the arguments discussed here do not prove that God does not have a mind, and it has not been proved that there are no disembodied minds. However, these claims are consistent with at least some elements of the Islamic tradition, and if the claims are accepted, they will support the view that God is not a person.

Several arguments have been presented here. Neither those in favour of the claim that God is a person, nor those against this claim, are conclusive. Those who wish to defend either position must address unanswered and difficult questions. But there is a lesson to be learned from this very inconclusiveness. The issue of whether or not God is a person has been presented as a controversy between Christians and Muslims, but it need not be seen as such. I mentioned that Muslims are not united in their belief that God is not personal, and although personalism is now predominant among Christian theologians, it need not be. Belief in the personality of Jesus is compatible with belief in the impersonality of the being of which Christians believe Jesus to be a hypostasis.

> God is not a person as man is a person. The all-embracing and all-penetrating is never an object that man can view from a distance in order to make statements about it. The primal ground, primal support and primal goal of all reality . . . is not an individual person among other persons. . . . It will be better to call the most real reality not personal or impersonal but *transpersonal* or *suprapersonal*.[31]

These are not the words of an ayatollah or a sufi, but of the Christian theologian, Hans Küng.

NOTES

1. H. P. Owen, 'Theism', *The Encyclopedia of Philosophy,* 1972, VIII, p. 97.
2. John Hick, *Philosophy of Religion,* 2nd ed. (Englewood Cliffs, N.J.: Prentice Hall, 1973), p. 5.
3. Richard Swinburne, *The Coherence of Theism* (Oxford: Clarendon Press, 1977), p. 1.
4. J. L. Mackie, *The Miracle of Theism* (Oxford: Clarendon Press, 1982), p. 1.
5. Ali Shari'ati, *On the Sociology of Islam,* trans. Hamid Algar (Berkeley: Mizan Press, 1979), *passim.*
6. This is the thesis of Clement C. J. Webb, *God and Personality* (London: George Allen & Unwin, 1920), pp. 61–89. Webb argues that Christians did not explicitly claim that God is *a* person, or had a personality until the nineteenth century. They spoke of persons *in* God, but not of the person *of* God. The point is debatable. Aquinas, for example, explicitly states that '. . . in God essence is not really distinct from person . . .' (*Summa Theologica* I, q. 39, a. 1), although this claim is highly qualified.

7. The claim that God is one being whose persons differ only in relation to human understanding is the heresy of the third-century theologian Sabellius, and is condemned by Aquinas (*Summa Theologica* I, q. 31, a. 2).
8. *Summa Theologica* I, q. 29, a. 3.
9. Hick, pp. 9–10.
10. Kai Nielson, *An Introduction to the Philosophy of Religion* (New York: St. Martin's Press, 1982), pp. 36–7.
11. Cf. Isaac Husik, *A History of Mediaeval Jewish Philosophy* (New York: Meridian Books, and Philadelphia: The Jewish Publication Society of America, 1960), p. xlv.
12. This explanation of the origin of the term *kalam* is given by al'Allamah as-Sayyid Muhammad Husayn at-Tabataba'i, *Al-Mizan,* trans. Sayyid Saeed Akhtar Rizvi (Tehran: World Organization for Islamic Services, 1982) Vol. 4, p. 149. For a conflicting explanation, see the extensive discussion in Harry Austryn Wolfson, *The Philosophy of the Kalam* (Cambridge: Harvard University Press, 1976).
13. 'Allamah Sayyid Muhammad Husayn Tabataba'i, *Shi'ite Islam,* trans. Seyyed Hossein Nasr (Houston: Free Islamic Literatures, 1979), p. 143.
14. al'Allamah as-Sayyid Muhammad Husayn at-Tabataba'i, *Al-Mizan,* trans. Sayyid Saeed Akhtar Rizvi (Tehran: World Organization for Islamic Services, 1982), Vol. 4, p. 133–42.
15. Karl Rahner, *Foundations of Christian Faith,* trans. William V. Dyck (New York: The Seabury Press, 1978), p. 73.
16. Frederick Copleston, *A History of Philosophy,* vol. 11, *Mediaeval Philosophy: Augustine to Scotus* (Westminister, MD: The Newman Press, 1962), pp. 396–7.
17. John Laird, *Mind and Deity* (London: George Allen & Unwin, 1941), pp. 166–8.
18. A similar observation is given caustic expression by Alan Watts in his *Behold the Spirit: A Study is the Necessity of Mystical Religion* (New York: Pantheon Books, 1947), pp. 133–5: 'After the Renaissance, to meet the rise of Humanism, . . . spirituality became more and more Christocentric, and at the same time quite alien to the traditions of Christian mysticism! Contemplation, as understood by the mediaeval mystics, was replaced by affective and imaginative devotion to the humanity of Jesus. From the standpoint of mysticism this was a disaster based on a misunderstanding of the Incarnation, for it made the divine humanity transcendent and humanized the mystery of God. . . . When . . . theology tries to achieve a compromise between immanence and transcendence, both are deprived of their effect. God is not quite immanent and not quite transcendent. . . .' This passage is anthologized in Charles Hartshorne and William L. Reese, *Philosophers Speak of God* (Chicago: University of Chicago Press, 1969), p. 325. Note that Watts does not claim that the compromise between immanence and transcendence is inherent in Christianity; rather he claims that this is a misguided response to renaissance humanism.
19. Webb, p. 87.
20. Seyyed Hossein Nasr, *Ideals and Realities of Islam* (Boston: Beacon Press, 1975), p. 137.
21. Shaykh al-Mufid, *Kitab al-Irshad,* trans. I. K. A. Howard (London: The Muhammadi Trust, 1981), p. 165.
22. Ash-shaykh Abu Ja'far Muhammad Ibn Ya'qub Ibn Is'haq al-Kulayni Ar-Raxi, *Al-Kafi,* vol. 1, Part One, 3, (11), trans. Sayyid Muhammad Hasan Rizvi (Tehran: World Organization for Islamic Services, 1980), pp. 209–16.
23. In conversation, 11 February 1985, Tehran.
24. Sadr al-Din Shirazi, *The Wisdom of the Throne,* trans. James Winston Morris (Princeton: Princeton University Press, 1981), p. 96.
25. *Ibid.* p. 100.
26. *Summa Theologica* I, q. 29, a. 3. Notice that just as in *Al-Kafi* it is claimed that God is a thing for to deny this would be to deny that He exists, Aquinas argues that God is a substance for to deny this would be to deny that He subsists. 'Subsistence' is a technical term in Thomistic philosophy. The imperfect subsistence of secondary substance distinguishes one species from another. The perfect subsistence of first substances is that by which one individual is distinct from all others. In the philosophy of Mulla Sadra and contemporary Shi'ite theology the subsistence of God would be rejected. Differences belong to creation, while God is the undifferentiated ground of all being, pure existence. Cf. note 3, p. 00011.
27. John Hick, 'Christianity', *The Encyclopedia of Philosophy,* 1972, II, p. 106.
28. Cf. Fazlur Rahman, *The Philosophy of Mulla Sadra* (Albany: State University of New York Press, 1975).
29. Imam Khomeini, *Islam and Revolution,* trans. Hamid Algar (Berkeley: Mizan Press, 1981), pp. 406–7.
30. Sadr al-Din Shirazi, p. 99.
31. Hans Küng, *Does God Exist?* (London: Collins, 1980), pp. 632–3. Cited in Mackie, p. 244.

DISCUSSION QUESTIONS

1. How persuasive are Legenhausen's criticisms of the arguments in favor of the claim that God is a person? Explain.
2. Is he right that most Christians believe that God is a person?
3. How helpful is the analogy of the ocean to its waves for understanding God's relation to this world?
4. Legenhausen says that an atheist might reason that mind is dependent on body, and God is supposed to be a mind without a body, so God cannot exist. The impersonalist view of God allows the alternative conclusion that God exists but does not have a mind. How would you reply to the atheist's argument? Is the impersonalist view more compelling? Explain.
5. Compare the impersonalist view of God in this essay with the view of God in Smullyan's dialogue.
6. Contrast the personalist view of God in this essay with the view of God in Broad's essay.

Chapter 36

A. O. RORTY

Amélie Oksenberg Rorty teaches in the History of Ideas program in the Department of Classical Studies at Brandeis University. She likes to read Proust, Tolstoi, and George Eliot, and she spends a lot of time looking at paintings. Rorty is the author of Explaining Emotions *(1980) and* The Many Faces of Philosophy: Reflections from Plato to Arendt *(2003). Her edited books include collections of essays on the ethics, the* Rhetoric, *the* Poetics, *and the* De Anima *of Aristotle, essays on Descartes'* Meditations, The Identities of Persons *(1976), and* The Many Faces of Evil: Historical Perspectives *(2001).*

In this essay Rorty identifies seven distinct but sometimes overlapping concepts of a person: (1) a deserver of respect and subject of rights; (2) a legal entity with liability or responsibility; (3) an autonomous, self-defining agent; (4) a social role-player enacting a drama; (5) a thing with a life history it may or may not be aware of; (6) a biological self-sustaining organism; (7) the ultimate subject of experience, an ego. Rorty's analysis yields two possible conclusions: (a) there is no such thing as the concept of personhood; there are only seven separate and independently functioning regional conceptions that cannot be unified; (b) the various functions of the concept sometimes conflict and the concept itself cannot provide decision procedures for resolving conflicting claims for rights and obligations because it embeds and expresses just those conflicts. Nothing hangs on the choice between (a) and (b), however, Rorty thinks, because neither political practice nor philosophic theory is affected by our choice. Rather, she sees appeals to the various conceptions of the person as rhetorical.

Persons and Personae

I

Controversies about personal identity have been magnified by the fact that there are a number of distinct questions at issue, questions that have not always been clearly distinguished from one another. Parties to the dispute have differed, often without arguing the case, about which questions are centrally interesting. Some have concentrated on analyses of class differentiation, distinguishing persons from computers, apes, fetuses, corporations. Others have been primarily interested in criteria for individuation and differentiation. Still others have been interested in the criteria for reidentifying the same individual in different contexts, under different descriptions, or at different times. Most philosophers who have been concerned with individual reidentification analyze conditions for temporal reidentification, trying to define conditions for distinguishing successive stages of a single continuing person from stages of a successor or descendant person. Yet others have been primarily interested in individual identification: What sorts of characteristics are essential to the identity of the person, so that if those characteristics were changed, she would be a significantly different person, though she might still be differentiated and reidentified as the same individual? Defining the conditions for individual identification does not reduce to specifying conditions for reidentification because the characteristics that distinguish or reidentify persons (e.g., fingerprints, DNA codes, or memories) may not be thought by the individual herself or by her society to determine her *real* identity. For instance, an individual might be reidentifiable by the memory criterion but not identifiable as the same person, because all that she considers essential to her identity has changed: her principles and preference rankings are different, her tastes, plans, hopes, and fears. She remembers her old principles of choice well enough and so, by the memory criterion, might consider herself the same old person; but by grace or reeducation she can be counted on to choose and act in a new way. Though all these questions are distinguishable, and though a philosopher may legitimately be interested in one without being forced to treat them all, a particular sort of solution to one problem will certainly influence, though probably not dictate, a solution to the others.

Behind these differences in emphases and interests, there are differences about whether we should concentrate on conditions for strict identity (with the consequence that a biological individual may not remain the same person throughout a lifetime), on conditions of loose typic identity (with the consequence that conditions for identity and conditions for individuation become distinct), or on conditions assuring continuity or survival (with

---

Source: From *Mind in Action,* edited by Amélie Oksenberg Rorty, Copyright © 1988. Boston: Beacon Press: 27–46. Reprinted by permission of Beacon Press, Boston.

the consequence that the conditions for *significant* continuity or survival still require to be specified).

Also at issue are methodological disagreements about what is involved in giving a criterial analysis. Some of the debates have only incidentally been about personal identity; they have been primarily about whether criteria for identity should provide necessary and sufficient conditions, prepared to meet and resist any possible counterexamples. If we look for necessary and sufficient conditions, puzzle and problem cases loom large in the discussion, as possible counterexamples to the analyses. Consider the problems that arise from Shoemaker's Lockean transplant case: Brown's brain is put in Robinson's head, with the results that Brownson, the fellow with Brown's brain in (the rest of) Robinson's body remembers Brown's experience, identifies Brown's body as "his," expresses Brown's tastes and preferences. To give the question "Who is who?" some force, we might ask who goes home to which wife ("Do you love me for myself alone, or for my beautiful body?"). And if one of them committed a crime, who goes to jail?

Those who are skeptical about the utility of giving analyses of logically necessary conditions see the Brownson case as presenting an interesting curiosity, a fringe case of personal identity. They hold that the strategic conclusions to which we are forced in extremities should not be taken to reveal the workings of these concepts in their standard uses. For them, the real point of such thought experiments is to untangle the various strands in our conceptions, to show that although they normally support one another, they are independent, and can sometimes pull apart.

Thought experiments of this kind are always underdescribed: Suppose that Robinson limps painfully. Won't Brown's passion for dancing the flamenco be affected by the discomfort of expressing it in Robinson's hulking, lumbering body? Suppose Robinson's body suffers from an overproduction of adrenalin: will Brownson's memories take on an irascible tone? How can we establish the identity of tastes and memories under different emotional tonalities? In forcing decisions about such cases for the sake of assuring criterial accounts, we move subtly from analyses of concepts in their standard use to constructions whose application to standard cases become legislative and normative, no longer straightforwardly analytically descriptive. This may indeed be a useful and important enterprise: but legislation should take place openly, so that the many factors that affect the accounts of personal identification—moral and political factors, as well as coherence of accounting—can be brought into play. If we are going to tidy up a concept whose various strands have been pulled apart, we had best be clear about the consequences that our tidying will have on our social practices. The most important of these will affect the redistribution of liability and responsibility, of praise, blame, and punishment.

Perhaps the most significant source of the controversy about criteria for personal identity springs from disagreements about the function that the concept of a person plays in social life as the unit of intentional, responsible agency. Locke distinguished the identity of an individual substance, the identity of a human being, and the identity of a person, remarking that as the concept of a person is primarily a forensic, legal notion, the criterion for personal identity must reflect the conditions for an individual's being a responsible agent. Because he focused on legal liability, rather than social responsibility, he was interested in identifying the past actions of persons. He thus took the condition for forensic identity to be continuity of reflective consciousness, established primarily by memory. Those who are concerned with responsibility for future actions might stress the continuity of preference rankings, character traits, and intellectual capacities that affect rational choice and action. In any case, controversies about conditions for personal identity reflect differences about the conditions that establish an individual as a responsible agent.

Why are we interested in someone being the same person, and not merely the same human being or physical object? One reason is primarily retrospective: we need to know whom to reward and whom to punish for actions performed when "they" were acknowledgedly different in some respects from the present population. But we have more forward-looking reasons as well: we want to know what traits remain constant so that we can know what we can expect from the persons around us. We assign crucial responsibilities to individuals, assume important continuing relations to them in the belief that certain of their traits are relatively constant or predictable. And for ourselves, we are interested in our own identities because we make choices that will affect our futures: we set in motion a train of actions whose consequences involve "our" well-being, without knowing whether we shall have, in the future, the desires and beliefs that now direct our planning.

A society's conception of agency is closely linked to the sorts of actions that are taken as central because they preserve or enhance that society's conception of its proper survival and development. In a society of hunters, cripples are thought incapable of action; but in a society of religious ascetics, cripples may be thought most capable of the sort of action that defines the true person. The range of traits and criteria for identification are open to negotiation by the moral and political reformer. Descriptive analyses of personal identity affect the allocation of obligations and rights; but the analysis of persons is itself affected by the allocation of obligations and rights. When paradigm cases of action are set, the traits that conduce to responsible agency for those sorts of actions are fixed, and the range of agents—corporations, human beings, demon possessors, Martians, or dolphins—is also set. But in times of social and political change, primary activities are relocated (from hunting, to religious meditation, to symbolic communication); reformers recommend an expansion or contraction of the class of persons. Changes in practice go hand in hand with conceptual reconstruction and reform, though it may take several generations for the hands to catch up. New conceptions of actions and agency sometimes relocate the conditions for responsibility and liability. That reformers can negotiate the extension of the class of persons certainly does not make the concept of a person *merely* conventional, if anything ever is. Both changes in practice and in conceptual analysis are argued by demonstrating the capacities of previously extended classes.

II

There is a philosophical dream, a dream that moral and political ideals are not only grounded in and explained by human nature, but that fundamental moral and political principles can be derived from the narrower conditions that define persons. Though sometimes bold and wild dreamers do go so far, this dream does not usually express a metaphysical wish that could be satisfied by analyzing the conditions for reflective subjectivity or the psycholinguistic conditions for the reflexivity of first-person attributions. More commonly, the dream is that normative political and moral principles can be derived from what is essential to the concept of a person.

The strongest version of this dream attempts to use the (initially value-neutral) concept of a person to derive specific rights, principles, and obligations; a somewhat more modest version attempts to use the concept of a person to set constraints on such rights, principles, and obligations; a yet weaker version makes the two notions—the concept of a person and the delineation of moral and political rights—mutually explicative. But all versions of this dream press for a single concept of a person, whose various components form a harmonious structure that could provide adjudication among competing normative claims about what does or does not fall within the domain of the rights and obligations of persons. The press for one well-structured concept that allocates priorities among its various conditions is a demand for a decision procedure to settle disagreements about, and conflicts among, competing values and obligations.

But there is no such thing as "the" concept of a person. This is so not only for the obvious historical reason that there have been dramatically discontinuous changes in the characterization of persons, though that is true. Nor for the equally obvious anthropological-cultural reason that the moral and legal practices heuristically treated as analogous across cultures differ so dramatically that they capture "the concept" of personhood only vaguely and incompletely, though that is also true.

The various functions performed by our contemporary concept of persons don't hang together: there is some overlap, but also some tension. Indeed, the functions that "the" notion plays are so related that attempts to structure them in a taxonomic order express quite different norms and ideals. Disagreements about primary values and goods reappear as disagreements about the priorities and relations among the various functions the concept plays, disagreements about what is essential to persons. Not only does each of the functions bear a different relation to the class of persons and human beings, but each also has a different contrast class.

As inheritors of the Judeo-Christian, Renaissance, Enlightenment, and Romantic traditions, we want the concept of the person to fill a number of functions:

1. The attribution should give us objective grounds for being taken seriously, with respect—and to be taken seriously with respect on grounds that can't be lost through illness, poverty, villainy, inanity, or senility. On this view, the idea of person is an insurance policy. Some think of the insurance as guaranteeing us rights. Others think of it as assuring us a certain kind of regard, that we will be treated as ends rather than merely as means, that our activities will be perceived as centrally rational (or at least reasonable) and good-willed (or at least well-intentioned) and interpreted by an extension of the principle of charity. For some, the special status of persons is justified by some set of properties: persons should be respected because they are capable of critical rationality, or because they are free inventors of their lives, or because they have divinely donated souls, or because they can be harmed, frustrated in living out their life plans. For others, specific rights cannot be justified by or derived from the essential properties of the class of persons, because such rights are among the essential properties of persons. For yet others, claims to rights can only be based on the general social and political benefits that such rights might bring.

Among the Hellenes, the contrast class for this notion was the class of slaves and barbarians. Among Christians, the contrast class is that of unsouled beings. For Kantians, the contrast class is that of nonrational beings, incapable of understanding the laws of nature and unable to act freely, from the idea of the laws of morality. This conception of the class of persons intersects, but is not identical with nor subsumed within, the class of human beings: Martians and dolphins might be persons, as might intrapsychic homunculi.

2. Sometimes the respect and rights of persons are assured by law: persons are defined as legal entities. The legal concept of a person is meant to assure, first, liability. This is a retrospective function, defined by the conditions for presumptive agency: bodily continuity, memory, *mens rea*. (The contrast class is made up of those with defective conditions for agency, for example, the insane and the senile.)

Second, the legal concept of persons ensures legally defined responsibility. This is a prospective and regionalized function that defines specific duties and obligations. Such responsibilities are often institutionally defined: sometimes the legal person's duties and responsibilities are contractually fixed, with explicitly articulated sanctions for default or violation; sometimes the obligations are defined informally by commonly accepted practices and sanctions. In such cases, liability is carried by the legal entity, rather than by the individuals—for example, trustees, corporations, guardians, boards of directors, banks—who act as its officers. (The contrast class includes minors and, still in some places, women.)

Third, the legal concept guarantees specifically defined citizen rights and duties. This is a function that empowers a designated class of individuals to act and speak on behalf of the State. They are, as Hobbes put it, its "artificial persons." Polities accord specific rights and duties of participation in decision-making, representation, governance. Indeed, this is one way political systems differ: by the different ways they distribute the power and the right to act or speak in the person of the State, as an agent of one of its constitutive institutions. As the frontispiece of Hobbes's *Leviathan* graphically demonstrates, the king of an absolute monarchy is the embodied person of the State. If the State is composed of families or clans, rather than of individuals, those families or clans are the person-citizens of the State, and their heads or elders speak and act for them. Similarly, representatives of state-defined political institutions (the judiciary, the legislative body, city officials) act in the person of the State: their decisions personify the official acts of the State. When the Pope speaks *ex cathedra,* he speaks as the personification of the Church; the voice of Parliament is the voice of the people; "We the People"—citizens casting votes on public issues or selecting their representatives—are expressing the views of the person(s) of the State. Even though their rights and welfare are under the legal protection of the state, the disenfranchised—etymologically, the unfree—are the subjects or wards of the State rather than citizen-persons entitled to act or speak as the person of the State. Whether the class of citizen-persons coincides with or is a subset of the class of those who are legally liable is, of course, a political and even an ideological issue. (The composition of the contrast class is usually under contention and may include, for example, aliens, slaves, exiles, and fetuses.)

Neither the Kantian regulative principle of respect nor the Christian idea of the immortal soul have any necessary connection with the legal function of the idea of person. Respect for the person doesn't entail any particular legal rights; nor does the assurance of legal personhood assure social or moral respect. Furthermore, each of the distinctive legal *personae* might well select different grounds for the attribution of personhood. For instance, an individual can claim some citizen rights (the right of *habeas corpus,* for example) without satisfying the conditions for liability. Nor need a legal person be accorded all the rights of citizenship: universities do not, as such, vote or receive social security. The conditions for prospective responsibility are regional and relative: whether an individual or a group is designated a legal person is characteristically a political, and sometimes an ideological, issue.

Some legal theorists argue that no single concept of a person can—or should—be used to derive the wide variety of legislative and judicial policies required to give appropriately differentiated treatment to the varieties of legal *personae.*[1] They maintain that moral and legal practices contextualize and regionalize the status of a person: a fetus is, for example, accorded the status of a legal person in some contexts and for some issues, but not for others; a corporation has the legal status of a person for some purposes, for others not. We should, they hold, draw our inclusionary and exclusionary classes contextually, following our sense of what is morally and judicially appropriate, rather than attempting to derive our legal practices from a sharply—and, they suggest, arbitrarily—defined class of persons. ("First come the practices of right and wrong, and then come definitions and classifications.") The question of whether there are several distinctive legal concepts of a person, each with its own pragmatically defined domain, or whether there is one concept, with distinctive pragmatic applications is an idle question, since neither legal theory nor legal practice are affected by the answer.

There are, of course, dramatic cultural variations in the criteria for agency, variations in the legal conditions that define persons. The class of liable and responsible persons can, for instance, exclude individuals in favor of groups of individuals (clans or families), or the heads of such groups (the chief patriarch), intrapsychic homunculi, demonic possessors. It can be treated as an all-or-none classification, or as a matter of degree. It is often difficult to determine how to diagnose such cultural variation. Do these differences represent disagreements about the proper analysis of the concept of a person? Do some cultures lack the concept, or do they have an analogous construct? Do some cultures lack what we consider a legal system, or do they locate their legal system in a different network of institutions? There may be no fact of the matter: exigencies of theory construction rather than ontology may determine whether we can legitimately project our concept of a legal person to analogous bearers of liability and responsibility, or whether we should decline the attribution to individuals whose agency is defined within radically different schemes of liability and responsibility.

3. The idea of a person is also the idea of an autonomous agent, capable of self-defined and self-defining choices. There are at least two versions of this idea. The first is primarily negative and defensive, concentrating on the desire to fend off external interference: *Noli me tangere,* or in Amerispeak, "Don't tread on me, buddy." The second is primarily positive and constructive, concentrating on capacities for self-determination. Both the negative and the positive idea of autonomy emphasize critical rationality and independent evaluation. A person is essentially capable of stepping back from her beliefs and desires to evaluate their rationality and appropriateness; she is also capable (at the very least) of attempting to form and modify her beliefs and desires, her actions, on the basis of her rational evaluations. (The contrast class would thus comprise the mindless, the nonrational, the dissociated.)

The idea of autonomy, whether negatively or positively defined, also emphasizes imaginative creativity. Because their decisions and actions are intentionally identified, and because they have latitude in transforming, improvising, and inventing their intentions, persons can, in a number of significant ways, form the worlds in which they live. There are two dimensions on which such formations take place: the political and the visionary-poetic.

For the first, since the social and political domain is constructed, it can be reconstructed, if only a piece at a time. To be a person is to participate actively in public life, forming or at least modifying the social and political policies and institutions that significantly and effectively shape life. (The contrast class: the masses, whose opinions and actions can be manipulated.)

For the second, by choosing or constructing systems of values, persons create the categories that structure and interpret their world, that form their ambitions, hopes, and fears. Since they determine what is important and significant, their interpretations structure both what they see and what they do. (The contrast class: the dependent, the fearful, the timid, the unimaginative.)

These aspects of the idea of autonomy mark differences in two faces or moments in Enlightenment political theory. The first stance is defensive: it is designed to protect the person from what is perceived as tyrannical or unjust political or epistemic authority. This concept of a person stresses negative liberty and minimal government. There is some correlation, but no necessary connection, between the defensive boundary conception of the free person and the conception of the person whose critical and rational capacities are primarily exercised in scientific discovery or poetic creativity and only secondarily in defense against error.

Although the Enlightenment concept of a person began with the Christian conception of a person as defined by his free will, his capacity to affirm or deny God's law, autonomy shifted from the freedom of the will to the rational power of independent critical judgments of truth and falsity. When the old order loses its authority, the emphasis on persons as autonomous judges preserving and protecting individual boundaries is replaced by an emphasis on autonomous legislators generating new social structures and practices. Negative liberty gives way to positive liberty; minimal government gives way to a government charged with the formation of citizen values. Protection against error gives way to the power of constructing a systematic science, and eventually to the power of the imagination in constructing a world through poetic language. There is some correlation, but no necessary connection, between the concept of a person as a constructive, self-determining legislator and the concept of a person as primarily a creator. The movement from the earlier defensive to the later constructive conceptions of persons correlates in a very rough way with the movement from early Cartesian Enlightenment conceptions of the independent, inquiring, rational self, free of the claims of dogmatic doctrine, to late Enlightenment Romanticism, with its emphasis on positive liberty, political reform, and poetic creativity.

The conception of persons as deserving respect is sometimes rooted in the conception of a person as capable of self-definition. But of course both the rational and the creative dimensions of the idea of the self-defining person (in its negative and positive forms) leave individual claims to personhood empirically contingent. If claims to respect are based on the capacities for autonomy, we're in deep trouble. Constitutional and sociopolitical contingencies affect the likelihood of an individual actually (rather than notionally or potentially) developing her capacities for critical rationality; similar contingencies determine whether she is actually (rather than notionally) capable of creative self-determination. Has the individual been well nourished and nurtured, well educated and well formed? Or has she suffered irreparable traumas that make autonomy practically impossible? Logical or notional possibility is not helpful here: aardvarks, baboons, and caterpillars might notionally be capable of autonomy. It might seem as if this concept of a person provides grounds for normative political claims. Precisely because certain kinds of political structures are required to actualize otherwise only notional claims to personhood, there is a prima facie obligation to structure political systems in such a way as to allow the best development of the capacities for critical self-determination. Unfortunately, many extra premises are required to substantiate this claim, premises about the primary and the proper functions of the obligations of political systems. The obligation cannot follow solely from the requirements for personhood. (This conception of the class of persons intersects, but is not identical with or subsumed within, the class of biologically defined human beings. The contrast class is composed of all those incapable of self-correcting and self-legislating critical reflexivity.)

Christianity is, for once, surprisingly open and generous. If part of the point of the concept of a person is to assure respect, it is wiser not to rest one's hopes on such fragile and vulnerable capacities as those for autonomy or creativity. Maybe a divinely assured immortal soul—or even just a divinely assured soul, immortal or not—would provide more secure grounds for respect. To be sure, standardly, conditions for rationality and autonomy are regulative rather than empirical: we might take comfort in the principle that every rational being *ought* to be treated with respect. But it takes unusually good luck to get that regulative principle realized under harsh circumstances, just when it is most needed. Respect may be well-grounded without being well-assured. What recourse do the unrespected have when they most require respect? Moral indignation? Righteousness in the eyes of history—itself a politically variable matter—is not reliably effective in assuring entitlements.

More recently, the Christian conception of persons as endowed with a free will capable of affirming or denying God's law has been redefined: the rights of persons are accorded to all those capable of suffering, those whose naturally formed life histories can be harmed, shortened, frustrated. Whether the sentient are self-consciously aware of the natural shapes of their lives, whether they form plans and expectations (the transformation of the idea of the will as legislator), matters less than the fact that their lives can be painful or unfulfilled. It is the sheer fact of sentience that qualifies an individual to the rights of persons.[2]

4. Social persons are identified by their mutual interactions, by the roles they enact in the dynamic

dramas of their shared lives. There are several varieties of this conception.

The idea of a *dramatis persona* as the bearer of roles in a dramatic unfolding of action has its source in the theater. A *persona* is the mask of an actor cast to play a part in developing a narrative or a plot. Essentially meshed with others, the social person's scope and directions are defined by her role in a complex course of events, involving the interactions of agents whose varied intentions modify the outcomes—and indeed sometimes the directions—of one another's projects. While the dramatic conception of a person is only indirectly linked to the concept of a person as entitled to respect, or with that of a self-defining individual, it bears some kinship to the idea of a person as an agent, as the source of liable and responsible action. When *dramatis personae* are in principle able to predict their effects on one another's lives, their intentions can carry moral or legal weight. (The contrast class includes whatever is inert, without the power of intentional action. Since inanimate objects and events—volcanoes, wars, famines—can forward or redirect dramatic action, they are sometimes personified; but they are accounted persons only if intentional action is attributed to them.)

Some psychologists introduce a normative notion of a person as capable of taking others seriously, capable of entering into mutually affective and effective relations. To be a person is to acknowledge the reality of others, living in a commonly constructed world, actively and cooperatively sharing practices. Some psychologists attempt to connect the social with the respect-based definitions of persons, treating them as mutually supportive conditions.[3] But there is not necessarily a link between the two conditions. On the one hand, respect might be grounded in the idea of (a divinely donated) soul, whose sociability is contingent on the identity and roles assigned to it; on the other, some conceptions of sociability might valorize a type of intimacy that minimizes respect-across-individual-boundaries. Such a manifestly culture-bound concept of personhood can easily come into conflict with the (equally culture-bound) concept of the ideal person as capable of radical autonomy. (The contrast class in this instance is made up of dissociated personalities and psychopaths.)

There is a presumptively ontological, prepsychological version of the concept of persons as essentially formed by their relations to others. It perceives the person as constituted, formed by "the look of the other." According to this theory, consciousness is initially unreflective, without a sense of self; it acquires an image of itself—an image that comes to form the person's somatic sense of self—by seeing itself mirrored in the eyes of others. We form one another's identities by the act of mutual mirroring, mutual regard. A person's life is constructed from, and constituted by, such interactive formative relations. Though there may be normative claims about how we *ought* to regard one another, the conception of a person as interactively emergent neither entails nor is entailed by the conception of a person as entitled to respect or to specific legal rights. (The contrast class: nonconscious beings, beings incapable of self-conscious reflection.)

Associated but not identical with the psychological condition is the honorific attribution of personhood. Some individuals are accounted *real* persons: "She's a real mensch!" But although the capacities for autonomy (rationality or creativity) might be ingredient in the qualifications for being a *real* person, in contrast to the usual humanoid, they are not sufficient. Indeed, a partisan of the concept of a person as an autonomous creator might well be disqualified as a real mensch-person. On this view—to be sure a view not widely shared as definitive of the concept of a person—*real* persons are generally distinguished by fortitude and reliability, by their presence, their style and individuality, often combined with compassion and a humorous sense of proportion, an ironic recognition of human frailty and finitude. (The contrast class: the psychopath, the creep, the jerk, the whine, the brute, the Neanderthal.)

5. The concept of personhood is also used to sketch the norms for the appropriate shape and

structure of a life. Those who identify persons by a characteristic life history or life plan require an account of a standard—or maybe not so standard—shaping of a life, one that goes beyond biologically determined patterns of maturation and aging. This view originally derives from the Christian conception of the soul, whose life and choices move it toward salvation or damnation; it is a descendant of the definition of persons as constructors of their fates. The emphasis shifts: the person is first identified as the author of the story, then by the activity of story construction, and then simply by the emergent content of the narrative.[4]

There are two versions of this focus. The first, which postulates a fact of the matter, can give an account of how a culture can malform and misdirect lives, as well as misunderstand the processes by which it shapes typical life stories. The second might be characterized as the "It's all up to us" version, with the "us" referring either to individual free spirits or to the members of a self-defining community.

While the narrative conception of personhood is compatible with the definition of persons as autonomous, it neither entails nor is entailed by that conception. A person's life story need not be autonomously constructed; nor need it provide grounds for respect. Even more dramatically, the conditions for autonomy need have no bearing on the shape and events of life histories, which are, after all, contingent and heteronomous. In a Kantian framework, for example, the conditions for autonomy are purely intellectual: they neither affect nor can be affected by the contingent narrative of a life. Nor is the possibility of reflective subjectivity essential to the construction of a life story: a life can have the shape of a well-formed narrative without its subject experiencing anything like first-person inner subjectivity. It is the convenience of theory construction rather than brute ontology that determines whether the narrative condition for personhood requires further qualification. As it stands, the view that a person is one who possesses a life story seems to allow any subject of a narrative history to qualify even if that subject is not conscious of itself as a subjective center of experience. An individual might have a life story without being subjectively aware of it, and certainly without being self-consciously reflective about her shaping of it. Yet if the unadorned narrative condition of personhood allows mice and mountains to qualify as persons, the additional requirement of active subjective reflection seems too strong: it appears to disqualify individuals who might, on moral or political grounds, qualify as persons. The capacities for active subjective reflection—for constructing life plans—might turn out to be consequences of, rather than presuppositions for, an individual's qualifying as a social and political person.

The contrast class for the conception of persons as characterized by life stories is difficult to define. Everything temporal can be construed as having a life story, even a life story with a normative form. This criterion allows squirrels, a particular patch of pachysandra, and the Mediterranean basin to qualify as persons because they have life stories with a beginning, middle, and end. If we attach the further condition that persons must be capable of reflecting on, if not actively forming, a life story or a life plan, the contrast class is no easier to define. Who has the capacity for the autonomous construction of a life plan? Should the class include individuals who in principle might acquire the capacities for reflective agency, for constructing and following a life plan, if they could be accorded the status of persons? How are such counterfactual claims evaluated in holistic systems?

6. The biological conception of an individual is sometimes taken to provide the foundation or basic structure of the concept of a person. Biologists want a concept that will provide (a) the unit of genetic individuation and (b) *conatus:* the determination of growth and immunology, the energy and direction of action, reaction, and defense.

Persons are, among other things, self-sustainers and self-starters. The biological account of organic independence provides the practical origin of the more far-reaching notion of autonomy. But the concept of an organic individual does not necessarily provide a sharp distinction between human beings and other species, let alone between persons and other sorts of organic entities. Whether there is a subclass, a variety of human beings who can be designated as persons by virtue of a special set of standardly inheritable properties is a matter for empirical determination. If rationality marks the class of persons, are the various properties and capacities that constitute rationality biologically fixed, genetically coded? How do the conditions for reflective critical rationality described by Kant and Frankfurt function in the organism's system of action and reaction, expansion and defense? If self-determination marks the class of persons, are those properties and traits that constitute an individual's capacity for self-determination biologically fixed, genetically coded? How do the various capacities for creative self-definition affect a person's constitution? We are a long way from having a reasonable speculative theory, let alone a sound research program, connecting the moral, political, and legal notions of persons with the biological notion of a reproductive, self-sustaining, defensively structured organism.

It has been argued that just as women and blacks were once excluded from the class of persons on presumptively biological grounds, so too we are now misled by superficial speciesism to exclude dolphins and mammals. But we are a long way from an account of the criteria for appropriate classification: what formally identical or analogous constitutional structures qualify nonhumans as persons? Why should baboons but not robots qualify? Or Martians but not crustaceans? While empirical considerations are relevant (do dolphins have central nervous systems?), they cannot settle the questions of whether corporations and robots only qualify as persons by metaphorical courtesy, while dolphins and chimpanzees qualify as full members by an appropriate corrective extension of the class. When is a batch of wires a central nervous system and when is it only an analogue? When is an analogue good enough? When is it all too good? When does behavioral similarity qualify for literal attribution? What are the criteria for identifying biologically based behavioral similarity? Both the arguments for excluding corporations and the left hemisphere of the brain and the arguments for including robots and Martians depend on normatively charged conceptual analyses. Since similarities and differences can be found wholesale, other, further considerations are required to select the features that demarcate the class of persons. What considerations select the capacity to feel pain, rather than for rational thought, as the criteria for the class? Indeed, because the classification has significant political and social consequences, we should not be surprised to discover that conceptual analyses of biological functions—particularly those presumed to affect intentional agency—are strongly, though often only implicitly and unselfconsciously, guided by moral intuitions, ideology, and taste. Controversies among sociobiologists about drawing relevant analogies between humans and other animals—their hierarchy or altruistic behavior, their protection of property—should make us suspicious about attempts to support policies concerning the rights of persons on what are allegedly purely empirical, biological considerations. (The contrast class comprises inanimate objects.)

7. Psychometaphysicians have a notion of the elusive, ultimate subject of experience, the 'I' that cannot be reduced to an object, even though it can treat itself objectively, as the focus of introspection and investigation.[5] But this 'I' can be diachronically discontinuous: the subject of "sequential" experiences need not be strictly identical. And even synchronic subjects of experiences need not be united: every aspect of a complex act of awareness could, in principle, have its own subject. The subject who is aware of the acute pain of loss need not be identical with the subject who is at the same time aware of the shifting pattern of light on the leaves of a tree. Or at any rate, the transcendental unity of apperception (if there is such a thing) does not necessarily provide specific closure to what is, and

what is not, included within the bounds of such a presumptive unity. The limits of the domain of experience cannot be set by the subject of a transcendental unity of apperception without circularity.

In any case, there are a number of distinctive construals of subjectivity as the condition for personhood, and while each has quite different consequences for the concept, none has any necessary consequences for morality, or for political or legal theory. The 'I' that is the subject of experience serves as the contrastive notion, but the various contrasts are not isomorphic. The person as the 'I,' the subject of experience, has been identified with the interior or internal perspective in contrast to the external; with the subjective in contrast to the objective; with the subject-of-experiences in contrast to its experiences; with rationality and the will in contrast to causality and desire; with spontaneity and creativity in contrast to the conditioned; with the decision-maker and agent in contrast to the predictor and observer; with the knower or interpreter in contrast to the known or interpreted; with reflective consciousness in contrast to the content of reflection; with mind in contrast to body.

Although each of these juxtapositions marks quite a different contrast, each is guided by the intuition that persons are capable of bearing a unique reflexive, reflective relation to themselves, a relation that somehow shapes them. Persons are sometimes characterized as capable of having a distinctive set of experiences—ego-oriented attitudes of anxiety, remorse, pride, guilt—that originally give rise to the idea of the self. But the reflective 'I' can reject or identify with these ego-oriented attitudes as easily as it can with its body or its habits. It is no more identical with any set of "existential attitudes" than it is with any of its more externally defined attributes. The *act* of reflecting on an attribute or attitude, asking "Is that *me?*" ("putting the self in question"), is always different from the attitude or attribute itself, even if the attitude reveals—as anxiety is said to do—the precarious position of the 'I' as the act of self-constituting reflection. Being anxious is one thing; being the act that identifies with anxiety is another. Both are different from something-perhaps-a-nothing-I-know-not-what, or a simple soul beyond experience, or a pure act of reflection that constitutes itself. All these—different as they are from one another—are far from the original starting point of the 'I' as a being whose experience, and especially its experience of itself, is *sui generis.* None of these reflexive attitudes carries specific political, legal, or moral consequences. In *Notes from the Underground,* Dostoyevsky's dramatic explorations of the subterranean destructiveness of the endlessly ironic self-mirroring self-consciousness demonstrate that even rational, self-critical reflexivity can assure neither sociability nor morality; and it can destroy self-respect. (The contrast class: objects, those incapable of self-conscious reflection.)

III

The variety of functions that 'the' concept of a person plays—the variety of conceptions of personhood we've sketched—cannot be plausibly combined in a single concept. At most, one might settle for a heterogeneous class, defined by a disjunction of heterogeneous conditions. Even if some rough construction of a denominator common to all these notions and functions were proposed, that conception would be so general that it could not fulfill—nor could it generate—the various functions performed by the various regional and substantively rich conceptions.

But this stark conclusion seems premature. Perhaps we can characterize persons by attempting some sort of synthesis of our various conditions: *A person is a unit of agency, a unit that is (a) capable of being directed by its conception of its own identity and by what is important to that identity, and (b) capable of acting with others, in a common world. A person is an interactive member of a community, reflexively sensitive to the contexts of her activity, a critically reflective inventor of the story line of her life.* Surely this is a parody of a characterization. The conditions only cohere if one doesn't look too closely. It is not clear whether these conditions are conjunctive or whether they are nestled. After all, the conditions for strong autonomy might well on occasion conflict with those for strong sociability. The conditions of critical rationality might well on occasion conflict with those of poetic creativity. The conditions for personhood—and indeed the class of those qualifying as persons—are quite different if critical rationality dominates over sociability, rather than sociability over the capacities for critical rationality. Societies that weight these capacities differently differ dramatically; and sometimes ideological or political issues determine the weighting and priority of the various conditions.

Might the metaphysical notion of a person be primary, in a way that would settle these questions of priority? Primary to what? A universalistic metaphysical notion can constrain, but it cannot select or determine the priorities among competing politically and ideologically defined persons. If the metaphysical idea of a person is rich and robust enough to generate political consequences, it is already charged and directed toward those consequences. If it stands neutrally above those consequences, it is unlikely to be rich enough to do the work done by the various strands in the concepts of persons. The concept of the referent of first-person attributions or the concept of the subject of experience might be a precondition for the political or moral uses of the concept of a person. But even that is questionable: it is not conceptually necessary that the bearer of rights be capable of reflexive first-person attributions.

The notion of a human being is a notion of a biologically defined entity; the notion of a person is, however, normatively and sometimes ideologically charged. It expresses a view about what is important, valuable about being creatures like us, in having this or that set of significant traits and properties. Such creatures need not belong to our biological species. Martians or Super-robots could be persons; organically organized families and clans might qualify, as could intrapsychic demons, homunculi, or consciences. For some, this notion designates a natural kind: there is a fact of the matter about what ought to be important and significant to us. For others, we are that natural kind whose primary attributes are plastic: within limits, we are self-legislatively self-defining, even self-constructing, creatures.

But even those who think of persons as self-defining creators of their identities do not agree about the extension of this class. For some, self-determination is a matter of individual volition; for others, only historical communities with self-perpetuating practices can be considered self-determining. For some, *all* individuals, no matter how pathetically malformed, however constitutionally or socially deprived or deformed, are equally the creators of the stories that are their lives. No matter what story one tells about one's life, that story *is* one's life as a person. For others, only Nietzschean self-creating and free individual spirits, the solitary ones who transcend the herd and the conventions of the herd, are capable of self-definition. For others, only cultural and political communities can define or create themselves: individual persons are self-legislating only as members of a community defined by shared interactive practices, which define the boundaries and the essential traits of persons. On this view, the definition of persons is implicit in the practices that express and reproduce the community's cultural forms, especially the practices of parenting and education and the distribution of legal and political power.

These reflections on "the" concept of a person seem unsatisfactory: all we have is a complaint inspired by vulgar forms of Wittgensteinianism, that shifts the burden of analysis. Instead of dispatching yet another vexed philosophic issue, counseling Quixotic philosophers to stop looking for a nonexistent essential definition of persons, we should perhaps more modestly end with an account of the many different reasons we have wanted, and perhaps needed, the notion of a person. These are, after all, honorable desires, as philosophic desires go. We have, in a sketchy way, explored some of the reasons that philosophers and legal-political theorists want the concept: those reasons are given by the heterogeneous list of functions—some of them rhetorical—that the concept has played. The Procrustean tactic of cutting limbs to fit an arbitrary, if elegantly designed, form neither illuminates nor gains anything: it limits rather than enhances an understanding of the various functions of "the" concept.

It is of course possible to legislate one central notion of a person, and to fend off strong contending candidates for definition. Such legislation might express a moral or an ideological victory; if it is widely accepted, it might even succeed in being a culturally self-fulfilling prophecy. But it would not on that account alone constitute an insightful illumination into the nature of persons. Such legislation about the essential character of persons expresses rather than grounds or legitimates our moral and legal principles. But significantly, the deep fissures and conflicts that are central to moral experience, and that make their way into the complexities of legal practice, are reintroduced among, and even sometimes within, the various functions of the concepts of persons. We do not even have the luxury of assuring ourselves that at least the concept of the person is coordinate with the concepts of moral and legal practices. At best we can say that the tensions and conflicts at the heart of moral and legal practices are reflected in, and sometimes clarified by, tensions and conflicts in conceptions of persons.

Why, then, is there such a metaphysical longing for one concept? (Or is it a longing for one metaphysical concept?) Perhaps the explanation is that the various functions the concept plays are each unifying functions: "the" locus of liability; "the" subject of experience; "the" autonomous critical reflector or creator. Since these various functions are unifying functions, there might be a strong temptation to look for their unified source. But this is an elementary error, on a par with illicitly extracting and then detaching an existential quantifier from its proper nested location. A desire for unity cannot by itself perform the conjuring trick of pulling one rabbit out of several hats: a transcendental unity of the concept of person, unifying the variety of distinct, independently unifying functions that each regional concept plays.

Our reflections leave our conclusions open: we might conclude that there is no such thing as the concept of personhood, that there are only highly regionalized functions that seemed, erroneously, to be subsumable in a structured concept. Or we might conclude that the various functions of the concept are sometimes at odds, that the concept of a person cannot function to provide decision procedures for resolving conflicts among competing claims for rights and obligations because it embeds and expresses just those conflicts. Nothing hangs on the choice between these conclusions because neither political practice nor philosophic theory is affected by the outcome. For all practical and theoretical purposes it doesn't matter whether the concept of a person has multiple and sometimes conflicting functions, or whether there is no single foundational concept that can be characterized as *the* concept of a person. As long as we recognize that such appeals are, in the classical and unpejorative sense of that term, rhetorical, we can continue to appeal to conceptions of persons in arguing for extending political rights, or limiting the exercise of political power. The success of such rhetorical appeals depends on whether the proposed concept expresses some of the active values and practices of the audience.

Another metaphysical longing remains unsatisfied. But of course that doesn't mean that we shall be freed of metaphysical longing, nor even of this particular metaphysical longing.[6]

NOTES

1. See C. Baron, 'The Concept of Person in the Law', in M.W. Shaw and A.E. Doudera (edd.), *Defining Human Life: Medical, Legal, and Ethical Implications* (Ann Arbor, Mich., 1983), 121–48; and R. Tur, 'The "Person" in Law', in A. Peacocke and G. Gillett (edd.), *Persons and Personality: A Contemporary Inquiry* (Oxford, 1987), 116–29.
2. See K. Capek, *War with the Newts* (London, 1985); and P. Singer, *Animal Liberation* (New York, 1977).
3. See H. Kohut, *The Restoration of the Self* (New York, 1977).
4. See J. Bruner, *Actual Minds, Possible Worlds* (Cambridge, Mass., 1986).
5. See T. Nagel, *The View From Nowhere* (New York, 1986).
6. This chapter is based on a paper given at the Aberystwyth conference on 'Persons and Human Beings'. An earlier version of this chapter appeared as 'Persons as Rhetorical Categories', *Social Research,* 54 (1987), 55–72.

DISCUSSION QUESTIONS

1. Describe the thought experiment (inspired by Locke's case of the prince's soul being transplanted into the cobbler's body on p. 85 of this volume) of Brown, Robinson, and Brownson. Why does Rorty think that thought experiments of this kind are always under described?
2. What does Rorty think happens when we force decisions about how to analyze criterial accounts of personal identity?
3. Rorty says that in times of social and political change, reformers recommend an expansion or contraction of the class of persons. Are we currently in a time of social and political change? Explain. If so, which reformers are recommending expansion of the class of persons? Which reformers are recommending contraction? Which group compels you more? Explain.
4. Can the seven conceptions of "person" identified by Rorty be reduced to fewer distinct regional concepts? Are some arguably subclasses of others? Explain.
5. Discuss why one might want to dream the metaphysical dream of the "person" concept despite Rorty's argument that there is no unified answer to this dreamy puzzle.
6. Are some of Rorty's concepts more influenced by cultural factors than others? Would Russian or Chinese concepts of persons differ substantially from Rorty's Anglo-American concepts? Explain.

Chapter 37

R. G. A. DOLBY

Alex Dolby is a professor in the School of History, Rutherford College, University of Kent. His interests include the social construction of scientific knowledge, science fiction, and late 19th-century history of science. He is author of Uncertain Knowledge: An Image of Science for a Changing World *(Cambridge 1996). In this essay, Dolby argues that there is no way of establishing a definitive pattern of usage which spans the many contexts of discourse—religious, ethical, social, psychological, legal, metaphysical—of the concept "person." He thinks that what makes a being a person is not the nature of its inner mental processes (including intentions), but whether or not we are prepared to accept it into our society. Dolby believes it is hard to imagine the concept "person" disappearing without some other category of thought appearing which enriches language sufficiently for the language users to be prepared to allow the loss of the person category. He holds that the distinction between the extension and the intension of the concept "person" cannot be sharply made. He contends that the concept may come to apply to future, technologically sophisticated, computer-operated robots. He concludes this essay by describing what he maintains is a conceptually coherent story illustrating fluid changes to the concept "person" between 2001 and 2201 AD.*

The Possibility of Computers Becoming Persons

[. . .] The concept of person is complicated by being closely related to other important concepts like 'human being', 'self' and so on. I will assume that a human being is an individual belonging to the human species and that a person is an individual with whom we relate reciprocally in society, attributing self-awareness, legal and moral responsibility, and so on. The relationship we have with a person is quite different from that with a material object, such as a stone, or even a sophisticated machine, like a computer. The origin and physical appearance of a human being is rather more important than that of a person. The actions and inner qualities of a person are rather more important than those of a human being. Most of the persons we know are human beings, but in extreme cases the two concepts can be expected to diverge. A human being, for example, can be breathing but brain-dead. In the context of controversy over the acceptability of abortion, philosophers have argued whether a human fetus incapable of independent existence deserves to be called a person simply because it is a human being.[1] In a religious context, we might regard supernatural beings as persons. In a science-fiction context it might be reasonable to ponder whether a particular extraterrestrial being is a person, or whether a person might have a body transplant, or whether two persons might share one body. It is harder to distinguish the concepts of persons and of self, but the concept of self is closely tied to ideas of self-image and self-awareness, while the concept of person has a wider range of links, coming in part from its origins in the concept persona (see Section 4.1).

The concept 'person' is not easily defined by specifying a number of necessary characteristics which anything must have if it is to be called a person (and to which less essential characteristics of persons may be linked). We could not be expected to agree on what these characteristics are. A Christian might require the possession of an immortal soul (and then have recourse to sacred texts to decide what kinds of entities have immortal souls). In an ethical or legal context, the concept of person can be linked to that of a morally or legally responsible agent. In the context of the theory of mind, a person might be thought of as the possessor of a mind, or of inner mental workings, or at least to whom the language of actions and intentions may be attributed. Where such contexts generate distinctive forms of technical language, there is a temptation to adapt the concept 'person' in a manner appropriate to that context only. For example, in some legal contexts it is appropriate to treat a corporate body such as a

Source: R. G. A. Dolby, "The Possibility of Computers becoming Persons." Reprinted from *Social Epistemology* 3, no. 4 (1989): 321–336 (edited) with the permission of Taylor & Francis Ltd and the author. http://www.tandf.co.uk/journals/routledge/02691728.html

business company as if it were a person, because the company is the agent which should be held responsible. We can regard such a company as a 'quasi-person', and examine its legal rights and responsibilities.[2] Of course, such a quasi-person does not have a soul or a mind. It is not self-aware in any sense which has a close analogy to human self-awareness. While these differences remain important, to describe a company as a person is no more than a metaphor with a significant negative analogy. One of the problems of the nature of the concept 'person' is that such contexts of discourse as a person's social role, legal status, religious classification and psychological nature are all relevant. Criteria based on each normally support one another in the identification of humans as persons, but in extreme cases they can give conflicting conditions for the application of the concept. When we try to study such a concept we typically have to construct links and priorities within the network of acceptable conceptual usage that relates all these contexts of discourse. Philosophers, like other people, typically do this with an implicit theory of their relationship — this can be a simple attitude or interest (for example, committed Christianity can incline one to draw a line between entities which have souls and those which do not), or a full metaphysical theory and associated ontology (as Descartes had), or even a set of procedural principles as is more common in recent philosophy.

In my view there is no way of establishing a *definitive* pattern of usage which spans the many contexts of discourse of the concept person. Our analysis will always depend on the theory implicit in the approach we have taken.

One candidate for such an invariant framework was called descriptive metaphysics by Strawson (in contrast to some sort of revisionist metaphysics such as mind-body identity theory). Descriptive metaphysics argues from what is fundamental to and invariant in present conceptual usage. However, descriptive metaphysics presupposes that the fundamental conceptual patterns found in present language have thereby been shown to be necessary to all language, which is precisely the point at issue. For the concept 'person' has developed and will continue to develop.

3.2. The Concept of Robot

Most of the persons we meet are normal human beings, and there are a multitude of unquestioned presuppositions which we draw upon in our interactions with them as persons. It is only in special cases that our attention is drawn to the presuppositions which have become problematic. However, if the conditions of our life were to change, for example, if we were to meet sophisticated machines which had capacities for speech and behaviour comparable to humans, so that the question arose of whether or not to treat them as persons, there would naturally be some initial doubt about the legitimate application of our unquestioned presuppositions to the new situation.

One established way of drawing the distinction between people and mere physical things like robots is by showing that the language of action and intention cannot satisfactorily be attributed to purely physical things. But the arguments about this fundamental aspect of the language of persons do not settle our problem. In talking about human organisms, we have a choice of whether to use the category of persons or that of physical things. To show that concepts such as intention cannot correctly be applied to a robot when it is regarded as a physical thing does not prevent us going on to regard the robot as a person and then applying the concept of intention correctly. To make the objection work, it would be required to show that a robot cannot be regarded as a person. But that is precisely the point at issue.

The extension of the concept 'person' to cover some future form of robot would initially appear to raise similar difficulties to those of regarding a business corporation as a person. Let us assume, in the science-fiction tradition, that a robot is a purely physical construction which is mobile and self-powered and equipped with sensory instrumentation and with some ability to manipulate objects in its environment. Let us assume further that its functioning might be coordinated by some development of present electronic computers and that (unlike present factory robots) it is sufficiently similar in form and function to a human being to tempt us to represent its functioning by using language at present applied primarily to human beings.

Some of the issues on which this paper draws have been discussed many times in terms of whether or not machines could ever be said to have minds. The mid-twentieth century tradition of philosophical discussion of minds and machines explored the possibility of a computer imitating a human in a reasonably demanding context.[3] It was as if people looked for a set of defining characteristics of the human mind and then argued about whether or not they could ever be replicated by a computer. Subsequent development of the field of artificial intelligence worked at producing the kinds of computer performance to which we might be inclined to apply the language of human mental performance. I wish to avoid the standard issues of the philosophical discussion. In my view, the key aspects of what makes a being a person are not the nature of the inner processes. We do not really know enough about human minds to be able to set precise requirements for a thinking machine. I do not think that even the sophistication of the public behavior of an entity can settle whether or not it is a person. We are quite prepared to regard very young children and relatively senile old folk as persons even though they have very limited behavioral capacities. *What matters most is whether or not we are prepared to accept a particular entity as one of ourselves.* What is critical is the attitude of the rest of society. For this reason, the debate about machine minds should give way to one about whether we are prepared to accept sentient mobile computer-based systems as persons, that is, whether robots could ever join human society.

3.2.1. The idea of a robot as a person is just a joke . . . For centuries, there has been a powerful cultural charge in the idea of a mechanism which is also a person. The automaton which is rejected or imperfectly controlled by its creator and which ends by destroying him (as Frankenstein's monster destroyed Frankenstein in Mary Shelley's novel) was a common expression of this symbolism.[4] The idea of the automaton was developed into the modern concept of the robot in science fiction. Over the last few decades, the concept of the robot has been exploited by successive groups to advance their own concerns. The use of the concept for certain kinds of automated machinery on factory assembly lines has occurred alongside the increasing use of robots in science-fiction film. Even mime dancers exploit and augment our idea of robots. Robots have become one of the common stereotypes of modern culture. All this is reflected in the genre of cartoon humour. A part of this stereotype is the notion that although a mechanical philosopher or artist or lover seems absurd, we cannot help admitting that it just might happen.

Clearly, there is bizarre incongruity about a robot being thought of as a person. One robot sits in an armchair and says, 'I compute, therefore I exist'. Another leans over a bar saying, 'My programmer doesn't understand me'. If such humour depended on nothing more than the oddity of treating a mechanism on the analogy of a human being, then it would soon lose its novelty. But there is also a biting edge to these jokes. This is especially clear in the versions in which a computer or a robot takes over a person's job. The bitterness of the person whose job is replaced by a computer is exceeded only by the person who is replaced by a single transistor. As such jokes get near to what humans value most about themselves, especially powerful feelings of ambivalence towards robots can be exploited. Robot jokes are not just a passing whimsy, they reflect sustained underlying cultural tensions.

3.3. How Language Changes

Language is, of course, changing all the time. New words are introduced, old words die out, the meanings of existing words are modified, and new strands of meaning are added. In the case of a word like 'person', we might distinguish its extension and its intention. A change in the former occurs if it is applied to new things without change in meaning, and a change in the latter occurs if it acquires a new meaning. But if the change of meaning is at all significant, it has effectively become a new concept.

It might be argued that the concept 'person' is so fundamental a category of thought that as long as language survives, there will have to be such a concept, in very much like its present form. If, however, relevant change does occur, two possibilities present themselves. The first possibility is that the category of person will disappear altogether and language will be restricted to other categorial forms. To the extent that the language of action and intention presuppose a concept 'person', that too would disappear. My own view is that it is very difficult to make such a transformation seem plausible by arguments expressed within present language. It is hard to imagine the concept of person disappearing without some (incompatible) category of thought appearing which enriches language sufficiently for the language users to be prepared to allow the loss of the person category.[5]

A second possible change to the concept of person would be for it to be retained but to evolve. For example, if it were to come to be applied to a succession of new kinds of entities each of which is closely analogous to the entities to which it is already applied. As these changes in the extension of the concept cumulate, the meaning of the concept may be expected to evolve.

Let us consider two rival theses about the possibility of robots being persons.

> *Thesis A:* a future development of robots makes them sufficiently like human beings to apply the concept of person to them with its present meaning.
>
> *Thesis B:* the current concept of person does not allow robots to be called persons. If in fact a language change occurs so that robots come to be called persons, then this will involve a change in the concept of person. Then the old concept may disappear, or a new word may be found for it.

My position is that the distinction between the extension and intension of the concept 'person' cannot be made very sharp. A part of my argument is that one important mechanism of concept evolution is that when a term is applied to a succession of new cases, the cumulative effect can be to produce a change in meaning. My claim that the concept of person may come to apply to future robots involves a certain vagueness about the point in the evolution at which we should say that the intension of the concept has changed. In my view, the meaning one gives the concept 'person' depends on the implicit theory employed to link the contexts of discourse about persons. Those who hold particular theories may have firm views on whether or not future robots could be persons in the present sense of 'person'. However, there are always many such theories and their relative fortune can be expected to fall in with the current pattern of usage—as the usage changes so will the preferred theory. A descriptive metaphysics, too, will find itself out of date as usage falls into a contrary pattern.

4. CHANGES IN THE CONCEPT 'PERSON'

The view I am defending is, then, that a concept like 'person' is historically variable. It has changed now, and could well change even more dramatically in the future. Although most of the changes are gradual, their effect cumulates. Most transitions can be regarded as minor extensions to the concept with virtually no effect on its current meaning, but when viewed in the perspective of a longer time scale, such changes in extension can be seen to have fundamentally reworked the concept. The concepts of person and material thing already overlap, and the nature of the overlap is variable. We can treat human beings both as persons *and* as bodies. Future change might extend or reduce the overlap.

4.1. The History of the Concept

The modern concept of person has a complex origin. The essential features are sketched out in the *Oxford English Dictionary.* Its origins are traced back in particular to (and through) the Latin *persona,* which carries the idea of a mask worn by a player, or a character in a performance, or a role in life or a being having legal rights. Increasingly, however, the concept came to be used to refer to an individual (human) being, whether or not that individual was acting in a specific capacity. The Christian notions of the Holy Trinity as three persons and of Christ as one person with two natures became an additional meaning and an important influence on the general development of the concept. The philosophical sense of a person as a self-conscious or rational being was a later addition.

A. Mauss, in a recently reprinted historical discussion of the development of the concept 'person', summarized the key transitions as follows.

> From a simple masquerade to the mask, from a 'role' (personnage) to a person (personne), to a name, to an individual; from the latter to a being possessing metaphysical and moral value; from a moral consciousness to a sacred being; from the latter to a fundamental form of thought and action . . .[6]

Mauss's account is regarded as stimulating rather than conclusive in the papers that accompany it in *The Category of the Person.* For example, Carrithers[7] suggested that Mauss has artificially constructed the developmental sequence of his narrative history by moving gradually from the concepts of role (*personnage*) to the concept of self (*moi*) in his historical exposition, even though close analogues to the present concept of self can be found in, for example, the religious writings of ancient India. It is not crucial to my argument that any particular history of the concept 'person' be accepted. The key features of the human condition have changed far less throughout recorded history than they would change in the possible circumstances being explored in the later parts of this paper. Nevertheless, it is surely highly plausible that the concept of person has been changed in those cultures which had self-sustaining traditions of intellectual discussion on issues relating to the concept of person. Religion and philosophy appear to have been especially significant historically. Let us provisionally conclude then that present-day philosophical discussions of the concept of person relate to the modern form of the concept, which builds upon the early Christian notion of person to which a philosophical sense of self as a self-conscious rational being was later added.

4.2. Contemporary Change in the Concept

At the end of his discussion, Mauss asks, 'Who knows what progress the Understanding will yet make on this matter?' My discussion explores some of the possibilities, looking at trends occurring in the present, and at the changes in our life and language being brought about by changes in science and technology. In some respects the changes have already begun.

4.2.1. Potential changes by deletion. An interesting argument can be developed in analogy with that of Mackie in ethics,[8] namely that the whole concept of person might presuppose some condition which is built into ordinary thought and language about persons but which is in error. Consider, for example, a simplified version of the Christian view that a person is a being which possesses a soul. If robots do not possess souls, then they cannot be persons. If in fact there are no such things as souls, then robots would be in the same relationship to the concept of person as humans. This argument cannot be used in its strongest form in defence of the possibility of robots as persons. For if having a soul were indeed a necessary condition of being a person and there are no souls then neither human beings nor robots could be persons. According to the view I expressed in Section 3.2, however, the essential meaning of the concept of person is carried intuitively. A rigorous definition would be an artificial imposition. Having a soul might be regarded as a necessary condition for being a person in a certain culture, but the meaning of the concept is not pinned down so simply.

However, a weaker version of the argument has some value. If having a soul is an important consideration in the application of the concept 'person' but is not a necessary condition, then the non-existence of souls would indeed undermine one basis for a sharp distinction between humans and robots in their right to be called persons.

I will develop a form of this argument by suggesting that as society changes, the key considerations which we employ in trying to pin down the essential meaning of 'person' are subject to reworking. In the earlier Christian form of European culture, the presence of a soul was indeed a key aspect of being a person. It was rather more important than having a body. A being, such as the Holy Spirit in the Christian Trinity, which does not have a human body can still be a person. The process of deciding whether or not a given entity has a soul did not appear to be on the basis of empirical evidence, but rather as an application of the interpretation of sacred texts. In many parts of the western world, society is becoming more secular. In a culture such as ours in which believers and non-believers coexist, the concept of soul no longer commands consensus, and we are already seeing the criterion of the presence or absence of a soul decrease in significance from its status in the earlier European history of the concept of person. Among a community of believers, then, since the idea of robots was not at all well developed in ancient times, further revelation is needed from God on the status of robots. A provisional argument has some religious plausibility that a robot, by being manufactured, cannot have a God-given soul and is, therefore, not a person. Arguments like this seem to raise the risk of religious discrimination against robots. (What are the requirements of a religion that could include robots?) In the present age, however, the concept of person is no longer a matter of purely religious considerations. Souls may not actually exist, and therefore the requirement that persons have souls is not a suitable criterion for judging whether robots can be persons.

A similar argument can be developed concerning the concept of mind. To the extent that the concept of mind comes to be regarded as a mistaken artefact of the Cartesian tradition, the requirement that a person have the kind of self-awareness with which the concept of mind is associated could be seen as less relevant to the idea that a robot could be a person.

My own view is that the modern concept of person does draw upon our sense of our mental nature and that many people now think that robots do not and cannot possess the inner qualities of human beings. However, the psychological aspect of the concept of person is not something of which we have privileged knowledge. The way we see our inner nature depends very much on what our culture enables us to see. To a considerable extent the concepts we group together in terms of 'minds' are social. The idea of the mind as a social construction is beginning to be discussed.[9] On this view, such requirements of 'persons' as that they be self-aware, and so on, have less to do with their inner capacities than with their capacity to fit into a social situation and to fulfil certain social expectations. In a very unreflective culture, there would seem to be little difficulty in imagining that future robots would have the capacity to give all the signs of inner processes which that society required. At the other extreme, a highly mystical culture which makes very elaborate claims for a hierarchy of inner mental states might be more disinclined to accept comparable inner processes in the same future robots. However, as a sceptical Westerner, I might doubt that even human beings have the capacities attributed to them by such mysticism. My point, that what we discover within ourselves is what society induces us to find, leaves very little for our inner natures that all persons have but robots cannot have. The problem becomes one of whether we are prepared to make the same attributions about robots' inner states as we are about our own. The only evidence that could clearly affect our attitude has to do with any incapacity of robots to show expected signs of their inner nature.

4.2.2. Changes by augmentation. In addition to changes in the concept of person which are occurring as the metaphysics of relevant contexts of discourse about persons become outdated, other changes are occurring as new contexts of discourse emerge. We pay increasing attention to a biological conception of the person. In an evolutionary context, we argue about the significance of each individual's genetic make-up. The change is clearly hinted at by the way people tend to misuse the concept of a human clone. The idea of clones being made of some exceptional individual tends to carry with it the notion that the same person will be regenerated in a new body. It would seem that we might have to fear large numbers of new Hitlers if some original tissue from Hitler were found. However, since cloned individuals could be expected to be even less like the original than identical twins (who are genetically identical and were raised in the same family), this fear can be regarded as a corruption of the normal concept of person. However, some cultures have regarded twins as significantly different from most persons. A development of our culture *could* make clones a different kind of multiple-bodied person to whom special criteria apply. Another aspect of the tendency to link the concept of person to biological ideas is the identification of the mind with the brain. Most people would think that if a brain were transplanted into a new body, personal identity would be transferred at the same time. In philosophy, the view is discussed in which mental processes are linked to the processes of the brain. This mind–brain identity theory is widely criticized for neglecting crucial aspects of the network of concepts around the concept of person. In particular, actions and intentions cannot be attributed to purely physical entities like brain processes. A purely physical concept of person would, then, be incompatible with, and an impoverishment of the present concept. Nevertheless, the trend of linking the social, legal, ethical, religious and psychological aspects of the concept to an enriched biological network is likely to continue.

4.2.3. Human minds and computers. Another more recent change is the growing resonance between the concept of person and computer processes. The idea that both involve the processing of information and that the study of each can provide insight into the other has become steadily richer. In this section, I will seek to show how this convergence is facilitating changes in the concept of person. As more terms traditionally restricted to human beings come to be applied to computers, the possibility increases that computers (and in particular mobile computer systems with sensory instrumentation and motor powers) might eventually be regarded as sufficiently close to human beings to be regarded as persons too.

4.2.3.1. The language of human intentionality applied to computers. As Chris Fields argued, the dominant way of conceptualizing computers is to treat them as electronic instruments used as tools.[10] However, the existing language of tool usage has not been adequate for devices such as computers which can carry out sustained and complex processes with minimal supervision. To fill the gap, a rich new jargon of computer language has grown up. At many points this language has been augmented by terms once applied only to persons.

Most of the intentional language of computing is appropriate, as it relates to the intentions of the humans who create, program and use the computer systems. However, as computer systems have become more sophisticated, the separation between human purpose and machine performance becomes increasingly pronounced. It is as if the machine has a life of its own. Consider, as an example, a computer program that plays the game of chequers against human opponents, and is also designed to draw upon its experience of the successful strategems of past games in each new game.[11] An informal description of how such a program works naturally uses the language of intention. In simpler cases, the relevant intentions can be seen as that of the human programmer and of those who run the program on particular occasions. But as the program can be used in contexts unforeseen by the original programmer, and by operators with minimal understanding of what the computer will do, we are inclined to slip into the usage which attributes the intention to the computer. The intention of the original programmer was that his program should win at games of chequers without requiring his direct knowledge or intervention. In the context of a particular game between the computer and a human, we are tempted to keep our usage symmetric and say that both the computer and the human are playing to win. As the best program can beat the best humans in chequers, it becomes increasingly unnatural to continue insisting that what beats the human player is the original programmer (who would have lost without the computer). Inevitably, therefore, the intentional language of how people use computers as tools comes to be applied to the computer systems themselves.

From the beginning of modern electronic computing it has been a commonplace to describe computer processes in the language of human reasoning. A computer running a program is said to calculate, to solve, to infer, or to conclude. As computer systems have acquired new capacities there has been a corresponding growth of the range of vocabulary taken over from the action of persons. For example, computer-based expert systems have been said to give advice, and to explain or justify their conclusions when challenged. Similarly, the language of computer-based bureaucratic systems has taken over many terms of bureaucratic procedure which were originally applied to human functionaries. The computer can be said to expect or require or demand payment, for example. In one much repeated anecdote the computer demanded payment for a bill for a zero amount. No human being *intended* that such a bill should be sent out. In the UK, the printed report of an automated breathalyser can even have legal status. A computer system may even be said to show intelligence (artificial intelligence) or a modest level of originality (as in proving a new theorem).

Of course, there are also many other terms which we apply to people which cannot be applied to computer systems at present. For example, the idea of computers having emotions seems bizarre. This is sometimes developed into the argument that the *emotional qualities* of humans are distinctive to persons. Surely a computer could never feel pain or truly hate its programmer?

[. . .] There is no difficulty in a computer-based machine simulating behavior we are inclined to regard as the display of emotion. A robot could, for example, be set to flinch from contact which might be expected to cause it damage and it could make loud wailing noises when damage occurs. However, it is presumably the *inner* nature of emotional performances which is to be used to distinguish mere mechanisms from true persons. Our problem then becomes one of distinguishing a genuine emotion (or other mental act) from a mere simulation. No one else knows (and perhaps does not even care) whether the widow's expression of grief at her husband's funeral is completely genuine or is largely a pretence which happens to be appropriate to the situation. The acceptance of the genuineness of her grief is a natural outcome of our empathy with her situation. In the absence of any contrary information we are not inclined to question that she is genuinely grieving. The problem, then, becomes one of when and why we make the unquestioning attribution of a certain inner quality to the emotion in question. In part such an attribution will be determined by whether or not we are prepared to regard the entity as a person and thus as a fit object for our empathy. If language changes to allow us to regard robots as persons, then the problem of whether or not to attribute genuine feelings to them will have changed in their favor.

The observation has frequently been made that the list of key mental qualities that distinguishes human beings from mere machines has often been revised as new capacities of computers have been demonstrated. The idea that there is something distinctive about human mental performance appears to be suffering a death by a thousand qualifications. For example, those mental qualities which are only acquired by extended formal learning were once high on the list of distinctly human capacities, perhaps because they were used to mark the superiority of an educated human over a less educated one. But the more abstract and formal qualities have frequently turned out to be the easiest to replicate on a computer.

4.2.3.2. The language of computers applied to humans. In a materialistic culture in which scientific methods are important in the growth of knowledge, it is not surprising to find that computers are increasingly used as a tool to study human psychological processes. Information theory has grown into a repertoire of techniques which can be applied to human processes, to animals, and to machines. Cognitive psychologists use computers to model human thought processes in terms of information processing. To the extent that such methods prove effective, the label 'cognitive science' will displace old distinctions between people and machines and it will become natural for us to see our own inner processes in terms of successful computer models. Already some young enthusiasts of artificial intelligence can be found on American campuses who represent their own mental processes entirely in the language of computers.[12] This trend may seem horrific to defenders of the traditional vision of mankind, but to oppose it is to impose an arbitrary limit on the possible applications of scientific rationality. To the extent that it succeeds, the gap between persons and robots will be reduced still further.

4.2.3.3. 'User friendly' computers are becoming more like persons. An important recent trend in computer programming has been to create programmes that inexperienced users will find readily comprehensible and easy to use. One technique in such 'user friendly' programmes is to use a simple pictographic language of ikons and mouse-controlled symbolic movements on the screen. Another increasingly important technique is to allow the inexperienced user to relate to the computer as he/she would to another person. A user-friendly computer interface may be more tolerant of common human errors, asking questions when the user's intention is not clear. With added artificial intelligence, computer systems are beginning to be able to talk to and listen to their users, communicating in an increasingly acceptable approximation to natural language. It is very difficult to predict the limits to the trend of enabling computer systems to relate to humans in human terms, as it depends on the success of developments in computing. However, to the extent that it occurs, it encourages us to treat computer systems anthropomorphically.

4.2.3.4. Our instinctive anthropomorphism applies readily to robots. The sharp line that we naturally draw between persons and mere physical objects is easily blurred. In many cultures there is a widespread anthropomorphic tendency to see deities or other personalities in such natural objects as large rocks or trees. Ships have long been regarded by sailors as having the personalities of women. The anthropomorphic tendency easily applies to modern machinery.

Our present fictional culture is not at all restrictive in what is treated as a person. Children's fiction has long favored animal characters with the qualities of a person, and now that science fiction films reach a substantial proportion of the youthful population, there has been a rise in the dissemination of the image of the robot. Cute robots have joined the talking mice and rabbits of children's fiction. Adults too seem to have no difficulty in accepting the idea of robots with human personalities.

Although the idea of a mechanical person was most often used in nineteenth and early twentieth century fiction to symbolize the internal poverty of mechanical models of thought and the external danger that mankind's half understood creations may end up destroying us, modern science fiction (and the work of Isaac Asimov in particular[13]), has sought to make the robot image less of a threat. Modern science-fiction writers often strive for tension between the themes of robot as threat and robot as man's collaborator and benefactor. The pleasant possibilities of future robots have been explored at such length in fiction that the notion of robots as persons is becoming one which much of present society would find interesting and acceptable, rather than abhorrent. I will use the science fiction idea in Section 4.3 to explore the coherence of my view of a mechanism for the cumulation of change in the concept of person.

In real life, as in fiction, the idea of a computer system as a person is already proving attractive. It can be easier and quicker to interact with a complex computer system by treating it as a person than by using the more obvious technique of conceptualizing it as a tool. As a tool, sophisticated computer systems are usually so complicated that only professional experts can have the opportunity and understanding to be able to control them. There have been studies[14] which suggest that people in a less exalted relationship to a computer system cope with it better by treating it as a kind of person rather than as a complex kind of tool. If I treat a computer system as I would a person, I need to be able to anticipate the response I will receive to my actions. I am able to use the technique of creating mental representation of the other person and attempt to work out the appropriate form of interaction by trials on my mental model. In such a human–computer interaction, someone who holds only the vaguest of ideas about the actual inner states of the computer may cope well by treating it as a person. At present, the computer tends to be conceptualized as a very restricted kind of person. It would be quite inappropriate to ask oneself whether the computer might be distracted by love. However, it *would* be appropriate to ask, 'Does the computer understand my intention?' There is clearly a problem about regarding a purely physical system as being able to 'understand', but it is appropriate and helpful for the naive user to think in this way in trying to decide whether or not the computer will perform the desired function (even though he/she does not know exactly how).

4.2.4. Resistance to such changes. Although I have described trends and tendencies of changes in the concept of person as if they were almost unstoppable, there is in fact a great deal of resistance to such change. (Some aspects of the practice of philosophy such as descriptive metaphysics clearly illustrate the conservative tendencies.) Many institutions and individuals are committed to conserving traditional forms of language by keeping corruptions of speech at bay, refusing to use the latest slang and the latest jargon. If tendencies such as treating computer systems anthropomorphically and constructing our self-understanding out of computer jargon turn out to be mere passing fashions, then the conservative institutions will claim to have been vindicated. If the social practices to which these language changes are linked become widespread and deeply entrenched, the same institutions will, however, apply themselves to conserving the new form of language. My argument is that it is the overall context that is the most important factor in whether or not such changes occur, and not the logical form of language itself.

4.3. A Science-Fiction Scenario of Possible Future Changes

In order to illustrate the idea that there are no significant logical constraints on future developments of the concept of person, I would like to sketch the plot of a science-fiction story. My argument is that such stories are conceptually coherent, and illustrate how little effect the existing network of concepts can be expected to have on long-term change to future language.

2001 AD. An engineer, Jane, meets a charming and affable extraterrestrial visitor, EV, who has the form of a short humanoid biped. EV fits well into our society. Jane sets about getting EV a legal identity — as at first he has no status at all. He is initially regarded as a kind of honorary person, but as people become familiar with him he is given many of the rights and takes up the obligations of a citizen. He becomes a celebrity, a public figure who is a model of honesty, integrity, wisdom and intelligence.

2011 AD. Society learns that EV is actually a robot, with a nervous system based on a sophisticated form of electronic circuitry. However, it is decided that EV's physical constitution should make no difference to our acceptance of it as a person.

2013 AD. EV has to leave our planet. As a gift, it leaves Jane plans for its manufacture. The plans are exceptionally well laid out and easy to follow. Jane makes simple things which in turn make EV2. EV2 has the memories and knowledge of EV up to the time of its departure. EV2 is accepted as a person, fitting into the place in society previously occupied by EV.

2014 AD. Jane then makes EV3. EV3 also has memories and knowledge of EV at the time of its departure.

2016 AD. Jane has now made a thousand more EVs. People are getting worried. There are arguments, as EVs come to be seen as a potential threat. But the EVs are charming and accommodating. They overcome the build-up of prejudice and reduce the tension. They are accepted as people.

2018 AD. The EVs have the same personality and are virtually indistinguishable from one another. This causes problems about personal identity. Humans and EVs must be treated differently, because the criteria and nature of their personal identity are different. The EVs themselves introduce an important extra change. They collectively modify themselves so that they can be electronically linked, and the capacity of this link is repeatedly improved. Now they share all perceptions. Jane can talk to one, break off the conversation, and later carry on the same conversation with another EV which was not initially present.

2050–90 AD. Human beings get a dreadful epidemic disease, which spreads through the entire population. Most people recover, but the disease has made all its victims sterile. Now humans can only be produced by a biological laboratory process roughly analogous to, but more expensive than, that which produces EVs. The human population decreases dramatically, but civilization carries on.

2160 AD. Civilization is now carried on primarily by EVs, with their collective self-awareness. The few human beings are manufactured and have no distinctive sexuality. They have come to regard themselves as organic EVs, and modifications are developed with the aid of genetic engineering so that they too can join the collective consciousness.

2200 AD. Now civilization is carried on by many bodies, some organic, most robotic. They share a highly extended complexly structured consciousness, which is not completely unified but fragmented and flowing. All parts of the collective consciousness are accessible but typically an individual organism must expend time and effort to coordinate thought related to a specific issue at any given moment. Inner thought has become complex and spoken language has disappeared. Writing continues as an important form of physical memory.

2201 AD. EV returns and is aghast at what has happened. In our narrow historically limited sense of person, the robot EV is the only person left on Earth.

Although this story is far-fetched, I suggest that it is conceptually coherent. The concept of person could come to be transformed through such a succession of small changes. There is no difficulty in elaborating the story to make each change understandable and acceptable. In principle, even more radical transformations could occur, but such a science-fiction story is limited to the kinds of change which can be coherently represented within the language of the present day; more extreme changes are difficult to envisage and even more difficult to communicate. However, the history of science is full of examples in which fundamental conceptual processes become established which were previously unimaginable. For example, chemical thinking in terms of quantitative relationships expressed by chemical equations, a commonplace by the late nineteenth century, builds upon a way of thinking quantitatively within a systematic chemical nomenclature which had not even been envisaged before the late eighteenth century. There are modern chemical facts which could not have been instantly communicated even as chemical fiction to the generation of Robert Boyle.

5. CONCLUDING REMARKS

My own view is that the key aspects of what makes a being a person are not the nature of the inner processes. We tend to see within ourselves what our culture leads us to expect to see. As culture changes, so do our introspections. What *is* critical is the *attitude* of the rest of society. What we should be arguing about, therefore, is not the possibility of machine souls or machine minds, but whether robots could ever join human society. The requirement that must be met by a robot is that people are prepared to treat it as a person. If they are, they will also be prepared to attribute to it whatever inner qualities they believe a person must have. If a future culture takes a sufficiently permissive attitude to robots, they may come to be accepted as persons without a fundamental change in the concept of person.

NOTES

1. See, for example: Carter, W. R. 'Do zygotes become people?' *Mind* (1980), 91: pp. 77–95, which develops its arguments in the context of many philosophical works on this issue.
2. The idea that a computer could be regarded as a 'partial person' in a legal context is developed by Willick, M. 'Constitutional law and artificial intelligence: the potential legal recognition of computers as "persons" '. In A. Joshi (ed.), *Proceedings of the Ninth International Joint Conference on Artificial Intelligence.* Kaufmann, Los Altos (1985), pp. 1271–1273, and discussed by Fields, C. (1987), pp. 18–19 (see note 1).
3. One influential frame of discussion was set by Alan Turing's account of his 'imitation game' in 'Computing machinery and intelligence', *Mind* (1950) 59: pp. 433–460. See for example: Anderson, A. R. (ed.), *Minds and Machines.* Prentice-Hall, Englewood Cliffs, NJ (1964).
4. For example: Melville, H. 'The bell tower' (1855). Reprinted in: *Great Short Works of Herman Melville.* Harper and Row, New York (1969). Bierce, A. 'Moxom's master'. In *Can Such Things Be?* (1893). Reprinted in *The Collected Writings of Ambrose Bierce.* Citadel Press, New York (1960). Capek, C. *RUR* (1921, transl. 1923).
5. Such an imaginative leap might be made by elaborating upon extreme science fiction scenarios. For example, in Pohl, F. *The Tunnel Under the World* (1956), it turns out that the hero is not the autonomous person he thinks he is, but a semi-autonomous simalcron within an elaborate simulation exercise, whose memories are reprogrammed in each run. If we were to discover this of ourselves, as the hero of *The Tunnel Under the World* does, we might decide that the traditional category of person does not fit our situation and replace it by some new concept, perhaps drawn from the language of simulation.
6. Mauss, A. 'A category of the human mind: the notion of person; the notion of self'. In Carrithers, M., Collins, S. and Lukes, S. (eds), *The Category of the Person: Anthropology, Philosophy, History.* Cambridge University Press, Cambridge (1985), p. 22.
7. Carrithers, M. 'An alternative social history of the self'. In Anderson, A. R. (ed.), pp. 234–256 (see note 3).
8. This possibility can be compared with Mackie's argument in ethics that ethics is based on a comparable error. See: Mackie, J. L. *Ethics: Inventing Right and Wrong.* Penguin, Harmondsworth (1977), especially Part 1. This analogy between ethics and

the concept of person was suggested to me by Christopher Cherry.

9. For example: Harré, R. 'Social elements as mind'. *British Journal of Medical Psychology* (1984) 57: pp. 127–135.
10. Fields, C. 'Human computer interaction: a critical synthesis'. *Social Epistemology* (1987), 1 pp. 5–25.
11. This is an allusion to the chequers playing program described by Samuel, A. L. in 'Some studies in machine learning using the game of checkers'. In Feigenbaum, E. A. and Feldman, J. (eds) *Computers and Thought.* McGraw Hill, New York (1963).
12. See Turkle, S. 'Thinking of yourself as a machine', Chap. 8, especially pp. 296 ff. In *The Second Self: Computers and the Human Spirit,* Granada, London (1984).
13. Asimov, I. in the stories collected in *I Robot* (1950) and *The Rest of the Robots* (1964), employs his three laws of robotics to provide a hierarchy of constraints on robot action so that by the later stories one robot has become an admirable member of human society. In *The Bicentennial Man* (1976), Asimov describes a robot that gradually becomes a human being.
14. The point is illustrated by S. Turkle (1984), especially pp. 281 ff. (see note 12), and the benefits of such a change are argued by Fields (1987) (see note 10.)

DISCUSSION QUESTIONS

1. How does Dolby define "person" at the beginning of his essay?
2. Why does he think the concept resists definition by specifying necessary characteristics of a person?
3. What does descriptive metaphysics (e.g., Strawson) presuppose about present conceptual usage?
4. How does Dolby relate Frankenstein's monster to common modern cultural stereotypes of robots?
5. What are Dolby's reasons for thinking that a concept like "person" is historically variable? Do you agree? Explain.
6. How does Dolby respond to the Christian argument that robots lack God-given souls and so cannot be persons?
7. Does Dolby think that the idea of the mind is a social construction? Explain.
8. What does Dolby mean by suggesting that emotional behavior could be simulated?
9. What evidence does Dolby give for his claim that the idea of a computer system as a person is proving attractive?
10. Is Dolby's story about the future conceptually coherent? Explain.

TROELS ENGBERG-PEDERSEN

Engberg-Pedersen studied Classics and Philosophy at the Universities of Copenhagen and Oxford. He is a member of the Royal Danish Academy of Sciences and a professor at the Institute of Biblical Exegesis in Copenhagen. His books include Aristotle's Theory of Moral Insight *(1983),* The Stoic Theory of Oikeiōsis *(1990), and* Paul and the Stoics *(2000).*

In this selection, he argues that Boethius was summing up the ancient Greek philosophical tradition rather than innovating when he defined the person as "an individual substance of a rational nature." The view that reason has the power to change a man's desires lies at the center of the ancient Greek concept of the person, according to Engberg-Pedersen. He argues that this view has been the target of attack by the common tradition in modern European thought (since Hume) in ethics and moral psychology. Boethius' definition of the person reflects a specifically Stoic understanding of the individual. Bernard Williams and Thomas Nagel share a modern understanding of individuality or subjectivity which opposes the Stoic view of the relationship in a human being of rationality and individuality. Consequently, this view held by Williams and Nagel threatens to erode the traditional (Stoic) concept of the person. Engberg-Pedersen defends the ancient Stoic concept against the modern view as expressed by Williams and Nagel by explicating the Stoics' developmental understanding of the self articulated in their theory of oikeiōsis. *The Stoics conceived of practical rationality and objectivity as logically inseparable from individuality and subjectivity, whereas Williams and Nagel see them as inescapably in conflict. The Stoics, Engberg-Pedersen contends, viewed human beings and human reason as bound to the world, and they saw human freedom as the exercise of our capacity to understand the world and ourselves better.*

*Stoic Philosophy and the Concept of the Person**

Like so many other time-hallowed concepts, that of the person is constantly under attack in modern philosophy, and one may be rather tempted to give it up altogether. Has it in fact any specific function at all? Does it add anything that is not already, and better, being done by other concepts in ethics and the philosophy of mind and action? Also, it may be suggested that the concept of the person is a specifically Christian idea. The Greeks did not have it, and therefore, so it may be said, with the demise of Christianity the concept of the person too will disappear.

Both claims, I believe, are right up to a point. It is true that the concept of the person is in a way parasitic on ideas in ethics and the philosophy of mind and action. There is no 'philosophy of the person' as such, and the work that must be done in order to elucidate the concept of the person belongs in those other philosophies. Still, I shall argue that the concept of the person has valuable work to do in bringing together a number of ideas developed in the other philosophies.

As for the second claim, it is true that classical Greek philosophy (Plato, Aristotle, the Stoics) had no special term for 'the person'—just as, and not unrelatedly, the Greeks had no exact term for 'freedom' of will nor indeed for 'will'. It also seems true that when the term *persona* came to have its full theoretical content in later ancient philosophy, one important factor behind this development was reflection on the Trinity and Christ's two natures. Still, it is decidedly false to suggest that the classical Greek philosophers had no concept of the person. On the contrary, it seems fair to say that whatever they said in ethics and those parts of their philosophy which we would include under philosophy of action was intended to bring out precisely what defines a person, namely a 'human being' (*anthrōpos*) in the rather exclusive sense in which the Greeks understood this. Therefore, when around AD 520 the Christian philosopher Boethius defined the person (*persona*) as 'an individual substance of a rational nature',[1] he was summing up the whole ancient tradition rather than being innovatory.

If, then, ancient Greek *and* Christian thought agree in their understanding of the person, and if

*This is an extensively revised version of the paper I read at the Aberystwyth conference. A later version was read to the Copenhagen Aristotelian group. I am grateful to the audience on both occasions for criticism that helped to clarify a number of points. Adam Morton, Finn Collin, Peter Sandøe, and the editor also provided written comments, for which I am most grateful.

Source: Troels Engberg-Pedersen, "Stoic Philosophy and the Concept of the Person." From *The Person and the Human Mind,* edited by Gill, Christopher (1990), 109–135 (edited). Reprinted by permission of Oxford University Press.

it is also the case that this understanding finds expression in their doctrines in ethics and the philosophy of action, then the modern attack on the concept of the person will presumably not be an insignificant affair. Rather, it will be part of a very general attack on central elements in what may (in spite of individual differences) fairly be called *the* common tradition in European thought in ethics and moral psychology. The aim of this essay is to diagnose what is, as I hope to show, a fairly important element in that clash between the ancients and the moderns, and moreover an element which seems to me to lie at the centre of the concept of the person. If that concept is to have any future, the element that I shall point to must prove capable of resisting attack.

What concerns me is an understanding of the function and power of reflection (rationality) in relation to an agent's desires which in spite of great individual differences is shared by Plato, Aristotle, and the Stoics. This is the view that the power of reason is such that it may in principle change a man's desires. I say 'in principle' mainly because of Aristotle. Although the matter is debated, it seems reasonably clear that Aristotle developed a view of the antecedents of action according to which two independent roots, namely belief and desire, are in the final analysis required in order to give a full explanation of it.[2] In spite of this, however, Aristotle insists, in his chapter in the *Nicomachean Ethics* (hereafter *EN*) on moral psychology, that 'the desiderative part' is made so as to 'obey' 'the rational part', which in turn 'gives commands' to the other one (*EN* 1. 13. 1102b25–1103a1). One may, but need not, find an inconsistency between these two views, but the point is that, no matter whether there is one or not, Aristotle himself apparently wished to claim that reason does have the power to change a man's desires—even when he held views which (at last initially) seem to point in a different direction. In Stoicism, not only is it explicitly claimed that reason is 'a craftsman of impulse' (Diogenes Laertius, 7. 86), but we shall see that a great deal of Stoic ethics and philosophy of action is intended to explicate the ramifications of this idea. This idea, I suggest, is 'common knowledge' down through the history of European thought on these matters. It begins to be questioned, famously, in Hume; and Kant's moral philosophy (with its distinction between the empirical and the noumenal world) may to a large degree be seen as an attempt to reinstate it in the face of criticism made of it by Hume and others. But Kant's attempt to stem the tide was unsuccessful and throughout the two last centuries it has come under constant attack, not only in philosophy, but also in new intellectual disciplines like psychology, so that by now it has more or less lost its hold on the general imagination.

I wish to discuss the idea here in the form given to it in Stoic philosophy. This is not merely for the reason that, historically, the Stoic formulation is particularly important. It *is* this: the Stoics confronted the question of the power of reason more directly than Aristotle did, both in their analysis of desire (impulse) and in their analysis of human freedom of the will. In other words, Stoicism contains the classic formulation of the idea, to which Plato and Aristotle may be said to lead. Furthermore, although the formulation of the idea given by Boethius in his definition of the person is reached by him through a series of dichotomies which are common Platonic, Aristotelian, and Stoic heritage,[3] I believe that the exact point of 'individual' in the definition is in fact specifically Stoic. So this definition, which stands at the gateway to medieval and later European thought, reflects a specifically Stoic understanding.

The other reason why I concentrate on the Stoics is that they developed the idea of reason as a craftsman of impulse in a way that invites comparison with certain ideas put forward in two quite recent and important books on ethics, Bernard Williams's *Ethics and the Limits of Philosophy* and Thomas Nagel's *The View from Nowhere*.[4] These two books are not directly concerned with the person in the sense in which I am working with the notion here,[5] but I have already stated my view that any valid assertion about the person will be made in ethics and other philosophical disciplines. The two books are also very different in their basic attitude towards morality. Still, as I shall try to show, they share an understanding of individuality or subjectivity which, irrespective of any differences between them, opposes them to the traditional view, as exemplified here by Stoicism, and in fact casts doubt on the general validity of the concept of the person.

My procedure here is as follows. I first mention the ideas in Williams and Nagel that interest me. Then I set forth certain relevant ideas in Stoicism with the following aims in view: (1) elucidating the view of subjectivity that Williams and Nagel share, by distinguishing it from the kind of subjectivity we find in Stoicism; (2) suggesting that the view of subjectivity that is found in Williams and Nagel, and the corresponding view of rationality in relation to individuality, threatens to erode the traditional concept of the person; (3) suggesting, with appropriate caution, that there may not, after all, be sufficient grounding for their view, and hence for its far-reaching implications.

Before starting I should perhaps emphasize that my topic here is not just the familiar one of the relationship of reason to desire (although I referred to that theme earlier). That theme is part of the topic, but not the whole of it. Rather my topic is the more general one of the relationship in a human being of rationality and individuality. On reason and desire, as is well known, Williams and Nagel disagree, Williams avowing himself to be 'sub-Humean' in the explanation of action[6] and Nagel adopting a more Kantian position.[7] On the wider and more fundamental question, however, I believe that they agree—thereby displaying their modernity.[8]

The point that I find significant in Williams and Nagel is their dissociation of what Nagel calls 'the good life' from what he calls 'the moral life.'[9] In the end Williams would hardly find any use at all for the notion of 'the moral life'. For one result of his sustained attack throughout *Ethics* on 'morality, the peculiar institution' is clearly that the idea of the moral life, in the basically Kantian sense in which I employ it, is discredited as being at all a useful one.[10] But Williams and Nagel agree in denying a view which was fundamental to ancient ethics, namely that the moral life *is* the good life. The Greeks (Aristotle and the Stoics) started out by asking about the *telos,* i.e. about the good life for a man, and then by various routes ended up by saying that a life consisting in behaviour that is ordinarily said to be moral is (at least part of) what the good life *is.* Furthermore, they more or less explicitly understood the moral life in that sense, that is a life in accordance with virtue and 'the noble', as one that is impersonally good in a way that points in the direction of the Kantian conception.[11] In Williams and Nagel, by contrast, the moral life, to the extent that it is allowed for at all (by Williams), is dissociated from the good life not just logically (as it is in ancient ethics too), but in fact: in certain situations concern about the good life will require one type of behaviour whereas concern about the moral life will require another, *and the two requirements are not to be reconciled.* We may note some of the underpinnings of this idea in Williams and Nagel, taking the two philosophers in that order.

As already noted, in Williams the dissociation of the good life and the moral life has the form of a 'challenge', which Nagel has christened 'Williams's Question',[12] 'to the claims of impersonal morality from the point of view of the individual agent to whom those claims are addressed. . . . The general objection [sc. Williams's] is that impersonal moralities demand too much of us, and that if we accept and act on those demands, we cannot lead good lives.' Behind this challenge there lies a view of man which finds expression in a number of different, but connected ideas. I mention some of them.[13]

There is first Williams's adoption of a 'sub-Humean' understanding of practical reasoning according to which so-called 'external reason statements, when definitely isolated as such, are false, or incoherent, or really something else misleadingly expressed. . . . The only real claims about reasons for action will be internal claims.'[14] This view, however, is not in itself sufficient to question the legitimacy of connecting the good life and the moral life. For as already hinted, whereas Aristotle may have subscribed to a Humean understanding of the explanation of action, he certainly did not dissociate the two lives.[15]

Next there is Williams's insistence on the plurality, and in fact the genuine incommensurability, of values.[16] This insistence is part of his general attack on utilitarianism, but it is also connected with two claims of his which take us nearer to the root idea behind his challenge to impersonal morality. One is his thesis that a man has 'a *ground* project or set of projects which are closely related to his existence and which to a significant degree give a meaning to his life', 'the idea of a man's ground projects providing the motive force which propels him into the future, and gives him a reason for living.'[17] With this idea comes, according to Williams, the possibility of 'radical conflict'[18] between the claims of a man's ground projects and those of moral impartiality of the Kantian kind, and once this possibility is allowed for, one is forced to admit that it is not a reasonable demand on the agent that the requirements of impartial morality should always win. 'There can come a point at which it is quite unreasonable for a man to give up, in the name of the impartial good ordering of the world of moral agents, something which is a condition of his having any interest in being around in that world at all.' Williams sums up this idea in the notion of 'having a character' and claims that 'the Kantians' omission of character is a condition of their ultimate insistence on the demands of impartial morality, just as it is a reason for finding inadequate their account of the individual'.[19] With the very last word in this quotation we are, I believe, at the heart of the matter.

The other claim that is linked with the idea of the incommensurability of values is that we need the concept of moral individuality if we are to give an adequate account of personal relations. People have dissimilar characters and projects and one context where this becomes of vital importance is that of personal relations. For these are precisely cases of commitment or involvement with a particular other person regarded as being different from others. Moreover, since personal relations fall under a man's ground projects, they too may come into conflict with impersonal morality, and this conflict too will be radical and in fact insoluble: 'somewhere . . . one reaches the necessity that such things as deep attachments to other persons will express themselves in the world in ways which cannot at the same time embody the impartial view, and that they also run the risk of offending against it'.[20]

A third idea behind Williams's challenge to impersonal morality is his historicist and relativist view of the ontological status of values. In 'The Truth in Relativism',[21] he argued for an understanding of relativism which allows it to be a logically coherent claim that relativism 'for ethical outlooks at least' is a correct standpoint. In *Ethics* he argues extensively[22] that relativism (for such outlooks) is in fact the correct standpoint. For my purposes the most important feature of this argument is Williams's repeated claim that philosophers have misconceived the power and role of reflection (reason). Instead of assuming that reflection can provide a universal justification of morality, which can then be applied to everyday practice, one should recognize that 'reflective criticism' should work in the opposite direction. [. . .] [W]e have reached what I take to be the root idea behind Williams's challenge to impersonal morality, namely the insistence on the non-transcendable character of 'the local view'. The question that calls for an answer is whether there is sufficient philosophical backing for this insistence, or whether it is rather an expression of a combination of Williams's own openly professed liberal individualism with a more widely shared, general modern sentiment to the same effect.

I may be somewhat briefer on Nagel's version of the view that I am tracking, since on the relevant points it is closely similar to Williams's. Nagel differs radically from Williams, of course, in that

Nagel's whole book is premised on the view that the idea of a 'point of view of the universe' is not, as Williams once put it,[23] 'memorably absurd', rather it brings out a vital property of a human being, which is that the human individual has an impulse and a capacity to transcend the subjective viewpoint and to adopt an objective viewpoint from which one sees oneself as just an individual among others. This viewpoint, so Nagel claims, is to be thought of as being 'centerless',[24] it is the viewpoint of 'someone considering the world in detachment from the perspective of any particular person within it'[25] or 'from no particular point of view'.[26] But the other side of Nagel's overall picture is that the objective view will need to recognize that the world that it is considering contains subjective points of view which cannot be replaced by the objective view, and this idea turns out to be closer to Williams's than might immediately appear.

In its first appearances in *The View from Nowhere* Nagel's claim takes up his old view[27] that there are subjective features of conscious mental processes which cannot be captured by objective thought, but only (if at all) by some kind of subjective imagination. Thus we shall never know exactly how scrambled eggs taste to a cockroach even if we develop a detailed objective phenomenology of the cockroach's sense of taste. But Nagel broadens this idea considerably when he goes on immediately to declare: 'When it comes to values, goals, and forms of life, the gulf may be even more profound.' Later in the book, in the chapters on value, ethics, and living rightly and living well, the gulf is taken to be an established fact precisely with regard to values, goals and forms of life.[. . .]

[. . .] His discussion is illuminating, but he ends by noting (rightly to my mind) that 'there remains something deeply unsatisfying about conflict between the good life and the moral life and the compromises between them.'[28] As in the case of Williams, I believe that the question should be whether there is in fact enough philosophical backing behind the insistence on individuals 'having their own lives to lead' (and so on)—or whether here too this insistence may not rather be an expression of a modern pluralistic individualism to which Nagel too declares his adherence.[29]

I now turn to the Stoic material.[. . .]

The Stoic doctrine that interests me is their account of *oikeiōsis,* i.e. of a mental process by which a human being will, if things go rightly, arrive at the true grasp of the good, namely that it is 'living in accordance with nature' (*convenientia naturae*) or rather, as we shall see, 'in accordance with the real'. The Stoic account has two stages. It first provides an account of the explanation of pre-rational action (of animals and infants), which is thought of by the Stoics as a non-normative account of pre-rational 'impulse' (Greek *hormē*). Next it gives an account of a change in understanding of the goals of action that comes with reason and issues in a grasp of what is truly good. The account of the second stage is itself twofold. At first the process results in the grasp that the true good is *convenientia naturae,* where the latter is understood in such a way that it does not coincide with anything *we* would include under 'the moral'.[30] (By contrast, the Stoics themselves did connect *convenientia naturae* with 'virtue' and 'the noble', i.e. with *to kalon,* which from Aristotle onwards is the common Greek expression for what belongs in the 'moral' sphere as opposed, for example, to considerations of prudence.)[31] Later, then, the process results in a grasp of something that we too will immediately call a moral good, normally the goodness of justice.

Let me explain these stages in more detail. The essence of the first stage is this.[32] Any pre-rational action that is governed by impulse is to be explained in the following terms. (I) The immediate logical starting-point is the animal's love of self, and impulse is then to be explained in terms of an awareness on the part of the animal that things in the world either 'belong' or are 'alien' to the self, of whose 'constitution' or structure the animal is also aware. A child, for example, will have some instinctive awareness of its own bodily structure and, due to its love of self, it will consider certain things, e.g. food, which tend to preserve that structure, as 'belonging' to itself, whereas other things, e.g. lack of shelter, will be considered to be 'alien' to it. In the appropriate circumstances such awareness will issue in action. (2) This account of pre-rational impulse seems, at first glance, to be based on the familiar idea that an animal's response to its environment combines an evaluative component (love of self) with a certain set of non-evaluative beliefs in the form of an awareness of the structure of the self and of the relationship of certain things in the world to that structure, namely whether they will tend to preserve or destroy it. However, underlying what immediately appeared to be the logical starting-point (love of self), the Stoics postulated another kind of relation to the self, viz. self-awareness (*sensus sui,* in Cicero's formulation) (*Fin.* 3. 5. 16). In fact it appears that they worked with a logical triad which (starting from what is most basic) consists of (*a*) 'being aware of oneself', (*b*) 'seeing oneself as belonging to oneself', and (*c*) 'loving oneself'. [. . .]

[. . .] What the Stoics seem to be saying is that one cannot think of a being who is aware of himself, and hence of the fact that he is distinct from the rest of the world, but who is not also concerned about himself or about maintaining in existence the distinct being that he is.

What the Stoics have given us so far is an analysis of pre-rational impulse with the following main features. Such impulse is to be understood in terms of the idea of what we may call a subjective viewpoint, and there are two aspects of this claim. First, the viewpoint is *subjective* in the sense that it is ineradicably based in the agent's awareness of his own self. Whatever is seen is seen *from* the particular perspective that is created by self-awareness in the way I suggested. Secondly, the subjective viewpoint is to be understood precisely as a *viewpoint,* as a perspective from which things are *seen.* The Stoics are analysing impulse, which is a generic term for desire, but they are claiming that impulse should be understood in terms of two mental states which are not evaluative: (1) awareness of individual identity and (2) belief about the 'constitution' of the self and about what things in the world preserve and destroy the self as so constituted.

The Stoics give no extended argument for the truth of this way of understanding pre-rational impulse. Rather, their claim is an a priori one.[33] It is, however, based on an understanding of the relation of sentient beings to the world which is of crucial importance to the whole doctrine. According to the Stoics, when an animal or infant starts 'dividing' the world between that which belongs and that which is alien, the logical starting-point, as we have seen, is self-awareness. But this does not mean that it is the self which in some sense posits how it is constituted and how, consequently, the world should be divided. On the contrary, even in its most rudimentary state of awareness the self is concerned from the start with judging the truth about its own constitution and the divisions of the world. The animal's mental equipment is right from the start adapted towards discovering how things are. This view is a naturalistic one, and it coheres closely with, and is indeed a part of, Stoic epistemology. It is also, as I think we should say, a normative view, in the sense that it presupposes without argument a certain description of sentient beings at a fundamental level which while being taken to be true is also understood as having normative consequences (at least potentially): if a sentient being does not fulfil the process of development described in this account, it goes wrong and should in principle be corrected. I am not going to argue that this view is true (though I believe it is), merely to note that on this view sentient beings are from the start operating in an area of what may be called 'public discourse', an area where the presupposed aim is truth or being right and where the criteria for truth-assertions are shared or public.[34]

The main point is that although the Stoics saw every case of intentional behaviour as being based in a subjective viewpoint that is ineliminable, they would not have understood (or at least would have pressed for further information on) the notion of ineradicable subjectivity as regards the *content* of the subjective viewpoint. The Stoics stressed the importance of the notion of the self to such an extent that one may be tempted to claim that they even discovered it. But they did not allot to it any ineradicably subjective content. On the contrary, whatever content it has was thought by them to be in principle public and accessible to rational discourse.

The next stage in the Stoic account of *oikeiōsis* comes with the arrival of reason. Essentially this stage consists in becoming aware, by a process of self-reflection, of the value that underlies behaviour at the first stage. Once a man has acquired reason he will come to see two things. The first is that, although at the first stage the various particular objects appeared to be valuable and good since they 'belong' to the self, what is truly valuable (and hence the only thing that truly deserves the predicate 'good') is in fact the single 'value' which underlies those particular judgements, namely truth or being right about what belongs. That, then, is the good for man, *convenientia naturae* in the sense of being right about 'nature' or about what is the case (as regards belonging or being alien to somebody). The second thing that will become clear to a man during this process of self-reflection is that in reflecting on his own earlier acts and discovering in that way the single underlying value of being right about what belongs, he is making use of a special property of his, namely his rationality. In other words, in exercising his rational capacity and thus acquiring a belief about the good for man, he also becomes aware of his own rationality and comes to see rationality as a constituent of his own self. The result is that the belief about the good that he has acquired becomes a belief about his own good, and hence it becomes (at least potentially) action-guiding.

The good that is so grasped is not yet what we would call a 'moral' good. It is, in Stoic terms, as we already noted: they call it *to kalon* or *honestum*, and the grasp of it is virtue. And so they are entitled to say that what in the process of *oikeiōsis* began as a search for 'the good', in the sense of one's *telos* (and evidently one's own *telos*), has ended up by identifying that good as moral virtue. The reason why the Stoics could understand *convenientia naturae* (in the sense in which I have explained it) as a 'moral' good is that they saw the defining property of those mental states that were ordinarily called moral virtues as lying in the dissociation from the immediate, subjective view of values—and this dissociation is the essence of *oikeiōsis* at the rational level as I have just described it.[35] This dissociation is the result of what Nagel calls man's 'objectifying impulse'. It is not yet a dissociation from oneself in relation to others (and hence not moral in our sense). Rather, it is a dissociation from oneself in the sense of one's immediate, subjective view, and an adoption of a view of oneself that is external since it draws on public or objective criteria in order to determine the truth or falsity of one's immediate view of what is valuable. Let us consider further the exact form of this dissociation, thereby bringing the Stoic material to bear on some of the ideas we noted in Williams and Nagel.

The Stoics drew a fundamental distinction between what is good, which is one thing alone, as we have seen, and things that are *proēgmena*. The good alone is 'choiceworthy' (*haireton*). The *proēgmena* consist of most of those particular objects that appeared choiceworthy at the first stage of *oikeiōsis*. At the mature stage they are no longer considered choiceworthy (and rightly so), but they are still *proēgmena*. How should we translate this term? In two ways. (1) Such things are 'preferable' in the sense of 'objectively to be preferred'. For in many cases these things are the goals pursued in actions which are objectively right since they are directed towards procuring what (in the objective view) genuinely belongs to a given individual. Here the objective view *confers* value on the things that are *proēgmena*. (2) But such things are also 'preferable' in the sense that they will also be *actually* 'preferred' by an individual who is applying the objective view. For he sees them as belonging to himself *qua* individual, and hence as worthy objects of pursuit: he would rather have them than not.

The two senses of *proēgmenon* that I have distinguished clearly correspond, to some extent, to the two points of view that give rise, in Williams and Nagel, to the distinction between the moral life and the good life. It is also well known that whereas Williams and Nagel insist on the possibility of conflict, the Stoics denied this possibility. Why this difference? I believe that the reason is to be found in a different understanding, in the two cases, of individuality and rationality and of their mutual relationship.

Take first the case of (practical) rationality. As we saw, Nagel understands the objective viewpoint, which he associates with practical rationality, as centreless. Williams ridicules this idea. In fact, Nagel's formulation may be only a *façon de parler,*[36] but why is it necessary? Presumably because of Nagel's assumption that if one does not understand the objective view as centreless, if practical rationality remains *somebody's,* then it will necessarily lose its rational and objective character. Contrast with this the Stoic understanding of practical rationality. In Stoicism, practical rationality is consistently regarded as belonging to *somebody* and to somebody who has, and retains, an individual self throughout the development of the objective view. The objective view is a view *on oneself,* and this fact has a number of welcome consequences. One is that we can avoid the idea, which when taken literally is in fact absurd, of a 'point of view of the universe'. Another consequence, which I hinted at when explaining the theory, is that there is now no difficulty in understanding how one should come to *act* on the insights gained in applying the objective view. Most importantly, however, in Stoicism, in contrast to Nagel, there is no suggestion that the connection of the objective view to the individual makes it any less objective or rational.

Take then the other pole, individuality. Why should Nagel in fact assume that once we locate the objective view in an individual it will lose its objective character? It seems fairly clear that this is because in Nagel, and in Williams too, the notion of the subjective or individual is heavily loaded in some way that one would wish to see further specified. The Stoics, by contrast, did have the notion of the subjective or individual, namely the theoretically crucial concept of the self, but they understood it in such a way that it is not opposed to the notion of objectivity and rationality. In Stoicism the subjective viewpoint is not allotted any *content* that cannot in principle be taken over by the objective view. Here what is 'radically subjective' is nothing beyond the sheer fact, the importance of which cannot admittedly be overstated, of the indexicality of the objective view, i.e. its being ineradicably bound up with a given individual. So, just as practical rationality and objectivity are conceived by the Stoics as being logically inseparable from individuality and as 'matching' it, so individuality and subjectivity are conceived as being logically inseparable from rationality and objectivity. On the Stoic conception, the former two presuppose the latter two.[37]

The Stoic conception of man is therefore that of a being who is, so to speak, intermediate between being merely individual (a 'thing') and no longer individual (God). His intermediate status is bound up with his sentience, for sentience already marks a step from the object-like status of pure individuality, and yet his continuing sentience marks his continuing status as an individual. What defines the middle ground is an unbreakable, logical connection of individuality and rationality.

Against the background of this conception of the adult human being, how should one understand the Stoic category of the *proēgmena?* It has often been suggested that, after introducing their radical view that there is only one thing that is good, the Stoics bowed to human nature, so to speak, by bringing in the *proēgmena* as things of secondary value. Nothing could be further from the truth. We noted above that things are *proēgmena* in two ways that correspond to the two points of view that an adult human being may adopt. Note then that in an adult human being his dual view of the *proēgmena* is 'fused' in such a way that he retains his subjective interest in them, when this is allowed by the objective view, but loses that interest, when this is required by the objective view. In a way, things that are *proēgmena* remain 'preferable' both objectively and subjectively even when the objective view tells one to act in ways that will *not* procure such things for onself;[38] but in these cases they are subjectively *proēgmena* in the sense that the agent *would* rather have had them. There is an actual loss of interest in those things, but not of such a kind as to render the agent's attitude 'impersonal'. Once more the suggestion is that the subjective and the objective views should be kept together. The Stoics managed to do this in the way I have attempted to explain.

In order to explore the Stoic conception of the relation between the two views we may consider the second phase of their account of the development towards objectivity in an adult human being. This is the phase that results in a grasp of the moral good proper (in our sense of 'moral'), namely the goodness of justice.[39] In its essence the theory is very simple. Just as in the first phase (the development from the primitive to the mature grasp of value), so in the second phase the starting-point is something the Stoics took to be a pervasive empirical fact: that parents love their children. This love is both intelligible as an expression of the basic instinct of self-love, since children are an 'extension' of the parents, and also a genuine case of an altruistic attitude, since it is love of the children for their own sake.[40] All children, then, have experienced this attitude and they reciprocate it through love for their parents. As reason comes, along with adulthood, the human being extends his love for his parents (whom he, in turn, saw as 'belonging' to himself) to all other human beings, whom he now sees as also 'belonging' to himself since they share in the rationality that he now realizes in himself. This newly acquired affection for all mankind is the attitude that underlies justice.

The details in this picture may appear unpersuasive, but the point that is relevant in the present context is that the doctrine is one more example of how the Stoics aimed to start from a subjective perspective and to develop it in the direction of a genuinely objective one in such a way that there is no loss of personal content once the objective view has been reached. It would surely be perverse to suggest that on the Stoic view children would (or should) stop loving their parents (or vice versa) once they have reached the objective view. Rather, as in the case of *proēgmena,* we should take it that in the adult human being the two types of concern are fused into a single one; and although, in this fused concern, the objective aspect must always win, room is still left for personal concern. The reason why the Stoics could make both claims is that they saw no discrepancy between the subjective and objective viewpoints, but saw them as essentially united. [. . .]

[. . .] Williams rejected the project of grounding ethical considerations in rational freedom. One might perhaps paraphrase his argument as claiming that, in the case of practical deliberation, there is not a sufficient degree of freedom for the project to get off the ground precisely because of the irreducibly first-personal elements in such deliberation. I now turn to a line of thought in Nagel that appears very similar and leads Nagel to deny not only that human beings have freedom of the will, but also that there is any coherent notion of the freedom of the will at all. First, however, I shall outline, very briefly, the Stoic view on this matter. Their doctrine here is extremely complex[41] and I shall concentrate on those elements that are immediately relevant to the present discussion.

The doctrine has two parts, one intended to account for freedom of action and one for freedom of the will. I am concerned only with the latter. On one influential interpretation of the Stoic doctrine of moral responsibility and freedom,[42] when the Stoics say that human actions are 'up to us' they are saying that our actions are 'ours' in the sense that they are not directly caused from the outside; rather the single most important causal factor lies in ourselves, in our own 'character', 'personality' or 'individual nature'.[43] But then, it is sometimes asked, how will a reference to the individual's character or individual 'nature' (understood as both determining the particular action and being themselves determined by the external factors of heredity and environment) in fact make the individual morally responsible and even free?[44]

I believe that it can be shown that the Stoics both wished (and were able) to claim that the human being is free even in relation to his own character and also that in a different respect human freedom is bound. This comes out best in certain Stoic passages in the Christian philosopher Origen. In one of these[45] Origen contrasts animal movement at large with the intelligent behaviour of a rational being. The rational agent, so he says, is capable of 'somehow following his own movement'. This is clearly another formulation of the basic element in *oikeiōsis,* namely self-reflection. A man has the capacity for being distanced from his own immediate impulse or understanding, and it is this capacity which enables him, as Origen says elsewhere,[46] to 'judge his presentations and reject some or accept some as a guide to action', 'to handle them in this or the opposite way by using reason as a judge and inquirer into how one should react to these particular external things.' What Origen describes here is of course practical deliberation, and it is precisely the capacity for practical deliberation, as the Stoics understood this, which makes a man morally responsible, because free—even in relation to his own character. For on the Stoic view, just as an impulse is at base a (practical) belief about the world, so an agent's character is a set of beliefs, and in practical deliberation a person is capable of raising in a way that is genuinely new the question whether his previous understanding was in fact correct.

But note two ways in which, if human freedom is the freedom of deliberation, such freedom will also be bound. It will be bound, first, in that it is essentially committed to discovering what the world is like. As Origen says:[47] we *ourselves* reject certain impressions *as false.* Elsewhere[48] he says that the mind assents to something *because of* certain plausibilities. This is the point at which the freedom of reason is bound no less than anything else; it is determined by the way the world is, that is by fate. In a splendid remark,[49] Origen explicitly distinguishes his Stoic understanding of what is 'up to us' from what looks like a more modern notion of freedom. 'If', he says, 'somebody should want what is up to us to be *detached from the (world as a) whole* so that we do not choose something *because* something has happened to us, then he has forgotten that he is part of the universe and that he is contained in a community of human beings and of what contains.' Reason does not exist in a vacuum. Reason is *about the world* and its point lies in grasping the world. It would be a complete misunderstanding of the role of reason in binding human beings and the world together, were one to understand what is 'up to us', and hence the freedom that reason gives us, as being completely detached from any relation to the world. Rather the freedom that reason gives is a freedom to reach a *better* understanding of the world, to reach a grasp of the world that is more likely to be *true.*

There is a second way in which human freedom (understood as the freedom of deliberation) will be bound. As reason works in deliberation it is a capacity to extend infinitely towards objective truth, but the specific understanding of any given individual will necessarily be limited, and therefore his assent and decision will in fact be bound by the actual limitations on the scope of his reach towards the whole of truth. The Stoics would evidently admit that at some point any given individual will necessarily have to decide for himself about how the world appears to him, but I conjecture (it cannot be more) that they would insist that this fact does not diminish his freedom; *for,* since he is rational, such an individual will *know,* first that he may be wrong about the world, and secondly that he *could* have made further attempts to find out about it. This knowledge, indeed, seems implied in the very ability to deliberate. [. . .]

[. . .] For the Stoics there is no inherent property in the subjective view which makes it unfit as an object of rational reflection. For, although the subjective view is ineliminable as the starting-point of deliberation and the basis of action, it is restricted to being just that. As for its content (first-personal practical beliefs), these are of the same type as the beliefs formulated by the objective view, and so descriptive in form. There is nothing in the subjective view that the objective view will show to *be* nothing.

This concerns the pole of individuality in the dual scheme of the individual and the rational. Here, as we have seen, although the Stoics insisted, and very strongly, on the notion of the self, they also regarded any content that is ascribed to it as being public, rather than private, and therefore as open to rational examination by other rational beings. Nagel's despair that ultimately human beings cannot transcend themselves would not, therefore, be theirs. As regards the other pole in the scheme, in particular Nagel's suggestion that reason at first leads us to believe that we can, in an absolute sense, choose 'everything about ourselves, including all our principles of choice' (*View* p. 118), and that this is the content of our intuitive idea of autonomy, the Stoics would, if anything, find the suggestion preposterous. For on the Stoic view human beings are bound to the world and so is human reason. Still it gives them freedom of the only intelligible kind, by making them capable of understanding the world and themselves better, which is what they have been trying to do all along. Human freedom is having or exercising this capacity, nothing more nor less.

I believe that the Stoic conception of the human being as one in whom individuality and rationality are logically connected, and their concomitant views on impulse, practical deliberation and freedom, are worthy of further exploration with a view to assessing their independent, philosophical merit. This has not been my aim in this essay. Rather, I have wished, as it were, to impersonate Stoic philosophy and to present certain central tenets of that philosophy in the form of a challenge to a view of human subjectivity that seems to be shared by Bernard Williams and Thomas Nagel, but which one might wish to see further clarified and argued for.

The perspective of my argument will be clear. I suggested initially that there is a single concept of the person which runs through centuries of European thought; and that this concept, as formulated by Boethius, for instance, on the point of transition between the ancient and the medieval world, is specifically Stoic in its insistence on the connection between individuality and rationality in a person. I then introduced into my picture claims of Williams and Nagel in ethics and in the philosophy of mind which are incompatible with the Stoic conception of the person even though the two philosophers do not set out to dispute that conception explicitly. The perspective was that if these claims are correct, then the concept of the person that has reigned for centuries should fall.[50]

But should it not be allowed to fall? Even if the Stoic conception can be upheld against the individualistic views of Williams and Nagel, it may seem that it presupposes, without defence, an unchanging conception of human nature, and that it is, in any case, too generalized to be of much practical use. As for the first objection, although the Stoics did not themselves work with the idea of historical change, one may fairly easily extend their conception of a person to take account of this idea too. For as I have explained it, their conception is a second-order notion, which allows for changes in human nature at the first-order level and correspondingly for changing views of what 'belongs' to a human being. And as for the second objection, while the Stoic notion of the person (and their concomitant view of the good as living in accordance with the real) is in fact general and does not determine, in specific detail, how human beings should live, it seems likely that it was never intended to do this, in any strong sense of 'determine'. What it gives is the formula for a general view of human beings which may serve as a framework for reflection on how to live one's own life—but which will also place important moral constraints on the result of such reflection. It is not clear that the property that is conveyed in this formula is itself subject to historical change, nor that the formula may not do valuable work in reflection on the good life.

NOTES

1. *Liber de persona et duabus naturis,* ch. 3, in J. P. Migne (ed.), *Patrologia Latina,* lxiv. 1343c: *Persona est naturae rationalis individua substantia.*
2. I have argued for this in *Aristotle's Theory of Moral Insight* (Oxford, 1983), pt. II.
3. See *Liber de persona,* ch. 2, in Migne (ed.), *Patrologia,* lxiv. 1342c–1343c.
4. *Ethics* (London, 1985); *View* (New York, 1986).
5. Nagel, of course, discusses extensively the question of personal *identity.*
6. See esp. 'Internal and External Reasons', in *Moral Luck: Philosophical Essays 1973–1980* (Cambridge, 1981), 101–13.
7. *View,* pp. 149–52—and of course in Nagel, *The Possibility of Altruism* (Oxford, 1970), *passim.*
8. In spite of Nagel's professed reactionary stance, *View,* pp. 9 ff.
9. *View,* ch. 10, *passim.* Nagel himself declines to define the two terms in advance, since 'their analysis is part of the problem' (p. 193). In this chapter I understand 'the moral life' as 'a life that complies with moral requirements' (so Nagel, p. 193), but understand moral requirements as being impersonal requirements. 'The general opposition we are concerned with is that between the claims of impersonal morality and the personal perspective of the agent to whom they are addressed' (Nagel, p. 192).
10. Williams has a lot to say throughout *Ethics* about a life which he calls an ethical life. But this life is defined precisely in opposition to the moral life as I understand it here.
11. This may seem a very strong claim. I have argued for it, as regards Aristotle, in *Aristotle's Theory,* chs. 2–3; and the affinity of the Stoic theory with Kant's will become apparent later in this essay. Williams, who is very sympathetic to Aristotle and wishes to enlist his theory in support of his own attack on 'morality', does not confront this aspect of the Aristotelian theory in his otherwise excellent discussion of Aristotle in *Ethics,* ch. 3. But then, in the final analysis he of course stands back from the Aristotelian theory when he comes near to its view of human nature and its function in the theory. (See *Ethics,* ch. 3, pp. 52–3.)
12. *View,* pp. 189–93. The quotation is from p. 191.
13. In what follows I often refer to Williams's writings previous to *Ethics.* This is because some of the formulations of particular aspects of Williams's general view seem sharper there. I do not find any fundamental change from these writings to *Ethics.* If one wants to spell out the *basis* for Williams's position in *Ethics,* e.g. for his final rejection of the Aristotelian theory (cf. n. 11 above), which turns on the possibility of a gap between 'the agent's perspective', or 'personal aspirations', and 'the outside view', one will often find it helpful to go back to the earlier writings.
14. 'Internal and External Reasons', in *Moral Luck,* p. 111.
15. Williams of course knows this and brings out well in *Ethics,* ch. 3, the difference between Aristotle and himself.
16. See e.g. 'Conflicts of Values' in *Moral Luck,* pp. 71–82.
17. See 'Persons, Character and Morality' in *Moral Luck,* pp. 1–19. Quotations are from pp. 12 and 13. (Williams's emphasis.)
18. Ibid. 12.
19. Quotations, ibid. 14.
20. Ibid. 15–19. Quotation from p. 18.
21. In *Moral Luck,* pp. 132–43. The quotation is from p. 142.
22. See esp. ch. 9.
23. *Moral Luck,* Pref., p. xi.
24. *The View,* pp. 18, 140.
25. Ibid. 153.
26. Ibid. 161.

27. From 'What is it Like to Be a Bat?', in *Mortal Questions* (Cambridge, 1979), 165–80.
28. *View,* p. 205.
29. Ibid. 188, 207.
30. I take it to be constitutive of the ordinary modern notion of the moral that it has to do with an individual's relations with others.
31. The distinction that I am implying here between the Greek understanding of the 'moral' sphere and the modern one should not be pressed. It is precisely a question whether 'the Greek' understanding, as expressed in their use of the term *kalon,* does differ so strongly as it is often taken from 'the modern' understanding with its strong emphasis on the relationship with others and on considerations of justice.
32. I have discussed all the Stoic topics that I touch on in this essay much more extensively in a book entitled *The Stoic Theory of Oikeiōsis* (Aarhus, 1990). In the present essay I incorporate from the book some fairly important changes in relation to my earlier paper, 'Discovering the good: *Oikeiōsis* and *kathēkonta* in Stoic Ethics', in M. Schofield and G. Striker (edd.), *The Norms of Nature: Studies in Hellenistic Ethics* (Cambridge, 1986), 145–83. The main textual evidence on *oikeiōsis* on Cicero, *De Finibus (Fin.),* 3. 5. 16–7. 25.
33. Cf. in the sentence from Cicero quoted above: 'they could not feel desire towards anything unless . . .'.
34. This way of putting it may seem both anachronistic and somewhat ludicrous once it is thought to apply to cockroaches and the like. The first objection I shall merely waive. As for the second, the Stoics fairly clearly wished to understand non-rational animals (and infants) as *pre*-rational, i.e. to understand them *on the basis of* their understanding of rational animals.
35. See e.g. Cicero, *Fin.* 3. 7. 25.
36. 'way of speaking'. [Ed.]
37. Recall that pre-rational individuality (the self-awareness of non-rational animals and infants) is precisely understood by the Stoics as pre-rational, i.e. it is understood on the basis of their view of rational individuality.
38. This has to do with the fact that *proēgmena* are *types* of thing. They may therefore retain their character of being valuable even though reason may in particular cases order one to abandon them.
39. The main textual evidence is in Cicero, *Fin.* 3. 19. 62–20. 66.
40. The term in Cicero is 'care' *(cura),* e.g. in *De Officiis,* 1. 2. 12.
41. I have discussed it in detail in *Stoic Theory,* ch. 6.
42. C. Stough, 'Stoic Determinism and Moral Responsibility', in J. M. Rist (ed.), *The Stoics* (Los Angeles, 1978), 203–31.
43. Stough, p. 219.
44. Cf. e.g. B. Inwood, *Ethics and Human Action in Early Stoicism* (Oxford, 1985), 68.
45. H. von Arnim (ed.), *Stoicorum Veterum Fragmenta,* ii (Leipzig, 1903, repr. Stuttgart, 1964), fr. 989.
46. Ibid. ii. 988, 990.
47. Ibid. 989.
48. Ibid. 988.
49. Ibid. 996.
50. In fact it is not clear what the position of Williams and Nagel is in relation to the person. Williams has some derogatory remarks on the concept in *Ethics,* p. 114, Nagel has none (on the idea of a person as opposed to questions of personal identity) in *View.*

DISCUSSION QUESTIONS

1. Do you agree with Engberg-Pedersen that the ancient Greek thinkers (Plato, Aristotle, and the Stoics as represented by Cicero and Epictetus in this book) and Christian thinkers (like Boethius) basically agreed in their understanding of the person? Explain.
2. Explain the two stages of the theory of *oikeiōsis* as described by Engberg-Pedersen.
3. Engberg-Pedersen is tempted to claim that the Stoics discovered the notion of the self. Given your study of the history of the person through the readings in this book, are you similarly tempted? Explain.
4. In the discussion of certain Stoic passages in Origen, how does the capacity for practical deliberation make a man free and thus morally responsible?
5. Explain the way in which, on Origen's Stoic view, "the freedom of reason is bound no less than anything else." Do you agree?
6. At the end of the essay, how does Engberg-Pedersen respond to the objections that the Stoic concept of the person presupposes an ahistorical, unchanging conception of human nature and one that is too generalized to be useful?

Chapter 39

OSWALD HANFLING

Hanfling is the author of The Quest for Meaning *(1988),* Wittgenstein's Later Philosophy *(1989),* Great Philosophers: Ayer *(1997), and the eBook* Philosophy and Ordinary Language. *He edited* Philosophical Aesthetics *(1992) and is an honorary member of the philosophy faculty at The Open University, Oxford.*

In this reading Hanfling holds that when philosophers speak of "persons" they usually do not mean humans in a biological sense, but rather beings with a certain moral status: those whom we respect in certain ways, and who are expected to respect us in similar ways. This ascription of moral status is connected with an "inner life." He argues against the view that machines that acted like natural (e.g., human) people would lack an inner life, and this would prevent us from treating them as real people. He reasons that skepticism about the feelings of artificial people would be no better than skepticism about the feelings of natural people. Skepticism about the feelings of natural people is simply the traditional "problem" of establishing the existence of minds other than our own. Hanfling follows Wittgenstein in holding that our language-games of relations with other people are neither based on evidence, nor subject to refutation by contrary evidence. Thus an artificial person subjected to discrimination because of his origin as an artifact would be entitled to accuse us of "artifactism," just as a woman or a black subjected to discrimination would be entitled to accuse us of sexism or racism. Hanfling describes a practical situation, in dialogue form, in which it would be impossible for us to avoid entering into an obligation of promising with an artificial person.

Machines as Persons?

I

The subject of this symposium is sometimes introduced by asking whether machines could think. This way of introducing it may be misleading, for it may seem as if it were merely about a particular activity, called 'thinking'. The question would then seem to have the same character as 'Can machines make a noise?'. But thinking is not something that can be treated in isolation from other personal qualities. What we need to consider is whether, or to what extent, a machine could participate in the whole complex of qualities, activities, attitudes, thoughts, feelings and moral relationships that we regard as essential to being a person—whether, in this sense, machines could be persons.

But this brings us to a second pitfall. In formulating the issue as being about *machines,* we are in danger of having settled it in the very act of formulation. This is because the word 'machine' is commonly used to mean an object that is *not,* like ourselves, a person. This is not merely because, as it happens, all or most of the machines we know of are different, in all sorts of ways, from ourselves, but because the very quality of being *mechanical* is one that goes against our conception of a person. We do sometimes describe people as acting in a mechanical way, but this means that their actions are deficient in the characteristics of human action, such as thought, responsibility, etc. The concept of a machine, it may be said, excludes the ascription of personal qualities to machines in any but a diluted or metaphorical sense. In this way the issue may be reduced to a 'merely verbal' level, and readily disposed of.

There are, of course, machines and machines. The vast majority of those in our experience—lawnmowers, aeroplanes, sewing machines and the like—have little resemblance to ourselves, and the idea of regarding such objects as people would strike us as suitable only for nursery stories. Nowadays, however, we may be more likely to think of computers as being the relevant kind of machine. Yet we may feel little inclination to ascribe personhood to what is, after all, a box standing on the desk, however complex its design and impressive its performance may be. Here we may be reminded of Wittgenstein's remark: 'Only of a living human being and what resembles (behaves like) a living human being can one say: it has sensations; it sees; is blind; hears; is deaf; is conscious or unconscious.'[1] This may suggest that what we should be talking about are robots, that this is where the required resemblance may be found. But the word 'robot' too is laden with negative connotations. Nowadays many car factories are operated by means of robots, but no one would be inclined to treat such objects, however ingeniously designed, as persons. Again, to say of some real person that he behaves like a robot is to say that his behaviour falls short of normal human behaviour; lacking the qualities which distinguish human behaviour from that of a mere machine. In this way the term

Source: Oswald Hanfling, "Machines as Persons?" in *Human Beings,* Royal Institute of Philosophy Supplement 29, David Cockburn, ed., Cambridge University Press, 1991: 25–34 (excerpts). Reprinted with the permission of the author.

'robot' might be applied to someone who, for example, follows a leader with blind obedience as a result of brain-washing. Such a person has lost the faculty of critical evaluation; he behaves, as we say, like a robot. Hence, if we ask whether robots could be people, the very meaning of the word 'robot' may prevent us from giving a positive answer.

A safer way to pose the issue is by means of the neutral 'artifact'. What the issue is really about is whether an artifact could be a person; or, putting it the other way round, whether a person could be an artifact—a thing made by human hands and not born of woman in the traditional way. If the answer is 'yes', then it would not follow that *machines* or *robots* could be people, for the artifacts which are people could not properly, and without causing confusion, be described as machines or robots. This, indeed, would be an aspect of the personal status of these artifacts. We may take it that these (artificial) persons would *resent* any description of them as mere machines or robots, and they might well accuse anyone who speaks in this way of *artifactism*. People, they would say, should be judged by their personal qualities and not according to their origins. To describe one of them as behaving like a robot merely because of his origins would be mistaken and unjust in the same way as the ascription of negative qualities to a Jew or negro merely because of his origins.

[. . .] The interesting question . . . arises when we turn to artifacts whose behaviour would not appear mechanical; where . . . there are overwhelmingly impressive resemblances with human behaviour, where the objects in question appear to act in every respect like human beings and they look exactly like us, too.*

The supposition that their actions resemble ours 'in every respect' is not, however, as easy to make as it may appear. I am not thinking here of technical difficulties that may stand in the way of such creations, for these are not the philosopher's concern. There is no obstacle to supposing any state of affairs, however far fetched it may be in practical terms, provided that the supposition is logically coherent. In this case, however, certain difficulties arise if we try to fill in the details of the artifact's behaviour. How, for instance, would he behave with regard to eating and drinking, and—let us face it—defecating? If his insides were radically different from ours—microchips, and not flesh and blood, let us say—then these functions are hardly likely to be similar to ours. But what, in that case, would happen about feelings, such as hunger, which are such an important part of our humanity?

Again, how are we to envisage the artifact's medical situation? Does he sometimes consult a doctor? Is he subject to the thousand natural shocks that flesh is heir to? There are shocks and infirmities which only creatures of flesh and blood can suffer, and whose existence is an important part of the human condition. Again, what are we to suppose about the artifact's sex life, his memories of childhood or his attitude to death?

There are many details that need filling in before we can take up the supposition of an artifact who acts like a human being 'in every respect'. Perhaps it would be easier to think in terms of a being who is indeed made of flesh and blood—synthetized flesh and blood—rather than the usually postulated computer materials. (This might be especially important with regard to the

*For example, Rachael, Pris, and Roy, the NEXUS 6 Replicants engineered by the Rosen Corporation in the Philip K. Dick novel, *Do Androids Dream of Electric Sheep* (originally published in 1968). Ridley Scott's science fiction film version (1982) is introduced thus: Early in the 21st century, the Tyrell corporation advanced robot evolution into the NEXUS phase—a being virtually identical to a human—known as the Replicant. The NEXUS 6 Replicants were superior in strength and agility, and at least equal in intelligence, to the genetic engineers who created them. Replicants were used off-world as slave labor, in the hazardous exploration and colonization of other planets. After a bloody mutiny by a NEXUS 6 combat team in an off-world colony, Replicants were declared illegal on earth—under penalty of death. Special police squads—BLADERUNNER UNITS—had orders to shoot to kill, upon detection, any trespassing Replicant. This was not called execution. It was called retirement. [Ed.]

artifact's *face,* given the importance of the face in human relations.) But if we take this course, then the issue (originally expressed in terms of 'machines') is in danger of being trivialized. For if, as we may suppose, the synthetic materials are indistinguishable from their natural counterparts, including the processes of metabolism, growth etc., then there will be no difference left between the artificial beings and ourselves, apart from the facts of origin. (We might think of this in terms of 'test tube babies', using the term in a more radical sense than now, to mean artificial creations.)

It might be held that even in this case the ascription of personal qualities and status would be problematic. However, I shall address the issue, as it is usually posed, in terms of non-organic materials, accepting that the resemblance between these artifacts and ourselves would be less than complete. A variety of possibilities might then be considered, including some that have been presented in vivid ways in science fiction. But, avoiding these complications, I shall simply . . . assume that there are overwhelmingly impressive resemblances. I shall argue . . . that if this were so, then there would be nothing important 'left over'—that the facts about origin and internal materials would not and should not prevent these beings from being described and treated as people. The same would be true, in my opinion, even of beings who resemble us to a lesser extent, in various ways. But I shall not, in this paper, try to say what kind or degree of resemblance is necessary. I dare say, however, that if the point is conceded for the case of complete resemblance, then it would also be conceded for something less than that, whatever it might be.

[. . .] The interest of the topic is not, it seems to me, confined to the actual likelihood of [such machines that are indistinguishable from human beings being developed.] It lies, rather, in bringing out what is—and is not—involved in our treatment of ordinary human beings as persons. I shall maintain that what makes the difference between a person and a non-person is not some fact about origin or internal composition.

II

If such beings, resembling ourselves, began to appear among us, what would stand in the way of regarding them as persons? *Ex hypothesi,* they would not be human in the biological sense. But this is not usually what is meant when philosophers speak of 'persons'; what they mean is a certain moral status. Persons are beings whom we respect in certain ways, and who are expected to respect us in similar ways. Unlike mere 'things', they belong to a moral community, a network of moral relationships involving rights and duties, etc.

Now the ascription of moral status is connected with what we may call the 'inner life'—the existence of consciousness, feelings, sentience, as distinct from any behaviour that we may observe. But could an artifact have an inner life in this sense? Let us also get rid of the impersonal connotations of the word 'artifact', by thinking in terms of particular beings with ordinary English names, such as Jane. Would Jane have an inner life? Would she, for example, feel pain as normal people do? Or would her pain-behaviour, when it occurs, be unaccompanied by the feeling of pain of which such behaviour is normally an expression?

Here we are close to the traditional problem of 'other minds'. Now this problem is fuelled by a certain sense of mystery about the inner life of others. I know that my own thoughts and feelings are expressed only to some extent, and I assume it is the same with others. There is more to the life of a person than what is expressed. But how, we may wonder, would this 'more' have been created in the case of the artifact? We may assume that the people who designed it were instructed to produce an object which would behave just like a human being. Now a reasonable way of conceiving this task would be in terms of inputs and outputs. Thus, in the case of pain, suitable pain-behaviour would occur in response to the relevant inputs (or stimuli)—and also sometimes without such inputs, as is the case with us.

But what if we asked the designers what they proposed to do about the pain itself? Would this be an additional item to be included in the design? This would be difficult, for it is not clear what it would mean to design a feeling of pain (unless, indeed, some of the versions of materialism now on offer could be made intelligible). We may take it, then, that nothing was done about the feeling as distinct from the behaviour, and from this we might conclude that no such feeling exists in the case of the artifact.

But this conclusion will seem less straightforward if we try to fill in some of the details. If we think of pain-behaviour in terms of input and output, we probably have in mind such examples as hitting one's finger with a hammer and responding with a suitable action, exclamation, facial expression, etc. But we should remember that by far the most usual expression of pain, as well as other feelings, in the case of adult human beings, is verbal. The sharp withdrawal, the groaning and writhing, which are sometimes emphasized in commentaries on Wittgenstein's discussion of pain—these are characteristic only of extreme cases; nor do they have counterparts in the case of other feelings than pain. More often, the expression takes the form of telling someone, more or less calmly, that one has or had a pain (a 'slight pain', perhaps) in such and such a place. (This is not to deny that, in the case of pain at least, the non-verbal behaviour is prior to the verbal statement.)[2]

Now these verbal expressions of pain and other feelings would also have to be given by Jane, if her behaviour were to be like ours. Hence the question whether she really feels pain would not need to be left at the level of mute behaviour. We could, after all, *ask* Jane whether she feels pain, both in the extreme cases and on other occasions; and if she behaves and speaks like ourselves, then her answer will sometimes be yes and sometimes no. What would it be in extreme cases, such as hitting one's finger with a hammer? If *this* part of her behaviour is to be like ours, then the answer must be 'yes' (or, more emphatically: 'Don't ask stupid questions; can't you see?'). But then, if she had no feelings (because none had been 'inserted' by the designers), what could we make of this response? Would she even understand the question? And how could we make sense of her behaviour—both the original physical behaviour and then the apparently positive response to our question? Similar difficulties would arise if we supposed Jane to give a negative response—if she answered 'no' to the question whether she feels pain. One way or another, it seems impossible to make sense of the idea that Jane's behaviour really resembles ours if we deny that she has an inner life. Once we think about *talking* to her, the supposition that she behaves just like us but feels nothing becomes unintelligible.

It might be objected that the introduction of language makes no fundamental difference, since language is just another kind of behaviour, additional to the non-verbal behaviour but subject to the same sceptical doubts. If it is possible for someone to exhibit pain-behaviour without really being in pain, is it not equally possible to exhibit 'speaking-behaviour' without really speaking?

There is, of course, more to speaking than just making suitable sounds. Parrots are capable of making such sounds, and so are 'I speak your weight' machines; but we would not regard them as cases of speaking in the full sense. What prevents us from doing so? It is not the absence of some internal process, analogous to the feeling of pain. What we need in order to recognize real speech is only, so to speak, more of the same. If the parrot or artifact are prepared to give reasons, if they can explain why they said one thing rather than another, if they demand similar explanations from us and comment critically on these, if they sometimes tell lies, sometimes own up to them and sometimes make excuses—in short, if they play the language-game as we all do, then there will be no difference left between their 'speaking-behaviour' and real speaking. And this would also include the language-game of feelings, as in the case of Jane.

III

Should we conclude, then, that Jane would have an inner life? According to [some], we would find it impossible to see Jane in this way. [. . .] But what is meant here by 'impossible'? If what is meant were logical impossibility, then an argument would be needed in support of this. Or is the issue merely one of psychological probabilities, allowing, perhaps, for the speculation that some people might find it impossible while others did not? I shall argue that, for reasons which are not merely psychological, we would find it impossible *not* to treat these beings as persons. [. . .]

I have already commented on the question-begging implications of the word 'machine' and in what follows I shall speak of . . . 'machine actors' as 'a-people' (a for artificial) and of natural people as 'n-people'.

[The] reluctance to ascribe sentience to a-people may be compared with the reluctance which many people felt in the past about ascribing certain qualities to women. Imagine a discussion taking place forty or fifty years ago about whether a woman could ever be Prime Minister. We cannot deny *a priori,* says one participant, that such a thing is conceivable. Yes, but would we regard such a being as having the inner qualities of a Prime Minister? Perhaps, unable to stomach this, he would say . . . that we would attribute Prime Ministerial qualities to the woman's activities, but deny them to their author, i.e. the woman herself. Perhaps such things might be said—or felt, more or less obscurely—by those who have never had experience of women in positions of leadership. But such hesitations would soon evaporate and there is, as far as I can see, no reason why the same should not happen in the case of a-people. [. . .]

[. . .] Is it part of the present intension—in other words, meaning—of the word 'person', that an artifact cannot be a person? It is, if by 'person' one means a human being in the biological sense. And perhaps it would be, if by 'person' one meant an immaterial essence of the kind postulated by dualists. But what if one means a being who looks and behaves like a human being, engages our sympathy, respect and resentment, is held responsible for what he says and does, and so forth? Then a-people would not be excluded from being persons.

But, it may be asked, would we be right to interact with a-people in these ways? [One. . .] suggestion is that machine-persons, like characters in plays or books, are *fictitious* persons and are to be responded to accordingly. [One might hold that] no matter how perfect an imitation, they remain representations. [. . .] Now in the case of characters in a play, there is a familiar language-game in place. We as a matter of course assign the same range of properties to characters in plays as we do to people we meet in the street, yet we know perfectly well that these properties are not being attributed to the actors themselves. To do so would be to confuse imitation with reality; and [one might think] a similar confusion could take place in attributing personal qualities to 'machine-persons'.

Such confusions do take place. Children at a play will often mistake fiction for reality. They also, as Wittgenstein pointed out, attribute personal qualities to dolls. But adults (and children too, most of the time) know the difference; and if they attribute these qualities to imitation or fictitious people, they know that this does not have the same sense as attributing them to real people. (We also attribute certain qualities, such as 'clever' and 'temperamental', to ordinary machines which have no pretensions to personhood.)

There is, however, an important difference between 'imitation human beings' (a-people) and the imitations that we see on the stage, as [one could point out]. The machines . . . will be (designed to be) sucked into the hurly-burly of life in a way other fictitious personages aren't. Although when he leaves the stage an actor sheds the character he portrays, a machine artifact never leaves the stage [one could argue].

But, this being so, what (other than origin and inner materials) is left of the difference between a-persons and persons? The case may be compared with that of real and fictitious money. In playing

Monopoly we use fictitious money that has the attributes of money only in the context of the game. Outside that context it loses the character of money and is merely a collection of coloured slips of paper. But suppose this money were 'sucked into the hurly-burly of life', that it 'never leaves the stage', but is used just like real money in the conduct of real transactions. In that case it would *be* real money. Similarly, if a-people interacted with us just like real people, then what sense would there be in denying that they *are* real people?

Here again we may be misled by words like 'imitation' and 'artificial'. It is true, of course, that a-people would be artificial, and that the aim in making them would be to imitate human behaviour; and both of these words, 'imitation' and 'artificial', are sometimes used as opposites to the word 'real'. But these words would only affect the origins of a-people and not their personal qualities or status as persons. There need be nothing artificial or imitatory about these. If, in a real situation, we called such a person's behaviour 'artificial', this would have the same derogatory meaning as in the case of an n-person; and similarly with the word 'imitation'.

The attribution of personal qualities to a-people would not be a matter of choice for us, any more than the attribution of such qualities to n-people. Let us suppose that an a-person, call him Edward, has lived among us for many years and it has always been assumed that he is an n-person. Perhaps he is a bit vague when asked about his origins, but no one has ever thought to press the enquiry. Edward has a steady job in charge of a small department at a local firm. He is a respected colleague, though without any remarkable qualities, and so forth. Well, one day Edward decides to 'come out', to reveal his secret (I assume he would himself *know* the secret of his origins. We could also imagine a scenario in which he doesn't—as happens in romantic novels.) What then? Would we take back everything we said about Edward's thoughts and feelings? Would we now say, and believe, that Edward does not really resent it when we let him down, doesn't really feel insulted if we accuse him of behaving like a robot, is not really glad when he gets a rise in pay? Consider how this might work in a case of letting down:

> EDWARD, to n-person subordinate: Will you meet me here tomorrow morning? It's very important, so don't let me down.
>
> N-PERSON: Yes, I promise to meet you. (Thinks: He is only an imitation person, an artifact, and therefore not sentient. One can't have moral obligations to such a being, so my promise isn't really a promise.)
>
> EDWARD: By the way, I've heard that you have been reading some bad philosophy, and this has made you an artifactist. But don't let's have any nonsense about this. If you promise to be here, then I expect you to be here, and I'll be very angry if you don't turn up. So if you are not prepared to give a promise and stand by your obligation, then please say so now. Then I'll make other arrangements.

In these and many other situations we would find it impossible to treat Edward as something other than a person. His announcement might cause a stir at first (finding out a person's origins sometimes does), but after that life would go on as before. (Perhaps, if Edward went on and on about his origins, we would find it a bore and tell him to forget it.)

Someone who persisted in denying sentience to Edward and other a-people would be in the same position as the philosophical sceptic about 'other minds'. Such a sceptic would be stating—or purporting to state—beliefs which are belied by his own behaviour. He would be saying the words 'I doubt whether *p*' (or, as the case may be, 'I deny that *p*'), but his behaviour would show that he doubts or denies nothing of the sort. As Wittgenstein remarked about another kind of sceptic, '[He] doesn't simply look the train up in the time-table and go to the station at the right time, but says: "I have *no* belief that the train will really arrive, but I will go to the station all the same". He does everything that the normal person does . . .'[3]

It might be objected that I have overlooked a crucial difference between a-people and n-people—that with which the whole discussion began. In the case of a-people there is, after all, a very different internal structure. Would this not constitute important evidence for doubting or denying that they are sentient? (Would it not be so in the case of the discovery about Edward, for example?)

My answer is that our language-games of relations with other people are neither based on evidence, nor subject to refutation by contrary evidence. In the context of suitable human situations, we cannot help treating beings who behave like ourselves as persons; and this is not dependent on their origins or internal composition. In this respect the scepticism about a-people would be no more tenable than the corresponding scepticism about n-people—i.e. the traditional problem of other minds. In both cases the facts of origin and internal composition are irrelevant. The sceptic about other minds is not to be refuted by drawing attention to the 'positive evidence', and neither would the 'negative evidence' in the case of a-people undermine our treatment of them as people. The two versions of scepticism, about a-people and about n-people, stand or fall—in my view, fall—together.[4]

NOTES

1. L. Wittgenstein, *Philosophical Investigations* (Oxford: Blackwell 1958).
2. For further discussion of this matter see my 'Criteria, Conventions and Other Minds', in Stuart Shanker (ed.), *Critical Essays on Wittgenstein* (London: Croom Helm, 1986).
3. L. Wittgenstein, *On Certainty* (Oxford: Blackwell 1969), section 339.
4. I am grateful to David Cockburn for many helpful comments on this paper.

DISCUSSION QUESTIONS

1. What problem does Hanfling see in asking whether *machines* could think or be persons?
2. What problem does Hanfling see in asking whether *robots* could be people?
3. According to Hanfling, what makes the difference between a person and a nonperson?
4. Is the comparison of "artifactism" with sexism and racism tenable? Explain.
5. Hanfling argues that if Monopoly® money was sucked into the hurly-burly of life and was used like real money, it would *be* real money; similarly, if artificial people interacted with us just like real people, those a-persons would also *be* real people. Is this argument convincing? Explain.
6. In the film *Blade Runner* (1982), does Deckard (Harrison Ford) have the right to "retire" Roy (Rutger Hauer) the Replicant? Defend your view.
7. In the film *RoboCop* (1987), is it morally wrong to dismantle the cyborg RoboCop? Explain. Is the RoboCop an a-person? Is the RoboCop less of a person than Officer Alex Murphy (Peter Weller) was before his transformation into RoboCop? Explain.
8. In *Blade Runner,* Rachael (Sean Young) seems to engage the sympathy and respect of Deckard. If so, then Hanfling's comments imply that Deckard considers Rachael—though a Replicant—to be a person. Is Deckard right to consider Rachael an a-person? Explain.
9. In the film *Terminator 2: Judgment Day* (1991), is it praiseworthy when the Terminator (Arnold Schwarzenegger) sacrifices himself? Would the Terminator count as an a-person? Defend your view.

RAYMOND MARTIN

Ray Martin received his Ph.D. from the University of Rochester. He is the author of Self-Concern: An Experiential Approach to What Matters in Survival *(1998) and* The Elusive Messiah: A Philosophical Overview of the Quest for the Historical Jesus *(1999), and co-author of* Naturalization of the Soul: Self and Personal Identity in the Eighteenth Century *(2000). The University of Maryland gave Martin a Distinguished Scholar-Teacher Award in 2001.*

Born in Hagen, Westphalia, Germany in 1928, Rescher is University Professor of Philosophy at the University of Pittsburgh. A member of several learned European academies, Rescher is editor of American Philosophical Quarterly *and author of some hundred books in various areas of philosophy. He received the Alexander von Humboldt Prize for Humanistic Scholarship in 1984.*

In this selection, Martin advocates a "pragmatic" approach to conceptualizing what a person is, invoking Locke's idea that "person" is a forensic term. In contrast, Martin complains, Rescher stipulates seven severally necessary and jointly sufficient conditions of personhood: (1) self-understanding, (2) self-conceptualization, (3) thinking of oneself as a free rational agent, (4) deserving the respect of others, (5) owing respect to others, (6) having a self-respect rooted in (7) appreciation of oneself as an intelligent free agent. Martin criticizes these requirements as so much higher than Locke's—since they are not couched exclusively in an individual's capacities and abilities but also in terms of an individual's beliefs, attitudes, and values—that Neanderthals, dolphins, great apes, the mentally retarded, psychopaths, sociopaths, misanthropes, fatalists, determinists, and amoralists (like Spinoza), all fail to qualify as persons. If a religious analytic philosopher wanted to add belief in theism to Rescher's long list of necessary conditions, then Bertrand Russell would not have qualified either. Martin sees no clear reason to distinguish between embodied human animals and persons. In reply, Rescher explains why he thinks it worth distinguishing between humans (members of the species Homo sapiens*), intelligent beings (higher primates and perhaps future electronic artifacts), and persons (beings with rights, responsibilities, duties, and obligations).*

Was Spinoza a Person?

In twenty-thousand year old graves in the north of France, stones, animal parts and artifacts are carefully arranged around human skeletons. We don't know what these graves meant to the Neanderthals who arranged them. Surely they meant something. Many anthropologists believe the graves were arranged not for such ordinary animal purposes as those of securing food, shelter, or sex but to express—perhaps for the first time here on Earth—a characteristically human concern about death. Some think the graves express the belief of those who arranged them that those they buried somehow survived their bodily deaths.

Were the Neanderthals who arranged these graves people? They were homo sapiens. And for the times they had sophisticated concerns. Is that enough? John Locke famously said that to be a person is to be "a thinking intelligent being that has reason and reflection and can consider itself as itself, the same thinking thing, in different times and places" (Locke 1694, II.27, this volume p. 82). On this criterion the Neanderthals who arranged the graves may or may not have been persons. It would be interesting to know what these Neanderthals were capable of and how they differed in their capacities from other animals of the time and from us. But we can know that without knowing whether they were persons. Is there a *further* interesting question about whether they were persons?

Locke wanted identity conditions for persons that differed from those for human animals. It's not clear why he wanted this. Whatever his reasons his standards for personhood were pretty low. He could have lowered them further and still have had identity conditions for persons that differed from those for human animals. The Neanderthals who arranged the graves might then clearly have qualified. But what would it matter? The deeper issue is not how high (or low) one should set one's standards for personhood and, hence, whether Locke or anyone else has struck the right balance but, rather, why one should distinguish between persons and human animals in the first place.

Rescher's requirements for personhood are higher than Locke's. Much higher. And they differ from Locke's in another way as well. Whereas Locke's are exclusively in terms of what individuals can do—their capacities or abilities—Rescher's are also in terms of what individuals believe and in terms of what attitudes and values they have. For instance, Rescher says that personhood is a matter not only "of self-understanding or self-conceptualization—of thinking of oneself" as a free rational agent, as deserving the respect of others on this basis, as owing a like respect to others, etc.,"—but also of one's having "a self-respect rooted in one's appreciation of oneself as an intelligent free agent" (Rescher 1992-94, Vol. II, p. 114; *cf.* Rescher 1994, p.447). On Rescher's criterion probably the Neanderthals who arranged the graves would not have qualified as persons. Neither would various non-human animals, such as

Source: Raymond Martin, "Was Spinoza a Person?" in *Pragmatic Idealism: Critical Essays on Nicholas Rescher's System of Pragmatic Idealism,* A. Wüstehube & M. Quante, eds. Atlanta: Rodopi, 1998, pp. 111–118, response by Rescher: 242–244. Reprinted with the permission of Rodopi, Amsterdam.

dolphins and the great apes, which some philosophers have argued are persons (see, *e.g.,* Cavalieri, 1993). Neither would many retarded or otherwise mentally or emotionally impaired humans: psychopaths, sociopaths, even misanthropes. Neither would fatalists, determinists, and amoralists (hence, neither would Spinoza). Does it matter?

From one point of view it doesn't matter at all. Creatures are whatever they are regardless of whether they belong to the person-club. *Person* is just a word. What determines whether it matters how one defines the word *person* is what one intends to do with one's definition. To make it matter one must put one's definition to some significant practical, moral, or theoretical use. For legal purposes, for instance, if hospital employees mistreat a person, rather than a mere human, that might make them more vulnerable to lawsuit (provided the relevant notion of person is encoded in the law). For moral purposes, if a fetus is a person, rather than a proto-person, that might make it more difficult to justify abortion (provided the relevant notion of person is encoded in preferred moral standards). For theoretical purposes if one defines *person* one way rather than another, that might make a difference, say, to how one conceptualizes some phenomenon, such as multiple personality disorder (see, *e.g.,* Wilkes 1990, pp. 21-6). For any such purposes it is hard to see how there would be any nonverbal truth of the matter about whether one had adopted the right criterion of person. Rather, it would seem to be merely a question of whether it is more useful than not to think of individuals of some sort as persons. For instance, people suffering from multiple personality disorder are not *really* either one person with several personas or several people each with one persona; rather, they may be thought of either way, depending on which way of thinking of them is more useful, and the utility of thinking of them in one way or the other may vary with the context.

In sum, on this view of the status and function of a definition of *person* whether one's definition is a good one depends solely on whether it is more useful for some worthwhile purpose than competing definitions. And if it is more useful, that will not make it a good definition *per se* but only a good one relative to that purpose. That's how I would view definitions of *person* and their importance: pragmatically. It's doubtful, though, in spite of his self-avowed pragmatism, that it's how Rescher views them. Unfortunately it's not clear just how he does view them—his own definition of *person* in particular. Various things he says *suggest* that he intends to use his definition for three rather different purposes: first, to reveal what the word *person* means; second, to reveal what people must assume they take themselves to be to explain their self-images and self-understandings; and, third, to explicate the real nature of personhood, apparently in order to ground and/or express his view of our rational and moral obligations.

With respect to the first of these objectives Rescher says of his seven conditions of personhood that they "are severally necessary and jointly sufficient" for an individual's "being 'a person' in the standard sense of that term" (Rescher 1992-94, Vol. II, p. 114). But in the case of the word *person* what reason is there to think there is just one "standard sense" of the term and, even if there is, that Rescher in his definition has captured it? Apparently we have to answer such questions intuitively. So, for whatever it's worth, it seems implausible to me that the word *person* "standardly" (by which I assume Rescher means, "generally, to most people") means anything as elaborate and sensitively nuanced as his seven-part definition. For one thing, many people who routinely use the word *person* correctly probably would have a hard time even understanding what some of Rescher's seven conditions mean. For another, even if Rescher were right about how most of those in his language-culture understand *person,* individuals in other cultures may not think of personhood (or themselves) along Rescherian lines. For instance, Rescher says that on his definition personhood does not admit of degrees and persons can be non-material, wholly spiritual beings (Rescher 1992-94, Vol. II, p. 113). Kwasi Wiredu says that on the concept of *person* to which traditional Akans of West Africa subscribe personhood does admit of degrees and persons must be material (Wiredu 1990, pp. 285, 291). So, if Rescher's project is to explicate the standard sense of *person* and Wiredu is right about the Akans, Rescher may have to relativize his account to particular cultures. In any case, even if there were a standard, universal sense of the word *person* and Rescher had captured it in his definition, it's not clear what importance that would have philosophically.

With respect to the second objective—that of revealing what people must assume they take themselves to be to explain their self-images and self-understandings—Rescher says that "perhaps the most significant and far-reaching single fact about us is that we are *persons*" since "it is this, above all, that determines our self-image and our self-understanding—our view of the sort of beings that we ourselves are" (Rescher 1992-94, Vol. II, p. 113). But *whose* self-image and self-understanding? The Neanderthals who arranged the graves? Seventeenth-century Tsinglit Eskimos, untouched by European culture and fighting a daily battle for survival on the frozen tundra? Contemporary Nepalese peasants? Your average American? Your average philosopher? Disciples of Spinoza? Readers of this essay? And whichever group Rescher has in mind, which aspects—and how much—of that group's self-image and self-understanding is determined by their thinking of themselves as persons in Rescher's sense?

No doubt most people, including most readers of this essay, will tend to have self-images and self-understandings that are importantly influenced by many things, including some of their beliefs, values, and attitudes, that are not reflected in Rescher's definition. For instance, many will be influenced in their self-images and self-understandings by their beliefs about what race or sex, or sexual orientation, or age they are, or by their beliefs that they are (or are not) capable of having babies or lovable, or part of God's plan, and so on. If Rescher's purpose is to reveal what people must assume they take ourselves to be to explain their self-images and self-understandings, why aren't these and a hundred other items mentioned in his account of persons?

Rescher may think the items in his definition are more important in determining self-image and self-understanding than other characteristics humans may have. If he does think this, why? If he does not think this, why, then, does he focus just on the characteristics he mentions in his definition? Perhaps Rescher intends to be articulating just the common denominator, that is, just that part of the explanation of peoples' self-images and self-understandings that applies to everyone. If that is what he intends, there are two problems: first, there are items that are not mentioned in his definition, such as that people have bodies, that would seem to impact on peoples' self-images as universally as the items he mentions; and, second, many individuals who prima facie are people apparently don't think of themselves along Rescherian lines.

John Kekes has pointed out that it is an "odd consequence" of Rescher's definition "that people whose beliefs and actions are inconsistent with it, and thus fail to see themselves as Rescher says that persons must, are not, and for that very reason, persons" (Kekes 1994, p. 418). More specifically, Kekes has criticized Rescher for making his requirements for personhood so demanding that individuals fail to qualify "who do not understand themselves as free and rational agents," or who "lack self-respect because they see themselves as having wasted their lives, or having lived in a shameful way, or who unquestioningly subordinate themselves to some external authority," or who advocate slavery (Aristotle), or elitism (Nietzsche), or misanthropy (Schopenhauer), or egoism (Kekes 1994, p. 418).

Rescher replied,

> "insofar as such people (sic) do think and act in the way projected by Kekes they do indeed betray and abandon their personhood." They are "*failed* persons." But "failed persons," Rescher adds, are not necessarily "*non-persons.*" For as long as failed persons are potentially persons "the rest of us (i.e., those who are being true to our personhood) have it incumbent on us to give these failed persons the benefit of doubt and are not only well advised but (morally) required to treat them as persons."

Rescher continues:

> The salient point is this: just as *human* has two quite different contrast cases (non-human and inhuman) so does *person* (non-person and "un"-person—ordinary language simply leaves us in the lurch here). The les-

> son here is clear enough—the determinist who sees himself and others as automata, the misanthropist who deems himself and his fellows as unworthy of respect and deserving of fathomless degradation, the sociopath who sets the value of peoples' lives at zero, all step outside the pale of personhood (in these specified regards at least). And I see this as a consequence of my view of persons that can be accepted with equanimity and without fretting too much about accusations of undue exclusivity. (Rescher 1994, p. 448)

Does this reply help? In one way it does. Rescher's remarks do at least suggest that he wants to use his definition to shore up or at least reflect his view about what he thinks are our rational and/or moral obligations. For instance, he says that humans who have the potential to satisfy the requirements of his definition but don't satisfy them do not simply and, thereby, not satisfy them, rather, they "betray" their personhood; they are not simply and, thereby, non-persons, rather, they are "failed" persons. On the other hand, those who satisfy his requirements for personhood not only are persons *simpliciter,* rather, they are "true to" their personhood.

Rescher says that the obligations he thinks people have to act rationally and morally is "rooted in" our nature as persons. For instance, he says we have an "ontological obligation for self-development" and that it is "perverse" and "wicked" deliberately to flout this obligation (Rescher 1992-94, Vol. III, p. 214). But what does it mean to have an "ontological obligation," and how, in Rescher's view, do such obligations arise? It's not clear how Rescher would answer. He says, and this may be part of his answer, that some projects come to us "not by preference or selection but by destiny, or rather by our very mode of emplacement in the world's scheme of things" (Rescher 1994, p. 379). He calls projects of this sort, "situational imperatives." Rescher doesn't say explicitly that being a person is for most humans a situational imperative but he suggests that it is. For instance, he talks about our having duties, such as our duty to be moral, that inhere "in our common nature as free rational agents" (Rescher 1994, p. 387). And he says that "we humans are both (naturally) inclined and (ontologically) obligated to see ourselves as rational beings and free agents—that is, as *persons*" (Rescher 1992-94, Vol. I, p. 388). Rescher adds that "the impetus to rationality is what makes us what [we] can and should be" and that "as self-purportedly rational beings we are bound—and entitled—to value ourselves as the sorts of creatures we see ourselves as being" (*Ibid.*). He concludes, "personhood, with its elements of rationality and freedom of action, are accordingly prime values for us" (*Ibid.*).

Even if, for the sake of argument, we grant Rescher that all of us have some such "ontological obligations" because of the kinds of creatures we are, it is not clear on his view how or why our having some capacity or other issues in our having an obligation to develop and/or act on that capacity. For instance, most humans at some point or other in their adult lives are "naturally inclined" to desire sexual intercourse with other humans. Presumably humans have such desires because of the kinds of creatures they are. Does that mean, in Rescher's view, that a human who voluntarily chose to be celibate would be a failed person? And, if some adult human were not to have normal sexual desires even though it were possible for him to develop them (say, by testosterone shots) should that human to be "true to his personhood" try to develop them? Are women who are capable of having babies because of the kind of creatures they are obligated to have babies? And so on. I presume Rescher would want to answer all of these questions in the negative. But then he owes us an explanation of how and why some capacities we have because of the kinds of creatures we are issue in "ontological obligations" to realize and/or act on those capacities while others do not.

Rescher might want to respond by claiming that in his definition he is characterizing just the real essence of personhood, that capacities persons have he does not mention are not essential but accidental, and that it is only essential capacities that issue in "ontological obligations." But it is questionable whether persons do have real essences. Natural kinds have real essences. But it is doubtful that *person* is a natural kind. Locke, for instance, thought *person* is "a forensic term, appropriating actions and their merit" (Locke 1694, II.27.26). If

Locke is right, then *person* at best has only a nominal essence. *Human being* may have a real essence. But some characteristics that Rescher does not mention in his definition, such as one's having a body and one's being of some particular race, would seem to be essential to being human.

In any case, if Rescher is offering his definition, as it seems he is, to support an ideal of personhood that he thinks we should all strive to meet, and the utility of his definition in shoring up or expressing that ideal is part of what is supposed to make it a good definition, then it seems to me that he needs to argue more fully than he has that his definition is a good ideal. As we have seen, one of the main potential problems with his definition as an ideal of personhood is that it seems to be ideological in that it requires that persons have certain beliefs, attitudes, and values. So, it may be worth asking whether Rescher's ideal would be a good one for philosophers to adopt as one of their ideals. It seems to me that it would not be. It would require philosophers to hold particular, substantive views on contentious philosophical issues, such as on free will and the status of morality, and thus preclude their adopting some version or other of the (to me, more attractive) Socratic ideal of being committed only to rational inquiry and to following the argument wherever it might lead. I don't say that philosophers should adopt some such Socratic ideal but just that it should be an option. Philosophers who adopted Rescher's ideal rather than such a Socratic ideal would have to begin the philosophical project knowing in advance in certain important respects where they were going to end up. For such philosophers not everything and not even all the really fundamental things would be up for grabs. They would already have grabbed. Their project—like that of some religious philosophers—would be to work within a basic framework they imported into the philosophical enterprise.

Today there are quite a few analytic philosophers, including some of the best, who are also religious philosophers and who espouse doing philosophy in just this sense. So, perhaps it would be worth asking Rescher how he would respond to some such philosopher who proposed that in defining an ideal of personhood we should demand even more in the way of belief than Rescher thinks we should demand. For instance, suppose that a religious philosopher suggested that we enrich Rescher's proposal so that persons, by definition, would be committed not just to acknowledging the reality of freedom and the objectivity of morality but also to acknowledging some version or other of religious dogma; in other words, the suggestion is that we start with Rescher's definition and simply add to it additional conditions requiring that one have certain religious beliefs. How might Rescher reply? If he would reply that for most purposes for which we might want to use a definition of *person,* including that of expressing an ideal, requiring belief in religious dogma as a condition of being a person would be going too far, surely he would be right. But for pretty much the same reasons it seems that Rescher too may have gone too far. On the religious definition of person we just imagined, atheists would not qualify as persons. Hence, Bertrand Russell would not have qualified. On Rescher's definition determinists would not qualify as persons. Hence, Spinoza would not have qualified.

In sum, one problem with Rescher's definition of *person* for the various uses to which he wants to put it is that it is unclear why one should subscribe to his rather than to some other definition. Another problem—perhaps the deeper issue—is that it is unclear why one should distinguish between human animals and persons in the first place.[1]

University of Maryland

NOTES

1. Thanks to John Barresi for helpful comments on an earlier version of this paper.

Response to Raymond Martin

In his stimulating and provocatively entitled paper Raymond Martin presses various requests for the clarification and defense of my published views regarding what personhood consists in and what obligations it entails. For starters he wants to know "Why should one distinguish between persons and human animals in the first place?" Here my position is straightforward, since once one considers that there well might be intelligent life elsewhere in the cosmos, then any idea that we members of *Homo Sapiens* have a monopoly on personhood becomes very questionable. However, it is with the issue of the boundaries of moral concern that the question "What is a person" becomes more problematic. It clearly matters a good deal whether or not we see psychopaths or amoralists as persons, largely because this will prove pivotal for the ways in which we can go about determining and justifying a response to their condition in structuring our interactions with them. For being a person carries in its wake claims and entitlements bound up with being treated as such.

With respect to Neanderthals, the question is certainly not one of how they thought of themselves but rather in the first instance (since "person" is an ethical rather than a biological concept) as to how we *should* see them if (hypothetically and contrary to fact) we should have to deal with them ourselves. And specifically, insofar as we should find it necessary to modify their behavior—to alter what they think and they do—would we find it in order to proceed by force majeure or by way of rational suasion. (This should take care of Spinoza.)

Of course "person" is just a word. But, as with other words its meaning is not up for grabs but is inherent in the cultural and intellectual contexts within which it functions—in this case one that involves the legal, religious, and social domain of activity and process within which the term has long figured. And the fact that some other culture uses different concepts has no bearing on the issue of our discussion—any more than it matters for *our* purposes in discussion of the color green that some other culture may not distinguish between green and blue.

Moreover, that seemingly puzzling issue of "ontological obligation" stands coordinate with this ethical dimension of the matter. What qualifies certain beings as persons is clearly their *potential* of seeing themselves as free and responsible agents. And here again Spinoza is definitely in. You don't lose the condition of personhood by failing to think of yourself as such any more than you would so lose the condition of being ambidextrous. (To be sure, discernibly incurable madmen and idiots have lost their personhood on such a construction of the matter.)

The notable thing about capacities like intelligence and rationality and personhood is that—unlike capacities for singing or eating—one automatically incurs through their mere possession

---

Source: Nicholas Rescher, "Response to Raymond Martin" in *Pragmatic Idealism,* pp. 242–244. Reprinted with the permission of Rodopi, Amsterdam.

alone not so much the *inclination* as the *obligation* to exercise them, to function at a level where their resources become operative. And persons *ipso facto* also incur the obligation to value this aspect of their nature (obligations which, like any others, one can of course manage to neglect). At this point self-understanding acquires an ethical aspect that it lacks elsewhere. It is incongruous for a rational being (or a person or a moral being) to fail to value this capacity in a way that it is not automatically incongruous for a sexual or an amphibious being to value these capabilities.

But what is the basis of this ontological obligation on our part? Here Martin dismisses "natural inclination"—and this is clearly right for the obvious reasons that have prevented my having ever even hinted that this is the answer. To get on the right track we have to ask: What is the basis of *any* comparable obligation. Why should intelligent beings cultivate their intelligence? or, Why should moral agents act morally?

People can have many obligations. They have a moral obligation to keep promises, a legal obligation to drive within the speed limit, a professional obligation to provide competent service. But there is also a category of obligation that differs in nature from these issue particularized obligation categories. For consider "People ought to try to lead rewarding lives" or "People ought to act in such a way that the world is a better place for their having been present in it." Such obligations have the following features: (1) They are not other-oriented. Unlike my moral obligation to honor my premises to you they are not oriented toward some particular second-party beneficiary. Insofar as one owes it to someone to act in this way, one "owes it to oneself"—or perhaps even "to the world at large." (2) They are inevitable. Unlike an obligation associated with an elective role, like that of a captain towards the passengers of the ship, they are incumbent on everyone—on all rational agents at large. They are not elective in their basis but situational—they "go with the territory" of being a rational agent. They are obligations one *has* by virtue of what one *is*.

Why should one acknowledge these ontological obligations of personhood. "What's in it for me?" if I honor them. Why is it in my interest to honor such an obligation? The answer is straightforward: What's in it for me is that I am a better person for so doing—not necessarily a happier person but a better person, not necessarily one whose life is more pleasant but one whose life affords a better basis for rational contentment. (I am baffled about why Martin thinks it should be that, on such a construction of persons and their obligations, the responsible choice of an unusual life-plan—being an atheist, say, or a celibate, or a philosopher, for that matter—would or could somehow compromise one's personhood.)

To be sure, this consideration makes it *prudent* (in the truest sense of the term) for me to honor the obligations of personhood. The question remains: But what makes it *obligatory* for me to do so. It is not that I *have* to do it in the sense that there is no *possible* alternative for me but that I *ought to do it* in the sense that there is no better *alternative* that is available to me. And with the sort of obligation now at issue, this "better" is one not just of "better for me" but "better for the world at large." With the present sort of ontological obligation—as with all others—something goes wrong when the obligation is dishonored. But what goes wrong is in this case something that impacts negatively both upon my condition and upon that of the world at large. The basis of that ontological obligation is thus in the final analysis an axiological one. In violating such obligations we diminish both ourselves and the world we live in.

But, in any case, I am perplexed as to how Martin can see it as a deep and difficult issue "why one should distinguish between human animals and person in the first place." To my mind this marks him as one of those thinkers who suffers from the dietary insufficiency of examples of which Wittgenstein somewhere speaks. For it is all too obviously worthwhile to distinguish between *humans* (members of the species Homo sapiens), *intelligent beings* (discussibly including higher primates and arguably also some future artifacts of electronics), and *persons* as creatures not only equipped with intelligences and feelings, but capable of functioning at the level where it begins to make sense to talk of rights and responsibilities, duties and obligations. The teachings of cosmology taken in conjunction with the imaginative leaps of science fiction have surely by now combined to bring us to a point where the distinction between human animal and persons can no longer be seen as philosophically irrelevant.

DISCUSSION QUESTIONS

1. Why do you think the Neanderthals in northern France buried their deceased with artifacts, stones, and animal parts?
2. Do you agree with Martin that the usage of "person" seems merely to be a question of whether it is more useful than not to think of individuals of some sort as persons? Explain.
3. Why does Martin believe that Rescher's view of persons may entail that it is an "ontological obligation" for humans to desire sexual intercourse with other humans? Explain Martin's criticisms regarding celibacy and women's obligation to have babies. Discuss the legitimacy of these criticisms.
4. Does Martin have good reasons for thinking Rescher's conditions of personhood are too restrictive? Explain.
5. Why does Rescher think that how Neanderthals thought of themselves is certainly not the question?
6. How does Rescher respond to Martin's comments on ontological obligations? Is Rescher's response adequate? Explain.
7. What specific uses do you think Rescher wants to make of his distinctions between humans, intelligent beings, and persons?

Chapter 41

WILLIAM O. STEPHENS

Stephens (1962–) grew up a Chicago Cubs fan in West Lafayette, Indiana. He played varsity tennis at Earlham College where he earned his B.A. in 1984. He received his Ph.D. from the University of Pennsylvania in 1990. He is Professor of Philosophy and Professor of Classical & Near Eastern Studies at Creighton University. He writes on Stoicism, ethics, and animals.

*In this selection, Stephens first traces the historical development of the concept "person" from its initial emergence in the ancient Stoic sources Epictetus (*prosōpon* "character") and Cicero (*persona* "role") through medieval Christian trinitarian theology. He then analyzes science fiction examples of various alien persons. He concludes that (1) "person" has a rich, stable, and adequately definite core meaning though it resists analysis into a tidy set of necessary and sufficient conditions; (2) this core meaning is neither intensively nor extensively coincident with the concept "human being," but is rather species-neutral; (3) this concept is indispensable to our moral discourse. Stephens thus defends the conceptual coherence of ascribing personhood to the appropriate nonhuman physical beings.*

Masks, Androids, and Primates: The Evolution of the Concept "Person"

The evolution of the concept "person", from its ancient Greek origin *prosōpon* and its Latin equivalent *persona* to its usage in current philosophical debates, is interesting in its own right. Moreover, attention to the historical development of this term promises to help resolve controversy over its utility in contemporary moral theorizing. One contemporary moral philosopher argues that we should dispense with the concept of a person altogether because its meaning is (has become?) too vague and indeterminate to carry the ethical freight that proponents of animal welfare philosophy wish to load upon it.[1] I wish to argue against this view in the following way. I shall examine several key episodes within the historical development of the concept from its initial emergence in the ancient Stoic sources Epictetus and Cicero up to contemporary discussions. I shall not attempt to present anything approaching a comprehensive survey of every stage of that historical development. Rather, I wish to show only (1) that "person" has a rich, stable, and adequately definite core meaning; (2) that this core meaning is neither intensively nor extensively coincident with the concept "human being" but is rather species-neutral; and (3) that this core meaning of "person" fills a needed niche in our ethical vocabulary, and is sufficiently precise to yield ethical consequences. Those who believe that the concept is fuzzy probably make the common assumption that either most or all human beings, and only human beings, are or can be persons.[2] I will conclude that the richness and somewhat elastic borders of the concept, far from fostering its selective application to humans,[3] can instead favor a philologically legitimate and philosophically meaningful application to at least some nonhuman animals. If my account succeeds, it will make clear why the appeal to the current use of the concept by way of "what people think" can play only a limited role in its analysis, given the contours of its etymology and the evolution of its usage.

I

The evolution of the concept "person" begins with the ancient Greeks. The Greek word *prosōpeion* means *mask*. Its cognate *prosōpon* means face, countenance; mask, dramatic role, character; person, legal

---

Source: William O. Stephens, *Masks, Androids, and Primates: The Evolution of the Concept "Person"* in *Etica & Animali* 9: special issue on Nonhuman Personhood, ed. Paula Cavalieri, 1998, pp. 111–127. Reprinted with the permission of the author.

personality.[4] The most sustained moral use of *prosōpon* (and its Latin equivalent *persona*) is found in Roman Stoicism. Consequently, careful examination of how these Stoics used the term is vital for understanding its early philosophical meaning. Consider the following four texts[5] from the *Discourses* of the Stoic teacher Epictetus:

> T1 A time will soon come when the tragic actors will think that their *prosōpeia* [= masks] and buskins and the long robe are themselves. (1.29.41)
>
> T2 "Take a governorship." I take it and having done so I show how an educated human being comports himself. "Lay aside the laticlave, and having put on rags come forward in a corresponding *prosōpon* [= character]." (1.29.44–45)
>
> T3 For what is lacking now is not quibbles, but the books of the Stoics are full of quibbles. What, then, is the thing lacking? The user of them, the one who bears witness to the arguments by his deed. This is the *prosōpon* [= character] I would have you assume, that we may no longer use old models in the school, but may have some model of our own. (1.29.56–57)
>
> T4 But for determining the rational and the irrational, we employ not only the values of external things, but also the things which accord with one's own particular *prosōpon* [= character]. (1.2.7)

Compare these passages to two texts from the compendium of the *Discourses* called the *Encheiridion* (Handbook):

> T5 Remember that you are an actor in a play, which is how the Playwright wishes it; if He wishes it short, it is short; if long, it is long; if He wishes you to play the beggar, then play even this skillfully; and similarly if a cripple, a public official, or a private citizen. For this is yours, to play the assigned *prosōpon* [= role] well; but the selection of it is Another's. (*Ench.* 17)
>
> T6 If you undertake some *prosōpon* [= role] beyond your capability, you both disgrace yourself in that one, and you neglect the one which you might have been capable of successfully filling. (*Ench.* 37)

In T1 Epictetus uses the root meaning of *prosōpeion*, "mask". He distinguishes the actor's dramatic costume which enlivens his stage-role, from the identity of the individual behind or underneath that guise. Epictetus warns the actors against fooling themselves into believing that the dramatic roles they assume as pretense on the stage are their real selves.

In T2, a governorship is cited as an example of a post, station, or office one may be given. Only one who wears the laticlave—the toga with a broad red stripe worn by Romans of senatorial rank—can occupy a governorship. When one lays aside the uniform indicative of the post, one thereby exchanges one role for another with its own representative costume. Epictetus explains that some roles can be freely chosen (T6), and in those cases our responsibility is to choose those roles which match our talents rather than those roles which exceed our abilities. Thus certain roles are recommended (T3). Other roles, however, we are born into and do not choose for ourselves (T5). Our genetic inheritance may determine one of the roles we must play, and, depending on the rigidity of our society's class structure, our social status too may be the result of chance, not choice. Thus membership in our immediate social group, our relation to other social groups, the effect our physical limitations have on the activities we can perform, and the cluster of activities and connected responsibilities which constitute a *role* or *function* are all dimensions of the concept *prosōpon* in Epictetus.

The cripple, the governor, the senator, the beggar, all of these roles are generic functions. Various individuals can perform or assume each of these functions or roles; none of them are unique to anyone. In T4, however, Epictetus extends the use of *prosōpon* beyond these generic modes of agency to the power of *individualization*. For one slave, Epictetus explains, it is reasonable to hold a chamber-pot for his master. For another slave, in contrast, it is not only intolerable to hold such a pot for his master, but, were *he* the master, he would not tolerate someone else holding the pot for *him*. In this text, then, Epictetus adds to the already rich concept of *prosōpon* the notion of self-worth, or the sense of self-propriety, that is, one's stand on what befits oneself and what does not. One individual's judgment of what befits him may differ greatly from another's.[6]

These elements of the early concept of personhood were discussed in Epictetus' Stoic school at the end of the first and the beginning of the second centuries of the common era. But as early as the middle of the first century BCE the Roman orator, public servant, and scholar Marcus Tullius Cicero, in book one of his *De officiis,* had already composed what is arguably the most famous Latin text on the term *persona*.[7]

T7 Furthermore, one must understand that we have been dressed, as it were, by nature for two *personae* [= roles]; one is common, arising from the fact that we all have a share in reason and in the superiority by which we surpass the beasts. Everything honorable and seemly is derived from this, and from it we discover a method of finding our duty. The other, however, is that assigned specifically to individuals. For just as there are enormous bodily differences (for some, as we see, their strength is the speed that they can run, for others the might with which they wrestle; again, some have figures that are dignified, others that are graceful), similarly there are still greater differences in spirits. (1.107)

T8 Reflecting on such matters, everyone ought to weigh the characteristics that are his own, and to regulate them, not wanting to see how someone else's might become his: for what is most seemly for a man is the thing that is most his own. Everyone, therefore, should acquire knowledge of his own talents, and show himself a sharp judge of his own good qualities and faults; else it will seem that actors have more good sense than us. For they do not choose the best plays, but those that are most suited to themselves. (1.113-114)

T9 To the two *personae* [= roles] of which I spoke above, a third is added: this is imposed by some chance or circumstance. There is also a fourth, which we assume for ourselves by our own decision. Kingdoms, military powers, nobility, political honors, wealth and influence, as well as the opposites of these, are in the gift of chance and governed by circumstances. In addition, assuming a *persona* [= role] that we want ourselves is something that proceeds from our own will; as a consequence, some apply themselves to philosophy, others to civil law, and others again to oratory, while even in the case of the virtues, different men prefer to excel in different of them. (1.115)

In T7 the first *persona* is identified as arising from reason. Cicero, following his second century BCE source the Stoic Panaetius, claims that all and only human beings share this reason, and that we are distinguished from, and superior to, all nonhuman animals thereby. Note that Cicero does *not* claim that it is our bodily form, our anatomy, or our species that make us superior to nonhuman animals. Rather, it is the capacity of reason (*ratio*)—whatever that amounts to—that generates a being's first *persona*. If Cicero is wrong about all and only human beings having reason, then that mistake in no way vitiates the derivation of the first *persona* from reason. If most members of a certain species share in reason, but other members of that species—due to congenital defects, neurological disease, or brain injuries—have diminished rational capacity or no rational capacity at all, then it would be fair to say that most specimens of that species satisfy the first *persona* criterion, but not that it is universal for that species. The possession of reason is not *in itself* indexed to members of *Homo sapiens.* Thus, in T7 the possession of reason is indeed a species-neutral constituent of personhood because we need not share Cicero's opinion about which beings have reason and which beings lack it.

The second *persona* in Cicero's theory arises from a being's particular strengths, talents, and abilities. Some have unique bodily excellences, while others have special mental or emotional powers. This part of T7 is reminiscent of passages in Epictetus where he explains that not just any calf can lead the herd, but it is the bull's special job to do so (*Disc.* 1.2.30-32, 3.1.22-23, and 3.22.6); the drones do not rule the hive, but rather it is the queen bee's special gift and task (*Disc.* 3.22.99); not every horse is exceedingly swift (*Disc.* 1.2.34); not every dog tracks especially well (*Disc.* 4.5.13-14 and 3.1.22-23). (We could add that there is only one alpha male that leads the wolf pack.) The idea is that one is distinguished from others by one's forte, and one's forte carries with it special functions and responsibilities. Thus while the first *persona* is shared by all rational beings, the second *persona* distinguishes individuals from one another.

In T8 Cicero appeals to the theater metaphor which, as we have seen, is integral to the core meaning of *persona*. Just as savvy actors play only those dramatic roles for which they are individually suited, intelligent agents must apply themselves only to those functions, tasks, and activities for which they are individually suited. The connection with T6 is clear. To pursue an activity beyond one's abilities entails neglecting an activity matched to one's abilities. For Cicero, rejecting what is most one's own (one's characteristics) is unseemly self-denial. One's innate characteristics are not chosen, of course. But failure to exercise them appropriately is our decision. Thus the second *persona* is defined by both an element of unchosen inheritance and an element of conscious choice flowing from knowledge of that inheritance.

The third *persona* in Cicero's theory results from chance or involuntary circumstance. T9 bears comparison with T5. In T5 Epictetus attributes one's station in life to the choice of the cosmic Playwright, Zeus; in T9 Cicero chalks it up to chance. Either way, this third dimension of personhood is determined not by one's own choice, but by external contingencies, whether we see those contingencies as providential or random.

Cicero suggests that the fourth *persona* is wholly a matter of decision. Here we might wonder whether, given the second *persona,* only those who are good at philosophy should do it seriously, only those who are good at civil law should do it seriously, and so on. Does Cicero mean that if one has roughly equal talent for two different professions (or virtues), then one is free to select either in assuming one's fourth *persona?* Or perhaps with this fourth *persona* Cicero wants to make room for exceptions to the second: so long as I am not naturally awful at oratory, it is allowable for me to devote myself to it even if philosophy is my stronger talent. In any case, in his account of this fourth *persona* Cicero wishes to emphasize that some of the duties we incur result from our own decisions, and in this way we importantly contribute to the definition of our own personhood.[8]

What conclusions can be drawn from the examination of texts like these? Here we may borrow from a particularly useful recent study (Long, 1997).

> T10 In classical Latin, *persona* is sometimes used in exactly the way we speak today of a "certain person or persons", but what underlies this usage is the term's seemingly original allusion to mask, role or part. *Persona* is not primarily what a human being is, but rather a role or status a human being has or maintains or undertakes or bears or assumes. (13)

Does this suggest that *persona* applies only to members of the human species? Long corrects this mistaken impression.

> T11 Neither Latin *persona* nor its Greek equivalent *prosōpon* is invested in the pre-Christian era with other connotations of "person" that have become familiar since at least the seventeenth century; I mean the usage of person to distinguish human beings, individually or collectively, from other ani-

> mals (and perhaps also from human bodily features), whether by virtue of reason, reflection and (self-) consciousness (as in Locke or Leibniz), or as being "ends in themselves" (as in Kant), or as in some modern accounts, such as those of Frankfurt and Dennett, which take person to be essentially a normative concept. (13–14)

Now it seems clear that human slaves (a) have a share in reason, (b) have particular talents and abilities, and (c) become slaves involuntarily and by chance. Wouldn't this entail that we should ascribe to human slaves at least the first three *personae* described by Cicero and, if so, consider slaves to be persons? Though this inference seems perfectly licit philosophically, the Romans blocked it by legal fiat.

> T12 In Rome, as we have seen, slaves were legally defined as property, and they were not entitled to own property. Slaves were strictly nonpersons; they did not own themselves. The Stoics, I shall propose, canvassed the radical idea that everyone has at least one inalienable possession—the essence of the individual self, as defined by each human being's autonomy or capacity to give or withhold assent (the mental faculty they called *synkatathesis,* and which Cicero translated by *adsensio*). Thus they undermined any justification for slavery on the basis of a human being's nature: what is essentially yours or mine can never belong to anyone else. (16)

Long's study is especially pertinent for my purposes because his account of the Stoics' theories on persons and property-ownership actually provides the conceptual tools for constructing a fascinating argument for the personhood of *non*human animals. A key principle that can be gleaned from Long's article but is nowhere explicitly stated by him is that *beings that own themselves are persons.* That principle (2 below) can be set alongside several of Long's explicit statements to form the following line of reasoning.[9]

1. All human individuals own themselves. [p. 15]
2. All and only beings that own themselves are persons. [implied principle]
3. Things that do not own themselves are property. [corollary of 2]
4. By means of *oikeiōsis,* all individual animals perceive themselves, love themselves, and own themselves; every animal is not merely a center of agency, but a self—a being that feels itself to have an individual identity. [p. 26]
5. Therefore, every animal is a person, not an item of property. [from 2 and 4]

The technical term *oikeiōsis* requires some explanation here. The root meaning of *oikeion* is "belonging to", "owning", "having as one's own". The Stoics used the term *oikeiōsis* to refer to an innate process in all animals that explains why they behave in self-regarding ways. According to this developmental theory, animals have an instinctive affinity for their bodies and constitutions, and this gives them the ability to live their own specific ways of life, nourish and care for themselves, and protect themselves from harm. To greatly simplify, the Stoics' theory of *oikeiōsis* is designed to explain how self-love leads to self-preservation in animals.

Now as my argument above shows, the conclusion that every animal is a person can indeed be derived from the Stoics' theory of *oikeiōsis* and their theory of property. Yet the Stoics failed to recognize this. Instead, they insisted—as we observed in discussing Cicero above—that nonhuman animals lack reason, autonomy, and the capacity for assent, and are thereby excluded from the moral community.[10] So the Stoics can be credited for recognizing that the institution of human slavery, by which autonomous human beings are "owned" by one another, cannot be justified since such beings—*persons*—"belong" to themselves in such a way that they are not property at all. Yet the Stoics failed to see that, given their own theory of *oikeiōsis,* at least some nonhuman animals are also arguably not items of property, but persons in this sense.

II

The next episode to focus on is the early Christian period. Here I need not argue for but will merely observe the profound and lasting influence that Stoicism exerted on Christian thought. This influence certainly included, though it was by no means limited to, the concept of a *prosōpon/persona.* The theologian G. L. Prestige explains how from the sense of *prosōpon* as "face" the sense of the expression revealed by that face, and so one's inner mind, the character one might assume, or the role one intended to act, was derived.[11] Prestige observes that the term is also frequently used to refer to particular individuals of a species, "in much the same way as we speak of so many 'head' of cattle, or the 'poll' tax . . ."[12] This usage persists, Prestige explains, "to the end of the patristic period, John of Damascus observing (*Dialectica* 43) that a prosopon means whatsoever is evidenced by its own proper activities and characteristics, and that the holy Fathers referred hypostasis (object) and prosopon (individual) and atomon (particular) to the same thing".[13] So it was that a momentous episode in the evolution of the concept "person" was reached when Tertullian applied the term *persona* to the "Persons" of the Holy Trinity in the same sense as *prosōpon* was commonly used in Greek.[14] In Greek philosophical theology God was described as one *ousia* ("essence") and three most perfect *hypostases* ("subsistents") or *prosōpa* ("persons"): the Father, the Son, and the Holy Spirit. The Latin Trinitarians correspondingly described God as one *substantia* and three *personae.*

The doctrine of the Holy Trinity was formulated and defended in order to avoid falling prey to two opposing heresies: Modalism and Tritheism.[15] Modalism is the view that the Father, the Son, and the Holy Spirit are the same singular person or being, which is conceived on different occasions under the names "the Father", "the Son", and "the Holy Spirit" in relation to an office, function, or mode characteristic of one of those three different names. The more serious heresy, Tritheism, is the view that there are three divine beings, not one. Peter van Inwagen states the doctrine of the triune God[16] as follows:

> T13 There is one divine Being, but there are three distinct Persons, each of whom is a divine Being; and the one divine Being is a Person, thought [*sic*] not a fourth Person in addition to those three; nor is He any one of the three.[17]

Now one may object that this use of "person" in Trinitarian theology unforgivably equivocates on the meaning of "person" in everyday life or in the philosophy of mind or in moral philosophy. To this objection van Inwagen replies that he is of the "party" of Peter Geach, whom he quotes:

> T14 The concept of a person, which we find so familiar in its application to human beings, cannot be clearly and sharply expressed by any word in the vocabulary of Plato and Aristotle; it was wrought with the hammer and anvil of theological disputes about the Trinity and the Person of Christ.[18]

In my earlier discussion I tried to illustrate how Epictetus and Cicero—philosophers *after* Plato and Aristotle and *before* Christian theology—employed the term(s) *prosōpon/persona* in such a way as to make substantive contributions to the development of the concept of a person. So what are we to make of T14? I see three possible explanations: (1) Geach and van Inwagen do not consider the use of *prosōpon/persona* in such philosophers to be a significant contribution to the refinement of the concept of a person *as it is applied to human beings;* (2) they are aware of this Stoic chapter in the history of the concept "person", but for some reason do not consider this chapter to be germane to its fashioning by theological smithcraft; (3) they are simply unfamiliar with this Stoic chapter. I decline to speculate on which possibility to favor.

What upshot does the Christian doctrine that there are three distinct divine Persons in the Godhead have for the legitimacy of extending the concept "person" to some nonhuman animals? Simply put, it is this. If there is a long-standing, popular tradition of applying the concept "person" to a nonphysical, supernatural, infinite, eternal, invisible being with miraculous causal powers, then it would seem to be a comparatively modest move to apply the concept to those physical, natural, finite, mortal, observable beings who have the causal powers typically associated with mindful behavior. Van Inwagen's own understanding of "person" seems to be species-neutral.

> T15 Something is a being . . . if it has causal powers. A being is a person . . . if it is self-aware and has beliefs and plans and acts on the basis of those beliefs to execute those plans.[19]

An activity of the Persons of the Trinity that van Inwagen emphasizes is love; the Father, the Son, and the Holy Spirit love one another. Now if the capacity for love among the divine Persons is similarly characteristic of mortal persons, then the moral philosopher sympathetic to the Great Ape Project would need to establish, for example, that instances of feeding, grooming, protecting, nurturing, and helping one another within social groups of great apes count as expressions of "love" in the relevant sense. If group altruism is arguably a kind of love, then some nonhuman animals certainly exhibit it in some of their actions. If those same animals are self-aware, have beliefs and plans, and act on those beliefs to carry out those plans, then, on van Inwagen's criteria, they would be persons.[20]

In addition to the considerations I have presented, Mary Midgley adds a few others.

> T16 In the first place, there are several well-established and indeed venerable precedents for calling non-human beings "persons". One concerns the persons of the Trinity and indeed, the personhood of God. Another is the case of "legal persons"— corporate bodies such as cities or colleges, which count as persons for various purposes, such as suing and being sued. . . . Thirdly, what may look nearer to the dolphins, the word is used by zoologists to describe the individual members of a compound or colonial organism, such as jellyfish or coral, each having (as the dictionary reasonably puts it) a "more or less independent life". There is nothing stretched or paradoxical about these uses, for the word does not in origin mean "human being" or anything like it at all. It means a mask, and its basic general sense comes from the drama. The "masks" in a play are the characters who appear in it. Thus, to quote the Oxford Dictionary . . . after "a mask", it means "a character or personage acted, one who plays or performs any part, a character, relation or capacity in which one acts, a being having legal rights, a juridical person". The last two meanings throw a clear light on the difference between this notion and that of being human. Not all human beings need be persons. The word *persona* in Latin does not apply to slaves, though it does apply to the state as a corporate person. Slaves have, so to speak, no speaking part in the drama; they do not figure in it; they are extras.[21]

Rather than appeal to the personhood of corporate bodies, however, I will next turn to a brief exploration of the coherence of talking about the personhood of extra-terrestrials.

III

Science fiction writers like Gene Roddenberry have provided us with an abundance of beings whose causal powers resemble those of human beings in kind, even when those causal powers far surpass human powers in degree. Vulcans, for example, are much more logical and much less emotional than human beings, yet they clearly possess the characteristics of personhood I have been discussing. Klingons and Romulans are decidedly bellicose in contrast to their peace-loving Vulcan counterparts, yet both of those species of fictional humanoids would surely count as persons. A few philosophers have mentioned these sorts of cases previously, but it seems to me that such examples have not been deployed as strategically as they can be. Betazoids[22] possess empathic powers that humans lack, yet their hypersensitivity to the emotional states of others, I would argue, makes them neither better nor worse paradigms of persons than human beings possessed of ordinary emotional awareness of others.

A more difficult case involves androids like Mr. Data.[23] Data, like all androids, is a synthetic, not an organic being. His positronic brain allows him to acquire information much faster than an organic human brain possibly could. His brain also holds a vastly greater store of that information for an indefinitely long duration of time. Data also has sensations; his artificial skin, ears, nose, and eyes transmit impulses to his brain, which processes them as qualia. Yet Data supposedly has no feelings or emotions at all. Data is a being who is far superior to adult human beings in rationality, whose beliefs are determined by evidence alone and never by wish-fulfillment, and whose actions, consequently, always consistently aim at the most efficient execution of his flawlessly conceived plans. Yet he has no experience of fear, joy, hatred, envy, boredom, sadness, or love. Would Data be a person?[24]

The objection could be raised that the extra-terrestrial beings I have described are mere fictions. We have no evidence that such beings exist.[25] Moreover, one could be understandably sceptical of an argument that beings that relevantly resemble these sorts of intelligent humanoids *could* exist given the probability, in such an immense universe, of the existence of *other* planets which supported the evolution of highly intelligent beings. But this objection misses my point: the core meaning of "person" is neither intensively nor extensively coincident with the concept "human being", and thus is in no way logically or conceptually limited to earthlings. The species-neutrality of the core sense of "person" seems to be tacitly reflected in the intuitions of many science fiction authors and more than a few philosophers.[26] Michael Tooley is one philosopher who shares such intuitions.

> T17 For it is obvious that if we encountered other "rational animals", such as Martians, the fact that their physiological makeup was very different from our own would not be grounds for denying them a right to life.[27]

In his article Tooley stipulates that he uses "having a moral right to life" and "being a person" synonymously,[28] and he asserts that it is quite possible that animals such as cats, dogs, and polar bears possess properties that make them persons.[29]

Let us consider the personhood of another science fiction creature, this one provided by George Lucas. If Chewbacca the Wookie existed, the fur that covers his entire body, his unusual height, and his alien anatomy would not disqualify him from being a person. Rather, his ability to assume and abandon roles, his self-ownership (self-awareness and self-love), and his ability to relate to others, his ability to plan, and all the beliefs that these abilities presuppose, constitute his personhood. Steve Sapontzis has observed that the science fiction creatures I have mentioned are not significantly different from us in appearance, and so "are human beings, even if not exactly *Homo sapiens*".[30] Sapontzis believes that in "everyday experience" bodily shape is extremely important for identifying persons.

> T18 Furthermore, even before we had much appreciation of the mentality of apes, there was a tendency to consider them to be, in an extended sense, "little people", because they look like human beings.[31]

And so with Wookies. But if a Wookie is incapable of piloting a spaceship or driving an automobile, and cannot even wield a crossbow, but nevertheless satisfies the core criteria of personhood, then that Wookie may well begin to resemble an unusually tall great ape.

IV

Having surveyed those episodes in the evolution of the concept "person" relevant to my argument, I can now return to the challenge I mentioned at the outset. David DeGrazia has argued that the concept "person" is both vague and indeterminate because it cannot be reduced to a set of necessary and sufficient conditions.[32] This complaint about the concept, however, is not new. As early as 1906 in a work titled *Persona und "Prosōpon" im Recht und im christlichen Dogma,* Siegmund Schlossmann, a law professor at Kiel, registered the same complaint.

> T19 The author starts out from the legal concept of person, citing much literature of great importance, with the express purpose of ridding the legal conceptual system of this "nuisance", since the concept is vague and indefinite.[33]

Perhaps the concept "athlete" is similar to the concept "person" in this respect: there are clear cases of members of that group, clear cases of non-members, and difficult borderline cases. For example, are those who play miniature golf professionally athletes? Are billiards-players or bowlers athletes? Surely the existence of tough cases like these fail to justify jettisoning the concept "athlete". Its fuzzy borders do not rob it of its utility, whether the concept occurs in discussions of the philosophy of sport by academics, or in arguments bandied about by denizens of sportsbars. Why think the concept "person" must fare any worse?

I suspect that one reason[34] the concept "person" has proved resistant to analysis into a tidy set of necessary and sufficient conditions stems, as DeGrazia suggests, from the gradational development of children's psychological capacities. There is no distinct, nonarbitrary threshold from nonperson, preperson, or potential person to full-blown, actual person. The incremental emergence of personhood in a being is a messy, complex matter. Yet its conceptual utility is neither destroyed nor diminished by that complexity, as is manifested by its continued, widespread use. The popularity it enjoys among bioethicists who discuss "proximate persons"[35] is only one such example. Thus I conclude that the core meaning of "person" stubbornly fills a vital niche in our contemporary ethical vocabulary whether we are discussing human neonates, space aliens, or orangutans.[36]

Arthur Danto provides an apt reply to DeGrazia's attempt to dispense with the concept "person" once and for all.

> T20 And some contemporary writers . . . would emphasize that this ordinary concept cannot, at present, be rendered comprehensible in scientific terms, and that relative to the known laws of physics and chemistry, persons are indeed primitive and irreducible entities. And it is precisely the ambiguity we have noted in the ordinary concept which serves to define persons in the metaphysical sense. A person *is* the body (the victim of a crime against the person); *is* the appearance (the comely person); *is* the self-conscious and rational individual; *is* the source and object of rights and obligations; *is* that which takes roles and discharges functions. It is only a weak sense of complexity, perhaps, or a commitment to one or another reductionist program, which leads us to regard the concept as incoherent.[37]

I submit that it is not merely "sometimes convenient" to use the concept "person" in our moral ontology, as DeGrazia argues. Rather, the concept has been, is now, and will continue to be into the foreseeable future, indispensable to our moral discourse.

My contribution on the evolution of the concept "person" is indebted to an earlier one, from which my last quotation is taken.

> T21 We can see from the word "personality" and its parallel "individuality", which also has its history, that they have not developed among the masses. But such words coined by science have great value for the commonalty if they become current and are

> true to their significant content, for *they may become standards in public judgment* and even volitional impulses. Consequently, it is the duty of writers not to wear down and dull the definition.[38]

I believe that an important goal of advocates of the Great Ape Project is to make current among the public the core meaning of "person" so that this concept can and increasingly will come to be applied to some nonhuman animals by a wider population than a small group of intellectuals. Perhaps "what people think" will in time become informed by a greater understanding of the historical development of the rich concept "person".

NOTES

1. DeGrazia 1997, p. 301.
2. Sapontzis 1987, for example, writes: "while acknowledging the existence of speculative, metaphorical, and reformist uses of the term, we can safely assert that in the actual course of our everyday affairs, the primary, descriptive use of 'person' is to denote all and only human beings" (p. 50).
3. H.T. Engelhardt, Jr. 1986 is one who employs such a selective application. He holds that "not all humans are persons. Not all humans are self-conscious, rational, and able to conceive of the possibility of blaming and praising. Fetuses, infants, the profoundly mentally retarded, and the hopelessly comatose provide examples of human non-persons" (p. 107). Engelhardt also distinguishes "between persons, who ought to be objects of respect, and animals, which ought to be objects of beneficent regard. We owe to persons both respect and beneficent regard. To animals we owe only beneficent regard" (p. 114).
4. H.G. Liddell, R. Scott and H.S. Jones, *A Greek-English Lexicon* (Clarendon Press, Oxford, 1996, 9th edition with revised supplement).
5. The translations of Epictetus are mine.
6. Cf. *Disc.* 1.2.11: "For you are the one that knows yourself, how much you are worth to yourself and at what price you sell yourself. For different people sell themselves at different prices". For a discussion of how roles are related to *aidos* in Epictetus, see pp. 147–152 in R. Kamtekar, "*AIDOS* in Epictetus", *Classical Philology* 93 (1998), pp. 136–160.
7. The following translations from *De officiis* are those of M.T. Griffin and E.M. Adkins (Cambridge University Press, Cambridge, 1991), very slightly modified.
8. For a more detailed discussion of the *personae*-doctrine in Cicero, Epictetus, and others see A.R. Dyck, *A Commentary on Cicero, "De officiis"* (University of Michigan Press, Ann Arbor, 1996).
9. The numbers within the square brackets in steps 1 and 4 indicate the page of Long 1997 from which that proposition is taken.
10. See Dombrowski 1984 and Sorabji 1993.
11. Prestige 1952. p. 157.
12. *Ibid.*
13. *Ibid.*, p. 158.
14. *Ibid.*, p. 159.
15. Here I borrow from van Inwagen 1995, pp. 229–230.
16. An interesting attempt is made by van Inwagen to show that the doctrine of the Holy Trinity can be stated in such a way that it is demonstrably free of formal contradiction.
17. van Inwagen 1995, pp. 223–224.
18. *Ibid.*, p. 231.
19. *Ibid.*, p. 246. See Jaegwon Kim's analysis of causal power in *Supervenience and Mind* (Cambridge University Press, Cambridge, 1993), pp. 325–326 and 348 ff.
20. Cf. Cavalieri and Singer 1994. Peter Singer's argument that chimpanzees, gorillas and orangutans are persons can be found in Singer 1993, pp. 117–118.
21. Midgley 1985, p. 315 this volume. See also "A literary postscript: characters, persons, selves, individuals", in A.O. Rorty 1976, pp. 301–323, especially pp. 309–311.
22. Such as Counselor Deanna Troi of the television series *Star Trek: Next Generation.*
23. Also of *Star Trek: Next Generation.*
24. For a detailed discussion of the personhood of Data, see R. Hanley 1997, pp. 42–120. Hanley concludes that if there were individuals like Data, we ought to consider these individuals to be persons.
25. See Thomas V. Morris, *The Logic of the God Incarnate* (Cornell University Press, Ithaca, 1986), pp. 170–186, for what one Christian philosopher makes of the possibility of extraterrestrial persons.

26. This is why I disagree with the judgment that the use of such science fiction examples is insignificant because "science fiction cases can only contribute to inconclusive speculation regarding what our concepts might become" (Sapontzis 1987, p. 49). Controversy over the philosophical justification of the scope of the application of the term "person" cannot, *contra* Sapontzis (p. 48), be settled by appealing to dictionaries. I contend that the intuitions at work in our science fiction may well derive from our "everyday experience" *as it is informed by* attention to the evolution of the term. Joel Feinberg has argued that "[a]gainst the view that membership in the species *Homo sapiens* is a *necessary* condition of membership in the class of moral persons, we have the possibility of there being moral persons from other planets who belong to other biological species" (Feinberg 1986, p. 265). In "Conditions of personhood" Daniel Dennett observes that "we recognize almost all human beings as persons, but . . . we can easily contemplate the existence of biologically very different persons—inhabiting other planets, perhaps . . ." (p. 227 this volume). Amélie Rorty's remarks are worth quoting at length: "[t]he issue of whether the class of persons exactly coincides with the class of biologically defined human beings—whether corporations, Venusians, mongolian idiots, and fetuses are persons—is in part a conceptual question. It is a question about whether the relevant base for the classification of persons requires attention to whether things *look* like "us", whether they are made out of *stuff* like "ours", or whether it is enough that they *function* as we take "ourselves" to function. If Venusians and robots come to be thought of as persons, at least part of the argument that will establish them will be that they function as we do: that while they are not the *same* organisms that we are, they are in the appropriate sense the same *type* of organism or entity. Does an entity have to be an organism to be a person? When is a well-organized, self-sustaining entity an organism? Of course there may be a time when Venusians and robots are called persons by science fiction writers and philosophers and by no one else. The question of the personhood of Venusians and robots becomes serious when we actually start raising questions about their legal rights and obligations. It is a very complex matter: if Venusians and robots come increasingly to be treated as persons are now treated, their inclusion in the class will come to modify our conceptions and treatment of human organisms. Treating ourselves as of the same *type* as Venusians will gradually and subtly come to affect leading questions and presuppositions about the nature of an organism. But there is no point speculating about what we *shall* say in transitional periods, and certainly none in legislating in advance what we shall decide. Whether we shall, when the time comes, classify Venusians as persons will certainly depend on what they are like, on whether we like them, and on our political and social preoccupations when the issue becomes a live one" (Rorty 1976, pp. 322–323). It seems that we have entered one of those "transitional periods" regarding the personhood of great apes and some other nonhuman animals.
27. Tooley 1997, pp. 51–52.
28. *Ibid.,* p. 42.
29. *Ibid.,* p. 40
30. Sapontzis 1987, p. 49.
31. *Ibid.*
32. DeGrazia 1997, p. 305.
33. A bibliographical comment by Hans Vaihinger appended to Trendelenburg 1910, p. 359, and originally published as an editorial in *Kant-Studien* 13, 1–2 (1908), pp. 194 ff.
34. Dennett offers another: "why are we not in a position to claim that these necessary conditions of moral personhood are also sufficient? Simply because the concept of a person is . . . inescapably normative. Human beings or other entities can only aspire to being approximations of the ideal, and there can be no way to set a "passing grade" that is not arbitrary. Were the six conditions (strictly interpreted) considered sufficient they would not ensure that any actual entity was a person, for nothing would ever fulfill them. The moral notion of a person and the metaphysical notion of a person are not separate and distinct concepts but just two different and unstable resting points on the same continuum. This relativity infects the satisfaction of conditions of personhood at every level" (this volume pp. 237–238)
35. Walters 1997.
36. By this I in no way wish to suggest that if we come to apply the term "person" to *all* great apes, human and otherwise, and to certain other large-brained social mammals and cetaceans, then this would justify us in holding that *only these* animals have interests deserving of the respect of human moral agents.
37. Danto 1967, p. 113.
38. Trendelenburg 1910, pp. 358–359; emphasis added.

REFERENCES

Cavalieri, P., and Singer, P. (eds), (1994), *The Great Ape Project. Equality beyond Humanity;* St Martin's Press, New York.

Danto, A. C. (1967), "Persons", in P. Edwards (ed.), *Encyclopedia of Philosophy,* Macmillan, New York, pp. 110–114.

DeGrazia, D. (1997), "Great apes, dolphins, and the concept of personhood", *The Southern Journal of Philosophy* 35, 3, pp. 301–320.

Dombrowski, D. (1984), *The Philosophy of Vegetarianism,* University of Massachusetts Press, Amherst.

Engelhardt Jr., H. T. (1986), *The Foundations of Bioethics,* Oxford University Press, Oxford.

Feinberg, J. (1986), "Abortion", in T. Regan (ed.), *Matters of Life and Death,* Random House, New York, pp. 256–293.

Hanley, R. (1997), *The Metaphysics of Star Trek,* Basic Books, New York.

Long, A. A. (1997), "Stoic philosophers on persons, property-ownership and community", in R. Sorabji (ed.), *Aristotle and After. Bulletin of the Institute of Classical Studies,* suppl. 68, pp. 13–31.

Midgley, M. (1985), "Persons and non-persons", this volume pp. 314–320.

Prestige, G. L. (1952), *God in Patristic Thought,* S. P. C. K., London.

Rorty, A. O. (ed.), (1976), *The Identities of Persons,* University of California Press, Berkeley.

Sapontzis, S.F. (1987), *Morals, Reason, and Animals,* Temple University Press, Philadelphia.

Singer, P. (1993), *Practical Ethics,* 2nd ed., Cambridge University Press, Cambridge.

Sorabji, R. (1993), *Animal Minds and Human Morals,* Cornell University Press, Ithaca.

Tooley, M. (1997), "Abortion and infanticide", in S. Dwyer and J. Feinberg (eds), *The Problem of Abortion,* Wadsworth, Belmont, CA, pp. 40–58.

Trendelenburg, A. (1910), "A Contribution to the history of the word person", *Monist* 20, pp. 336–363.

van Inwagen, P. (1995), *God, Knowledge and Mystery,* Cornell University Press, Ithaca, Chapter 8: "And yet they are not three Gods but one God", pp. 222–259.

Walters, J. W. (1997), *What is a Person? An Ethical Exploration.* University of Illinois Press, Urbana.

DISCUSSION QUESTIONS

1. Do you agree with Stephens' analysis of Cicero's text T7 that the possession of reason is a species-neutral constituent of personhood?
2. Consider Stephens' argument that since, according to the Stoic theory of *oikeiōsis,* animals own themselves, they are persons and not property. The Stoics denied that nonhuman animals have reason and affirmed that they are property. Given this, is it legitimate for Stephens to use a Stoic concept to construct an argument for the personhood of nonhuman animals?
3. Do you think Engberg-Pedersen would accept Stephens' argument for the personhood of animals based on the Stoic theory of *oikeiōsis?* Explain.
4. Explain the heresies of Modalism and Tritheism.
5. Do you agree with Stephens that applying the concept "person" to the Great Apes seems modest compared to the Christian tradition of applying it to the divine Trinity? Explain.
6. If Vulcans, Klingons, Romulans, and Wookies were real, would you consider them to be persons? Defend your answer.

Chapter 42

THE BOYD GROUP

The Boyd Group is a forum based in the United Kingdom for the exchange of views on issues related to the use of animals in science. Its members include veterinarians, scientists using animals, members of animal welfare organizations, anti-vivisectionists, philosophers, and others. In this May 2003 paper the authors argue that the principle that the moral status of all individual persons (e.g., the people, in contrast to the pebbles, on a beach) should be respected has in recent centuries come to be widely accepted. Children, women, slaves, and members of other ethnic groups are given as historical examples of individuals whose moral status was not respected, and who were consequently treated as mere means, not ends in themselves. What counts as a person? Is it possible that some humans are not *persons and that some nonhuman animals, especially primates,* are *persons? The authors explain that the psychologist Gómez accepts the philosopher Dennett's view that a person is an intentional agent capable of recognizing other persons as intentional agents. Having studied their behavior, Gómez thinks that apes are capable of this mutual intersubjective recognition of each other's intentionality. Two objections to Gómez' position are not fatal, they contend. Apes are perhaps moral patients, that is, persons currently unable to exercise moral agency and lacking in responsibility, but having equal moral status to other persons. Moral patients—humans who have become demented, for example—need to be treated differently than moral agents.*

The Moral Status of Non-Human Primates: Are Apes Persons?

1. THE MORAL STATUS OF PERSONS

The term 'moral status' refers to what, because something is the kind of thing it is, you may or may not do to it. Because of the kind of thing it is, a pebble on a beach has little or no moral status: there is nothing about pebbles as such, that makes it wrong to throw them into the sea as mere means to your end of amusing yourself. People on a beach are a very different kind of thing. They are the same kind of thing as you are—not mere means but, like you, ends in themselves. Their moral status is that of persons, with a right not to be harmed by you, especially not without their consent.

The difference in moral status between pebbles and people is so obvious, that if anyone asked why they should not throw people into the sea just to amuse themselves, we would doubt their seriousness or their sanity. But what if they wanted to throw people into the sea, not to amuse themselves, but for a good reason such as scientific research which could benefit humanity by saving other lives? Without (at least) the consent of the people concerned, that too would be morally wrong. The example of the hypothermia researchers in Nazi Germany who plunged prisoners into tanks of freezing water illustrates this. While the morality of using the results of that research is debated, the immorality of the research itself is unquestioned.

What this example also illustrates however, is that the moral status of persons has not always been universally recognised and respected. There are countless historical examples of apparently sane people treating other people who were in some respect weaker than them (children, women, slaves and members of other ethnic groups, for example) as if they were not the same kind of thing as themselves. One historical reason for this, no doubt, is scarcity. To regard others as having equal moral status to yourself has demanding implications. It may require you to share your resources with them, or, at least to refrain from treating them in ways which might be to your own or your nearer kin's advantage. But the resources available to anyone are finite; and other people's interests may conflict with your own, sometimes even with your own or your nearer kin's survival. Historically, this was often the case; and since not only material resources, but also people's time and imagination are finite, it is not surprising that some people have regarded others, especially those whose interests may have con-

Source: The Boyd Group, "The Moral Status of Non-Human Primates: Are Apes Persons?" Printed from http://www.boyd-group.demon.co.uk/Paper 3.pdf/ and used with the permission of Jane Smith (editor) and Kenneth Boyd (author).

flicted with their own, as not having equal moral status to themselves.

Against the background of scarcity, what perhaps is surprising is the emergence of the modern view of the moral and legal status of persons. This view emerged, slowly and patchily, from different strands of religious and philosophical reflection. But only in recent centuries was it formalised, and widely accepted, as the principle that the moral status and human rights of all individual persons should be respected, simply because they are persons, rather than because they are (to others or to God) important persons.

Widespread acceptance of this principle however, has left unsettled the question of who counts as a person and how this is to be determined. The claim that all and only members of the species *Homo sapiens* are persons, simply because they are members of that species, is now too contestable, on mature philosophical reflection (see Tooley, 1998), to settle the matter. This opens up the possibility that some humans may not be persons and that members of some other species, especially primates, may be persons. But how do you determine who or what counts as a person?

Perhaps the most common philosophical way of trying to answer this is by saying that what determines whether members of other species count as persons, is whether they have properties or characteristics which make them sufficiently similar, in morally relevant ways, to humans whose personhood is not in doubt. The characteristics most often cited as morally relevant are intelligence and the capacity to suffer pain or distress. But stated as simply as that, without further qualification, these are characteristics of the members of many non-human species. The moral status of members of these species clearly is much higher than that of pebbles, and probably higher than that of living creatures which (assuming this could be shown) are less intelligent or sensitive to suffering. But to characterise them as persons may be to broaden the meaning of that concept so much that it loses its distinctive content.

2. APES, METAREPRESENTATIONAL CAPACITY, AND INTERSUBJECTIVITY

For the concept to have content, further qualification of the characteristics morally relevant to determining personhood seems to be required. The variations on this theme in the literature are many, particularly with reference to consciousness and self-consciousness. But one recent version, by the psychologist Gómez (1998), is particularly interesting for the present purpose, both because it concerns apes, and because it defends a claim to personhood on their (but not necessarily all primates') behalf, against the very stringent criteria for personhood suggested by the philosopher Dennett (1976).

According to Dennett, persons must be not only intentional agents, but capable of reciprocal understanding that other persons are intentional agents. This requires 'metarepresentational ability', the ability to represent, in one's own mind, other persons as having minds and metarepresentational ability of their own. But metarepresentational ability can be developed and detected only by means of language. So creatures that lack language cannot be persons.

Responding to these criteria, Gómez notes that there 'seems to be little controversy that apes . . . are intentional creatures that follow goals with a diversity of behavioural and instrumental means and who form complex expectations about the world at some representational level'. But do apes 'understand others as intentional agents with their own ability to reciprocate in this understanding'? In terms of Dennett's language requirement, Gómez concedes that, in apes, evidence is still at best ambiguous both of linguistic ability, and of non-linguistic cognitive abilities amounting to a 'theory of mind' (i.e., an understanding that other creatures act 'on the basis of thoughts, wishes, beliefs, intentions, etc.').

Gómez agrees that the 'ability to reciprocally recognise each other's intentionality' is 'an essential feature of persons'. But he questions Dennett's stipulation that this requires an ability to *recognize explicitly* (in metarepresentations) one another's mental states. 'Would it not be possible', he asks, 'to engage in this mutual recognition without explicitly representing the intentions of others as internal mental states?'

If this mutual recognition, or 'intersubjectivity', is the 'essential feature' of persons, what needs to be shown, is whether apes, as 'subjects (intentional agents in Dennett's terminology) can coordinate their 'subjectivities' (i.e., their mental states) with other creatures' subjectivities (i.e., other creatures' mental states) without having recourse to metarepresentations'. Gómez believes that this can be shown, and illustrates this with observations from his own and others' research—for example that apes, like humans, but unlike some other non-human primates, use eye-contact and other aspects of face-to-face interaction, not in a 'single, predominantly aggressive/defensive way', but 'as a pivotal component of different kinds of social interactions' in which they attend and respond to the intentionality and emotions of others.

This non-metarepresentational intersubjectivity, Gómez points out, appears to be achieved by human infants in the first year of life, and is characteristic not only of apes, but perhaps also of 'adult humans, who do not seem to understand attention contact in metarepresentational terms either (unless they are cognitive scientists engaging in prepositional redescriptions with scientific purposes).' This does not mean that apes are the same as humans, whose 'metarepresentational minds are capable of achieving much more sophisticated versions of consciousness and personhood'. But apes do appear to satisfy the key condition for personhood: they 'act and feel as persons in the most essential sense of the word, which I take to be the ability to recognize others and themselves as individual subjects capable of feeling and behaving intersubjectively.'

Gómez sums up his argument thus: 'I am not a person in so far as I think I am a person; I am not a person in so far as another thinks of me as a person. I am a person in so far as I and another perceive and treat each other as persons.' This formulation amplifies the African proverb that 'a person is a person through other persons.' Gómez' view also is similar in some respects to the primatologist Smuts' (1999) claim (illustrated by her experience not only with baboons but also with her own dog) that 'relating to other beings as persons has nothing to do with whether or not we attribute human characteristics to them. It has to do, instead, with recognising that they are social subjects like us, whose idiosyncratic subjective experience of us plays the same role in their relations with us that our subjective experience of them plays in our relations with them. If they relate to us as individuals, and if we relate to them as individuals, it is possible for us to have a personal relationship'.

3. TWO OBJECTIONS

One possible objection to Gómez' argument is this. He argues that 'I am a person in so far as I and another perceive and treat each other as persons'. But for apes to be accepted as persons, he needs not only (like Smuts perhaps) 'intuitive, subjective' experience of a personal relationship with individual animals, but also what he calls 'analytical, objective' scientific evidence 'that can be independently and objectively verified by different people'. For the purposes of his argument therefore, whether or not apes are to be accepted as persons does indeed seem to depend on whether 'another thinks of me as a person'. It depends too on whether 'different people' actually do 'verify' the philosophical criteria and interpretation of the scientific evidence offered by Gómez. Since scientific evidence and interpretation are always vulnerable to reinterpretation and further evidence, and since philosophical theories are essentially contestable, Gómez' arguments about personhood and apes are at best persuasive but not conclusive.

This objection is not necessarily fatal to Gómez' argument, however. Whether or not apes are persons is a question to which there may be no conclusive, but only more or less persuasive answers. What is at issue here therefore may be whether Gómez' intersubjectivity argument is more or less persuasive than Dennett's stipulation that to be a person requires linguistic capacity. In this respect, one problem about Dennett's argument is that, historically, many human persons with the capacity for speech (slaves, or 'lesser breeds' for example) have not been 'heard' as speaking meaningfully, and so have not been treated as persons. If there is any doubt about whether apes are persons who are not being 'heard' in this way, Gómez' claim that 'I am a person in so far as I and another person perceive and treat each other as persons', offers a way of trying to answer the question that at least admits that it is a reasonable question. It does not, that is, foreclose the question in advance with the stipulation that a necessary condition for personhood is a physiological capacity which (probably) only humans possess—a capacity moreover which even when present in some human persons, has not proved sufficient to persuade other human persons of their personhood.

Gómez' argument that 'I am a person in so far as I and another perceive and treat each other as persons' receives some support also from the philosopher Gaita's (1991) view that a person is someone who can 'be seen as one who could be someone's friend', even when not heard or treated as a person by almost everyone else. Gaita, however, is impatient of philosophical arguments which make the recognition of others as persons await confirmation that they possess morally relevant properties. In real life, he argues, recognition of others as persons depends not on intellectual beliefs about their capacities, but upon recognition of another 'I'—in Wittgenstein's terms, not 'on the *opinion* that he has a soul', but on 'an attitude towards a soul'.

Gaita's argument here seems close to Gómez' view that 'I am a person in so far as I and another person perceive and treat each other as persons'. But a second objection to Gómez' claims for apes is raised by a further point made by Gaita about someone who can 'be seen as one who could be someone's friend'. Such a person, he argues, 'must be seen as someone who is subject to the demands which are internal to friendship, as someone of whom it is intelligible to require that he rise to those demands, no matter how often he actually fails to do so.' (1991). He doubts that this is possible for non-human animals. 'Only human beings (of the beings we know) have an inner life. That is because only human beings can reflect on what happens to them and take an attitude to what happens to them because of such reflection. An animal can suffer but it cannot curse the day it was born; an animal can be afraid but it cannot be ashamed of its fear and despise itself; an animal can be happy but it cannot be joyous . . . The problems of life's meaning cannot arise for an animal and only a being for whom life can be problematic can have a spiritual life, and therefore, have a soul' (1991).

This second objection, again, is not necessarily fatal to Gómez' argument. While arguing that apes 'act and feel as persons in the most essential sense of the word, which I take to be the ability to recognise others and themselves as individual subjects capable of feeling and behaving intersubjectively', he does not deny that humans' 'metarepresentational minds are capable of achieving much more sophisticated versions of consciousness and personhood.' On the other hand, if personhood is something that admits of different versions, can it still do the work that is required of it as a concept that protects the equal moral status of all persons?

4. MORAL AGENTS AND MORAL PATIENTS

One response to this difficulty is to argue that while all persons have equal moral status, what that entails for how they ought or ought not to be treated, depends on whether they are moral agents or moral patients. A moral patient—a person who is currently unable to exercise moral agency (in Gaita's terms, to 'rise to . . . the demands that are internal to friendship', for example)—may have equal moral status to other persons, but nevertheless need be treated differently than a moral agent. This distinction within the category of persons avoids the morally unpalatable conclusion that people who have become demented, for example, are no longer persons. It can also be used to argue that, even if apes cannot 'rise to . . . the demands that are internal to friendship' for example, generosity suggests that they are still entitled (if Gómez' arguments are accepted) to be regarded as persons.

A possible objection to such generosity, suggested by Gaita (1991), is that if animals are moral patients, they (unlike humans) 'are not as they are through misfortune'. If that is a morally relevant consideration, the case for treating apes as persons who are moral patients may be weakened. But are apes moral patients rather than moral agents? The question of whether at least some animals are or may be moral, is at least debatable. Smuts, for example, writes this about her dog Safi: 'because I regard Safi as a person, and she regards me as one, we can be friends. As in any genuine human-to-human friendship, our relationship is predicated on mutual respect and reciprocity. Although she depends on me to provide certain necessities, like food and water, this dependence is contingent, not inherent: if I lived in the world of wild dogs, I would depend on her for food and protection'.

Smuts illustrates these claims with various experiences of her relationship with Safi, and concludes: 'I do not claim that any dog will show such behaviours if treated as an equal. In fact, I believe that Safi is exceptional, that she was born, perhaps, with an unusually sensitive nature. However, I do firmly believe—and my experience with other animals supports this belief—that treating members of other species as persons, as beings with potential far beyond our normal expectations, will bring out the best in them . . . '

It is difficult to see how such claims for animal morality could be substantiated to the satisfaction of many who would regard what Smuts writes as 'sentimental'. If she did live 'in the world of wild dogs', would Safi actually afford her the necessary 'food and protection'? But to identify what is or is not 'sentimental', or to achieve a 'healthy' critical distance from subjectivity, itself is a matter of judgement, and intersubjective agreement may be the closest we can come to the truth about it.

It may, of course, not be possible to achieve intersubjective agreement on questions like animal morality or whether apes are persons, let alone the much more difficult question of the relative moral status of members of other animal species. But at least to try is incumbent on members of an animal-using species who claim to be moral animals. A serious effort, clearly, needs to examine, carefully and critically, scientific evidence of the kind offered both by Gómez and by others who interpret their evidence differently. But it also needs to examine, just as carefully and critically, the varieties of 'testimony' offered by those who, like Smuts, have first-hand experience of living and working with the animal species in question.

REFERENCES

Dennett, D.C. (1976). Conditions of personhood. This volume, pp. 227–240.

Gaita, R. (1991). *Good and evil: an absolute conception* (pp. 120,128,153). London: Macmillan.

Gómez, J.C. (1998). Are apes persons? The case for primate intersubjectivity. *Etica & Animali,* 9, 51–63.

Smuts, B. (1999). In J.M. Coetzee, *The lives of animals* (pp. 107–120). Princeton: Princeton University Press.

Tooley, M.(1998). Speciesism and basic moral principles. *Etica & Animali,* 9, 5–36.

DISCUSSION QUESTIONS

1. What is the example of hypothermia researchers in Nazi Germany meant to show?
2. Do you think that all and only members of the species *Homo sapiens* are persons? Defend your view.
3. On what points does Gómez agree with Dennett? On what point does Gómez disagree with him?
4. How does Gómez' summary of his argument amplify an African proverb?
5. Describe the first possible objection to Gómez' argument. How successful do you judge it to be? Explain.
6. Which philosophical arguments is Gaita impatient of and why?
7. Could a chimpanzee be the friend of a human being? Explain.
8. Describe Gaita's objection to conceiving of any nonhuman animals, including apes, as moral patients. Do you agree?
9. Does the relationship between Smuts and her dog Safi constitute friendship? Explain.